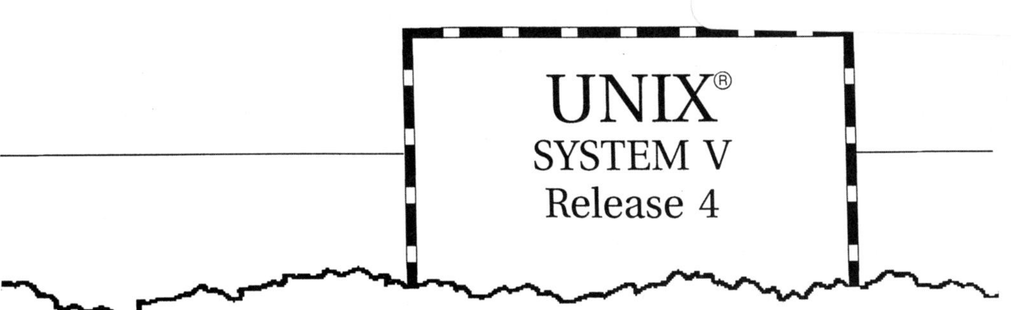

Commands Reference Manual

VOLUME 2

(Commands m-z)

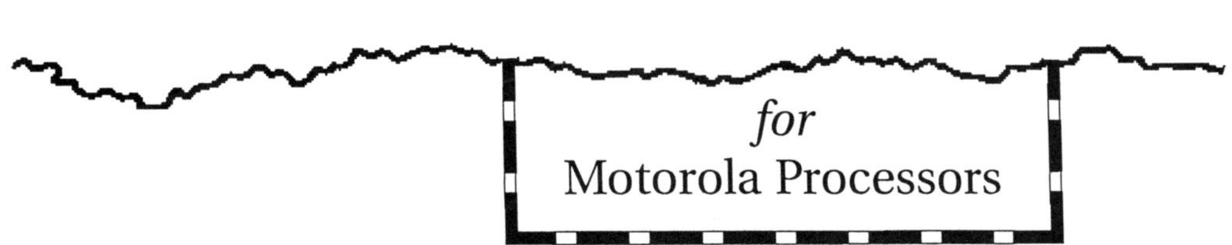

Published by PTR Prentice-Hall, Inc.
A Simon & Schuster Company
Englewood Cliffs, New Jersey 07632

10 9 8 7 6 5 4 3

Table of Contents

Commands(1) and Miscellaneous Facilities(5)

Commands Reference Manual

Introduction

Reference Manuals

Description

Manual pages provide technical reference information about the interfaces and execution behavior of each UNIX SYSTEM V Release 4 component.

Organization

The *type* of component being described is indicated by the numerical section suffix. Within each section there may be subsections indicated by a single letter. Related sections are organized into reference manuals and alphabetized by name. The following table shows the contents of the reference manuals and their section suffixes.

Title and Contents	Sections
Commands Reference Manual Volumes 1 and 2	
General-purpose user commands	1
Basic networking commands	1C
Form and Menu Language Interpreter (FMLI)	1F
System maintenance commands	1M
Enhanced networking commands	1N
Miscellaneous reference information related to commands.	5
System Calls and Library Functions Reference Manual	
System calls	2
BSD system compatibility library	3
Standard C library	3C
Executable and linking format library	3E

Continued on next page

Reference Manuals, Continued

Contents	Sections
System Calls and Library Functions Reference Manual (continued)	
General-purpose library	3G
Math library	3M
Networking library	3N
Standard I/O library	3S
Specialized library	3X
Miscellaneous reference information related to programming.	5
System Files and Devices Reference Manual	
System file formats	4
Special files (devices)	7
Device Driver Interface/Driver - Kernel Interface Reference Manual	
Driver Data Definitions	D1
Driver Entry Point Routines	D2
Kernel Utility Routines	D3
Kernel Data Structures	D4
Kernel Defines	D5
Master Permuted Index	
Permuted index of all manual pages	All

Retitled Reference Manuals

Background Four reference manuals for this release have been restructured and/or retitled to more accurately describe their contents. The following table shows these changes.

Previous Titles	**Current Titles**	**Current Sections**
User's Reference Manual/ System Administrator's Reference Manual (Commands a - l) (Commands m - z)	*Commands Reference Manual* *(Volume 1, a - l)* *(Volume 2, m - z)*	1, 1C, 1F, 1M, 1N, 5
Programmer's Reference Manual: Operating System API Part 1: Programming Commands and System Calls Part 2: Functions	*System Calls and Library Functions Reference Manual*	2, 3, 3C, 3E, 3G, 3M, 3N, 3S, 3X, 5
System Files and Devices Reference Manual	*System Files and Devices Reference Manual (section 5 removed)*	4, 7
Permuted Index	*Master Permuted Index*	All

Manual Page Format

Main headings used

All UNIX manual pages have a common format. The following main headings are used:

Heading	Section Contents
NAME	Name of the component and brief statement of its purpose
SYNOPSIS	Syntax of the component
DESCRIPTION	General discussion of functionality
EXAMPLE	Example(s) of usage
FILES	File names built into the component
SEE ALSO	Cross-references to related components

Note: Not all manual pages use all headings.

Typographical Conventions

Style and conventions used

The following typographical and formatting conventions are used.

Convention	Indicates ...
`Constant width`	a literal that should be entered just as it appears
Italic	a substitutable argument
Square brackets around an argument [ ]	an optional argument
name or *file*	a file name
Ellipses ...	previous argument may be repeated

Argument beginning with
   - minus
   + plus
   = equal
	a flag argument

Permuted Index

Definition

A permuted index is an alphabetical listing of all the keywords in the **NAME** line of a manual page.

Certain common words are not considered keywords and are not recognized. In the example below, the common words *of*, *to*, and *the* are not recognized.

Example

The **NAME** line of the `adjtime`(2) manual page appears below.

adjtime(2)   **adjtime(2)**

NAME

`adjtime`- correct the time to allow synchronization of the system clock

The `adjtime`(2) entries from the permuted index are shown below. These entries appear in the a, c, and s sections of the permuted index respectively.

Remainder of **NAME** line	Keyword and **NAME** line	Manual Page
synchronization of the system/	adjtime correct the time to allow.	adjtime(2)
clock adjtime correct the time to	allow synchronization of the system . . .	adjtime(2)
allow synchronization of the system	clock adjtime correct the time to . . .	adjtime(2)
synchronization of the/ adjtime	correct the time to allow	adjtime(2)
adjtime correct the time to allow	synchronization of the system clock . . .	adjtime(2)
to allow synchronization of the	system clock / correct the time	adjtime(2)

Continued on next page

Permuted Index, Continued

**How a
permuted
index is
constructed**

The center column lists each keyword followed by all or a
portion of the **NAME** line, as space permits. The left column
lists the remainder of the **NAME** line. The right column
indicates the manual page being referenced.

Omitted words are indicated with a slash (/).

**Identification
of entries**

Manual page entries are identified with their section suffixes
shown in parentheses.

<u>Example</u>: man(1) and man(5)

Section suffixes eliminate confusion caused by duplication of
names among the sections.

**Master
Permuted
Index**

Each reference manual has a permuted index for the manual
pages contained in that book.

The *Master Permuted Index* covers all the manual pages of this
documentation library.

Request for Comment

Description

A Request for Comment (RFC) is a document that describes some aspect of networking technology. The RFCs cited in the **SEE ALSO** section of these manual pages are available in hard copy for a small fee from:

> Network Information System Center
> SRI International
> 333 Ravenswood Avenue
> Menlo Park, CA 94025
> 415-859-6387 fax: 415-859-6028
> email:`nisc@nisc.sri.com`

Online versions of RFCs

Online versions of the RFCs are available by `ftp` from `nic.ddn.mil`.To retrieve an on-line RFC, do the following:

Step	Action
1	Connect to the RFC host by entering: `ftp nic.ddn.mil` `user name:` anonymous `password:` guest

2	Retrieve the RFC by entering:
	`get rfc/rfc`*num*
	
	`where `*num*` is the number of the RFC`
	
	<u>Example</u>:
	`get rfc:rfc1171.txt`

3	End the `ftp` session by entering: `quit`

NAME

Uutry - try to contact remote system with debugging on

SYNOPSIS

/usr/lib/uucp/Uutry [*options*] *system_name*

DESCRIPTION

Uutry is a shell that is used to invoke uucico to call a remote site. Debugging is initially turned on and is set to the default value of 5. The debugging output is put in file /tmp/*system_name*. Here are the options:

-c*type*   The first field in the Devices file is the "Type" field. The -c option forces uucico to only use entries in the "Type" field that match the user specified *type*. The specified *type* is usually the name of a local area network.

-r   This option overrides the retry time that is set in file /var/uucp/.Status/*system_name*.

-x*debug_level*
             debug_level is a number from 0 to 9. Higher numbers give more detailed debugging information.

FILES

/etc/uucp/Systems
/etc/uucp/Permissions
/etc/uucp/Devices
/etc/uucp/Limits
/var/spool/uucp/*
/var/spool/locks/*
/var/spool/uucppublic/*
/tmp/system_name

SEE ALSO

uucico(1M), uucp(1C), uux(1C).

NAME

m323rd - read disk resident manufacturer's bad track list (For M68K only)

SYNOPSIS

m323rd -L *maxcylinder heads maxbads file rawdevice*

m323rd -l *maxcylinder heads maxbads file rawdevice*

DESCRIPTION

The MVME323 devices have a manufacturer's bad track list on the disk in addition to the one written by the dinit(1M) utility. This command is used to read the manufacturer's list from the disk and write it to *file*. (The MVME323 devices are supported only on the M68000 family of processors.)

The L option writes the bad track list in *head/cylinder* format. The l option writes the bad track list in *head/cylinder/bfi* (bytes from index) format.

maxcylinder   is the maximum number of cylinders. Typically the last cylinder contains the manufacturer's defect list.

heads   is the number of surfaces per drive.

maxbads   is the maximum number of bad spots that are allowable on the disk.

file   is the name of the bad track file to create after reading the manufacturer's list.

rawdevice   is the name of the device for the selected drive, for example, /dev/rdsk/m328_c8d0s7 for drive 0.

SEE ALSO

dinit(1M), ddefs(1M).

NAME

m332xctl - a control utility

SYNOPSIS

m332xctl {-t|-r|-R|-D|-h< on|off|info> |-g| -s|[-d<*dlfile*> {-x<*sname*>
]...-l|-e<*fname*> }}dev

DESCRIPTION

m332xctl provides a functional control interface to the MVME332XT Communications Controller. Note that m332xctl provides no support for the MVME332 hardware and firmware architecture. The following options and fields are interpreted by m332xctl:

-t   Test the existence of the MVME332XT. Return if it exists, else return ENXIO.

-r   Get firmware and driver version and revision numbers. The designated dev should be the printer device.

-R   Get firmware version number in short format. The designated dev should be the printer device.

-D   Debug mode.

-g   Get downloadable area information from the MVME332XT controller. The address and size of the download area is displayed. The designated dev should be the printer device.

-s   Get symbol table of the MVME332XT firmware and display. The designated dev should be the printer device.

-h   Hardware flow control handshaking can be enabled or disabled, and hardware flow control port status can be queried. Hardware flow control is implemented with the RS232C RTS and CTS handshakes. The default is disabled.

-d   Download a coff file to the MVME332XT. The designated dev should be the printer device.

-x   Exclude a section when downloading. Up to sixteen sections may be excluded for a particular download operation. This option must be preceded by the -d option in the command invocation.

-l   Instruct the MVME332XT firmware to copy the the download line switch table to its internal data structure. This option must be preceded by the -d option in the command invocation.

-e   Instruct the MVME332XT firmware to execute a user function in a downloaded file. This option must be preceded by the -d option in the command invocation.

dev   MVME332XT serial I/O or printer device. dev should be the printer device for the -g, -d, -r, -R, -s, -l, and -x options.

dlfile   Coff compatible file that is to be linked to the MVME332XT symbol table before downloading.

sname Section names to be excluded when *dlfile* is downloaded.

fname Function within the *dlfile* that is to be executed.

To obtain the MVME332XT firmware version and revision number, execute the following `m332xctl` command, x is the controller number in `cxd8`:

```
m332xctl -R /dev/printer/m332_cxd8
```

This command issues a message of the form:
> *VR*

where *V* and *R* are the MVME332XT firmware version and revision numbers, respectively. For example, "129" would be 12.9.

The `m332xctl` command

```
m332xctl -h on /dev/port/m332_cxdy
```

enables hardware flow control option for the specified serial I/O port. The I/O device to be set is designated by the *cxdy* field throughout this document, where *x* and *y* refer to the MVME332XT controller and port device numbers, respectively.

Hardware flow control for any MVME332XT serial port may be disabled by issuing

```
m332xctl -h off /dev/port/m332_cxdy
```

Hardware flow control is implemented with the RS-232 RTS/CTS signal pairs. In this mode, a serial port transmitter is disabled when its CTS input negates and a receiver negates its RTS output when the associated receive channel character high water mark has been reached. A MVME332XT serial port hardware flow control configuration may be determined with the following `m332xctl` command.

```
m332xctl -h info /dev/port/m332_cxdy
```

In this example, if hardware flow control is enabled for the specified port, the following message will be sent to standard output.

```
hardware handshake is enabled
```

If hardware flow control is disabled for the specified port, the following message will be sent to standard output:

```
hardware handshake is disabled
```

To get the start address and size of the MVME332XT download area, use the following `m332xctl` command:

```
m332xctl -g /dev/printer/m332_cxd8
```

where `/dev/printer/m332_cxd8` must be the MVME332XT printer device. This restricts downloading and download area information access to `root`.

The following information is displayed in response to the previous command:

```
Downloadable area start address = AAAA, size = SSSS
```

The downloadable `coff` file should be linked to the displayed start address before downloading to the MVME332XT firmware, using the following syntax:

```
m332xctl -d dlfile /dev/printer/m332_cxd8
```

where *dlfile* is the `coff` file to be downloaded and `/dev/printer/m332_cxd8` is the

MVME332XT printer device name, required for security purposes.

To exclude sections of *dlfile* during the download operation, use

```
m332xctl    -d    dlfile    -x    sname1    ...    -x    snamen
/dev/printer/m332_cxd8
```

where *sname1*, ..., and *snamen* are the section names that are to be excluded during the download operation. The `m332xctl` command supports up to 16 excluded section names using the syntax shown.

The MVME332XT firmware supports user supplied line disciplines via the `m332xctl -d` and `-l` options, which allow the downloaded line switch table to be copied to the MVME332XT firmware data structures, as follows:

```
m332xctl -d dlfile -l /dev/printer/m332_cxd8
```

where *dlfile* is the download file name and `/dev/printer/m332_cxd8` is the MVME332XT printer device special file name, as before. The downloaded *dlfile* must contain the following symbols:

Symbol	Description
-linetable:	Linesw lineswitch table
-linecount:	Number of lines to be downloaded

Refer to `mvme332xt`(7) for discussion regarding linesw table structure. Notice that the linesw table structure defined in `mvme332xt`(7) differs from that described in `/usr/include/sys/conf.h`. Intimate familiarity with the MVME332XT firmware architecture is required to successfully port a user developed line discipline.

To download a `coff` file, *dlfile*, to the MVME332XT and execute a downloaded function, *fname*, use the following syntax:

```
m332xctl -d dlfile -e fname /dev/printer/m332_cxd8
```

where *dlfile* is the downloaded file, *fname* is the function to be executed by the MVME332XT firmware, and `/dev/printer/m332_cxd8` is the MVME332XT printer device name. Refer to `mvme332xt`(7) for more information regarding special file naming conventions.

The `-D` option enables the debug mode. Option `-DD` enables the debug mode at level 2, which results in more comprehensive debug messages. Either mode is useful for monitoring a downloading operation and for debugging user developed lineswitch and function routines.

FILES

```
/dev/port/m332_c*d*,  /dev/printer/m332_c*d8
```

SEE ALSO

`stty`(1), `ioctl`(2), `mvme332xt`(7). `termio`(7), `tty`(7).
MVME332XT Serial Intelligent Peripheral Controller Firmware User's Manual.

NAME

m4 - macro processor

SYNOPSIS

m4 [*options*] [*files*]

DESCRIPTION

The m4 command is a macro processor intended as a front end for C, assembler, and other languages. Each of the argument files is processed in order; if there are no files, or if a file name is -, the standard input is read. The processed text is written on the standard output.

The options and their effects are as follows:

-e
Operate interactively. Interrupts are ignored and the output is unbuffered.

-s
Enable line sync output for the C preprocessor (#line ...)

-B*int*
Change the size of the push-back and argument collection buffers from the default of 4,096.

-H*int*
Change the size of the symbol table hash array from the default of 199. The size should be prime.

-S*int*
Change the size of the call stack from the default of 100 slots. Macros take three slots, and non-macro arguments take one.

-T*int*
Change the size of the token buffer from the default of 512 bytes.

To be effective, the above flags must appear before any file names and before any -D or -U flags:

-D*name*[=*val*]
Defines *name* to *val* or to null in *val*'s absence.

-U*name*
undefines *name*.

Macro calls have the form:

name(*arg1,arg2,. . ., argn*)

The (must immediately follow the name of the macro. If the name of a defined macro is not followed by a (, it is deemed to be a call of that macro with no arguments. Potential macro names consist of alphanumeric characters and underscore (_), where the first character is not a digit.

Leading unquoted blanks, tabs, and new-lines are ignored while collecting arguments. Left and right single quotes are used to quote strings. The value of a quoted string is the string stripped of the quotes.

When a macro name is recognized, its arguments are collected by searching for a matching right parenthesis. If fewer arguments are supplied than are in the macro definition, the trailing arguments are taken to be null. Macro evaluation proceeds normally during the collection of the arguments, and any commas or right parentheses that happen to turn up within the value of a nested call are as effective as those in the original input text. After argument collection, the value of the macro is pushed back onto the input stream and rescanned.

m4 makes available the following built-in macros. These macros may be redefined, but once this is done the original meaning is lost. Their values are null unless otherwise stated.

define	the second argument is installed as the value of the macro whose name is the first argument. Each occurrence of n in the replacement text, where n is a digit, is replaced by the n-th argument. Argument 0 is the name of the macro; missing arguments are replaced by the null string; $\# is replaced by the number of arguments; $* is replaced by a list of all the arguments separated by commas; $@ is like $*, but each argument is quoted (with the current quotes).
undefine	removes the definition of the macro named in its argument.
defn	returns the quoted definition of its argument(s). It is useful for renaming macros, especially built-ins.
pushdef	like define, but saves any previous definition.
popdef	removes current definition of its argument(s), exposing the previous one, if any.
ifdef	if the first argument is defined, the value is the second argument, otherwise the third. If there is no third argument, the value is null. The word unix is predefined.
shift	returns all but its first argument. The other arguments are quoted and pushed back with commas in between. The quoting nullifies the effect of the extra scan that will subsequently be performed.
changequote	change quote symbols to the first and second arguments. The symbols may be up to five characters long. changequote without arguments restores the original values (that is, ` ´).
changecom	change left and right comment markers from the default # and new-line. With no arguments, the comment mechanism is effectively disabled. With one argument, the left marker becomes the argument and the right marker becomes new-line. With two arguments, both markers are affected. Comment markers may be up to five characters long.
divert	m4 maintains 10 output streams, numbered 0-9. The final output is the concatenation of the streams in numerical order; initially stream 0 is the current stream. The divert macro changes the current output stream to its (digit-string) argument. Output diverted to a stream other than 0 through 9 is discarded.
undivert	causes immediate output of text from diversions named as arguments, or all diversions if no argument. Text may be undiverted into another diversion. Undiverting discards the diverted text.
divnum	returns the value of the current output stream.
dnl	reads and discards characters up to and including the next new-line.

ifelse

has three or more arguments. If the first argument is the same string as the second, then the value is the third argument. If not, and if there are more than four arguments, the process is repeated with arguments 4, 5, 6 and 7. Otherwise, the value is either the fourth string, or, if it is not present, null.

incr

returns the value of its argument incremented by 1. The value of the argument is calculated by interpreting an initial digit-string as a decimal number.

decr

returns the value of its argument decremented by 1.

eval

evaluates its argument as an arithmetic expression, using 32-bit arithmetic. Operators include +, -, *, /, %, ** (exponentiation), bit-wise &, |, ^, and ~; relationals; parentheses. Octal and hex numbers may be specified as in C. The second argument specifies the radix for the result; the default is 10. The third argument may be used to specify the minimum number of digits in the result.

len

returns the number of characters in its argument.

index

returns the position in its first argument where the second argument begins (zero origin), or -1 if the second argument does not occur.

substr

returns a substring of its first argument. The second argument is a zero origin number selecting the first character; the third argument indicates the length of the substring. A missing third argument is taken to be large enough to extend to the end of the first string.

translit

transliterates the characters in its first argument from the set given by the second argument to the set given by the third. No abbreviations are permitted.

include

returns the contents of the file named in the argument.

sinclude

is identical to include, except that it says nothing if the file is inaccessible.

syscmd

executes the UNIX System command given in the first argument. No value is returned.

sysval

is the return code from the last call to syscmd.

maketemp

fills in a string of XXXXX in its argument with the current process ID.

m4exit

causes immediate exit from m4. Argument 1, if given, is the exit code; the default is 0.

m4wrap

argument 1 will be pushed back at final EOF; example: m4wrap(`cleanup()')

errprint

prints its argument on the diagnostic output file.

dumpdef

prints current names and definitions, for the named items, or for all if no arguments are given.

traceon
: with no arguments, turns on tracing for all macros (including built-ins). Otherwise, turns on tracing for named macros.

traceoff
: turns off trace globally and for any macros specified. Macros specifically traced by traceon can be untraced only by specific calls to traceoff.

INTERNATIONAL FUNCTIONS

m4 can process characters from supplementary code sets. Characters from supplementary code sets can be included in comments and literals in the given C program.

SEE ALSO

as(1), cc(1)

NAME
    `mach` - display the processor type of the current host

SYNOPSIS
    `/usr/ucb/mach`

DESCRIPTION
    The `mach` command displays the processor-type of the current host.

SEE ALSO
    `arch`(1), `machid`(1), `uname`(1), `uname`(2), `sysinfo`(2).

NAME

`machid`: `m68k`, `m88k`, `pdp11`, `u3b`, `u3b5`, `u3b15`, `vax`, `u370` - get processor type truth value

SYNOPSIS

`u3b`

`u3b2`

`u3b5`

`u3b15`

`m68k`

`m88k`

`pdp11`

`vax`

`u370`

DESCRIPTION

The following commands will return a true value (exit code of 0) if you are on a processor that the command name indicates.

`m68k`	True if you are on a M68000 family of processors computer.
`m88k`	True if you are on a M88000 family of processors computer.
`pdp11`	True if you are on a PDP-11/45™ or PDP-11/70™.
`u3b`	True if you are on a 3B20 computer.
`u3b2`	True if you are on a 3B2 computer.
`u3b5`	True if you are on a 3B5 computer.
`u3b15`	True if you are on a 3B15 computer.
`vax`	True if you are on a VAX-11/750™ or VAX-11/780™.
`u370`	True if you are on an IBM® System/370™ computer.

The commands that do not apply will return a false (non-zero) value. These commands are often used within makefiles [see `make`(1)] and shell procedures [see `sh`(1)] to increase portability.

SEE ALSO

`sh`(1), `test`(1), `true`(1), `uname`, `make`(1)

NOTES

The `machid` family of commands is obsolescent. Use `uname -p` and `uname -m` instead.

NAME

   mail, rmail - read mail or send mail to users

SYNOPSIS

Sending mail:

   mail [-tw] [-m *message_type*] *recipient* . . .

   rmail [-tw] [-m *message_type*] *recipient* . . .

Reading mail:

   mail [-ehpPqr] [-f *file*]

Forwarding mail:

   mail -F *recipient* . . .

Debugging:

   mail [-x*debug_level*] [*other_mail_options*] *recipient* . . .

   mail -T *mailsurr_file recipient* . . .

DESCRIPTION

A *recipient* is usually a user name recognized by login(1). When *recipients* are named, mail assumes a message is being sent (except in the case of the -F option). It reads from the standard input up to an end-of-file (CTRL-d) or, if reading from a terminal device, until it reads a line consisting of just a period. When either of those indicators is received, mail adds the *letter* to the *mailfile* for each *recipient*.

A *letter* is composed of some *header lines* followed by a blank line followed by the *message content*. The *header lines* section of the letter consists of one or more UNIX postmarks:

   From *sender date_and_time* [remote from *remote_system_name*]

followed by one or more standardized message header lines of the form:

   keyword-name : [*printable text*]

where *keyword-name* is comprised of any printable, non-whitespace, characters other than colon (':'). A Content-Length: header line, indicating the number of bytes in the *message content* will always be present. A Content-Type: header line that describes the type of the *message content* (such as text, binary, multipart, and so on) will always be present unless the letter consists of only header lines with no message content. Header lines may be continued on the following line if that line starts with white space.

Sending mail:

The following command-line arguments affect SENDING mail:

-m	causes a Message-Type: line to be added to the message header with the value of *message_type*.
-t	causes a To: line to be added to the message header for each of the intended recipients.
-w	causes a letter to be sent to a remote recipient without waiting for the completion of the remote transfer program.

If a letter is found to be undeliverable, it is returned to the sender with diagnostics that indicate the location and nature of the failure. If mail is interrupted during input, the message is saved in the file dead.letter to allow editing and resending. dead.letter is always appended to, thus preserving any previous contents. The initial attempt to append to (or create) dead.letter will be in the current directory. If this fails, dead.letter will be appended to (or created in) the user's login directory. If the second attempt also fails, no dead.letter processing will be done.

rmail only permits the sending of mail; uucp(1C) uses rmail as a security precaution. Any application programs that generate mail messages should be sure to invoke rmail rather than mail for message transport and/or delivery.

If the local system has the Basic Networking Utilities installed, mail may be sent to a recipient on a remote system. There are numerous ways to address mail to recipients on remote systems depending on the transport mechanisms available to the local system. The two most prevalent addressing schemes are UUCP-style and Domain-style. With UUCP-style addressing, remote recipients are specified by prefixing the recipient name with the remote system name and an exclamation point (such as sysa!user). A series of system names separated by exclamation points can be used to direct a letter through an extended network (such as sysa!sysb!sysc!user). With Domain-style addressing, remote recipients are specified by appending an '@' and domain (and possibly sub-domain) information to the recipient name (such as user@sf.att.com). (The local System Administrator should be consulted for details on which addressing conventions are available on the local system.)

Reading Mail:

The following command-line arguments affect READING mail:

-e   causes mail not to be printed. An exit value of 0 is returned if the user has mail; otherwise, an exit value of 1 is returned.

-h   causes a window of headers to be initially displayed rather than the latest message. The display is followed by the '?' prompt.

-p   causes all messages to be printed without prompting for disposition.

-P   causes all messages to be printed with *all* header lines displayed, rather than the default selective header line display.

-q   causes mail to terminate after interrupts. Normally an interrupt causes only the termination of the message being printed.

-r   causes messages to be printed in first-in, first-out order.

-f *file* causes mail to use *file* (such as mbox) instead of the default *mailfile*.

mail, unless otherwise influenced by command-line arguments, prints a user's mail messages in last-in, first-out order. The default mode for printing messages is to display only those header lines of immediate interest. These include, but are not limited to, the UNIX From and >From postmarks, From:, Date:, Subject:, and Content-Length: header lines, and any recipient header lines such as To:, Cc:, Bcc:, and so on. After the header lines have been displayed, mail will display the contents (body) of the message only if it contains no unprintable characters. Otherwise, mail will issue a warning statement about the message having binary content and not display the content. (This may be overridden via the p command. See below.)

For each message, the user is prompted with a ?, and a line is read from the standard input. The following commands are available to determine the disposition of the message:

#	Print the number of the current message.
–	Print previous message.
<new-line>, +, or n	Print the next message.
! *command*	Escape to the shell to do *command*.
a	Print message that arrived during the mail session.
d, or dp	Delete the current message and print the next message.
d *n*	Delete message number *n*. Do not go on to next message.
dq	Delete message and quit mail.
h	Display a window of headers around current message.
h *n*	Display a window of headers around message number *n*.
h a	Display headers of all messages in the user's *mailfile*.
h d	Display headers of messages scheduled for deletion.
m [*persons*]	Mail (and delete) the current message to the named *person(s)*.
n	Print message number *n*.
p	Print current message again, overriding any indications of binary (that is, unprintable) content.
P	Override default brief mode and print current message again, displaying all header lines.
q, or CTRL-D	Put undeleted mail back in the *mailfile* and quit mail.
r [*users*]	Reply to the sender, and other *user(s)*, then delete the message.
s [*files*]	Save message in the named *file(s)* (mbox is default) and delete the message.
u [*n*]	Undelete message number *n* (default is last read).
w [*files*]	Save message contents, without any header lines, in the named *files* (mbox is default) and delete the message.
x	Put all mail back in the *mailfile* unchanged and exit mail.
y [*files*]	Same as save.
?	Print a command summary.

When a user logs in, the presence of mail, if any, is usually indicated. Also, notification is made if new mail arrives while using mail.

The permissions of *mailfile* may be manipulated using chmod in two ways to alter the function of mail. The other permissions of the file may be read-write (0666), read-only (0664), or neither read nor write (0660) to allow different levels of privacy. If changed to other than the default (mode 0660), the file will be preserved even when empty to perpetuate the desired permissions. (The administrator may override this file preservation using the DEL_EMPTY_MAILFILE option of mailcnfg.)

The group id of the mailfile must be `mail` to allow new messages to be delivered, and the mailfile must be writable by group `mail`.

Forwarding mail:

The following command-line argument affects FORWARDING of mail:

`-F` *recipients*   Causes all incoming mail to be forwarded to *recipients*. The mailbox must be empty.

The `-F` option causes the *mailfile* to contain a first line of:

    Forward to *recipient* . . .

Thereafter, all mail sent to the owner of the *mailfile* will be forwarded to each *recipient*.

An `Auto-Forwarded-From: . . .` line will be added to the forwarded message's header. This is especially useful in a multi-machine environment to forward all a person's mail to a single machine, and to keep the recipient informed if the mail has been forwarded.

Installation and removal of forwarding is done with the `-F` invocation option. To forward all your mail to `systema!user` enter:

    mail -F systema!user

To forward to more than one recipient enter:

    mail -F "user1,user2@att.com,systemc!systemd!user3"

Note that when more than one recipient is specified, the entire list should be enclosed in double quotes so that it may all be interpreted as the operand of the `-F` option. The list can be up to 1024 bytes; either commas or white space can be used to separate users.

If the first character of any forwarded-to recipient name is the pipe symbol (`'|'`), the remainder of the line will be interpreted as a command to pipe the current mail message to. The command, known as a *Personal Surrogate*, will be executed in the environment of the recipient of the message (that is, basename of the *mailfile*). For example, if the mailfile is `/var/mail/foo`, `foo` will be looked up in `/etc/passwd` to determine the correct userID, groupID, and `HOME` directory. The command's environment will be set to contain only `HOME`, `LOGNAME`, `TZ`, `PATH` (= `/usr/usr/bin:`), and `SHELL` (= `/usr/bin/sh`), and the command will execute in the recipient's `HOME` directory. If the message recipient cannot be found in `/etc/passwd`, the command will not be executed and a non-delivery notification with appropriate diagnostics will be sent to the message's originator.

After the pipe symbol, escaped double quotes should be used to have strings with embedded whitespace be considered as single arguments to the command being executed. No shell syntax or metacharacters may be used unless the command specified is `/usr/bin/sh`. For example,

    mail -F "|/bin/sh -c \"shell_command_line\""

will work, but is not advised since using double quotes and backslashes within the shell_command_line is difficult to do correctly and becomes tedious very quickly.

Certain %keywords are allowed within the piped-to command specification and will be textually substituted for *before* the command line is executed.

%R   Return path to the message originator.
%c   Value of the `Content-Type:` header line if present.
%S   Value of the `Subject:` header line if present.

If the command being piped to exits with any non-zero value, `mail` will assume that message delivery failed and will generate a non-delivery notification to the message's originator. It is allowable to forward mail to other recipients and pipe it to a command, as in

```
mail -F "carol,joe,|myvacationprog %R"
```

Two UNIX System facilities that use the forwarding of messages to commands are `notify`(1), which causes asynchronous notification of new mail, and `vacation`(1), which provides an auto-answer capability for messages when the recipient will be unavailable for an extended period of time.

To remove forwarding enter:

```
mail -F ""
```

The pair of double quotes is mandatory to set a NULL argument for the -F option.

In order for forwarding to work properly the *mailfile* should have `mail` as group ID, and the group permission should be read-write.

`mail` will exit with a return code of 0 if forwarding was successfully installed or removed.

Debugging:

The following command-line arguments cause `mail` to provide DEBUGGING information:

-T *mailsurr_file*   causes `mail` to display how it will parse and interpret the `mailsurr` file.

-x*debug_level*   causes `mail` to create a trace file containing debugging information.

The -T option requires an argument that will be taken as the pathname of a test `mailsurr` file. If NULL (as in -T ""), the system `mailsurr` file will be used. To use, type 'mail -T *test_file recipient*' and some trivial message (like "testing"), followed by a line with either just a dot ('.') or a CTRL-D. The result of using the -T option will be displayed on standard output and show the inputs and resulting transformations as `mailsurr` is processed by the `mail` command for the indicated recipient. Mail messages will never actually be sent or delivered when the -T option is used.

The -x option causes `mail` to create a file named `/tmp/MLDBG`*process_id* that contains debugging information relating to how `mail` processed the current message. The absolute value of *debug_level* controls the verboseness of the debug information. Zero implies no debugging. If *debug_level* is greater than zero, the debug file will be retained `only` if `mail` encountered some problem while processing the message. If *debug_level* is less than zero the debug file will always be retained. The *debug_level* specified via -x overrides any specification of DEBUG in `/etc/mail/mailcnfg`. The information provided by the -x option is esoteric and is probably only useful to System Administrators. The output produced by the -x option is a superset of that provided by the -T option.

Delivery Notification

Several forms of notification are available for mail by including one of the following lines in the message header.

```
Transport-Options: [ /options ]
Default-Options: [ /options ]
>To: recipient [ /options ]
```

where the "/options" may be one or more of the following:

/delivery   Inform the sender that the message was successfully delivered to the *recipient*'s mailbox.

/nodelivery Do not inform the sender of successful deliveries.

/ignore   Do not inform the sender of unsuccessful deliveries.

/return   Inform the sender if mail delivery fails. Return the failed message to the sender.

/report   Same as /return except that the original message is not returned.

The default is /nodelivery/return. If contradictory options are used, the first will be recognized and later, conflicting, terms will be ignored.

FILES

dead.letter	unmailable text
/etc/passwd	to identify sender and locate recipients
/etc/mail/mailsurr	routing / name translation information
/etc/mail/mailcnfg	initialization information
$HOME/mbox	saved mail
$MAIL	variable containing path name of *mailfile*
/tmp/ma*	temporary file
/tmp/MLDBG*	debug trace file
/var/mail/*.lock	lock for mail directory
/var/mail/:saved	directory for holding temp files to prevent loss of data in the event of a system crash.
/var/mail/*user*	incoming mail for *user*; that is, the *mailfile*

SEE ALSO

chmod(1), login(1), mailx(1), notify(1), write(1), vacation(1), vacation_bsd(1), mail_pipe(1M), mailsurr(4), mailcnfg(4).

NOTES

The "Forward to recipient" feature may result in a loop. Local loops (messages sent to usera, which are forwarded to userb, which are forwarded to usera) will be detected immediately. Remote loops (mail sent to sys1!usera1 which is forwarded to sys2!userb, which is forwarded to sys1!usera) will also be detected, but only after the message has exceeded the built-in hop count limit of 20. Both cases of forwarding loops will result in a non-delivery notification being sent to the message originator.

As a security precaution, the equivalent of a `chmod s+g` is performed on the *mailfile* whenever forwarding is activated via the `-F` option, and a `chmod s-g` is done when forwarding is removed via the `-F` option. If the setGID mode bit is not set when `mail` attempts to forward an incoming message to a command, the operation will fail and a non-delivery report with appropriate diagnostics will be sent to the message's originator.

The interpretation and resulting action taken because of the header lines described in the Delivery Notifications section above will only occur if this version of `mail` is installed on the system where the delivery (or failure) happens. Earlier versions of `mail` may not support any types of delivery notification.

Conditions sometimes result in a failure to remove a lock file.

After an interrupt, the next message may not be printed; printing may be forced by typing a p.

NAME

mail_pipe - invoke recipient command for incoming mail

SYNOPSIS

mail_pipe [-x *debug_level*] -r *recipient* -R *path_to_sender* -c *content_type*
-S *subject*

DESCRIPTION

When a new mail message arrives, the mail command first checks if the recipient's mailbox indicates that the message is to be forwarded elsewhere (to some other recipient or as the input to some command). If the message is to be piped into a recipient-specified command, mail invokes mail_pipe to do some validation and then execute the command in the context of the recipient.

Command-line arguments are:

-x *debug_level*	Turn on debugging for this invocation. See the description of the -x option for the mail command for details.
-r *recipient*	The recipient's login id.
-R *path_to_sender*	The return address to the message's originator.
-c *content_type*	The value of the Content-Type: header line in the message.
-S *subject*	The value of the Subject: header line in the message if present.

mail_pipe is installed as a setuid-to-root process, thus enabling itself to change it's user and group ids to that of the recipient as necessary.

When invoked, mail_pipe performs the following steps (if a step fails, the exit code is noted as [N]):

- Validate invocation arguments [1].
- Verify that recipient name is ≤ 14 characters long [2].
- Verify that the setgid flag for the recipient mailbox is set [3].
- Open /var/mail/*recipient* [4].
- Verify that recipient's mailbox starts with the string Forward to [5].
- Find pipe symbol indicating start of command string in recipient mailbox [6].
- Find entry for recipient in /etc/passwd [7].
- Set gid to recipient's gid [8].
- Set uid to recipient's uid [9].
- Change current directory to recipient's login directory [10].
- Allocate space to hold newly exec'ed environment for recipient command [11].
- Parse the recipient command, performing any *%keyword* expansions required. See the 'Forwarding mail' section of mail(1), for more information regarding *%keyword* substitutions [12].
- Execute recipient command [13 if exec fails, otherwise exit code from recipient command itself].

FILES

`/etc/passwd`	to identify sender and locate recipients
`/var/mail/`*recipient*	incoming mail for *recipient*; that is, the mail file
`/tmp/MLDBG*`	debug trace file
`/usr/lib/mail/mail_pipe`	mail_pipe program

SEE ALSO

mail(1), notify(1), vacation(1)

NAME

`mailalias` - translate mail alias names

SYNOPSIS

`mailalias` [`-s`] [`-v`] *name* ...

DESCRIPTION

`mailalias` is called by `mail`. It places on the standard output a list of mail addresses corresponding to *name*. The mail addresses are found by performing the following steps:

1. Look for a match in the user's local alias file `$HOME/lib/names`. If a line is found beginning with the word *name*, print the rest of the line on standard output and exit.

2. Look for a match in the system-wide alias files, which are listed in the master path file `/etc/mail/namefiles`. If a line is found beginning with the word *name*, print the rest of the line on standard output and exit. If an alias file is a directory name *dir*, then search the file *dir/name*. By default, the file `/etc/mail/namefiles` lists the directory `/etc/mail/lists` and the file `/etc/mail/names`.

3. Otherwise print *name* and exit.

The alias files may contain comments (lines beginning with #) and information lines of the form:

> *name list-of-addresses*

Tokens on these lines are separated by white-space. Lines may be continued by placing a backslash (\) at the end of the line.

If the `-s` option is not specified and more than one name is being translated, each line of output will be prefixed with the name being translated.

The `-v` option causes debugging information to be written to standard output.

FILES

`$HOME/lib/names`	private aliases
`/etc/mail/namefiles`	list of files to search
`/etc/mail/names`	standard file to search

SEE ALSO

`uucp`(1), `mail`(1)
`smtp`(1M), `smtpd`(1M), `smtpqer`(1M), `smtpsched`(1M), `tosmtp`(1M).

NAME

`mailstats` - print statistics collected by sendmail

SYNOPSIS

`/usr/ucb/mailstats` [*filename*]

DESCRIPTION

`mailstats` prints out the statistics collected by the `sendmail` program on mailer usage. These statistics are collected if the file indicated by the `S` configuration option of `sendmail` exists. `mailstats` first prints the time that the statistics file was created and the last time it was modified. It will then print a table with one row for each mailer specified in the configuration file. The first column is the mailer number, followed by the symbolic name of the mailer. The next two columns refer to the number of messages received by *sendmail*, and the last two columns refer to messages sent by *sendmail*. The number of messages and their total size (in 1024 byte units) is given. No numbers are printed if no messages were sent (or received) for any mailer.

You might want to add an entry to `/var/spool/cron/crontab/root` to reinitialize the statistics file once a night. Copy `/dev/null` into the statistics file or otherwise truncate it to reset the counters.

FILES

`/var/spool/cron/crontab/root`
`/dev/null`

SEE ALSO

`sendmail`(1M)

NOTES

`mailstats` should read the configuration file instead of having a hard-wired table mapping mailer numbers to names.

NAME

mailx - interactive message processing system

SYNOPSIS

mailx [*options*] [*name . . .*]

DESCRIPTION

The command mailx provides a comfortable, flexible environment for sending and receiving messages electronically. When reading mail, mailx provides commands to facilitate saving, deleting, and responding to messages. When sending mail, mailx allows editing, reviewing and other modification of the message as it is entered.

Many of the remote features of mailx work only if the Basic Networking Utilities are installed on your system.

Incoming mail is stored in a standard file for each user, called the mailbox for that user. When mailx is called to read messages, the mailbox is the default place to find them. As messages are read, they are marked to be moved to a secondary file for storage, unless specific action is taken, so that the messages need not be seen again. This secondary file is called the mbox and is normally located in the user's HOME directory [see MBOX (ENVIRONMENT VARIABLES) for a description of this file]. Messages can be saved in other secondary files named by the user. Messages remain in a secondary file until forcibly removed.

The user can access a secondary file by using the -f option of the mailx command. Messages in the secondary file can then be read or otherwise processed using the same COMMANDS as in the primary mailbox. This gives rise within these pages to the notion of a current mailbox.

On the command line, *options* start with a dash (-) and any other arguments are taken to be destinations (recipients). If no recipients are specified, mailx attempts to read messages from the mailbox. Command-line options are:

-d	Turn on debugging output.
-e	Test for presence of mail. mailx prints nothing and exits with a successful return code if there is mail to read.
-f [*filename*]	Read messages from *filename* instead of mailbox. If no *filename* is specified, the mbox is used.
-F	Record the message in a file named after the first recipient. Overrides the record variable, if set (see ENVIRONMENT VARIABLES).
-h *number*	The number of network "hops" made so far. This is provided for network software to avoid infinite delivery loops. This option and its argument is passed to the delivery program.
-H	Print header summary only.
-i	Ignore interrupts. See also ignore (ENVIRONMENT VARIABLES).

-I	Include the newsgroup and article-id header lines when printing mail messages. This option requires the -f option to be specified.
-n	Do not initialize from the system default *mailx.rc* file.
-N	Do not print initial header summary.
-r *address*	Use *address* as the return address when invoking the delivery program. All tilde commands are disabled. This option and its argument is passed to the delivery program.
-s *subject*	Set the Subject header field to *subject*.
-T *file*	Message-id and article-id header lines are recorded in *file* after the message is read. This option will also set the -I option.
-u *user*	Read *user*'s mailbox. This is only effective if *user*'s mailbox is not read protected.
-U	Convert uucp style addresses to internet standards. Overrides the conv environment variable.
-V	Print the mailx version number and exit.

When reading mail, mailx is in *command mode*. A header summary of the first several messages is displayed, followed by a prompt indicating mailx can accept regular commands (see COMMANDS below). When sending mail, mailx is in *input mode*. If no subject is specified on the command line, a prompt for the subject is printed. (A subject longer than 1024 characters causes mailx to print the message *mail: ERROR signal 10*; the mail will not be delivered.) As the message is typed, mailx reads the message and store it in a temporary file. Commands may be entered by beginning a line with the tilde (˜) escape character followed by a single command letter and optional arguments. See TILDE ESCAPES for a summary of these commands.

At any time, the behavior of mailx is governed by a set of *environment variables*. These are flags and valued parameters which are set and cleared via the set and unset commands. See ENVIRONMENT VARIABLES below for a summary of these parameters.

Recipients listed on the command line may be of three types: login names, shell commands, or alias groups. Login names may be any network address, including mixed network addressing. If mail is found to be undeliverable, an attempt is made to return it to the sender's *mailbox*. If the recipient name begins with a pipe symbol (|), the rest of the name is taken to be a shell command to pipe the message through. This provides an automatic interface with any program that reads the standard input, such as lp(1) for recording outgoing mail on paper. Alias groups are set by the alias command (see COMMANDS below) and are lists of recipients of any type.

Regular commands are of the form

    [*command*] [*msglist*] [*arguments*]

If no command is specified in *command mode*, print is assumed. In *input mode*, commands are recognized by the escape character, and lines not treated as commands are taken as input for the message.

Each message is assigned a sequential number, and there is at any time the notion of a current message, marked by a right angle bracket (>) in the header summary. Many commands take an optional list of messages (*msglist*) to operate on. The default for *msglist* is the current message. A *msglist* is a list of message identifiers separated by spaces, which may include:

n	Message number n.
.	The current message.
^	The first undeleted message.
$	The last message.
*	All messages.
n-m	An inclusive range of message numbers.
user	All messages from user.
/string	All messages with string in the subject line (case ignored).
:c	All messages of type c, where c is one of:

d	deleted messages
n	new messages
o	old messages
r	read messages
u	unread messages

Note that the context of the command determines whether this type of message specification makes sense.

Other arguments are usually arbitrary strings whose usage depends on the command involved. File names, where expected, are expanded via the normal shell conventions [see sh(1)]. Special characters are recognized by certain commands and are documented with the commands below.

At start-up time, `mailx` tries to execute commands from the optional system-wide file (`/etc/mail/mailx.rc`) to initialize certain parameters, then from a private start-up file (`$HOME/.mailrc`) for personalized variables. With the exceptions noted below, regular commands are legal inside start-up files. The most common use of a start-up file is to set up initial display options and alias lists. The following commands are not legal in the start-up file: !, Copy, edit, followup, Followup, hold, mail, preserve, reply, Reply, shell, and visual. An error in the start-up file causes the remaining lines in the file to be ignored. The `.mailrc` file is optional, and must be constructed locally.

COMMANDS

The following is a complete list of `mailx` commands:

! shell-command
     Escape to the shell. See SHELL (ENVIRONMENT VARIABLES).

comment
      Null command (comment). This may be useful in `.mailrc` files.

=   Print the current message number.

?   Prints a summary of commands.

alias *alias name* . . .
group *alias name* . . .
      Declare an alias for the given names. The names are substituted when *alias*
      is used as a recipient. Useful in the `.mailrc` file.

alternates *name* . . .
      Declares a list of alternate names for your login. When responding to a
      message, these names are removed from the list of recipients for the
      response. With no arguments, alternates prints the current list of alternate
      names. See also `allnet` (ENVIRONMENT VARIABLES).

cd [*directory*]
chdir [*directory*]
      Change directory. If *directory* is not specified, $HOME is used.

copy [*filename*]
copy [*msglist*] *filename*
      Copy messages to the file without marking the messages as saved. Other-
      wise equivalent to the save command.

Copy [*msglist*]
      Save the specified messages in a file whose name is derived from the author
      of the message to be saved, without marking the messages as saved. Other-
      wise equivalent to the Save command.

delete [*msglist*]
      Delete messages from the mailbox. If autoprint is set, the next message
      after the last one deleted is printed (see ENVIRONMENT VARIABLES).

discard [*header-field* . . .]
ignore [*header-field* . . .]
      Suppresses printing of the specified header fields when displaying mes-
      sages on the screen. Examples of header fields to ignore are status and cc.
      The fields are included when the message is saved. The Print and Type
      commands override this command. If no header is specified, the current list
      of header fields being ignored will be printed. See also the undiscard and
      unignore commands.

dp [*msglist*]
dt [*msglist*]
      Delete the specified messages from the mailbox and print the next message
      after the last one deleted. Roughly equivalent to a delete command fol-
      lowed by a print command.

echo *string* . . .
      Echo the given strings [like echo(1)].

edit [*msglist*]
> Edit the given messages. The messages are placed in a temporary file and the EDITOR variable is used to get the name of the editor (see ENVIRON-MENT VARIABLES). Default editor is ed(1).

exit
xit
> Exit from mailx, without changing the mailbox. No messages are saved in the mbox (see also quit).

file [*filename*]
folder [*filename*]
> Quit from the current file of messages and read in the specified file. Several special characters are recognized when used as file names, with the following substitutions:
>
> | | |
> |---|---|
> | % | the current mailbox. |
> | %*user* | the mailbox for *user*. |
> | # | the previous file. |
> | & | the current mbox. |
>
> Default file is the current mailbox.

folders
> Print the names of the files in the directory set by the folder variable (see ENVIRONMENT VARIABLES).

followup [*message*]
> Respond to a message, recording the response in a file whose name is derived from the author of the message. Overrides the record variable, if set. See also the Followup, Save, and Copy commands and outfolder (ENVIRONMENT VARIABLES).

Followup [*msglist*]
> Respond to the first message in the *msglist*, sending the message to the author of each message in the *msglist*. The subject line is taken from the first message and the response is recorded in a file whose name is derived from the author of the first message. See also the followup, Save, and Copy commands and outfolder (ENVIRONMENT VARIABLES).

from [*msglist*]
> Prints the header summary for the specified messages.

group *alias name* . . .
alias *alias name* . . .
> Declare an alias for the given names. The names are substituted when *alias* is used as a recipient. Useful in the .mailrc file.

headers [*message*]
> Prints the page of headers which includes the message specified. The screen variable sets the number of headers per page (see ENVIRONMENT VARIABLES). See also the z command.

help   Prints a summary of commands.

hold [*msglist*]

preserve [*msglist*]
>   Holds the specified messages in the `mailbox`.

if *s* | *r*
mail-commands
else
mail-commands
endif   Conditional execution, where *s* executes following *mail-commands*, up to an
>   else or endif, if the program is in *send* mode, and *r* causes the *mail-
>   commands* to be executed only in *receive* mode. Useful in the `.mailrc` file.

ignore [*header-field* ...]
discard [*header-field* ...]
>   Suppresses printing of the specified header fields when displaying mes-
>   sages on the screen. Examples of header fields to ignore are `status` and `cc`.
>   All fields are included when the message is saved. The `Print` and `Type` com-
>   mands override this command. If no header is specified, the current list of
>   header fields being ignored will be printed. See also the `undiscard` and
>   `unignore` commands.

list   Prints all commands available. No explanation is given.

mail *name* ...
>   Mail a message to the specified users.

Mail *name*
>   Mail a message to the specified user and record a copy of it in a file named
>   after that user.

mbox [*msglist*]
>   Arrange for the given messages to end up in the standard `mbox` save file
>   when `mailx` terminates normally. See MBOX (ENVIRONMENT VARIABLES)
>   for a description of this file. See also the `exit` and `quit` commands.

next [*message*]
>   Go to next message matching *message*. A *msglist* may be specified, but in
>   this case the first valid message in the list is the only one used. This is use-
>   ful for jumping to the next message from a specific user, since the name
>   would be taken as a command in the absence of a real command. See the
>   discussion of *msglist*s above for a description of possible message
>   specifications.

pipe [*msglist*] [*shell-command*]
| [*msglist*] [*shell-command*]
>   Pipe the message through the given *shell-command*. The message is treated
>   as if it were read. If no arguments are given, the current message is piped
>   through the command specified by the value of the `cmd` variable. If the
>   `page` variable is set, a form feed character is inserted after each message (see
>   ENVIRONMENT VARIABLES).

preserve [*msglist*]
hold [*msglist*]
>   Preserve the specified messages in the `mailbox`.

Print [*msglist*]
Type [*msglist*]
>   Print the specified messages on the screen, including all header fields. Over-
>   rides suppression of fields by the `ignore` command.

print [*msglist*]
type [*msglist*]
>   Print the specified messages. If `crt` is set, the messages longer than the
>   number of lines specified by the `crt` variable are paged through the com-
>   mand specified by the `PAGER` variable. The default command is `pg`(1) (see
>   ENVIRONMENT VARIABLES).

quit
>   Exit from `mailx`, storing messages that were read in `mbox` and unread mes-
>   sages in the `mailbox`. Messages that have been explicitly saved in a file are
>   deleted.

Reply [*msglist*]
Respond [*msglist*]
>   Send a response to the author of each message in the *msglist*. The subject
>   line is taken from the first message. If `record` is set to a file name, the
>   response is saved at the end of that file (see ENVIRONMENT VARIABLES).

reply [*message*]
respond [*message*]
>   Reply to the specified message, including all other recipients of the mes-
>   sage. If `record` is set to a file name, the response is saved at the end of that
>   file (see ENVIRONMENT VARIABLES).

Save [*msglist*]
>   Save the specified messages in a file whose name is derived from the author
>   of the first message. The name of the file is taken to be the author's name
>   with all network addressing stripped off. See also the `Copy`, `followup`, and
>   `Followup` commands and `outfolder` (ENVIRONMENT VARIABLES).

save [*filename*]
save [*msglist*] *filename*
>   Save the specified messages in the given file. The file is created if it does not
>   exist. The file defaults to `mbox`. The message is deleted from the `mailbox`
>   when `mailx` terminates unless `keepsave` is set (see also ENVIRONMENT
>   VARIABLES and the `exit` and `quit` commands).

set
set *name*
set *name=string*
set *name=number*
>   Define a variable called *name*. The variable may be given a null, string, or
>   numeric value. `Set` by itself prints all defined variables and their values.
>   See ENVIRONMENT VARIABLES for detailed descriptions of the `mailx` vari-
>   ables.

shell
>   Invoke an interactive shell [see also `SHELL` (ENVIRONMENT VARIABLES)].

size [*msglist*]

Print the size in characters of the specified messages.

source *filename*
>   Read commands from the given file and return to command mode.

top [*msglist*]
>   Print the top few lines of the specified messages. If the toplines variable is set, it is taken as the number of lines to print (see ENVIRONMENT VARI-ABLES). The default is 5.

touch [*msglist*]
>   Touch the specified messages. If any message in *msglist* is not specifically saved in a file, it is placed in the mbox, or the file specified in the MBOX environment variable, upon normal termination. See exit and quit.

Type [*msglist*]
Print [*msglist*]
>   Print the specified messages on the screen, including all header fields. Over-rides suppression of fields by the ignore command.

type [*msglist*]
print [*msglist*]
>   Print the specified messages. If crt is set, the messages longer than the number of lines specified by the crt variable are paged through the command specified by the PAGER variable. The default command is pg(1) (see ENVIRONMENT VARIABLES).

undelete [*msglist*]
>   Restore the specified deleted messages. Will only restore messages deleted in the current mail session. If autoprint is set, the last message of those restored is printed (see ENVIRONMENT VARIABLES).

undiscard *header-field* . . .
unignore *header-field* . . .
>   Remove the specified header fields from the list being ignored.

unset *name* . . .
>   Causes the specified variables to be erased. If the variable was imported from the execution environment (for example, a shell variable) then it can-not be erased.

version
>   Prints the current version.

visual [*msglist*]
>   Edit the given messages with a screen editor. The messages are placed in a temporary file and the VISUAL variable is used to get the name of the edi-tor (see ENVIRONMENT VARIABLES).

write [*msglist*] *filename*
>   Write the given messages on the specified file, minus the header and trailing blank line. Otherwise equivalent to the save command.

xit

exit   Exit from `mailx`, without changing the `mailbox`. No messages are saved in
the `mbox` (see also `quit`).

z[+ | -]
Scroll the header display forward or backward one screen-full. The number
of headers displayed is set by the `screen` variable (see ENVIRONMENT
VARIABLES).

TILDE ESCAPES

The following commands may be entered only from *input mode,* by beginning a line
with the tilde escape character (˜). See `escape` (ENVIRONMENT VARIABLES) for
changing this special character.

~! *shell-command*
Escape to the shell.

~.   Simulate end of file (terminate message input).

~ : *mail-command*
~_ *mail-command*
Perform the command-level request. Valid only when sending a message
while reading mail.

~?   Print a summary of tilde escapes.

~A   Insert the autograph string `Sign` into the message (see ENVIRONMENT VARI-
ABLES).

~a   Insert the autograph string `sign` into the message (see ENVIRONMENT VARI-
ABLES).

~b *names* . . .
Add the *name*s to the blind carbon copy (Bcc) list.

~c *names* . . .
Add the *name*s to the carbon copy (Cc) list.

~d   Read in the `dead.letter` file. See DEAD (ENVIRONMENT VARIABLES) for a
description of this file.

~e   Invoke the editor on the partial message. See also EDITOR (ENVIRONMENT
VARIABLES).

~f [*msglist*]
Forward the specified messages. The messages are inserted into the message without alteration.

~h   Prompt for Subject line and To, Cc, and Bcc lists. If the field is displayed
with an initial value, it may be edited as if you had just typed it.

~i *string*
Insert the value of the named variable into the text of the message. For
example, ˜A is equivalent to '˜i Sign'. Environment variables set and
exported in the shell are also accessible by ˜i.

~m [*msglist*]
Insert the specified messages into the letter, shifting the new text to the
right one tab stop. Valid only when sending a message while reading mail.

~p   Print the message being entered.

~q   Quit from input mode by simulating an interrupt. If the body of the message is not null, the partial message is saved in `dead.letter`. See DEAD (ENVIRONMENT VARIABLES) for a description of this file.

~r *filename*
~< *filename*
~< *!shell-command*
> Read in the specified file. If the argument begins with an exclamation point (!), the rest of the string is taken as an arbitrary shell command and is executed, with the standard output inserted into the message.

~s *string* . . .
> Set the subject line to *string*.

~t *names* . . .
> Add the given *names* to the To list.

~v   Invoke a preferred screen editor on the partial message. See also VISUAL (ENVIRONMENT VARIABLES).

~w *filename*
> Write the message into the given file, without the header.

~x   Exit as with ˜q except the message is not saved in `dead.letter`.

~ | *shell-command*
> Pipe the body of the message through the given *shell-command*. If the *shell-command* returns a successful exit status, the output of the command replaces the message.

ENVIRONMENT VARIABLES

The following are environment variables taken from the execution environment and are not alterable within `mailx`.

HOME=*directory*
> The user's base of operations.

MAILRC=*filename*
> The name of the start-up file. Default is `$HOME/.mailrc`.

The following variables are internal `mailx` variables. They may be imported from the execution environment or set via the `set` command at any time. The `unset` command may be used to erase variables.

allnet
> All network names whose last component (login name) match are treated as identical. This causes the *msglist* message specifications to behave similarly. Default is `noallnet`. See also the `alternates` command and the `metoo` variable.

append
> Upon termination, append messages to the end of the `mbox` file instead of prepending them. Default is `noappend`.

askcc   Prompt for the Cc list after the Subject is entered. Default is noaskcc.

askbcc
     Prompt for the Bcc list after the Subject is entered. Default is noaskbcc.

asksub
     Prompt for subject if it is not specified on the command line with the -s option. Enabled by default.

autoprint
     Enable automatic printing of messages after delete and undelete commands. Default is noautoprint.

bang   Enable the special-casing of exclamation points (!) in shell escape command lines as in vi(1). Default is nobang.

cmd=*shell-command*
     Set the default command for the pipe command. No default value.

conv=*conversion*
     Convert uucp addresses to the specified address style. The only valid conversion now is internet, which uses domain-style addressing. Conversion is disabled by default. See also the -U command-line option.

crt=*number*
     Pipe messages having more than *number* lines through the command specified by the value of the PAGER variable [pg(1) by default]. Disabled by default.

DEAD=*filename*
     The name of the file in which to save partial letters in case of untimely interrupt. Default is $HOME/dead.letter.

debug   Enable verbose diagnostics for debugging. Messages are not delivered. Default is nodebug.

dot   Take a period on a line by itself during input from a terminal as end-of-file. Default is nodot.

EDITOR=*shell-command*
     The command to run when the edit or ~e command is used. Default is ed(1).

escape=*c*
     Substitute *c* for the ~ escape character. Takes effect with next message sent.

folder=*directory*
     The directory for saving standard mail files. User-specified file names beginning with a plus (+) are expanded by preceding the file name with this directory name to obtain the real file name. If *directory* does not start with a slash (/), $HOME is prepended to it. In order to use the plus (+) construct on a mailx command line, folder must be an exported sh environment variable. There is no default for the folder variable. See also outfolder below.

header
     Enable printing of the header summary when entering mailx. Enabled by

default.

hold   Preserve all messages that are read in the `mailbox` instead of putting them in the standard `mbox` save file. Default is `nohold`.

ignore

Ignore interrupts while entering messages. Handy for noisy dial-up lines. Default is `noignore`.

ignoreeof

Ignore end-of-file during message input. Input must be terminated by a period (.) on a line by itself or by the ~. command. Default is `noig-noreeof`. See also `dot` above.

keep   When the `mailbox` is empty, truncate it to zero length instead of removing it. Disabled by default.

keepsave

Keep messages that have been saved in other files in the `mailbox` instead of deleting them. Default is `nokeepsave`.

MBOX=*filename*

The name of the file to save messages which have been read. The xit command overrides this function, as does saving the message explicitly in another file. Default is `$HOME/mbox`.

metoo If your login appears as a recipient, do not delete it from the list. Default is `nometoo`.

LISTER=*shell-command*

The command (and options) to use when listing the contents of the `folder` directory. The default is `ls(1)`.

onehop

When responding to a message that was originally sent to several recipients, the other recipient addresses are normally forced to be relative to the originating author's machine for the response. This flag disables alteration of the recipients' addresses, improving efficiency in a network where all machines can send directly to all other machines (for example, one hop away).

outfolder

Causes the files used to record outgoing messages to be located in the directory specified by the `folder` variable unless the path name is absolute. Default is `nooutfolder`. See `folder` above and the `Save`, `Copy`, `followup`, and `Followup` commands.

page   Used with the `pipe` command to insert a form feed after each message sent through the pipe. Default is `nopage`.

PAGER=*shell-command*

The command to use as a filter for paginating output. This can also be used to specify the options to be used. Default is `pg(1)`.

prompt=*string*

Set the *command mode* prompt to *string*. Default is "? ".

quiet Refrain from printing the opening message and version when entering `mailx`. Default is `noquiet`.

`record=`*filename*
Record all outgoing mail in *filename*. Disabled by default. See also `out-folder` above. If you have the `record` and `outfolder` variables set but the `folder` variable not set, messages are saved in +*filename* instead of *filename*.

save Enable saving of messages in `dead.letter` on interrupt or delivery error. See DEAD for a description of this file. Enabled by default.

`screen=`*number*
Sets the number of lines in a screen-full of headers for the `headers` command. It must be a positive number.

`sendmail=`*shell-command*
Alternate command for delivering messages. Default is `/usr/bin/rmail`.

`sendwait`
Wait for background mailer to finish before returning. Default is `nosendwait`.

`SHELL=`*shell-command*
The name of a preferred command interpreter. Default is `sh`(1).

`showto`
When displaying the header summary and the message is from you, print the recipient's name instead of the author's name.

`sign=`*string*
The variable inserted into the text of a message when the ~a (autograph) command is given. No default [see also ~i (TILDE ESCAPES)].

`Sign=`*string*
The variable inserted into the text of a message when the ~A command is given. No default [see also ~i (TILDE ESCAPES)].

`toplines=`*number*
The number of lines of header to print with the `top` command. Default is 5.

`VISUAL=`*shell-command*
The name of a preferred screen editor. Default is `vi`(1).

FILES

`$HOME/.mailrc`	personal start-up file
`$HOME/mbox`	secondary storage file
`/var/mail/*`	post office directory
`/usr/share/lib/mailx/mailx.help*`	help message files
`/etc/mail/mailx.rc`	optional global start-up file
`/tmp/R[emqsx]*`	temporary files

SEE ALSO

`ls`(1), `mail`(1), `pg`(1)

NOTES

The -h and -r options can be used only if `mailx` is using a delivery program other than `/usr/bin/rmail`.

Where *shell-command* is shown as valid, arguments are not always allowed. Experimentation is recommended.

Internal variables imported from the execution environment cannot be unset.

The full internet addressing is not fully supported by `mailx`. The new standards need some time to settle down.

Attempts to send a message having a line consisting only of a "." are treated as the end of the message by `mail`(1) (the standard mail delivery program).

NAME

`make` - maintain, update, and regenerate groups of programs

SYNOPSIS

`make` [`-f` *makefile*] [`-eiknpqrstu`] [*names*]

DESCRIPTION

`make` allows the programmer to maintain, update, and regenerate groups of computer programs. `make` executes commands in *makefile* to update one or more target *names* (*names* are typically programs). If the `-f` option is not present, then `makefile`, `Makefile`, and the Source Code Control System (SCCS) files `s.makefile`, and `s.Makefile` are tried in order. If *makefile* is -, the standard input is taken. More than one `-f` *makefile* argument pair may appear.

`make` updates a target only if its dependents are newer than the target. All prerequisite files of a target are added recursively to the list of targets. Missing files are deemed to be outdated.

The following list of four directives can be included in *makefile* to extend the options provided by `make`. They are used in *makefile* as if they were targets:

`.DEFAULT:`	If a file must be made but there are no explicit commands or relevant built-in rules, the commands associated with the name `.DEFAULT` are used if it exists.
`.IGNORE:`	Same effect as the `-i` option.
`.PRECIOUS:`	Dependents of the `.PRECIOUS` entry will not be removed when quit or interrupt are hit.
`.SILENT:`	Same effect as the `-s` option.

The options for `make` are listed below:

`-e`	Environment variables override assignments within makefiles.
`-f` *makefile*	Description filename (*makefile* is assumed to be the name of a description file).
`-i`	Ignore error codes returned by invoked commands.
`-k`	Abandon work on the current entry if it fails, but continue on other branches that do not depend on that entry.
`-n`	No execute mode. Print commands, but do not execute them. Even command lines beginning with an @ are printed.
`-p`	Print out the complete set of macro definitions and target descriptions.
`-q`	Question. `make` returns a zero or non-zero status code depending on whether or not the target file has been updated.
`-r`	Do not use the built-in rules.
`-s`	Silent mode. Do not print command lines before executing.
`-t`	Touch the target files (causing them to be updated) rather than issue the usual commands.

-u   Unconditionally make the target, ignoring all timestamps.

Creating the makefile

The makefile invoked with the -f option is a carefully structured file of explicit instructions for updating and regenerating programs, and contains a sequence of entries that specify dependencies. The first line of an entry is a blank-separated, non-null list of targets, then a :, then a (possibly null) list of prerequisite files or dependencies. Text following a ; and all following lines that begin with a tab are shell commands to be executed to update the target. The first non-empty line that does not begin with a tab or # begins a new dependency or macro definition. Shell commands may be continued across lines with a backslash-new-line (\ new-line) sequence. Everything printed by make (except the initial tab) is passed directly to the shell as is. Thus,

```
echo a\
b
```

will produce

```
ab
```

exactly the same as the shell would.

Sharp (#) and new-line surround comments including contained \ new-line sequences.

The following makefile says that pgm depends on two files a.o and b.o, and that they in turn depend on their corresponding source files (a.c and b.c) and a common file incl.h:

```
pgm: a.o b.o
        cc a.o b.o -o pgm
a.o: incl.h a.c
        cc -c a.c
b.o: incl.h b.c
        cc -c b.c
```

Command lines are executed one at a time, each by its own shell. The SHELL environment variable can be used to specify which shell make should use to execute commands. The default is /usr/bin/sh. The first one or two characters in a command can be the following: @, -, @-, or -@. If @ is present, printing of the command is suppressed. If - is present, make ignores an error. A line is printed when it is executed unless the -s option is present, or the entry .SILENT: is included in *makefile*, or unless the initial character sequence contains a @. The -n option specifies printing without execution; however, if the command line has the string $(MAKE) in it, the line is always executed (see the discussion of the MAKEFLAGS macro in the "Environment" section below). The -t (touch) option updates the modified date of a file without executing any commands.

Commands returning non-zero status normally terminate make. If the -i option is present, if the entry .IGNORE: is included in *makefile*, or if the initial character sequence of the command contains -, the error is ignored. If the -k option is present, work is abandoned on the current entry, but continues on other branches that do not depend on that entry.

Interrupt and quit cause the target to be deleted unless the target is a dependent of the directive .PRECIOUS.

Environment

The environment is read by make. All variables are assumed to be macro definitions and are processed as such. The environment variables are processed before any makefile and after the internal rules; thus, macro assignments in a makefile override environment variables. The -e option causes the environment to override the macro assignments in a makefile. Suffixes and their associated rules in the makefile will override any identical suffixes in the built-in rules.

The MAKEFLAGS environment variable is processed by make as containing any legal input option (except -f and -p) defined for the command line. Further, upon invocation, make "invents" the variable if it is not in the environment, puts the current options into it, and passes it on to invocations of commands. Thus, MAKEFLAGS always contains the current input options. This feature proves very useful for "super-makes". In fact, as noted above, when the -n option is used, the command $(MAKE) is executed anyway; hence, one can perform a make -n recursively on a whole software system to see what would have been executed. This result is possible because the -n is put in MAKEFLAGS and passed to further invocations of $(MAKE). This usage is one way of debugging all of the makefiles for a software project without actually doing anything.

Include Files

If the string include appears as the first seven letters of a line in a *makefile,* and is followed by a blank or a tab, the rest of the line is assumed to be a filename and will be read by the current invocation, after substituting for any macros.

Macros

Entries of the form *string1* = *string2* are macro definitions. *string2* is defined as all characters up to a comment character or an unescaped new-line. Subsequent appearances of $(*string1*[:*subst1*=[*subst2*]]) are replaced by *string2*. The parentheses are optional if a single-character macro name is used and there is no substitute sequence. The optional :*subst1*=*subst2* is a substitute sequence. If it is specified, all non-overlapping occurrences of *subst1* in the named macro are replaced by *subst2*. Strings (for the purposes of this type of substitution) are delimited by blanks, tabs, new-line characters, and beginnings of lines. An example of the use of the substitute sequence is shown in the "Libraries" section below.

Internal Macros

There are five internally maintained macros that are useful for writing rules for building targets.

$*   The macro $* stands for the filename part of the current dependent with the suffix deleted. It is evaluated only for inference rules.

$@   The $@ macro stands for the full target name of the current target. It is evaluated only for explicitly named dependencies.

$<   The $< macro is only evaluated for inference rules or the .DEFAULT rule. It is the module that is outdated with respect to the target (the "manufactured" dependent file name). Thus, in the .c.o rule, the $< macro would evaluate to the .c file. An example for making optimized .o files from .c files is:

```
        .c.o:
                cc -c -O $*.c
or:
        .c.o:
                cc -c -O $<
```

$? The `$?` macro is evaluated when explicit rules from the makefile are evaluated. It is the list of prerequisites that are outdated with respect to the target, and essentially those modules that must be rebuilt.

$% The `$%` macro is only evaluated when the target is an archive library member of the form `lib(file.o)`. In this case, `$@` evaluates to `lib` and `$%` evaluates to the library member, `file.o`.

Four of the five macros can have alternative forms. When an upper case `D` or `F` is appended to any of the four macros, the meaning is changed to "directory part" for `D` and "file part" for `F`. Thus, `$(@D)` refers to the directory part of the string `$@`. If there is no directory part, `./` is generated. The only macro excluded from this alternative form is `$?`.

Suffixes

Certain names (for instance, those ending with `.o`) have inferable prerequisites such as `.c`, `.s`, etc. If no update commands for such a file appear in *makefile*, and if an inferable prerequisite exists, that prerequisite is compiled to make the target. In this case, make has inference rules that allow building files from other files by examining the suffixes and determining an appropriate inference rule to use. The current default inference rules are:

```
.c       .c~      .f       .f~      .s       .s~      .sh      .sh~     .C       .C~
.c.a     .c.o     .c~.a    .c~.c    .c~.o    .f.a     .f.o     .f~.a    .f~.f    .f~.o
.h~.h    .l.c     .l.o     .l~.c    .l~.l    .l~.o    .s.a     .s.o     .s~.a    .s~.o
.s~.s    .sh~.sh  .y.c     .y.o     .y~.c    .y~.o    .y~.y    .C.a     .C.o     .C~.a
.C~.C    .C~.o    .L.C     .L.o     .L~.C    .L~.L    .L~.o    .Y.C     .Y.o     .Y~.C
.Y~.o    .Y~.Y
```

The internal rules for make are contained in the source file `rules.c` for the make program. These rules can be locally modified. To print out the rules compiled into the make on any machine in a form suitable for recompilation, the following command is used:

```
        make -pf - 2>/dev/null </dev/null
```

A tilde in the above rules refers to an SCCS file [see `sccsfile`(4)]. Thus, the rule `.c~.o` would transform an SCCS C source file into an object file (`.o`). Because the `s.` of the SCCS files is a prefix, it is incompatible with the make suffix point of view. Hence, the tilde is a way of changing any file reference into an SCCS file reference.

A rule with only one suffix (for example, `.c:`) is the definition of how to build x from $x.c$. In effect, the other suffix is null. This feature is useful for building targets from only one source file, for example, shell procedures and simple C programs.

Additional suffixes are given as the dependency list for `.SUFFIXES`. Order is significant: the first possible name for which both a file and a rule exist is inferred as a prerequisite. The default list is:

```
.SUFFIXES: .o .c .c~ .y .y~ .l .l~ .s .s~ .sh .sh~ .h .h~ .f .f~ .C
.C~ .Y .Y~ .L .L~
```

Here again, the above command for printing the internal rules will display the list of suffixes implemented on the current machine. Multiple suffix lists accumulate; `.SUFFIXES:` with no dependencies clears the list of suffixes.

Inference Rules

The first example can be done more briefly.

```
pgm: a.o b.o
        cc a.o b.o -o pgm
a.o b.o: incl.h
```

This abbreviation is possible because `make` has a set of internal rules for building files. The user may add rules to this list by simply putting them in the *makefile*.

Certain macros are used by the default inference rules to permit the inclusion of optional matter in any resulting commands. For example, `CFLAGS`, `LFLAGS`, and `YFLAGS` are used for compiler options to `cc`(1), `lex`(1), and `yacc`(1), respectively. Again, the previous method for examining the current rules is recommended.

The inference of prerequisites can be controlled. The rule to create a file with suffix `.o` from a file with suffix `.c` is specified as an entry with `.c.o:` as the target and no dependents. Shell commands associated with the target define the rule for making a `.o` file from a `.c` file. Any target that has no slashes in it and starts with a dot is identified as a rule and not a true target.

Libraries

If a target or dependency name contains parentheses, it is assumed to be an archive library, the string within parentheses referring to a member within the library. Thus, `lib(file.o)` and `$(LIB)(file.o)` both refer to an archive library that contains `file.o`. (This example assumes the `LIB` macro has been previously defined.) The expression `$(LIB)(file1.o file2.o)` is not legal. Rules pertaining to archive libraries have the form `.XX.a` where the *XX* is the suffix from which the archive member is to be made. An unfortunate by-product of the current implementation requires the *XX* to be different from the suffix of the archive member. Thus, one cannot have `lib(file.o)` depend upon `file.o` explicitly. The most common use of the archive interface follows. Here, we assume the source files are all C type source:

```
lib: lib(file1.o) lib(file2.o) lib(file3.o)
        @echo lib is now up-to-date
.c.a:
        $(CC) -c $(CFLAGS) $<
        $(AR) $(ARFLAGS) $@ $*.o
        rm -f $*.o
```

In fact, the `.c.a` rule listed above is built into `make` and is unnecessary in this example. A more interesting, but more limited example of an archive library maintenance construction follows:

```
lib: lib(file1.o) lib(file2.o) lib(file3.o)
        $(CC) -c $(CFLAGS) $(?:.o=.c)
        $(AR) $(ARFLAGS) lib $?
        rm $?
```

```
                    @echo lib is now up-to-date
            .c.a:;
```

Here the substitution mode of the macro expansions is used. The `$?` list is defined
to be the set of object filenames (inside `lib`) whose C source files are outdated. The
substitution mode translates the `.o` to `.c`. (Unfortunately, one cannot as yet
transform to `.c~`; however, this transformation may become possible in the future.)
Also note the disabling of the `.c.a:` rule, which would have created each object
file, one by one. This particular construct speeds up archive library maintenance
considerably. This type of construct becomes very cumbersome if the archive
library contains a mix of assembly programs and C programs.

FILES

`[Mm]akefile` and `s.[Mm]akefile`
`/usr/bin/sh`

SEE ALSO

`cc`(1), `lex`(1), `yacc`(1), `printf`(3S), `sccsfile`(4)
`cd`(1), `sh`(1)

NOTES

Some commands return non-zero status inappropriately; use `-i` or the `-` command
line prefix to overcome the difficulty.

Filenames with the characters `=  :  @` will not work. Commands that are directly
executed by the shell, notably `cd`(1), are ineffectual across new-lines in `make`. The
syntax `lib(file1.o  file2.o  file3.o)` is illegal. You cannot build
`lib(file.o)` from `file.o`.

NAME

makedbm - make a Network Information Service (NIS) dbm file

SYNOPSIS

/usr/sbin/makedbm [-l] [-s] [-i *yp_input_file*] [-o *yp_output_name*]
     [-d *yp_domain_name*] [-m *yp_master_name*] *infile outfile*

makedbm [-u *dbmfilename*]

DESCRIPTION

The makedbm command takes *infile* and converts it to a pair of files in dbm(3) format, namely *outfile*.pag and *outfile*.dir. Each line of the input file is converted to a single dbm record. All characters up to the first TAB or SPACE form the key, and the rest of the line is the data. If a line ends with '\', then the data for that record is continued on to the next line. It is left for NIS clients to interpret '#'; makedbm does not itself treat it as a comment character. *infile* can be '-', in which case the standard input is read.

makedbm is meant to be used in generating dbm files for NIS and it generates a special entry with the key *yp_last_modified*, which is the date of *infile* (or the current time, if *infile* is '-').

The following options are available:

-l   Lowercase. Convert the keys of the given map to lower case, so that host name matches, for example, can work independent of upper or lower case distinctions.

-s   Secure map. Accept connections from secure NIS networks only.

-i *yp_input_file*
        Create a special entry with the key *yp_input_file*.

-o *yp_output_name*
        Create a special entry with the key *yp_output_name*.

-d *yp_domain_name*
        Create a special entry with the key *yp_domain_name*.

-m *yp_master_name*
        Create a special entry with the key *yp_master_name*. If no master host name is specified, *yp_master_name* will be set to the local host name.

-u *dbmfilename*
        Undo a dbm file. That is, print out a dbm file one entry per line, with a single space separating keys from values.

SEE ALSO

dbm(3)

NAME

makedev - adds /dev entries for generic devices table

SYNOPSIS

`/sbin/auto-device/makedev`

DESCRIPTION

`makedev` performs the following steps:

1. Any generic device names in the `/dev/SA`, `/dev/rSA`, `/dev/term`, `/dev/rmt`, `/dev/printer` directories are deleted.

2. The `/dev/dsk`, `/dev/rdsk`, `/dev/rmt`, and `/dev/port` directories are scanned for the controller-specific device names present (for example, `m328_*`). For each unique device found, its Extended EDT information is examined to determine if it is a hard disk, floppy, CDROM, archive-compatible tape, nine-track tape, serial port, or printer port.

3. Generic device names for each device type [for example, hard disk (`disk`), archive (`ctape`), nine track (`ninetrack`)] will be assigned numbers (starting with 1) in the order that the devices were scanned if the file `/etc/device-map` is not found. If this file is present, device numbers are assigned in the order that the controller-specific names are listed in the file. Any devices found that are not specified in the file have their device numbers assigned in scanned order.

4. The generic names are created in the `/dev/SA`, `/dev/rSA`, `/dev/term`, `/dev/rmt`, and `/dev/printer` directories.

5. The `/etc/device.tab` file is examined and modified if any entries refer to devices which no longer exist or if new devices must be added.

`makedev` is called each time the system is automatically reconfigured, but after all other device naming programs have been run. It must also be called after `sysadm rmdisk` to restore the `/dev` entries so a disk can be resliced.

FILES

`/dev/SA/*`	entries for the hard disks for use by system administration
`/dev/rSA/*`	entries for the hard disks and tapes for use by system administration
`/dev/rmt/*`	entries for the generic tape names
`/dev/term/*`	entries for the generic port names
`/dev/printer/*`	entries for the generic printern ames
`/etc/device_map`	forces a particular ordering when naming generic devices

SEE ALSO

`mvme323`(1M) (For M68K only), `mvme328`(1M), `mvme350`(1M) (For M68K only), `mvme376`(1M), `sysadm`(1M), `device-map`(4)

NAME

makefsys - create a file system

SYNOPSIS

makefsys

DESCRIPTION

The makefsys command allows you to create a file system.

The command invokes a visual interface (the make task available through the sysadm command).

The initial prompt allows you to select the device on which to create the file system. After selecting the device, you are asked some further questions before the file system is created.

The identical function is available under the sysadm menu:

sysadm make

DIAGNOSTICS

The makefsys command exits with one of the following values:

0   Normal exit.

2   Invalid command syntax. A usage message is displayed.

7   The visual interface for this command is not available because it cannot invoke fmil. (The FMLI package is not installed or is corrupted.)

SEE ALSO

checkfsys(1M), labelit(1M), mkfs(1M), mountfsys(1M), sysadm(1M)

NAME

makekey - generate encryption key

SYNOPSIS

`/usr/lib/makekey`

DESCRIPTION

makekey improves the usefulness of encryption schemes depending on a key by increasing the amount of time required to search the key space. It attempts to read 8 bytes for its *key* (the first eight input bytes), then it attempts to read 2 bytes for its *salt* (the last two input bytes). The output depends on the input in a way intended to be difficult to compute (that is, to require a substantial fraction of a second).

The first eight input bytes (the *input key*) can be arbitrary ASCII characters. The last two (the *salt*) are best chosen from the set of digits, ., /, and upper- and lower-case letters. The salt characters are repeated as the first two characters of the output. The remaining 11 output characters are chosen from the same set as the salt and constitute the *output key*.

The transformation performed is essentially the following: the salt is used to select one of 4,096 cryptographic machines all based on the National Bureau of Standards DES algorithm, but broken in 4,096 different ways. Using the *input key* as key, a constant string is fed into the machine and recirculated a number of times. The 64 bits that come out are distributed into the 66 *output key* bits in the result.

makekey is intended for programs that perform encryption. Usually, its input and output will be pipes.

SEE ALSO

ed(1), crypt(1), vi(1), passwd(4).

NOTES

makekey can produce different results depending upon whether the input is typed at the terminal or redirected from a file.

This command is provided with the Encryption Utilities, which is only available in the United States.

NAME

man - display reference manual pages; find reference pages by keyword

SYNOPSIS

/usr/ucb/man [-] [-t] [-M *path*] [-T *macro-package*] [-v *version*]
[[*section*] *title*...] *title* ...

/usr/ucb/man [-M *path*] -k *keyword* ...

/usr/ucb/man [-M *path*] -f *filename* ...

DESCRIPTION

The man command displays information from the reference manuals. It can display complete manual pages that you select by *title*, or one-line summaries selected either by *keyword* (-k), or by the name of an associated file (-f).

A *section*, when given, applies to the *titles* that follow it on the command line (up to the next *section*, if any). man looks in the indicated section of the manual for those *title*s. *section* is either a digit, or one of the words new, local, old, or public. If *section* is a digit, it can be followed by a single letter indicating the type of manual page. man is not sensitive to the case of the letter, i.e. the letter can be in either upper case or lower case. If *section* is omitted, man searches all reference sections (giving preference to commands over functions) and prints the first manual page it finds. If no manual page is located, man prints an error message.

The reference page sources are typically located in the /usr/share/man/man? directories. Since these directories are optionally installed, they may not reside on your host; you may have to mount /usr/share/man from a host on which they do reside. If there are preformatted, up-to-date versions in corresponding cat? or fmt? directories, man simply displays or prints those versions. If the preformatted version of interest is out-of-date or missing, man reformats it prior to display. If directories for the preformatted versions are not provided, man reformats a page whenever it is requested, using a temporary file to store the formatted text during display.

If the standard output is not a terminal, or if the - flag is given, man pipes its output through cat. Otherwise, man pipes its output through more to handle paging and underlining on the screen.

The following options are available:

-t   man arranges for the specified manual pages to be troffed to a suitable raster output device (see troff or vtroff). If both the - and -t flags are given, man updates the troffed versions of each named *title* (if necessary), but does not display them.

-M *path*

Change the search path for manual pages. *path* is a colon-separated list of directories that contain manual page directory subtrees. When used with the -k or -f options, the -M option must appear first. Each directory in the *path* is assumed to contain subdirectories of the form man[1-81-p].

-T *macro-package*

man uses *macro-package* rather than the standard -man macros defined in /usr/ucblib/doctools/tmac/tmac.an for formatting manual pages.

-k *keyword* ...
> man prints out one-line summaries from the whatis database (table of contents) that contain any of the given *keyword*s.

-f *filename* ...
> man attempts to locate manual pages related to any of the given *filename*s. It strips the leading pathname components from each *filename* and then prints one-line summaries containing the resulting basename or names.

-v *version* ...
> man displays the manpage for version *version*. For example, enter:

```
$ man -v bsd ls
```

> to see the BSD version of the ls(1) manual page.
>
> Versions include:

bsd	BSD
xen	XENIX
s5	s5 file system
nfs	nfs file system
bfs	bfs file system
ufs	ufs file system

MANUAL PAGES

Manual pages are troff or nroff source files prepared with the -man macro package.

When formatting a manual page, man examines the first line to determine whether it requires special processing.

Preprocessing Manual Pages

If the first line is a string of the form:

```
´ \" X
```

where *X* is separated from the '"' by a single space and consists of any combination of characters in the following list, man pipes its input to troff or nroff through the corresponding preprocessors.

e	eqn, or neqn for nroff
r	refer
t	tbl, and col for nroff

If eqn or neqn is invoked, it will automatically read the file /usr/ucblib/pub/eqnchar [see eqnchar(5)].

ENVIRONMENT

MANPATH
> If set, its value overrides /usr/share/man as the default search path. The -M flag, in turn, overrides this value.

PAGER   A program to use for interactively delivering man's output to the screen. If not set, 'more -s' (see more(1)) is used.

TCAT   The name of the program to use to display troffed manual pages. If not set, 'lp -Ttroff' (see lp(1)) is used.

TROFF   The name of the formatter to use when the -t flag is given. If not set, troff is used.

NOTES

Related manual pages for commands on one manual page may be directly accessed. For example enter:

```
$ man strcat
```

to see the manual page for string where strcat is documented.

A manual page is reproducible either on a phototypesetter or on an ASCII terminal. However, on a terminal some information (indicated by font changes, for instance) is necessarily lost.

Some dumb terminals cannot process the vertical motions produced by the e [eqn(1)] preprocessing flag. To prevent garbled output on these terminals, when you use e , also use t to invoke col(1) implicitly. This workaround has the disadvantage of eliminating superscripts and subscripts — even on those terminals that can display them. CTRL-Q will clear a terminal that gets confused by eqn(1) output.

Online manual pages are provided as part of this product. If you have any trouble finding the online documentation for a command, use the apropos(1) command.

If the manual page was not found, man exits with 1 , otherwise 0.

FILES

/usr/share/man	root of the standard manual page directory subtree
/usr/share/man/man?/*	unformatted manual entries
/usr/share/man/cat?/*	nroffed manual entries
/usr/share/man/fmt?/*	troffed manual entries
/usr/share/man/whatis	table of contents and keyword database
/usr/ucblib/doctools/tmac/man.macs	
	standard -man macro package
/usr/ucblib/pub/eqnchar	

SEE ALSO

apropos(1), cat(1), catman(1M), col(1), eqn(1), eqnchar(5), lp(1), more(1) nroff(1), refer(1), tbl(1), troff(1), whatis(1),

NAME

man - macros to format Reference Manual pages

SYNOPSIS

`nroff` `-man` *filename*...

`troff` `-man` *filename*...

DESCRIPTION

These macros are used to lay out the reference pages in this manual. Note: if *filename* contains format input for a preprocessor, the commands shown above must be piped through the appropriate preprocessor. This is handled automatically by man(1). See the "Conventions" section.

Any text argument *t* may be zero to six words. Quotes may be used to include SPACE characters in a word. If *text* is empty, the special treatment is applied to the next input line with text to be printed. In this way `.I` may be used to italicize a whole line, or `.SB` may be used to make small bold letters.

A prevailing indent distance is remembered between successive indented paragraphs, and is reset to default value upon reaching a non-indented paragraph. Default units for indents *i* are ens.

Type font and size are reset to default values before each paragraph, and after processing font and size setting macros.

These strings are predefined by `-man`:

`*R`	'®', '(Reg)' in `nroff`.
`*S`	Change to default type size.

Requests

* n.t.l. = next text line; p.i. = prevailing indent

Request	Cause Break	If no Argument	Explanation
`.B` *t*	no	*t*=n.t.l.*	Text is in bold font.
`.BI` *t*	no	*t*=n.t.l.	Join words, alternating bold and italic.
`.BR` *t*	no	*t*=n.t.l.	Join words, alternating bold and roman.
`.DT`	no	.5i 1i...	Restore default tabs.
`.HP` *i*	yes	*i*=p.i.*	Begin paragraph with hanging indent. Set prevailing indent to *i*.
`.I` *t*	no	*t*=n.t.l.	Text is italic.
`.IB` *t*	no	*t*=n.t.l.	Join words, alternating italic and bold.
`.IP` *x i*	yes	*x*=""	Same as `.TP` with tag *x*.
`.IR` *t*	no	*t*=n.t.l.	Join words, alternating italic and roman.
`.IX` *t*	no	-	Index macro.
`.LP`	yes	-	Begin left-aligned paragraph. Set prevailing indent to .5i.
`.PD` *d*	no	*d*=.4v	Set vertical distance between paragraphs.
`.PP`	yes	-	Same as `.LP`.

`.RE`	yes	-	End of relative indent. Restores prevailing indent.
`.RB` *t*	no	*t*=n.t.l.	Join words, alternating roman and bold.
`.RI` *t*	no	*t*=n.t.l.	Join words, alternating roman and italic.
`.RS` *i*	yes	*i*=p.i.	Start relative indent, increase indent by *i*. Sets prevailing indent to .5i for nested indents.
`.SB` *t*	no	-	Reduce size of text by 1 point, make text bold.
`.SH` *t*	yes	-	Section Heading.
`.SM` *t*	no	*t*=n.t.l.	Reduce size of text by 1 point.
`.SS` *t*	yes	*t*=n.t.l.	Section Subheading.
`.TH` *n s d f m*	yes	-	Begin reference page *n*, of of section *s*; *d* is the date of the most recent change. If present, *f* is the left page footer; *m* is the main page (center) header. Sets prevailing indent and tabs to .5i.
`.TP` *i*	yes	*i*=p.i.	Begin indented paragraph, with the tag given on the next text line. Set prevailing indent to *i*.
`.TX` *t p*	no	-	Resolve the title abbreviation *t*; join to punctuation mark (or text) *p*.

Conventions

When formatting a manual page, `man` examines the first line to determine whether it requires special processing. For example a first line consisting of:

```
'\" t
```

indicates that the manual page must be run through the `tbl`(1) preprocessor.

A typical manual page for a command or function is laid out as follows:

`.TH` *title* [1-8]
> The name of the command or function, which serves as the title of the manual page. This is followed by the number of the section in which it appears.

`.SH` NAME
> The name, or list of names, by which the command is called, followed by a dash and then a one-line summary of the action performed. All in roman font, this section contains no `troff`(1) commands or escapes, and no macro requests. It is used to generate the `whatis`(1) database.

`.SH` SYNOPSIS
> Commands:
>
>> The syntax of the command and its arguments, as typed on the command line. When in boldface, a word must be typed exactly as printed. When in italics, a word can be replaced with an argument that you supply. References to bold or italicized items are not capitalized in other sections, even when they begin a sentence.

Syntactic symbols appear in roman face:

[ ] An argument, when surrounded by brackets is optional.

| Arguments separated by a vertical bar are exclusive. You can supply only one item from such a list.

. . . Arguments followed by an elipsis can be repeated. When an elipsis follows a bracketed set, the expression within the brackets can be repeated.

Functions:

If required, the data declaration, or `#include` directive, is shown first, followed by the function declaration. Otherwise, the function declaration is shown.

`.SH DESCRIPTION`

A narrative overview of the command or function's external behavior. This includes how it interacts with files or data, and how it handles the standard input, standard output and standard error. Internals and implementation details are normally omitted. This section attempts to provide a succinct overview in answer to the question, "what does it do?"

Literal text from the synopsis appears in constant width, as do literal filenames and references to items that appear elsewhere in the reference manuals. Arguments are italicized.

If a command interprets either subcommands or an input grammar, its command interface or input grammar is normally described in a USAGE section, which follows the OPTIONS section. The DESCRIPTION section only describes the behavior of the command itself, not that of subcommands.

`.SH OPTIONS`

The list of options along with a description of how each affects the command's operation.

`.SH FILES`

A list of files associated with the command or function.

`.SH SEE ALSO`

A comma-separated list of related manual pages, followed by references to other published materials.

`.SH DIAGNOSTICS`

A list of diagnostic messages and an explanation of each.

`.SH NOTES`

A description of limitations, known defects, and possible problems associated with the command or function.

FILES

        /usr/ucblib/doctools/man

SEE ALSO

        man(1), nroff(1), troff(1), whatis(1)

NAME

mcs - manipulate the comment section of an object file

SYNOPSIS

mcs [-a *string*] [-c] [-d] [-n *name*] [-p] [-V] *file* . . .

DESCRIPTION

The mcs command is used to manipulate a section, by default the .comment section, in an ELF object file. It is used to add to, delete, print, and compress the contents of a section in an ELF object file, and only print the contents of a section in a COFF object file. mcs must be given one or more of the options described below. It applies each of the options in order to each file.

The following options are available:

-a *string*   Append *string* to the comment section of the object files. If *string* contains embedded blanks, it must be enclosed in quotation marks.

-c   Compress the contents of the comment section of the ELF object files. All duplicate entries are removed. The ordering of the remaining entries is not disturbed.

-d   Delete the contents of the comment section from the ELF object files. The section header for the comment section is also removed.

-n *name*   Specify the name of the comment section to access if other than .comment. By default, mcs deals with the section named .comment. This option can be used to specify another section.

-p   Print the contents of the comment section on the standard output. Each section printed is tagged by the name of the file from which it was extracted, using the format *filename* [*member_name*] : for archive files; and *filename* : for other files.

-V   Print, on standard error, the version number of mcs.

If the input file is an archive [see ar(4)], the archive is treated as a set of individual files. For example, if the -a option is specified, the string is appended to the comment section of each ELF object file in the archive; if the archive member is not an ELF object file, it is left unchanged.

If mcs is executed on an archive file, the archive symbol table will be removed unless only the -p option has been specified. The archive symbol table must be restored by executing the ar command with the -s option before the archive can be linked by the ld command. mcs will produce appropriate warning messages when this situation arises.

EXAMPLES

```
        mcs -p file        # Print file's comment section

        mcs -a string file # Append string to file's comment section
```

FILES

TMPDIR/mcs*	temporary files
TMPDIR	usually /var/tmp but can be redefined by setting the environment variable TMPDIR [see tempnam in tmpnam(3S)]

INTERNATIONAL FUNCTIONS

Characters from supplementary code sets can be used in *object-files*. Comments using characters from supplementary code sets can be specified with the -a option.

The section name specified in *name* with the -n option must contain ASCII characters only.

SEE ALSO

ar(1), as(1), cc(1), ld(1), tmpnam(3S), a.out(4), ar(4).

NOTES

mcs cannot add to, delete or compress the contents of a section that is contained within a segment.

NAME

me - macros for formatting papers

SYNOPSIS

`nroff -me` [*options*] *filename ...*
`troff -me` [*options*] *filename ...*

DESCRIPTION

This package of `nroff` and `troff` macro definitions provides a canned formatting facility for technical papers in various formats. When producing 2-column output on a terminal, filter the output through *col*(1).

The macro requests are defined below. Many `nroff` and `troff` requests are unsafe in conjunction with this package, however, these requests may be used with impunity after the first `.pp`:

`.bp`	begin new page
`.br`	break output line here
`.sp` n	insert n spacing lines
`.ls` n	(line spacing) n=1 single, n=2 double space
`.na`	no alignment of right margin
`.ce` n	center next n lines
`.ul` n	underline next n lines
`.sz` +n	add n to point size

Output of the `eqn`, `meqn`, `mefer`, and `tbl`(1) preprocessors for equations and tables is acceptable as input.

REQUESTS

In the following list, initialization refers to the first `.pp`, `.lp`, `.ip`, `.np`, `.sh`, or `.uh` macro. This list is incomplete.

Request	Initial Value	Cause Break	Explanation
`.(c`	-	yes	Begin centered block
`.(d`	-	no	Begin delayed text
`.(f`	-	no	Begin footnote
`.(l`	-	yes	Begin list
`.(q`	-	yes	Begin major quote
`.(x`x	-	no	Begin indexed item in index x
`.(z`	-	no	Begin floating keep
`.)c`	-	yes	End centered block
`.)d`	-	yes	End delayed text
`.)f`	-	yes	End footnote
`.)l`	-	yes	End list
`.)q`	-	yes	End major quote
`.)x`	-	yes	End index item
`.)z`	-	yes	End floating keep

Request	Initial Value	Cause Break	Explanation
.++ m H	-	no	Define paper section. m defines the part of the paper, and can be C (chapter), A (appendix), P (preliminary, for instance, abstract, table of contents, and so on), B (bibliography), RC (chapters renumbered from page one each chapter), or RA (appendix renumbered from page one).
.+c T	-	yes	Begin chapter (or appendix, and so on, as set by .++). T is the chapter title.
.1c	1	yes	One column format on a new page.
.2c	1	yes	Two column format.
.EN	-	yes	Space after equation produced by eqn or meqn.
.EQ x y	-	yes	Precede equation; break out and add space. Equation number is y. The optional argument x may be I to indent equation (default), L to left-adjust the equation, or C to center the equation.
.GE	-	yes	End *gremlin* picture.
.GS	-	yes	Begin *gremlin* picture.
.PE	-	yes	End pic picture.
.PS	-	yes	Begin pic picture.
.TE	-	yes	End table.
.TH	-	yes	End heading section of table.
.TS x	-	yes	Begin table; if x is H table has repeated heading.
.ac A N	-	no	Set up for ACM style output. A is the Author's name(s), N is the total number of pages. Must be given before the first initialization.
.b x	no	no	Print x in boldface; if no argument switch to boldface.
.ba +n	0	yes	Augments the base indent by n. This indent is used to set the indent on regular text (like paragraphs).
.bc	no	yes	Begin new column
.bi x	no	no	Print x in bold italics (nofill only)
.bu	-	yes	Begin bulleted paragraph
.bx x	no	no	Print x in a box (nofill only).
.ef 'x'y'z	′′′′′	no	Set even footer to x y z
.eh 'x'y'z	′′′′′	no	Set even header to x y z
.fo 'x'y'z	′′′′′	no	Set footer to x y z
.hx	-	no	Suppress headers and footers on next page.
.he 'x'y'z	′′′′′	no	Set header to x y z
.hl	-	yes	Draw a horizontal line
.i x	no	no	Italicize x; if x missing, italic text follows.

Request	Initial Value	Cause Break	Explanation
.ip x y	no	yes	Start indented paragraph, with hanging tag x. Indentation is y ens (default 5).
.lp	yes	yes	Start left-blocked paragraph.
.lo	-	no	Read in a file of local macros of the form .*x. Must be given before initialization.
.np	1	yes	Start numbered paragraph.
.of ´x´y´z	´´´´´	no	Set odd footer to x y z
.oh ´x´y´z	´´´´´	no	Set odd header to x y z
.pd	-	yes	Print delayed text.
.pp	no	yes	Begin paragraph. First line indented.
.r	yes	no	Roman text follows.
.re	-	no	Reset tabs to default values.
.sc	no	no	Read in a file of special characters and diacritical marks. Must be given before initialization.
.sh n x	-	yes	Section head follows, font automatically bold. n is level of section, x is title of section.
.sk	no	no	Leave the next page blank. Only one page is remembered ahead.
.sm x	-	no	Set x in a smaller pointsize.
.sz +n	10p	no	Augment the point size by n points.
.th	no	no	Produce the paper in thesis format. Must be given before initialization.
.tp	no	yes	Begin title page.
.u x	-	no	Underline argument (even in `troff`). (Nofill only).
.uh	-	yes	Like .sh but unnumbered.
.xp x	-	no	Print index x.

FILES

    /usr/ucblib/doctools/tmac/e
    /usr/ucblib/doctools/tmac/*.me

SEE ALSO

    eqn(1), nroff(1), troff(1), refer(1), tbl(1)

NAME

mesg - permit or deny messages

SYNOPSIS

mesg [-n] [-y]

DESCRIPTION

mesg with argument -n forbids messages via write(1) by revoking non-user write permission on the user's terminal. mesg with argument -y reinstates permission. All by itself, mesg reports the current state without changing it.

FILES

/dev/tty*

SEE ALSO

write(1)

DIAGNOSTICS

Exit status is 0 if messages are receivable, 1 if not, 2 on error.

NAME

message - put arguments on FMLI message line

SYNOPSIS

message [-t] [-b [*num*]] [-o] [-w] [*string*]
message [-f] [-b [*num*]] [-o] [-w] [*string*]
message [-p] [-b [*num*]] [-o] [-w] [*string*]

DESCRIPTION

The message command puts *string* out on the FMLI message line. If there is no string, the *stdin* input to message will be used. The output of message has a duration (length of time it remains on the message line). The default duration is "transient": it or one of two other durations can be requested with the following mutually-exclusive options:

-t   explicitly defines a message to have transient duration. Transient messages remain on the message line only until the user presses another key or a CHECKWORLD occurs. The descriptors itemmsg, fieldmsg, invalidmsg, choicemsg, the default-if-not-defined value of oninterrupt, and FMLI generated error messages (for example, from syntax errors) also output transient duration messages. Transient messages take precedence over both frame messages and permanent messages.

-f   defines a message to have "frame" duration. Frame messages remain on the message line as long as the frame in which they are defined is current. The descriptor framemsg also outputs a frame duration message. Frame messages take precedence over permanent messages.

-p   defines a message to have "permanent" duration. Permanent messages remain on the message line for the length of the FMLI session, unless explicitly replaced by another permanent message or temporarily superseded by a transient message or frame message. A permanent message is not affected by navigating away from, or by closing, the frame which generated the permanent message. The descriptor permanentmsg also outputs a permanent duration message.

Messages displayed with message -p will replace (change the value of) any message currently displayed or stored via use of the permanentmsg descriptor. Likewise, message -f will replace any message currently displayed or stored via use of the framemsg descriptor. If more than one message in a frame definition file is specified with the -p option, the last one specified will be the permanent duration message.

The *string* argument should always be the last argument. Other options available with message are the following:

-b [*num*]   rings the terminal bell *num* times, where *num* is an integer from 1 to 10. The default value is 1. If the terminal has no bell, the screen will flash *num* times instead, if possible.

-o   forces message to duplicate its message to *stdout*.

-w   turns on the working indicator.

EXAMPLES

When a value entered in a field is invalid, ring the bell 3 times and then display `Invalid Entry: Try again!` on the message line:

```
invalidmsg=`message -b 3 "Invalid Entry: Try again!"`
```

Display a message that tells the user what is being done:

```
done=`message EDITOR has been set in your environment` close
```

Display a message on the message line and *stdout* for each field in a form (a pseudo-"field duration" message).

```
fieldmsg="`message -o -f "Enter a filename."`"
```

Display a blank transient message (effect is to "remove" a permanent or frame duration message).

```
done=`message  ""` nop
```

NOTES

If `message` is coded more than once on a single line, it may appear that only the right-most instance is interpreted and displayed. Use `sleep(1)` between uses of `message` in this case, to display multiple messages.

`message -f` should not be used in a stand-alone backquoted expression or with the `init` descriptor because the frame is not yet current when these are evaluated.

In cases where `message -f "string"` is part of a stand-alone backquoted expression, the context for evaluation of the expression is the previously current frame. The previously current frame can be the frame that issued the `open` command for the frame containing the backquoted expression, or it can be a frame given as an argument when `fmli` was invoked. That is, the previously current frame is the one whose frame message will be modified.

Permanent duration messages are displayed when the user navigates to the command line.

SEE ALSO

`sleep(1)`.

NAME

migration - move an archive from one set of volumes to another

SYNOPSIS

migration -B [-dlmotuvAENS] *bkjobid ofsname ofsdev ofslab descript*

DESCRIPTION

migration is invoked as a child process by bkdaemon(1M) to move an existing archive made by some other arbitrary method to a new set of volumes. The existing backup history log entry of the archive is updated to reflect the new volumes and destination information of the archive.

bkjobid is the job id assigned by backup(1M). *ofsdev* is the name of the UNIX raw (character) device on which the archive resides. *ofslab* is the volume label on the archive [see labelit(1M)]. *descript* is a description for a destination device in the form:

dgroup:dname:dchar:dlabels

dgroup specifies a device group. dname specifies a device name. *dchars* specifies characteristics for the specified device and group (see device.tab(4) for a further description of device characteristics). *dlabels* specifies the media names for the media to be used for the archive.

Options

d*   Do not update the backup history log entry for the archive.

l*   Create a long form of the backup history log that includes a table-of-contents for the archive. This includes the data used to generate an *ls -l*-like listing of each file in the archive.

m*   Mount the originating filesystem read-only before starting the backup and remount it with its original permissions after completing the backup.

o   Permit the user to override media insertion requests (see getvol(1M) -o).

t*   Create a table of contents for the backup on additional media instead of in the backup history log.

u*   Unmount the originating filesystem before performing the backup and remount it with its original permissions after completing the backup.

v*   Validate the archive as it is written. A checksum is computed as the archive is being written; as each medium is completed, it is re-read and the checksum recomputed to verify that each block is readable and correct. If either check fails, the medium is considered unreadable. If -A has been specified, the archiving operation fails; otherwise, the operator is prompted to replace the failed medium.

A   Do not prompt the user for removable media operations (automated operation).

E*   Report an estimate of media usage for the archive; then perform the backup.

N*   Report an estimate of media usage for the archive; do not perform the backup.

S*   Generate a period (.) for every 100 (512 byte) blocks read-from or written-to the archive on the destination device.

User Interactions

The connection between an archiving method and backup(1M) is more complex than a simple fork/exec or pipe. backup(1M) is responsible for all interactions with the user, either directly, or through bkoper(1M). Therefore, migration neither reads from standard-input nor writes to standard-output or standard-error. A method library must be used [see libbrmeth(3)] to communicate reports (estimates, periods, status, and so on) to backup(1M).

DIAGNOSTICS

If migration successfully completes its task, it exits with a 0 status. If any of the parameters to migration are invalid, it exits with a 1 status. If any error occurs which causes migration to fail to complete *all* portions of its task, it exits with a 2 status.

Errors are reported if any of the following occur:

1.   -t is specified together with -A.

2.   -A is specified together with -o.

3.   -t is specified and the destination device does not support removable media.

4.   -A is specified and more than one removable medium is required.

5.   Unrecoverable errors occurred in trying to read or write the destination device.

6.   -m is specified and the originating filesystem could not be mounted read-only.

7.   -m is specified and the originating filesystem could not be unmounted.

8.   -o is not specified and insufficient media names are supplied in *descript*.

9.   -u is specified and the filesystem could not be unmounted.

10.   -u is specified and the filesystem could not be remounted.

FILES

/usr/oam/bkrs/tables/bkhist.tab
$TMP/filelist$$

SEE ALSO

awk(1), backup(1M), device.tab(4), getvol(1M), grep(1), labelit(1M), libbrmeth(3), ls(1), prtvtoc(1M), restore(1M), rsoper(1M), sed(1), time(2), urestore(1M)

NAME

mk - remake the binary system and commands from source code

DESCRIPTION

All source code for the UNIX system is distributed in the directory /usr/src. The directory tree rooted at /usr/src includes source code for the operating system, libraries, commands, miscellaneous data files necessary for the system and procedures to transform this source code into an executable system.

Within the /usr/src directory are the cmd, lib, uts, head, and stand directories, as well as commands to remake the parts of the system found under each of these sub-directories. These commands are named :mk and :mk*dir* where *dir* is the name of the directory to be recreated. Each of these :mk*dir* commands rebuilds all or part of the directory it is responsible for. The :mk command runs each of the other commands in order and thus recreates the whole system. The :mk command is distributed only to source code licensees.

Each command, with its associated directory, is described below.

:mklib
: The lib directory contains the source code for the system libraries. The most important of these is the C library. Each library is in its own sub-directory. If any arguments are specified on the :mklib command line then only the given libraries are rebuilt. The argument * causes it to rebuild all libraries found under the lib directory.

:mkhead
: The head directory contains the source code versions of the header files found in the /usr/include directory. The :mkhead command installs the header files given as arguments. The argument * causes it to install all header files.

:mkuts
: The uts directory contains the source code for the UNIX Operating System. The :mkuts command takes no arguments and invokes a series of makefiles that recreates the operating system.

    Associated with the operating system is a set of header files that describe the user interface to the operating system. The source for these header files is found in a sub-directory within the uts directory tree. The user-accessible versions of these header files are found in the /usr/include/sys directory. The :mksyshead command installs these header files into the /usr/include/sys directory.

:mkstand
: The stand directory contains stand-alone commands and boot programs. The :mkstand command rebuilds and installs these programs. Note that these stand-alone programs are only applicable to the DEC processors and are not built for any other machine.

:mkcmd
: The cmd directory contains the source code for all the commands available on the system. There are two types of entries within the cmd directory: commands whose source code consists of only one file with one of the following suffixes: .l, .y, .c, .s, .sh, or a sub-directory that contains the multiple source files that comprise a particular command or subsystem. Each sub-directory is assumed to have a makefile [see make(1)] with the name *command*.mk that takes care of creating everything associated with that directory and its sub-directories.

The `:mkcmd` command transforms source code into an executable command based on a set of predefined rules. If the `:mkcmd` command encounters a sub-directory within the `cmd` directory then it runs the makefile found in that sub-directory. If no makefile is found then an error is reported. For single-file commands, the predefined rules are dependent on the file's suffix. C programs (`.c`) are compiled by the C compiler and loaded stripped with shared text. Assembly language programs (`.s`) are assembled and loaded stripped. Yacc programs (`.y`) and lex programs (`.l`) are processed by `yacc`(1) and `lex`(1) respectively, before C compilation. Shell programs (`.sh`) are copied to create the command. Each of these operations leaves a command in the `./cmd` directory which is then installed into a user-accessible directory by using `/usr/sbin/install`.

The arguments to `:mkcmd` are either command names or subsystem names. Some subsystems distributed with the UNIX system are: `acct`, `graf`, `sgs`, `sccs`, and `text`. Prefacing the `:mkcmd` command with an assignment to the shell variable `$ARGS` causes the indicated components of the subsystem to be rebuilt.

For example, the entire `sccs` subsystem can be rebuilt by:

```
/usr/src/:mkcmd sccs
```

while the `delta` component of `sccs` can be rebuilt by:

```
ARGS="delta" /usr/src/:mkcmd sccs
```

The `log` command, which is a part of the `stat` package, which is itself a part of the `graf` package, can be rebuilt by:

```
ARGS="stat log" /usr/src/:mkcmd graf
```

The argument `*` causes all commands and subsystems to be rebuilt.

Makefiles throughout the system, and particularly in the `cmd` directory, have a standard format. In particular, `:mkcmd` depends on each makefile having target entries for `install` and `clobber`. The `install` target should cause everything over which the makefile has jurisdiction to be built and installed by `/usr/sbin/install`. The `clobber` target should cause a complete cleanup of all unnecessary files resulting from the previous invocation. The commands that use the `CLOBBER` environment variable are `:mkcmd`, `:mklib`, and `:mkuts`. These commands all check the `CLOBBER` variable before executing `make clobber`. If this variable is set to `OFF`, then `make clobber` is *not* performed. If the variable is *not* set or is set to anything other than `OFF`, the `make clobber` *is* performed.

An effort has been made to separate the creation of a command from source and its installation on the running system. The command `/usr/sbin/install` is used by `:mkcmd` and most makefiles to install commands in standard directories on the system. The use of `install` allows maximum flexibility in the administration of the system. The `install` command makes very few assumptions about where a command is located, who owns it, and what modes are in effect. All assumptions may be overridden on invocation of the command, or more permanently by redefining a few variables in `install`. The purpose of `install` is to install a new version of a command in the same place, with the same attributes as the prior version.

In addition, the use of a separate command to perform installation allows for the creation of test systems in other than standard places, easy movement of commands to balance load, and independent maintenance of makefiles.

SEE ALSO

install(1M), lex(1), make(1), yacc(1).

NAME

mkapropos - create apropos list of manpage descriptions

SYNOPSIS

mkapropos [*-w* | *-m*] [*file ...*] [*directory ...*]

DESCRIPTION

mkapropos prints a one-line description per manpage on standard output. The output of mkapropos is similar to that of the whatis file found on BSD systems. Typically, the output is redirected to a file that can be searched for keyword strings. The output can be used as the aproposfile resource of xman(1).

mkapropos searches manpage files for the descriptive text. The manpage may be formatted or nroff source. If formatted, the manpage file may be optionally packed or compressed. See compress(1) or pack(1).

The description is the text of the "NAME" section of the manpage. The description section is delimited by the keyword "NAME" at the beginning of the section and by a blank line preceding the next manpage section. mkapropos filters out newlines found in the "NAME" section to produce the one-line format, so that a simple grep(1) search can find all the information associated with a given manpage.

Either manpage filenames or directory names may be given as arguments. If individual filenames are given, only the specified files will be searched. If directory names are given, mkapropos will recursively search those directories.

If no command line arguments are given, mkapropos first checks whether the MAN-PATH environment variable is set. If so, mkapropos recursively searches for manpages in each directory specified by MANPATH. If not, mkapropos recursively searches for manpages in the directory /usr/catman.

The following options are available:

-w   mkapropos prints a one line description similar to the output given by mkapropos without -w option, except that the suffixes of the file are enclosed in parentheses. Hyphenated words due to the line breaks are combined.

-m   mkapropos prints lines of mapping associations for commands on one manpage. One line of mapping includes the command name, file name where the command is documented, and the description.

SEE ALSO

compress(1), grep(1), man(1), pack(1), xman(1)

NAME

mkboot - convert an object file to a bootable object file

SYNOPSIS

/usr/sbin/mkboot [-m *master*] [-d *directory*] -k *kernel_obj* [-f *kernel_master*]

/usr/sbin/mkboot [-m *master*] [-d *directory*] *obj_file*

DESCRIPTION

The mkboot command is used to create a new object file from a previous object file and its associated master file; the new object file can be used by the cunix program to configure a new bootable operating system.

Typically, a user makes changes to one or more files in the directory /etc/master.d [files in this directory are called master files, and are in the format specified in the master(4) manual page].

Then, the user executes a mkboot command (with appropriate options) from the /boot directory; the /boot directory is used to hold all device driver object files that must be configured into the bootable operating system so that the operating system correctly reflects the current configuration of the machine.

One mkboot command must be executed for each master file changed. The mkboot command updates the existing object file in /boot with the changes made to its associated master file.

After executing all necessary mkboot commands, the user then either configures a new bootable operating system from firmware mode and reboots the system, or uses the cunix command to configure a new bootable operating system at the user level.

The user must specify either the -k option with the kernel object file name (usually KERNEL), or the name of another object file to be changed (usually a file in /boot). The object file name used can be a relative or full pathname, and can have an optional .o suffix.

If the -k option is used, the master file name kernel is assumed; -f can be used to specify a master file other than kernel to build the *kernel_obj* object.

If *obj_file* is specified instead of -k, the named *obj_file* must have an associated file in /etc/master.d; the name of the associated master file is the name of the *obj_file* in lowercase letters, without any path prefix or .o suffix.

If you are making a new object file for the kernel, you must use the -k option to specify the kernel object file; if you process a kernel object file without the -k option, the resulting object file will be unusable by cunix (an error is returned by cunix that says that no object was flagged as the kernel; this flag is added to the object file only when -k is specified).

The -m and -d options are used to specify alternate locations for master files and object files output by mkboot:

-m *master*   This option specifies the directory containing the master files to be used for the object file. The default *master* directory is /etc/master.d.

-d *directory*   This option specifies the directory to be used for storing the new object file. The default output *directory* is /boot.

To create a new object file, the applicable master file is read and the configuration information is extracted. Then, the old object file is read from the current directory, and changed to reflect the new configuration information. The resulting new object file is written to the output directory specified by the -d option or to /boot. It is given the same name as specified by *obj_file* or *kernel_obj*, in uppercase letters and without any .o suffix.

Note that if the output directory is the same as the current working directory when mkboot is executed, then the output object file overwrites the previous object file residing in the directory.

EXAMPLE

    mkboot -m newmaster gentty.o

This will read the file named gentty from the directory newmaster for the gentty device configuration data, take the file gentty.o from the current directory, and create the object file /boot/GENTTY for use in configuring a new operating system.

    cd /boot; mkboot -k KERNEL

This will read the file named kernel from the directory /etc/master.d for the new kernel configuration data, take the file KERNEL from the current directory, and create the /boot/KERNEL object file.

    cd /boot; mkboot sem

This will read the file named sem from the /etc/master.d directory, take the file SEM from the current directory (/boot), and place the output file in /boot/SEM.

DIAGNOSTICS

    mkboot FILE   (FILE does not exist)

    mkboot: FILE: cannot open: No such file or directory

    mkboot -d dir SEM   (dir does not exist)

    mkboot: dir: cannot open: No such file or directory
    mkboot: SEM; not processed

SEE ALSO

    cunix(1M), master(4).

NAME

mkdir - make directories

SYNOPSIS

mkdir [-m *mode*] [-p] *dirname* ...

DESCRIPTION

mkdir creates the named directories in mode 777 (possibly altered by umask(1)).

Standard entries in a directory (for example, the files ., for the directory itself, and .., for its parent) are made automatically. mkdir cannot create these entries by name. Creation of a directory requires write permission in the parent directory.

The owner ID and group ID of the new directories are set to the process's real user ID and group ID, respectively.

Two options apply to mkdir:

-m   This option allows users to specify the mode to be used for new directories. Choices for modes can be found in chmod(1).

-p   With this option, mkdir creates dirname by creating all the non-existing parent directories first.

EXAMPLE

To create the subdirectory structure ltr/jd/jan, type:

```
mkdir -p ltr/jd/jan
```

SEE ALSO

sh(1), rm(1), umask(1)
intro(2), mkdir(2).

DIAGNOSTICS

mkdir returns exit code 0 if all directories given in the command line were made successfully. Otherwise, it prints a diagnostic and returns non-zero.

NAME

`mkfifo` - make FIFO special file

SYNOPSIS

`mkfifo path...`

DESCRIPTION

`mkfifo` creates the FIFO special files named by its argument list. The arguments are taken sequentially, in the order specified; and each FIFO special file is either created completely or, in the case of an error or signal, not created at all.

For each *path* argument, the `mkfifo` command behaves as if the function `mkfifo` [see `mkfifo`(3C)] was called with the argument *path* set to *path* and the *mode* set to the bitwise inclusive OR of `S_IRUSR`, `S_IWUSR`, `S_IRGRP`, `S_IWGRP`, `S_IROTH` and `S_IWOTH`.

If errors are encountered in creating one of the special files, `mkfifo` writes a diagnostic message to the standard error and continues with the remaining arguments, if any.

SEE ALSO

`mkfifo`(3C).

DIAGNOSTICS

`mkfifo` returns exit code `0` if all FIFO special files were created normally; otherwise it prints a diagnostic and returns a value greater than `0`.

NAME

mkfs (generic) - construct a file system

SYNOPSIS

mkfs [-F *FSType*] [-V] [-m] [*current_options*] [-o *specific_options*] *special* [*operands*]

DESCRIPTION

mkfs constructs a file system by writing on the *special* file; *special* must be the first argument. The file system is created based on the *FSType, specific_options* and *operands* specified on the command line. mkfs waits 10 seconds before starting to construct the file system. During this time the command can be aborted by entering a delete (DEL).

operands are *FSType*-specific and the *FSType* specific manual page of mkfs should be consulted for a detailed description.

current_options are options supported by the s5-specific module of mkfs. Other *FSTypes* do not necessarily support these options. *specific_options* indicate suboptions specified in a comma-separated list of suboptions and/or keyword-attribute pairs for interpretation by the *FSType*-specific module of the command. See mkfs_*FSType*(1M) for details.

The options are:

-F   Specify the *FSType* to be constructed. The *FSType* should either be specified here or be determinable from /etc/vfstab by matching the *special* with an entry in the table.

-V   Echo the complete command line, but do not execute the command. The command line is generated by using the options and arguments provided by the user and adding to them information derived from /etc/vfstab. This option should be used to verify and validate the command line.

-m   Return the command line which was used to create the file system. The file system must already exist. This option provides a means of determining the command used in constructing the file system. It cannot be used with *current_options, specific_options*, or *operands*. It must be invoked by itself.

-o   Specify *FSType*-specific options.

NOTES

This command may not be supported for all *FSTypes*.

FILES

/etc/vfstab   list of default parameters for each file system

SEE ALSO

makefsys(1M), mkfs_bfs(1M), mkfs_s5(1M), mkfs_ufs(1M), vfstab(4).

NAME

mkfs (bfs) - construct a boot file system

SYNOPSIS

mkfs [-F bfs] *special blocks* [*inodes*]

DESCRIPTION

mkfs is used to create a boot file system, which is a contiguous flat file system, to hold the bootable programs and data files necessary for the boot procedure.

The argument *special* is the device special file that refers to the slice on which the file system is to be created. The *blocks* argument is used to specify the size of the file system. The block size is automatically 512 bytes.

The *inodes* argument specifies the number of files that the file system will hold.

NOTES

This file system is intended to hold the bootable files and data files for the boot procedure. Use as a general purpose file system is not recommended.

NAME

mkfs (s5) - construct an s5 file system

SYNOPSIS

mkfs [-F s5] [*generic_options*] [-b *block_size*] *special blocks*[:*i-nodes*] [*gap blocks/cyl*]
mkfs [-F s5] [*generic_options*] [-b *block_size*] *special proto* [*gap blocks/cyl*]

DESCRIPTION

generic_options are options supported by the generic mkfs command.

mkfs constructs an s5 file system by writing on the *special* file using the values found in the remaining arguments of the command line. mkfs builds a file system with a root directory and a lost+found directory.

The options are:

-F s5   Specifies an s5-FSType.

-b *blocksize*

> Specifies the logical block size for the file system. The logical block size is the number of bytes read or written by the operating system in a single I/O operation. Valid values for *blocksize* are 512, 1024, and 2048. The default is 1024.

If the second argument to mkfs is a string of digits, the size of the file system is the value of *blocks* interpreted as a decimal number. This is the number of *physical* (512 byte) disk blocks the file system will occupy. If the number of i-nodes is not given, the default is approximately the number of *logical* blocks divided by 4. mkfs builds a file system with a single empty directory on it. The boot program block (block zero) is left uninitialized.

If the second argument is the name of a file that can be opened, mkfs assumes it to be a prototype file *proto*, and will take its directions from that file. The prototype file contains tokens separated by spaces or new-lines. A sample prototype specification follows (line numbers have been added to aid in the explanation):

```
1    /dev/c1d0s0
2    4872 110
3    d--777 3 1
4    usr   d--777 3 1
5          sh      ---755 3 1 /sbin/sh
6          ken     d--755 6 1
7                  $
8          b0      b--644 3 1 0 0
9          c0      c--644 3 1 0 0
10         slnk    l--777 2 2 /var/tmp
11                 $
12   $
```

Line 1 in the example is the name of a file to be copied onto block zero as the bootstrap program.

Line 2 specifies the number of *physical* (512 byte) blocks the file system is to occupy and the number of i-nodes in the file system.

Lines 3-10 tell mkfs about files and directories to be included in this file system.

Line 3 specifies the root directory.

Lines 4-6 and 8-10 specify other directories and files.

Line 10 specifies the symbolic link slnk set up in /usr and containing /var/tmp.

The $ on line 7 tells mkfs to end the branch of the file system it is on, and continue from the next higher directory. The $ on lines 11 and 12 end the process, since no additional specifications follow.

File specifications give the mode, the user ID, the group ID, and the initial contents of the file. Valid syntax for the contents field depends on the first character of the mode.

The mode for a file is specified by a 6-character string. The first character specifies the type of the file. The character range is -bcdl to specify regular, block special, character special, directory, and symbolic link files respectively. The second character of the mode is either u or - to specify set-user-id mode or not. The third is g or - for the set-group-id mode. The rest of the mode is a 3 digit octal number giving the owner, group, and other read, write, execute permissions [see chmod(1)].

Two decimal number tokens come after the mode; they specify the user and group IDs of the owner of the file.

If the file is a regular file, the next token of the specification may be a path name whence the contents and size are copied. If the file is a block or character special file, two decimal numbers follow which give the major and minor device numbers. If the file is a directory, mkfs makes the entries . and .. and then reads a list of names and (recursively) file specifications for the entries in the directory. As noted above, the scan is terminated with the token $.

The *gap blocks/cyl* argument in both forms of the command specifies the rotational gap and the number of blocks/cylinder. The following values are recommended for the devices available:

Device	Gap Size 512-byte FS	Gap Size 1K FS	Gap Size 2K FS	Blks/Cyl	
10M Hard Disk	8	10	12	72	
30M Hard Disk	8	10	12	90	
72M Hard Disk	8	10	12	162	(CDC Wren II)
72aM Hard Disk	8	10	12	144	(Micropolis)
72bM Hard Disk	8	10	12	162	(Priam)
72cM Hard Disk	8	10	12	198	(Fujitsu)

If the *gap* and *blocks/cyl* are not specified or are invalid values a default value of gap size 10 and 162 blocks/cyl is used.

NOTES

With a prototype file there is no way to specify hard links.

FILES

/etc/vtoc/*

SEE ALSO

chmod(1), dir(4), fs(4), generic mkfs(1M)

NAME

mkmsgs - create message files for use by gettxt

SYNOPSIS

mkmsgs [-o] [-i *locale*] *inputstrings msgfile*

DESCRIPTION

The mkmsgs utility is used to create a file of text strings that can be accessed using the text retrieval tools [see gettxt(1), srchtxt(1), exstr(1), and gettxt(3C)]. It will take as input a file of text strings for a particular geographic locale [see setlocale(3C)] and create a file of text strings in a format that can be retrieved by both gettxt(1) and gettxt(3C). By using the -i option, you can install the created file under the /usr/lib/locale/*locale*/LC_MESSAGES directory (*locale* corresponds to the language in which the text strings are written).

inputstrings   the name of the file that contains the original text strings.

msgfile   the name of the output file where mkmsgs writes the strings in a format that is readable by gettxt(1) and gettxt(3C). The name of *msgfile* can be up to 14 characters in length, but may not contain either \0 (null) or the ASCII code for / (slash) or : (colon).

-i *locale*   install *msgfile* in the /usr/lib/locale/*locale*/LC_MESSAGES directory. Only someone who is super-user or a member of group bin can create or overwrite files in this directory. Directories under /usr/lib/locale will be created if they don't exist.

-o   overwrite *msgfile*, if it exists.

The input file contains a set of text strings for the particular geographic locale. Text strings are separated by a new-line character. Nongraphic characters must be represented as alphabetic escape sequences. Messages are transformed and copied sequentially from *inputstrings* to *msgfile*. To generate an empty message in *msgfile*, leave an empty line at the correct place in *inputstrings*.

Strings can be changed simply by editing the file *inputstrings*. New strings must be added only at the end of the file; then a new *msgfile* file must be created and installed in the correct place. If this procedure is not followed, the retrieval function will retrieve the wrong string and software compatibility will be broken.

EXAMPLES

The following example shows an input message source file c.str:

```
File %s:\t cannot be opened\n
%s: Bad directory\n
          .
          .
          .
write error\n
          .
          .
```

The following command uses the input strings from c.str to create text strings in the appropriate format in the file UX in the current directory:

```
mkmsgs C.str UX
```

The following command uses the input strings from FR.str to create text strings in the appropriate format in the file UX in the directory /usr/lib/locale/french/LC_MESSAGES/UX.

```
mkmsgs -i french FR.str UX
```

These text strings would be accessed if you had set the environment variable LC_MESSAGES=french and then invoked one of the text retrieval tools listed at the beginning of the DESCRIPTION section.

FILES

/usr/lib/locale/*locale*/LC_MESSAGES/*   message files created by mkmsgs(1M)

SEE ALSO

exstr(1), gettxt(1), gettxt(3C), setlocale(3C), srchtxt(1)

NAME

montbl - create monetary database

SYNOPSIS

montbl [-o *outfile*] *infile*

DESCRIPTION

The montbl command takes as input a specification file, *infile*, that describes the formatting conventions for monetary quantities for a specific locale.

-o *outfile*　　　Write the output on *outfile*; otherwise, write the output on a file named LC_MONETARY.

The output of montbl is suitable for use by the localeconv( ) function [see localeconv(3C)]. Before *outfile* can be used by localeconv( ), it must be installed in the /usr/lib/locale/*locale* directory with the name LC_MONETARY by someone who is super-user or a member of group bin. *locale* is the locale whose monetary formatting conventions are described in *infile*. This file must be readable by user, group, and other; no other permissions should be set. To use formatting conventions for monetary quantities described in this file, use setlocale(3C) to change the locale for category LC_MONETARY to *locale* [see setlocale(3C)].

Once installed, this file will be used by the localeconv( ) function to initialize the monetary specific fields of a structure of type struct lconv. For a description of each field in this structure, see localeconv(3C).

```
struct        lconv        {
        char *decimal_point;          /* "." */
        char *thousands_sep;          /* "" (zero length string) */
        char *grouping;               /* "" */
        char *int_curr_symbol;        /* "" */
        char *currency_symbol;        /* "" */
        char *mon_decimal_point;      /* "" */
        char *mon_thousands_sep;      /* "" */
        char *mon_grouping;           /* "" */
        char *positive_sign;          /* "" */
        char *negative_sign;          /* "" */
        char int_frac_digits;         /* CHAR_MAX */
        char frac_digits;             /* CHAR_MAX */
        char p_cs_precedes;           /* CHAR_MAX */
        char p_sep_by_space;          /* CHAR_MAX */
        char n_cs_precedes;           /* CHAR_MAX */
        char n_sep_by_space;          /* CHAR_MAX */
        char p_sign_posn;             /* CHAR_MAX */
        char n_sign_posn;             /* CHAR_MAX */
    };
```

The specification file specifies the value of each struct lconv member, except for the first three members, *decimal_point*, *thousands_sep*, and *grouping* which are set by the LC_NUMERIC category of setlocale(3C). Each member's value is given on a line with the following format:

value

where *value* is a string for those fields that are a `char` * and an integer for those fields that are an `int`. For example,

```
ITL.
```

will set the international currency symbol to be displayed in an internationally formatted monetary quantity to `ITL`.

Lines starting with a # are taken to be comments and are ignored. A character in a string may be in octal or hex representation. For example, `\141` or `\x61` could be used to represent the letter 'a'. If there is no specification line for a given structure member, then the default 'C' locale value for that member is used (see the values in comments in the `struct lconv` definition above).

Given below is an example of what the specification file for Italy would look like:

```
# Italy
ITL.
L.


\3

 _
 0
 0
 1
 0
 1
 0
 1
 1
```

FILES

```
/usr/lib/locale/locale/LC_MONETARY
```
LC_MONETARY database for *locale*

```
/usr/lib/locale/C/montbl_C
```
input file used to construct LC_MONETARY in the default locale.

SEE ALSO

`localeconv`(3C), `setlocale`(3C)

NAME

`more`, `page` - browse or page through a text file

SYNOPSIS

`more` [*-cdflrsuw*] [*-lines*] [*+linenumber*] [*+/pattern*] [*filename* . . .

`page` [*-cdflrsuw*] [*-lines*] [*+linenumber*] [*+/pattern*] [*filename* . . .

DESCRIPTION

`more` is a filter that displays the contents of a text file on the terminal, one screenful at a time. It normally pauses after each screenful, and prints `--More--` at the bottom of the screen. `more` provides a two-line overlap between screens for continuity. If `more` is reading from a file rather than a pipe, the percentage of characters displayed so far is also shown.

`more` scrolls up to display one more line in response to a RETURN character; it displays another screenful in response to a SPACE character. Other commands are listed below.

`page` clears the screen before displaying the next screenful of text; it only provides a one-line overlap between screens.

`more` sets the terminal to *noecho* mode, so that the output can be continuous. Commands that you type do not normally show up on your terminal, except for the `/` and `!` commands.

If the standard output is not a terminal, `more` acts just like `cat`(1V), except that a header is printed before each file in a series.

OPTIONS

The following options are available with `more`:

`-c`	Clear before displaying. Redrawing the screen instead of scrolling for faster displays. This option is ignored if the terminal does not have the ability to clear to the end of a line.
`-d`	Display error messages rather than ringing the terminal bell if an unrecognized command is used. This is helpful for inexperienced users.
`-f`	Do not fold long lines. This is useful when lines contain nonprinting characters or escape sequences, such as those generated when `nroff`(1) output is piped through `ul`(1).
`-l`	Do not treat FORMFEED characters (CTRL-d) as page breaks. If `-l` is not used, `more` pauses to accept commands after any line containing a `^L` character (CTRL-d). Also, if a file begins with a FORMFEED, the screen is cleared before the file is printed.
`-r`	Normally, `more` ignores control characters that it does not interpret in some way. The `-r` option causes these to be displayed as `^C` where C stands for any such control character.
`-s`	Squeeze. Replace multiple blank lines with a single blank line. This is helpful when viewing `nroff`(1) output, on the screen.
`-u`	Suppress generation of underlining escape sequences. Normally, `more` handles underlining, such as that produced by `nroff`(1), in a manner appropriate to the terminal. If the terminal can perform underlining or has a stand-out mode, `more` supplies appropriate

escape sequences as called for in the text file.

-w   Normally, more exits when it comes to the end of its input. With -w, however, more prompts and waits for any key to be struck before exiting.

-lines   Display the indicated number of *lines* in each screenful, rather than the default (the number of lines in the terminal screen less two).

+linenumber   Start up at *linenumber*.

+/pattern   Start up two lines above the line containing the regular expression *pattern*. Note: unlike editors, this construct should *not* end with a '/'. If it does, then the trailing slash is taken as a character in the search pattern.

USAGE
Environment
more uses the terminal's termcap(5) entry to determine its display characteristics, and looks in the environment variable for any preset options. For instance, to page through files using the -c mode by default, set the value of this variable to -c. (Normally, the command sequence to set up this environment variable is placed in the .login or .profile file).

Commands
The commands take effect immediately; it is not necessary to type a carriage return. Up to the time when the command character itself is given, the user may type the line kill character to cancel the numerical argument being formed. In addition, the user may type the erase character to redisplay the '--More--(*xx*%)' message.

In the following commands, *i* is a numerical argument (1 by default).

*i*SPACE   Display another screenful, or *i* more lines if *i* is specified.

*i*RETURN   Display another line, or *i* more lines, if specified.

i^D   (CTRL-d) Display (scroll down) 11 more lines. If *i* is given, the scroll size is set to *i* .

*i*d   Same as ^D.

*i*z   Same as SPACE, except that *i* , if present, becomes the new default number of lines per screenful.

*i*s   Skip *i* lines and then print a screenful.

*i*f   Skip *i* screenfuls and then print a screenful.

i^B   (CTRL-b) Skip back *i* screenfuls and then print a screenful.

b   Same as ^B (CTRL-d).

q
Q   Exit from more.

=   Display the current line number.

v   Drop into the editor indicated by the EDITOR environment variable, at the current line of the current file. The default editor is ed(1).

h	Help. Give a description of all the more commands.
i/*pattern*	Search forward for the *i* th occurrence of the regular expression *pattern*. Display the screenful starting two lines before the line that contains the *i* th match for the regular expression *pattern*, or the end of a pipe, whichever comes first. If more is displaying a file and there is no such match, its position in the file remains unchanged. Regular expressions can be edited using erase and kill characters. Erasing back past the first column cancels the search command.
in	Search for the *i* th occurrence of the last *pattern* entered.
´	Single quote. Go to the point from which the last search started. If no search has been performed in the current file, go to the beginning of the file.
!*command*	Invoke a shell to execute *command* . The characters % and !, when used within *command* are replaced with the current filename and the previous shell command, respectively. If there is no current filename, % is not expanded. Prepend a backslash to these characters to escape expansion.
i:n	Skip to the *i* th next filename given in the command line, or to the last filename in the list if *i* is out of range.
i:p	Skip to the *i* th previous filename given in the command line, or to the first filename if *i* is out of range. If given while more is positioned within a file, go to the beginning of the file. If more is reading from a pipe, more simply rings the terminal bell.
:f	Display the current filename and line number.
:q :Q	Exit from more (same as q or Q).
.	Dot. Repeat the previous command.
^\	Halt a partial display of text. more stops sending output, and displays the usual --More-- prompt. Unfortunately, some output is lost as a result.

FILES

/usr/share/lib/termcap   terminal data base
/usr/lib/more.help   help file

SEE ALSO

cat(1), csh(1), man(1), script(1), sh(1)
environ(5V), termcap(5).

NOTES

Skipping backwards is too slow on large files.

NAME

mount, umount (generic) - mount or unmount file systems and remote resources

SYNOPSIS

    mount [-v |-p]
    mount [-F *FSType*] [-V] [*current_options*] [-o *specific_options*] {*special* | *mount_point*}
    mount [-F *FSType*] [-V] [*current_options*] [-o *specific_options*] *special mount_point*
    umount [-V] [-o *specific_options*] {*special* | *mount_point*}

DESCRIPTION

File systems other than root (/) are considered removable in the sense that they can be either available to users or unavailable. mount notifies the system that *special*, a block special device or a remote resource, is available to users from the *mount_point* which must already exist; it becomes the name of the root of the newly mounted *special* or resource.

mount, when entered with arguments, validates all arguments except for the device name and invokes a *FSType* specific mount module. If invoked with no arguments, mount lists all the mounted file systems from the mount table. If invoked with any of the following partial argument lists, for example, one of *special* or *mount_point* or when both arguments are specified but no *FSType* is specified mount will search /etc/vfstab to fill in the missing arguments: *FSType*, *special*, *mount_point*, and *specific_options*. It will then invoke the *FSType*-specific mount module. See mount_*FSType*(1M) for details.

Most *FSTypes* do not have a umount specific module. If one exists it is executed otherwise the generic unmounts the file systems. If the -o option is specified the umount specific module is always executed.

current_options are options supported by the s5-specific module of mount and umount. Other *FSTypes* do not necessarily support these options. *specific_options* indicate suboptions specified in a comma-separated list of suboptions and/or keyword-attribute pairs for interpretation by the *FSType*-specific module of the command.

The options are:

-v   Print the output in a new style. The new output has the *FSType* and flags displayed in addition to the old output. The *mount_point* and *special* fields are reversed.

-p   Print the list of mounted file systems in the /etc/vfstab format.

-F   used to specify the *FSType* on which to operate. The *FSType* must be specified or must be determinable from /etc/vfstab while mounting a file system.

-V   Echo the complete command line, but do not execute the command. The command line is generated by using the options and arguments provided by the user and adding to them information derived from /etc/vfstab. This option should be used to verify and validate the command line.

-o   used to specify *FSType*-specific options.

mount can be used by any user to list mounted file systems and resources. Only a super-user can mount or unmount file systems.

NOTES

The old output format will be phased out in a future release and all output will be in the new -v format. The most significant changes are the addition of two new fields to show the *FSType* and flags and the reversal of the *mount_point* and *special* name.

If a special device in the mount table /etc/mnttab is not found in /etc/vfstab, the -p format will print a "—" as the corresponding fsck device.

mount adds an entry to the mount table /etc/mnttab; umount removes an entry from the table.

FILES

/etc/mnttab   mount table
/etc/vfstab   list of default parameters for each file system.

SEE ALSO

mount_bfs(1M),   mount_nfs(1M),   mount_rfs(1M),   mount_s5(1M), mount_ufs(1M), mountfsys(1M), setmnt(1M), umountfsys(1M), mnttab(4), vfstab(4).

NAME

mount (bfs) - mount bfs file systems

SYNOPSIS

mount [-F bfs] [*generic_options*] [-r] [-o *specific_options*] {*special* | *mount_point*}
mount [-F bfs] [*generic_options*] [-r] [-o *specific_options*] *special mount_point*

DESCRIPTION

generic_options are options supported by the generic mount command.

mount attaches a bfs file system, referenced by *special*, to the file system hierarchy at the pathname location *mount_point*, which must already exist. If *mount_point* has any contents prior to the mount operation, these are hidden until the file system is unmounted.

The options are:

-F bfs   Specify the bfs-FSType

-r   Mount the file system read-only

-o   Specify the options specific to the bfs file system. Available options are:

              rw | ro   Read/write or read-only. Default is read/write.

Only a privileged user can mount file systems.

FILES

/etc/mnttab   mount table

SEE ALSO

generic mount(1M), mountfsys(1M), mount(2), mnttab(4).

NAME

mount - mount remote NFS resources

SYNOPSIS

mount [-F nfs] [-r] [-o *specific_options*] {*resource* | *mountpoint*}
mount [-F nfs] [-r] [-o *specific_options*] *resource mountpoint*

DESCRIPTION

The mount command attaches a named *resource* to the file system hierarchy at the pathname location *mountpoint*, which must already exist. If *mountpoint* has any contents prior to the mount operation, the contents remain hidden until the *resource* is once again unmounted.

If the resource is listed in the vfstab file, the command line can specify either *resource* or *mountpoint*, and mount will consult vfstab for more information. If the -F option is omitted, mount will take the file system type from vfstab.

mount maintains a table of mounted file systems in /etc/mnttab, described in mnttab(4).

The following options are available to the mount command:

-r   Mount the specified file system read-only.

-o   Specify the nfs file-specific options in a comma-separated list. The available options are:

rw | ro	*resource* is mounted read-write or read-only. The default is rw.
suid | nosuid	Setuid execution allowed or disallowed. The default is suid.
remount	If a file system is mounted read-only, remounts the file system read-write.
bg | fg	If the first attempt fails, retry in the background, or, in the foreground. The default is fg.
retry=*n*	The number of times to retry the mount operation. The default is 10000.
port=*n*	The server IP port number. The default is NFS_PORT.
grpid	Create a file with its GID set to the effective GID of the calling process. This behavior may be overridden on a per-directory basis by setting the set-GID bit of the parent directory; in this case, the GID is set to the GID of the parent directory [see open(2) and mkdir(2)]. Files created on file systems that are *not* mounted with the grpid option will obey BSD semantics; that is, the GID is unconditionally inherited from that of the parent directory.
rsize=*n*	Set the read buffer size to *n* bytes.
wsize=*n*	Set the write buffer size to *n* bytes.
timeo=*n*	Set the NFS timeout to *n* tenths of a second.
retrans=*n*	Set the number of NFS retransmissions to *n*.
soft | hard	Return an error if the server does not respond, or continue the retry request until the server responds.

`intr`	Allow keyboard interrupts to kill a process that is hung while waiting for a response on a hard-mounted file system.
`secure`	Use a more secure protocol for NFS transactions.
`noac`	Suppress attribute caching.
`acregmin=n`	Hold cached attributes for at least n seconds after file modification.
`acregmax=n`	Hold cached attributes for no more than n seconds after file modification.
`acdirmin=n`	Hold cached attributes for at least n seconds after directory update.
`acdirmax=n`	Hold cached attributes for no more than n seconds after directory update.
`actimeo=n`	Set *min* and *max* times for regular files and directories to n seconds.

NFS FILE SYSTEMS

Background vs. Foreground

If the mount is initially unsuccessful, `mount` retries the attempt up to as many times as specified in the `retry=n` option (default 10000). File systems mounted with the `bg` option indicate that `mount` is to retry in the background if the server's mount daemon [`mountd(1M)`] does not respond, otherwise the retry will occur in the foreground. Between retry attempts `mount` sleeps for an interval that begins at 5 seconds and doubles each time until the interval reaches 120 seconds, where it remains until the mount succeeds or the retry count is exhausted.

NOTE: If you specify that the mount is to occur in the forground and the number of retries is large, your system may hang when attempting to mount file systems on unresponsive servers. E.g., a retry count of 500 will cause `mount` to retry for more than 16 hours.

Once the file system is mounted, each NFS request waits `timeo=n` tenths of a second for a response. If no response arrives, the time-out is multiplied by 2 and the request is retransmitted. The timeout will not increase beyond 20 seconds. When the number of retransmissions has reached the number specified in the `retrans=n` option, a file system mounted with the `soft` option returns an error on the request; one mounted with the `hard` option prints a warning message and continues to retry the request.

Read-Write vs. Read-Only

File systems that are mounted `rw` (read-write) should use the `hard` option.

Secure File Systems

The `secure` option must be given if the server requires secure mounting for the file system.

File Attributes

The attribute cache retains file attributes on the client. Attributes for a file are assigned a time to be flushed. If the file is modified before the flush time, then the flush time is extended by the time since the last modification (under the assumption that files that changed recently are likely to change soon). There is a minimum and maximum flush time extension for regular files and for directories. Setting `actimeo=n` extends flush time by n seconds for both regular files and directories.

EXAMPLES

To mount a remote file system: `mount -F nfs serv:/usr/src /usr/src`
To hard mount a remote file system: `mount -o hard serv:/usr/src /usr/src`

FILES

`/etc/mnttab`	mount table
`/etc/dfs/fstypes`	default distributed file system type
`/etc/vfstab`	table of automatically mounted resources

SEE ALSO

`mountall`(1M), `mount`(2), `umount`(2), `mnttab`(4).

NOTES

If the directory on which a file system is to be mounted is a symbolic link, the file system is mounted on *the directory to which the symbolic link refers,* rather than being mounted on top of the symbolic link itself.

NAME

mount - mount remote resources

SYNOPSIS

mount [-F rfs] [-o *suboption*] [-cr] *resource directory*

DESCRIPTION

The mount command makes a remote *resource* available to users from the mount point *directory*. The command adds an entry to the table of mounted devices, /etc/mnttab.

If multiple transport providers are installed and administrators attempt to mount a resource over them, the transport providers should be specified as network IDs in the /etc/netconfig file. The NETPATH environment variable can be used to specify the sequence of transport providers mount will use to attempt a connection to a server machine (NETPATH=tcp:starlan). If only one transport provider is installed and /etc/netconfig has not been set up, all resources will be mounted over this transport provider by default.

The following options are available:

-o *suboption*

nocaching	Disable client caching.
[rw|ro]	*resource* is to be mounted read/write or read-only. The default is read/write.
[suid|nosuid]	set-uid bits are to be obeyed or ignored, respectively, on execution. The default is nosuid.

-c Disable client caching. This is the same as -o nocaching.

-r *resource* is to be mounted read-only. If the *resource* is write-protected, this flag, or the -o ro flag, must be used.

FILES

/etc/mnttab
/etc/netconfig
/etc/vfstab

SEE ALSO

umount(1M), share(1M), fuser(1M), unshare(1M), dfshares(1M), dfmounts(1M), netconfig(4), mnttab(4), vfstab(1M)

NAME

mount (s5) - mount an s5 file system

SYNOPSIS

mount [-F s5] [*generic_options*] [-r] [-o *specific_options*] {*special | mount_point*}
mount [-F s5] [*generic_options*] [-r] [-o *specific_options*] *special mount_point*

DESCRIPTION

generic_options are options supported by the generic mount command.

mount notifies the system that *special*, an s5 block special device, is available to users from the *mount_point* which must exist before mount is called; it becomes the name of the root of the newly mounted *special*.

The options are:

-F s5   Specify an s5 FSType.

-r   Mount the file system read-only.

-o   Specify s5-specific suboptions. The suboptions are:

       rw | ro   Read/write or read-only. Default is rw.

       suid | nosuid   Setuid is honored or ignored on execution Default is suid.

       remount   Used in conjunction with rw. A file system mounted read-only can be *remounted* read-write. Fails if the file system is not currently mounted or if the file system is mounted rw. Option is in force only when specified.

Only a privileged user can mount file systems.

FILES

/etc/mnttab   mount table

SEE ALSO

generic mount(1M), mountfsys(1M), setmnt(1M), mount(2), setuid(2), mnttab(4).

NAME

mount (ufs) - mount ufs file systems

SYNOPSIS

mount [-F ufs] [*generic_options*] [-r] [-o *specific_options*] { *special* | *mount_point* }

mount [-F ufs] [*generic_options*] [-r] [-o *specific_options*] *special mount_point*

DESCRIPTION

generic_options are options supported by the generic mount command. mount attaches a ufs file system, referenced by *special*, to the file system hierarchy at the pathname location *mount_point*, which must already exist. If *mount_point* has any contents prior to the mount operation, these remain hidden until the file system is once again unmounted.

The options are:

-F ufs   Specifies the ufs-FSType.

-r   Mount the file system read-only.

-o   Specify the ufs file system specific options in a comma-separated list. If invalid options are specified, a warning message is printed and the invalid options are ignored. The following options are available:

f	Fake an /etc/mnttab entry, but do not actually mount any file systems. Parameters are not verified.
n	Mount the file system without making an entry in /etc/mnttab.
rw | ro	Read/write or read-only. Default is rw.
nosuid	By default the file system is mounted with setuid execution allowed. Specifying nosuid overrides the default and causes the file system to be mounted with setuid execution disallowed.
remount	Used in conjunction with rw. A file system mounted read-only can be *remounted* read-write. Fails if the file system is not currently mounted or if the file system is mounted rw.

NOTES

If the directory on which a file system is to be mounted is a symbolic link, the file system is mounted on the directory to which the symbolic link refers, rather than on top of the symbolic link itself.

FILES

/etc/mnttab   mount table

SEE ALSO

generic mount(1M), mountfsys(1M), umountfsys(1M), mkdir(2), mount(2), open(2), unmount(2), mnttab(4)

NAME

mountall, umountall - mount, unmount multiple file systems

SYNOPSIS

mountall [-F *FSType*] [-1 | -r] [-s *strategy*] [-n *number*] [*file-system-table*]
umountall [-F *FSType*] [-k] [-1 | -r]

DESCRIPTION

These commands may be executed only by a privileged user.

mountall is used to mount file systems according to a *file-system-table*. (/etc/vfstab is the default file system table.) The special file name "-" reads from the standard input. If the dash is specified, then the standard input must be in the same format as /etc/vfstab.

Before each file system is mounted, a sanity check is done using fsck [see fsck(1M)] to see if it appears mountable. If the file system does not appear mountable, it is fixed, using fsck, before the mount is attempted.

umountall causes all mounted file systems except root, /proc, /var, and /usr to be unmounted. If the *FSType* is specified mountall and umountall limit their actions to the *FSType* specified.

The options are:

-F   Specify the File System type to be mounted or unmounted. If *FSType* is specified the action is limited to file systems of this *FSType*.

-k   Send a *SIGKILL* signal to processes that have files opened.

-1   Limit the action to local file systems.

-n   Specify a numeric argument. This may only be used with the *disk-busy* strategy: it specifies the maximum number of disks that may be checked in parallel. If it is not specified, all disks with file systems requiring checking will be checked in parallel.

-r   Limit the action to remote file system types.

-s   Specifies the strategy to be used when checking file systems. More information on the mountall strategies can be found in the mountall section below.

MOUNTALL

The mountall program is capable of checking and repairing file systems using several different strategies.

The basic strategy is *sequential*: file systems are checked one at a time in the order they are found in the *file-system-table*.

The next strategy is *fsck-pass*; it is the default strategy. The *fsck-pass* strategy checks the file systems with their *file-system-table* fsck pass numbers of two or greater in parallel, grouped by the fsck pass numbers. Only local file systems may be checked in parallel; the fsck pass number information will be ignored for remote file systems.

File systems with fsck pass numbers of 0 and 1 will be checked in sequential order in the fashion of the *sequential* strategy; those with fsck pass numbers of two or greater will be checked in parallel.

All file systems assigned to the same fsck pass number will have their fsck(1M) operations started simultainiously. *mountall* will then wait for all of the fsck(1M) operations started at the beginning of a pass to be completed before it starts the next pass.

To obtain the best performance, only one fsck(1M) operation should be performed on a disk at one time. The file systems being checked in parallel should be grouped by size as closely as possible. Checking too many file systems in parallel may actually slow down the overall process; start with 2 or 3 at a time.

The final strategy is *disk-busy*. The *disk-busy* strategy ignores the fsck pass number information and attempts to determine if all of the local file systems are located on properly named, real disk devices. If all of the local file systems aren't located on properly named, read disk devices, `mountall` will switch to the *fsck-pass* strategy. If all of the local file systems are acceptable, the *disk-busy* strategy will attempt to keep one fsck operation running on each disk device as long as there is a file system that needs to be checked.

If all of the file systems on a system are located on real disk drives, this strategy should perform the required fsck operations in the minimum amount of time.

To change the strategy used when the system checks its file systems on reboot, edit the file */etc/rc2.d/S01MOUNTFSYS* and add the −s option with the desired strategy argument to the line that starts with */sbin/mountall*.

DIAGNOSTICS

No messages are printed if the file systems are mountable and clean.

Error and warning messages come from `fsck`(1M) and `mount`(1M).

SEE ALSO

`fsck`(1M), `fuser`(1M), `mount`(1M), `vfstab`(4), `mnttab`(4).

NAME

mountd - NFS mount request server

SYNOPSIS

mountd [-n]

DESCRIPTION

mountd is an RPC server that answers file system mount requests. It reads the file /etc/dfs/sharetab, described in sharetab(4), to determine which file systems are available for mounting by which machines. It also provides information as to what file systems are mounted by which clients. This information can be printed using the dfmounts(1M) command.

The mountd daemon is automatically invoked in run level 3.

With the -n option, mountd does not check that the clients are root users. Though this option makes things slightly less secure, it does allow older versions (pre-3.0) of client NFS to work.

FILES

/etc/dfs/sharetab

SEE ALSO

dfmounts(1M), sharetab(4)

NAME

`mountfsys`, `umountfsys` - mount, unmount a file system

SYNOPSIS

`mountfsys`
`umountfsys`

DESCRIPTION

The `mountfsys` command mounts a file system so that users can read from it and write to it. The `umountfsys` command unmounts the file system.

The command invokes a visual interface (the `mount` or `unmount` tasks available through the `sysadm` command).

The initial prompt for both commands allows you to select the device on which to mount/unmount the file system.

For the `mountfsys` command, you are asked to select how the file system is to be mounted; for example, read-only or read/write.

The identical functions are available under the `sysadm` menu:

`sysadm mount`

`sysadm unmount`

DIAGNOSTICS

Both `mountfsys` and `umountfsys` exit with one of the following values:

0   Normal exit.

2   Invalid command syntax. A usage message is displayed.

7   The visual interface for this command is not available because it cannot invoke `fmli`. (The `fmli` package is not installed or is corrupt.)

NOTES

For a removable medium, once the disk is mounted it must not be removed from the disk drive until it has been unmounted. Removing the disk while it is still mounted can cause severe damage to the data on the disk.

SEE ALSO

`checkfsys`(1M), `labelit`(1M), `makefsys`(1M), `mkfs`(1M), `mount`(1M), `sysadm`(1M)

NAME

ms - text formatting macros

SYNOPSIS

nroff -ms [*options*] *filename* ...

troff -ms [*options*] *filename* ...

DESCRIPTION

This package of nroff(1) and troff(1) macro definitions provides a formatting facility for various styles of articles, theses, and books. When producing 2-column output on a terminal or lineprinter, or when reverse line motions are needed, filter the output through col(1V). All external -ms macros are defined below.

Note: this -ms macro package is an extended version written at Berkeley and is a superset of the standard -ms macro packages as supplied by Bell Labs. Some of the Bell Labs macros have been removed; for instance, it is assumed that the user has little interest in producing headers stating that the memo was generated at Whippany Labs.

Many nroff and troff requests are unsafe in conjunction with this package. However, the first four requests below may be used with impunity after initialization, and the last two may be used even before initialization:

.bp	begin new page
.br	break output line
.sp *n*	insert n spacing lines
.ce *n*	center next n lines
.ls *n*	line spacing: $n=1$ single, $n=2$ double space
.na	no alignment of right margin

Font and point size changes with \f and \s are also allowed; for example, \fIword\fR will italicize *word*. Output of the tbl(1), eqn(1) and refer(1) preprocessors for equations, tables, and references is acceptable as input.

REQUESTS

Macro Name	Initial Value	Break? Reset?	Explanation
.AB *x*	-	y	begin abstract; if *x*=no do not label abstract
.AE	-	y	end abstract
.AI	-	y	author's institution
.AM	-	n	better accent mark definitions
.AU	-	y	author's name
.B *x*	-	n	embolden *x*; if no *x*, switch to boldface
.B1	-	y	begin text to be enclosed in a box
.B2	-	y	end boxed text and print it
.BT	date	n	bottom title, printed at foot of page
.BX *x*	-	n	print word *x* in a box
.CM	if t	n	cut mark between pages
.CT	-	y,y	chapter title: page number moved to CF (TM only)
.DA *x*	if n	n	force date *x* at bottom of page; today if no *x*

Macro Name	Initial Value	Break? Reset?	Explanation
.DE	-	y	end display (unfilled text) of any kind
.DS x y	I	y	begin display with keep; x=I, L, C, B; y=indent
.ID y	8n,.5i	y	indented display with no keep; y=indent
.LD	-	y	left display with no keep
.CD	-	y	centered display with no keep
.BD	-	y	block display; center entire block
.EF x	-	n	even page footer x (3 part as for .tl)
.EH x	-	n	even page header x (3 part as for .tl)
.EN	-	y	end displayed equation produced by eqn
.EQ x y	-	y	break out equation; x=L,I,C; y=equation number
.FE	-	n	end footnote to be placed at bottom of page
.FP	-	n	numbered footnote paragraph; may be redefined
.FS x	-	n	start footnote; x is optional footnote label
.HD	undef	n	optional page header below header margin
.I x	-	n	italicize x; if no x, switch to italics
.IP x y	-	y,y	indented paragraph, with hanging tag x; y=indent
.IX x y	-	y	index words x y and so on (up to 5 levels)
.KE	-	n	end keep of any kind
.KF	-	n	begin floating keep; text fills remainder of page
.KS	-	y	begin keep; unit kept together on a single page
.LG	-	n	larger; increase point size by 2
.LP	-	y,y	left (block) paragraph.
.MC x	-	y,y	multiple columns; x=column width
.ND x	if t	n	no date in page footer; x is date on cover
.NH x y	-	y,y	numbered header; x=level, x=0 resets, x=S sets to y
.NL	10p	n	set point size back to normal
.OF x	-	n	odd page footer x (3 part as for .tl)
.OH x	-	n	odd page header x (3 part as for .tl)
.P1	if TM	n	print header on first page
.PP	-	y,y	paragraph with first line indented
.PT	- % -	n	page title, printed at head of page
.PX x	-	y	print index (table of contents); x=no suppresses title
.QP	-	y,y	quote paragraph (indented and shorter)
.R	on	n	return to Roman font
.RE	5n	y,y	retreat: end level of relative indentation
.RP x	-	n	released paper format; x=no stops title on first page
.RS	5n	y,y	right shift: start level of relative indentation
.SH	-	y,y	section header, in boldface
.SM	-	n	smaller; decrease point size by 2
.TA	8n,5n	n	set TAB characters to 8n 16n ... (nroff) 5n 10n ... (troff)
.TC x	-	y	print table of contents at end; x=no suppresses title
.TE	-	y	end of table processed by tbl
.TH	-	y	end multi-page header of table

Macro Name	Initial Value	Break? Reset?	Explanation
.TL	-	y	title in boldface and two points larger
.TM	off	n	UC Berkeley thesis mode
.TS x	-	y,y	begin table; if x=H table has multi-page header
.UL x	-	n	underline x, even in `troff`
.UX x	-	n	UNIX; trademark message first time; x appended
.XA x y	-	y	another index entry; x=page or no for none; y=indent
.XE	-	y	end index entry (or series of .IX entries)
.XP	-	y,y	paragraph with first line exdented, others indented
.XS x y	-	y	begin index entry; x=page or no for none; y=indent
.1C	on	y,y	one column format, on a new page
.2C	-	y,y	begin two column format
.] -	-	n	beginning of `refer` reference
.[0	-	n	end of unclassifiable type of reference
.[N	-	n	N= 1:journal-article, 2:book, 3:book-article, 4:report

REGISTERS

Formatting distances can be controlled in –ms by means of built-in number registers. For example, this sets the line length to 6.5 inches:

```
.nr  LL  6.5i
```

Here is a table of number registers and their default values:

Name	Register Controls	Takes Effect	Default
PS	point size	paragraph	10
VS	vertical spacing	paragraph	12
LL	line length	paragraph	6i
LT	title length	next page	same as LL
FL	footnote length	next .FS	5.5i
PD	paragraph distance	paragraph	1v (if n), .3v (if t)
DD	display distance	displays	1v (if n), .5v (if t)
PI	paragraph indent	paragraph	5n
QI	quote indent	next .QP	5n
FI	footnote indent	next .FS	2n
PO	page offset	next page	0 (if n), ~1i (if t)
HM	header margin	next page	1i
FM	footer margin	next page	1i
FF	footnote format	next .FS	0 (1, 2, 3 available)

When resetting these values, make sure to specify the appropriate units. Setting the line length to 7, for example, will result in output with one character per line. Setting FF to 1 suppresses footnote superscripting; setting it to 2 also suppresses indentation of the first line; and setting it to 3 produces an .IP-like footnote paragraph.

Here is a list of string registers available in –ms; they may be used anywhere in the text:

Name	String's Function
*Q	quote (" in nroff, '' in troff)
*U	unquote (" in nroff, '' in troff)
*-	dash (-- in nroff, — in troff)
*(MO	month (month of the year)
*(DY	day (current date)
**	automatically numbered footnote
*´	acute accent (before letter)
*`	grave accent (before letter)
*^	circumflex (before letter)
*,	cedilla (before letter)
*:	umlaut (before letter)
*~	tilde (before letter)

When using the extended accent mark definitions available with .AM, these strings should come after, rather than before, the letter to be accented.

FILES

    /usr/ucb/lib/doctools/tmac/s
    /usr/ucblib/doctools/tmac/ms.???

SEE ALSO

    col(1V), eqn(1), nroff(1), refer(1), tbl(1), troff(1)

NOTES

Floating keeps and regular keeps are diverted to the same space, so they cannot be mixed together with predictable results.

NAME

mt - magnetic tape control

SYNOPSIS

`/usr/ucb/mt` `[-f` *tapename*`]` *command* `[`*count*`]`

DESCRIPTION

`mt` sends commands to a magnetic tape drive. If *tapename* is not specified, the environment variable `TAPE` is used. If `TAPE` does not exist, `mt` uses the device `/dev/rmt/ctape1n`. *tapename* must refer to a raw (not block) tape device. By default, `mt` performs the requested operation once; multiple operations may be performed by specifying *count*.

The available commands are listed below. Only as many characters as are required to uniquely identify a command need be specified.

`mt` returns a 0 exit status when the operation(s) were successful, 1 if the command was unrecognized or if `mt` was unable to open the specified tape drive, and 2 if an operation failed.

the following commands are available to `mt`:

`eof, weof`	Write *count* EOF marks at the current position on the tape.
`rewind`	Rewinds the tape.
`fsf`	Forward space *count* files.
`fsr`	Forward space *count* records.
`bsf`	Back space *count* files.
`bsr`	Back space *count* records.

For the following commands, *count* is ignored:

`offline, rewoffl`
    Rewind, unload, and place the tape drive unit off-line.

`status`
    Print status information about the tape unit.

`retension`
    Wind the tape to the end of the reel and then rewind it, smoothing out the tape tension.

`erase` Erase the entire tape.

`eod` Space to the end of the data. This positions the tape at the end of the data so that additional files may be appended.

FILES

`/dev/rmt*`	raw magnetic tape interface
`dev/rmt/ctape*`	raw cartridge tape interface
`dev/rmt/ninetrack*`	
	raw 9-track tape interface

SEE ALSO

`ar`(4), `dd`(1M), `environ`(5), and `tape`(7)

NOTES
      Not all devices support all options.

NAME

mv - move files

SYNOPSIS

mv [-f] [-i] *file1* [*file2* ...] *target*

DESCRIPTION

The mv command moves *filen* to *target*. *filen* and *target* may not have the same name. (Care must be taken when using sh(1) metacharacters). If *target* is not a directory, only one file may be specified before it; if it is a directory, more than one file may be specified. If *target* does not exist, mv creates a file named *target*. If *target* exists and is not a directory, its contents are overwritten. If *target* is a directory the file(s) are moved to that directory. *target* and *filen* do not have to share the same parent directory.

If mv determines that the mode of *target* forbids writing, it will print the mode [see chmod(2)], ask for a response, and read the standard input for one line. If the line begins with y, the mv occurs, if permissible; otherwise, the command exits. When the parent directory of *filen* is writable and has the sticky bit set, one or more of the following conditions must be true:

    the user must own the file
    the user must own the directory
    the file must be writable by the user
    the user must be a privileged user

The following options are recognized:

-i   mv will prompt for confirmation whenever the move would overwrite an existing *target*. A y answer means that the move should proceed. Any other answer prevents mv from overwriting the *target*.

-f   mv will move the file(s) without prompting even if it is writing over an existing *target*. This option overrides the -i option. Note that this is the default if the standard input is not a terminal.

You can use mv to move directories as well as files. If *filen* is a directory, *target* must be a directory in the same physical file system.

If *filen* is a file and *target* is a link to another file with links, the other links remain and *target* becomes a new file.

NOTES

If *filen* and *target* are on different file systems, mv copies the file and deletes the original; any links to other files are lost.

A -- permits the user to mark explicitly the end of any command line options, allowing mv to recognize filename arguments that begin with a -. As an aid to BSD migration, mv will accept - as a synonym for --. This migration aid may disappear in a future release. If a -- and a - both appear on the same command line, the second will be interpreted as a filename.

SEE ALSO

chmod(1), cp(1), cpio(1), ln(1), rm(1)

NAME

mvdir - move a directory

SYNOPSIS

/usr/sbin/mvdir *dirname name*

DESCRIPTION

mvdir moves directories within a file system. *dirname* must be a directory. If *name* does not exist, it will be created as a directory. If *name* does exist, and is a directory, *dirname* will be created as *name/dirname*. *dirname* and *name* may not be on the same path; that is, one may not be subordinate to the other. For example:

    mvdir x/y x/z

is legal, but

    mvdir x/y x/y/z

is not.

SEE ALSO

mkdir(1), mv(1).

NOTE

Only the super-user can use mvdir.

NAME

mvme323 - adds `/dev` entries for hard disks in the Equipped Device Table (EDT) (For M68K only)

SYNOPSIS

`/sbin/auto-device/mvme323`

DESCRIPTION

`mvme323` performs the following steps:

1. The EDT is searched to see if any `mvme323` ESDI disk controllers are equipped. If none are found, the program deletes any existing related device nodes and exits.

2. Any existing device nodes for controllers that are not present are deleted.

3. The Extended EDT information for each controller present is examined to determine the peripheral compliment attached to each controller. All non-present devices with existing device nodes have their device nodes deleted.

4. The existing device nodes are compared against the Extended EDT information and device nodes are created for all devices that do not have device nodes.

`mvme323` is called each time the system is re-configured. It must also be called after `sysadm rmdisk` is executed, to restore the `/dev` entries so a disk can be resliced.

FILES

`/dev/dsk/*`   entries for the hard disk and floppies for general use
`/dev/rdsk/*`

SEE ALSO

`makedev`(1M), `mvme328`(1M), `mvme350`(1M) (For M68K only), `sysadm`(1M), `intro`(7)

NAME

mvme328 - add /dev entries for SCSI devices in the Equipped Device Table (EDT)

SYNOPSIS

/sbin/auto-device/mvme328

DESCRIPTION

mvme328 performs the following steps:

1. The EDT is searched to see if any mvme328 SCSI host adapters are equipped. If none are found, the program deletes any existing related device nodes and exits.

2. Any existing device nodes for controllers that are not present are deleted.

3. The Extended EDT information for each controller present is examined to determine the peripheral complement attached to each controller. All non-present devices with existing device nodes have their device nodes deleted.

4. The existing device nodes are compared against the Extended EDT information and device nodes are created for all devices that do not have device nodes. Devices that may have changed type (for example, tape to disk) will have their device nodes deleted and recreated.

mvme328 is called each time the system is re-configured. It must also be called after sysadm rmdisk is executed, to restore the /dev entries so a disk can be resliced.

FILES

/dev/dsk/*   entries for the hard disk and floppies for general use
/dev/rdsk/*
/dev/rmt/*   entries for the tapes for general use

SEE ALSO

makedev(1M), mvme323(1M) (For M68K only), mvme350(1M) (For M68K only), sysadm(1M), intro(7)

NAME

mvme332xt - create character device files

SYNOPSIS

```
/sbin/auto-device/mvme332xt [-v]
```

DESCRIPTION

The `mvme332xt` command creates character device files in `/dev/term`, `/dev/port` and `/dev/printer`. The `mvme332xt` command created character device files in `/dev/port` for eight asynchronous RS-232 ports and in `/dev/printer` for one parallel printer port for every mvme332xt board in the kernel's Equip Device Table (EDT). The entries in `/dev/port` are the controller specific namings of the above mentioned ports. Their format is `/dev/port/m332_cXdY` where X is the controller number and Y is the port number. `/dev/printer` contains the parallel printer controller specific naming `/dev/printer/m332_cXd8` where X is the controller number. A port is named *sn*, where *s* is the board number and *n* is a number from 0 to 8. Board numbers start at 0 and increment by 1.

When `mvme332xt` is invoked, it does the following:

removes any `/dev/port` and `/dev/printer` controller specific device files for boards that no longer exist

makes new `/dev/port` and `/dev/printer` printer files for the `mvme332xt` boards as needed

The `mvme332xt` command is invoked only upon system installation or when reconfiguration and reboot of the system prompts a new kernel to be created. The `-v` option sets the output to verbose.

Any devices, such as a printer or a modem, that are added to a `mvme332xt` board should link the names that are to be used for the devices to the corresponding tty device files that were created [see `ln`(1)]. The command can be used only by the super-user.

EXAMPLE

A parallel printer is added to a `mvme332xt` board that is board number 1. The corresponding slot is `/dev/printer/m332_c0d8`. The user should use `ln` to link an appropriate name such as `lp1` to the tty device file.

```
ln /dev/printer/m332_c0d8 /dev/lp1
```

FILES

```
/dev/port
/dev/printer
```

SEE ALSO

`ln`(1)

NAME

mvme350 - adds /dev entries for tapes in the Equipped Device Table (EDT)   (For M68K only)

SYNOPSIS

/sbin/auto-device/mvme350

DESCRIPTION

mvme350 performs the following steps:

1. The EDT is searched to see if any mvme350 tape controllers are equipped. If none are found, the program deletes any existing related device nodes and exits.

2. Any existing device nodes for controllers that are not present are deleted.

3. The Extended EDT information for each controller present is examined to determine the peripheral compliment attached to each controller. All non-present devices with existing device nodes have their device nodes deleted.

4. The existing device nodes are compared against the Extended EDT information and device nodes are created for all devices that do not have device nodes.

mvme350 is called each time the system is re-configured.

FILES

/dev/rmt/*

SEE ALSO

makedev(1M), mvme323(1M) (For M68K only), mvme328(1M), sysadm(1M), intro(7)

NAME

mvme376 - adds /dev entries for the MVME376 Ethernet Board in the Equipped Device Table

SYNOPSIS

/sbin/auto-device/mvme376

DESCRIPTION

mvme376 performs the following steps:

1. Any MVME376 device names in the /dev directory are deleted.

2. The Equipped Device Table (EDT) is searched to see if any MVME376 Ethernet controllers are equipped. If none are found, the program exits at this point.

3. For each MVME376 found in the EDT, a hardware device node is created as /dev/m376_c*, where * is the cpu number of the MVME376.

mvme376 is called each time the system is booted.

FILES

/dev/m376_c*

SEE ALSO

makedev(1M), sysadm(1M)

NAME

mvmecpu - create /dev entries for cpu related devices

SYNOPSIS

/sbin/auto-device/mvmecpu

DESCRIPTION

mvmecpu performs the following steps:

1. Determines which cpu board is being used by the running system.

2. Deletes any existing device nodes for devices not appropriate for the cpu being used (for example, non-volatile RAM, special console ports) by the running system.

3. Creates device nodes for devices appropriate for the cpu being used (for example, non-volatile RAM, special console ports) by the running system if they do not already exist.

4. Searches the kernel configuration table for configurable device support functions (for example, line printer, ethernet) appropriate for the cpu used by the running system. Device nodes for these devices are created or deleted as necessary.

5. Searchs the kernel memory region table for regions that require device nodes. Device nodes are created or deleted as necessary.

FILES

/dev/nvr*
/dev/printer/*
/dev/contty*
/dev/memregion/*

SEE ALSO

makedev(1M), sysadm(1M), intro(7)

NAME

named, in.named - Internet domain name server

SYNOPSIS

in.named [-d *debug_level*] [-p *port#*] [-b *bootfile*]

DESCRIPTION

The named command is the Internet domain name server. See RFC 1035 for more information on the Internet name-domain system. Without any arguments, named will read the default boot file /etc/named.boot, read any initial data, and then listen for queries.

The available options are:

-d *debug_level*
> Print debugging information; the *debug_level* will determine the level of messages printed.

-p *port#*   Use a different port number, *port#*; the default is the standard port number as listed in /etc/services.

-b *bootfile*   Use the alternate boot file *bootfile*. This is optional and will allow you to specify a file with a leading dash. The default value is /etc/named.boot.

Any additional argument is taken as the name of the boot file. The boot file contains information about where the name server is to get its initial data. If multiple boot files are specified, only the last one is used. Lines in the boot file cannot be continued on subsequent lines.

The following is a small example:

```
;
;       boot file for name server
;
directory    /var/named

; type       domain                source host/file              backup file

cache        .                                                   root.cache
primary      Berkeley.EDU          berkeley.edu.zone
primary      32.128.IN-ADDR.ARPA   ucbhosts.rev
secondary    CC.Berkeley.EDU       128.32.137.8 128.32.137.3 cc.zone.bak
secondary    6.32.128.IN-ADDR.ARPA 128.32.137.8 128.32.137.3 cc.rev.bak
primary      0.0.127.IN-ADDR.ARPA                              localhost.rev
forwarders 10.0.0.78 10.2.0.78
; slave
```

The directory line causes the server to change its working directory to the specified directory. This can be important for the correct processing of $INCLUDE files in the primary zone files.

The cache line specifies that data in root.cache is to be placed in the backup cache. Its main use is to specify data such as locations of root domain servers. This cache is not used during normal operation, but is used as ''hints'' to find the current root servers. The file root.cache is in the same format as berkeley.edu.zone.

More than one cache file can be specified. The cache files are processed to preserve the time-to-live (TTL) values for all the data dumped out. The data for the root nameservers will be kept artificially valid if necessary.

The first `primary` line states that the file `berkeley.edu.zone` contains authoritative data for the `Berkeley.EDU` zone. The file `berkeley.edu.zone` contains data in the master file format described in RFC 1035. All domain names are relative to the origin, in this case, `Berkeley.EDU` (see below for a more detailed description).

The second `primary` line states that the file `ucbhosts.rev` contains authoritative data for the domain `32.128.IN-ADDR.ARPA`, which is used to translate addresses in network 128.32 to hostnames. Each master file should begin with an SOA record for the zone (see below).

The first `secondary` line specifies that all authoritative data under `CC.Berkeley.EDU` is to be transferred from the name server at 128.32.137.8. If this transfer fails, the system will try 128.32.137.3 and continue trying the addresses, up to 10, listed on this line. The secondary copy is also authoritative for the specified domain. The first non-dotted-quad address on this line will be taken as a filename in which to backup the transferred zone. The name server will load the zone from this backup file if it exists when it boots, thus providing a complete copy even if the master servers are unreachable. Whenever a new copy of the domain is received by automatic zone transfer from one of the master servers, this file will be updated. The second "secondary" line states that the address-to-hostname mapping for the subnet 128.32.136 should be obtained from the same list of master servers as the previous zone.

The `forwarders` line specifies the addresses of sitewide servers that will accept recursive queries from other servers. If the boot file specifies one or more forwarders, then the server will send all queries for data not in the cache to the forwarders first. Each forwarder will be asked in turn until an answer is returned or the list is exhausted. If no answer is forthcoming from a forwarder, the server will continue as it would have without the forwarders line unless it is in `slave` mode. The forwarding facility is useful for generating a large site-wide cache on a master, as well as for reducing traffic over links to outside servers. It can also be used to allow servers to run that do not have access directly to the Internet, but wish to act as though they do.

The `slave` line (shown commented out) is used to put the server in slave mode. In this mode, the server will only make queries to forwarders. This option is normally used on machines that wish to run a server, but for physical or administrative reasons cannot be given access to the Internet, but have access to a host which does have access.

The `sortlist` line can be used to indicate networks that are to be preferred over other, unlisted, networks. Queries for host addresses from hosts on the same network as the server will receive responses with the local network addresses listed first, then the addresses on the sort list, and then the other addresses. This line is only acted on at initial startup. This line will be ignored when reloading the nameserver with a SIGHUP.

The master file consists of control information and a list of resource records for objects in the zone using the following formats:

```
$INCLUDE <filename> <opt_domain>
$ORIGIN <domain>
<domain> <opt_ttl> <opt_class> <type> <resource_record_data>
```

where domain is "." for root, "@" for the current origin, or a standard domain name. If domain is a standard domain name that does not end with ".", the current origin will be appended to the domain. Domain names ending with "." will remain unmodified. The opt_domain field is used to define an origin for the data in an included file. It is equivalent to placing a $ORIGIN statement before the first line of the included file. (This field is optional.) Neither the opt_domain field nor the $ORIGIN statements in the included file will modify the current origin for this file. The opt_ttl field is an optional integer number for the time-to-live field. It defaults to zero, meaning the minimum value specified in the SOA record for the zone. The opt_class field is the object address type; currently only one type is supported, IN, for objects connected to the DARPA Internet. The type field contains one of the following tokens (the data expected in the resource_record_data field is shown within parentheses).

A   a host address (dotted quad)

NS   an authoritative name server (domain)

MX   a mail exchanger (domain)

CNAME
         the canonical name for an alias (domain)

SOA   marks the start of a zone of authority (domain of originating host, domain address of maintainer, a serial number and the following parameters in seconds: refresh, retry, expire and minimum TTL [see RFC 1035])

MB   a mailbox domain name (domain)

MG   a mail group member (domain)

MR   a mail rename domain name (domain)

NULL   a null resource record (no format or data)

WKS   a well-known service description (not implemented yet)

PTR   a domain name pointer (domain)

HINFO   host information (cpu_type OS_type)

MINFO   mailbox or mail list information (request_domain error_domain)

Resource records normally end at the end of a line, but may be continued across lines between opening and closing parentheses. Comments are introduced by semicolons and continue to the end of the line.

Each master zone file should begin with an SOA record for the zone. An example SOA record is as follows:

```
@      IN    SOA    ucbvax.Berkeley.EDU. rwh.ucbvax.Berkeley.EDU. (
                        2.89   ; serial
                        10800  ; refresh
                        3600   ; retry
                        3600000        ; expire
                        86400  )       ; minimum
```

The SOA lists a serial number which should be changed whenever the master file is changed. Secondary servers will check the serial number at intervals specified by the refresh time in seconds; if the serial number changes, a zone transfer will be done to load the new data. If a master server cannot be contacted when a refresh is due, the retry time will specify the interval at which refreshes should be attempted until successful. If a master server cannot be contacted within the interval given by the expire time, all data from that zone will be discarded by the secondary servers. The minimum value is the "time-to-live" used by records in the file which contain no explicit "time-to-live" value.

NOTES

The boot file directives "domain" and "suffixes" have been obsoleted by a more useful resolver-based implementation of suffixing for partially qualified domain names. The prior mechanisms could fail under a number of situations, especially when the local nameserver did not have complete information.

The following signals have the specified effect when sent to the server process using the `kill`(1) command:

SIGHUP

    Causes the server to read `named.boot` and to reload the database.

SIGINT

    Dumps the the contents of the current data base and cache to `/var/tmp/named_dump.db`.

SIGIOT

    Will dump statistics data into `/var/tmp/named.stats` if the server is compiled with the `-DSTATS` flag. The statistics data will be appended to this file.

SIGSYS

    Will dump the profiling data in `/var/tmp` if the server is compiled with profiling (server forks, chdirs and exits).

SIGTERM

    Will dump the primary and secondary database files; used to save modified data on shutdown if the server is compiled with dynamic updating enabled.

SIGUSR1

    Turns on debugging; each SIGUSR1 will increment the debug level. (SIGEMT on older systems without SIGUSR1.)

SIGUSR2
>
> Turns off debugging completely. (SIGFPE on older systems without SIGUSR2.)

FILES

`/etc/named.boot`	name server configuration boot file
`/etc/named.pid`	the process id
`/var/tmp/named.run`	debug output
`/var/tmp/named_dump.db`	dump of the name server database
`/var/tmp/named.stats`	statistical data for nameserver

SEE ALSO

`kill`(1), `gethostbyname`(3N), `signal`(3C), `resolver`(3N), `resolv.conf`(4).
RFC 1035, RFC 1034, RFC 974.

NAME

nawk - pattern scanning and processing language

SYNOPSIS

nawk [-F *re*] [-v *var=value*] ['*prog*'] [*file* ...]

nawk [-F *re*] [-v *var=value*] [-f *progfile*] [*file* ...]

DESCRIPTION

nawk scans each input *file* for lines that match any of a set of patterns specified in *prog*. The *prog* string must be enclosed in single quotes (') to protect it from the shell. For each pattern in *prog* there may be an associated action performed when a line of a *file* matches the pattern. The set of pattern-action statements may appear literally as *prog* or in a file specified with the -f *progfile* option. Input files are read in order; if there are no files, the standard input is read. The file name - means the standard input.

Each input line is matched against the pattern portion of every pattern-action statement; the associated action is performed for each matched pattern. Any *file* of the form var=*value* is treated as an assignment, not a filename, and is executed at the time it would have been opened if it were a filename, and is executed at the time it would have been opened if it were a filename. The option -v followed by var=*value* is an assignment to be done before *prog* is executed; any number of -v options may be present.

An input line is normally made up of fields separated by white space. (This default can be changed by using the FS built-in variable or the -F *re* option.) The fields are denoted $1, $2, ...; $0 refers to the entire line.

A pattern-action statement has the form:

pattern { action }

Either pattern or action may be omitted. If there is no action with a pattern, the matching line is printed. If there is no pattern with an action, the action is performed on every input line. Pattern-action statements are separated by newlines or semicolons.

Patterns are arbitrary Boolean combinations (!, | |, &&, and parentheses) of relational expressions and regular expressions. A relational expression is one of the following:

expression relop expression
expression matchop regular_expression
expression in *array-name*
(*expression, expression, ...)* in *array-name*

where a *relop* is any of the six relational operators in C, and a *matchop* is either ~ (contains) or !~ (does not contain). An *expression* is an arithmetic expression, a relational expression, the special expression

var in *array*

or a Boolean combination of these.

Regular expressions are as in egrep(1). In patterns they must be surrounded by slashes. Isolated regular expressions in a pattern apply to the entire line. Regular expressions may also occur in relational expressions. A pattern may consist of two patterns separated by a comma; in this case, the action is performed for all lines between an occurrence of the first pattern and the next occurrence of the second pattern.

The special patterns BEGIN and END may be used to capture control before the first input line has been read and after the last input line has been read respectively. These keywords do not combine with any other patterns.

A regular expression may be used to separate fields by using the -F *re* option or by assigning the expression to the built-in variable FS. The default is to ignore leading blanks and to separate fields by blanks and/or tab characters. However, if FS is assigned a value, leading blanks are no longer ignored.

Other built-in variables include:

ARGC	command line argument count
ARGV	command line argument array
ENVIRON	array of environment variables; subscripts are names
FILENAME	name of the current input file
FNR	ordinal number of the current record in the current file
FS	input field separator regular expression (default blank and tab)
NF	number of fields in the current record
NR	ordinal number of the current record
OFMT	output format for numbers (default %.6g)
OFS	output field separator (default blank)
ORS	output record separator (default new-line)
RS	input record separator (default new-line)
SUBSEP	separates multiple subscripts (default is 034)

An action is a sequence of statements. A statement may be one of the following:

```
if ( expression ) statement [ else statement ]
while ( expression ) statement
do statement while ( expression )
for ( expression ; expression ; expression ) statement
for ( var in array ) statement
delete array[subscript] #delete an array element
break
continue
{ [ statement ] ... }
expression     # commonly variable = expression
print [ expression-list ] [ >expression ]
printf format [ , expression-list ] [ >expression ]
next        # skip remaining patterns on this input line
exit [expr] # skip the rest of the input; exit status is expr
return [expr]
```

Statements are terminated by semicolons, new-lines, or right braces. An empty expression-list stands for the whole input line. Expressions take on string or numeric values as appropriate, and are built using the operators +, -, *, /, %, ^ and concatenation (indicated by a blank). The operators ++ -- += -= *= /= %= ^= > >= < <= == != ?: are also available in expressions. Variables may be scalars, array elements (denoted x[i]), or fields. Variables are initialized to the null string or zero. Array subscripts may be any string, not necessarily numeric; this allows for a form of associative memory. Multiple subscripts such as [i,j,k] are permitted; the constituents are concatenated, separated by the value of SUBSEP. String constants are quoted (" "), with the usual C escapes recognized within.

The `print` statement prints its arguments on the standard output, or on a file if >*expression* is present, or on a pipe if | *cmd* is present. The arguments are separated by the current output field separator and terminated by the output record separator. The `printf` statement formats its expression list according to the format in the printf(3S) manpage. The built-in function close(*expr*) closes the file or pipe *expr*.

The mathematical functions: atan2, cos, exp, log, sin, sqrt, are built-in.

Other built-in functions include:

gsub(*for*, *repl*, *in*) behaves like sub (see below), except that it replaces successive occurrences of the regular expression (like the ed global substitute command).

index (*s*, *t*) returns the position in string *s* where string *t* first occurs, or 0 if it does not occur at all.

int truncates to an integer value.

length (*s*) returns the length of its argument taken as a string, or of the whole line if there is no argument.

match (*s*, *re*) returns the position in string *s* where the regular expression *re* occurs, or 0 if it does not occur at all. RSTART is set to the starting position (which is the same as the returned value), and RLENGTH is set to the length of the matched string.

rand random number on $(0, 1)$.

split (*s*, *a*, *fs*) splits the string *s* into array elements $a[1]$, $a[2]$, . . ., $a[n]$, and returns n. The separation is done with the regular expression *fs* or with the field separator FS if *fs* is not given.

srand sets the seed for rand

sprintf (*fmt*, *expr*, *expr*, ...)
formats the expressions according to the printf(3S) format given by *fmt* and returns the resulting string.

sub(*for*, *repl*, *in*) substitutes the string *repl* in place of the first instance of the regular expression *for* in string *in* and returns the number of substitutions. If *in* is omitted, nawk substitutes in the current record ($0).

substr(*s*, *m*, *n*) returns the n-character substring of *s* that begins at position m.

The input/output built-in functions are:

close (*filename*)   closes the file or pipe named *filename*.

cmd | `getline`   pipes the output of *cmd* into `getline`; each successive call to *get-line* returns the next line of output from *cmd*.

`getline`   sets $0 to the next input record from the current input file.

`getline` <*file*   sets $0 to the next record from *file*.

`getline` *x*   sets variable *x* instead.

`getline` *x* <*file*   sets *x* from the next record of *file*.

`system` (*cmd*)   executes *cmd* and returns its exit status.

All forms of `getline` return 1 for successful input, 0 for end of file, and -1 for an error.

`nawk` also provides user-defined functions. Such functions may be defined (in the pattern position of a pattern-action statement) as

```
function name (args, . . . ) { stmts }
```

Function arguments are passed by value if scalar and by reference if array name. Argument names are local to the function; all other variable names are global. Function calls may be nested and functions may be recursive. The `return` statement may be used to return a value.

EXAMPLES

Print lines longer than 72 characters:

```
length > 72
```

Print first two fields in opposite order:

```
{ print $2, $1 }
```

Same, with input fields separated by comma and/or blanks and tabs:

```
BEGIN { FS = ",[ \t]*|[ \t]+" }
      { print $2, $1 }
```

Add up first column, print sum and average:

```
      { s += $1 }
END   { print "sum is", s, " average is", s/NR }
```

Print fields in reverse order:

```
{ for (i = NF; i > 0; --i) print $i }
```

Print all lines between start/stop pairs:

```
/start/, /stop/
```

Print all lines whose first field is different from previous one:

```
$1 != prev { print; prev = $1 }
```

Simulate echo(1):

```
BEGIN {
      for (i = 1; i < ARGC; i++)
            printf "%s", ARGV[i]
      printf "\n"
```

```
        exit
        }
```
Print a file, filling in page numbers starting at 5:

```
/Page/     { $2 = n++; }
        { print }
```

Assuming this program is in a file named `prog`, the following command line prints the file `input` numbering its pages starting at 5: `nawk -f prog n=5 input`.

SEE ALSO

`egrep`(1), `grep`(1), `sed`(1)
`lex`(1), `printf`(3S).

NOTES

`nawk` is a new version of `awk` that provides capabilities unavailable in previous versions. This version will become the default version of `awk` in the next major UNIX system release.

Input white space is not preserved on output if fields are involved.

There are no explicit conversions between numbers and strings. To force an expression to be treated as a number add 0 to it; to force it to be treated as a string concatenate the null string (" ") to it.

NAME

ncheck (generic) - generate a list of path names vs i-numbers

SYNOPSIS

ncheck [-F *FSType*] [-V] [*current_options*] [-o *specific_options*] [*special* ...]

DESCRIPTION

ncheck with no options generates a path-name vs. i-number list of all files on *special*. If *special* is not specified on the command line the list is generated for all *specials* in /etc/vfstab for entries which have a numeric *fsckpass*. *special* is a block special device on which the file system exists.

current_options are options supported by the s5-specific module of ncheck. Other *FSTypes* do not necessarily support these options. *specific_options* indicate suboptions specified in a comma-separated list of suboptions and/or keyword-attribute pairs for interpretation by the *FSType*-specific module of the command. See ncheck_*FSType*(1M) for details.

The options are:

-F   Specify the *FSType* on which to operate. The *FSType* should either be specified here or be determinable from /etc/vfstab by finding an entry in the table that has a numeric *fsckpass* field and a matching *special* if specified.

-V   Echo the complete command line, but do not execute the command. The command line is generated by using the options and arguments provided by the user and adding to them information derived from /etc/vfstab. This option should be used to verify and validate the command line.

-o   used to specify *FSType* specific options if any.

FILES

/etc/vfstab   list of default parameters for each file system

SEE ALSO

ncheck_s5(1M), ncheck_ufs(1M), vfstab(4).

NOTES

This command may not be supported for all *FSTypes*.

NAME

ncheck (s5) - generate path names versus i-numbers for s5 file systems

SYNOPSIS

ncheck [-F s5] [*generic_options*] [-i *i-number* . . .] [-a] [-s] [*special* . . .]

DESCRIPTION

generic_options are options supported by the generic ncheck command.

ncheck generates a path-name vs. i-number list of all files on the specified *special* device(s). Names of directory files are followed by "/." .

The options are:

-F s5   Specifies the s5-FSType.

-i *i-number*

> Limits the report to those files whose i-numbers follow. The *i-numbers* must be separated by commas without spaces.

-a   Allows printing of the names "." and "..", which are ordinarily suppressed.

-s   Limits the report to special files and files with set-user-ID mode. This option may be used to detect violations of security policy.

DIAGNOSTICS

If the file system structure is not consistent, ?? denotes the parent of a parentless file and a path-name beginning with . . . denotes a loop.

SEE ALSO

generic ncheck(1M)

NAME
ncheck (ufs) - generate pathnames versus i-numbers for ufs file systems

SYNOPSIS
ncheck [-F ufs] [*generic_options*] [-i *i-list*] [-a] [-s] [-o m] [*special* ...]

DESCRIPTION
generic_options are options supported by the generic ncheck command.

ncheck generates a pathname versus i-number list of files for the ufs file system. Names of directory files are followed by "/ . ".

The options are:

-F ufs   Specifies the ufs-FSType.

-i *i-list*   Limits the report to the files on the i-list that follows. The i-list must be separated by commas without spaces.

-a   Allows printing of the names "." and "..", which are ordinarily suppressed.

-s   Limits the report to special files and files with set-user-ID mode. This option may be used to detect violations of security policy.

-o   Specify ufs file system specific options. The available option is:

m   Print mode information.

DIAGNOSTICS
When the file system structure is improper, ?? denotes the parent of a parentless file and a pathname beginning with ... denotes a loop.

SEE ALSO
generic ncheck(1M)

NAME

netstat - show network status

SYNOPSIS

netstat [-aAn] [-f *addr_family*] [*system*] [*core*]

netstat [-n] [-s] [-h | -i | -m | -r] [-f *addr_family*] [*system*] [*core*]

netstat [-n] [-I *interface*] *interval* [*system*] [*core*]

DESCRIPTION

netstat displays the contents of various network-related data structures in various formats, depending on the options you select.

The first form of the command displays a list of active sockets for each protocol. The second form selects one from among various other network data structures. The third form displays running statistics of packet traffic on configured network interfaces; the *interval* argument indicates the number of seconds in which to gather statistics between displays.

The default value for the system argument is /stand/unix; for *core*, the default is /dev/kmem.

The following options are available:

-a   Show the state of all sockets; normally sockets used by server processes are not shown.

-A   Show the address of any protocol control blocks associated with sockets; used for debugging.

-h   Show the state of the IMP host table. This does not work in an environment where the IMP host tables do not exist.

-i   Show the state of interfaces that have been auto-configured. Interfaces that are statically configured into a system, but not located at boot time, are not shown.

-m   Show the statistics recorded by management routines for the network's private buffer pool.

-n   Show network addresses as numbers. netstat normally displays addresses as symbols. This option may be used with any of the display formats.

-r   Show the routing tables. When used with the -s option, show routing statistics instead.

-s   Show per-protocol statistics. When used with the -r option, show routing statistics.

-f *addr_family*
    Limit statistics or address control block reports to those of the specified *addr_family*, which can be one of:

        inet   For the AF_INET address family, or
        unix   For the AF_UNIX family.

-I *interface*

> Highlight information about the indicated *interface* in a separate column; the default (for the third form of the command) is the interface with the most traffic since the system was last rebooted. *interface* can be any valid interface listed in the system configuration file, such as emd1 or lo0.

DISPLAYS

Active Sockets (First Form)

The display for each active socket shows the local and remote address, the send and receive queue sizes (in bytes), the protocol, and the internal state of the protocol.

The symbolic format normally used to display socket addresses is either:

> *hostname.port*

when the name of the host is specified, or:

> *network.port*

if a socket address specifies a network but no specific host. Each hostname and *network* is shown according to its entry in the /etc/hosts or the /etc/networks file, as appropriate.

If the network or hostname for an address is not known (or if the -n option is specified), the numerical network address is shown. Unspecified, or wildcard, addresses and ports appear as *. For more information regarding the Internet naming conventions, refer to inet(7).

TCP Sockets

The possible state values for TCP sockets are as follows:

CLOSED	Closed. The socket is not being used.
LISTEN	Listening for incoming connections.
SYN_SENT	Actively trying to establish connection.
SYN_RECEIVED	Initial synchronization of the connection under way.
ESTABLISHED	Connection has been established.
CLOSE_WAIT	Remote shut down; waiting for the socket to close.
FIN_WAIT_1	Socket closed; shutting down connection.
CLOSING	Closed, then remote shutdown; awaiting acknowledgement.
LAST_ACK	Remote shut down, then closed; awaiting acknowledgement.
FIN_WAIT_2	Socket closed; waiting for shutdown from remote.
TIME_WAIT	Wait after close for remote shutdown retransmission.

Network Data Structures (Second Form)

The form of the display depends upon which of the -m, -i, -h or -r, options you select. If you specify more than one of these options, netstat selects one in the order listed here.

Routing Table Display

The routing table display lists the available routes and the status of each. Each route consists of a destination host or network, and a gateway to use in forwarding packets. The *flags* column shows the status of the route as follows:

D -	Route created dynamically by a redirect
G -	Destination is a gateway
H -	Destination is a host
S -	Route must be switched
T -	A gateway switched the route
U -	Route is useable
V -	A slave switched the route

Direct routes are created for each interface attached to the local host; the gateway field for such entries shows the address of the outgoing interface.

The `refcnt` column gives the current number of active uses per route. Connection-oriented protocols normally hold on to a single route for the duration of a connection, whereas connectionless protocols obtain a route while sending to the same destination.

The `use` column displays the number of packets sent per route.

The *interface* entry indicates the network interface utilized for the route.

Cumulative Traffic Statistics (Third Form)

When the *interval* argument is given, `netstat` displays a table of cumulative statistics regarding packets transferred, errors and collisions, the network addresses for the interface, and the maximum transmission unit (mtu). The first line of data displayed, and every 24th line thereafter, contains cumulative statistics from the time the system was last rebooted. Each subsequent line shows incremental statistics for the *interval* (specified on the command line) since the previous display.

SEE ALSO

`trpt`(1M), `hosts`(4), `networks`(4), `protocols`(4), `services`(4).

NOTES

The notion of errors is ill-defined.

The kernel's tables can change while `netstat` is examining them, creating incorrect or partial displays.

NAME

`newaliases` - rebuild the data base for the mail aliases file

SYNOPSIS

`/usr/ucb/newaliases`

DESCRIPTION

`newaliases` rebuilds the random access data base for the mail aliases file `/etc/aliases`. `newaliases` should be run whenever the `/etc/aliases` file is updated.

FILES

```
/etc/aliases
/etc/aliases.dir
/etc/aliases.pag
```

SEE ALSO

`sendmail`(1M), `aliases`(4)

NAME

newform - change the format of a text file

SYNOPSIS

newform [-s] [-i tabspec] [-o tabspec] [-bn] [-en] [-pn] [-an] [-f] [-c char] [-ln]
[*files*]

DESCRIPTION

newform reads lines from the named *files*, or the standard input if no input file is named, and reproduces the lines on the standard output. Lines are reformatted in accordance with command line options in effect.

Except for -s, command line options may appear in any order, may be repeated, and may be intermingled with the optional *files*. Command line options are processed in the order specified. This means that option sequences like "-e15 -l60" will yield results different from "-l60 -e15". Options are applied to all *files* on the command line.

-s   Shears off leading characters on each line up to the first tab and places up to 8 of the sheared characters at the end of the line. If more than 8 characters (not counting the first tab) are sheared, the eighth character is replaced by a * and any characters to the right of it are discarded. The first tab is always discarded.

An error message and program exit will occur if this option is used on a file without a tab on each line. The characters sheared off are saved internally until all other options specified are applied to that line. The characters are then added at the end of the processed line.

For example, to convert a file with leading digits, one or more tabs, and text on each line, to a file beginning with the text, all tabs after the first expanded to spaces, padded with spaces out to column 72 (or truncated to column 72), and the leading digits placed starting at column 73, the command would be:

newform -s -i -l -a -e *file*

-i*tabspec*   Input tab specification: expands tabs to spaces, according to the tab specifications given. *tabspec* accepts four types of tab specifications: canned, repetitive, arbitrary and file. *-n* represents the repetitive tab specification. This format can be used to replace each tab in a file with *n* spaces. For example,

newform -i-4 *file*

replaces tabs with 4 spaces. For more information about the *tabspec* formats see tabs(1). In addition, *tabspec* may be --, in which newform assumes that the tab specification is to be found in the first line read from the standard input (see fspec(4)). If no *tabspec* is given, *tabspec* defaults to -8. A *tabspec* of -0 expects no tabs; if any are found, they are treated as -1.

-o*tabspec*   Output tab specification: replaces spaces by tabs, according to the tab specifications given. The tab specifications are the same as for -i*tabspec*. If no *tabspec* is given, *tabspec* defaults to -8. A *tabspec* of -0 means that no spaces will be converted to tabs on output.

-b*n*   Truncate *n* columns from the beginning of the line when the line length is greater than the effective line length (see -l*n*). Default is to truncate the number of columns necessary to obtain the effective line length. The default value is used when -b with no *n* is used. This option can be used to delete the sequence numbers from a COBOL program as follows:

```
newform -l1 -b7 file
```

-e*n*   Same as -b*n* except that columns are truncated from the end of the line.

-p*n*   Prefix *n* columns (see -c*k*) to the beginning of a line when the line length is less than the effective line length. Default is to prefix the number of columns necessary to obtain the effective line length.

-a*n*   Same as -p*n* except columns are appended to the end of a line.

-f   Write the tab specification format line on the standard output before any other lines are output. The tab specification format line which is printed will correspond to the format specified in the *last* -o option. If no -o option is specified, the line which is printed will contain the default specification of -8.

-c*k*   Change the prefix/append character to *k*. The prefix/append character *k* must be one single-byte character. Default character for *k* is a space.

-l*n*   Set the effective line length to *n* columns. If *n* is not entered, -l defaults to 72. The default line length without the -l option is 80 columns. Note that tabs and backspaces are considered to be one column (use -i to expand tabs to spaces).

     The -l1 must be used to set the effective line length shorter than any existing line in the file so that the -b option is activated.

DIAGNOSTICS

All diagnostics are fatal.

`usage:  . . .`	newform was called with a bad option.
`"not -s format"`	There was no tab on one line.
`"can't open file"`	Self-explanatory.
`"internal line too long"`	

     A line exceeds 512 characters after being expanded in the internal work buffer.

`"tabspec in error"`   A tab specification is incorrectly formatted, or specified tab stops are not ascending.

`"tabspec indirection illegal"`

     A *tabspec* read from a file (or standard input) may not contain a *tabspec* referencing another file (or standard input).

0 - normal execution
1 - for any error

INTERNATIONAL FUNCTIONS

newform can process characters from supplementary code sets as well as ASCII characters.

SEE ALSO

csplit(1), tabs(1)
fspec(4).

NOTES

newform normally only keeps track of physical characters; however, for the -i and -o options, newform will keep track of backspaces in order to line up tabs in the appropriate logical columns.

newform will not prompt the user if a *tabspec* is to be read from the standard input (by use of -i-- or -o--).

If the -f option is used, and the last -o option specified was -o--, and was preceded by either a -o-- or a -i--, the tab specification format line will be incorrect.

NAME

newfs - construct a new file system

SYNOPSIS

/usr/ucb/newfs [-nNv] [*mkfs-options*] *block-special-file*

DESCRIPTION

newfs is a friendly front-end to the mkfs(1M) program.

block-special-file is the name of a block special device residing in /dev. If you want to make a file system on sd0, you can specify sd0 rsd0 or /dev/rsd0; if you only specify sd0, newfs will find the proper device.

newfs then calculates the appropriate parameters to use in calling mkfs, builds the file system by forking mkfs and, if the file system is a root slice, installs the necessary bootstrap programs in its initial 16 sectors.

OPTIONS

-n   Do not install the bootstrap programs.

-N   Print out the file system parameters without actually creating the file system.

-v   Verbose. newfs prints out its actions, including the parameters passed to mkfs.

mkfs-options

Options that override the default parameters passed to mkfs(1M) are:

-b *block-size*

The block size of the file system in bytes.

-c *#cylinders/group*

The number of cylinders per cylinder group in a file system. The default value used is 16.

-d *rotdelay*

This specifies the expected time (in milliseconds) to service a transfer completion interrupt and initiate a new transfer on the same disk. It is used to decide how much rotational spacing to place between successive blocks in a file.

-f *frag-size*

The fragment size of the file system in bytes.

-i *bytes/inode*

This specifies the density of inodes in the file system. The default is to create an inode for each 2048 bytes of data space. If fewer inodes are desired, a larger number should be used; to create more inodes a smaller number should be given.

-m *free-space%*

The percentage of space reserved from normal users; the minimum free space threshold. The default value used is 10%.

-o *optimization*

(space or time). The file system can either be instructed to try to minimize the time spent allocating blocks, or to try to minimize the space fragmentation on the disk. If the minimum free space threshold (as specified by the −m option) is less than 10%, the default is to optimize for space; if the minimum free space threshold is greater than or equal to 10%, the default is to optimize for time.

−r *revolutions/minute*
The speed of the disk in revolutions per minute (normally 3600).

−s *size*　The size of the file system in sectors.

−t *#tracks/cylinder*
The number of tracks per cylinders on the disk.

FILES

    /usr/mdec   for boot strapping programs
    /dev

SEE ALSO

    fsck(1M), mkfs(1M), tunefs(1M), fs(4).

NAME

newgrp - log in to a new group

SYNOPSIS

newgrp [-] [group]

DESCRIPTION

newgrp changes a user's real and effective group ID. The user remains logged in and the current directory is unchanged. The user is always given a new shell, replacing the current shell, by newgrp, regardless of whether it terminated successfully or due to an error condition (i.e., unknown group).

Exported variables retain their values after invoking newgrp; however, all unexported variables are either reset to their default value or set to null. System variables (such as PS1, PS2, PATH, MAIL, and HOME), unless exported by the system or explicitly exported by the user, are reset to default values. For example, a user has a primary prompt string (PS1) other than $ (default) and has not exported PS1. After an invocation of newgrp, successful or not, the user's PS1 will now be set to the default prompt string $. Note that the shell command export [see the sh(1) manual page] is the method to export variables so that they retain their assigned value when invoking new shells.

With no arguments, newgrp changes the user's group IDs (real and effective) back to the group specified in the user's password file entry. This is a way to exit the effect of an earlier newgrp command.

If the first argument to newgrp is a -, the environment is changed to what would be expected if the user actually logged in again as a member of the new group.

A password is demanded if the group has a password and the user is not listed in /etc/group as being a member of that group.

FILES

/etc/group   system's group file

/etc/passwd   system's password file

NOTES

The ability of the user to enter a password when using this command will be removed in a future release.

SEE ALSO

login(1), sh(1), group(4), passwd(4), environ(5).

NAME

newkey - create a new key in the publickey database

SYNOPSIS

newkey -h *hostname*

newkey -u *username*

DESCRIPTION

The newkey command is normally run by the RPC administrator on the machine that contains the publickey(4) database, to establish public keys for users and privileged users on the network. These keys are needed when using secure RPC or secure NFS.

newkey will prompt for a password for the given *username* or *hostname* and then create a new public/secret key pair for the user or host in /etc/publickey, encrypted with the given password.

The following options are available:

-h *hostname*   Create a new public/secret key pair for the privileged user at the given *hostname*. Prompts for a password for the given *hostname*.

-u *username*   Create a new public/secret key pair for the given *username*. Prompts for a password for the given *username*.

SEE ALSO

chkey(1), keylogin(1), keylogout(1), keyserv(1M), publickey(4)

NAME

news - print news items

SYNOPSIS

news [-a] [-n] [-s] [*items*]

DESCRIPTION

news is used to keep the user informed of current events. By convention, these events are described by files in the directory /var/news.

When invoked without arguments, news prints the contents of all current files in /var/news, most recent first, with each preceded by an appropriate header. news stores the "currency" time as the modification date of a file named .news_time in the user's home directory (the identity of this directory is determined by the environment variable $HOME); only files more recent than this currency time are considered "current."

-a   option causes news to print all items, regardless of currency. In this case, the stored time is not changed.

-n   option causes news to report the names of the current items without printing their contents, and without changing the stored time.

-s   option causes news to report how many current items exist, without printing their names or contents, and without changing the stored time. It is useful to include such an invocation of news in one's .profile file, or in the system's /etc/profile.

All other arguments are assumed to be specific news items that are to be printed.

If a *delete* is typed during the printing of a news item, printing stops and the next item is started. Another *delete* within one second of the first causes the program to terminate.

FILES

/etc/profile
/var/news/*
$HOME/.news_time

SEE ALSO

profile(4), environ(5).

NAME

nfsd - NFS daemon

SYNOPSIS

nfsd [*nservers*]

DESCRIPTION

nfsd starts the daemons that handle client file system requests. *nservers* is the number of file system request daemons to start. This number should be based on the load expected on this server. Four is the usual number of *nservers*.

The nfsd daemons are automatically invoked in run level 3.

FILES

.nfs*XXX*   client machine pointer to an open-but-unlinked file

SEE ALSO

biod(1M), mountd(1M), sharetab(4).

NAME

nfsstat - Network File System statistics

SYNOPSIS

nfsstat [-csnrz]

DESCRIPTION

nfsstat displays statistical information about the NFS (Network File System) and RPC (Remote Procedure Call), interfaces to the kernel. It can also be used to reinitialize this information. If no options are given the default is

nfsstat -csnr

That is, display everything, but reinitialize nothing.

Options

The options for nfsstat are as follows:

-c   Display client information. Only the client side NFS and RPC information will be printed. Can be combined with the -n and -r options to print client NFS or client RPC information only.

-s   Display server information.

-n   Display NFS information. NFS information for both the client and server side will be printed. Can be combined with the -c and -s options to print client or server NFS information only.

-r   Display RPC information.

-z   Zero (reinitialize) statistics. This option is for use by the super-user only, and can be combined with any of the above options to zero particular sets of statistics after printing them.

Displays

The server RPC display includes the fields:

calls   total number of RPC calls received

badcalls total number of calls rejected

nullrecv number of times no RPC packet was available when trying to receive

badlen   number of packets that were too short

xdrcall   number of packets that had a malformed header

The server NFS display shows the number of NFS calls received (calls) and rejected (badcalls), and the counts and percentages for the various calls for file system primitive operations that were made.

The client RPC display includes the following fields:

calls   total number of RPC calls sent

badcalls total of calls rejected by a server

retrans   number of times a call had to be retransmitted

badxid   number of times a reply did not match the call

          `timeout`   number of times a call timed out

          `wait`   number of times a call had to wait on a busy `CLIENT` handle

          `newcred` number of times authentication information had to be refreshed

The client NFS display shows the number of calls sent (`calls`) and rejected (`badcalls`), as well as the number of times a `CLIENT` handle was received (`nclget`), the number of times a call had to sleep while awaiting a handle (`nclsleep`), as well as a count of the various calls and their respective percentages.

FILES

    `/stand/unix`   system namelist
    `/dev/kmem`   kernel memory

NAME

nice - run a command at low priority

SYNOPSIS

nice [*-increment*] *command* [*arguments*]

DESCRIPTION

nice executes *command* with a lower CPU scheduling priority. The priocntl command is a more general interface to scheduler functions.

The invoking process (generally the user's shell) must be in the time-sharing scheduling class. The *command* is executed in the time-sharing class.

If the *increment* argument (in the range 1-19) is given, it is used; if not, an increment of 10 is assumed.

The super-user may run commands with priority higher than normal by using a negative increment, for example, --10.

SEE ALSO

nohup(1), priocntl(1)
nice(2).

DIAGNOSTICS

nice returns the exit status of *command*.

NOTES

An *increment* larger than 19 is equivalent to 19.

NAME

nl - line numbering filter

SYNOPSIS

nl [-b*type*] [-f*type*] [-h*type*] [-v*start#*] [-i*incr*] [-p] [-l*num*] [-s*sep*] [-w*width*]
[-n*format*] [-d*delim*] [*file*]

DESCRIPTION

nl reads lines from the named *file*, or the standard input if no *file* is named, and
reproduces the lines on the standard output. Lines are numbered on the left in
accordance with the command options in effect.

nl views the text it reads in terms of logical pages. Line numbering is reset at the
start of each logical page. A logical page consists of a header, a body, and a footer
section. Empty sections are valid. Different line numbering options are independently available for header, body, and footer. For example, -bt (the default)
numbers non-blank lines in the body section and does not number any lines in the
header and footer sections.

The start of logical page sections are signaled by input lines containing nothing but
the following delimiter character(s):

Line contents	Start of
\:\:\:	header
\:\:	body
\:	footer

Unless optioned otherwise, nl assumes the text being read is in a single logical
page body.

Command options may appear in any order and may be intermingled with an
optional file name. Only one file may be named. The options are:

-b*type*   Specifies which logical page body lines are to be numbered. Recognized
*type*s and their meanings are:

        a   number all lines
        t   number lines with printable text only
        n   no line numbering
        p*exp*   number only lines that contain the regular expression
                 specified in *exp* (see ed(1))

     Default *type* for logical page body is t (text lines numbered). All charac-
ters from supplementary code sets are considered printable.

-f*type*   Same as -b*type* except for footer. Default *type* for logical page footer is n
(no lines numbered).

-h*type*   Same as -b*type* except for header. Default *type* for logical page header is
n (no lines numbered). All characters from supplementary code sets are
considered printable.

-v*start#*   *start#* is the initial value used to number logical page lines. Default *start#* is 1.

-i*incr*   *incr* is the increment value used to number logical page lines. Default *incr* is 1.

-p   Do not restart numbering at logical page delimiters.

-l*num*   *num* is the number of blank lines to be considered as one. For example, -12 results in only the second adjacent blank being numbered (if the appropriate -ha, -ba, and/or -fa option is set). Default *num* is 1.

-s*sep*   *sep* is the character(s) used in separating the line number and the corresponding text line. Default *sep* is a tab. Characters used for *sep* must be single-byte characters.

-w*width*   *width* is the number of characters to be used for the line number. The default for *width* is 6. The maximum for *width* is 100. If a number greater than the maximum is specified for *width*, the maximum is automatically used.

-n*format*   *format* is the line numbering format. Recognized values are: ln, left justified, leading zeroes suppressed; rn, right justified, leading zeroes suppressed; rz, right justified, leading zeroes kept. Default *format* is rn (right justified).

-d*delim*   The two delimiter characters specifying the start of a logical page section may be changed from the default characters (\:) to two user-specified characters. If only one character is entered, the second character remains the default character (:). No space should appear between the -d and the delimiter characters. To enter a backslash, use two backslashes. Characters used for *delim* must be single-byte characters.

EXAMPLE

The command:

```
nl -v10 -i10 -d!+ file1
```

will cause the first line of the page body to be numbered 10, the second line of the page body to be numbered 20, the third 30, and so forth. The logical page delimiters are !+.

INTERNATIONAL FUNCTIONS

nl can process files containing characters from supplementary code sets. Searches are performed on characters, not on bytes.

SEE ALSO

pr(1), ed(1)

NAME

nlsadmin - network listener service administration

SYNOPSIS

```
/usr/sbin/nlsadmin -x
/usr/sbin/nlsadmin [ options ] net_spec
/usr/sbin/nlsadmin [ options ] -N port_monitor_tag
/usr/sbin/nlsadmin -V
/usr/sbin/nlsadmin -c cmd | -o streamname [ -p modules ]
    [ -A address | -D ] [ -R prognum : versnum  ]
```

DESCRIPTION

nlsadmin is the administrative command for the network listener process(es) on a machine. Each network has at least one instance of the network listener process associated with it; each instance (and thus, each network) is configured separately. The listener process "listens" to the network for service requests, accepts requests when they arrive, and invokes servers in response to those service requests. The network listener process may be used with any network (more precisely, with any connection-oriented transport provider) that conforms to the transport provider specification.

nlsadmin can establish a listener process for a given network, configure the specific attributes of that listener, and start and kill the listener process for that network. nlsadmin can also report on the listener processes on a machine, either individually (per network) or collectively.

The list below shows how to use nlsadmin. In this list, *net_spec* represents a particular listener process. Specifically, *net_spec* is the relative path name of the entry under /dev for a given network (that is, a transport provider). *address* is a transport address on which to listen and is interpreted using a syntax that allows for a variety of address formats. By default, *address* is interpreted as the symbolic ASCII representation of the transport address. An *address* preceded by a \x will let you enter an address in hexadecimal notation. Note that *address* must appear as a single word to the shell and thus must be quoted if it contains any blanks.

Changes to the list of services provided by the listener or the addresses of those services are put into effect immediately.

nlsadmin may be used with the following combinations of options and arguments:

nlsadmin   Gives a brief usage message.

nlsadmin -x   Reports the status of all of the listener processes installed on this machine.

nlsadmin *net_spec*
                Prints the status of the listener process for *net_spec*.

nlsadmin -q *net_spec*
                Queries the status of the listener process for the specified network, and reflects the result of that query in its exit code. If a listener process is active, nlsadmin will exit with a status of 0; if no process is active, the exit code will be 1; the exit code will be greater than 1 in case of error.

`nlsadmin` -v *net_spec*
> Prints a verbose report on the servers associated with *net_spec*, giving the service code, status, command, and comment for each. It also specifies the `uid` the server will run as and the list of modules to be pushed, if any, before the server is started.

`nlsadmin` -z *service_code net_spec*
> Prints a report on the server associated with *net_spec* that has service code *service_code*, giving the same information as in the -v option.

`nlsadmin` -q -z *service_code net_spec*
> Queries the status of the service with service code *service_code* on network *net_spec*, and exits with a status of 0 if that service is enabled, 1 if that service is disabled, and greater than 1 in case of error.

`nlsadmin` -l *address net_spec*
> Changes or sets the transport address on which the listener listens (the general listener service). This address can be used by remote processes to access the servers available through this listener (see the -a option, below). If *address* is just a dash (-), `nlsadmin` will report the address currently configured, instead of changing it.
>
> A change of address takes effect immediately.

`nlsadmin` -t *address net_spec*
> Changes or sets the address on which the listener listens for requests for terminal service but is otherwise similar to the -l option above. A terminal service address should not be defined unless the appropriate remote login software is available; if such software is available, it must be configured as service code 1 (see the -a option, below).

`nlsadmin` -i *net_spec*
> Initializes an instance of the listener for the network specified by *net_spec*; that is, creates and initializes the files required by the listener as well as starting that instance of the listener. Note that a particular instance of the listener should be initialized only once. The listener must be initialized before assigning addresses or services.

`nlsadmin` -a *service_code* [-p *modules*] [-w *name*] -c *cmd* -y *comment net_spec*
> Adds a new service to the list of services available through the indicated listener. *service_code* is the code for the service, *cmd* is the command to be invoked in response to that service code, comprised of the full path name of the server and its arguments, and *comment* is a brief (free-form) description of the service for use in various reports. Note that *cmd* must appear as a single word to the shell; if arguments are required, the *cmd* and its arguments must be enclosed in quotation marks. The *comment* must also appear as a single word to the shell. Characters from supplementary code sets can be used for *cmd* and *comment*. When a service is added, it is initially enabled (see the -e and -d options, below).

Service codes are alphanumeric strings, and are administered by pmadm(1M). The numeric service codes 0 through 100 are reserved for internal use by the listener. Service code 0 is assigned to the nlps server, which is the service invoked on the general listening address. In particular, code 1 is assigned to the remote login service, which is the service automatically invoked for connections to the terminal login address.

If the -p option is specified, then *modules* will be interpreted as a list of STREAMS modules for the listener to push before starting the service being added. The modules are pushed in the order they are specified. *modules* should be a comma-separated list of modules, with no white space included.

If the -w option is specified, then *name* is interpreted as the user name from /etc/passwd that the listener should look up. From the user name, the listener obtains the user ID, the group ID(s), and the home directory for use by the server. If -w is not specified, the default is to use the user name listen.

A service must explicitly be added to the listener for each network on which that service is to be available. This operation will normally be performed only when the service is installed on a machine, or when populating the list of services for a new network.

nlsadmin -r *service_code net_spec*
> Removes the entry for the *service_code* from that listener's list of services. This is normally done only in conjunction with the deinstallation of a service from a machine.

nlsadmin -e *service_code net_spec*
nlsadmin -d *service_code net_spec*
> Enables or disables (respectively) the service indicated by *service_code* for the specified network. The service must previously have been added to the listener for that network (see the -a option, above). Disabling a service will cause subsequent service requests for that service to be denied, but the processes from any prior service requests that are still running will continue unaffected.

nlsadmin -s *net_spec*
nlsadmin -k *net_spec*
> Starts and kills (respectively) the listener process for the indicated network. These operations will normally be performed as part of the system startup and shutdown procedures. Before a listener can be started for a particular network, it must first have been initialized (see the -i option, above). When a listener is killed, processes that are still running as a result of prior service requests will continue unaffected.

nlsadmin [*options*] -N *port_monitor_tag*
> Under the Service Access Facility, it is possible to have multiple instances of the listener on a single *net_spec*. In any of the above commands, the option -N *port_monitor_tag* may be used in place of the *net_spec* argument. This argument specifies the tag by which an

instance of the listener is identified by the Service Access Facility. If the -N option is not specified (i.e., the *net_spec* is specified in the invocation), then it will be assumed that the last component of the *net_spec* represents the tag of the listener for which the operation is destined. In other words, it is assumed that there is at least one listener on a designated *net_spec*, and that its tag is identical to the last component of the *net_spec*. This listener may be thought of as the primary, or default, listener for a particular *net_spec*.

nlsadmin is also used in conjunction with the Service Access Facility commands.

In that capacity, the following combinations of options can be used:

nlsadmin -V   Writes the current version number of the listener's administrative file to the standard output. It is used as part of the sacadm command line when sacadm adds a port monitor to the system.

nlsadmin -c *cmd* | -o *streamname* [-p *modules*] [-A *address* | -D]
        [-R *prognum* : *versnum*]
        Formats the port monitor-specific information to be used as an argument to pmadm(1M).

        The -c option specifies the full path name of the server and its arguments. *cmd* must appear as a single word to the shell, and its arguments must therefore be surrounded by quotes. Characters from supplementary code sets can be used for *cmd*.

        The -o option specifies the full path name of a FIFO or named STREAM through which a standing server is actually receiving the connection.

        If the -p option is specified, then *modules* will be interpreted as a list of STREAMS modules for the listener to push before starting the service being added. The modules are pushed in the order in which they are specified. *modules* must be a comma-separated list, with no white space included.

        If the -A option is specified, then *address* will be interpreted as the server's private address. The listener will monitor this address on behalf of the service and will dispatch all calls arriving on this address directly to the designated service. This option may not be used in conjunction with the -D option.

        If the -D option is specified, then the service is assigned a private address dynamically, that is, the listener will have the transport provider select the address each time the listener begins listening on behalf of this service. For RPC services, this option will often be used in conjunction with the -R option to register the dynamically assigned address with the rpcbinder. This option may not be used in conjunction with the -A option.

        When the -R option is specified, the service is an RPC service whose address, program number, and version number should be registered with the rpcbinder for this transport provider. This registration is performed each time the listener begins listening on behalf of the service. *prognum* and *versnum* are the program number and version number, respectively, of the RPC service.

`nlsadmin` may be invoked by any user to generate reports but all operations that affect a listener's status or configuration are restricted to privileged users.

The options specific to the Service Access Facility may not be mixed with any other options.

INTERNATIONAL FUNCTIONS

net_spec must be in ASCII .

The module name *modules* with option -p must consist of ASCII characters only.

SEE ALSO

`listen`(1M), `pmadm`(1M), `rpcbind`(1M), `sacadm`(1M).

NOTES

Dynamically assigned addresses are not displayed in reports as are statically assigned addresses.

The -m option of the SVR3.2 `nlsadmin` command is now ignored.

NAME

nm - print name list of an object file

SYNOPSIS

nm [-oxhvnefurplVT] *files*

DESCRIPTION

The nm command displays the symbol table of each ELF or COFF object file, specified by *file(s)*. The file may be a relocatable or absolute ELF or COFF object file; or it may be an archive of relocatable or absolute ELF or COFF object files. For each symbol, the following information will be printed:

Index
: The index of the symbol. (The index appears in brackets.)

Value
: The value of the symbol is one of the following: a section offset for defined symbols in a relocatable file; alignment constraints for symbols whose section index is SHN_COMMON; a virtual address in executable and dynamic library files.

Size
: The size in bytes of the associated object.

Type
: A symbol is of one of the following types: NOTYPE (no type was specified), OBJECT (a data object such as an array or variable), FUNC (a function or other executable code), SECTION (a section symbol), or FILE (name of the source file).

Bind
: The symbol's binding attributes. LOCAL symbols have a scope limited to the object file containing their definition; GLOBAL symbols are visible to all object files being combined; and WEAK symbols are essentially global symbols with a lower precedence than GLOBAL.

Other
: A field reserved for future use, currently containing 0.

Shndx
: Except for three special values, this is the section header table index in relation to which the symbol is defined. The following special values exist: ABS indicates the symbol's value will not change through relocation; COMMON indicates an unallocated block and the value provides alignment constraints; and UNDEF indicates an undefined symbol.

Name
: The name of the symbol.

The output of nm may be controlled using the following options:

-o
: Print the value and size of a symbol in octal instead of decimal.

-x
: Print the value and size of a symbol in hexadecimal instead of decimal.

-h
: Do not display the output heading data.

-v
: Sort external symbols by value before they are printed.

-n
: Sort external symbols by name before they are printed.

-e
: See NOTES below.

-f
: See NOTES below.

-u
: Print undefined symbols only.

-r   Prepend the name of the object file or archive to each output line.

-p   Produce easily parsable, terse output. Each symbol name is preceded by
            its value (blanks if undefined) and one of the letters U (undefined), N
            (symbol has no type), D (data object symbol), T (text symbol), S (section
            symbol), or F (file symbol). If the symbol's binding attribute is LOCAL, the
            key letter is lower case; if the symbol's binding attribute is WEAK, the key
            letter is upper case; if the -l modifier is specified, the upper case key
            letter is followed by a *; if the symbol's binding attribute is GLOBAL, the
            key letter is upper case.

-l   Distinguish between WEAK and GLOBAL symbols by appending a * to the
            key letter for WEAK symbols.

-V   Print the version of the nm command executing on the standard error out-
            put.

-T   See NOTES below.

Options may be used in any order, either singly or in combination, and may appear
anywhere in the command line. When conflicting options are specified (such as nm
-v -n) the first is taken and the second ignored with a warning message to the
user.

SEE ALSO

as(1), cc(1), dump(1), ld(1), a.out(4), ar(4)

NOTES

The following options are obsolete because of changes to the object file format and
will be deleted in a future release.

-e   Print only external and static symbols. The symbol table now contains
            only static and external symbols. Automatic symbols no longer appear in
            the symbol table. They do appear in the debugging information pro-
            duced by cc -g, which may be examined using dump(1).

-f   Produce full output. Redundant symbols (such as .text, .data, and so on)
            which existed previously do not exist and producing full output will be
            identical to the default output.

-T   By default, nm prints the entire name of the symbols listed. Since symbol
            names have been moved to the last column, the problem of overflow is
            removed and it is no longer necessary to truncate the symbol name.

NAME

nohup - run a command immune to hangups and quits

SYNOPSIS

nohup *command* [*arguments*]

DESCRIPTION

nohup executes *command* with hangups and quits ignored. If output is not re-directed by the user, both standard output and standard error are sent to nohup.out. If nohup.out is not writable in the current directory, output is redirected to $HOME/nohup.out.

EXAMPLE

It is frequently desirable to apply nohup to pipelines or lists of commands. This can be done only by placing pipelines and command lists in a single file, called a shell procedure. One can then issue:

    nohup sh *file*

and the nohup applies to everything in *file*. If the shell procedure *file* is to be executed often, then the need to type sh can be eliminated by giving *file* execute permission. Add an ampersand and the contents of *file* are run in the background with interrupts also ignored (see sh(1)):

    nohup *file* &

An example of what the contents of *file* could be is:

    sort ofile > nfile

SEE ALSO

chmod(1), nice(1), sh(1)
signal(2).

NOTES

In the case of the following command

    nohup command1; command2

nohup applies only to command1. The command

    nohup (command1; command2)

is syntactically incorrect.

NAME

notify - notify user of the arrival of new mail

SYNOPSIS

notify -y [-m *mailfile*]
notify [-n]

DESCRIPTION

When a new mail message arrives, the mail command first checks if the recipient's mailbox indicates that the message is to be forwarded elsewhere (to some other recipient or as the input to some command). notify is used to set up forwarding on the user's mailbox so that the new message is saved into an alternative mailbox and, if the user is currently logged in, he or she is notified immediately of the arrival of new mail.

Command-line options are:

-m *mailfile*　　File to save mail messages into while automatic notification is activated. If not specified, it defaults to *$HOME/.mailfile*.
-n　　Remove mail notification facility
-y　　Install mail notification facility

If invoked with no arguments, notify reports whether automatic mail notification is activated or not.

The notification is done by looking in /var/adm/utmp to determine if the recipient is currently logged in, and if so, on which terminal device. Then the terminal device is opened for writing and the user is notified about the new message. The notification will indicate who the message is from. If the message contains a Sub-ject: header line it will be included. (For security, all unprintable characters within the header will be converted to an exclamation point.)

If the user is logged in multiple times he or she will get multiple notifications, one per terminal. To disable notifications to a particular login session, the mesg(1) command can be used to disable writing to that terminal.

If there are multiple machines connected together via RFS or NFS, notify will look up the /var/adm/utmp files on the other systems as well. To do this, the file /etc/mail/notify.sys will be consulted, which will contain two columns, the first being the name of a system and the second being a path to find the root filesystem for that machine.

If notify has troubles delivering the mail to the specified mailfile, notify will look up the directory of the mailfile in /etc/mail/notify.fsys. If the file's directory is found in the first column of the file, the mail will be forwarded to the system listed in the second column instead of being returned to the sender.

FILES

/tmp/notif*	temporary file
/var/mail/*	users' standard mailboxes
/usr/lib/mail/notify2	program that performs the notification
/etc/mail/notify.fsys	list of file systems and home systems
/etc/mail/notify.sys	list of machines and paths to their root filesystems

`/var/adm/utmp`   list of users who are logged in

SEE ALSO

`mail`(1), `mesg`(1).

NOTES

Because `notify` uses the "`Forward to  |`*command*" facility of `mail` to implement notifications, `/var/mail/`*username* should not be specified as the place to put newly arrived messages via the `-m` invocation option. The `mail` command uses `/var/mail/`*username* to hold either mail messages, or indications of mail forwarding, but not both simultaneously.

If the user is using `layers`(1), the notification will `only` appear in the `login` window.

NAME

nroff - format documents for display or line-printer

SYNOPSIS

/usr/ucb/nroff [-ehiqz] [-F*dir*] [-m*name*] [-n*N*] [-o*pagelist*] [-r*aN*]
          [-s*N*] [-T*name*] [-u*N*] [*filename* . . .]

DESCRIPTION

nroff formats text in the named *filename* for typewriter-like devices. See also troff.

If no *filename* argument is present, nroff reads the standard input. An argument consisting of a '-' is taken to be a file name corresponding to the standard input.

The following options may appear in any order, but must appear *before* the files.

-e	Produce equally-spaced words in adjusted lines, using full terminal resolution.
-h	Use output TAB characters during horizontal spacing to speed output and reduce output character count. TAB settings are assumed to be every 8 nominal character widths.
-i	Read the standard input after the input files are exhausted.
-q	Invoke the simultaneous input-output mode of the rd request.
-F*dir*	Search directory *dir* for font tables instead of the system-dependent default.
-m*name*	Prepend the macro file /usr/share/lib/tmac/tmac.*name* to the input files.
-n*N*	Number first generated page N.
-o*pagelist*	Print only pages whose page numbers appear in the comma-separated *list* of numbers and ranges. A range N- M means pages N through M; an initial -N means from the beginning to page N; and a final N- means from N to the end.
-r*aN*	Set register a (one-character) to N.
-s*N*	Stop every N pages. nroff will halt prior to every N pages (default $N=1$) to allow paper loading or changing, and will resume upon receipt of a NEWLINE.
-T*name*	Prepare output for a device of the specified name. Known names are:

37	Teletype Corporation Model 37 terminal — this is the default.
crt I lpr I tn300	GE TermiNet 300, or any line printer or terminal without half-line capability.
300	DASI-300.
300-12	DASI-300 — 12-pitch.

    300S | 302 | dtc
                DASI-300S.

    300S-12 | 302-12 | dtc12
                DASI-300S.

    382   DASI-382 (fancy DTC 382).

    382-12   DASI-82 (fancy DTC 382 — 12-pitch).

    450 | ipsi DASI-450 (Diablo Hyterm).

    450-12 | ipsi12
                DASI-450 (Diablo Hyterm) — 12-pitch.

    450-12-8   DASI-450 (Diablo Hyterm) — 12-pitch and 8 lines-per-inch.

    450X   DASI-450X (Diablo Hyterm).

    832   AJ 832.

    833   AJ 833.

    832-12   AJ 832 — 12-pitch.

    833-12   AJ 833 — 12-pitch.

    epson   Epson FX80.

    itoh   C:ITOH Prowriter.

    itoh-12   C:ITOH Prowriter — 12-pitch.

    nec   NEC 55?0s0 or NEC 77?0s0 Spinwriter.

    nec12   NEC 55?0 or NEC 77?0 Spinwriter — 12-pitch.

    nec-t   NEC 55?0/77?0 Spinwriter — Tech-Math/Times-Roman thimble.

    qume   Qume Sprint — 5 or9.

    qume12   Qume Sprint — 5 or 9,12-pitch.

    xerox   Xerox 17?0 or Diablo 16?0.

    xerox12   Xerox 17?0 or Diablo 16?0 — 12-pitch.

    x-ecs   Xerox/Diablo 1730/630 — Extended Character Set.

    x-ecs12   Xerox/Diablo 1730/630 — Extended Character Set, 12-pitch.

-u*N*   Set emboldening factor for the font mounted on position 3 to N. Emboldening is accomplished by overstriking the specified number of times.

-z   Suppress formatted output. The only output will consist of diagnostic messages from nroff and messages output with the .tm request.

EXAMPLE

The following command:

```
nroff -s4 -me users.guide
```

formats `users.guide` using the `-me` macro package, and stopping every 4 pages.

FILES

`/tmp/ta*`	temporary file
`/usr/ucblib/doctools/tmac/tmac.*`	standard macro files
`/usr/ucblib/doctools/term/*`	terminal driving tables for `nroff`
`/usr/ucblib/doctools/term/README`	index to terminal description files

SEE ALSO

`checknr`(1), `col`(1), `eqn`(1), `tbl`(1), `troff`(1), `term`(4), man(7), me(7), ms(7).

NAME

`nslookup` - query DARPA Internet name servers interactively

SYNOPSIS

`nslookup` [*-opt ...*]   # interactive mode using default server

`nslookup` [*-opt ...*] - *server*   # interactive mode using "server"

`nslookup` [*-opt ...*] *host*   # just look up host using default server

`nslookup` [*-opt ...*] *host server*   # just look up "host" using "server"

DESCRIPTION

The `nslookup` program can be used interactively to query ARPA Internet domain name servers. When `nslookup` is utilized "interactively", the user can query name servers for information about specific hosts and domains; in the "non-interactive" mode, a user can only print a list of hosts within a domain.

INTERACTIVE MODE vs NON-INTERACTIVE MODE

The "interactive" mode will be entered for the following cases:

a)   if no arguments are given (i.e., the default name server is to be used),

b)   if the first argument is a hyphen (-) and the second argument is the host name or the Internet address of a name server.

The program enters the "non-interactive" mode when the first argument specifies the name or (Internet address) of the host to be looked up; the optional second argument then would specify the host name or address of a name server.

The options listed under the "`set`" command below can be specified in the `.nslookuprc` file in the user's home directory if they are listed there in a one-per-line format. These options can also be specified on the command line if they precede the arguments and are prefixed with a hyphen. For example, to change the default query type to host information and the initial timeout to 10 seconds, the user would enter:

```
nslookup -query=hinfo  -timeout=10
```

NON-INTERACTIVE OPTIONS

host   The default server will be used, depending upon the existence of the `/etc/resolv.conf` file.

host server
             Look up host using the specified server.

OVERVIEW

The DARPA Internet "domain name-space" is tree-structured, with four top-level domains at present:

COM   commercial establishments

EDU   educational institutions

      GOV   government agencies

      MIL   MILNET hosts

When looking for a specific host, you need to know something about the host's organization in order to determine the top-level domain it belongs to. For instance, if you want to find the Internet address of a machine at UCLA, do the following:

- Connect with the root server using the `root` command. The root server of the name space has knowledge of the top-level domains.

- Since UCLA is a university, its domain name is `ucla.edu`. Connect with a server for the `ucla.edu` domain with the command `server ucla.edu`. The response will print the names of hosts that act as servers for that domain.

- To request information about a particular host in the domain (for example, `locus`), just type the host name. To request a listing of hosts in the UCLA domain, use the `ls` command. The `ls` command will need a domain name (in this case, `ucla.edu`) as an argument.

If you are connected with a name server that handles more than one domain, all lookups for host names must be fully specified with its domain. For instance, the domain `harvard.edu` is served by `seismo.css.gov`, which also services the `css.gov` and `cornell.edu` domains. Therefore, a lookup request for the host `aiken` in the `harvard.edu` domain must be specified as `aiken.harvard.edu`. However, the

      `set domain=`*name*

and

      `set defname`

commands can be used to append a domain name to each request on an automatic basis.

After a successful lookup of a host, you may use the `finger` command to see who is on the system or to "finger" a specific person. You can get other information about the host by using

      `set querytype=`*value*

command to change the type of information desired and to request another lookup. (`finger` requires the type to be A.)

INTERACTIVE COMMANDS

The following basic rules apply to an "interactive" command line:

a)   The command line length must be less than 256 characters;

b)   to end a command line, enter <^D> (EOF);

c)   a built-in command can be used as a host name by preceding it with an escape character ("\");

d)   any unrecognized command will be interpreted as a host name.

The following commands and command options are provided:

host [*server*]
> Look up information for *host* using the current default server or using *server*, if specified. To look up a host name not in the current domain, append a period to this host name.
>
> If *host* is an Internet address and if the "query type" is A or PTR, the host name will be returned. If *host* is a name and does not have a trailing period, the default domain name will be appended to this name.
>
> **NOTE:** This behavior depends of the state of the set options domain, srchlist, defname, and search.

server *domain*
lserver *domain*
> Change the default server to *domain*. The lserver command will use the initial server to look up information about *domain* while the server command will use the current default server. If an authoritative answer cannot be found, the names of servers that might have the answer are returned.

root
> Changes the default server to the server for the root of the "domain name space". Currently, the host ns.nic.ddn.mil is used; this command is a synonym for lserver ns.nic.ddn.mil.) The name of the root server can be changed with the set root command (see below).

finger [*name*]
> Connect with the finger server on the current host, which a previous lookup for a host was successful and returned address information (see the set *querytype*=A command). The *name* argument is optional. As with the shell, output can be redirected to a named file using > and >>.

ls [*option*] *domain* [> *filename*]

ls [*option*] *domain* [>> *filename*]
> List the information available for *domain*. The default output contains host names and their respective Internet addresses; as a option, this output can be created as (or appended to) *filename*. The following *option* types are available:
>
> -t *querytype*
>> lists all records of the specified type (see *querytype* below)
>
> -a   lists aliases of hosts in the domain (a synonym for -t CNAME).
>
> -h   lists the CPU and Operating System information for the domain (a synonym for -t HINFO.)
>
> -s   lists the "well-known services" of the hosts in this domain (a synonym for -t WKS).
>
> When output is directed to a file, a hash mark (#) is printed for every 50 records received from the server.

view *filename*
> Sort and list the output of the `ls` command with `more`(1).

`help`

`?` Print a brief summary of commands.

`exit`
> Exits the program.

`set` *keyword* [= *value*] This command is used to change state information that affects the lookups. The valid keywords are:

> `all` Prints the current values of the various options to `set`. Information about the current default server and host is also printed.

> `class=`*value*
>> Change the query class to one of the following:

>> `IN` the Internet class.

>> `CHAOS` the Chaos class.

>> `HESIOD`
>>> the MIT Athena Hesiod class.

>> `ANY` wildcard (i.e., any of the above): The class specifies the protocol group of the information.
>> The default value is `IN`, abbreviation = cl.

[`no`] `deb` [`ug`]
> Enable debugging mode. A lot more information is printed about the packet sent to the server and the resulting answer. The default is `nodebug`.

[`no`] `def` [*name*]
> Append the default domain *name* to every lookup. The default is `nodefname`.

`do` [`main`] =*filename*
> Change the default domain name to *filename*. The default domain name will be appended to all lookup requests if the `defname` option has been set. The default is the value in `/etc/resolv.conf`.

`q` [`uerytype`] =*value*
> Change the type of information returned from a query to one of:

> `A` The host's Internet address (the default value).

> `CNAME` The canonical name for an alias.

> `HINFO` The host `CPU` and its Operating System type.

> `MD` The mail destination.

> `MX` The mail exchanger.

> `MB` The mailbox domain name.

> `MG` The mail group member.

> `MINFO` The mailbox or mail list information.

(Other types specified in the RFC 1035 document are valid, but are not very useful.)

[no]rec[urse]
Tell the name server to query other servers if it does not have the information. The default is recurse.

ret[ry]=*count*
Set the number of times to retry a request before giving up to count. When a reply to a request is not received within a certain amount of time (changed with set timeout), the request will be re-sent. The default value of count is 2.

ro[ot]=*host*
Change the name of the root server to host. This affects the root command. The default root server is ns.nic.ddn.mil.

t[imeout l]=*interval*
Change the timeout interval for a reply to *interval* seconds. The default *interval* is 10 seconds.

[no]v[c]
Always use a virtual circuit when sending requests to the server. The default is novc.

DIAGNOSTICS

If the lookup request was not successful, an error message will be printed. The possible errors are:

Time-out
The server did not respond to a request after a certain amount of time (changed with set timeout=*value*) and a certain number of retries (changed with set retry=*value*).

No information
Depending on the query type set with the set querytype command, no information about the host was available, but the host name is valid.

Non-existent domain
The host or domain name does not exist.

Connection refused
Network is unreachable
The connection to the name or finger server could not be made at the current time. This error commonly occurs with finger requests.

Server failure
The name server found an internal inconsistency in its database and could not return a valid answer.

Refused
The name server refused to service the request.

The following error should not occur: this indicates a bug in the program.

Format error
The name server found that the request packet was not in the proper format.

FILES

    `/etc/resolv.conf`   initial domain name and name server addresses.

SEE ALSO

    `named`(1M), `resolver`(3N), `resolv.conf`(4).
    RFC 1035, RFC 1183.

NOTES

    The root server does not have information about `ucla.edu`, but knows the names and addresses of hosts that do. Once located by the root server, all future queries will be sent to the UCLA name server.

    The *host* behavior depends of the state of the `set` options `domain`, `srchlist`, `defname`, and `search`.

NAME

nsquery - Remote File Sharing name server query

SYNOPSIS

nsquery [-h] [*name*]

DESCRIPTION

nsquery provides information about resources available to the host from both the local domain and from other domains. All resources are reported, regardless of whether the host is authorized to access them. When used with no options, nsquery identifies all resources in the domain that have been advertised as sharable. A report on selected resources can be obtained by specifying *name*, where *name* is:

nodename The report will include only those resources available from *nodename*.

domain. The report will include only those resources available from *domain*.

domain.nodename The report will include only those resources available from *domain.nodename*.

When the name does not include the delimiter ".", it will be interpreted as a *nodename* within the local domain. If the name ends with a delimiter ".", it will be interpreted as a domain name.

The information contained in the report on each resource includes its advertised name (*domain.resource*), the read/write permissions, the server (*nodename.domain*) that advertised the resource, and a brief textual description.

When -h is used, the header is not printed.

A remote domain must be listed in your rfmaster file in order to query that domain.

EXIT STATUS

If no entries are found when nsquery is executed, the report header is printed.

SEE ALSO

adv(1M), unadv(1M), rfmaster(4)

NOTES

If your host cannot contact the domain name server, an error message will be sent to standard error.

NAME
>   od - octal dump

SYNOPSIS
>   od [-bcDdFfOoSsvXx] [*file*] [[+]*offset*[. | b]]

DESCRIPTION
>   od displays *file* in one or more formats, as selected by the first argument. If the first argument is missing, -o is default. If no *file* is specified, the standard input is used. For the purposes of this description, "word" refers to a 16-bit unit, independent of the word size of the machine; "long word" refers to a 32-bit unit, and "double long word" refers to a 64-bit unit. The meanings of the format options are:

>   -b   Interpret bytes in octal.

>   -c   Interpret bytes as single-byte characters. Multibyte characters are treated as non-graphic characters. Certain non-graphic characters appear as C-language escapes: null=\0, backspace=\b, form-feed=\f, new-line=\n, return=\r, tab=\t; others appear as 3-digit octal numbers. For example:

```
echo "hello world" | od -c
0000000    h   e   l   l   o       w   o   r   l   d  \n
0000014
```

>   -D   Interpret long words in unsigned decimal.

>   -d   Interpret words in unsigned decimal.

>   -F   Interpret double long words in extended precision.

>   -f   Interpret long words in floating point.

>   -O   Interpret long words in unsigned octal.

>   -o   Interpret words in octal.

>   -S   Interpret long words in signed decimal.

>   -s   Interpret words in signed decimal.

>   -v   Show all data (verbose).

>   -X   Interpret long words in hex.

>   -x   Interpret words in hex.

>   *offset* specifies an offset from the beginning of *file* where the display will begin. The value of the *offset* argument must be specified in bytes. *offset* is normally interpreted as octal bytes. If . is appended, *offset* is interpreted in decimal. If x is appended, *offset* is interpreted in hexadecimal. If b is appended, *offset* is interpreted in blocks of 512 bytes. If *file* is omitted, *offset* must be preceded by +.

>   The display continues until an end-of-file is reached.

INTERNATIONAL FUNCTIONS
>   od can process characters from supplementary code sets.

NAME

`offline` - take a processor offline

SYNOPSIS

`offline` [`-v`] [*processor-id* ...]

DESCRIPTION

`offline` takes each processor that is specified on the command line offline. If no processors are specified, all processors in the system are taken offline. In either case, some processors may not be taken offline because of hardware restrictions. At least one processor must remain online at all times. Processors that have bound processes can not be taken offline. If the `-v` flag is specified, the status of the processor is displayed before and after the attempt to take it offline.

SEE ALSO

`online`(1M), `p_online`(2)

NOTES

This command may not be supported in future releases.

NAME

`online` - bring a processor online

SYNOPSIS

`online` [`-v`] [*processor-id . . .*]

DESCRIPTION

`online` brings each processor that is specified on the command line online. If no processors are listed, all processors are brought online. If the `-v` flag is specified, the status of the processor is displayed before and after the attempt to turn it on.

SEE ALSO

`offline`(1M), `p_online`(2)

NOTES

This command may not be supported in future releases.

NAME

pack, pcat, unpack - compress and expand files

SYNOPSIS

pack [-] [-f] *name ...*

pcat *name ...*

unpack *name ...*

DESCRIPTION

pack attempts to store the specified files in a compressed form. Wherever possible (and useful), each input file *name* is replaced by a packed file *name*.z with the same access modes, access and modified dates, and owner as those of *name*. The -f option will force packing of *name*. This is useful for causing an entire directory to be packed even if some of the files will not benefit. If pack is successful, *name* will be removed. Packed files can be restored to their original form using unpack or pcat.

pack uses Huffman (minimum redundancy) codes on a byte-by-byte basis. If the - argument is used, an internal flag is set that causes the number of times each byte is used, its relative frequency, and the code for the byte to be printed on the standard output. Additional occurrences of - in place of *name* will cause the internal flag to be set and reset.

The amount of compression obtained depends on the size of the input file and the character frequency distribution. Because a decoding tree forms the first part of each .z file, it is usually not worthwhile to pack files smaller than three blocks, unless the character frequency distribution is very skewed, which may occur with printer plots or pictures.

Typically, text files are reduced to 60-75% of their original size. Load modules, which use a larger character set and have a more uniform distribution of characters, show little compression, the packed versions being about 90% of the original size.

pack returns a value that is the number of files that it failed to compress.

No packing will occur if:

> the file appears to be already packed;
> the file name has more than 12 characters;
> the file has links;
> the file is a directory;
> the file cannot be opened;
> no disk storage blocks will be saved by packing;
> a file called *name*.z already exists;
> the .z file cannot be created;
> an I/O error occurred during processing.

The last segment of the file name must contain no more than 12 characters to allow space for the appended .z extension. Directories cannot be compressed.

pcat does for packed files what cat(1) does for ordinary files, except that pcat cannot be used as a filter. The specified files are unpacked and written to the standard output. Thus to view a packed file named name.z use:

    pcat name.z
or just:
    pcat name

To make an unpacked copy, say nnn, of a packed file named name.z (without destroying name.z) use the command:

    pcat name >nnn

pcat returns the number of files it was unable to unpack. Failure may occur if:

> the file name (exclusive of the .z) has more than 12 characters;
> the file cannot be opened;
> the file does not appear to be the output of pack.

unpack expands files created by pack. For each file *name* specified in the command, a search is made for a file called *name*.z (or just *name*, if *name* ends in .z). If this file appears to be a packed file, it is replaced by its expanded version. The new file has the .z suffix stripped from its name, and has the same access modes, access and modification dates, and owner as those of the packed file.

Unpack returns a value that is the number of files it was unable to unpack. Failure may occur for the same reasons that it may in pcat, as well as for the following:

> a file with the "unpacked" name already exists;
> if the unpacked file cannot be created.

SEE ALSO

    cat(1), compress(1).

NAME

pagesize - display the size of a page of memory

SYNOPSIS

`/usr/ucb/pagesize`

DESCRIPTION

`pagesize` prints the size of a page of memory in bytes, as returned by `get-pagesize`. This program is useful in constructing portable shell scripts.

SEE ALSO

`getpagesize(3)`

NAME

passmgmt - password files management

SYNOPSIS

passmgmt -a *options name*
passmgmt -m *options name*
passmgmt -d *name*

DESCRIPTION

The passmgmt command updates information in the password files. This command works with both /etc/passwd and /etc/shadow.

passmgmt -a adds an entry for user *name* to the password files. This command does not create any directory for the new user and the new login remains locked (with the string *LK* in the password field) until the passwd(1) command is executed to set the password.

passmgmt -m modifies the entry for user *name* in the password files. The name field in the /etc/shadow entry and all the fields (except the password field) in the /etc/passwd entry can be modified by this command. Only fields entered on the command line will be modified.

passmgmt -d deletes the entry for user *name* from the password files. It will not remove any files that the user owns on the system; they must be removed manually.

The following options are available:

-c *comment* A short description of the login. It is limited to a maximum of 128 characters and defaults to an empty field.

-h *homedir* Home directory of *name*. It is limited to a maximum of 256 characters and defaults to /usr/*name*.

-u *uid* UID of the *name*. This number must range from 0 to the maximum non-negative value for the system. It defaults to the next available UID greater than 99. Without the -o option, it enforces the uniqueness of a UID.

-o This option allows a UID to be non-unique. It is used only with the -u option.

-g *gid* GID of the *name*. This number must range from 0 to the maximum non-negative value for the system. The default is 1.

-s *shell* Login shell for *name*. It should be the full pathname of the program that will be executed when the user logs in. The maximum size of *shell* is 256 characters. The default is for this field to be empty and to be interpreted as /usr/bin/sh.

-l logname
This option changes the *name* to logname. It is used only with the -m option.

The total size of each login entry is limited to a maximum of 511 bytes in each of the password files.

FILES

/etc/passwd,
/etc/shadow,
/etc/opasswd,
/etc/oshadow

SEE ALSO

useradd(1M), userdel(1M), usermod(1M), passwd(1), passwd(4), shadow(4)

DIAGNOSTICS

The passmgmt command exits with one of the following values:

0   Success.

1   Permission denied.

2   Invalid command syntax. Usage message of the passmgmt command will be displayed.

3   Invalid argument provided to option.

4   UID in use.

5   Inconsistent password files (for example, *name* is in the /etc/passwd file and not in the /etc/shadow file, or vice versa).

6   Unexpected failure. Password files unchanged.

7   Unexpected failure. Password file(s) missing.

8   Password file(s) busy. Try again later.

9   *name* does not exist (if -m or -d is specified), already exists (if -a is specified), or logname already exists (if -m -l is specified).

NOTES

You cannot use a colon or carriage return as part of an argument because it is interpreted as a field separator in the password file.

This command will be removed in a future release. Its functionality has been replaced and enhanced by useradd, userdel, and usermod. These commands are currently available.

NAME

passwd - change login password and password attributes

SYNOPSIS

passwd [*login_name*]

passwd [-l | -d] [-f] [-n *min*] [-x *max*] [-w *warn*] *login_name*

passwd -s [-a]

passwd -s [*login_name*]

DESCRIPTION

The passwd command changes the password or lists password attributes associated with the user's *login_name*. Additionally, privileged-users may use passwd to install or change passwords and attributes associated with any *login_name.*

If *login_name* is not specified, passwd uses getlogin() to obtain the user's *login_name* from /etc/utmp. If the user has obtained a shell on the system in a way that does not create a *login_name* entry in /etc/utmp, passwd will return a usage error when invoked without *login_name* specified.

If the user has used su(1) to change to a new name, passwd will return Permission denied when invoked without *login_name* specified.

When used to change a password, passwd prompts ordinary users for their old password, if any. It then prompts for the new password twice. When the old password is entered, passwd checks to see if it has "aged" sufficiently. If aging is insufficient, passwd terminates [see shadow(4)].

Assuming aging is sufficient, a check is made to ensure that the new password meets construction requirements. When the new password is entered a second time, the two copies of the new password are compared. If the two copies are not identical the cycle of prompting for the new password is repeated for at most two more times.

Passwords must be constructed to meet the following requirements:

> Each password must have at least six characters. Only the first eight characters are significant. PASSLENGTH is found in /etc/default/passwd and is set to 6.

> Each password must contain at least two alphabetic characters and at least one numeric or special character. In this case, "alphabetic" refers to all upper or lower case letters.

> Each password must differ from the user's *login_name* and any reverse or circular shift of that *login_name*. For comparison purposes, an upper case letter and its corresponding lower case letter are equivalent.

> New passwords must differ from the old by at least three characters. For comparison purposes, an upper case letter and its corresponding lower case letter are equivalent.

Super-users (for example, real and effective UID equal to zero) [see id(1M) and su(1M)] may change any password; hence, passwd does not prompt privileged-users for the old password. Privileged-users are not forced to comply with password aging and password construction requirements. A privileged-user can create a null password by entering a carriage return in response to the prompt for a new password. (This differs from `passwd -d` because the "password" prompt will still be displayed.)

Any user may use the `-s` option to show password attributes for his or her own *login_name*.

The format of the display will be:

> *login_name status mm/dd/yy min max warn*

or, if password aging information is not present,

> *login_name status*

where

login_name	The login ID of the user.
status	The password status of *login_name*: `PS` stands for passworded or locked, `LK` stands for locked, and `NP` stands for no password.
mm/dd/yy	The date password was last changed for *login_name*. (Note that all password aging dates are determined using Greenwich Mean Time and, therefore, may differ by as much as a day in other time zones.)
min	The minimum number of days required between password changes for *login_name*. MINWEEKS is found in `/etc/default/passwd` and is set to NULL.
max	The maximum number of days the password is valid for *login_name*. MAXWEEKS is found in `/etc/default/passwd` and is set to NULL.
warn	The number of days relative to *max* before the password expires that the *login_name* will be warned. WARNWEEKS is found in `/etc/default/passwd` and is the number of weeks before password expiration when the user should start being warned.

Only a privileged-user can use the following options:

`-l`	Locks password entry for *login_name*.
`-d`	Deletes password for *login_name*. The *login_name* will not be prompted for password.
`-n`	Set minimum field for *login_name*. The *min* field contains the minimum number of days between password changes for *login_name*. If *min* is greater than *max*, the user may not change the password. Always use this option with the `-x` option, unless *max* is set to -1 (aging turned off). In that case, *min* need not be set.
`-x`	Set maximum field for *login_name*. The *max* field contains the number of days that the password is valid for *login_name*. The aging for *login_name* will be turned off immediately if *max* is set to -1. If it is set to 0, then the user is forced to change the password at the next login session and aging is turned off.
`-w`	Set warn field for *login_name*. The *warn* field contains the number of days before the password expires that the user will be warned.

`-a`	Show password attributes for all entries. Use only with `-s` option; *login_name* must not be provided.
`-f`	Force the user to change password at the next login by expiring the password for *login_name*.

FILES

/etc/shadow, /etc/passwd, /etc/oshadow

DIAGNOSTICS

The `passwd` command exits with one of the following values:

0	SUCCESS.
1	Permission denied.
2	Invalid combination of options.
3	Unexpected failure. Password file unchanged.
4	Unexpected failure. Password file(s) missing.
5	Password file(s) busy. Try again later.
6	Invalid argument to option.

SEE ALSO

`id`(1M), `login`(1), `passmgmt`(1M), `pwconv`(1M), `su`(1M), `useradd`(1M), `userdel`(1M), `usermod`(1M), `crypt`(3C), `passwd`(4), `shadow`(4).

NAME

`paste` - merge same lines of several files or subsequent lines of one file

SYNOPSIS

```
paste - | file1  - | file2 ...
paste -d list - | file1  - | file2 ...
paste -s  [-d list ] - | file1 ...
```

DESCRIPTION

In the first two forms, `paste` concatenates corresponding lines of the given input files *file1*, *file2*, etc. It treats each file as a column or columns of a table and pastes them together horizontally (parallel merging). `paste` is the counterpart of `cat`(1) which concatenates vertically, that is, one file after the other. In the last form above, `paste` replaces the function of an older command with the same name by combining subsequent lines of the input file (serial merging). If more than one file is specified with the `-s` option, `paste`(1) concatenates the merged files one below the other. In all cases, lines are glued together with the *tab* character, or with characters from an optionally specified *list*. Output is to the standard output, so it can be used as the start of a pipe, or as a filter, if – is used in place of a filename.

The meanings of the options are:

`-d`   Without this option, the newline characters of each but the last file (or last line in case of the `-s` option) are replaced by a *tab* character. This option allows replacing the *tab* character by one or more alternate characters (see below).

list   One or more characters immediately following `-d` replace the default *tab* as the line concatenation character. The list is used sequentially and circularly: first, the first element on the list is used to concatenate the lines, then the next, and so on; when all elements have been used, the list is reused starting from the first element. In parallel merging (that is, no `-s` option), the lines from the last file are always terminated with a newline character, not from the *list*. The list may contain the special escape sequences: \n (newline), \t (tab), \\ (backslash), and \0 (empty string, not a null character). Quoting may be necessary, if characters have special meaning to the shell (e.g., to get one backslash, use *-d* \\\\ ″″). Characters from supplementary code sets can be specified for *list*.

`-s`   Merge subsequent lines rather than one from each input file. Use *tab* for concatenation, unless a *list* is specified with the `-d` option. Regardless of the *list*, the very last character of the file is forced to be a newline.

–   May be used in place of any filename, to read a line from the standard input. (There is no prompting.)

EXAMPLES

```
ls | paste -d" " -          lists directory in one column
ls | paste - - - -          lists directory in four columns
paste -d"\t\n" file1 file2  lists file1 in column 1 and file2 in column 2; the
                            columns are separated by a tab
```

```
paste -s -d"\t\n" file1 file2
```
merges pairs of subsequent lines first in *file1*, then in *file2*; concatenates the merged *file2* below *file1*

DIAGNOSTICS

```
line too long
```
Output lines are restricted to 511 characters.

```
too many files
```
Except for `-s` option, no more than 12 input files may be specified.

INTERNATIONAL FUNCTIONS

`paste` can process characters from supplementary code sets as well as ASCII characters.

SEE ALSO

`cut`(1), `grep`(1), `pr`(1).

NAME

pathconv - search FMLI criteria for filename

SYNOPSIS

pathconv [-f] [-v *alias*]
pathconv [-t] [-l] [-n*num*] [-v *string*]

DESCRIPTION

The pathconv function converts an alias to its pathname. By default, it takes the alias as a string from *stdin*.

-f   If -f is specified, the full path will be returned (this is the default).

-t   If -t is specified, pathconv will truncate a pathname specified in *string* in a format suitable for display as a frame title. This format is a shortened version of the full pathname, created by deleting components of the path from the middle of the string until it is under DISPLAYW - 6 characters in length, and then inserting ellipses (. . .) between the remaining pieces. Ellipses are also used to show truncation at the ends of the strings if necessary, unless the -l option is given.

    -l   If -l is specified, < and > will be used instead of ellipses (. . .) to indicate truncation at the ends of the string generated by the -t option. Truncation in the middle of the string is still indicated with ellipses. Using -l allows display of the longest possible string while still notifying users it has been truncated.

    -n*num*   If -n is specified, *num* is the maximum length of the string (in characters) generated by the -t option. The argument *num* can be any integer from 1 to 255.

-v *arg*   If the -v option is used, then *alias* or *string* can be specified when pathconv is called. The argument *alias* must be an alias defined in the *alias_file* named when fmli was invoked. The argument *string* can only be used with the -t option and must be a pathname.

EXAMPLES

Here is a menu descriptor that uses pathconv to construct the menu title. It searches for MYPATH in the *alias_file* named when fmli was invoked:

```
menu=`pathconv -v MYPATH/ls`
     .
     .
     .
```

where there is a line in *alias_file* that defines MYPATH. For example, MYPATH=$HOME/bin:/usr/bin.

Here is a menu descriptor that takes *alias* from *stdin*.

```
menu=`echo MYPATH/ls | pathconv`
     .
     .
     .
```

SEE ALSO
        fmli(1)

NAME

pbind - bind a process to a processor

SYNOPSIS

pbind -b *processor-id pid* . . .

pbind -u *pid* . . .

pbind -q [*pid* . . .]

DESCRIPTION

If the -b option is specified, pbind binds the processes specified by the process ID (*pid*) arguments to the processor specified by *processor-id*. Processes that are bound to a processor will run only on that processor, except briefly when the process requires a resource that only another processor can provide. The processor may run other processes in addition to those which are bound to it.

If there are already processes exclusively bound to the specified processor (for example, by pexbind), the pbind command will fail.

If a process specified by *pid* is already bound to a different processor, the binding for that process shall be changed to the specified processor. If, however, a process specified by *pid* is bound exclusively (for example, by pexbind) the pbind command will fail.

If the -u option is specified, any binding will be removed for the specified processes.

Users can control only those processes they own unless the user is a super-user.

If the -q option is specified, pbind displays binding information for the specified *pid*s. If no *pid*s are specified, pbind displays binding information for the entire system.

NOTES

The format of the output displayed by pbind -q may change significantly in a future release. Applications and shell scripts should not depend on this format.

SEE ALSO

pexbind(1M)
processor_bind(2) in the *Programmer's Supplement*

NAME

pexbind - exclusively bind processes to a processor

SYNOPSIS

pexbind -b *processor-id pid* ...

pexbind -u *pid* ...

pexbind -q [*pid* ...]

DESCRIPTION

If the -b option is specified pexbind exclusively binds the process(es) specified by the *pid* arguments to the processor specified by *processor-id*. Processes that are exclusively bound to a processor will execute only on that processor. However, an exclusively bound process will execute briefly on another processor if the process requires a resource that only that other processor can provide. In general, the processor will execute only those processes that are exclusively bound to it. However, the processor can briefly execute other processes in the system if it must provide a resource to the other processes that no other processor can provide.

If there are already processes bound to the specified processor, either exclusively or non-exclusively, the pexbind(1M) command will fail. Note, to exclusively bind several processes to a processor, all processes must be specified in one invocation of pexbind.

If a process specified by *pid* is already exclusively bound to a different processor, the exclusive binding for that process will be changed to the specified processor. If, however, a process specified by *pid* is bound non-exclusively (for example, with pbind) the previous non-exclusive binding will remain in effect for that process (the pexbind call will have no effect on that process).

If the -u option is specified, any exclusive binding will be removed for the specified processes.

Only the super-user can change the exclusive binding of processes using the pexbind command.

If the -q option is specified, pexbind displays exclusive binding information for the specified *pids*. If no *pids* are specified, pexbind displays exclusive binding information for the entire system.

NOTES

This command may not be supported in future releases. The format of the output displayed by pexbind -q may change significantly in a future release. Applications and shell scripts should not depend on this format.

SEE ALSO

pbind(1M)

processor_bind(2) in the *Programmer's Supplement*

NAME

pfmt - display error message in standard format

SYNOPSIS

```
pfmt [-llabel] [-sseverity] [-gcatalog:msgid] format [args]
```

DESCRIPTION

`pfmt` uses *format* for `printf` style formatting of *args*. If the `-g` option is specified, `pfmt` retrieves a localized version of the *format* string from a locale-specific message database. The output is displayed on *stderr*.

`pfmt` encapsulates the output in the standard error message format. The `-l`*label* option specifies the label string to be displayed with the message (e.g. `"UX:cat"`). *label* is a character string no more than 25 characters in length; it will be automatically suffixed with a colon (`:`). When unspecified, no label is displayed as part of the message.

The `-s`*severity* option specifies the severity string to be displayed with the message. Acceptable strings include the standard severities in either their print string (i.e. `HALT`, `ERROR`, `INFO`, `WARNING`, and `"TO FIX"`) or keyword (i.e. `halt`, `error`, `info`, `warn`, and `action`) forms, or any other user-defined string. A user-defined string will be assigned the integer severity value of 5. The severity will be suffixed with a colon (`:`). The `ERROR` severity will be used if no severity is specified.

The `-g`*catalog*:*msgnum* option specifies that a localized version of the *format* should be retrieved from a message database. *catalog* is used to indicate the message database that contains the localized version of the *format* string. *catalog* must be limited to 14 characters. These characters must be selected from a set of all characters values, excluding `\0` (null) and the ASCII codes for `/` (slash) and `:` (colon).

msgnum is a positive number that indicates the index of the string into the message database.

If the catalog does not exist in the current locale (identified by the `LC_MESSAGES` or `LANG` environment variables), or if the message number is out of bound, `pfmt` will attempt to retrieve the message from the C locale. If this second retrieval fails, `pfmt` uses the *format* string as passed on the command line.

`pfmt` will output `Message not found!!\n` as *format* string if *catalog* is not a valid catalog name, or if *msgnum* is not a valid number.

STANDARD ERROR MESSAGE FORMAT

`pfmt` displays error messages in the following format:

> *label*: *severity*: *text*

If no *label* was defined using the `-l`*label* option, the message is displayed in the format:

> *severity*: *text*

If `pfmt` is called twice to display an error message and a helpful *action* or recovery message, the output can look like:

> *label*: *severity*: *text*
> *label*: `TO FIX`: *text*

ERRORS

Upon success, `pfmt` exits with code 0. Upon failure, `pfmt` exits with the following codes:

1   write error.

3   syntax error.

EXAMPLE

```
pfmt -l UX:test -s error "Syntax error\n"
```

displays the message:

```
UX:test: ERROR: Syntax error
```

SEE ALSO

environ(5), gettxt(1), lfmt(1), pfmt(3C), printf(1),

NAME

pg - file perusal filter for CRTs

SYNOPSIS

pg [*-number*] [-p *string*] [-cefnrs] [*+linenumber*] [+/*pattern*/] [*file . . .*]

DESCRIPTION

The pg command is a filter that allows the examination of *files* one screenful at a time on a CRT. (If no *file* is specified or if it encounters the file name -, pg reads from standard input.) Each screenful is followed by a prompt. If the user types a carriage return, another page is displayed; other possibilities are listed below.

This command is different from previous paginators in that it allows you to back up and review something that has already passed. The method for doing this is explained below.

To determine terminal attributes, pg scans the terminfo(4) data base for the terminal type specified by the environment variable TERM. If TERM is not defined, the terminal type dumb is assumed.

The command line options are:

-number	An integer specifying the size (in lines) of the window that pg is to use instead of the default. (On a terminal containing 24 lines, the default window size is 23).
-c	Home the cursor and clear the screen before displaying each page. This option is ignored if clear_screen is not defined for this terminal type in the terminfo(4) data base.
-e	Causes pg *not* to pause at the end of each file.
-f	Normally, pg splits lines longer than the screen width, but some sequences of characters in the text being displayed (for example, escape sequences for underlining) generate undesirable results. The -f option inhibits pg from splitting lines.
-n	Normally, commands must be terminated by a *<newline>* character. This option causes an automatic end of command as soon as a command letter is entered.
-p *string*	Causes pg to use *string* as the prompt. If the prompt string contains a %d, the first occurrence of %d′ in the prompt will be replaced by the current page number when the prompt is issued. The default prompt string is " : ".
-r	Restricted mode. The shell escape is disallowed. pg will print an error message but does not exit.
-s	Causes pg to print all messages and prompts in standout mode (usually inverse video).
+linenumber	Start up at *linenumber*.
+/*pattern*/	Start up at the first line containing the regular expression pattern.

The responses that may be typed when pg pauses can be divided into three categories: those causing further perusal, those that search, and those that modify the perusal environment.

Commands that cause further perusal normally take a preceding *address*, an optionally signed number indicating the point from which further text should be displayed. This *address* is interpreted in either pages or lines depending on the command. A signed *address* specifies a point relative to the current page or line, and an unsigned *address* specifies an address relative to the beginning of the file. Each command has a default address that is used if none is provided.

The perusal commands and their defaults are as follows:

(+1)<*newline*> or <*blank*>

      This causes one page to be displayed. The address is specified in pages.

(+1) l   With a relative address this causes pg to simulate scrolling the screen, forward or backward, the number of lines specified. With an absolute address this command prints a screenful beginning at the specified line.

(+1) d or ^D   Simulates scrolling half a screen forward or backward.

*i*f   Skip *i* screens of text.

*i*z   Same as <*newline*> except that *i*, if present, becomes the new default number of lines per screenful.

The following perusal commands take no *address*.

. or ^L   Typing a single period causes the current page of text to be redisplayed.

$ Displays the last windowful in the file. Use with caution when the input is a pipe.

The following commands are available for searching for text patterns in the text. The regular expressions described in ed(1) are available. They must always be terminated by a <*newline*>, even if the -*n* option is specified.

i/*pattern*/   Search forward for the *i*th (default *i*=1) occurrence of *pattern*. Searching begins immediately after the current page and continues to the end of the current file, without wrap-around.

i^*pattern*^
i?*pattern*?   Search backwards for the *i*th (default *i*=1) occurrence of *pattern*. Searching begins immediately before the current page and continues to the beginning of the current file, without wrap-around. The ^ notation is useful for Adds 100 terminals which will not properly handle the ?.

After searching, pg will normally display the line found at the top of the screen. This can be modified by appending m or b to the search command to leave the line found in the middle or at the bottom of the window from now on. The suffix t can be used to restore the original situation.

The user of pg can modify the environment of perusal with the following commands:

*i*n   Begin perusing the *i*th next file in the command line. The *i* is an unsigned number, default value is 1.

*i*p   Begin perusing the *i*th previous file in the command line. *i* is an unsigned number, default is 1.

*i*w   Display another window of text. If *i* is present, set the window size to *i*.

s *filename*
        Save the input in the named file. Only the current file being perused is saved. The white space between the s and *filename* is optional. This command must always be terminated by a *<newline>*, even if the *-n* option is specified.

h   Help by displaying an abbreviated summary of available commands.

q or Q   Quit pg.

! *command*
        Command is passed to the shell, whose name is taken from the SHELL environment variable. If this is not available, the default shell is used. This command must always be terminated by a *<newline>*, even if the *-n* option is specified.

At any time when output is being sent to the terminal, the user can hit the quit key (normally CTRL-\) or the interrupt (break) key. This causes pg to stop sending output, and display the prompt. The user may then enter one of the above commands in the normal manner. Unfortunately, some output is lost when this is done, because any characters waiting in the terminal's output queue are flushed when the quit signal occurs.

If the standard output is not a terminal, then pg acts just like cat(1), except that a header is printed before each file (if there is more than one).

EXAMPLE
The following command line uses pg to read the system news:

```
news | pg -p "(Page %d):"
```

FILES
/usr/share/lib/terminfo/?/*   terminal information database

/tmp/pg*   temporary file when input is from a pipe

SEE ALSO
ed(1), grep(1), more(1), terminfo(4).

NOTES
While waiting for terminal input, pg responds to BREAK, DEL, and CTRL-\ by terminating execution. Between prompts, however, these signals interrupt pg's current task and place the user in prompt mode. These should be used with caution when input is being read from a pipe, since an interrupt is likely to terminate the other commands in the pipeline.

The terminal /, ^, or ? may be omitted from the searching commands.

If terminal tabs are not set every eight positions, undesirable results may occur.

When using pg as a filter with another command that changes the terminal I/O options, terminal settings may not be restored correctly.

INTERNATIONAL FUNCTIONS

pg can process files containing characters from supplementary code sets. Searches are performed on characters, not on individual bytes.

The prompt *string* with option -p can include characters from supplementary code sets.

NAME
pinfo - get information about processors

SYNOPSIS
pinfo [-v] [*processor-id* . . .]

DESCRIPTION
pinfo displays information about the processors named in the command line by
their *processor-id*s. If no processors are specified, information is displayed about all
processors in the system. The online/offline status of the processor is displayed. If
the processor is online and the -v flag is specified, the type of the processor is also
displayed, along with the clock rate (in megahertz) of the processor, and the types
of any floating point units attached to the processor.

SEE ALSO
processor_info(2) in the *Programmer's Supplement*

NOTES
This command may not be supported in future releases.

NAME

ping - send ICMP ECHO_REQUEST packets to network hosts

SYNOPSIS

/usr/sbin/ping *host* [*timeout*]

/usr/sbin/ping -s [-lrRv] *host* [*packetsize*] [*count*]

DESCRIPTION

ping utilizes the ICMP protocol's ECHO_REQUEST datagram to elicit an ICMP ECHO_RESPONSE from the specified *host* or network gateway. If *host* responds, ping will print *host* is alive on the standard output and exit. Otherwise after *timeout* seconds, it will write no answer from *host*. The default value of *timeout* is 20 seconds.

When the -s flag is specified, ping sends one datagram per second, and prints one line of output for every ECHO_RESPONSE that it receives. No output is produced if there is no response. In this second form, ping computes round trip times and packet loss statistics; it displays a summary of this information upon termination or timeout. The default datagram packet size is 64 bytes, or you can specify a size with the *packetsize* command-line argument. If an optional *count* is given, ping sends only that number of requests.

When using ping for fault isolation, first ping the local host to verify that the local network interface is running.

OPTIONS

-l   Loose source route. Use this option in the IP header to send the packet to the given host and back again. Usually specified with the -R option.

-r   Bypass the normal routing tables and send directly to a host on an attached network. If the host is not on a directly-attached network, an error is returned. This option can be used to ping a local host through an interface that has been dropped by the router daemon [see routed(1M)].

-R   Record route. Sets the IP record route option, which will store the route of the packet inside the IP header. The contents of the record route will only be printed if the -v option is given, and only be set on return packets if the target host preserves the record route option across echos, or the -l option is given.

-v   Verbose output. List any ICMP packets, other than ECHO_RESPONSE, that are received.

SEE ALSO

ifconfig(1M), netstat(1M), rpcinfo(1M), icmp(7)

NAME

pkgadd - transfer software package to the system

SYNOPSIS

pkgadd [-d *device*] [-r *response*] [-n] [-a *admin*] [*pkginst1* [*pkginst2*[...]]]

pkgadd -s *spool* [-d *device*] [*pkginst1* [*pkginst2*[...]]]

DESCRIPTION

pkgadd transfers the contents of a software package from the distribution medium or directory to install it onto the system. Used without the -d option, pkgadd looks in the default spool directory for the package (var/spool/pkg). Used with the -s option, it reads the package to a spool directory instead of installing it.

-d	Installs or copies a package from *device*. *device* can be a full path name to a directory or the identifiers for cartridge tape or removable disk (for example, /var/tmp, /dev/ctape1, or ctape1). It can also be the device alias. See putdev(1M) for information on device aliases.
-r	Identifies a file or directory, *response*, which contains output from a previous pkgask session. This file supplies the interaction responses that would be requested by the package in interactive mode. *response* must be a full pathname. See "NOTES" below.
-n	Installation occurs in non-interactive mode. The default mode is interactive.
-a	Defines an installation administration file, *admin*, to be used in place of the default administration file. The token none overrides the use of any *admin* file, and thus forces interaction with the user. Unless a full path name is given, pkgadd looks in the /var/sadm/install/admin directory for the file. See admin(4) for more information.
pkginst	Specifies the package instance or list of instances to be installed. The token all may be used to refer to all packages available on the source medium. The format *pkginst*. * can be used to indicate all instances of a package.
-s	Reads the package into the directory *spool* instead of installing it.

When executed without options, pkgadd uses var/spool/pkg (the default spool directory).

EXIT CODES

The following are successful exit codes:

0	No reboot is necessary.
10	Reboot is necessary after installation of other packages.
20	Reboot is necessary immediately.

Exit codes other than those shown above indicate various errors.

NOTES

When transferring a package to a spool directory, the -r, -n, and -a options cannot be used.

The `-r` option can be used to indicate a directory name as well as a filename. The directory can contain numerous *response* files, each sharing the name of the package with which it should be associated. This would be used, for example, when adding multiple interactive packages with one invocation of `pkgadd`. Each package would need a *response* file. If you create response files with the same name as the package (*i.e. package1* and *package2*), provide the name of the directory in which these files reside after the `-r`.

The `-n` option will cause the installation to halt if any interaction is needed to complete it.

SEE ALSO

`pkgask`(1M), `pkgchk`(1M), `pkgmk`(1), `pkgparam`(1), `pkgproto`(1), `pkgrm`(1M), `pkgtrans`(1), `putdev`(1M), `removef`(1M), `admin`(4), `pkginfo`(4).

NAME

pkgask - stores answers to a request script

SYNOPSIS

pkgask [-d *device*] -r *response pkginst* [*pkginst* [...]]

DESCRIPTION

pkgask allows the administrator to store answers to an interactive package (one with a request script). Invoking this command generates a *response* file that is then used as input at installation time. The use of this *response* file avoids any interaction from occurring during installation since the file already contains all of the information the package needs.

-d   Runs the request script for a package on *device*. *device* can be a directory pathname or the identifiers for a tape, (for example, /var/tmp, /dev/rmt/ctape1, and /dev/dsk/c8d0s0). The default device is the installation spool directory.

-r   Identifies a file or directory, which should be created to contain the responses to interaction with the package. The name must be a full pathname. The file, or directory of files, can later be used as input to the pkgadd command.

pkginst   Specifies the package instance or list of instances for which request scripts will be created. The token all may be used to refer to all packages available on the source medium.

NOTES

The -r option can be used to indicate a directory name as well as a filename. The directory name is used to create numerous *response* files, each sharing the name of the package with which it should be associated. This would be used, for example, when you will be adding multiple interactive packages with one invocation of pkgadd. Each package would need a *response* file. To create multiple response files with the same name as the package instance, name the directory in which the files should be created and supply multiple instance names with the pkgask command. When installing the packages, you will be able to identify this directory to the pkgadd command.

SEE ALSO

pkgadd(1M), pkgchk(1), pkgmk(1), pkgparam(1), pkgproto(1), pkgtrans(1), pkgrm(1M), removef(1M), pkginfo(4).

NAME

pkgchk - check accuracy of installation

SYNOPSIS

pkgchk [-l | -acfqv] [-nx] [-p *path1*[, *path2* ...] [-i *file*] [*pkginst*...]

pkgchk -d *device* [-l | v] [-p *path1*[, *path2* ...] [-i *file*] [*pkginst*...]

pkgchk -m *pkgmap* [-e *envfile*] [-l | -acfqv] [-nx] [-i *file*]
     [-p *path1*[, *path2* ...]]

DESCRIPTION

pkgchk checks the accuracy of installed files or, by use of the -l option, displays information about package files. The command checks the integrity of directory structures and the files. Discrepancies are reported on stderr along with a detailed explanation of the problem.

The first synopsis defined above is used to list or check the contents and/or attributes of objects that are currently installed on the system. Package names may be listed on the command line, or by default the entire contents of a machine will be checked.

The second synopsis is used to list or check the contents of a package which has been spooled on the specified device, but not installed. Note that attributes cannot be checked for spooled packages.

The third synopsis is used to list or check the contents and/or attributes of objects which are described in the indicated *pkgmap*.

The option definitions are:

-l   Lists information on the selected files that make up a package. It is not compatible with the a, c, f, g, and v options.

-a   Audits the file attributes only, does not check file contents. Default is to check both.

-c   Audits the file contents only, does not check file attributes. Default is to check both.

-f   Corrects file attributes if possible. If used with the -x option, it removes hidden files. When pkgchk is invoked with this option it creates directories, named pipes, links and special devices if they do not already exist.

-q   Quiet mode. Does not give messages about missing files.

-v   Verbose mode. Files are listed as processed.

-n   Does not check volatile or editable files. This should be used for most post-installation checking.

-x   Searches exclusive directories, looking for files which exist that are not in the installation software database or the indicated *pkgmap* file. Exclusive directories are directories created by and for a package, and no other files should be in these directories.

-p   Only checks the accuracy of the pathname or pathnames listed. *pathname* can be one or more pathnames separated by commas (or by white space, if the list is quoted).

-i   Reads a list of pathnames from *file* and compares this list against the installation software database or the indicated *pkgmap* file. Pathnames which are not contained in *inputfile* are not checked.

-d   Specifies the device on which a spooled package resides. *device* can be a directory pathname or the identifiers for tape, floppy disk or removable disk (for example, `/var/tmp` or `/dev/rmt/ctape1`).

-m   Requests that the package be checked against the pkgmap file *pkgmap*.

-e   Requests that the pkginfo file named as *envfile* be used to resolve parameters noted in the specified pkgmap file.

pkginst

Specifies the package instance or instances to be checked. The format *pkginst*.* can be used to check all instances of a package. The default is to display all information about all installed packages.

SEE ALSO

pkgadd(1M), pkgask(1M), pkgrm(1M), pkgtrans(1), pkginfo(4), pkgmap(4).

NAME

pkginfo - display software package information

SYNOPSIS

pkginfo [-q] [-x |-l] [-p |-i] [-a *arch*] [-v *version*]
        [-c *category1* , [*category2*[, ...]]] [*pkginst*[, *pkginst*[, ...]]]

pkginfo -d *device* [-q] [-x |-l] [-a *arch*] [-v *version*]
        [-c *category1* , [*category2*[, ...]]] [*pkginst*[, *pkginst*[, ...]]]

DESCRIPTION

pkginfo displays information about software packages that are installed on the
system (as requested in the first synopsis) or that reside on a particular device or
directory (as requested in the second synopsis). A package is a collection of related
files and executables that can be independently installed.

When run without options, pkginfo displays one line of information about every
installed package (whether installed completely or partially). The information
displayed includes the primary category, package instance, and name of the package. For UNIX software packages produced before UNIX System V Release 4,
pkginfo displays only the package name and abbreviation. For XENIX software
packages, pkginfo identifies the package as a XENIX software package and
displays only the package name and abbreviation.

The -p and -i options are meaningless if used in conjunction with the -d option.
The -p and -i options are mutually exclusive. The -x and -l options are mutually
exclusive.

The options for this command are:

-q   Do not list any information. This option overrides the -x, -l, -p, and -i
            options. (Can be invoked by a program to query whether or not a pack-
            age has been installed.)

-x   Extract and display the following information about the specified pack-
            age: abbreviation, name, and, if available, architecture and version.

-l   Display a "long format" report (that is, one that includes all available
            information) about the specified package(s).

-p   Display information only for partially installed packages.

-i   Display information only for fully installed packages.

-a *arch*   Specify the architecture of the package as *arch*.

-v *version* Specify the version of the package as *version*. All compatible versions
            can be requested by preceding the version name with a tilde (~). The list
            produced by -v will include pre-Release 4 and XENIX software pack-
            ages (with which no version numbers are associated). Multiple white
            spaces are replaced with a single space during version comparison.

-c *category* ...

            Display information about packages that belong to category *category*.
            (Categories are defined in the category field of the pkginfo file; see
            pkginfo(4) for details.) More than one category may be specified (as
            long as they are separated by white space). A package is required to
            belong to only one category, however, even when multiple categories
            are specified. The package-to-category match is case specific.

pkginst   A short string used to designate a package. It is composed of one or two parts: *pkg* (an abbreviation for the package name) or, if more than one instance of that package exists, *pkg* plus *inst* (an instance identifier). (The term "package instance" is used loosely: it refers to all instantiations of *pkginst*, even those that do not include instance identifiers.)

The package name abbreviation (*pkg*) is the mandatory part of *pkginst*. [See `pkginfo`(4).]

The second part (*inst*), which is required only if you have more than one instance of the package in question, is a suffix that identifies the instance. This suffix is either a number (preceded by a period) or any short mnemonic string you choose. If you do not assign your own instance identifier when one is required, the system assigns a numeric one by default. For example, if you have three instances of the Software Distribution Service package and you do not create your own mnemonic identifiers (such as `old` and `beta`), the system adds the suffixes `.2` and `.3` to the second and third packages, automatically.

To indicate all instances of a package, specify `inst.*`. (When using this format, enclose the command line in single quotes to prevent the shell from interpreting the `*` character.) Use the token `all` to refer to all packages available on the source medium.

`-d` *device*   Display information from packages that reside on *device*. *device* can be (a) the full pathname to a directory (such as `/var/tmp`), (b) the full pathname to a device (such as `/dev/rmt/*` or `/dev/dsk/*`) [see `intro`(7)], or (c) a device alias. The default device is the installation spool directory (`/var/spool/pkg`).

An alias is the unique name by which a device is known. (For example, the alias for a cartridge tape drive might be `ctape1`.) The name must be limited in length to 64 characters (`DDB_MAXALIAS`) and may contain only alphanumeric characters and/or any of the following special characters: underscore (`_`), dollar sign (`$`), hyphen (`-`), and period (`.`). No two devices in the database may share the same alias.

NOTES

`pkginfo` cannot tell if a pre-UNIX System V Release 4 or XENIX software package is only partially installed. It is assumed that all pre-Release 4 and XENIX software packages are fully installed.

FILES

`/var/spool/pkg`   default spool directory

SEE ALSO

`pkgadd`(1M), `pkgask`(1M), `pkgchk`(1M), `pkgrm`(1M), `pkgtrans`(1), `pkginfo`(4), `intro`(7).

NAME

pkgmk - produce an installable package

SYNOPSIS

pkgmk [-o] [-d *device*] [-r *rootpath*] [-b *basdir*] [-l *limit*] [-a *arch*]
     [-v *version*] [-p *pstamp*] [-f *prototype*] [*variable=value* ...] [*pkginst*]

DESCRIPTION

pkgmk produces an installable package to be used as input to the pkgadd command.
The package contents will be in directory structure format.

The command uses the package prototype file as input and creates a pkgmap file.
The contents for each entry in the prototype file is copied to the appropriate output location. Information concerning the contents (checksum, file size,
modification date) is computed and stored in the pkgmap file, along with attribute
information specified in the prototype file.

-o	Overwrites the same instance, package instance will be overwrit-ten if it already exists.
-d	Creates the package on *device*. *device* can be a directory pathname or the identifiers for a tape (for example, /dev/rmt/ctape). The default device is the installation spool directory.
-r	Ignores destination paths in the prototype file. Instead, uses the indicated *rootpath* with the source pathname appended to locate objects on the source machine.
-b	Prepends the indicated *basedir* to locate relocatable objects on the source machine.
-l	Specifies the maximum size in 512 byte blocks of the output dev-ice as *limit*. By default, if the output file is a directory or a mount-able device, pkgmk will employ the df command to dynamically calculate the amount of available space on the output device. Useful in conjunction with pkgtrans to create package with datastream format.
-a	Overrides the architecture information provided in the pkginfo file with *arch*.
-v	Overrides version information provided in the pkginfo file with *version*.
-p	Overrides the production stamp definition in the pkginfo file with *pstamp*.
-f	Uses the file prototype as input to the command. The default prototype filename is [Pp]rototype.
variable=value	Places the indicated variable in the packaging environment. [See prototype(4) for definitions of packaging variables.]
pkginst	Specifies the package by its instance. An instance can be the pack-age abbreviation or a specific instance (for example, inst.1).

NOTES

Architecture information is provided on the command line with the `-a` option or in the `prototype` file. If no architecture information is supplied at all, the output of `uname -m` will be used.

Version information is provided on the command line with the `-v` option or in the `prototype` file. If no version information is supplied, a default based on the current date will be provided.

Command line definitions for both architecture and version override the `prototype` definitions.

SEE ALSO

`pkgparam`(1), `pkgproto`(1), `pkgtrans`(1).

NAME

pkgparam - displays package parameter values

SYNOPSIS

pkgparam [-v][-d *device*] *pkginst* [*param*[. . .]]

pkgparam -f *file* [-v] [*param*[. . .]]

DESCRIPTION

pkgparam displays the value associated with the parameter or parameters requested on the command line. The values are located in either the pkginfo file for *pkginst* or from the specific file named with the -f option.

One parameter value is shown per line. Only the value of a parameter is given unless the -v option is used. With this option, the output of the command is in this format:

> *parameter1*=' *value1* '
> *parameter2*=' *value2* '
> *parameter3*=' *value3* '

If no parameters are specified on the command line, values for all parameters associated with the package are shown.

Options and arguments for this command are:

-v   Specifies verbose mode. Displays name of parameter and its value.

-d   Specifies the *device* on which a *pkginst* is stored. It can be a full pathname to a directory or the identifiers for tape, floppy disk or removable disk (for example, /var/tmp, /dev/dsk/f0t, and /dev/dsk/0s2). The default device is the installation spool directory. If no instance name is given, parameter information for all packages residing in *device* is shown.

-f   Requests that the command read *file* for parameter values.

pkginst   Defines a specific package instance for which parameter values should be displayed. The format *pkginst*.* can be used to indicate all instances of a package. When using this format, enclose the command line in single quotes to prevent the shell from interpreting the * character.

param   Defines a specific parameter whose value should be displayed.

ERRORS

If parameter information is not available for the indicated package, the command exits with a non-zero status.

NOTES

The -f synopsis allows you to specify the file from which parameter values should be extracted. This file should be in the same format as a pkginfo file. As an example, such a file might be created during package development and used while testing software during this stage.

SEE ALSO

install f(1M), pkgmk(1), pkgparam(3x), pkgproto(1), pgktrans(1)

NAME

pkgproto - generate a prototype file

SYNOPSIS

pkgproto [-i] [-c *class*] [*path1*[=*path2*] ...]

DESCRIPTION

pkgproto scans the indicated paths and generates a prototype file that may be used as input to the pkgmk command.

-i   Ignores symbolic links and records the paths as ftype=f (a file) versus ftype=s(symbolic link)

-c   Maps the class of all paths to *class*.

path1   Path of directory where objects are located.

path2   Path that should be substituted on output for *path1*.

If no paths are specified on the command line, standard input is assumed to be a list of paths. If the path listed on the command line is a directory, the contents of the directory are searched. if input is read from stdin, a directory specified as a path will not be searched.

path2 could be substituted with an installation parameter to make a relocatable package.

NOTES

By default, pkgproto creates symbolic link entries for any symbolic link encountered (ftype=s). When you use the -i option, pkgproto creates a file entry for symbolic links (ftype=f). The prototype file would have to be edited to assign such file types as v (volatile), e (editable), or x (exclusive directory). pkgproto detects linked files. If multiple files are linked together, the first path encountered is considered the source of the link.

EXAMPLE

The following two examples show uses of pkgproto and a parial listing of the output produced.

Example 1:

```
$ pkgproto /usr/bin=bin /usr/usr/bin=usrbin /etc=etc
f none bin/sed=/bin/sed 0775 bin bin
f none bin/sh=/bin/sh 0755 bin daemon
f none bin/sort=/bin/sort 0755 bin bin
f none usrbin/sdb=/usr/bin/sdb 0775 bin bin
f none usrbin/shl=/usr/bin/shl 4755 bin bin
d none etc/master.d 0755 root daemon
f none etc/master.d/kernel=/etc/master.d/kernel 0644 root daemon
f none etc/rc=/etc/rc 0744 root daemon
```

Example 2:

```
$ find / -type d -print | pkgproto
d none / 755 root root
d none /usr/bin 755 bin bin
d none /usr 755 root root
d none /usr/bin 775 bin bin
d none /etc 755 root root
```

```
      d none /tmp 777 root root
```
SEE ALSO

      installf(1M), pkgmk(1), pkgparam(1), pkgtrans(1)

NAME

pkgquest - formats and asks package questions

SYNOPSIS

pkgquest *questions pkginst > output_file*

DESCRIPTION

pkgquest allows the packager to store questions for an interactive package in a common format and retrieve easily into a request script. Invoking this command generates output compatible with that of a request script. The format of the questions file is compatible with the installation and upgrade pkgparam routines.

pkgquest searches in /inst/pkg/*pkginst*/install/answers for the pre-installation file that matches this package. If found, it will simply copy the contents of the file to stdout. Otherwise, it will display the questions and ask for responses. The results are then copied to stdout.

questions   is the source file for the questions, pkgquest(4) describes its format.

pkginst   specifies the package instance for which responses will be created.

output_file   is formatted the same as would be generated by a request script.

NOTES

The system installation and upgrade procedures share the question files with pkgquest and generate answer files during the initial installation.

SEE ALSO

pkgadd(1M), pkgask(1M), pkgchk(1), pkgmk(1), pkgparam(1), pkgproto(1), pkgrm(1), pkgtrans(1), removef(1M), pkginfo(4).

NAME

pkgrm - removes a package from the system

SYNOPSIS

pkgrm [-n] [-a *admin*] [*pkginst1* [*pkginst2* [...]]]

pkgrm -s *spool* [*pkginst*]

DESCRIPTION

pkgrm will remove a previously installed or partially installed package from the system. A check is made to determine if any other packages depend on the one being removed. The action taken if a dependency exists is defined in the admin file.

The default mode for the command is in interactive mode, meaning that prompt messages are given during processing to allow the administrator to confirm the actions being taken. Non-interactive mode can be requested with the -n option.

The -s option can be used to specify the directory from which spooled packages should be removed.

The options and arguments for this command are:

-n
    Non-interactive mode. If there is a need for interaction, the command will exit. Use of this option requires that at least one package instance be named upon invocation of the command.

-a
    Defines an installation administration file, *admin*, to be used in place of the default *admin* file.

-s
    Removes the specified package(s) from the directory "spool."

pkginst
    Specifies the package to be removed. The format *pkg_abbrev.* * can be used to remove all instances of a package.

SEE ALSO

pkgadd(1M), pkgask(1M), pkgchk(1), pkgmk(1), pkgparam(1), pkgproto(1), pkgtrans(1), removef(1M), pkginfo(4).

NAME

pkgtrans - translate package format

SYNOPSIS

pkgtrans [-ions] *device1 device2* [*pkginst1*[*pkginst2*[...]]]

DESCRIPTION

pkgtrans translates an installable package from one format to another. It will translate the following:

- a directory to a datastream,

- a datastream to a directory.

The options and arguments for this command are:

-i	Copies only the pkginfo and pkgmap files.
-o	Overwrites the same instance on the destination device, package instance will be overwritten if it already exists.
-n	Creates a new instance if any instance of this package already exists.
-s	Indicates that the package should be written to *device2* as a datastream rather than as a file system. The default behavior is to write a file system format on devices that support both formats.
device1	Indicates the source device. The package or packages on this device will be translated and placed on *device2*.
device2	Indicates the destination device. Translated packages will be placed on this device.
pkginst	Specifies which package instance or instances on *device1* should be translated. The token all may be used to indicate all packages. *pkginst*.* can be used to indicate all instances of a package. If no packages are defined, a prompt shows all packages on the device and asks which to translate.

NOTES

Device specifications can be either the special node name (/dev/rmt/ctape) or the device alias (ctape1). The device spool indicates the default spool directory. Source and destination devices may not be the same.

By default, pkgtrans will not transfer any instance of a package if any instance of that package already exists on the destination device. Use of the -n option will create a new instance if an instance of this package already exists. Use of the -o option will overwrite the same instance if it already exists. Neither of these options are useful if the destination device is a datastream.

EXAMPLE

The following example translates all packages on the tape drive /dev/rmt/ctape and places the translations on /tmp.

```
pkgtrans /dev/rmt/ctape /tmp all
```

The next example translates packages pkg1 and pkg2 on /tmp and places their translations (i.e., a datastream) on the 9track1 output device.

```
pkgtrans /tmp 9track1 pkg1 pkg2
```

The next example translates `pkg1` and `pkg2` on `tmp` and places them on the tape in a data stream format.

```
pkgtrans -s /tmp /dev/rmt/ctape pkg1 pkg2
```

SEE ALSO

installf(1M), pkgadd(1M), pkgask(1M), pkginfo(1), pkgmk(1), pkgparam(1), pkgproto(1), pkgrm(1M), removef(1M)

NAME

plot, aedplot, bgplot, crtplot, dumbplot, gigiplot, hpplot, implot, t300, t300s, t4013, t450, tek - graphics filters for various plotters

SYNOPSIS

/usr/ucb/plot [-T*terminal*]

DESCRIPTION

plot reads plotting instructions [see plot(4)] from the standard input and produces plotting instructions suitable for a particular *terminal* on the standard output.

If no *terminal* is specified, the environment variable TERM is used. The default *terminal* is tek.

ENVIRONMENT

Except for ver, the following terminal-types can be used with 'lpr -g' (see lpr) to produce plotted output:

2648 | 2648a | h8 | hp2648 | hp2648a
       Hewlett Packard® 2648 graphics terminal.

300   DASI 300 or GSI terminal (Diablo® mechanism).

300s | 300S   DASI 300s terminal (Diablo mechanism).

450   DASI Hyterm 450 terminal (Diablo mechanism).

4013   Tektronix® 4013 storage scope.

4014 | tek   Tektronix 4014 and 4015 storage scope with Enhanced Graphics Module. (Use 4013 for Tektronix 4014 or 4015 without the Enhanced Graphics Module).

aed   AED 512 color graphics terminal.

bgplot | bitgraph
       BBN bitgraph graphics terminal.

crt   Any crt terminal capable of running vi(1).

dumb | un | unknown
       Dumb terminals without cursor addressing or line printers.

gigi | vt125
       DEC® vt125 terminal.

h7 | hp7 | hp7221
       Hewlett Packard 7221 graphics terminal.

implot   Imagen plotter.

var   Benson Varian printer-plotter

ver   Versatec® D1200A printer-plotter. The output is scan-converted and suitable input to 'lpr -v'.

FILES

/usr/ucb/aedplot
/usr/ucb/bgplot

```
/usr/ucb/crtplot
/usr/ucb/dumbplot
/usr/ucb/gigiplot
/usr/ucb/hpplot
/usr/ucb/implot
/usr/ucb/plot
/usr/ucb/t300
/usr/ucb/t300s
/usr/ucb/t4013
/usr/ucb/t450
/usr/ucb/tek
/usr/ucb/vplot
/var/ucb/vplotnnnnnn
```

SEE ALSO

lpr(1), vi(1), plot(3X), plot(4).

NAME

pmadm - port monitor administration

SYNOPSIS

pmadm -a [-p *pmtag* | -t *type*] -s *svctag* -i id -m *pmspecific*
     -v *ver* [-f xu] [-y *comment*] [-z *script*]

pmadm -r -p *pmtag* -s *svctag*

pmadm -e -p *pmtag* -s *svctag*

pmadm -d -p *pmtag* -s *svctag*

pmadm -l [-t *type* | -p *pmtag*] [-s *svctag*]

pmadm -L [-t *type* | -p *pmtag*] [-s *svctag*]

pmadm -g -p *pmtag* -s *svctag* [-z *script*]

pmadm -g -s *svctag* -t *type* -z *script*

DESCRIPTION

pmadm is the administrative command for the lower level of the Service Access
Facility hierarchy, that is, for service administration. A port may have only one service associated with it although the same service may be available through more
than one port. In order to uniquely identify an instance of a service the pmadm command must identify both the port monitor or port monitors through which the service is available (-p or -t) and the service (-s). See the option descriptions below.

pmadm performs the following functions:

    - add or remove a service

    - enable or disable a service

    - install or replace a per-service configuration script

    - print requested service information

Any user on the system may invoke pmadm to request service status (-l or -L) or to
print per-service configuration scripts (-g without the -z option). pmadm with
other options may be executed only by a privileged user.

The options have the following meanings:

-a   Add a service. pmadm adds an entry for the new service to the port
       monitor's administrative file. Because of the complexity of the options
       and arguments that follow the -a option, it may be convenient to use a
       command script or the menu system to add services. If you use the menu
       system, enter sysadm ports, then choose the port_services option.

-d   Disable a service. Add x to the flag field in the entry for the service *svctag*
       in the port monitor's administrative file. This is the entry used by port
       monitor *pmtag*. See the -f option, below, for a description of the flags
       available.

-e   Enable a service. Remove x from the flag field in the entry for the service
       svctag in the port monitor administrative file. This is the entry used by
       port monitor *pmtag*. See the -f option, below, for a description of the flags
       available.

-f xu The -f option specifies one or both of the following two flags which are then included in the flag field of the entry for the new service in the port monitor's administrative file. If the -f option is not included, no flags are set and the default conditions prevail. By default, a new service is enabled and no utmp entry is created for it. A -f option without a following argument is illegal.

    x   Do not enable the service *svctag* available through port monitor *pmtag*.

    u   Create a utmp entry for service *svctag* available through port monitor *pmtag*.

-g Print, install, or replace a per-service configuration script. The -g option with a -p option and a -s option prints the per-service configuration script for service *svctag* available through port monitor *pmtag*. The -g option with a -p option, a -s option, and a -z option installs the per-service configuration script contained in the file *script* as the per-service configuration script for service *svctag* available through port monitor *pmtag*. The -g option with a -s option, a -t option, and a -z option installs the file *script* as the per-service configuration script for service *svctag* available through any port monitor of type *type*. Other combinations of options with -g are invalid.

-i id id is the identity that is to be assigned to service *svctag* when it is started. id must be an entry in /etc/passwd.

-l The -l option requests service information. Used by itself and with the options described below it provides a filter for extracting information in several different groupings.

    -l   By itself, the -l option lists all services on the system.

    -l -p *pmtag*   Lists all services available through port monitor *pmtag*.

    -l -s *svctag*   Lists all services with tag *svctag*.

    -l -p *pmtag* -s *svctag*
    Lists service *svctag*.

    -l -t *type*   Lists all services available through port monitors of type *type*.

    -l -t *type* -s *svctag*
    Lists all services with tag *svctag* available through a port monitor of type *type*.

Other combinations of options with -l are invalid.

-L The -L option is identical to the -l option except that output is printed in a condensed format.

-m *pmspecific*
    pmspecific is the port monitor-specific portion of the port monitor administrative file entry for the service.

-p *pmtag*
> Specifies the tag associated with the port monitor through which a service (specified as -s *svctag*) is available.

-r
> Remove a service. When pmadm removes a service, the entry for the service is removed from the port monitor's administrative file.

-s *svctag*
> Specifies the service tag associated with a given service. The service tag is assigned by the system administrator and is part of the entry for the service in the port monitor's administrative file.

-t *type*   Specifies the the port monitor type.

-v *ver*   Specifies the version number of the port monitor administrative file. The version number may be given as

        -v `pmspec -V`

> where *pmspec* is the special administrative command for port monitor *pmtag*. This special command is ttyadm for ttymon and nlsadmin for listen. The version stamp of the port monitor is known by the command and is returned when *pmspec* is invoked with a -V option.

-y *comment*
> Associate *comment* with the service entry in the port monitor administrative file.

-z *script*
> Used with the -g option to specify the name of the file that contains the per-service configuration script. Modifying a configuration script is a three-step procedure. First a copy of the existing script is made (-g alone). Then the copy is edited. Finally, the copy is put in place over the existing script (-g with -z).

OUTPUT

If successful, pmadm will exit with a status of 0. If it fails for any reason, it will exit with a nonzero status.

Options that request information write the requested information to the standard output. A request for information using the -l option prints column headers and aligns the information under the appropriate headings. In this format, a missing field is indicated by a hyphen. A request for information in the condensed format using the -L option prints the information in colon-separated fields; missing fields are indicated by two successive colons. # is the comment character.

EXAMPLES

Add a service to a port monitor with tag pmtag. Give the service the tag svctag. Port monitor-specific information is generated by specpm. The service defined by svctag will be invoked with identity root.

```
pmadm -a -p pmtag -s svctag -i root -m `specpm -a arg1 -b arg2` \
    -v `specpm -V`
```

Add a service with service tag svctag, identity guest, and port monitor-specific information generated by specpm to all port monitors of type type:

```
pmadm -a -s svctag -i guest -t type -m `specpm -a arg1 -b arg2` \
```

```
        -v `specpm -V`
```

Remove the service `svctag` from port monitor `pmtag`:

```
pmadm -r -p pmtag -s svctag
```

Enable the service `svctag` available through port monitor `pmtag`:

```
pmadm -e -p pmtag -s svctag
```

Disable the service `svctag` available through port monitor `pmtag`:

```
pmadm -d -p pmtag -s svctag
```

List status information for all services:

```
pmadm -l
```

List status information for all services available through the port monitor with tag `ports`:

```
pmadm -l -p ports
```

List the same information in condensed format:

```
pmadm -L -p ports
```

List status information for all services available through port monitors of type `listen`:

```
pmadm -l -t listen
```

Print the per-service configuration script associated with the service `svctag` available through port monitor `pmtag`:

```
pmadm -g -p pmtag -s svctag
```

FILES

```
/etc/saf/pmtag/_config
/etc/saf/pmtag/svctag
/var/saf/pmtag/*
```

SEE ALSO

doconfig(3n), sacadm(1M), sac(1M)

NAME

postdaisy - PostScript translator for Diablo 630 files

SYNOPSIS

/usr/lib/lp/postscript/postdaisy [*options*] [*files*]

DESCRIPTION

The postdaisy filter translates Diablo 630 daisy-wheel *files* into PostScript and writes the results on the standard output. If no *files* are specified, or if - is one of the input *files*, the standard input is read. The following *options* are understood:

-c *num*	Print *num* copies of each page. By default only one copy is printed.
-f *name*	Print *files* using font *name*. Any PostScript font can be used, although the best results will be obtained only with constant-width fonts. The default font is Courier.
-h *num*	Set the initial horizontal motion index to *num*. Determines the character advance and the default point size, unless the -s option is used. The default is 12.
-m *num*	Magnify each logical page by the factor *num*. Pages are scaled uniformly about the origin, which is located near the upper left corner of each page. The default magnification is 1.0.
-n *num*	Print *num* logical pages on each piece of paper, where *num* can be any positive integer. By default, *num* is set to 1.
-o *list*	Print pages whose numbers are given in the comma-separated *list*. The list contains single numbers N and ranges $N1 - N2$. A missing $N1$ means the lowest numbered page, a missing $N2$ means the highest.
-p *mode*	Print *files* in either portrait or landscape *mode*. Only the first character of *mode* is significant. The default *mode* is portrait.
-r *num*	Selects carriage return and line feed behavior. If *num* is 1, a line feed generates a carriage return. If *num* is 2, a carriage return generates a line feed. Setting *num* to 3 enables both modes.
-s *num*	Use point size *num* instead of the default value set by the initial horizontal motion index.
-v *num*	Set the initial vertical motion index to *num*. The default is 8.
-x *num*	Translate the origin *num* inches along the positive x axis. The default coordinate system has the origin fixed near the upper left corner of the page, with positive x to the right and positive y down the page. Positive *num* moves everything right. The default offset is 0.25 inches.
-y *num*	Translate the origin *num* inches along the positive y axis. Positive *num* moves text up the page. The default offset is -0.25 inches.

DIAGNOSTICS

An exit status of 0 is returned if *files* were successfully processed.

FILES

```
/usr/lib/lp/postscript/postdaisy.ps
/usr/lib/lp/postscript/forms.ps
/usr/lib/lp/postscript/ps.requests
```

SEE ALSO

download(1), dpost(1), postdmd(1), postio(1), postmd(1), postprint(1), postreverse(1), posttek(1)

NAME

`postdmd` - PostScript translator for DMD bitmap files

SYNOPSIS

`/usr/lib/lp/postscript/postdmd` [*options*] [*files*]

DESCRIPTION

`postdmd` translates DMD bitmap *files*, as produced by *dmdps*, or *files* written in the Ninth Edition `bitfile`(9.5) format into PostScript and writes the results on the standard output. If no *files* are specified, or if - is one of the input *files*, the standard input is read. The following *options* are understood:

`-b` *num*	Pack the bitmap in the output file using *num* byte patterns. A value of 0 turns off all packing of the output file. By default, *num* is 6.
`-c` *num*	Print *num* copies of each page. By default only one copy is printed.
`-f`	Flip the sense of the bits in *files* before printing the bitmaps.
`-m` *num*	Magnify each logical page by the factor *num*. Pages are scaled uniformly about the origin, which by default is located at the center of each page. The default magnification is 1.0.
`-n` *num*	Print *num* logical pages on each piece of paper, where *num* can be any positive integer. By default *num* is set to 1.
`-o` *list*	Print pages whose numbers are given in the comma-separated *list*. The list contains single numbers N and ranges N1 - N2. A missing N1 means the lowest numbered page, a missing N2 means the highest.
`-p` *mode*	Print *files* in either portrait or landscape *mode*. Only the first character of *mode* is significant. The default *mode* is portrait.
`-x` *num*	Translate the origin *num* inches along the positive x axis. The default coordinate system has the origin fixed at the center of the page, with positive x to the right and positive y up the page. Positive *num* moves everything right. The default offset is 0 inches.
`-y` *num*	Translate the origin *num* inches along the positive y axis. Positive *num* moves everything up the page. The default offset is 0.

Only one bitmap is printed on each logical page, and each of the input *files* must contain complete descriptions of at least one bitmap. Decreasing the pattern size using the `-b` option may help throughput on printers with fast processors (such as PS-810s), while increasing the pattern size will often be the right move on older models (such as PS-800s).

DIAGNOSTICS

An exit status of 0 is returned if *files* were successfully processed.

FILES

```
/usr/lib/lp/postscript/postdmd.ps
/usr/lib/lp/postscript/forms.ps
/usr/lib/lp/postscript/ps.requests
```

SEE ALSO
download(1), dpost(1), postdaisy(1), postio(1), postmd(1), postprint(1),
postreverse(1), posttek(1)

NAME

`postio` - serial interface for PostScript printers

SYNOPSIS

`postio` -l *line* [*options*] [*files*]

DESCRIPTION

`postio` sends *files* to the PostScript printer attached to *line*. If no *files* are specified the standard input is sent. The first group of *options* should be sufficient for most applications:

-b *speed*
Transmit data over *line* at baud rate *speed*. Recognized baud rates are 1200, 2400, 4800, 9600, and 19200. The default *speed* is 9600 baud.

-l *line*
Connect to the printer attached to *line*. In most cases there is no default and `postio` must be able to read and write *line*. If the *line* doesn't begin with a / it may be treated as a Datakit destination.

-q
Prevents status queries while *files* are being sent to the printer. When status queries are disabled a dummy message is appended to the log file before each block is transmitted.

-B *num*
Set the internal buffer size for reading and writing *files* to *num* bytes. By default *num* is 2048 bytes.

-D
Enable debug mode. Guarantees that everything read on *line* will be added to the log file (standard error by default).

-L *file*
Data received on *line* gets put in *file*. The default log *file* is standard error. Printer or status messages that don't show a change in state are not normally written to *file* but can be forced out using the -D option.

-P *string*
Send *string* to the printer before any of the input files. The default *string* is simple PostScript code that disables timeouts.

-R *num*
Run *postio* as a single process if *num* is 1 or as separate read and write processes if *num* is 2. By default `postio` runs as a single process.

The next two *options* are provided for users who expect to run `postio` on their own. Neither is suitable for use in spooler interface programs:

-i
Run the program in interactive mode. Any *files* are sent first and followed by the standard input. Forces separate read and write processes and overrides many other options. To exit interactive mode use your interrupt or quit character. To get a friendly interactive connection with the printer type `executive` on a line by itself.

-t
Data received on *line* and not recognized as printer or status information is written to the standard output. Forces separate read and write processes. Convenient if you have a PostScript program that will be returning useful data to the host.

The last option is not generally recommended and should only be used if all else fails to provide a reliable connection:

-S   Slow the transmission of data to the printer. Severely limits throughput, runs as a single process, disables the -q option, limits the internal buffer size to 1024 bytes, can use an excessive amount of CPU time, and does nothing in interactive mode.

The best performance will usually be obtained by using a large internal buffer (the -B option) and by running the program as separate read and write processes (the -R 2 option). Inability to fork the additional process causes postio to continue as a single read/write process. When one process is used, only data sent to the printer is flow controlled.

The *options* are not all mutually exclusive. The -i option always wins, selecting its own settings for whatever is needed to run interactive mode, independent of anything else found on the command line. Interactive mode runs as separate read and write processes and few of the other *options* accomplish anything in the presence of the -i option. The -t option needs a reliable two way connection to the printer and therefore tries to force separate read and write processes. The -S option relies on the status query mechanism, so -q is disabled and the program runs as a single process.

In most cases postio starts by making a connection to *line* and then attempts to force the printer into the IDLE state by sending an appropriate sequence of ^T (status query), ^C (interrupt), and ^D (end of job) characters. When the printer goes IDLE, *files* are transmitted along with an occasional ^T (unless the -q option was used). After all the *files* are sent the program waits until it's reasonably sure the job is complete. Printer generated error messages received at any time except while establishing the initial connection (or when running interactive mode) cause postio to exit with a non-zero status. In addition to being added to the log file, printer error messages are also echoed to standard error.

EXAMPLES

Run as a single process at 9600 baud and send *file1* and *file2* to the printer attached to /dev/tty01:

```
postio -l /dev/tty01 file1 file2
```

Same as above except two processes are used, the internal buffer is set to 4096 bytes, and data returned by the printer gets put in file *log*:

```
postio -R2 -B4096 -l/dev/tty01 -Llog file1 file2
```

Establish an interactive connection with the printer at Datakit destination *my/printer*:

```
postio -i -l my/printer
```

Send file program to the printer connected to /dev/tty22, recover any data in file results, and put log messages in file *log*:

```
postio -t -l /dev/tty22 -L log program >results
```

NOTES

The input *files* are handled as a single PostScript job. Sending several different jobs, each with their own internal end of job mark (^D) is not guaranteed to work properly. `postio` may quit before all the jobs have completed and could be restarted before the last one finishes.

All the capabilities described above may not be available on every machine or even across the different versions of the UNIX system that are currently supported by the program. For example, the code needed to connect to a Datakit destination may work only on System V and may require that the DKHOST software package be available at compile time.

There may be no default *line*, so using the -l option is strongly recommended. If omitted, `postio` may attempt to connect to the printer using the standard output. If Datakit is involved, the -b option may be ineffective and attempts by `postio` to impose flow control over data in both directions may not work. The -q option can help if the printer is connected to RADIAN. The -S option is not generally recommended and should be used only if all other attempts to establish a reliable connection fail.

DIAGNOSTICS

An exit status of 0 is returned if the files ran successfully. System errors (such as an inability to open the line) set the low order bit in the exit status, while PostScript errors set bit 1. An exit status of 2 usually means the printer detected a PostScript error in the input *files.*

SEE ALSO

`download`(1), `dpost`(1), `postdaisy`(1), `postdmd`(1), `postmd`(1), `postprint`(1), `postreverse`(1), `posttek`(1)

NAME

postmd - matrix display program for PostScript printers

SYNOPSIS

/usr/lib/lp/postscript/postmd [*options*] [*files*]

DESCRIPTION

The postmd filter reads a series of floating point numbers from *files*, translates them into a PostScript gray scale image, and writes the results on the standard output. In a typical application the numbers might be the elements of a large matrix, written in row major order, while the printed image could help locate patterns in the matrix. If no *files* are specified, or if - is one of the input *files*, the standard input is read. The following *options* are understood:

-b *num*　　Pack the bitmap in the output file using *num* byte patterns. A value of 0 turns off all packing of the output file. By default, *num* is 6.

-c *num*　　Print *num* copies of each page. By default, only one copy is printed.

-d *dimen*　　Sets the default matrix dimensions for all input *files* to *dimen*. The *dimen* string can be given as rows or rowsxcolumns. If *columns* is omitted it will be set to rows. By default, postmd assumes each matrix is square and sets the number of rows and columns to the square root of the number of elements in each input file.

-g *list*　　*List* is a comma or space separated string of integers, each lying between 0 and 255 inclusive, that assigns PostScript gray scales to the regions of the real line selected by the -i option. 255 corresponds to white, and 0, to black. The postmd filter assigns a default gray scale that omits white (that is, 255) and gets darker as the regions move from left to right along the real line.

-i *list*　　*List* is a comma, space or slash(/) separated string of N floating point numbers that slice the real line into $2N+1$ regions. The *list* must be given in increasing numerical order. The slices are used to map floating point numbers read from the input *files* into gray scale integers that are either assigned automatically by postmd or arbitrarily selected using the -g option. The default interval *list* is -1,0,1, which partions the real line into seven regions.

-m *num*　　Magnify each logical page by the factor *num*. Pages are scaled uniformly about the origin which, by default, is located at the center of each page. The default magnification is 1.0.

-n *num*　　Print *num* logical pages on each piece of paper, where *num* can be any positive integer. By default, *num* is set to 1.

-o *list*　　Print pages whose numbers are given in the comma separated *list*. The list contains single numbers N and ranges $N1$ - $N2$. A missing $N1$ means the lowest numbered page, a missing $N2$ means the highest.

-p *mode*　　　　Print *files* in either portrait or landscape *mode*. Only the first character of *mode* is significant. The default *mode* is portrait.

-w *window*　　　*Window* is a comma or space separated list of four positive
integers that select the upper left and lower right corners of a
submatrix from each of the input *files*. Row and column indices
start at 1 in the upper left corner and the numbers in the input
files are assumed to be written in row major order. By default, the
entire matrix is displayed.

-x *num*　　　　Translate the origin *num* inches along the positive x axis. The
default coordinate system has the origin fixed at the center of the
page, with positive x to the right and positive y up the page.
Positive *num* moves everything right. The default offset is 0
inches.

-y *num*　　　　Translate the origin *num* inches along the positive y axis. Positive
num moves everything up the page. The default offset is 0.

Only one matrix is displayed on each logical page, and each of the input *files* must
contain complete descriptions of exactly one matrix. Matrix elements are floating
point numbers arranged in row major order in each input file. White space, including newlines, is not used to determine matrix dimensions. By default, `postmd`
assumes each matrix is square and sets the number of rows and columns to the
square root of the number of elements in the input file. Supplying default dimensions on the command line with the -d option overrides this default behavior, and
in that case the dimensions apply to all input *files*.

An optional header can be supplied with each input file and is used to set the
matrix dimensions, the slice of the real line, the gray scale map, and a window into
the matrix. The header consists of keyword/value pairs, each on a separate line. It
begins on the first line of each input file and ends with the first unrecognized string,
which should be the first matrix element. Values set in the header take precedence,
but apply only to the current input file. Recognized header keywords are `dimen-
sion`, `interval`, `grayscale`, and `window`. The syntax of the value string that fol-
lows each keyword parallels what's accepted by the -d, -i, -g, and -w options.

EXAMPLES

For example, suppose file initially contains the 1000 numbers in a 20x50 matrix.
Then you can produce exactly the same output by completing three steps. First,
issue the following command line:

```
postmd -d20x50 -i"-100 100" -g0,128,254,128,0 file
```

Second, prepend the following header to *file*:

```
dimension 20x50
interval  -100.0 .100e+3
grayscale 0 128 254 128 0
```

Third, issue the following command line:

```
postmd file
```

The interval list slices the real line into five regions and the gray scale list maps numbers less than -100 or greater than 100 into 0 (that is, black), numbers equal to -100 or 100 into 128 (that is, 50 percent black), and numbers between -100 and 100 into 254 (that is, almost white).

NOTES

The largest matrix that can be adequately displayed is a function of the interval and gray scale lists, the printer resolution, and the paper size. A 600x600 matrix is an optimistic upper bound for a two element interval list (that is, five regions) using 8.5x11 inch paper on a 300 dpi printer.

Using white (that is, 255) in a gray scale list is not recommended and won't show up in the legend and bar graph that postmd displays below each image.

DIAGNOSTICS

An exit status of 0 is returned if *files* were successfully processed.

FILES

```
/usr/lib/lp/postscript/postmd.ps
/usr/lib/lp/postscript/forms.ps
/usr/lib/lp/postscript/ps.requests
```

SEE ALSO

dpost(1), postdaisy(1), postdmd(1), postio(1), postprint(1), postreverse(1), posttek(1)

NAME

postplot - PostScript translator for plot graphics files

SYNOPSIS

/usr/lib/lp/postscript/postplot [*options*] [*files*]

DESCRIPTION

The postplot filter translates plot(4) graphics *files* into PostScript and writes the results on the standard output. If no *files* are specified, or if - is one of the input *files*, the standard input is read. The following *options* are understood:

-c *num*
: Print *num* copies of each page. By default, only one copy is printed.

-f *name*
: Print text using font *name*. Any PostScript font can be used, although the best results will be obtained only with constant width fonts. The default font is Courier.

-m *num*
: Magnify each logical page by the factor *num*. Pages are scaled uniformly about the origin which, by default, is located at the center of each page. The default magnification is 1.0.

-n *num*
: Print *num* logical pages on each piece of paper, where *num* can be any positive integer. By default, *num* is set to 1.

-o *list*
: Print pages whose numbers are given in the comma-separated *list*. The list contains single numbers N and ranges N1 - N2. A missing N1 means the lowest numbered page, a missing N2 means the highest.

-p *mode*
: Print *files* in either portrait or landscape *mode*. Only the first character of *mode* is significant. The default *mode* is landscape.

-w *num*
: Set the line width used for graphics to *num* points, where a point is approximately 1/72 of an inch. By default, *num* is set to 0 points, which forces lines to be one pixel wide.

-x *num*
: Translate the origin *num* inches along the positive x axis. The default coordinate system has the origin fixed at the center of the page, with positive x to the right and positive y up the page. Positive *num* moves everything right. The default offset is 0.0 inches.

-y *num*
: Translate the origin *num* inches along the positive y axis. Positive *num* moves everything up the page. The default offset is 0.0.

DIAGNOSTICS

An exit status of 0 is returned if *files* were successfully processed.

NOTES

The default line width is too small for write-white print engines, such as the one used by the PS-2400.

FILES

```
/usr/lib/lp/postscript/postplot.ps
/usr/lib/lp/postscript/forms.ps
/usr/lib/lp/postscript/ps.requests
```

SEE ALSO
download(1), dpost(1), postdaisy(1), postdmd(1), postio(1), postmd(1), post-
print(1), postreverse(1), plot(4)

NAME

postprint - PostScript translator for text files

SYNOPSIS

/usr/lib/lp/postscript/postprint [*options*] [*files*]

DESCRIPTION

The postprint filter translates text *files* into PostScript and writes the results on the standard output. If no *files* are specified, or if - is one of the input *files*, the standard input is read. The following *options* are understood:

-c *num*
: Print *num* copies of each page. By default, only one copy is printed.

-f *name*
: Print *files* using font *name*. Any PostScript font can be used, although the best results will be obtained only with constant width fonts. The default font is Courier.

-l *num*
: Set the length of a page to *num* lines. By default, *num* is 66. Setting *num* to 0 is allowed, and will cause *postprint* to guess a value, based on the point size that's being used.

-m *num*
: Magnify each logical page by the factor *num*. Pages are scaled uniformly about the origin, which is located near the upper left corner of each page. The default magnification is 1.0.

-n *num*
: Print *num* logical pages on each piece of paper, where *num* can be any positive integer. By default, *num* is set to 1.

-o *list*
: Print pages whose numbers are given in the comma-separated *list*. The *list* contains single numbers N and ranges N1 - N2. A missing N1 means the lowest numbered page, a missing N2 means the highest.

-p *mode*
: Print *files* in either portrait or landscape *mode*. Only the first character of *mode* is significant. The default *mode* is portrait.

-r *num*
: Selects carriage return behavior. Carriage returns are ignored if *num* is 0, cause a return to column 1 if *num* is 1, and generate a newline if *num* is 2. The default *num* is 0.

-s *num*
: Print *files* using point size *num*. When printing in landscape mode *num* is scaled by a factor that depends on the imaging area of the device. The default size for portrait mode is 10.

-t *num*
: Assume tabs are set every *num* columns, starting with the first column. By default, tabs are set every 8 columns.

-x *num*
: Translate the origin *num* inches along the positive x axis. The default coordinate system has the origin fixed near the upper left corner of the page, with positive x to the right and positive y down the page. Positive *num* moves everything right. The default offset is 0.25 inches.

-y *num*
: Translate the origin *num* inches along the positive y axis. Positive *num* moves text down the page. The default offset is 0.25 inches.

−A *file*	Append a simple accounting record to *file* after all the input *files* have been successfully translated. By default, no accounting data is produced.
−L *file*	Use *file* as the PostScript prologue, which, by default, is `/usr/lib/lp/postscript/postprint.ps`.

In addition, three options allow the insertion of arbitrary PostScript at controlled points in the translation process:

−C *file*	Copy *file* to the output file. *File* follows the prologue but precedes any job initialization commands. *File* becomes part of the job's global environment and must contain legitimate PostScript commands.
−P *string*	Add *string* to the output file. *String* follows the prologue but precedes any job initialization commands. *String* becomes part of the job's global environment and must be legitimate PostScript.
−R *action*	Requests special *action* (e.g. manualfeed) on a per page or global basis. The *action* string can be given as request, `request:page`, or `request:page:file`. If page is omitted or given as 0 the request applies to all pages. If file is omitted the request lookup is done in `/usr/lib/lp/postscript/ps.requests`. The collection of recognized requests can be modified or extended by changing `/usr/lib/lp/postscript/ps.requests`. Multiple occurrences of the −R option behave as expected.

A new logical page is started after 66 lines have been printed on the current page, or whenever an ASCII form feed character is read. The number of lines per page can be changed using the −l option. Unprintable ASCII characters are ignored, and lines that are too long are silently truncated by the printer.

INTERNATIONAL FUNCTIONS

In order to support non-ASCII characters, two additional options are available when the European Language Supplement package is installed. These allow `postprint` to use the font files, normally used by `troff(1)` and `dpost(1)`, to obtain codeset mappings and PostScript descriptions of unsupported characters. By selecting the font files appropriate to a particular codeset, a text file composed of characters from that codeset can be correctly translated.

−F *dir*	Use *dir* as the font directory. The default *dir* is `/usr/lib/font` and `postprint` reads binary font files from directory `/usr/lib/font/devpost`.
−T *name*	Use font files for device *name* as the best description of available Postscript fonts. By default, *name* is set to `post` and `postprint` reads binary files from `/usr/lib/font/devpost`.

EXAMPLES

To print *file1* and *file2* in landscape mode, issue the following command:

```
postprint -pland file1 file2
```

To print three logical pages on each physical page in portrait mode:

    postprint -n3 *file*

To print *file* which is composed of characters from the ISO 8859/1 codeset,

    postprint -Tps88591 *file*

DIAGNOSTICS

An exit status of 0 is returned if *files* were successfully processed.

FILES

    /usr/lib/lp/postscript/postprint.ps
    /usr/lib/lp/postscript/forms.ps
    /usr/lib/lp/postscript/ps.requests
    /usr/lib/font/dev*/*.out
    /usr/lib/font/dev*/charlib/*

SEE ALSO

download(1), dpost(1), postdaisy(1), postdmd(1), postio(1), postmd(1), postreverse(1), posttek(1)

NAME

postreverse - reverse the page order in a PostScript file

SYNOPSIS

/usr/lib/lp/postscript/postreverse [*options*] [*file*]

DESCRIPTION

The postreverse filter reverses the page order in files that conform to Adobe's Version 1.0 or Version 2.0 file structuring conventions, and writes the results on the standard output. Only one input *file* is allowed and if no *file* is specified, the standard input is read. The following *options* are understood:

-o *list*   Select pages whose numbers are given in the comma-separated *list*. The *list* contains single numbers *N* and ranges *N1 - N2*. A missing *N1* means the lowest numbered page, a missing *N2* means the highest.

-r   Don't reverse the pages in *file*.

The postreverse filter can handle a limited class of files that violate page independence, provided all global definitions are bracketed by %%BeginGlobal and %%EndGlobal comments. In addition, files that mark the end of each page with %%EndPage: label ordinal comments will also reverse properly, provided the prologue and trailer sections can be located. If postreverse fails to find an %%EndProlog or %%EndSetup comment, the entire *file* is copied, unmodified, to the standard output.

Because global definitions are extracted from individual pages and put in the prologue, the output file can be minimally conforming, even if the input *file* wasn't.

EXAMPLES

To select pages 1 to 100 from *file* and reverse the pages:

    postreverse -o1-100 *file*

To print four logical pages on each physical page and reverse all the pages:

    postprint -n4 *file* | postreverse

To produce a minimally conforming file from output generated by dpost without reversing the pages:

    dpost *file* | postreverse -r

DIAGNOSTICS

An exit status of 0 is returned if *file* was successfully processed.

NOTES

No attempt has been made to deal with redefinitions of global variables or procedures. If standard input is used, the input *file* will be read three times before being reversed.

SEE ALSO

download(1), dpost(1), postdaisy(1), postdmd(1), postio(1), postmd(1), postprint(1), posttek(1)

NAME

posttek - PostScript translator for tektronix 4014 files

SYNOPSIS

/usr/lib/lp/postscript/posttek [*options*] [*files*]

DESCRIPTION

The posttek filter translates tektronix 4014 graphics *files* into PostScript and writes the results on the standard output. If no *files* are specified, or if - is one of the input *files*, the standard input is read. The following *options* are understood:

-c *num*	Print *num* copies of each page. By default, only one copy is printed.
-f *name*	Print text using font *name*. Any PostScript font can be used, although the best results will be obtained only with constant width fonts. The default font is Courier.
-m *num*	Magnify each logical page by the factor *num*. Pages are scaled uniformly about the origin which, by default, is located at the center of each page. The default magnification is 1.0.
-n *num*	Print *num* logical pages on each piece of paper, where *num* can be any positive integer. By default, *num* is set to 1.
-o *list*	Print pages whose numbers are given in the comma-separated *list*. The *list* contains single numbers *N* and ranges *N1* - *N2*. A missing *N1* means the lowest numbered page, a missing *N2* means the highest.
-p *mode*	Print *files* in either portrait or landscape *mode*. Only the first character of *mode* is significant. The default *mode* is landscape.
-w *num*	Set the line width used for graphics to *num* points, where a point is approximately 1/72 of an inch. By default, *num* is set to 0 points, which forces lines to be one pixel wide.
-x *num*	Translate the origin *num* inches along the positive x axis. The default coordinate system has the origin fixed at the center of the page, with positive x to the right and positive y up the page. Positive *num* moves everything right. The default offset is 0.0 inches.
-y *num*	Translate the origin *num* inches along the positive y axis. Positive *num* moves everything up the page. The default offset is 0.0.

DIAGNOSTICS

An exit status of 0 is returned if *files* were successfully processed.

NOTES

The default line width is too small for write-white print engines, such as the one used by the PS-2400.

FILES

/usr/lib/lp/postscript/posttek.ps
/usr/lib/lp/postscript/forms.ps
/usr/lib/lp/postscript/ps.requests

SEE ALSO
download(1), dpost(1), postdaisy(1), postdmd(1), postio(1), postmd(1), post-
print(1), postreverse(1)

NAME

powerdown - stop all processes and turn off the power

SYNOPSIS

powerdown [-y | -Y]

DESCRIPTION

The powerdown command brings the system to a state where nothing is running.

The command invokes a visual interface (the powerdown task available through the sysadm(1M) command).

You are asked questions that control how much warning the other users are given. The options are:

-y   prevents the questions from being asked and just gives the warning messages. There is a 60-second pause between the warning messages.

-Y   is the same as -y except that it has no pause between messages. It is the fastest way to bring the system down.

The identical function is available under the sysadm menu:

sysadm powerdown

This command may be assigned a password with the sysadm systemsetup password command.

FILES

/usr/sbin/shutdown - invoked by powerdown

DIAGNOSTICS

The powerdown command exits with one of the following values:

0   Normal exit.

2   Invalid command syntax. A usage message is displayed.

7   The visual interface for this command is not available because it cannot invoke fmli. (The FMLI package is not installed or is corrupt.)

SEE ALSO

shutdown(1M), sysadm(1M)

NAME

ppp - login shell for the Point-to-Point Protocol

SYNOPSIS

`/usr/lib/ppp/ppp`

DESCRIPTION

`/usr/lib/ppp/ppp` is executed by `login`(1) upon receipt of an incoming PPP connection request.

`ppp` then passes the name of its controlling tty to `in.pppd` through the named pipe `/usr/lib/ppp/named_ppp` and then waits for the PPP datagram traffic on this link to stop, either through a timeout or an active close of the link. When the tty is released, `in.pppd` will kill the `ppp` process and break the IP connection to the remote host.

FILES

`/usr/lib/ppp/named_ppp`

SEE ALSO

`login`(1), `pppd`(1M), `ttymon`(1M), `ppp`(7).

USER CONSIDERATIONS

As cited in the description for the "Basic Networking Utilities," this login shell will need appropriate entries in the `/etc/passwd` and `/etc/group` files for each PPP host.

The typical entries in `/etc/passwd` will look like this:

```
nppp:x:11:9:0000-ppp(0000):/var/spool/uucppublic:/usr/lib/ppp/ppp
```

In addition, a corresponding entry will be needed for `ppp` in `/etc/group`:

```
ppp::9:root,ppp
```

The remote login request needs to use `nppp` as its login user name since the named pipe, `/usr/lib/ppp/named_ppp`, is created with uid `nppp`.

Note that when `ppp` is killed, this action will also cause `in.pppd` to break the IP connection for this PPP path.

NAME
pppd - Point-to-Point Protocol Daemon

SYNOPSIS
`/usr/sbin/in.pppd`

DESCRIPTION
The `in.pppd` daemon manages the Point-to-Point physical connection between the *local* and *remote* host. `in.pppd` uses the login-password technique to establish PPP connections to remote hosts. `in.pppd` uses the configuration files associated with the "Basic Network Utilities." The method for configuring the serial IP link is similar to that used for `uucp`(1) or `cu`(1). The serial lines may be used interchangeably for standard user logins, uucp logins, and PPP logins, and the standard `uucp` lock file techniques are used to share these resources.

`in.pppd` opens a contol channel to the kernel PPP through `/dev/ppcid`, and listens on the named pipe, `/usr/lib/ppp/named_ppp` for incoming PPP connection requests. The PPP user shell, `ppp`(1), sends a PPP service request over `/usr/lib/ppp/named_ppp` for each incoming PPP connection request. When PPP needs to attach a remote host before initiating PPP packet traffic, it will send a request over the control channel with the desired IP address. `in.pppd` searches `/etc/inet/ppphosts` [see `ppphosts`(4)] for an entry with a host name corresponding to this IP address. This entry in conjunction with the `/usr/lib/uucp/Systems` file is used to dial the modem (if necessary) and perform a login into the *remote* host.

When the remote login process completes, `in.pppd` links the connected tty beneath the PPP multiplexing driver and informs PPP that the link is established.

USER CONSIDERATIONS
If an outgoing PPP connection request fails, the IP Service Provider (IPSP) will be "temporarily" marked down; however, any subsequent successful incoming connections will cause the IPSP to be marked up.

FILES
```
/dev/ppcid
/etc/inet/ppphosts
/usr/lib/ppp/named_ppp
/usr/lib/uucp/Systems
/usr/lib/uucp/Devices
```

SEE ALSO
`cu`(1), `ppp`(1), `syslog`(1M), `uucp`(1), `ppphosts`(4), `ppp`(7).

NAME

pr - print files

SYNOPSIS

pr [[-*columns*] [-w*width*] [-a]] [-e*ck*] [-i*ck*] [-drtfp] [+*page*] [-n*ck*] [-o*offset*]
[-l*length*] [-s*separator*] [-h*header*] [-F] [*file* ...]

pr [[-m] [-w*width*]] [-e*ck*] [-i*ck*] [-drtfp] [+*page*] [-n*ck*] [-o*offset*] [-l*length*]
[-s*separator*] [-h*header*] [-F] [*file1* *file2* ...]

DESCRIPTION

The pr command formats and prints the contents of a file. If *file* is -, or if no files
are specified, pr assumes standard input. pr prints the named files on standard
output.

By default, the listing is separated into pages, each headed by the page number, the
date and time that the file was last modified, and the name of the file. Page length
is 66 lines which includes 10 lines of header and trailer output. The header is composed of 2 blank lines, 1 line of text (can be altered with -h), and 2 blank lines; the
trailer is 5 blank lines. For single column output, line width may not be set and is
unlimited. For multicolumn output, line width may be set and the default is 72
columns. Diagnostic reports (failed options) are reported at the end of standard
output associated with a terminal, rather than interspersed in the output. Pages are
separated by series of line feeds rather than form feed characters.

By default, columns are of equal width, separated by at least one space; lines which
do not fit are truncated. If the -s option is used, lines are not truncated and
columns are separated by the *separator* character.

Either -*columns* or -m should be used to produce multi-column output. -a should
only be used with -*columns* and not -m.

Command line options are:

+*page*   Begin printing with page numbered *page* (default is 1).

-*columns*   Print *columns* columns of output (default is 1). Output appears as if -e
and -i are on for multi-column output. May not use with -m.

-a   Print multi-column output across the page one line per column. *columns*
must be greater than one. If a line is too long to fit in a column, it is
truncated.

-m   Merge and print all files simultaneously, one per column. The maximum number of files that may be specified is eight. If a line is too long
to fit in a column, it is truncated. May not use with -*columns*.

-d   Double-space the output. Blank lines that result from double-spacing
are dropped when they occur at the top of a page.

-e*ck*   Expand input tabs to column positions $k+1$, $2*k+1$, $3*k+1$, etc. If k is 0
or is omitted, default tab settings at every eighth position are assumed.
Tab characters in the input are expanded into the appropriate number of
spaces. If c (any non-digit character) is given, it is treated as the input
tab character (default for c is the tab character). The tab character c must
be a single byte character.

−i*ck*	In output, replace white space wherever possible by inserting tabs to column positions $k+1$, $2*k+1$, $3*k+1$, etc. If k is 0 or is omitted, default tab settings at every eighth position are assumed. If c (any non-digit character) is given, it is treated as the output tab character (default for c is the tab character). The tab character c must be a single byte character.
−n*ck*	Provide k-digit line numbering (default for k is 5). The number occupies the first $k+1$ character positions of each column of single column output or each line of −m output. If c (any non-digit character) is given, it is appended to the line number to separate it from whatever follows (default for c is a tab). The character c to be appended to the line number must be a single byte character.
−w*width*	Set the width of a line to *width* column positions (default is 72). This is effective only for multi-column output (−*column* and −m). There is no line limit for single column output.
−o*offset*	Offset each line by *offset* character positions (default is 0). The number of character positions per line is the sum of the width and offset.
−l*length*	Set the length of a page to *length* lines (default is 66). A *length* of 0 specifies the default length. By default, output contains 5 lines of header and 5 lines of trailer leaving 56 lines for user-supplied text. When −l*length* is used and *length* exceeds 10, then *length*-10 lines are left per page for user supplied text. When *length* is 10 or less, header and trailer output is omitted to make room for user supplied text; see the −t option.
−h *header*	Use *header* as the text line of the header to be printed instead of the file name. −h is ignored when −t is specified or −l*length* is specified and the value of *length* is 10 or less. (−h is the only pr option requiring space between the option and argument.) characters from supplementary code sets can be used in the page header, *header*.
−p	Pause before beginning each page if the output device is a terminal. pr rings the terminal bell and waits for a carriage return.
−f	Use a single form-feed character for new pages (default is to use a sequence of line feeds). Pause before beginning the first page if the standard output is associated with a terminal.
−r	Print no diagnostic reports on files that cannot be opened.
−t	Print neither the five-line identifying header nor the five-line trailer normally supplied for each page. Quit printing after the last line of each file without spacing to the end of the page. Use of −t overrides the −h option.
−s*separator*	Separate columns by the single character *separator* instead of by the appropriate number of spaces (default for *separator* is a tab). Prevents truncation of lines on multi-column output unless −w is specified. The column separator, *separator*, must be a single byte character.

　　　-F　　　　　　Fold the lines of the input file. When used in multi-column mode (with
　　　　　　　　　　the -a or -m options) lines will be folded to fit the current column's
　　　　　　　　　　width, otherwise they will be folded to fit the current line width (80
　　　　　　　　　　columns).

EXAMPLES

Print file1 and file2 as a double-spaced, three-column listing headed by "file
list":

```
pr -3dh "file list" file1 file2
```

Copy file1 to file2, expanding tabs to columns 10, 19, 28, 37, ... :

```
pr -e9 -t < file1 > file2
```

Print file1 and file2 simultaneously in a two-column listing with no header or
trailer where both columns have line numbers:

```
pr -t -n file1 | pr -t -m -n file2 -
```

FILES

/dev/tty*　　　If standard output is directed to one of the special files /dev/tty*,
　　　　　　　　then other output directed to this terminal is delayed until standard
　　　　　　　　output is completed. This prevents error messages from being
　　　　　　　　interspersed throughout the output.

INTERNATIONAL FUNCTIONS

pr can process characters from supplementary code sets in addition to ASCII characters.

SEE ALSO

cat(1), fold(1), more(1), page(1), pg(1).

NAME

printenv - display environment variables currently set

SYNOPSIS

/usr/ucb/printenv [*variable*]

DESCRIPTION

printenv prints out the values of the variables in the environment. If a *variable* is specified, only its value is printed.

SEE ALSO

tset(1)

csh(1), echo(1), sh(1), stty(1), environ(5).

DIAGNOSTICS

If a *variable* is specified and it is not defined in the environment, printenv returns an exit status of 1.

NAME

printf - print formatted output

SYNOPSIS

printf *format* [*arg* . . .]

DESCRIPTION

The printf command converts, formats, and prints its *args* under control of the *format*. It fully supports conversion specifications for strings (%s descriptor); however, the results are undefined for the other conversion specifications supported by printf(3S).

format   a character string that contains three types of objects: 1) plain characters, which are simply copied to the output stream; 2) conversion specifications, each of which results in fetching zero or more *args*; and 3) C-language escape sequences, which are translated into the corresponding characters.

arg   string(s) to be printed under the control of *format*. The results are undefined if there are insufficient *args* for the format. If the format is exhausted while *args* remain, the excess *args* are simply ignored.

Each conversion specification is introduced by the character %. After the %, the following appear in sequence:

An optional field, consisting of a decimal digit string followed by a $, specifying the next *arg* to be converted. If this field is not provided, the *arg* following the last *arg* converted is used.

An optional decimal digit string specifying a minimum *field width*. If the converted value has fewer characters than the field width, it is padded on the left (or right, if the left-adjustment flag '-' has been given) to the field width. The padding is with blanks unless the field width digit string starts with a zero, in which case the padding is with zeros.

An optional *precision* that gives the maximum number of characters to be printed from a string in %s conversion. The precision takes the form of a period (.) followed by a decimal digit string; a null digit string is treated as zero (nothing is printed). Padding specified by the precision overrides the padding specified by the field width. That is, if *precision* is specified, its value is used to control the number of characters printed.

A field width or precision or both may be indicated by an asterisk (*) instead of a digit string. In this case, an integer *arg* supplies the field width or precision. The *arg* that is actually converted is not fetched until the conversion letter is seen, so the *args* specifying field width or precision must appear *before* the *arg* (if any) to be converted. A negative field width argument is taken as a '-' (left-adjustment) flag followed by a positive field width. If the precision argument is negative, it is changed to zero (nothing is printed). In no case does a non-existent or small field width cause truncation of a field; if the result of a conversion is wider than the field width, the field is simply expanded to contain the conversion result.

The conversion characters and their meanings are:

`%s`   The *arg* is taken to be a string and characters from the string are printed until a null character (`\0`) is encountered or the number of characters indicated by the precision specification is reached. If the precision is missing, it is taken to be infinite, so all characters up to the first null character are printed. A null value for *arg* yields undefined results.

`%%`   Print a `%`; no argument is converted.

EXAMPLES

The command

```
printf '%s %s %s\n' Good Morning World
```

results in the output:

```
Good Morning World
```

The following command produces the same output.

```
printf '%2$s %s %1$s\n' World Good Morning
```

Here is an example that prints the first 6 characters of `$PATH` left-adjusted in a 10-character field:

```
printf 'First 6 chars of %s are %-10.6s.\n' $PATH $PATH
```

If `$PATH` has the value `/usr/bin:/usr/local/bin`, then the above command would print the following output:

```
First 6 chars of /usr/bin:/usr/local/bin are /usr/b    .
```

SEE ALSO

`printf`(3S).

NAME

priocntl - process scheduler control

SYNOPSIS

```
priocntl -l
priocntl -d [-i idtype] [idlist]
priocntl -s [-c class] [class-specific options] [-i idtype] [idlist]
priocntl -e [-c class] [class-specific options] command [argument(s)]
```

DESCRIPTION

The `priocntl` command displays or sets scheduling parameters of the specified process(es). It can also be used to display the current configuration information for the system's process scheduler or execute a command with specified scheduling parameters.

Processes fall into distinct classes with a separate scheduling policy applied to each class. The two process classes currently supported are the real-time class and the time-sharing class. The characteristics of these two classes and the class-specific options they accept are described below under the headings REAL-TIME CLASS and TIME-SHARING CLASS. With appropriate permissions, the `priocntl` command can change the class and other scheduling parameters associated with a running process.

In the default configuration, a runnable real-time process runs before any other process. Therefore, inappropriate use of real-time processes can have a dramatic negative impact on system performance.

The command

```
priocntl -l
```

displays a list of classes currently configured in the system along with class-specific information about each class. The format of the class-specific information displayed is described under the appropriate heading below.

The `-d` and `-s` options to `priocntl` allow the user to display or set the scheduling parameters associated with a set of processes. The `-i` option and its associated *idtype* argument, together with the *idlist* arguments to `priocntl` (if any), specify one or more processes to which the `priocntl` command is to apply. The interpretation of *idlist* depends on the value of *idtype*. The valid *idtype* arguments and corresponding interpretations of *idlist* are as follows:

`-i pid`   *idlist* is a list of process IDs. The `priocntl` command applies to the specified processes.

`-i ppid`   *idlist* is a list of parent process IDs. The `priocntl` command applies to all processes whose parent process ID is in the list.

`-i pgid`   *idlist* is a list of process group IDs. The `priocntl` command applies to all processes in the specified process groups.

`-i sid`   *idlist* is a list of session IDs. The `priocntl` command applies to all processes in the specified sessions.

`-i class`   *idlist* consists of a single class name (RT for real-time or TS for time-sharing). The `priocntl` command applies to all processes in the specified class.

-i uid   *idlist* is a list of user IDs. The `priocntl` command applies to all processes with an effective user ID equal to an ID from the list.

-i gid   *idlist* is a list of group IDs. The `priocntl` command applies to all processes with an effective group ID equal to an ID from the list.

-i all   The `priocntl` command applies to all existing processes. No *idlist* should be specified (if one is it is ignored). The permission restrictions described below still apply.

If the -i *idtype* option is omitted when using the -d or -s options the default *idtype* of pid is assumed.

If an *idlist* is present it must appear last on the command line and the elements of the list must be separated by white space. If no *idlist* is present an *idtype* argument of pid, ppid, pgid, sid, class, uid, or gid specifies the process ID, parent process ID, process group ID, session ID, class, user ID, or group ID respectively of the `priocntl` command itself.

The command

    `priocntl -d` [-i *idtype*] [*idlist*]

displays the class and class-specific scheduling parameters of the process(es) specified by *idtype* and *idlist*.

The command

    `priocntl -s` [-c *class*] [*class-specific options*] [-i *idtype*] [*idlist*]

sets the class and class-specific parameters of the specified processes to the values given on the command line. The -c *class* option specifies the class to be set. (The valid *class* arguments are RT for real-time or TS for time-sharing). The class-specific parameters to be set are specified by the class-specific options as explained under the appropriate heading below. If the -c *class* option is omitted, *idtype* and *idlist* must specify a set of processes which are all in the same class, otherwise an error results. If no class-specific options are specified the process's class-specific parameters are set to the default values for the class specified by -c *class* (or to the default parameter values for the process's current class if the -c *class* option is also omitted).

In order to change the scheduling parameters of a process using `priocntl` the real or effective user ID of the user invoking `priocntl` must match the real or effective user ID of the receiving process or the effective user ID of the user must be superuser. These are the minimum permission requirements enforced for all classes. An individual class may impose additional permissions requirements when setting processes to that class or when setting class-specific scheduling parameters.

When *idtype* and *idlist* specify a set of processes, `priocntl` acts on the processes in the set in an implementation-specific order. If `priocntl` encounters an error for one or more of the target processes, it may or may not continue through the set of processes, depending on the nature of the error. If the error is related to permissions, `priocntl` prints an error message and then continue through the process set, resetting the parameters for all target processes for which the user has appropriate permissions. If `priocntl` encounters an error other than permissions, it does not continue through the process set but prints an error message and exits immediately.

A special sys scheduling class exists for the purpose of scheduling the execution of certain special system processes (such as the swapper process). It is not possible to change the class of any process to sys. In addition, any processes in the sys class that are included in the set of processes specified by *idtype* and *idlist* are disregarded by priocntl. For example, if *idtype* were uid, an *idlist* consisting of a zero would specify all processes with a UID of zero except processes in the sys class and (if changing the parameters using the -s option) the init process.

The init process (process ID 1) is a special case. In order for the priocntl command to change the class or other scheduling parameters of the init process, *idtype* must be pid and *idlist* must be consist of only a 1. The init process may be assigned to any class configured on the system, but the time-sharing class is almost always the appropriate choice.

The command

> priocntl -e [-c *class*] [*class-specific options*] *command* [*argument(s)*]

executes the specified command with the class and scheduling parameters specified on the command line (*arguments* are the arguments to the command). If the -c *class* option is omitted the command is run in the user's current class.

REAL-TIME CLASS

The real-time class provides a fixed priority preemptive scheduling policy for those processes requiring fast and deterministic response and absolute user/application control of scheduling priorities. If the real-time class is configured in the system it should have exclusive control of the highest range of scheduling priorities on the system. This ensures that a runnable real-time process is given CPU service before any process belonging to any other class.

The real-time class has a range of real-time priority (*rtpri*) values that may be assigned to processes within the class. Real-time priorities range from 0 to x, where the value of x is configurable and can be displayed for a specific installation by using the command

> priocntl -l

The real-time scheduling policy is a fixed priority policy. The scheduling priority of a real-time process never changes except as the result of an explicit request by the user/application to change the *rtpri* value of the process.

For processes in the real-time class, the *rtpri* value is, for all practical purposes, equivalent to the scheduling priority of the process. The *rtpri* value completely determines the scheduling priority of a real-time process relative to other processes within its class. Numerically higher *rtpri* values represent higher priorities. Since the real-time class controls the highest range of scheduling priorities in the system it is guaranteed that the runnable real-time process with the highest *rtpri* value is always selected to run before any other process in the system.

In addition to providing control over priority, priocntl provides for control over the length of the time quantum allotted to processes in the real-time class. The time quantum value specifies the maximum amount of time a process may run assuming that it does not complete or enter a resource or event wait state (sleep). Note that if another process becomes runnable at a higher priority the currently running process may be preempted before receiving its full time quantum.

The command

    priocntl -d [-i *idtype*] [*idlist*]

displays the real-time priority and time quantum (in millisecond resolution) for each real-time process in the set specified by *idtype* and *idlist*.

The valid class-specific options for setting real-time parameters are:

-p *rtpri*	Set the real-time priority of the specified process(es) to *rtpri*.
-t *tqntm* [-r *res*]	Set the time quantum of the specified process(es) to *tqntm*. You may optionally specify a resolution as explained below.

Any combination of the -p and -t options may be used with priocntl -s or priocntl -e for the real-time class. If an option is omitted and the process is currently real-time the associated parameter is unaffected. If an option is omitted when changing the class of a process to real-time from some other class, the associated parameter is set to a default value. The default value for *rtpri* is 0 and the default for time quantum is dependent on the value of *rtpri* and on the system configuration; see rt_dptbl(4).

When using the -t *tqntm* option you may optionally specify a resolution using the -r *res* option. (If no resolution is specified, millisecond resolution is assumed.) If *res* is specified it must be a positive integer between 1 and 1,000,000,000 inclusive and the resolution used is the reciprocal of *res* in seconds. For example, specifying -t 10 -r 100 would set the resolution to hundredths of a second and the resulting time quantum length would be 10/100 seconds (one tenth of a second). Although very fine (nanosecond) resolution may be specified, the time quantum length is rounded up by the system to the next integral multiple of the system clock's resolution. Requests for time quantums of zero or quantums greater than the (typically very large) implementation-specific maximum quantum result in an error.

In order to change the class of a process to real-time (from any other class) the user invoking priocntl must have super-user privileges. In order to change the *rtpri* value or time quantum of a real-time process the user invoking priocntl must either be super-user, or must currently be in the real-time class (shell running as a real-time process) with a real or effective user ID matching the real or effective user ID of the target process.

The real-time priority and time quantum are inherited across the fork(2) and exec(2) system calls.

Examples

    priocntl -s -c RT -t 1 -r 10 -i *idtype idlist*

sets the class of any non-real-time processes selected by *idtype* and *idlist* to real-time and sets their real-time priority to the default value of 0. The real-time priorities of any processes currently in the real-time class are unaffected. The time quantums of all of the specified processes are set to 1/10 seconds.

```
priocntl -e -c RT -p 15 -t 20 command
```

executes *command* in the real-time class with a real-time priority of 15 and a time quantum of 20 milliseconds.

TIME-SHARING CLASS

The time-sharing scheduling policy provides for a fair and effective allocation of the CPU resource among processes with varying CPU consumption characteristics. The objectives of the time-sharing policy are to provide good response time to interactive processes and good throughput to CPU-bound jobs while providing a degree of user/application control over scheduling.

The time-sharing class has a range of time-sharing user priority (*tsupri*) values that may be assigned to processes within the class. User priorities range from -x to +x, where the value of x is configurable. The range for a specific installation can be displayed by using the command

```
priocntl -l
```

The purpose of the user priority is to provide some degree of user/application control over the scheduling of processes in the time-sharing class. Raising or lowering the *tsupri* value of a process in the time-sharing class raises or lowers the scheduling priority of the process. It is not guaranteed, however, that a time-sharing process with a higher *tsupri* value will run before one with a lower *tsupri* value. This is because the *tsupri* value is just one factor used to determine the scheduling priority of a time-sharing process. The system may dynamically adjust the internal scheduling priority of a time-sharing process based on other factors such as recent CPU usage.

In addition to the system-wide limits on user priority (displayed with `priocntl -l`), there is a per process user priority limit (*tsuprilim*), which specifies the maximum *tsupri* value that may be set for a given process.

The command

```
priocntl -d [-i idtype] [idlist]
```

displays the user priority and user priority limit for each time-sharing process in the set specified by *idtype* and *idlist*.

The valid class-specific options for setting time-sharing parameters are:

-m *tsuprilim*   Set the user priority limit of the specified process(es) to *tsuprilim*.

-p *tsupri*   Set the user priority of the specified process(es) to *tsupri*.

Any time-sharing process may lower its own *tsuprilim* (or that of another process with the same user ID). Only a time-sharing process with super-user privileges may raise a *tsuprilim*. When changing the class of a process to time-sharing from some other class, super-user privileges are required in order to set the initial *tsuprilim* to a value greater than zero.

Any time-sharing process may set its own *tsupri* (or that of another process with the same user ID) to any value less than or equal to the process's *tsuprilim*. Attempts to set the *tsupri* above the *tsuprilim* (and/or set the *tsuprilim* below the *tsupri*) result in the *tsupri* being set equal to the *tsuprilim*.

Any combination of the -l and -p options may be used with priocntl -s or priocntl -e for the time-sharing class. If an option is omitted and the process is currently time-sharing the associated parameter is normally unaffected. The exception is when the -p option is omitted and -l is used to set a *tsuprilim* below the current *tsupri*. In this case the *tsupri* is set equal to the *tsuprilim* which is being set. If an option is omitted when changing the class of a process to time-sharing from some other class, the associated parameter is set to a default value. The default value for *tsuprilim* is 0 and the default for *tsupri* is to set it equal to the *tsuprilim* value which is being set.

The time-sharing user priority and user priority limit are inherited across the fork(2) and exec(2) system calls.

Examples

        priocntl -s -c TS -i *idtype idlist*

sets the class of any non-time-sharing processes selected by *idtype* and *idlist* to time-sharing and sets both their user priority limit and user priority to 0. Processes already in the time-sharing class are unaffected.

        priocntl -e -c TS -l 0 -p -15 *command* [*arguments*]

executes *command* with the arguments *arguments* in the time-sharing class with a user priority limit of 0 and a user priority of -15.

SEE ALSO

        ps(1), nice(1), priocntl(2), rt_dptbl(4).

DIAGNOSTICS

        priocntl prints the following error messages:

        Process(es) not found: None of the specified processes exists.

        Specified processes from different classes: The -s option is being used to set parameters, the -c *class* option is not present, and processes from more than one class are specified.

        Invalid option or argument: An unrecognized or invalid option or option argument is used.

NAME

prof - display profile data

SYNOPSIS

prof [-t | c | a | n] [-o | x] [-g | l] [-z] [-h] [-s] [-m *mdata*] –V [*prog*]

DESCRIPTION

The prof command interprets a profile file produced by the monitor function. The symbol table in the object file *prog* (a.out by default) is read and correlated with a profile file (mon.out by default). For each external text symbol the percentage of time spent executing between the address of that symbol and the address of the next is printed, together with the number of times that function was called and the average number of milliseconds per call.

The mutually exclusive options -t, -c, -a, and -n determine the type of sorting of the output lines:

-t   Sort by decreasing percentage of total time (default).

-c   Sort by decreasing number of calls.

-a   Sort by increasing symbol address.

-n   Sort lexically by symbol name.

The mutually exclusive options -o and -x specify the printing of the address of each symbol monitored:

-o   Print each symbol address (in octal) along with the symbol name.

-x   Print each symbol address (in hexadecimal) along with the symbol name.

The mutually exclusive options -g and -l control the type of symbols to be reported. The -l option must be used with care; it applies the time spent in a static function to the preceding (in memory) global function, instead of giving the static function a separate entry in the report. If all static functions are properly located (see example below), this feature can be very useful. If not, the resulting report may be misleading.

Assume that A and B are global functions and only A calls static function S. If S is located immediately after A in the source code (that is, if S is properly located), then, with the -l option, the amount of time spent in A can easily be determined, including the time spent in S. If, however, both A and B call S, then, if the -l option is used, the report will be misleading; the time spent during B's call to S will be attributed to A, making it appear as if more time had been spent in A than really had. In this case, function S cannot be properly located.

-g   Include static (non-global) functions.

-l   Do not include static (non-global) functions (default).

The following options may be used in any combination:

-z   Include all symbols in the profile range, even if associated with zero number of calls and zero time.

-h   Suppress the heading normally printed on the report. (This is useful if the report is to be processed further.)

-s   Print a summary of several of the monitoring parameters and statistics on the standard error output.

-m *mdata*
    Use file *mdata* instead of mon.out as the input profile file.

-V   Print prof version information on the standard error output.

A program creates a profile file if it has been link edited with the -p option of cc. This option to the cc command arranges for calls to monitor at the beginning and end of execution. It is the call to monitor at the end of execution that causes the system to write a profile file. The number of calls to a function is tallied if the -p option was used when the file containing the function was compiled.

The name of the file created by a profiled program is controlled by the environmental variable PROFDIR. If PROFDIR is not set, mon.out is produced in the directory current when the program terminates. If PROFDIR=*string*, *string*/*pid*.*progname* is produced, where *progname* consists of argv[0] with any path prefix removed, and *pid* is the process ID of the program. If PROFDIR is set, but null, no profiling output are produced.

A single function may be split into subfunctions for profiling by means of the MARK macro [see prof(5)].

FILES

    mon.out   default profile file
    a.out   default namelist (object) file

SEE ALSO

    cc(1), lprof(1), exit(2), profil(2), monitor(3C), prof(5).

NOTES

The times reported in successive identical runs may show variances because of varying cache-hit ratios that result from sharing the cache with other processes. Even if a program seems to be the only one using the machine, hidden background or asynchronous processes may blur the data. In rare cases, the clock ticks initiating recording of the program counter may ''beat'' with loops in a program, grossly distorting measurements. Call counts are always recorded precisely, however.

Only programs that call exit or return from main are guaranteed to produce a profile file, unless a final call to monitor is explicitly coded.

The times for static functions are attributed to the preceding external text symbol if the -g option is not used. However, the call counts for the preceding function are still correct; that is, the static function call counts are not added to the call counts of the external function.

If more than one of the options -t, -c, -a, and -n is specified, the last option specified is used and the user is warned.

Profiling may be used with dynamically linked executables, but care must be applied. Currently, shared objects cannot be profiled with prof. Thus, when a profiled, dynamically linked program is executed, only the ''main'' portion of the image is sampled. This means that all time spent outside of the ''main'' object, that is, time spent in a shared object, will not be included in the profile summary; the total time reported for the program may be less than the total time used by the program.

Because the time spent in a shared object cannot be accounted for, the use of shared objects should be minimized whenever a program is profiled with `prof`. If possible, the program should be linked statically before being profiled.

Consider an extreme case. A profiled program dynamically linked with the shared C library spends 100 units of time in some `libc` routine, say, `malloc`. Suppose `malloc` is called only from routine B and B consumes only 1 unit of time. Suppose further that routine A consumes 10 units of time, more than any other routine in the "main" (profiled) portion of the image. In this case, `prof` will conclude that most of the time is being spent in A and almost no time is being spent in B. From this it will be almost impossible to tell that the greatest improvement can be made by looking at routine B and not routine A. The value of the profiler in this case is severely degraded; the solution is to use archives as much as possible for profiling.

NAME

profiler: `prfld`, `prfstat`, `prfdc`, `prfsnap`, `prfpr` - UNIX system profiler

SYNOPSIS

`/usr/sbin/prfld` [*system_namelist*]
`/usr/sbin/prfstat on`
`/usr/sbin/prfstat off`
`/usr/sbin/prfdc` *file* [*period* [*off_hour*]]
`/usr/sbin/prfsnap` *file*
`/usr/sbin/prfpr` [-P] *file* [*cutoff* [*system_namelist*]]

DESCRIPTION

`prfld`, `prfstat`, `prfdc`, `prfsnap`, and `prfpr` form a system of programs to facilitate an activity study of the UNIX operating system.

`prfld` is used to initialize the recording mechanism in the system. It generates a table containing the starting address of each system subroutine as extracted from *system_namelist*.

`prfstat` is used to enable or disable the sampling mechanism. Profiler overhead is less than 1% as calculated for 500 text addresses. `prfstat` will also reveal the number of text addresses being measured.

`prfdc` and `prfsnap` perform the data collection function of the profiler by copying the current value of all the text address counters to a file where the data can be analyzed. `prfdc` will store the counters into *file* every *period* minutes and will turn off at *off_hour* (valid values for *off_hour* are 0-24). `prfsnap` collects data at the time of invocation only, appending the counter values to *file*.

`prfpr` formats the data collected by `prfdc` or `prfsnap`. Each text address is converted to the nearest text symbol (as found in *system_namelist*) and is printed if the percent activity for that range is greater than *cutoff*. By default, system-wide totals are printed.

Specifying the -P option prints the per-processor total.

FILES

`/dev/prf`   interface to profile data and text addresses

`/stand/unix`   default for system namelist file

NAME

prs - print an SCCS file

SYNOPSIS

prs [-d[*dataspec*]] [-r[*SID*]] [-e] [-1] [-c[*date-time*]] [-a] *files*

DESCRIPTION

prs prints, on the standard output, parts or all of an SCCS file [see sccsfile(4)] in a user-supplied format. If a directory is named, prs prints the files in that directory, except the non-SCCS files (last component of the path name does not begin with s.) and unreadable files. If a name of - is given, the standard input is read; each line of the standard input is taken to be the name of an SCCS file or directory to be processed. prs silently ignores non-SCCS files and unreadable files.

Arguments to prs, which may appear in any order, consist of keyletter arguments and file names.

The keyletter arguments apply independently to each named file:

-d[*dataspec*]	Specifies the output data specification. The *dataspec* is a string consisting of SCCS file data keywords (see the DATA KEYWORDS section) interspersed with optional user-supplied text.
-r[*SID*]	Specifies the SCCS identification (SID) string of a delta for which information is desired. The default is the top delta.
-e	Requests information for all deltas created earlier than and including the delta designated via the -r keyletter or the date given by the -c option.
-1	Requests information for all deltas created later than and including the delta designated via the -r keyletter or the date given by the -c option.
-c[*date-time*]	The cutoff date-time in the form:

YY[MM[DD[HH[MM[SS]]]]]

Units omitted from the date-time default to their maximum possible values; for example, -c7502 is equivalent to -c750228235959. Any number of non-numeric characters may separate the fields of the cutoff date; for example, "-c77/2/2 9:22:25".

-a	Requests printing of information for both removed, that is, delta type = R, [see rmdel(1)] and existing, that is, delta type = D, deltas. If the -a keyletter is not specified, information for existing deltas only is provided.

DATA KEYWORDS

Data keywords specify those parts of an SCCS file that are to be retrieved and output. All parts of an SCCS file [see sccsfile(4)] have an associated data keyword. There is no limit on the number of times a data keyword may appear in a *dataspec*.

The information printed by prs consists of: (1) the user-supplied text; and (2) appropriate values (extracted from the SCCS file) substituted for the recognized data keywords in the order of appearance in the *dataspec*. The format of a data keyword value is either "Simple" (S), in which keyword substitution is direct, or

"Multi-line" (M), in which keyword substitution is followed by a carriage return.

User-supplied text is any text other than recognized data keywords. A tab is specified by \t and carriage return/new-line is specified by \n. The default data keywords are:

```
":Dt:\t:DL:\nMRs:\n:MR:COMMENTS:\n:C:"
```

Keyword	Data Item	File Section	Value	Format
:Dt:	Delta information	Delta Table	See below*	S
:DL:	Delta line statistics	"	:Li:/:Ld:/:Lu:	S
:Li:	Lines inserted by Delta	"	*nnnnn*	S
:Ld:	Lines deleted by Delta	"	*nnnnn*	S
:Lu:	Lines unchanged by Delta	"	*nnnnn*	S
:DT:	Delta type	"	D *or* R	S
:I:	SCCS ID string (SID)	"	:R:.:L:.:B:.:S:	S
:R:	Release number	"	*nnnn*	S
:L:	Level number	"	*nnnn*	S
:B:	Branch number	"	*nnnn*	S
:S:	Sequence number	"	*nnnn*	S
:D:	Date Delta created	"	:Dy:/:Dm:/:Dd:	S
:Dy:	Year Delta created	"	*nn*	S
:Dm:	Month Delta created	"	*nn*	S
:Dd:	Day Delta created	"	*nn*	S
:T:	Time Delta created	"	:Th:::Tm:::Ts:	S
:Th:	Hour Delta created	"	*nn*	S
:Tm:	Minutes Delta created	"	*nn*	S
:Ts:	Seconds Delta created	"	*nn*	S
:P:	Programmer who created Delta	"	*logname*	S
:DS:	Delta sequence number	"	*nnnn*	S
:DP:	Predecessor Delta seq-no.	"	*nnnn*	S
:DI:	Seq-no. of deltas incl., excl., ignored	"	:Dn:/:Dx:/:Dg:	S
:Dn:	Deltas included (seq #)	"	:DS: :DS:...	S
:Dx:	Deltas excluded (seq #)	"	:DS: :DS:...	S
:Dg:	Deltas ignored (seq #)	"	:DS: :DS:...	S
:MR:	MR numbers for delta	"	*text*	M
:C:	Comments for delta	"	*text*	M
:UN:	User names	User Names	*text*	M
:FL:	Flag list	Flags	*text*	M

Keyword	Data Item	File Section	Value	Format
:Y:	Module type flag	"	*text*	S
:MF:	MR validation flag	"	yes *or* no	S
:MP:	MR validation pgm name	"	*text*	S

:KF:	Keyword error/warning flag	"	yes **or** no	S
:KV:	Keyword validation string	"	*text*	S
:BF:	Branch flag	"	yes **or** no	S
:J:	Joint edit flag	"	yes **or** no	S
:LK:	Locked releases	"	:R: ...	S
:Q:	User-defined keyword	"	*text*	S
:M:	Module name	"	*text*	S
:FB:	Floor boundary	"	:R:	S
:CB:	Ceiling boundary	"	:R:	S
:Ds:	Default SID	"	:I:	S
:ND:	Null delta flag	"	yes **or** no	S
:FD:	File descriptive text	Comments	*text*	M
:BD:	Body	Body	*text*	M
:GB:	Gotten body	"	*text*	M
:W:	A form of what(1) string	N/A	:Z::M:\t:I:	S
:A:	A form of what(1) string	N/A	:Z::Y: :M: :I::Z:	S
:Z:	what(1) string delimiter	N/A	@(#)	S
:F:	SCCS file name	N/A	*text*	S
:PN:	SCCS file path name	N/A	*text*	S

```
* :Dt: = :DT: :I: :D: :T: :P: :DS: :DP:
```

EXAMPLES

The command

```
prs -d"Users and/or user IDs for :F: are:\n:UN:" s.file
```

may produce on the standard output:

```
Users and/or user IDs for s.file are:
xyz
131
abc
```

The command

```
prs -d"Newest delta for pgm :M:: :I: Created :D: By :P:" -r
s.file
```

may produce on the standard output:

```
Newest delta for pgm main.c: 3.7 Created 77/12/1 By cas
```

The default case:

```
prs s.file
```

produces on the standard output:

```
D 1.1 77/12/1 00:00:00 cas 1 000000/00000/00000
MRs:
b178-12345
b179-54321
COMMENTS:
this is the comment line for s.file initial delta
```

for each delta table entry of the "D" type. The only keyletter argument allowed to be used with the "special case" is the -a keyletter.

FILES

`/var/tmp/pr?????`

SEE ALSO

`admin`(1), `delta`(1), `get`(1), `help`(1), `sccsfile`(4)

DIAGNOSTICS

Use `help`(1) for explanations.

NAME

prt - display the delta and commentary history of an SCCS file

SYNOPSIS

/usr/ucb/prt [-abdefistu] [-y[*SID*]] [-c[*cutoff*]] [-r[*rev-cutoff*]] *filename* ...

DESCRIPTION

Note: the prt command is an older version of prs(1) that in most circumstances is more convenient to use, but is less flexible than prs.

prt prints part or all of an SCCS file in a useful format. If a directory is named, prt behaves as though each file in the directory were specified as a named file, except that non-SCCS files (last component of the pathname does not begin with s.) and unreadable files are silently ignored. If a name of '-' is given, the standard input is read; each line of the standard input is taken to be the name of an SCCS file to be processed. Again, non-SCCS files and unreadable files are silently ignored.

The following options are available with prt :

-a   Print those types of deltas normally not printed by the d keyletter. These are types R (removed). This keyletter is effective only if the d keyletter is also specified (or assumed).

-b   Print the body of the SCCS file.

-d   This keyletter normally prints delta table entries of the D type.

-e   This keyletter implies the d, i, u, f, and t keyletters and is provided for convenience.

-f   Print the flags of the named file.

-i   Print the serial numbers of those deltas included, excluded, and ignored. This keyletter is effective only if the d keyletter is also specified (or assumed).

The following format is used to print those portions of the SCCS file as specified by the above keyletters. The printing of each delta table entry is preceded by a NEWLINE.

- Type of delta (D or R).
- SPACE.
- SCCS identification string (SID).
- TAB.
- Date and time of creation (in the form YY/MM/DD HH:MM:SS).
- SPACE.
- Creator.
- TAB.
- Serial number.
- SPACE.
- Predecessor delta's serial number.
- TAB.
- Statistics (in the form inserted/deleted/unchanged).
- NEWLINE.

- "Included:TAB", followed by SID's of deltas included, followed by NEWLINE (only if there were any such deltas and if i keyletter was supplied).
- "Excluded:TAB", followed by SID's of deltas excluded, followed by NEWLINE (see note above).
- "Ignored:TAB", followed by SID's of deltas ignored, followed by NEW-LINE (see note above).
- "MRs:TAB", followed by MR numbers related to the delta, followed by NEWLINE (only if any MR numbers were supplied).
- Lines of comments (delta commentary), followed by newline (if any were supplied).

-s   Print only the first line of the delta table entries; that is, only up to the statistics. This keyletter is effective only if the d keyletter is also specified (or assumed).

-t   Print the descriptive text contained in the file.

-u   Print the login-names and/or numerical group IDs of those users allowed to make deltas.

-y[*SID*]

Print the delta table entries to stop when the delta just printed has the specified SID. If no delta in the table has the specified SID, the entire table is printed. If no SID is specified, the first delta in the delta table is printed. This keyletter will print the entire delta table entry for each delta as a single line (the NEWLINE in the normal multi-line format of the d keyletter are replaced by SPACE characters) preceded by the name of the SCCS file being processed, followed by a :, followed by a TAB. This keyletter is effective only if the d keyletter is also specified (or assumed).

-c[*cutoff*]

Stop printing the delta table entries if the delta about to be printed is older than the specified cutoff date-time (see get(1) for the format of date-time). If no date-time is supplied, the epoch 0000 GMT Jan. 1, 1970 is used. As with the y keyletter, this keyletter will cause the entire delta table entry to be printed as a single line and to be preceded by the name of the SCCS file being processed, followed by a :, followed by a tab. This keyletter is effective only if the d keyletter is also specified (or assumed).

-r[*rev-cutoff*]

Begin printing the delta table entries when the delta about to be printed is older than or equal to the specified cutoff date-time (see get(1) for the format of date-time). If no date-time is supplied, the epoch 0000 GMT Jan. 1, 1970 is used. (In this case, nothing will be printed). As with the y keyletter, this keyletter will cause the entire delta table entry to be printed as a single line and to be preceded by the name of the SCCS file being processed, followed by a :, followed by a tab. This keyletter is effective only if the d keyletter is also specified (or assumed).

If any keyletter but y, c, or r is supplied, the name of the file being processed (preceded by one NEWLINE and followed by two NEWLINE characters) is printed before its contents.

If none of the u, f, t, or b keyletters is supplied, the d keyletter is assumed.

Note: the s and i keyletters, and the c and r keyletters are mutually exclusive; therefore, they may not be specified together on the same prt command.

The form of the delta table as produced by the y, c, and r keyletters makes it easy to sort multiple delta tables in chronological order.

When both the y and c or the y and r keyletters are supplied, prt will stop printing when the first of the two conditions is met.

SEE ALSO

admin(1), get(1), delta(1), prs(1), what(1), sccs(1), sccsfile(5).

NAME

`prtconf` - print system configuration

SYNOPSIS

`/usr/sbin/prtconf` [`-l`] [`-c`]

DESCRIPTION

The `prtconf` command prints the system configuration information which includes the memory and peripheral configuration. This information is displayed every time the system is initialized to multiuser mode.

The `-l` flag prints all fields of the Equipped Device Table (EDT) and Extended Device Table (XEDT), with the exception of the size field of the XEDT.

The `-c` flag causes the size field of the XEDT to be printed.

SEE ALSO

`scsiscan`(1M).

NAME

prtvtoc - print the VTOC of a block device

SYNOPSIS

/sbin/prtvtoc *device*

DESCRIPTION

The prtvtoc command allows the contents of the VTOC (volume table of contents) to be viewed. The command can be used only by the super-user.

The *device* name must be the filename of a raw device in the form of *prefix_cXdYsZ*, where *prefix* uniquely defines the type of device, *X* specifies the controller number (starting from zero) of the stated device type, *Y* specifies the logical device number (starting from zero) for the device attached to the stated controller, and *Z* specifies device dependent information.

EXAMPLE

The command line entry and system response shown below are for a 72-megabyte hard disk:

```
# prtvtoc /dev/rdsk/m328_c0d0s7
* /dev/rdsk/m328_c0d0s7 slice map
*
* Dimension:
*       512 bytes/sector
*        18 sectors/track
*        11 tracks/cylinder
*       198 sectors/cylinder
*       754 cylinders
*       754 accessible cylinders
*
* Flags:
*     1: unmountable
*    10: read-only
*
* Unallocated space:
*          First       Sector      Last
*          Sector      Count       Sector
*              0         100          99
*
*
*                      First   Sector  Last
* Slice Tag   Flags    Sector  Count   Sector   Mount Directory
    0     2     00     19040   23460   42499    /
    1     3     01       100   18940   19039
    2     4     00     29552  119344  148895    /usr
    3     6     00     24552    5000   29551    /stand
    6     0     01         0  148896  148895
    7     1     01         0     100      99

#
```

Codes for TAG are:

NAME	NUMBER
UNASSIGNED	0
BOOT	1
ROOT	2
SWAP	3
USR	4
BACKUP	5
STAND	6

FLAG indicates how the slice is to be mounted.

NAME	NUMBER
MOUNTABLE, READ AND WRITE	00
NOT MOUNTABLE	01
MOUNTABLE, READ ONLY	10

SEE ALSO

fmthard(1M)

CAVEAT

The mount command does not check the "not mountable" bit.

The unallocated space information contains all of the unallocated space on the device. This may also include the space at the very beginning of the disk that is reserved by Motorola for media identification, boot blocks, and bad block location.

NAME

ps - report process status

SYNOPSIS

ps [-Pedajflc] [-t *termlist*] [-p *proclist*] [-u *uidlist*] [-g *grplist*] [-s *sesslist*]

DESCRIPTION

ps prints information about active processes. Without *options*, ps prints information about processes associated with the controlling terminal. The output contains only the process ID, terminal identifier, cumulative execution time, and the command name. Otherwise, the information displayed is controlled by the *options*.

Some options accept lists as arguments. Items in a list can be either separated by commas or else enclosed in double quotes and separated by commas or spaces. Values for *proclist* and *grplist* must be numeric.

The *options* are:

-P Prints the processor ID number of the processor on which a process is executing, in the case of processor binding. The processor ID number appears under the PSR column heading. If the process is not bound to a specific processor, a dash appears in the field. The -P option applies to multiprocessing only.

-e Prints information about every process now executing.

-d Prints information about all processes except session leaders.

-a Prints information about all processes most frequently requested: all those except process group leaders and processes not associated with a terminal.

-j Prints session ID and process group ID.

-f Generates a full listing. (See below for significance of columns in a full listing.)

-l Generates a long listing.

-c Prints information in a format that reflects scheduler properties as described in priocntl(1). The -c option affects the output of the -f and -l options, as described below.

-t *termlist*
  Lists only process data associated with the terminal given in *termlist*. Terminal identifiers may be specified in one of two forms: the device's file name (for example, tty04) or, if the device's file name starts with tty, just the digit identifier (for example, 04).

-p *proclist*
  Lists only process data whose process ID numbers are given in *proclist*.

-u *uidlist*
  Lists only the process data for those user IDs or login names given in *uidlist*. In the listing, the numerical user ID will be printed unless you give the -f option, which prints the login name.

-g *grplist*
  Lists only the process data for those group leader's ID number(s) that appear in *grplist*. (A group leader is a process whose process ID number is identical to its process group ID number.)

    -s *sesslist*
        Lists information on all session leaders whose IDs appear in *sesslist*.

Under the -f option, ps tries to determine the command name and arguments given when the process was created by examining the user block. Failing this, the command name is printed as it would have appeared without the -f option, in square brackets.

The column headings and the meaning of the columns in a ps listing are given below; the letters f, l, and P indicate the option (full, long, or processor respectively) that causes the corresponding heading to appear; all means that the heading always appears. Note that these two options determine only what information is provided for a process; they do not determine which processes will be listed.

F	(1)	Flags (hexadecimal and additive) associated with the process:

        00   Process has terminated: process table entry now available.
        01   A system process: always in primary memory.
        02   Parent is tracing process.
        04   Tracing parent's signal has stopped process: parent is waiting [ptrace(2)].
        10   Process is currently in primary memory.
        20   Process currently in primary memory: locked until an event completes.

S	(1)	The state of the process:

        O   Process is executing on a processor.
        S   Sleeping: process is waiting for an event to complete.
        R   Runnable: process is on run queue.
        I   Idle: process is being created.
        Z   Zombie state: process terminated and parent not waiting.
        T   Traced: process stopped by a signal because parent is tracing it.
        X   SXBRK state: process is waiting for more primary memory.

UID	(f,l)	The user ID number of the process owner (the login name is printed under the -f option).
PID	(all)	The process ID of the process (the PID is necessary in order to kill a process).
PPID	(f,l)	The process ID of the parent process.
C	(f,l)	Processor utilization for scheduling. Not printed when the -c option is used.
CLS	(f,l)	Scheduling class. Printed only when the -c option is used.
PRI	(1)	The priority of the process. Without the -c option, higher numbers mean lower priority. With the -c option, higher numbers mean higher priority.

NI	(1)	Nice value, used in priority computation. Not printed when the -c option is used. Only processes in the time-sharing class have a nice value.
ADDR	(1)	The memory address of the process.
SZ	(1)	The size (in pages or clicks) of the swappable process's image in main memory.
WCHAN	(1)	The address of an event for which the process is sleeping, or in SXBRK state, (if blank, the process is executing).
STIME	(f)	The starting time of the process, given in hours, minutes, and seconds. (A process begun more than twenty-four hours before the ps inquiry is executed is given in months and days.)
TTY	(all)	The controlling terminal for the process. A ? is printed when there is no controlling terminal.
TIME	(all)	The cumulative execution time for the process.
COMMAND	(all)	The command name (the full command name and its arguments are printed under the -f option).
PSR	(P)	The processor binding. (For multi-processing only.)

A process that has exited and has a parent, but has not yet been waited for by the parent, is marked <defunct>.

FILES

```
/dev
/dev/sxt/*
/dev/tty*
/dev/xt/*       terminal ("tty") names searcher files
/dev/kmem       kernel virtual memory
/dev/swap       the default swap device
/dev/mem        memory
/etc/passwd     UID information supplier
/etc/ps_data    internal data structure
```

SEE ALSO

getty(1M), kill(1), nice(1), priocntl(1), ps(1).

NOTES

Your environment can change while ps is executing; the snap-shot it gives is true only for a split second, and it may not be accurate by the time you see it. Some data printed for defunct processes is irrelevant.

If no *termlist*, *proclist*, *uidlist*, or *grplist* is specified, ps checks stdin, stdout, and stderr in that order, looking for the controlling terminal, and will attempt to report on processes associated with the controlling terminal. In this situation, if stdin, stdout, and stderr are all redirected, ps will not find a controlling terminal, so there will be no report.

ps may report an lseek error and exit. ps may seek an invalid user area address: having obtained the address of a process' user area, ps may not be able to seek that address before the process exits and the address becomes invalid.

`ps -ef` may not report the actual start of a tty login session, but rather an earlier time, when a `getty` was last respawned on the tty line.

NAME

ps - display the status of current processes

SYNOPSIS

/usr/ucb/ps [-acglnrSuUvwx] [-t*term*] [*num*]

DESCRIPTION

The ps command displays information about processes. Normally, only those processes that are running with your effective user ID and are attached to a controlling terminal (see termio(4)) are shown. Additional categories of processes can be added to the display using various options. In particular, the -a option allows you to include processes that are not owned by you (that do not have your user ID), and the -x option allows you to include processes without control terminals. When you specify both -a and -x, you get processes owned by anyone, with or without a control terminal. The -r option restricts the list of processes printed to running and runnable processes.

ps displays the process ID, under PID; the control terminal (if any), under TT; the cpu time used by the process so far, including both user and system time, under TIME; the state of the process, under S; and finally, an indication of the COMMAND that is running.

The state is given by a single letter from the following:

O	Process is running on a processor.
S	Sleeping. Process is waiting for an event to complete.
R	Runnable. Process is on run queue.
I	Idle. Process is being created.
Z	Zombie state. Process terminated and parent not waiting.
T	Traced. Process stopped by a signal because parent is tracing it.
X	SXBRK state. Process is waiting for more primary memory.

The following options must all be combined to form the first argument:

-a   Include information about processes owned by others.

-c   Display the command name, as stored internally in the system for purposes of accounting, rather than the command arguments, which are kept in the process' address space. This is more reliable, if less informative, since the process is free to destroy the latter information.

-g   Display all processes. Without this option, ps only prints interesting processes. Processes are deemed to be uninteresting if they are process group leaders. This normally eliminates top-level command interpreters and processes waiting for users to login on free terminals.

-l   Display a long listing, with fields F, PPID, CP, PRI, NI, SZ, RSS and WCHAN as described below.

-n   Produce numerical output for some fields. In a user listing, the USER field is replaced by a UID field.

-r   Restrict output to running and runnable processes.

-S   Display accumulated CPU time used by this process and all of its reaped children.

-u	Display user-oriented output. This includes fields USER, SZ, RSS and START as described below.
-U	Update a private database where ps keeps system information.
-v	Display a version of the output containing virtual memory. This includes fields SIZE and RSS, described below.
-w	Use a wide output format (132 columns rather than 80); if repeated, that is, -ww, use arbitrarily wide output. This information is used to decide how much of long commands to print.
-x	Include processes with no controlling terminal.
-t*term*	List only process data associated with the terminal, *term*. Terminal identifiers may be specified in one of two forms: the device's file name (for example, tty04 or term/14) or, if the device's file name starts with tty, just the digit identifier (for example, 04).
num	A process number may be given, in which case the output is restricted to that process. This option must be supplied last.

DISPLAY FORMATS

Fields that are not common to all output formats:

USER	Name of the owner of the process.
NI	Process scheduling increment [see getpriority(3) and nice(3C)].
SIZE SZ	The combined size of the data and stack segments (in kilobyte units)
RSS	Real memory (resident set) size of the process (in kilobyte units).
UID	Numerical user-ID of process owner.
PPID	Numerical ID of parent of process.
CP	Short-term CPU utilization factor (used in scheduling).
PRI	The priority of the process (higher numbers mean lower priority).
START	The starting time of the process, given in hours, minutes, and seconds. A process begun more than 24 hours before the ps inquiry is executed is given in months and days.
WCHAN	The address of an event for which the process is sleeping, or in SXBRK state (if blank, the process is running).
F	Flags (hexadecimal and additive) associated with the process:

         00   Process has terminated. Process table now available.
         01   A system process, always in primary memory.
         02   Parent is tracing process.
         04   Tracing parent's signal has stopped process. Parent is waiting, see ptrace(2).
         08   Process is currently in primary memory.
         10   Process currently in primary memory, locked until an event is completed.

A process that has exited and has a parent, but has not yet been waited for by the parent is marked <defunct>; otherwise, ps tries to determine the command name and arguments given when the process was created by examining the user block.

FILES

```
/dev
/dev/sxt/*
/dev/tty*
/dev/xt/*                 terminal (tty) names searcher files
/dev/kmem                 kernel virtual memory
/dev/swap                 default swap device
/dev/mem                  memory
/etc/passwd               UID information supplier
/etc/ps_data              internal data structure
```

SEE ALSO

kill(1), whodo(1), lseek(2), getpriority(3), nice(3C).

NOTES

Things can change while ps is running; the picture it gives is only a close approximation to the current state. Some data printed for defunct processes is irrelevant.

If no *term* or *num* is specified, ps checks the standard input, the standard output, and the standard error in that order, looking for the controlling terminal and will attempt to report on processes associated with the controlling terminal. In this situation, if the standard input, the standard output, and the standard error are all redirected, ps will not find a controlling terminal, so there will be no report.

On a heavily loaded system, ps may report an lseek(2) error and exit. ps may seek to an invalid user area address, having obtained the address of process' user area, ps may not be able to seek to that address before the process exits and the address becomes invalid.

NAME

putdev - edits device table

SYNOPSIS

putdev -a *alias* [*attribute=value* [. . .]]

putdev -m *device attribute=value* [*attribute=value* [. . .]]

putdev -d *device* [*attribute* [. . .]]

DESCRIPTION

putdev can add a new device to the device table, modify an existing device description or remove a device entry from the table. The first synopsis is used to add a device. The second synopsis is used to modify existing entries by adding or changing attributes. If a specified attribute is not defined, this option adds that attribute to the device definition. If it is already defined, it modifies the attribute definition. The third synopsis is used to delete either an entire device entry or, if the attribute argument is used, to delete an attribute assignment for a device.

The options and arguments for this command are:

-a	Adds a device to the device table using the specified attributes. The device must be referenced by its *alias*.
-m	Modifies a device entry in the device table. If an entry already exists, it adds any specified attributes that are not defined. It also modifies any attributes which already have a value with the value specified with this command.
-d	Removes a device from the device table, when executed without the *attributes* argument. Used with the *attribute* argument, it deletes the given attribute specification for *device* from the table.
alias	Designates the alias of the device to be added.
device	Designates the pathname or alias of the device whose attribute is to be added, modified, or removed.
attribute	Designates a device attribute to be added or modified. Can be any of the device attributes described under NOTES except alias. This prevents an accidental modification or deletion of a device's alias from the table.
value	Designates the value to be assigned to a device's attribute.

NOTES

The following list shows all of the attributes which can be defined for a device:

alias	The unique name by which a device is known. No two devices in the database may share the same alias name. The name is limited in length to 14 characters and should contain only alphanumeric characters and also the following special characters if they are escaped with a backslash: underscore (_), dollar sign ($), hyphen (-), and period (.).
bdevice	The pathname to the block special device node associated with the device, if any. The associated major/minor combination should be unique within the database and should match that associated with the cdevice field, if any. (It is the administrator's responsibility to ensure that these major/minor numbers are unique in the database.)

capacity	The capacity of the device or of the typical volume, if removable.
cdevice	The pathname to the character special device node associated with the device, if any. The associated major/minor combination should be unique within the database and should match that associated with the bdevice field, if any. (It is the administrator's responsibility to ensure that these major/minor numbers are unique in the database.)
cyl	Used by the command specified in the mkfscmd attribute.
desc	A description of any instance of a volume associated with this device (such as floppy diskette).
dpartlist	The list of disk slices associated with this device. Used only if type=disk. The list should contain device aliases, each of which must have type=dpart.
dparttype	The type of disk slice represented by this device. Used only if type=dpart. It should be either fs (for filesystem) or dp (for data slice).
erasecmd	The command string that, when executed, erases the device.
fmtcmd	The command string that, when executed, formats the device.
fsname	The filesystem name on the file system administered on this slice, as supplied to the /usr/sbin/labelit command. This attribute is specified only if type=dpart and dparttype=fs.
gap	Used by the command specified in the mkfscmd attribute.
mkfscmd	The command string that, when executed, places a file system on a previously formatted device.
mountpt	The default mount point to use for the device. Used only if the device is mountable. For disk slices where type=dpart and dparttype=fs, this attribute should specify the location where the slice is normally mounted.
nblocks	The number of blocks in the filesystem administered on this slice. Used only if type=dpart and dparttype=fs.
ninodes	The number of inodes in the filesystem administered on this slice. Used only if type=dpart and dparttype=fs.
norewind	The name of the character special device node that allows access to the serial device without rewinding when the device is closed.
pathname	Defines the pathname to an i-node describing the device (used for non-block or character device pathnames, such as directories).
type	A token that represents inherent qualities of the device. Standard types include: 9-track, ctape, disk, directory, diskette, dpart, and qtape.
volname	The volume name on the filesystem administered on this slice, as supplied to the /usr/sbin/labelit command. Used only if type=dpart and dparttype=fs.

volume   A text string used to describe any instance of a volume associated with this device. This attribute should not be defined for devices which are not removable.

ERRORS

The command will exit with one of the following values:

0 =   successful completion of the task.

1 =   command syntax incorrect, invalid option used, or internal error occurred.

2 =   device table could not be opened for reading or new device table could not be created.

3 =   if executed with the -a option, indicates that an entry in the device table with the alias *alias* already exits. If executed with the -m or -d options, indicates that no entry exists for device *device*.

4 =   indicates that -d was requested and one or more of the specified attributes were not defined for the device.

FILES

/etc/device.tab

SEE ALSO

devattr(1), putdgrp(1M)

NAME

putdgrp - edits device group table

SYNOPSIS

putdgrp [-d] *dgroup* [*device* [. . .]]

DESCRIPTION

putdgrp modifies the device group table. It performs two kinds of modification. It can modify the table by creating a new device group or removing a device group. It can also change group definitions by adding or removing a device from the group definition.

When the command is invoked with only a *dgroup* specification, the command adds the specified group name to the device group table if it does not already exist. If the -d option is also used with only the *dgroup* specification, the command deletes the group from the table.

When the command is invoked with both a *dgroup* and a *device* specification, it adds the given device name (or names) to the group definition. When invoked with both arguments and the -d option, the command deletes the device name (or names) from the group definition.

When the command is invoked with both a *dgroup* and a *device* specification and the device group does not exist, it creates the group and adds the specified devices to that new group.

The options and arguments for this command are:

-d   Deletes the group or, if used with *device*, the device from a group definition.

dgroup   Specifies a device group name.

device   Specifies the pathname or alias of the device that is to added to or deleted from the device group.

ERRORS

The command will exit with one of the following values:

0 = successful completion of the task.

1 = command syntax incorrect, invalid option used, or internal error occurred.

2 = device group table could not be opened for reading or a new device group table could not be created.

3 = if executed with the -d option, indicates that an entry in the device group table for the device group *dgroup* does not exist and so cannot be deleted. Otherwise, indicates that the device group *dgroup* already exists and cannot be added.

4 = if executed with the -d option, indicates that the device group *dgroup* does not have as members one or more of the specified devices. Otherwise, indicates that the device group *dgroup* already has one or more of the specified devices as members.

EXAMPLE

To add a new device group:

```
putdgrp floppies
```

To add a device to a device group:

```
putdgrp floppies diskette2
```

To delete a device group:

```
putdgrp -d floppies
```

To delete a device from a device group:

```
putdgrp -d floppies diskette2
```

FILES

```
/etc/dgroup.tab
```

SEE ALSO

listdgrp(1), putdev(1M).

NAME

pwck, grpck - password/group file checkers

SYNOPSIS

/usr/sbin/pwck [*file*]
/usr/sbin/grpck [*file*]

DESCRIPTION

pwck scans the password file and notes any inconsistencies. The checks include validation of the number of fields, login name, user ID, group ID, and whether the login directory and the program-to-use-as-shell exist. The default password file is /etc/passwd.

grpck verifies all entries in the group file. This verification includes a check of the number of fields, group name, group ID, whether any login names belong to more than NGROUPS_MAX groups and that all login names appear in the password file. The default group file is /etc/group.

FILES

/etc/group
/etc/passwd

SEE ALSO

group(4), passwd(4)

DIAGNOSTICS

Group entries in /etc/group with no login names are flagged.

NAME

pwck - check password database entries

SYNOPSIS

/usr/ucb/pwck [*filename*]

DESCRIPTION

pwck checks a password file for errors. If specified, *filename* is checked, otherwise /etc/passwd is checked.

This command differs from /usr/sbin/pwck in its ability to correctly parse YP entries in /etc/passwd.

DIAGNOSTICS

Too many/few fields
> An entry in the password file does not have the proper number of fields.

No login name
> The login name field of an entry is empty.

Bad character(s) in login name
> The login name in an entry contains characters other than lower-case letters and digits.

First char in login name not lower case alpha
> The login name in an entry does not begin with a lower-case letter.

Login name too long
> The login name in an entry has more than 8 characters.

Invalid UID
> The user ID field in an entry is not numeric or is greater than 65535.

Invalid GID
> The group ID field in an entry is not numeric or is greater than 65535.

No login directory
> The login directory field in an entry is empty.

Login directory not found
> The login directory field in an entry refers to a directory that does not exist.

Optional shell file not found.
> The login shell field in an entry refers to a program or shell script that does not exist.

No netgroup name
> The entry is a Yellow Pages entry referring to a netgroup, but no netgroup is present.

Bad character(s) in netgroup name
> The netgroup name in a Yellow Pages entry contains characters other than lower-case letters and digits.

First char in netgroup name not lower case alpha
> The netgroup name in a Yellow pages entry does not begin with a lower-case letter.

FILES

    /etc/passwd

SEE ALSO

    group(4), passwd(4).

NAME

    pwconv - install and update `/etc/shadow` with information from `/etc/passwd`

SYNOPSIS

    pwconv

DESCRIPTION

    The pwconv command creates and updates `/etc/shadow` with information from `/etc/passwd`.

    If the `/etc/shadow` file does not exist, pwconv creates `/etc/shadow` with information from `/etc/passwd`. The command populates `/etc/shadow` with the user's login name, password, and password aging information. If password aging information does not exist in `/etc/passwd` for a given user, none is added to `/etc/shadow`. However, the last changed information is always updated.

    If the `/etc/shadow` file does exist, the following tasks are performed:

        Entries that are in the `/etc/passwd` file and not in the `/etc/shadow` file are added to the `/etc/shadow` file.

        Entries that are in the `/etc/shadow` file and not in the `/etc/passwd` file are removed from `/etc/shadow`.

        Password attributes (for example, password and aging information) in an `/etc/passwd` entry are moved to the corresponding entry in `/etc/shadow`.

    The pwconv program is a privileged system command that cannot be executed by ordinary users.

FILES

    `/etc/passwd`, `/etc/shadow`, `/etc/opasswd`, `/etc/oshadow`

SEE ALSO

    passwd(1), passmgmt(1M)

DIAGNOSTICS

    The pwconv command exits with one of the following values:

        0   Success.
        1   Permission denied.
        2   Invalid command syntax.
        3   Unexpected failure. Conversion not done.
        4   Unexpected failure. Password file(s) missing.
        5   Password file(s) busy. Try again later.

NAME

pwd - working directory name

SYNOPSIS

pwd

DESCRIPTION

pwd prints the path name of the working (current) directory.

SEE ALSO

cd(1)

DIAGNOSTICS

"Cannot open .." and "Read error in .." indicate possible file system trouble and should be referred to a UNIX system administrator.

NOTES

If you move the current directory or one above it, pwd may not give the correct response. Use the cd(1) command with a full path name to correct this situation.

NAME

quot - summarize file system ownership

SYNOPSIS

quot [-acfhnv] [*filesystem*]

DESCRIPTION

quot displays the number of blocks (1024 bytes) in the named *filesystem* currently owned by each user. There is a limit of 2048 blocks. Files larger than this will be counted as a 2048 block file, but the total blocks count will be correct.

The options are:

-a   Generate a report for all mounted file systems.

-c   Display three columns giving a file size in blocks, the number of files of that size, and a cumulative total of blocks containing files of that size or a smaller size. Files exceeding 499 blocks are listed as 499 blocks. The last line always lists 499 blocks, even if there are no files of that size.

-f   Display count of number of files as well as space owned by each user. This option is incompatible with the -c and -v options.

-h   Estimate the number of blocks in the file — this does not account for files with holes in them.

-n   Attach names to the list of files read from standard input. quot -n cannot be used alone, because it expects data from standard input. For example, the pipeline

```
ncheck filesystem | sort +0n | quot -n filesystem
```

will produce a list of all files and their owners. This option is incompatible with all other options.

-v   In addition to the default output, display three columns containing the number of blocks not accessed in the last 30, 60, and 90 days.

NOTES

This command may only be used by a privileged user.

FILES

/etc/mnttab	mounted file systems
/etc/passwd	to get user names

SEE ALSO

du(1M)

NAME

quota - display a user's disk quota and usage

SYNOPSIS

quota [-v] [*username*]

DESCRIPTION

quota displays users' disk usage and limits. Only a privileged user may use the optional *username* argument to view the limits of other users.

quota without options displays only warnings about mounted file systems where usage is over quota. Remotely mounted file systems which do not have quotas turned on are ignored.

username can be numeric, corresponding to the uid of a user.

The -v option displays user's quotas on all mounted file systems where quotas exist.

FILES

/etc/mnttab   list of currently mounted filesystems

SEE ALSO

edquota(1M), quotaon(1M)

NAME

random - generate a random number

SYNOPSIS

random [-s] [*scale*]

DESCRIPTION

random generates a random number on the standard output, and returns the number as its exit value. By default, this number is either 0 or 1. If *scale* is given a value between 1 and 255, then the range of the random value is from 0 to *scale*. If *scale* is greater than 255, an error message is printed.

When the -s (silent) option is given, then the random number is returned as an exit value, but is not printed on the standard output. If an error occurs, random returns an exit value of zero.

SEE ALSO

rand(3C)

NOTES

This command does not perform any floating point computations. random uses the time of day as a seed.

NAME

rarpd - DARPA Reverse Address Resolution Protocol server

SYNOPSIS

rarpd *interface* [*hostname*]

```
/usr/sbin/rarpd -a
```

DESCRIPTION

rarpd starts a daemon that responds to Reverse Address Resolution Protocol (RARP) requests. The daemon forks a copy of itself that runs in background. It must be run as root.

RARP is used by machines at boot time to discover their Internet Protocol (IP) address. The booting machine provides its Ethernet Address in a RARP request message. Using the ethers and hosts databases, rarpd maps this Ethernet Address into the corresponding IP address which it returns to the booting machine in an RARP reply message. The booting machine must be listed in both databases for rarpd to locate its IP address. rarpd issues no reply when it fails to locate an IP address.

In the first synopsis, the *interface* parameter names the network interface upon which rarpd is to listen for requests. The *interface* parameter takes the "name unit" form used by ifconfig(1M). The second argument, *hostname*, is used to obtain the IP address of that interface. An IP address in "decimal dot" notation may be used for *hostname*. If *hostname* is omitted, the address of the interface will be obtained from the kernel. When the first form of the command is used, rarpd must be run separately for each interface on which RARP service is to be supported. A machine that is a router may invoke rarpd multiple times, for example:

```
/usr/sbin/rarpd 374_0 host
/usr/sbin/rarpd 374_1 host-backbone
```

In the second synopsis, rarpd locates all of the network interfaces present on the system and starts a daemon process for each one that supports RARP.

FILES

```
/etc/ethers
/etc/hosts
```

SEE ALSO

ifconfig(1M), ethers(4), hosts(4), netconfig(4), boot(8).

Finlayson, Ross, Timothy Mann, Jeffrey Mogul, and Marvin Theimer, *A Reverse Address Resolution Protocol*, RFC 903, Network Information Center, SRI International, Menlo Park, Calif., June 1984.

NAME

rc0 - run commands performed to stop the operating system

SYNOPSIS

`/sbin/rc0`

DESCRIPTION

This file is executed at each system state change that needs to have the system in an inactive state. It is responsible for those actions that bring the system to a quiescent state, traditionally called "shutdown".

There are three system states that require this procedure. They are state 0 (the system halt state), state 5 (the firmware state), and state 6 (the reboot state). Whenever a change to one of these states occurs, the rc0 procedure is run. The entry in `/etc/inittab` might read:

```
s0:056:wait:/sbin/rc0 >/dev/console 2>&1 </dev/console
```

Some of the actions performed by rc0 are carried out by files in the directory `/usr/sbin/shutdown.d` and files beginning with K in `/sbin/rc0.d`. These files are executed in ASCII order (see FILES below for more information), terminating some system service. The combination of commands in rc0 and files in `/usr/sbin/shutdown.d` and `/sbin/rc0.d` determines how the system is shut down.

The recommended sequence for rc0 is:

Stop System Services and Daemons.

> Various system services (such as LP Spooler) are gracefully terminated.

> When new services are added that should be terminated when the system is shut down, the appropriate files are installed in `/usr/sbin/shutdown.d` and `/sbin/rc0.d`.

Terminate Processes

> SIGTERM signals are sent to all running processes by killall(1M). Processes stop themselves cleanly if sent SIGTERM.

Kill Processes

> SIGKILL signals are sent to all remaining processes; no process can resist SIGKILL.

> At this point the only processes left are those associated with rc0 and processes 0 and 1, which are special to the operating system.

Unmount All File Systems

> Only the root file system (/) remains mounted.

Depending on which system state the systems end up in (0, 5, or 6), the entries in `/etc/inittab` will direct what happens next. If the `/etc/inittab` has not defined any other actions to be performed as in the case of system state 0, then the operating system will have nothing to do. It should not be possible to get the

system's attention. The only thing that can be done is to turn off the power or possibly get the attention of a firmware monitor. The command can be used only by
the super-user.

FILES

The execution by `/usr/bin/sh` of any files in `/usr/sbin/shutdown.d` occurs in
ASCII sort-sequence order. See `rc2`(1M) for more information.

SEE ALSO

`killall`(1M), `rc2`(1M), `shutdown`(1M), `inittab`(4)

NAME

`rc1` - run commands to bring system to administrative state

SYNOPSIS

`/sbin/rc1`

DESCRIPTION

The shell script `rc1` is run whenever a transition to run state 1 is requested either through `init 1` or `shutdown -i 1`.

File systems required for multi-user operations will be mounted at the end of `rc1`.

Entering this state is only meaningful when the system is coming up from the firmware state or the single-user state. When entering this state from the multi-user state [see rc2(1M)], no processes are killed and no services are stopped.

Note that in this state, logins requiring access to multi-user file systems can be used, but other multi-user services are unavailable.

SEE ALSO

`init`(1M), `rc0`(1M), `rc2`(1M), `shutdown`(1M), `inittab`(4).

NAME

rc2 - run commands performed for multi-user environment

SYNOPSIS

```
/sbin/rc2
```

DESCRIPTION

This file is executed via an entry in `/etc/inittab` and is responsible for those initializations that bring the system to a ready-to-use state, traditionally state 2, called the "multi-user" state.

The actions performed by `rc2` are found in files in the directory `/etc/rc.d` and files beginning with S in `/etc/rc2.d`. These files are executed by `/usr/bin/sh` in ASCII sort-sequence order (see FILES for more information). When functions are added that need to be initialized when the system goes multi-user, an appropriate file should be added in `/etc/rc2.d`.

The functions done by the `rc2` command and associated `/etc/rc2.d` files include:

Setting and exporting the TIMEZONE variable.

Setting-up and mounting the user (`/usr`) file system.

Cleaning up (remaking) the `/tmp` and `/var/tmp` directories.

Loading the network interface and ports cards with program data and starting the associated processes.

Starting the `cron` daemon by executing `/usr/sbin/cron`.

Cleaning up (deleting) uucp locks status, and temporary files in the `/var/spool/uucp` directory.

Other functions can be added, as required, to support the addition of hardware and software features.

EXAMPLES

The following are prototypical files found in `/etc/rc2.d`. These files are prefixed by an S and a number indicating the execution order of the files.

```
MOUNTFILESYS
        #    Set up and mount file systems
        cd /
        /sbin/mountall /etc/fstab

RMTMPFILES
        #  clean up /tmp
        rm -rf /tmp
        mkdir /tmp
        chmod 777 /tmp
        chgrp sys /tmp
        chown sys /tmp

uucp
        #    clean-up uucp locks, status, and temporary files
        rm -rf /var/spool/locks/*
```

The file `/etc/TIMEZONE` is included early in `rc2`, thus establishing the default time zone for all commands that follow.

FILES

Here are some hints about files in `/etc/rc.d`:

The order in which files are executed is important. Since they are executed in ASCII sort-sequence order, using the first character of the file name as a sequence indicator will help keep the proper order. Thus, files starting with the following characters would be:

[0-9].	very early
[A-Z].	early
[a-n].	later
[o-z].	last

Files in `/etc/rc.d` that begin with a dot (`.`) will not be executed. This feature can be used to hide files that are not to be executed for the time being without removing them. The command can be used only by a privileged user.

Files in `/etc/rc2.d` must begin with an `S` or a `K` followed by a number and the rest of the file name. Upon entering run level 2, files beginning with `S` are executed with the `start` option; files beginning with `K`, are executed with the `stop` option. Files beginning with other characters are ignored.

SEE ALSO

`shutdown`(1M), `inittab`(4)

NAME

rc3 - run commands to start distributed file sharing

SYNOPSIS

/sbin/rc3

DESCRIPTION

The shell script rc3 is run whenever a transition to run state 3 is requested either through init 3 or shutdown -i 3.

This state initializes networking and distributed file sharing operations.

SEE ALSO

init(1M), rc0(1M), rc2(1M), shutdown(1M), inittab(4).

NAME

rc6 - run commands performed to stop and reboot the operating system

SYNOPSIS

`/sbin/rc6`

DESCRIPTION

The shell script rc6 is run whenever a transition to run state 6 is requested either through `init 6` or `shutdown -i6`.

The sequence of events in rc6 is as follows:

Unmount all file systems.

`init` executes the `initdefault` entry in the `/etc/inittab` file to bring the system to the operating state defined by that entry.

SEE ALSO

init(1M), rc0(1M), rc2(1M), shutdown(1M), inittab(4).

NAME

rcp - remote file copy

SYNOPSIS

rcp [-p] *filename1 filename2*
rcp [-pr] *filename...directory*

DESCRIPTION

The rcp command copies files between machines. Each *filename* or *directory* argument is either a remote file name of the form:

hostname:path

or a local file name (containing no : characters, or a / before any : characters).

If a *filename* is not a full path name, it is interpreted relative to your home directory on *hostname*. A *path* on a remote host may be quoted (using \ , " , or ') so that the metacharacters are interpreted remotely.

rcp does not prompt for passwords; your current local user name must exist on *hostname* and allow remote command execution by rsh(1).

rcp handles third party copies, where neither source nor target files are on the current machine. Hostnames may also take the form

username@hostname:filename

to use *username* rather than your current local user name as the user name on the remote host. rcp also supports Internet domain addressing of the remote host, so that:

username@host.domain:filename

specifies the username to be used, the hostname, and the domain in which that host resides. Filenames that are not full path names will be interpreted relative to the home directory of the user named *username*, on the remote host.

The destination hostname may also take the form *hostname.username:filename* to support destination machines that are running older versions of rcp.

The following options are available:

-p   Attempt to give each copy the same modification times, access times, and modes as the original file.

-r   Copy each subtree rooted at *filename*; in this case the destination must be a directory.

FILES

$HOME/.profile

SEE ALSO

ftp(1), rlogin(1), rsh(1), hosts.equiv(4).

NOTES

rcp is meant to copy between different hosts; attempting to rcp a file onto itself, as with:

```
rcp tmp/file myhost:/tmp/file
```

results in a severely corrupted file.

rcp does not detect all cases where the target of a copy might be a file in cases where only a directory should be legal.

rcp can become confused by output generated by commands in a $HOME/.profile on the remote host.

rcp requires that the source host have permission to execute commands on the remote host when doing third-party copies.

If you forget to quote metacharacters intended for the remote host you get an incomprehensible error message.

If you are copying a directory to a remote machine, rcp -r behaves differently if the directory name ends with a slash (/). If the directory name is specified without a slash, rcp creates a new directory with that name on the remote machine and puts the contents of the local directory into the newly created remote directory. If the directory name ends with a slash, rcp copies the contents of the local directory but does not create a new directory on the remote machine.

For example, assume that your local machine has the directory stuff that contains file1 and file2. You are copying this directory to /tmp/things on the remote machine. The command

```
rcp -r stuff remote:/tmp/things
```

would create this directory structure:

```
remote:/tmp/things/stuff/file1
remote:/tmp/things/stuff/file2
```

On the other hand, the command

```
rcp -r stuff/ remote:/tmp/things
```

would create this directory structure:

```
remote:/tmp/things/file1
remote:/tmp/things/file2
```

NAME

rdate - set system date from a remote host

SYNOPSIS

rdate *hostname*

DESCRIPTION

rdate sets the local date and time from the *hostname* given as an argument. You must be super-user on the local system. Typically rdate can be inserted as part of a startup script.

NAME

readfile, longline - reads file, gets longest line

SYNOPSIS

readfile *file*

longline [*file*]

DESCRIPTION

The readfile function reads *file* and copies it to *stdout*. No translation of NEW-LINE is done. It keeps track of the longest line it reads and if there is a subsequent call to longline, the length of that line, including the NEWLINE character, is returned.

The longline function returns the length, including the NEWLINE character, of the longest line in *file*. If *file* is not specified, it uses the file named in the last call to readfile.

EXAMPLES

Here is a typical use of readfile and longline in a text frame definition file:

```
        .
        .
        .
    text="`readfile myfile`"
    columns=`longline`
        .
        .
        .
```

DIAGNOSTICS

If *file* does not exist, readfile will return FALSE (that is, the expression will have an error return).

longline returns 0 if a readfile has not previously been issued.

NOTES

More than one descriptor can call readfile in the same frame definition file. In text frames, if one of those calls is made from the text descriptor, then a subsequent use of longline will always get the longest line of the file read by the readfile associated with the text descriptor, even if it was not the most recent use of readfile.

SEE ALSO

cat(1)

NAME

reboot - restart the operating system

SYNOPSIS

`/usr/ucb/reboot` [`-dnq`] [*boot arguments*]

DESCRIPTION

`reboot` restarts the kernel. The kernel is loaded into memory by the PROM monitor, which transfers control to it.

Although `reboot` can be run by the privileged user at any time, `shutdown`(1M) is normally used first to warn all users logged in of the impending loss of service. See `shutdown`(1M) for details.

`reboot` performs a `sync`(1) operation on the disks, and then a multiuser reboot is initiated. See `init`(1M) for details.

`reboot` normally logs the reboot to the system log daemon, `syslogd`(1M), and places a shutdown record in the login accounting file `/var/adm/wtmp`. These actions are inhibited if the `-n` or `-q` options are present.

The following options are available:

`-d`   Dump system core before rebooting. This option is provided for compatibility, but is not supported by the underlying `reboot`(3) call.

`-n`   Avoid the `sync`(1). It can be used if a disk or the processor is on fire.

`-q`   Quick. Reboots quickly and ungracefully, without first shutting down running processes.

boot arguments
These arguments are accepted for compatibility, but are ignored by `reboot`. See `boot`(1M) for details.

Power Fail and Crash Recovery

Normally, the system will reboot itself at power-up or after crashes.

FILES

`/var/adm/wtmp`   login accounting file

SEE ALSO

`halt`(1M), `syslogd`(1M), `boot`(1M), `crash`(1M), `fsck`(1M), `init`(1M), `shutdown`(1M), `sync`(1M), `reboot`(3).

NAME

refer - expand and insert references from a bibliographic database

SYNOPSIS

/usr/ucb/refer [-b] [-e] [-n] [-a*r*] [-c*string*] [-k*x*] [-l*m,n*]
    [-p *filename*] [-s*keys*] *filename* . . .

DESCRIPTION

refer is a preprocessor for nroff(1), or troff(1), that finds and formats references. The input files (standard input by default) are copied to the standard output, except for lines between '. [' and '.]' command lines. Such lines are assumed to contain keywords as for lookbib(1), and are replaced by information from a bibliographic data base. The user can avoid the search, override fields from it, or add new fields. The reference data, from whatever source, is assigned to a set of troff strings. Macro packages such as ms(7) print the finished reference text from these strings. A flag is placed in the text at the point of reference. By default, the references are indicated by numbers.

When refer is used with eqn(1), neqn, or tbl(1), refer should be used first in the sequence, to minimize the volume of data passed through pipes.

The following options are available:

-b   Bare mode — do not put any flags in text (neither numbers or labels).

-e   Accumulate references instead of leaving the references where encountered, until a sequence of the form:

          . [
          $LIST$
          .]

      is encountered, and then write out all references collected so far. Collapse references to the same source.

-n   Do not search the default file.

-a*r*   Reverse the first *r* author names (Jones, J. A. instead of J. A. Jones). If *r* is omitted, all author names are reversed.

-c*string*
      Capitalize (with SMALL CAPS) the fields whose key-letters are in *string*.

-k*x*   Instead of numbering references, use key labels as specified in a reference data line beginning with the characters %*x*; By default, %*x* is %L.

-l*m,n* Instead of numbering references, use labels from the senior author's last name and the year of publication. Only the first *m* letters of the last name and the last *n* digits of the date are used. If either of *m* or *n* is omitted, the entire name or date, respectively, is used.

-p *filename*
      Take the next argument as a file of references to be searched. The default file is searched last.

-s*keys* Sort references by fields whose key-letters are in the *keys* string, and permute reference numbers in the text accordingly. Using this option implies the -e option. The key-letters in *keys* may be followed by a number indicating how many such fields are used, with a + sign taken as a very large number. The default is AD, which sorts on the senior author and date. To sort on all authors and then the date, for instance, use the options '-sA+T'.

FILES

```
/usr/ucblib/reftools/papers    default publication lists and indexes
/usr/ucblib/reftools           programs
```

SEE ALSO

addbib(1), eqn(1), indxbib(1), lookbib(1), nroff(1), roffbib(1), sortbib(1), tbl(1), troff(1)

NAME

regcmp - regular expression compile

SYNOPSIS

regcmp [-] *file* ...

DESCRIPTION

The regcmp command performs a function similar to regcmp(3G) and, in most cases, precludes the need for calling regcmp from C programs. Bypassing regcmp saves on both execution time and program size. The command regcmp compiles the regular expressions in *file* and places the output in *file*.i. If the - option is used, the output is placed in *file*.c. The format of entries in *file* is a name (C variable) followed by one or more blanks followed by one or more regular expressions enclosed in double quotes. The output of regcmp is C source code. Compiled regular expressions are represented as extern char vectors. *file*.i files may be #included in C programs, or *file*.c files may be compiled and later loaded. In the C program that uses the regcmp output, regex(abc,line) applies the regular expression named abc to line. Diagnostics are self-explanatory.

EXAMPLES

```
name      "([A-Za-z][A-Za-z0-9_]*)$0"

telno     "\({0,1}([2-9][01][1-9])$0\){0,1} *"
          "([2-9][0-9]{2})$1[ -]{0,1}"
          "([0-9]{4})$2"
```

The three arguments to telno shown above must all be entered on one line.

In the C program that uses the regcmp output,

```
regex(telno, line, area, exch, rest)
```

applies the regular expression named telno to line.

INTERNATIONAL FUNCTIONS

regcmp compiles regular expressions based on characters, not bytes, as regcmp(3G) in the *Programmer's Reference Manual* does. Regular expression in the *file* can include characters from supplementary code sets.

SEE ALSO

regcmp(3G).

NAME

regex - match patterns against a string

SYNOPSIS

regex [-e] [-v "*string*"] [*pattern template*] ... *pattern* [*template*]

DESCRIPTION

The regex command takes a string from *stdin*, and a list of *pattern* / *template* pairs, and runs regex(3X) to compare the string against each *pattern* until there is a match. When a match occurs, regex writes the corresponding *template* to *stdout* and returns TRUE. The last (or only) *pattern* does not need a template. If that is the pattern that matches the string, the function simply returns TRUE. If no match is found, regex returns FALSE.

-e   means regex will evaluate the corresponding template and write the result to *stdout*.

-v "*string*"   If -v is specified, *string* will be used instead of *stdin* to match against patterns.

The argument *pattern* is a regular expression of the form described in regex(3X). In most cases *pattern* should be enclosed in single quotes to turn off special meanings of characters. Note that only the final *pattern* in the list may lack a *template*.

The argument *template* may contain the strings $m0 through $m9, which will be expanded to the part of *pattern* enclosed in (...)$0 through (...)$9 constructs (see examples below). Note that if you use this feature, you must be sure to enclose *template* in single quotes so that FMLI doesn't expand $m0 through $m9 at parse time. This feature gives regex much of the power of cut(1), paste(1), and grep(1), and some of the capabilities of sed(1). If there is no *template*, the default is "$m0$m1$m2$m3$m4$m5$m6$m7$m8$m9".

EXAMPLES

To cut the 4th through 8th letters out of a string (this example will output strin and return TRUE):

```
`regex -v "my string is nice" '^.{3}(.{5})$0' '$m0'`
```

In a form, to validate input to field 5 as an integer:

```
valid=`regex -v "$F5" '^[0-9]+$'`
```

In a form, to translate an environment variable which contains one of the numbers 1, 2, 3, 4, 5 to the letters a, b, c, d, e:

```
value=`regex -v "$VAR1" 1 a 2 b 3 c 4 d 5 e '.*' 'Error'`
```

Note the use of the pattern '.*' to mean "anything else."

In the example below, all three lines constitute a single backquoted expression. This expression, by itself, could be put in a menu definition file. Since backquoted expressions are expanded as they are parsed, and output from a backquoted expression (the cat command, in this example) becomes part of the definition file being parsed, this expression would read /etc/passwd and make a dynamic menu of all the login ids on the system.

```
`cat /etc/passwd | regex '^([^:]*)$0.*$' '
name=$m0
action=`message "$m0 is a user"`'`
```

DIAGNOSTICS

If none of the patterns matches, regex returns FALSE, otherwise TRUE.

NOTES

Patterns and templates must often be enclosed in single quotes to turn off the special meanings of characters. Especially if you use the $m0 through $m9 variables in the template, since FMLI will expand the variables (usually to "") before regex even sees them.

Single characters in character classes (inside [ ]) must be listed before character ranges, otherwise they will not be recognized. For example, [a-zA-Z_/] will not find underscores (_) or slashes (/), but [_/a-zA-Z] will.

The regular expressions accepted by regcmp differ slightly from other utilities (that is, sed, grep, awk, ed, and so on).

regex with the -e option forces subsequent commands to be ignored. In other words if a backquoted statement appears as follows:

```
`regex -e ...; command1; command2`
```

command1 and *command2* would never be executed. However, dividing the expression into two:

```
`regex -e ...``command1; command2`
```

would yield the desired result.

SEE ALSO

awk(1), cut(1), grep(1), paste(1), sed(1), regcmp(3), regex(3X).

NAME

reinit - runs an initialization file

SYNOPSIS

reinit *file*

DESCRIPTION

The reinit command is used to change the values of descriptors defined in the initialization file that was named when fmli was invoked and/or define additional descriptors. FMLI will parse and evaluate the descriptors in *file,* and then continue running the current application. The argument *file* must be the name of a valid FMLI initialization file.

The reinit command does not re-display the introductory frame or change the layout of screen labels for function keys.

NAME

removef - remove a file from software database

SYNOPSIS

```
removef pkginst path1 [path2 ...]
removef -f pkginst
```

DESCRIPTION

removef informs the system that the user, or software, intends to remove a pathname. Output from removef is the list of input pathnames that may be safely removed (no other packages have a dependency on them).

After all files have been processed, removef should be invoked with the -f option to indicate that the removal phase is complete.

EXAMPLE

The following shows the use of removef in an optional pre-install script:

```
echo "The following files are no longer part of this package
      and are being removed."
removef $PKGINST /dev/xt[0-9][0-9][0-9] |
while read pathname
do
      echo "$pathname"
      rm -f $pathname
done
removef -f $PKGINST || exit 2
```

SEE ALSO

pkgmk(1), pkgproto(1), pkgtrans(1), pkgparam(3X), pkginfo(4).

NAME

renice - alter priority of running processes

SYNOPSIS

`/usr/ucb/renice` *priority pid* ...

`/usr/ucb/renice` *priority* [-p *pid* ...] [-g *pgrp* ...] [-u *username* ...]

DESCRIPTION

The `renice` command alters the scheduling priority of one or more running processes. By default, the processes to be affected are specified by their process IDs. *priority* is the new priority value.

The following options are available:

-p *pid* ...   Specify a list of process IDs.

-g *pgrp* ...   Specify a list of process group IDs. The processes in the specified process groups have their scheduling priority altered.

-u *user* ...   Specify a list of user IDs or usernames. All processes owned by each *user* have their scheduling altered.

Users other than the privileged user may only alter the priority of processes they own, and can only monotonically increase their nice value within the range 0 to 20. This prevents overriding administrative fiats. The privileged user may alter the priority of any process and set the priority to any value in the range -20 to 20. Useful priorities are: 19 (the affected processes will run only when nothing else in the system wants to), 0 (the base scheduling priority) and any negative value (to make things go very fast).

If only the priority is specified, the current process (alternatively, process group or user) is used.

FILES

`/etc/passwd`   map user names to user ID's

SEE ALSO

`priocntl`(1).

NOTES

If you make the priority very negative, then the process cannot be interrupted.

To regain control you must make the priority greater than zero.

Users other than the privileged user cannot increase scheduling priorities of their own processes, even if they were the ones that decreased the priorities in the first place.

The `priocntl` command subsumes the function of `renice`.

NAME

repquota - summarize quotas for a file system

SYNOPSIS

repquota [-v] *filesystem* . . .
repquota [-av]

DESCRIPTION

repquota prints a summary of the disk usage and quotas for the specified file systems. For each user the current number of files and amount of space (in kilobytes) is printed, along with any quotas created with edquota.

The options are:

-a   Report on all file systems that have "rq" in the mntopts field of the /etc/vfstab file.

-v   Report all quotas, even if there is no usage.

Only privileged users may view quotas which are not their own.

SEE ALSO

edquota(1M), quota(1M), quotacheck(1M), quotaon(1M)

NAME

reset - reset the current form field to its default values

SYNOPSIS

reset

DESCRIPTION

The reset function changes the entry in a field of a form to its default value; that is, the value displayed when the form was opened.

NAME

restore - initiate restores of filesystems, data slices, or disks

SYNOPSIS

restore [-o *target*] [-d *date*] [-mn] [-s | v] -P *partdev*

restore [-o *target*] [-d *date*] [-mn] [-s | v] -S *odevice*

restore [-o *target*] [-d *date*] [-mn] [-s | v] -A *partdev*

DESCRIPTION

restore posts requests for the restore of a data slice, a filesystem slice, or a disk from system-maintained archives. If the appropriate archive containing the required slice is online, the slice is restored immediately. If not, a request to restore the specified archive of the slice is posted to a restore status table. The restore status table is /etc/bkup/rsstatus.tab. The restore request is assigned a restore jobid that can be used to monitor the progress of the restore or to cancel it. A restore request that has been posted must later be resolved by an operator [see rsoper(1M)].

restore may be executed only by a user with superuser privilege.

If restore -A *partdev* is issued, the fdisk(1M) (full disk recovery) method is used to reslice and repopulate disk *partdev*. *partdev* is the name of the device that refers to the entire disk. For the supported DeltaSERIES reference platforms, it is /dev/rdsk/m328_c0d2s7.

Options

-d *date*	Restores the slice as of *date*. This may or may not be the latest archive. See getdate(1M) for valid date formats.
-m	If the restore cannot be carried out immediately, this option notifies the invoking user [via mail(1M)] when the request has been completed.
-n	Displays a list of all archived versions of the object contained in the backup history log, but does not attempt to restore the object.
-o *target*	Instead of restoring directly to the specified object (*partdev* or *fsdev*), this option restores the archive to *target*. *target* is of the form: [*oname*][: *odev*] where *oname* is the name of the filesystem to be restored to (for -S archives) and *odev* is the name of the slice to be restored to (for -P and -A archives).
-s	While a restore operation is occurring, displays a "." for each 100 (512-byte) blocks transferred from the destination device.
-v	Displays the name of each object as it is restored. Only those archiving methods that restore named directories and files (incfile, ffile) support this option.
-A *partdev*	Initiates restore of the entire disk *partdev*.
-P *partdev*	Initiates restore of the data slice *partdev*.
-S *odevice*	Initiates restore of the filesystem slice *odevice*.

DIAGNOSTICS

The exit codes for restore are the following:

0 = the task completed successfully
1 = one or more parameters to restore are invalid
2 = an error has occurred, causing restore to fail to
    complete *all* portions of its task

EXAMPLES

Example 1:

```
restore -m -S /usr
```

posts a request to restore the most current archived version of /usr. If the restore cannot be carried out immediately, notify the invoking user when the request has been completed.

Example 2:

```
restore -o /dev/rdsk/m328_c0d2s7 -P /dev/rdsk/m328_c0d3s7
```

posts a request that the archived data slice /dev/rdsk/m328_c0d3s7 be restored to the target device slice /dev/rdsk/m328_c0d2s7.

Example 3:

```
restore -d "december 1, 1987" -A /dev/rdsk/m328_c0d2s7
```

posts a request for the restore of the entire disk */dev/rdsk/m328_c0d2s7*. The restore should be made as of December 1, 1987.

Example 4:

```
restore -n -P /dev/rdsk/m328_c0d2s7
```

requests the system to display the backup date and an ls -1 listing from the backup history log of all archived versions of the data slice /dev/rdsk/m328_c0d2s7. The data slice is not restored.

FILES

/etc/bkup/bkhist.tab	lists the labels of all volumes that have been used for backup operations
/etc/bkup/rsstatus.tab	lists the status of all restore requests from users
/etc/bkup/rsnotify.tab	lists the email address of the operator to be notified whenever restore requests require operator intervention

SEE ALSO

fdisk(1M), mail(1M), rsnotify(1M), rsoper(1M), rsstatus(1M), urestore(1M), ursstatus(1M), getdate(3C).

NAME

rexecd - remote execution server

SYNOPSIS

in.rexecd *host.port*

DESCRIPTION

rexecd is the server for the rexec(3N) routine. The server provides remote execution facilities with authentication based on user names and encrypted passwords. It is invoked automatically as needed by inetd(1M), and then executes the following protocol:

1) The server reads characters from the socket up to a null (\0) byte. The resultant string is interpreted as an ASCII number, base 10.

2) If the number received in step 1 is non-zero, it is interpreted as the port number of a secondary stream to be used for the stderr. A second connection is then created to the specified port on the client's machine.

3) A null terminated user name of at most 16 characters is retrieved on the initial socket.

4) A null terminated, encrypted, password of at most 16 characters is retrieved on the initial socket.

5) A null terminated command to be passed to a shell is retrieved on the initial socket. The length of the command is limited by the upper bound on the size of the system's argument list.

6) rexecd then validates the user as is done at login time and, if the authentication was successful, changes to the user's home directory, and establishes the user and group protections of the user. If any of these steps fail the connection is aborted with a diagnostic message returned.

7) A null byte is returned on the connection associated with the stderr and the command line is passed to the normal login shell of the user. The shell inherits the network connections established by rexecd.

SEE ALSO

inetd(1M)

DIAGNOSTICS

All diagnostic messages are returned on the connection associated with the stderr, after which any network connections are closed. An error is indicated by a leading byte with a value of 1 (0 is returned in step 7 above upon successful completion of all the steps prior to the command execution).

username too long
: The name is longer than 16 characters.

password too long
: The password is longer than 16 characters.

command too long
: The command line passed exceeds the size of the argument list (as configured into the system).

`Login incorrect.`
> No password file entry for the user name existed.

`Password incorrect.`
> The wrong password was supplied.

`No remote directory.`
> The `chdir` command to the home directory failed.

`Try again.`
> A `fork` by the server failed.

`/usr/bin/sh: ...`
> The user's login shell could not be started.

NOTES

Indicating `Login incorrect` as opposed to `Password incorrect` is a security breach which allows people to probe a system for users with null passwords.

A facility to allow all data exchanges to be encrypted should be present.

NAME

`rfadmin` - Remote File Sharing domain administration

SYNOPSIS

`rfadmin`

`rfadmin` `-a` *hostname*

`rfadmin` `-r` *hostname*

`rfadmin` `-p` [-t *transport1,transport2, . . .*]

`rfadmin` `-q`

`rfadmin` `-o` *option*

DESCRIPTION

`rfadmin` is used to add and remove hosts, and their associated authentication information, from a *domain*/`passwd` file on a Remote File Sharing primary domain name server. It is also used to transfer domain name server responsibilities from one machine to another. Used with no options, `rfadmin` returns the *hostname* of the current domain name server for the local domain on each of the transport providers that span the domain.

`rfadmin` can only be used to modify domain files on the primary domain name server (`-a` and `-r` options). If domain name server responsibilities are temporarily passed to a secondary domain name server, that computer can use the `-p` option to pass domain name server responsibility back to the primary. The command can be directed to a specific set of transport providers by using the `-t` option with a comma-separated list of transport providers. Any host can use `rfadmin` with no options to print information about the domain. The user must have `root` permissions to use this command, except in the case when the -q option is used.

-a *hostname*	Add a host to a domain that is served by this domain name server. *hostname* must be of the form *domain.nodename*. It creates an entry for *hostname* in the *domain*/`passwd` file and prompts for an initial authentication password; the password prompting process conforms with that of `passwd`(1).
-r *hostname*	Remove a host, *hostname*, from its domain by removing it from the *domain*/`passwd file`.
-p	Used to pass the domain name server responsibilities back to a primary or to a secondary name server.
-t *transport1, transport2 . . .*	Select transport provider(s). The -t option is used only with the -p option.
-q	Tells if RFS is running.
-o *option*	Sets RFS system option. *option* is one of the following:
	`loopback` Enable loop back facility. This allows a resource advertised by a computer to be mounted by the same computer. `loopback` is off by default.

    `noloopback`   Turn off the loop back facility. `noloopback` is the default.

    `loopmode`   Check if the loop back facility is on or off.

ERRORS

When used with the *-a* option, if *hostname* is not unique in the domain, an error message will be sent to standard error.

When used with the *-r* option, if (1) *hostname* does not exist in the domain, (2) *hostname* is defined as a domain name server, or (3) there are resources advertised by *hostname*, an error message will be sent to standard error.

When used with the *-p* option to change the domain name server, if there are no backup name servers defined for *domain*, an error message will be sent to standard error.

FILES

`/etc/rfs/auth.info/`*domain*`/passwd`

For each *domain*, this file is created on the primary, copied to all secondaries, and copied to all hosts that want to do password verification of hosts in the *domain*.

SEE ALSO

`passwd`(1), `dname`(1M), `rfstart`(1M), `rfstop`(1M), `umount`(1M)

NAME

rfpasswd - change Remote File Sharing host password

SYNOPSIS

rfpasswd

DESCRIPTION

rfpasswd updates the Remote File Sharing authentication password for a host; processing of the new password follows the same criteria as passwd(1). The updated password is registered at the domain name server (/etc/rfs/auth.info/*domain*/passwd) and replaces the password stored at the local host (/etc/rfs/loc.passwd file).

This command is restricted to the super-user.

NOTE: If you change your host password, make sure that hosts that validate your password are notified of this change. To receive the new password, hosts must obtain a copy of the *domain*/passwd file from the domain's primary name server. If this is not done, attempts to mount remote resources may fail!

ERRORS

If (1) the old password entered from this command does not match the existing password for this machine, (2) the two new passwords entered from this command do not match, (3) the new password does not satisfy the security criteria in passwd(1), (4) the domain name server does not know about this machine, or (5) the command is not run with super-user privileges, an error message will be sent to standard error. Also, Remote File Sharing must be running on your host and your domain's primary name server. A new password cannot be logged if a secondary is acting as the domain name server.

FILES

/etc/rfs/auth.info/*domain*/passwd
/etc/rfs/loc.passwd

SEE ALSO

passwd(1), rfstart(1M), rfadmin(1M)

NAME

rfstart - start Remote File Sharing

SYNOPSIS

rfstart [-v] [-p *primary_addr*]

DESCRIPTION

rfstart starts Remote File Sharing and defines an authentication level for incoming requests. [This command can only be used after the domain name server is set up and your computer's domain name and network specification have been defined using dname(1M).]

-v   Specifies that verification of all clients is required in response to initial incoming mount requests; any host not in the file /etc/rfs/auth.info/*domain*/passwd for the domain they belong to, will not be allowed to mount resources from your host. If -v is not specified, hosts named in *domain*/passwd will be verified. Other hosts will be allowed to connect without verification.

-p *primary_addr*

Indicates the primary domain name server for your domain. *primary_addr* can specify any of the following: the network address of the primary name server for a domain (*addr*); a list of address tuples when RFS is used over multiple transport providers (*transport1:addr1,transport2:addr2, . . .*). An example of each type of specification follows:

-p *addr*
-p *transport1:addr1,transport2:addr2, . . .*

If the -p option is not specified, the address of the domain name server is taken from the associated rfmaster files. The -p *addr* specification is valid only when one transport provider is being used. See the rfmaster(1M) manual page for a description of the valid address syntax.

If the host password has not been set, rfstart will prompt for a password. The password prompting process must match the password entered for your machine at the primary domain name server [see rfadmin(1M)]. If you remove the loc.passwd file or change domains, you will also have to reenter the password.

Also, when rfstart is run on a domain name server, entries in the rfmaster(4) file are syntactically validated.

This command is restricted to the super-user.

ERRORS

If syntax errors are found when validating an rfmaster(4) file, a warning describing each error will be sent to standard error.

An error message will be sent to standard error if any of the following conditions are true:

1. remote file sharing is already running
2. there is no communications network
3. a domain name server cannot be found
4. a domain name server does not recognize the machine
5. the command is run without super-user privileges

Remote file sharing will not start if a host password in `/etc/rfs/<transport>/loc.passwd` is corrupted. If you suspect this has happened, remove the file and run `rfstart` again to reenter your password.

Note: `rfstart` will not fail if your host password does not match the password on the domain name server. You will simply receive a warning message. However, if you try to mount a resource from the primary, or any other host that validates your password, the mount will fail if your password does not match the one that the host has listed for your machine.

FILES

```
/etc/rfs/<transport>/rfmaster
/etc/rfs/<transport>/loc.passwd
```

SEE ALSO

`share`(1M), `dname`(1M), `idload`(1M), `mount`(1M), `rfadmin`(1M), `rfstop`(1M), `unshare`(1M), `rfmaster`(4).

NOTES

You must run `idload`(1M) to put any non-default user and group mappings into place.

NAME

`rfstop` - stop the Remote File Sharing environment

SYNOPSIS

`rfstop`

DESCRIPTION

`rfstop` disconnects a host from the Remote File Sharing environment until another `rfstart`(1M) is executed.

When executed on the domain name server, the domain name server responsibility is moved to a secondary name server as designated in the `rfmaster`(4) file. If there is no designated secondary name server `rfstop` will issue a warning message, Remote File Sharing will be stopped, and name service will no longer be available to the domain.

This command is restricted to the super-user.

ERRORS

If (1) there are resources currently advertised by this host, (2) resources from this machine are still remotely mounted by other hosts, (3) there are still remotely mounted resources in the local file system tree, (4) `rfstart`(1M) had not previously been executed, or (5) the command is not run with super-user privileges, an error message will be sent to standard error and Remote File Sharing will not be stopped.

SEE ALSO

`adv`(1M), `mount`(1M), `rfadmin`(1M), `rfstart`(1M), `unadv`(1M), `rfmaster`(4)

NAME

rfuadmin - Remote File Sharing notification shell script

SYNOPSIS

/etc/rfs/rfuadmin *message remote_resource* [*seconds*]

DESCRIPTION

The rfuadmin administrative shell script responds to unexpected Remote File Sharing events, such as broken network connections and forced unmounts, picked up by the rfudaemon process. This command is not intended to be run directly from the shell.

The response to messages received by rfudaemon can be tailored to suit the particular system by editing the rfuadmin script. The following paragraphs describe the arguments passed to rfuadmin and the responses.

disconnect *remote_resource*

> A link to a remote resource has been cut. rfudaemon executes rfuadmin, passing it the message disconnect and the name of the disconnected resource. rfuadmin sends this message to all terminals using wall(1):

> *Remote_resource* has been disconnected from the system.

> Then it executes fuser(1M) to kill all processes using the resource, unmounts the resource [umount(1M)] to clean up the kernel, and starts rmount to try to remount the resource.

fumount *remote_resource*

> A remote server machine has forced an unmount of a resource a local machine has mounted. The processing is similar to processing for a disconnect.

fuwarn *remote_resource seconds*

> This message notifies rfuadmin that a resource is about to be unmounted. rfudaemon sends this script the fuwarn message, the resource name, and the number of seconds in which the forced unmount will occur. rfuadmin sends this message to all terminals:

> *Remote_resource* is being removed from the system in # seconds.

INTERNATIONAL FUNCTIONS

The *message* can include characters from supplementary code sets.

SEE ALSO

fumount(1M), rmount(1M), rfudaemon(1M), rfstart(1M), wall(1).

NOTES

The console must be on when Remote File Sharing is running. If it's not, rfuadmin will hang when it tries to write to the console (wall) and recovery from disconnected resources will not complete.

NAME

rfudaemon - Remote File Sharing daemon process

SYNOPSIS

`/etc/rfs/rfudaemon`

DESCRIPTION

The `rfudaemon` command is started automatically by `rfstart`(1M) and runs as a daemon process as long as Remote File Sharing is active. Its function is to listen for unexpected events, such as broken network connections and forced unmounts, and execute appropriate administrative procedures.

When such an event occurs, `rfudaemon` executes the administrative shell script `rfuadmin`, with arguments that identify the event. This command is not intended to be run from the shell. Here are the events:

DISCONNECT A link to a remote resource has been cut. `rfudaemon` executes `rfuadmin`, with two arguments: `disconnect` and the name of the disconnected resource.

FUMOUNT A remote server machine has forced an unmount of a resource a local machine has mounted. `rfudaemon` executes `rfuadmin`, with two arguments: `fumount` and the name of the disconnected resource.

GETUMSG A remote user-level program has sent a message to the local `rfudae-mon`. Currently the only message sent is *fuwarn*, which notifies `rfuadmin` that a resource is about to be unmounted. It sends `rfuad-min` the *fuwarn*, the resource name, and the number of seconds in which the forced unmount will occur.

LASTUMSG The local machine wants to stop the `rfudaemon` [`rfstop`(1M)]. This causes `rfudaemon` to exit.

SEE ALSO

`rfstart`(1M), `rfuadmin`(1M)

NAME

`rlogin` - remote login

SYNOPSIS

`rlogin` [`-L`] [`-8`] [`-e` *c*] [`-l` *username*] *hostname*

DESCRIPTION

`rlogin` establishes a remote login session from your terminal to the remote machine named *hostname*.

Hostnames are listed in the *hosts* database, which may be contained in the `/etc/hosts` file, the Internet domain name server, or in both. Each host has one official name (the first name in the database entry), and optionally one or more nicknames. Either official hostnames or nicknames may be specified in *hostname*.

Each remote machine may have a file named `/etc/hosts.equiv` containing a list of trusted hostnames with which it shares usernames. Users with the same username on both the local and remote machine may `rlogin` from the machines listed in the remote machine's `/etc/hosts.equiv` file without supplying a password. Individual users may set up a similar private equivalence list with the file `.rhosts` in their home directories. Each line in this file contains two names: a *hostname* and a *username* separated by a space. An entry in a remote user's `.rhosts` file permits the user named *username* who is logged into *hostname* to log in to the remote machine as the remote user without supplying a password. If the name of the local host is not found in the `/etc/hosts.equiv` file on the remote machine, and the local username and hostname are not found in the remote user's `.rhosts` file, then the remote machine will prompt for a password. Hostnames listed in `/etc/hosts.equiv` and `.rhosts` files must be the official hostnames listed in the hosts database; nicknames may not be used in either of these files.

To counter security problems, the `.rhosts` file must be owned by either the remote user or by root.

The remote terminal type is the same as your local terminal type (as given in your environment TERM variable). The terminal or window size is also copied to the remote system if the server supports the option, and changes in size are reflected as well. All echoing takes place at the remote site, so that (except for delays) the remote login is transparent. Flow control using CTRL-S and CTRL-Q and flushing of input and output on interrupts are handled properly.

The following options are available:

`-L`   Allow the `rlogin` session to be run in litout mode.

`-8`   Pass eight-bit data across the net instead of seven-bit data.

`-e` *c*   Specify a different escape character, *c*, for the line used to disconnect from the remote host.

`-l` *username*
     Specify a different *username* for the remote login. If you do not use this option, the remote username used is the same as your local username.

Escape Sequences

Lines that you type which start with the tilde character are escape sequences (the escape character can be changed using the -e options):

~ .   Disconnect from the remote host — this is not the same as a logout, because the local host breaks the connection with no warning to the remote end.

susp   Suspend the login session (only if you are using a shell with Job Control). susp is your suspend character, usually CTRL-Z, see tty(1).

FILES

```
/etc/passwd
/usr/hosts/*          for hostname version of the command
/etc/hosts.equiv      list of trusted hostnames with shared usernames
$HOME/.rhosts         private list of trusted hostname/username combinations
```

SEE ALSO

rsh(1), stty(1), tty(1), named(1M), hosts(4), hosts.equiv(4).

NOTES

When a system is listed in hosts.equiv, its security must be as good as local security. One insecure system listed in hosts.equiv can compromise the security of the entire system.

If you use a windowing terminal and you intend to run layers(1) on the remote system, then you must invoke rlogin with the -8 option.

This implementation can only use the TCP network service.

NAME

rlogind - remote login server

SYNOPSIS

in.rlogind *host.port*

DESCRIPTION

rlogind is the server for the rlogin(1) program. The server provides a remote login facility with authentication based on privileged port numbers.

rlogind is invoked by inetd(1M) when a remote login connection is established, and executes the following protocol:

1)   The server checks the client's source port. If the port is not in the range 0-1023, the server aborts the connection. The client's address and port number are passed as arguments to rlogind by inetd in the form *host.port* with host in hexadecimal and port in decimal.

2)   The server checks the client's source address. If an entry for the client exists is both /etc/hosts and /etc/hosts.equiv, a user logging in from the client is not prompted for a password. If the address is associated with a host for which no corresponding entry exists in /etc/hosts, the user is prompted for a password, regardless of whether or not an entry for the client is present in /etc/hosts.equiv [see hosts(4) and hosts.equiv(4)].

Once the source port and address have been checked, rlogind allocates a pseudo-terminal and manipulates file descriptors so that the slave half of the pseudo-terminal becomes the stdin, stdout, and stderr for a login process. The login process is an instance of the login(1) program, invoked with the -r option. The login process then proceeds with the authentication process as described in rshd(1M), but if automatic authentication fails, it reprompts the user to login as one finds on a standard terminal line.

The parent of the login process manipulates the master side of the pseudo-terminal, operating as an intermediary between the login process and the client instance of the rlogin program. In normal operation, a packet protocol is invoked to provide Ctrl-S / Ctrl-Q type facilities and propagate interrupt signals to the remote programs. The login process propagates the client terminal's baud rate and terminal type, as found in the environment variable, TERM; see environ(4).

SEE ALSO

inetd(1M), hosts(4), hosts.equiv(4), resolv.conf(4).

DIAGNOSTICS

All diagnostic messages are returned on the connection associated with the stderr, after which any network connections are closed. An error is indicated by a leading byte with a value of 1.

Hostname for your address unknown.

No entry in the host name database existed for the client's machine.

Try again.

A *fork* by the server failed.

```
/usr/bin/sh: ...
```
The user's login shell could not be started.

NOTES

The authentication procedure used here assumes the integrity of each client machine and the connecting medium. This is insecure, but is useful in an ''open'' environment.

A facility to allow all data exchanges to be encrypted should be present.

It is possible for `rlogind` to respond slowly when Domain Name Service is in place and the primary nameserver is unreachable or slow to respond. If your nameserver or network is heavily loaded, refer to the `resolv.conf`(4) man page for details on how to configure DNS under these conditions.

NAME

rm, rmdir - remove files or directories

SYNOPSIS

rm [-f] [-i] *file* ...

rm -r [-f] [-i] dirname ... [*file* ...]

rmdir [-p] [-s] dirname ...

DESCRIPTION

rm removes the entries for one or more files from a directory. If a file has no write permission and the standard input is a terminal, the full set of permissions (in octal) for the file are printed followed by a question mark. This is a prompt for confirmation. If the answer begins with y (for yes), the file is deleted, otherwise the file remains.

If *file* is a symbolic link, the link will be removed, but the file or directory to which it refers will not be deleted. A user does not need write permission on a symbolic link to remove it, provided they have write permissions in the directory.

Note that if the standard input is not a terminal, the command will operate as if the -f option is in effect.

Three options apply to rm:

-f   This option causes the removal of all files (whether write-protected or not) in a directory without prompting the user. In a write-protected directory, however, files are never removed (whatever their permissions are), but no messages are displayed. If the removal of a write-protected directory is attempted, this option will not suppress an error message.

-r   This option causes the recursive removal of any directories and subdirectories in the argument list. The directory will be emptied of files and removed. Note that the user is normally prompted for removal of any write-protected files which the directory contains. The write-protected files are removed without prompting, however, if the -f option is used, or if the standard input is not a terminal and the -i option is not used.

Symbolic links that are encountered with this option will not be traversed.

If the removal of a non-empty, write-protected directory is attempted, the command will always fail (even if the -f option is used), resulting in an error message.

-i   With this option, confirmation of removal of any write-protected file occurs interactively. It overrides the -f option and remains in effect even if the standard input is not a terminal.

Two options apply to rmdir:

-p   This option allows users to remove the directory *dirname* and its parent directories which become empty. A message is printed on standard output about whether the whole path is removed or part of the path remains for some reason.

-s   This option is used to suppress the message printed on standard error when
      -p is in effect.

DIAGNOSTICS

All messages are generally self-explanatory.

It is forbidden to remove the files "." and ".." in order to avoid the consequences
of inadvertently doing something like the following:

```
rm -r .*
```

Both rm and rmdir return exit codes of 0 if all the specified directories are removed
successfully. Otherwise, they return a non-zero exit code.

SEE ALSO

unlink(2), rmdir(2).

NOTES

A -- permits the user to mark explicitly the end of any command line options,
allowing rm to recognize filename arguments that begin with a -. As an aid to BSD
migration, rm will accept - as a synonym for --. This migration aid may disappear
in a future release. If a -- and a - both appear on the same command line, the
second will be interpreted as a filename.

NAME
>   rmdel - remove a delta from an SCCS file

SYNOPSIS
>   rmdel -r*SID files*

DESCRIPTION
>   rmdel removes the delta specified by the *SID* (SCCS identification string) from each named SCCS file. The delta to be removed must be the newest (most recent) delta in its branch in the delta chain of each named SCCS file. In addition, the delta specified must not be that of a version being edited for the purpose of making a delta; that is, if a p-file exists for the named SCCS file [see get(1)], the delta specified must not appear in any entry of the p-file.
>
>   The -r option specifies the *SID* level of the delta to be removed.
>
>   If a directory is named, rmdel behaves as though each file in the directory were specified as a named file, except that non-SCCS files (last component of the path name does not begin with s.) and unreadable files are silently ignored. If a name of - is given, the standard input is read; each line of the standard input is taken to be the name of an SCCS file to be processed; non-SCCS files and unreadable files are silently ignored.
>
>   The rules governing the removal of a delta are as follows: if you make a delta and have appropriate file permissions, you can remove it; if you own the file and directory in which a new delta file resides, you can remove the delta.

FILES
>   x.file   [See delta(1)]
>   z.file   [See delta(1)]

SEE ALSO
>   delta(1), get(1), help(1), prs(1), sccsfile(4)

DIAGNOSTICS
>   Use help(1) for explanations.

NAME

rmntstat - display mounted resource information

SYNOPSIS

rmntstat [-h] [*resource*]

DESCRIPTION

When used with no options, rmntstat displays a list of all local Remote File Sharing resources that are remotely mounted, the local path name, and the corresponding clients. rmntstat returns the remote mount data regardless of whether a
resource is currently advertised; this ensures that resources that have been unad-
vertised but are still remotely mounted are included in the report. When a *resource*
is specified, rmntstat displays the remote mount information only for that
resource. The -h option causes header information to be omitted from the display.

EXIT STATUS

If no local resources are remotely mounted, rmntstat will return a successful exit
status.

ERRORS

If *resource* (1) does not physically reside on the local machine or (2) is an invalid
resource name, an error message will be sent to standard error.

SEE ALSO

mount(1M), fumount(1M), unadv(1M).

NAME

`rmnttry` - attempt to mount queued remote resources

SYNOPSIS

`/etc/rfs/rmnttry` [*resource...*]

DESCRIPTION

`rmnttry` sequences through the pending mount requests stored in `/etc/rfs/rmnttab`, trying to mount each resource. If a mount succeeds, the resource entry is removed from the `/etc/rfs/rmnttab` file.

If one or more resource names are supplied, mounts are attempted only for those resources, rather than for all pending mounts. Mounts are not attempted for resources not present in the `/etc/rfs/rmnttab` file (see `rmount`(1M)). If a mount invoked from `rmnttry` takes over 3 minutes to complete, `rmnttry` aborts the mount and issues a warning message.

`rmnttry` is typically invoked from a cron entry in `/var/spool/cron/crontabs/root` to attempt mounting queued resources at periodic intervals. The default strategy is to attempt mounts at 15 minute intervals. The cron entry for this is:

```
10,25,40,55 * * * * /etc/rfs/rmnttry >/dev/null
```

FILES

`/etc/rfs/rmnttab` pending mount requests

SEE ALSO

`crontab`(1), `mount`(1M), `rmount`(1M), `rumount`(1M), `mnttab`(4).

DIAGNOSTICS

An exit code of 0 is returned if all requested mounts succeeded, 1 is returned if one or more mounts failed, and 2 is returned for bad usage.

NAME

rmount - queue remote resource mounts

SYNOPSIS

`/usr/sbin/rmount` [-d[r] *resource directory*]

DESCRIPTION

`rmount` queues a remote resource for mounting. The command enters the resource request into `/etc/rfs/rmnttab`, which is formatted identically to `mnttab`(4). `rmnttry`(1M) is used to poll entries in this file.

When used without arguments, `rmount` prints a list of resources with pending mounts along with their destined directories, modes, and date of request. The resources are listed chronologically, with the oldest resource request appearing first.

The following options are available:

-d   indicates that the *resource* is a remote resource to be mounted on `directory`.

-r   indicates that the *resource* is to be mounted read-only. If the *resource* is write-protected, this flag must be used.

FILES

`/etc/rfs/rmnttab`   pending mount requests

SEE ALSO

`mount`(1M), `rmnttry`(1M), `rumount`(1M), `rmountall`(1M), `mnttab`(4)

DIAGNOSTICS

An exit code of 0 is returned upon successful completion of `rmount`. Otherwise, a non-zero value is returned.

NAME

rmountall, rumountall - mount, unmount Remote File Sharing resources

SYNOPSIS

/usr/sbin/rmountall [-] "*file-system-table*" [...]
/usr/sbin/rumountall [-k]

DESCRIPTION

rmountall is a Remote File Sharing command used to mount remote resources according to a *file-system-table*. (/etc/vfstab is the recommended *file-system-table*.) rmountall also invokes the rmnttry command, which attempts to mount queued resources. The special file name "-" reads from the standard input.

rumountall causes all mounted remote resources to be unmounted and deletes all resources that were queued from rmount. The -k option sends a SIGKILL signal, via fuser, to processes that have files open.

These commands may be executed only by the super-user.

The format of the *file-system-table* is as follows:

column 1   block special file name of file system

column 2   mount-point directory

column 3   -r if to be mounted read-only; -d if remote resource

column 4   file system type (not used with Remote File Sharing)

column 5+   ignored

Columns are separated by white space. Lines beginning with a pound sign (#) are comments. Empty lines are ignored.

SEE ALSO

fuser(1M), mount(1M), rfstart(1M), rmnttry(1M), rmount(1M), sysadm(1), signal(2).

DIAGNOSTICS

No messages are printed if the remote resources are mounted successfully.

Error and warning messages come from mount(1M).

NAME

roffbib - format and print a bibliographic database

SYNOPSIS

/usr/ucb/roffbib [-e] [-h] [-Q] [-x] [-m *filename*] [-np] [-o*list*]
      [-ra*N*] [-s*N*] [-T*term*] [*filename*] . . .

DESCRIPTION

The roffbib command prints out all records in a bibliographic database, in bibliography format rather than as footnotes or endnotes. Generally it is used in conjunction with sortbib(1):

      example% sortbib database | roffbib

If abstracts or comments are entered following the %X field key, roffbib will format them into paragraphs for an annotated bibliography. Several %X fields may be given if several annotation paragraphs are desired.

roffbib accepts all options understood by nroff(1) except -i and -q, as well as those listed below:

-e	Produce equally-spaced words in adjusted lines using full terminal resolution.
-h	Use output tabs during horizontal spacing to speed output and reduce output character count. TAB settings are assumed to be every 8 nominal character widths.
-Q	Queue output for the phototypesetter. Page offset is set to 1 inch.
-x	Suppress printing of abstracts.
-m *filename*	Prepend the macro file /usr/ucblib/doctools/tmac/tmac.name to the input files. There should be a space between the -m and the macro filename. This set of macros will replace the ones defined in /usr/ucblib/doctools/tmac/tmac.bib.
-n*p*	Number first generated page *p*.
-o*list*	Print only page numbers that appear in the comma-separated *list* of numbers and ranges. A range *N-M* means pages *N* through *M*; an initial -*N* means from the beginning to page *N*; a final *N*- means from page *N* to end.
-ra*N*	Set register *a* (one-character) to *N*. The command-line argument -rN1 will number the references starting at 1.
	Four command-line registers control formatting style of the bibliography, much like the number registers of ms(7). The flag -rV2 will double space the bibliography, while -rV1 will double space references but single space annotation paragraphs. The line length can be changed from the default 6.5 inches to 6 inches with the -rL6i argument, and the page offset can be set from the default of 0 to one inch by specifying -rO1i (capital O, not zero).
-s*N*	Halt prior to every *N* pages for paper loading or changing (default *N* =1). To resume, enter NEWLINE or RETURN.

-T*term*   Specify *term* as the terminal type.

FILES

`/usr/ucblib/doctools/tmac/tmac.bib`   file of macros used by `nroff/troff`

SEE ALSO

`addbib`(1), `indxbib`(1), `lookbib`(1), `nroff`(1) `refer`(1), `sortbib`(1), `troff`(1)

NOTES

Users have to rewrite macros to create customized formats.

NAME

    `route` - manually manipulate the routing tables

SYNOPSIS

    `route` [`-f`] [`-n`] [*command destination gateway* [*metric*]]

DESCRIPTION

The `route` program is used to manipulate the network routing tables manually. Normally, `route` is not needed, since the routing daemon, `routed` will manage the system Routing Table and therefore would handle this function.

If the `-f` option is specified, `route` will "flush" the Routing Tables of all `gateway` entries. If this is used in conjunction with one of the *commands* described below, the Routing Tables will be flushed prior to the command's execution.

The `-n` option will prevent any attempt to print host and network names symbolically when reporting the actions.

The *route* command will accept three command options:

    add - to add a route,
    delete - to delete a route, and
    change - to change a route (not supported).

All commands have the following syntax:

    `route` *command destination gateway* [*metric*]

where

command has the following options:

    ''`add` [*host* | *network*] *name*: `gateway` *host flags metric*''
    The specified route is being added to the tables.
    The printed values are from the Routing Table entry supplied in the
    ioctl call.

    ''`delete` *host: gateway host* `flags` *metric*''
    As *add*, but when deleting an entry.

destination
    is a host or network for which the route is "to",

gateway
    is the gateway to which packets should be addressed, and

metric is an optional count indicating the number of hops to the *destination*. If *metric* is unspecified, `route` assumes a default value of 0 for *metric* .

Any routes to a particular host can be distinguished from those to a network by interpreting the Internet address associated with *destination* . If the *destination* has a "local address part" of `INADDR_ANY` , this route will be assumed to be to a network; otherwise, it will be presumed to be a route to a host.

route will use a "raw socket" and the `SIOCADDRT` and `SIOCDELRT` *ioctl*'s to do its work. As such, only the super-user may modify the Routing Tables.

DIAGNOSTICS

"host host done*"*

When the -f flag is specified, each routing table entry deleted will appear with a message of this form.

"not in table"

A delete operation was attempted for an entry which did not appear in the Routing Tables.

"routing table overflow"

An add operation was attempted, but the system was low on resources and could not allocate memory to create the new entry.

SEE ALSO

routed(1M), hosts(4), intro(4), networks(4).

NOTE

If the route is to a destination connected via a gateway, *metric* should be greater than 0. All symbolic names specified for a *destination* or for a *gateway* will be looked up first in the host name database [see hosts(4)]. If this lookup fails, then the name will be looked for in the network name database [see networks(4)].

NAME

routed - network routing daemon

SYNOPSIS

in.routed [-d] [-g] [-q] [-s] [-t] [*logfile*]

DESCRIPTION

The routed daemon is invoked by the super-user at boot time to manage the Internet Routing Tables (usually during init 2). The routed daemon uses a variant of the Xerox NS Routing Information Protocol to maintain up-to-date kernel Routing Table entries.

In normal operation, routed listens on the udp(7) socket 520 (decimal) to provide the route service [see services(4)] for routing information packets. If the host is an internetwork router, it periodically supplies copies of its Routing Tables to any directly connected hosts and networks.

When routed is started, it uses the SIOCGIFCONF ioctl(2) to find those directly connected interfaces configured into the system and marked "up" (the software loopback interface will be ignored). If multiple interfaces are present, it is assumed that the host will forward packets between networks. Then routed transmits a REQUEST packet on each interface (using a broadcast packet if the interface supports it) and enters a loop, listening for REQUEST and RESPONSE packets from other hosts.

When a REQUEST packet is received, routed formulates a reply based on the information maintained in its internal tables. The generated RESPONSE packet contains a list of known routes, each marked with a "hop count" metric (a count of 16, or greater, is considered "infinite"). The metric associated with each route returned provides a metric "relative to the sender".

Any RESPONSE packets received by routed are used to update the Routing Tables if one of the following conditions is satisfied:

(1)   No Routing Table entry exists for the destination network or host, and the metric indicates the destination is "reachable" (i.e., the hop count is not infinite).

(2)   The source host of the packet is the same as the router in the existing Routing Table entry; that is, updated information is being received from the very internetwork router through which packets for the destination are being routed.

(3)   The existing entry in the Routing Table has not been updated for some time (defined to be 90 seconds) and the route is at least as cost-effective as the current route.

(4)   The new route describes a shorter route to the destination than the one currently stored in the Routing Tables; the metric of the new route is compared against the one stored in the table to decide this.

When an update is applied, routed records the change in its internal tables and updates the kernel Routing Table and generates a RESPONSE packet reflecting these changes to all directly connected hosts and networks. The routed daemon will wait a short period of time (no more than 30 seconds) before the kernel's Routing Tables to allow any possible unstable situations to settle.

In addition to processing incoming packets, routed also checks the Routing Table entries periodically. If an entry has not been updated for 3 minutes, this entry's metric is set to infinity and marked for deletion. Deletions are delayed for an additional 60 seconds to insure the invalidation is propagated throughout the local internet.

Any hosts acting as internetwork routers gratuitously supply their routing tables every 30 seconds to all directly connected hosts and networks. The response is sent to the broadcast address on nets capable of that function, to the destination address on point-to-point links, and to the router's own address on other networks. The normal Routing Tables are bypassed when sending gratuitous responses. The reception of responses on each network is used to determine that the network and interfaces are functioning correctly. If no response is received on an interface, another route may be chosen to route around the interface, or the route may be dropped if no alternative route is available.

The routed daemon supports several options:

-d   This option will stop *routed* going into background, and releasing itself from the controlling terminal, so that interrupts from the keyboard will kill the process.

-g   This flag is used on internetwork routers to offer a route to the "default" destination. Typically, this is used on a gateway to the Internet, or on a gateway that uses another routing protocol whose routes are not reported to other local routers.

-s   When used, this option forces routed to supply routing information whether it is acting as an internetwork router or not. This is the default if multiple network interfaces are present, or if a point-to-point link is in use.

-q   This is the opposite of the -s option.

-t   The -t option increments the tracing level, successive levels are:

routed -t	trace actions only
routed -t -t	trace actions and packets
routed -t -t -t	trace actions and history of packets and contents after change.
routed -t -t -t -t	trace actions, packets and contents.

This tracing level may also be incremented by sending a SIGUSR1 signal to the routed process. SIGUSR2 sets the tracing level to zero (off). All tracing is sent to standard output unless routed has divorced itself from a controlling terminal, or a *logfile* has been specified.

Any other argument supplied is interpreted as the name of file in which routed 's actions should be logged. This log contains information about any changes to the Routing Tables and - if not tracing all packets - a history of recent messages sent and received which are related to the changed route.

In addition to the facilities described above, routed supports the notion of "distant" passive and active gateways. When routed is started up, it reads the file /etc/gateways to find gateways which may not be located using only information from the SIOCGIFCONF ioctl. Gateways specified in this manner should be marked passive if they are not expected to exchange routing information, while gateways marked active should be willing to exchange routing information (i.e., they should have a routed process running on the machine). Routes through passive gateways will be installed in the kernel's routing tables once upon startup. Such routes are not included in any routing information transmitted. The active gateways will be treated the same as network interfaces. Routing information will be distributed to the gateway; if no routing information is received for a period of time, the associated route will be deleted. External gateways are also passive, but will not placed into the kernel Routing Table nor will they be included in the routing updates. The function of these external entries is to inform routed that another routing process will install such a route and that alternate routes to that destination should not be installed. Such entries are required only when both routers may learn of routes to the same destination.

The /etc/gateways table consists of a series of lines, each of the following format:

<net | host> *name1* gateway *name2* metric *value* <passive | active | external>

where

net

host   indicates if the route is to a network or to a specific host.

name1   the name of the destination network or host. This may be a symbolic name located in /etc/networks or /etc/hosts [or, if started after named(1M), known to the name server], or an Internet address specified in "dot notation" [see hosts(4) and inet(7)].

name2   the name or address of the gateway to which messages should be forwarded.

value   is a metric indicating the hop count to the destination host or network.

passive, active, or external
One of these keywords indicates if the gateway should be treated as passive or active (as described above), or whether the gateway is external to the scope of the routed protocol.

USER CONSIDERATIONS

The kernel's Routing Tables may not correspond to those of routed for short time intervals while processes utilizing the existing routes exit; the only remedy for these temporary discrepancies would be to place the routing process into the kernel.

In addition, routed should listen to any "intelligent interfaces" (such as an IMP) and to error protocols (such as ICMP). For example, routed should listen for any "redirects" included with ICMP packets received via a raw socket where these ICMP "redirects" will cause changed or added routes.

FILES

```
/etc/gateways   for distant gateways
/etc/networks
/etc/hosts
```

SEE ALSO

`ioctl`(2), `inet`(7), `udp`(7).
RFC 1058.

NAME

rpcbind - universal addresses to RPC program number mapper

SYNOPSIS

rpcbind

DESCRIPTION

rpcbind is a server that converts RPC program numbers into universal addresses. It must be running to make RPC calls.

When an RPC service is started, it will tell rpcbind at what address it is listening, and what RPC program numbers it is prepared to serve. When a client wishes to make an RPC call to a given program number, it will first contact rpcbind on the server machine to determine the address where RPC packets should be sent.

Normally, standard RPC servers are started by port monitors, so rpcbind must be started before port monitors are invoked.

rpcbind is restricted to users with appropriate privileges.

NOTES

If rpcbind crashes, all RPC servers must be restarted.

SEE ALSO

rpcinfo(1M)

NAME

rpcgen - an RPC protocol compiler

SYNOPSIS

rpcgen *infile*
rpcgen [-D*name*[=*value*]] [-T] [-K *secs*] *infile*
rpcgen -c|-h|-l|-m|-t [-o *outfile*] *infile*
rpcgen -s *nettype* [-o *outfile*] *infile*
rpcgen -n *netid* [-o *outfile*] *infile*

DESCRIPTION

rpcgen is a tool that generates C code to implement an RPC protocol. The input to rpcgen is a language similar to C known as RPC Language (Remote Procedure Call Language).

rpcgen is normally used as in the first synopsis where it takes an input file and generates up to four output files. If the *infile* is named proto.x, then rpcgen will generate a header file in proto.h, XDR routines in proto_xdr.c, server-side stubs in proto_svc.c, and client-side stubs in proto_clnt.c. With the -T option, it will also generate the RPC dispatch table in proto_tbl.i.

The server created can be started both by the port monitors (for example, inetd or listen) or by itself. When it is started by a port monitor, it creates servers only for the transport for which the file descriptor 0 was passed. The name of the transport must be specified by setting up the environment variable PM_TRANSPORT. When the server generated by rpcgen is executed, it creates server handles for all the transports specified in NETPATH environment variable, or if it is not set, it creates server handles for all the visible transports from /etc/netconfig file. Note: the transports are chosen at run time and not at compile time. When the server is self-started, it backgrounds itself by default. A special symbol, RPC_SVC_FG, can be defined at compilation time to make the server process run in foreground.

The second synopsis provides special features which allow for the creation of more sophisticated RPC servers. These features include support for user provided #defines and RPC dispatch tables. The entries in the RPC dispatch table contain:

- pointers to the service routine corresponding to that procedure,
- a pointer to the input and output arguments
- the size of these routines

A server can use the dispatch table to check authorization and then to execute the service routine; a client library may use it to deal with the details of storage management and XDR data conversion.

The other three synopses shown above are used when one does not want to generate all the output files, but only a particular one. Some examples of their usage is described in the EXAMPLE section below. When rpcgen is executed with the -s option, it creates servers for that particular class of transports. When executed with the -n option, it creates a server for the transport specified by *netid*. If *infile* is not specified, rpcgen accepts the standard input.

The C preprocessor, cc -E [see cc(1)], is run on the input file before it is actually interpreted by rpcgen. For each type of output file, rpcgen defines a special preprocessor symbol for use by the rpcgen programmer:

```
RPC_HDR     defined when compiling into header files
RPC_XDR     defined when compiling into XDR routines
RPC_SVC     defined when compiling into server-side stubs
RPC_CLNT    defined when compiling into client-side stubs
RPC_TBL     defined when compiling into RPC dispatch tables
```

Any line beginning with '%' is passed directly into the output file, uninterpreted by rpcgen.

For every data type referred to in *infile*, rpcgen assumes that there exists a routine with the string xdr_ prepended to the name of the data type. If this routine does not exist in the RPC/XDR library, it must be provided. Providing an undefined data type allows customization of XDR routines.

The following options are available:

-c   Compile into XDR routines.

-D*name*[=*value*]
         Define a symbol *name*. Equivalent to the #define directive in the source. If no *value* is given, *value* is defined as 1. This option may be specified more than once.

-h   Compile into C data-definitions (a header file). -T option can be used in conjunction to produce a header file which supports RPC dispatch tables.

-K *secs*
         By default, services created using rpcgen wait 120 seconds after servicing a request before exiting. That interval can be changed using the -K flag. To create a server that exits immediately upon servicing a request, -K 0 can be used. To create a server that never exits, the appropriate argument is -K -1.

         When monitoring for a server, some portmonitors, like listen(1M), *always* spawn a new process in response to a service request. If it is known that a server will be used with such a monitor, the server should exit immediately on completion. For such servers, rpcgen should be used with -K -1.

-l   Compile into client-side stubs.

-m   Compile into server-side stubs, but do not generate a main routine. This option is useful for doing callback-routines and for users who need to write their own main routine to do initialization.

-n *netid*
         Compile into server-side stubs for the transport specified by *netid*. There should be an entry for *netid* in the netconfig database. This option may be specified more than once, so as to compile a server that serves multiple transports.

-o *outfile*
         Specify the name of the output file. If none is specified, standard output is used (-c, -h, -l, -m, -n, -s and -t modes only).

-s *nettype*
         Compile into server-side stubs for all the transports belonging to the class *nettype*. The supported classes are netpath, visible, circuit_n, circuit_v, datagram_n, datagram_v, tcp, and udp [see rpc(3N) for the meanings associated with these classes]. This option may be specified more

than once. Note: the transports are chosen at run time and not at compile time.

-t   Compile into RPC dispatch table.

-T   Generate the code to support RPC dispatch tables.

The options -c, -h, -l, -m, -s and -t are used exclusively to generate a particular type of file, while the options -D and -T are global and can be used with the other options.

NOTES

The RPC Language does not support nesting of structures. As a work-around, structures can be declared at the top-level, and their name used inside other structures in order to achieve the same effect.

Name clashes can occur when using program definitions, since the apparent scoping does not really apply. Most of these can be avoided by giving unique names for programs, versions, procedures and types.

The server code generated with -n option refers to the transport indicated by *netid* and hence is very site specific.

EXAMPLE

The following example:

```
$ rpcgen -T prot.x
```

generates all the five files: prot.h, prot_clnt.c, prot_svc.c, prot_xdr.c and prot_tbl.i.

The following example sends the C data-definitions (header file) to the standard output.

```
$ rpcgen -h prot.x
```

To send the test version of the -DTEST, server side stubs for all the transport belonging to the class datagram_n to standard output, use:

```
$ rpcgen -s datagram_n -DTEST prot.x
```

To create the server side stubs for the transport indicated by *netid* tcp, use:

```
$ rpcgen -n tcp -o prot_svc.c prot.x
```

SEE ALSO

cc(1)

NAME

rpcinfo - report RPC information

SYNOPSIS

```
rpcinfo [host]
rpcinfo -p [host]
rpcinfo -T transport host program version
rpcinfo [-n portnum] -u host program version
rpcinfo [-n portnum] -t host program version
rpcinfo -a serv_address -T transport program [version]
rpcinfo -b [-T transport] program version
rpcinfo -d [-T transport] program version
```

DESCRIPTION

rpcinfo makes an RPC call to an RPC server and reports what it finds.

In the first synopsis, it lists all the registered RPC services with rpcbind on *host*. If *host* is not specified, it defaults to the local host.

In the second synopsis, it lists all the RPC services registered with portmapper. Also note that the format of the information is different in the first and the second synopsis; this is because in the first case, rpcbind (version 3) is contacted, while in the second case portmap (version 2) is contacted for information.

The third synopsis makes an RPC call to procedure 0 of *program* and *version* on the specified *host* and reports whether a response was received. *transport* is the transport which has to be used for contacting the given service. The remote address of the service is obtained by making a call to remote rpcbind.

The other ways of using rpcinfo are described below. See EXAMPLES.

The following options are available:

-T *transport*   Specify the transport on which the service is required. If this option is not specified, rpcinfo uses the transport specified in the NETPATH environment variable, or if that is unset or null, in the netconfig database. This is a generic option, and can be used in conjunction with any other option, except the -b option.

-a *serv_address*   Use *serv_address* as the (universal) address for the service on *transport*, to ping procedure 0 of the specified *program* and report whether a response was received. The use of -T option is required with -a option.

   If version number is not specified, rpcinfo tries to ping all the available version numbers for that program number. This option avoids calls to remote rpcbind to find the address of the service. The *serv_address* is specified in universal address format of the given transport.

-b   Make an RPC broadcast to procedure 0 of the specified *program* and *version* and report all hosts that respond. If *transport* is specified, it broadcasts its request only on the transport specified through *transport*. If broadcasting is not supported by any transport, an error message is printed. Only UDP transports support broadcasting.

-d	Delete registration for the RPC service of the specified *program* and *version*. If *transport* is specified, unregister the service on only that transport, otherwise unregister the services on all the transports on which it was registered. This option can be exercised only by the privileged user.
-n	Use *portnum* as the port number for the -t and -u options instead of the port number given by the portmapper. Use of this option avoids a call to the remote portmapper to find out the address of the service.
-p	Probe the portmapper on *host*, and print a list of all registered RPC programs. If *host* is not specified, it defaults to the local host.
-t	Make an RPC call to procedure 0 of *program* on the specified *host* using TCP, and report whether a response was received.
-u	Make an RPC call to procedure 0 of *program* on the specified *host* using UDP, and report whether a response was received.

The *program* argument is a number.

If a *version* is specified, rpcinfo attempts to call that version of the specified *program*. Otherwise, rpcinfo attempts to find all the registered version numbers for the specified *program* by calling version 0, which is presumed not to exist; if it does exist, rpcinfo attempts to obtain this information by calling an extremely high version number instead, and attempts to call each registered version. Note: the version number is required for -b and -d options.

EXAMPLES

To show all of the RPC services registered on the local machine use:

    $ rpcinfo

To show all of the RPC services registered with rpcbind on the machine named klaxon use:

    $ rpcinfo klaxon

To show if the RPC service with program number *prog_no* and version *vers* is registered on the machine named klaxon for the transport tcp use:

    $ rpcinfo -T tcp klaxon *prog_no vers*

To show all of the RPC services registered with the portmapper on the local machine use:

    $ rpcinfo -p

To ping version 2 of rpcbind (program number 100000) on host sparky:

    $ rpcinfo -t sparky 100000 2

To delete the registration for version 1 of the walld (program number 100008) service for all transports use:

```
# rpcinfo -d 100008 1
```

SEE ALSO

rpcbind(1M), rpc(4)

NAME

`rsh` - remote shell

SYNOPSIS

`rsh` [`-n`] [`-l` *username*] *hostname command*

`rsh` *hostname* [`-n`] [`-l` *username*] *command*

hostname [`-n`] [`-l` *username*] *command*

DESCRIPTION

`rsh` connects to the specified *hostname* and executes the specified *command*. `rsh` copies its standard input to the remote command, the standard output of the remote command to its standard output, and the standard error of the remote command to its standard error. Interrupt, quit and terminate signals are propagated to the remote command; `rsh` normally terminates when the remote command does.

If you omit *command*, instead of executing a single command, `rsh` logs you in on the remote host using `rlogin`(1). Shell metacharacters which are not quoted are interpreted on the local machine, while quoted metacharacters are interpreted on the remote machine. See EXAMPLES.

Hostnames are given in the *hosts* database, which may be contained in the `/etc/hosts` file, the Internet domain name database, or both. Each host has one official name (the first name in the database entry) and optionally one or more nicknames. Official hostnames or nicknames may be given as *hostname*.

If the name of the file from which `rsh` is executed is anything other than `rsh`, `rsh` takes this name as its *hostname* argument. This allows you to create a symbolic link to `rsh` in the name of a host which, when executed, will invoke a remote shell on that host. By creating a directory and populating it with symbolic links in the names of commonly used hosts, then including the directory in your shell's search path, you can run `rsh` by typing *hostname* to your shell.

Each remote machine may have a file named `/etc/hosts.equiv` containing a list of trusted hostnames with which it shares usernames. Users with the same username on both the local and remote machine may `rsh` from the machines listed in the remote machine's `/etc/hosts` file. Individual users may set up a similar private equivalence list with the file `.rhosts` in their home directories. Each line in this file contains two names: a *hostname* and a *username* separated by a space. The entry permits the user named *username* who is logged into *hostname* to use `rsh` to access the remote machine as the remote user. If the name of the local host is not found in the `/etc/hosts.equiv` file on the remote machine, and the local username and hostname are not found in the remote user's `.rhosts` file, then the access is denied. The hostnames listed in the `/etc/hosts.equiv` and `.rhosts` files must be the official hostnames listed in the `hosts` database; nicknames may not be used in either of these files.

`rsh` will not prompt for a password if access is denied on the remote machine unless the *command* argument is omitted.

OPTIONS

`-l` *username*

    Use *username* as the remote username instead of your local username. In the absence of this option, the remote username is the same as your local username.

  -n　　　Redirect the input of `rsh` to `/dev/null`. You sometimes need this option to avoid unfortunate interactions between `rsh` and the shell which invokes it. For example, if you are running `rsh` and invoke a `rsh` in the background without redirecting its input away from the terminal, it will block even if no reads are posted by the remote command. The -n option will prevent this.

The type of remote shell (`sh`, the restricted shell—`/usr/lib/rsh`, or other) is determined by the user's entry in the file `/etc/passwd` on the remote system.

EXAMPLES

The command:

```
rsh lizard cat lizard.file >> example.file
```

appends the remote file `lizard.file` from the machine called "lizard" to the file called `example.file` on the local machine, while the command:

```
rsh lizard cat lizard.file ">>" lizard.file2
```

appends the file `lizard.file` on the machine called "lizard" to the file `lizard.file2` which also resides on the machine called "lizard."

FILES

```
/etc/hosts
/etc/passwd
```

SEE ALSO

`rlogin`(1), `vi`(1), `named`(1M), `hosts`(4), `hosts.equiv`(4)

NOTES

When a system is listed in `hosts.equiv`, its security must be as good as local security. One insecure system listed in `hosts.equiv` can compromise the security of the entire system.

You cannot run an interactive command [such as `vi`(1)]; use `rlogin` if you want to do so.

Stop signals stop the local `rsh` process only; this is arguably wrong, but currently hard to fix for reasons too complicated to explain here.

The current local environment is not passed to the remote shell.

Sometimes the -n option is needed for reasons that are less than obvious. For example, the command:

```
rsh somehost dd if=/dev/nrmt0 bs=20b | tar xvpBf -
```

will put your shell into a strange state. Evidently, what happens is that the `tar` terminates before the `rsh`. The `rsh` then tries to write into the "broken pipe" and, instead of terminating neatly, proceeds to compete with your shell for its standard input. Invoking `rsh` with the -n option avoids such incidents.

This bug occurs only when `rsh` is at the beginning of a pipeline and is not reading standard input. Do not use the -n if `rsh` actually needs to read standard input. For example,

```
tar cf - . | rsh sundial dd of=/dev/rmt0 obs=20b
```

does not produce the bug. If you were to use the -n in a case like this, rsh would incorrectly read from /dev/null instead of from the pipe.

Prior to Release 4, the rsh command invoked the restricted shell. This restricted shell command is /usr/lib/rsh and can be executed by using the full pathname.

NAME

rshd - remote shell server

SYNOPSIS

in.rshd *host.port*

DESCRIPTION

rshd is the server for the rsh(1) program. The server provides remote execution facilities with authentication based on privileged port numbers.

rshd is invoked by inetd(1M) each time a shell service is requested, and executes the following protocol:

1) The server checks the client's source port. If the port is not in the range 0-1023, the server aborts the connection. The clients host address (in hex) and port number (in decimal) are the argument passed to rshd.

2) The server reads characters from the socket up to a null (\0) byte. The resultant string is interpreted as an ASCII number, base 10.

3) If the number received in step 1 is non-zero, it is interpreted as the port number of a secondary stream to be used for the stderr. A second connection is then created to the specified port on the client's machine. The source port of this second connection is also in the range 0-1023.

4) The server checks the client's source address. If the address is associated with a host for which no corresponding entry exists in the host name data base [see hosts(4)], the server aborts the connection.

5) A null terminated user name of at most 16 characters is retrieved on the initial socket. This user name is interpreted as a user identity to use on the server's machine.

6) A null terminated user name of at most 16 characters is retrieved on the initial socket. This user name is interpreted as the user identity on the client's machine.

7) A null terminated command to be passed to a shell is retrieved on the initial socket. The length of the command is limited by the upper bound on the size of the system's argument list.

8) rshd then validates the user according to the following steps. The remote user name is looked up in the password file and a chdir is performed to the user's home directory. If the lookup or fails, the connection is terminated. If the chdir fails, it does a chdir to / (root). If the user is not the super-user, (user ID 0), the file /etc/hosts.equiv is consulted for a list of hosts considered equivalent. If the client's host name is present in this file, the authentication is considered successful. If the lookup fails, or the user is the super-user, then the file .rhosts in the home directory of the remote user is checked for the machine name and identity of the user on the client's machine. If this lookup fails, the connection is terminated.

9) A null byte is returned on the connection associated with the stderr and the command line is passed to the normal login shell of the user. The shell inherits the network connections established by rshd.

FILES

    /etc/hosts.equiv

SEE ALSO

    rsh(1)

DIAGNOSTICS

The following diagnostic messages are returned on the connection associated with the `stderr`, after which any network connections are closed. An error is indicated by a leading byte with a value of 1 (0 is returned in step 9 above upon successful completion of all the steps prior to the command execution).

`locuser too long`
> The name of the user on the client's machine is longer than 16 characters.

`remuser too long`
> The name of the user on the remote machine is longer than 16 characters.

`command too long`
> The command line passed exceeds the size of the argument list (as configured into the system).

`Hostname for your address unknown.`
> No entry in the host name database existed for the client's machine.

`Login incorrect.`
> No password file entry for the user name existed.

`Permission denied.`
> The authentication procedure described above failed.

`Can't make pipe.`
> The pipe needed for the `stderr` was not created.

`Try again.`
> A *fork* by the server failed.

NOTES

The authentication procedure used here assumes the integrity of each client machine and the connecting medium. This is insecure, but is useful in an open environment.

A facility to allow all data exchanges to be encrypted should be present.

NAME

rsnotify - display or modify the information identifying the individual in charge of restore requests

SYNOPSIS

rsnotify [-u *user*]

DESCRIPTION

rsnotify without options displays the name of the person who is to receive mail(1M) notifications whenever restore requests require operator intervention. The display includes the date the individual was assigned.

rsnotify may only be executed by a user with superuser privileges.

Options

-u *user*

assigns *user* to be the one to receive restore notifications. *user* is the user's login ID. If *user* is null, rsnotify mails the notices to root. *user* must be in the passwd file.

DIAGNOSTICS

The exit codes for rsnotify are the following:

0 = the task completed successfully
1 = one or more parameters to rsnotify are invalid
2 = an error has occurred, causing rsnotify to fail to
    complete all portions of its task

EXAMPLES

Example 1:

```
rsnotify -u oper3
```

assigns the individual with login ID oper3 as the one to be notified when a restore request needing operator intervention is initiated.

FILES

/etc/bkup/rsnotify.tab   provides the electronic mail address of the operator to be notified whenever restore requests require operator intervention

/etc/bkup/rsstatus.tab   tracks the status of all restore requests from users

SEE ALSO

getvol(1M), restore(1M), rsstatus(1M), urestore(1M).

NAME

rsoper - service pending restore requests and service media insertion prompts

SYNOPSIS

rsoper $-d$ *ddev* [$-j$ *jobids*] [$-u$ *user*] [$-m$ *method*] [$-n$] [$-s\,|\,v$] [$-t$]
        [$-o$ *oname*[:*odevice*]]

rsoper $-r$ *jobid*

rsoper $-c$ *jobid*

DESCRIPTION

rsoper $-d$ identifies media containing backup archives of file systems and data slices, and allows an operator to complete pending restore(1M) and urestore(1M) requests. rsoper takes information about the archive entered on the command line and matches it against pending restore or urestore requests in the restore status table. rsoper then invokes the proper archiving method to read the archive and extract requested files, directories, and data slices. As subsequent archive volumes are needed, the operator is requested to insert or mount the appropriate archive volumes. See getvol(1M).

Depending on the information available in bkhist.tab and the volume labeling technique (internal or external), all options and arguments listed below may not be required. If required fields are omitted, rsoper issues an error message indicating the information that is needed. The command can then be reissued with the appropriate fields specified.

rsoper may be executed only by a user with superuser privileges.

rsoper $-r$ removes a pending restore job from the restore status table (see rsstatus(1M) and ursstatus(1M)) and notifies the requesting user that the job has been marked complete.

rsoper $-c$ removes a pending restore job from the restore status table (see rsstatus(1M) and ursstatus(1M)) and notifies the requesting user that the job has been canceled.

Options

$-c$ *jobid*   Cancels a pending restore request and notifies the originating user that the request has been canceled.

$-d$ *ddev*   Describes the device that will be used to read the archive containing the required file system or data slice. *ddev* is of the form:

        ddevice[: [*dchar*][: [*dmnames*]]]

    ddevice is the device name for the device; see device.tab(4). *dchar* describes characteristics associated with the device. *dchar* is of the form:

        [density=*density*] [blk_fac=*blockingfactor*] [mntpt=*dir*]

    If mntpt=*dir* is specified, *ddevice* is assumed to be a file system slice and *dir* is the place in the UNIX system directory structure where *ddevice* will be mounted. This is valid only for fimage(1M) archives. *dmnames* is a list of volume labels, separated by either commas or blanks. If the list is blank separated, the entire *ddev* argument must be surrounded by quotes.

-j *jobids*   Limits the scope of the request to the jobs specified. *jobids* is a list of restore job IDs (either comma separated or blank separated and surrounded by quotes).

-m *method*   Assumes the archive on the first volume in the destination device was created by the *method* archiving operation. Valid *methods* are: `incfile`, `ffile`, `fimage`, `fdp`, `fdisk`, and any customized methods in the `/etc/bkup/method` directory. This option is required if the backup history log is not available, if the log does not include information about the specified archive or if `rsoper` cannot determine the format of the archive.

-n   Displays attributes of the specified destination device but does not attempt to service pending restore requests.

-o *oname*[: *odevice*]
                Specifies the originating file system slice or data slice to be restored. *oname* is the name of the the originating file system. It may be null. *odevice* is the device name of the originating file system or data slice. This option is required if the backup history log is not available or does not include information about the specified archive.

-r *jobid*   Removes the restore request for the specified job.

-s   While a restore operation is occurring, this option displays a period (.) for each 100 (512-byte) blocks transferred from the destination device.

-t   Assumes that the volume inserted in the destination device contains a table of contents for an archive. This option is required if the backup history log is not available, if the log does not include information about the specified archive, or if `rsoper` cannot determine the format of the volume.

-u *user*   Restricts restores to those requested by the user specified.

-v   Displays the name of each object as it is restored. Only those archiving methods that restore named directories and files (`incfile` and `ffile`) support this option.

DIAGNOSTICS

The exit codes for `rsoper` are the following:

0 = the task completed successfully
1 = one or more parameters to `rsoper` are invalid
2 = an error has occurred, causing `rsoper` to fail to
    complete all portions of its task

If a method reports that no part of a restore request was completed, `rsoper` reports this fact to the user.

EXAMPLES

    Example 1:

```
rsoper -d /dev/rmt/ctape1
```

asks the restore service to read the archive volume that has been inserted into the device `/dev/rmt/ctape1`. The service will attempt to resolve any restore requests that can be satisfied by the archive volume.

Example 2:

The following example assumes that the backup history table contains a record of backups performed and that the restore status table contains a record of the restore requests. The command line

```
rsoper -d /dev/rmt/ctape1:density=1600:USRLBL1 -v -u clerk1
```

instructs the restore service to perform only pending restore requests from the `rsstatus.tab` table issued by `clerk1`. The restore procedures are to be done from the cartridge tape labeled USRLBL1, with a density of 1600 bps. The restore service will display on the operator terminal the names of the files and directories as they are successfully restored.

Example 3:

```
rsoper -c rest-737b
```

cancels the restore request with the job ID `rest-737b`.

FILES

`/etc/bkup/bkhist.tab`	lists the labels of all volumes that have been used for backup operations
`/etc/bkup/rsstatus.tab`	lists the status of all restore requests from users
`/etc/bkup/rsnotify.tab`	lists the electronic mail address of the operator to be notified whenever restore requests require operator intervention
`/etc/bkup/method`	a directory that contains the programs used for various backup methods

SEE ALSO

    `fdisk`(1M), `fdp`(1M), `ffile`(1M), `fimage`(1M), `getvol`(1M), `incfile`(1M), `restore`(1M), `rsnotify`(1M), `rsstatus`(1M), `urestore`(1M), `ursstatus`(1M), `mail`(1), `getdate`(3C), `device.tab`(4).

NAME

rsstatus - report the status of posted restore requests

SYNOPSIS

rsstatus [-h] [-d *ddev*] [-f *field_separator*] [-j *jobids*] [-u *users*]

DESCRIPTION

With no options, rsstatus reports the status of all pending restore requests that are posted in the restore status table.

rsstatus may be executed only by a user with superuser privileges.

Volume labels marked with an asterisk in the output of this command are table of contents volumes.

Options

-d *ddev* Restricts the report to pending restore jobs that could be satisfied by the specified device type or volumes. *ddev* describes the device or volumes used to select requests to be restored. *ddev* is of the form:

[*dtype*][: *dlabels*]

dtype is a device type (such as cartridge tape). If specified, restrict the report to posted requests that could be satisfied by volumes of the type specified.

dlabels is a list of volume names corresponding to the *volumename* displayed by the labelit command. *dlabels* may be either comma-separated or blank-separated and surrounded by quotes. If specified, restrict the report to posted requests that could be satisfied by an archive residing on the specified volumes.

-f *field_separator*

Suppresses field wrap and specifies an output field separator to be used. *field_separator* is the character that will appear as the field separator in the output displayed. To make sure the output is clear, avoid using a character (for a separator) that is likely to appear in a field. For example, do not use a colon as a field separator if the display will contain dates in which a colon is used to separate hours from minutes.

-h   Suppresses the header for the report.

-j *jobids* Restricts the report to the jobs specified. *jobids* is a list of restore job IDs (either comma-separated or blank-separated and surrounded by quotes).

-u *users* Restricts the report to requests submitted by the specified *users* (either comma-separated or blank-separated and surrounded by quotes). *users* must be listed in the passwd file.

DIAGNOSTICS

The exit codes for rsstatus are the following:

0 = successful completion of the task
1 = one or more parameters to rsstatus are invalid.
2 = an error has occurred which caused rsstatus to fail to
    complete all portions of its task.

EXAMPLES

Example 1:

```
rsstatus -d ctape1
```

reports the status of those posted restore requests that can be satisfied by inserting a cartridge tape into a cartridge tape drive.

Example 2:

```
rsstatus -j rest-354a,rest-429b
```

reports the status of only the two posted restore requests for which job IDs are specified.

FILES

`/etc/bkup/rsstatus.tab` — tracks the status of all restore requests from users

SEE ALSO

restore(1M), urestore(1M), ursstatus(1M), dgroup.tab(4), device.tab(4).

NAME

rumount - cancel queued remote resource request

SYNOPSIS

`/etc/rfs/rumount` *resource* ...

DESCRIPTION

`rumount` cancels a request for one or more resources that are queued for mount. The entries for the resources are deleted from `/etc/rfs/rmnttab`.

FILES

`/etc/rfs/rmnttab` — pending mount requests

SEE ALSO

`mount`(1M), `rmnttry`(1M), `rmount`(1M), `rumountall`(1M), `mnttab`(4)

DIAGNOSTICS

An exit code of 0 is returned if `rumount` completes successfully. A 1 is returned if the resource requested for dequeuing is not in `/etc/rfs/rmnttab`. A 2 is returned for bad usage or an error in reading or writing `/etc/rfs/rmnttab`.

NAME

run - run an executable

SYNOPSIS

run [-s] [-e] [-n] [-t *string*] *program*

DESCRIPTION

The run function runs *program*, using the PATH variable to find it. By default, when *program* has completed, the user is prompted (Press ENTER to continue:), before being returned to FMLI. The argument *program* is a UNIX system executable followed by its options (if any).

-e   If -e is specified the user will be prompted before returning to FMLI only if there is an error condition

-n   If -n is specified the user will never be prompted before returning to FMLI (useful for programs like vi, in which the user must do some specific action to exit in the first place).

-s   The -s option means "silent", implying that the screen will not have to be repainted when *program* has completed. NOTE: The -s option should only be used when *program* does not write to the terminal. In addition, when -s is used, *program* cannot be interrupted, even if it recognizes interrupts.

-t *string*   If -t is specified, *string* is the name this process will have in the pop-up menu generated by the frm-list command. This feature requires the executable facesuspend, (currently only available with the FACE product), to suspend the UNIX system process and return to the FMLI application.

EXAMPLE

Here is a menu that uses run:

```
menu="Edit special System files"

name="Password file"
action=`run -e vi /etc/passwd`

name="Group file"
action=`run -e vi /etc/group`

name="My .profile"
action=`run -n vi $HOME/.profile`
```

NAME

runacct - run daily accounting

SYNOPSIS

/usr/lib/acct/runacct [*mmdd* [*state*]]

DESCRIPTION

runacct is the main daily accounting shell procedure. It is normally initiated via cron. runacct processes connect, fee, disk, and process accounting files. It also prepares summary files for prdaily or billing purposes. runacct is distributed only to source code licensees.

runacct takes care not to damage active accounting files or summary files in the event of errors. It records its progress by writing descriptive diagnostic messages into *active*. When an error is detected, a message is written to /dev/console, mail [see mail(1)] is sent to root and adm, and runacct terminates. runacct uses a series of lock files to protect against re-invocation. The files lock and lock1 are used to prevent simultaneous invocation, and lastdate is used to prevent more than one invocation per day.

runacct breaks its processing into separate, restartable *states* using *statefile* to remember the last *state* completed. It accomplishes this by writing the *state* name into *statefile*. runacct then looks in *statefile* to see what it has done and to determine what to process next. *states* are executed in the following order:

SETUP　　　　　Move active accounting files into working files.

WTMPFIX　　　　Verify integrity of wtmp file, correcting date changes if necessary.

CONNECT　　　　Produce connect session records in tacct.h format.

PROCESS　　　　Convert process accounting records into tacct.h format.

MERGE　　　　　Merge the connect and process accounting records.

FEES　　　　　　Convert output of chargefee into tacct.h format and merge with connect and process accounting records.

DISK　　　　　　Merge disk accounting records with connect, process, and fee accounting records.

MERGETACCT

Merge the daily total accounting records in daytacct with the summary total accounting records in /var/adm/acct/sum/tacct.

CMS　　　　　　Produce command summaries.

USEREXIT　　　　Any installation dependent accounting programs can be included here.

CLEANUP　　　　Clean up temporary files and exit.

To restart runacct after a failure, first check the *active* file for diagnostics, then fix any corrupted data files, such as pacct or wtmp. The lock, lock1, and lastdate files must be removed before runacct can be restarted. The argument *mmdd* is necessary if runacct is being restarted, and specifies the month and day for which runacct will rerun the accounting. The entry point for processing is based on the contents of *statefile*; to override this, include the desired *state* on the command line to designate where processing should begin.

EXAMPLES

To start runacct:

```
nohup runacct 2> /var/adm/acct/nite/fd2log &
```

To restart runacct:

```
nohup runacct 0601 2>> /var/adm/acct/nite/fd2log &
```

To restart runacct at a specific *state*:

```
nohup runacct 0601 MERGE 2>> /var/adm/acct/nite/fd2log &
```

FILES

```
/var/adm/wtmp
/var/adm/pacctincr
/usr/src/cmd/acct/tacct.h
/usr/src/cmd/acct/ctmp.h
/var/adm/acct/nite/active
/var/adm/acct/nite/daytacct
/var/adm/acct/nite/lock
/var/adm/acct/nite/lock1
/var/adm/acct/nite/lastdate
/var/adm/acct/nite/statefile
```

SEE ALSO

acct(1M), acctcms(1M), acctcom(1), acctcon(1M), acctmerg(1M), acctprc(1M), acctsh(1M), cron(1M), fwtmp(1M), mail(1), acct(2), acct(4), utmp(4).

NOTES

Normally it is not a good idea to restart runacct in the SETUP *state*. Run SETUP manually and restart via:

```
runacct mmdd WTMPFIX
```

If runacct failed in the PROCESS *state*, remove the last ptacct file because it will not be complete.

NAME

ruptime - show host status of local machines

SYNOPSIS

ruptime [-alrtu]

DESCRIPTION

ruptime gives a status line like uptime for each machine on the local network; these are formed from packets broadcast by each host on the network once a minute.

Machines for which no status report has been received for 5 minutes are shown as being down.

Normally, the listing is sorted by host name, but this order can be changed by specifying one of the options listed below.

The following options are available:

-a   Count even those users who have been idle for an hour or more.

-l   Sort the display by load average.

-r   Reverse the sorting order.

-t   Sort the display by up time.

-u   Sort the display by number of users.

FILES

/var/spool/rwho/whod.*   data files

SEE ALSO

rwho(1), rwhod(1M)

NOTES

Ruptime shows a remote sytem up only if rwhod(1M) is running on both the local machine and the remote machine, and they both are on the same physical network or if their bridge/router passes rwhod broadcasts between subnets, and if the remote system has been up long enough to generate its first rwho broadcast.

NAME

rusers - who's logged in on local machines

SYNOPSIS

rusers [-ahilu] *host ...*

DESCRIPTION

The rusers command produces output similar to who(1), but for remote machines. The listing is in the order that responses are received, but this order can be changed by specifying one of the options listed below.

The default is to print out the names of the users logged in. When the -l flag is given, additional information is printed for each user, including idle time, when user logged in, and tty.

A remote host will only respond if it is running the rusersd(1M) daemon, which may be started up from inetd(1M) or listen(1M).

The following options are available:

-a   Give a report for a machine even if no users are logged on.

-h   Sort alphabetically by host name.

-i   Sort by idle time.

-l   Give a longer listing in the style of who(1).

-u   Sort by number of users.

SEE ALSO

inetd(1M), listen(1M), pmadm(1M), rusersd(1M), sacadm(1M), who(1)

NAME

rpc.rusersd - network username server

SYNOPSIS

/usr/lib/netsvc/rusers/rpc.rusersd

DESCRIPTION

rusersd is a server that returns a list of users on the host. The rusersd daemon may be started by inetd(1M) or listen(1M).

SEE ALSO

inetd(1M), listen(1M), pmadm(1M), sacadm(1M)

NAME

rwall - write to all users over a network

SYNOPSIS

/usr/sbin/rwall *hostname* . . .

DESCRIPTION

rwall reads a message from standard input until EOF. It then sends this message, preceded by the line:

    Broadcast Message . . .

to all users logged in on the specified host machines.

A machine can only receive such a message if it is running rwalld(1M), which may be started by inetd(1M) or listen(1M).

NOTES

The timeout is fairly short to allow transmission to a large group of machines (some of which may be down) in a reasonable amount of time. Thus the message may not get through to a heavily loaded machine.

SEE ALSO

inetd(1M), listen(1M), pmadm(1M), rwalld(1M), sacadm(1M), wall(1)

NAME

    rpc.rwalld - network rwall server

SYNOPSIS

    /usr/lib/netsvc/rwall/rpc.rwalld

DESCRIPTION

    rwalld is a server that handles rwall(1M) requests. It is implemented by calling
    wall(1M) on all the appropriate network machines. The rwalld daemon may be
    started by inetd(1M) or listen(1M).

SEE ALSO

    inetd(1M), listen(1M), rwall(1M), wall(1M)

NAME

rwho - who's logged in on local machines

SYNOPSIS

rwho [-a]

DESCRIPTION

The rwho command produces output similar to who(1), but for all machines on your network. If no report has been received from a machine for 5 minutes, rwho assumes the machine is down, and does not report users last known to be logged into that machine.

If a user has not typed to the system for a minute or more, rwho reports this idle time. If a user has not typed to the system for an hour or more, the user is omitted from the output of rwho unless the -a flag is given.

The -a option reports all users whether or not they have typed to the system in the past hour.

FILES

/var/spool/rwho/whod.*   information about other machines

SEE ALSO

finger(1), ruptime(1), who(1), rwhod(1M)

NOTES

Does not work through gateways.

This is unwieldy when the number of machines on the local net is large.

The rwho service daemon, rwhod(1M), must be enabled for this command to return useful results.

Rwho shows users on a remote machine only if rwhod(1M) is running on both the local machine and the remote machine and the remote machine has been up long enough to generate its first rwho broadcast.

NAME

rwhod, in.rwhod - system status server

SYNOPSIS

in.rwhod

DESCRIPTION

rwhod is the server which maintains the database used by the rwho(1) and ruptime(1) programs. Its operation is predicated on the ability to broadcast messages on a network.

rwhod operates as both a producer and consumer of status information. As a producer of information it periodically queries the state of the system and constructs status messages which are broadcast on a network. As a consumer of information, it listens for other rwhod servers' status messages, validating them, then recording them in a collection of files located in the directory /var/spool/rwho.

The rwho server transmits and receives messages at the port indicated in the rwho service specification, see services(4). The messages sent and received, are of the form:

```
struct      outmp {
        char  out_line[8];      /* tty name */
        char  out_name[8];      /* user id */
        long  out_time;  /* time on */
};

struct      whod {
        char  wd_vers;
        char  wd_type;
        char  wd_fill[2];
        int   wd_sendtime;
        int   wd_recvtime;
        char  wd_hostname[32];
        int   wd_loadav[3];
        int   wd_boottime;
            struct      whoent {
            struct      outmp we_utmp;
            int   we_idle;
        } wd_we[1024 / sizeof (struct whoent)];
};
```

All fields are converted to network byte order prior to transmission. The load averages are as calculated by the w(1) program, and represent load averages over the 5, 10, and 15 minute intervals prior to a server's transmission. The host name included is that returned by the gethostname(2) system call. The array at the end of the message contains information about the users logged in to the sending machine. This information includes the contents of the utmp(4) entry for each non-idle terminal line and a value indicating the time since a character was last received on the terminal line.

Messages received by the rwho server are discarded unless they originated at a rwho server's port. In addition, if the host's name, as specified in the message, contains any unprintable ASCII characters, the message is discarded. Valid messages received by rwhod are placed in files named whod.*hostname* in the directory

/var/spool/rwho. These files contain only the most recent message, in the format described above.

Status messages are generated approximately once every 60 seconds. rwhod performs an nlist(3) on /stand/unix every 10 minutes to guard against the possibility that this file is not the system image currently operating.

FILES

/var/spool/rwho

SEE ALSO

rwho(1), ruptime(1), w(1), gethostname(3), nlist(3), utmp(4)

NOTES

This service takes up progressively more network bandwidth as the number of hosts on the local net increases. For large networks, the cost becomes prohibitive.

rwhod should relay status information between networks. People often interpret the server dying as a machine going down.

For rwho to work properly, the directory /var/spool/rwho must exist on the system.

NAME

sac - service access controller

SYNOPSIS

sac -t *sanity_interval*

DESCRIPTION

The Service Access Controller (SAC) is the overseer of the server machine. It is started when the server machine enters multiuser mode. The SAC performs several important functions as explained below.

Customizing the SAC environment. When sac is invoked, it first looks for the per-system configuration script /etc/saf/_sysconfig. sac interprets _sysconfig to customize its own environment. The modifications made to the SAC environment by _sysconfig are inherited by all the children of the SAC. This inherited environment may be modified by the children.

Starting port monitors. After it has interpreted the _sysconfig file, the sac reads its administrative file /etc/saf/_sactab. _sactab specifies which port monitors are to be started. For each port monitor to be started, sac forks a child [fork(2)] and creates a utmp entry with the *type* field set to LOGIN_PROCESS. Each child then interprets its per-port monitor configuration script /etc/saf/*pmtag*/_config, if the file exists. These modifications to the environment affect the port monitor and will be inherited by all its children. Finally, the child process execs the port monitor, using the command found in the _sactab entry. (See sacadm; this is the command given with the -c option when the port monitor is added to the system.)

Polling port monitors to detect failure. The -t option sets the frequency with which sac polls the port monitors on the system. This time may also be thought of as half of the maximum latency required to detect that a port monitor has failed and that recovery action is necessary.

Administrative functions. The Service Access Controller represents the administrative point of control for port monitors. Its administrative tasks are explained below.

When queried (sacadm with either -l or -L), the Service Access Controller returns the status of the port monitors specified, which sacadm prints on the standard output. A port monitor may be in one of six states:

ENABLED
: The port monitor is currently running and is accepting connections. See sacadm(1M) with the -e option.

DISABLED
: The port monitor is currently running and is not accepting connections. See sacadm with the -d option, and see NOTRUNNING, below.

STARTING
: The port monitor is in the process of starting up. STARTING is an intermediate state on the way to ENABLED or DISABLED.

FAILED
: The port monitor was unable to start and remain running.

STOPPING
: The port monitor has been manually terminated but has not completed its shutdown procedure. STOPPING is an intermediate state on the way to NOTRUNNING.

NOTRUNNING   The port monitor is not currently running. (See sacadm with -k.) This is the normal "not running" state. When a port monitor is killed, all ports it was monitoring are inaccessible. It is not possible for an external user to tell whether a port is not being monitored or the system is down. If the port monitor is not killed but is in the DISABLED state, it may be possible (depending on the port monitor being used) to write a message on the inaccessible port telling the user who is trying to access the port that it is disabled. This is the advantage of having a DISABLED state as well as the NOTRUNNING state.

When a port monitor terminates, the SAC removes the utmp entry for that port monitor.

The SAC receives all requests to enable, disable, start, or stop port monitors and takes the appropriate action.

The SAC is responsible for restarting port monitors that terminate. Whether or not the SAC will restart a given port monitor depends on two things:

- the restart count specified for the port monitor when the port monitor was added by sacadm; this information is included in /etc/saf/*pmtag*/_sactab

- the number of times the port monitor has already been restarted

SEE ALSO
sacadm(1M), pmadm(1M).

FILES
/etc/saf/_sactab
/etc/saf/_sysconfig
/var/adm/utmp
/var/saf/_log

NAME

sacadm - service access controller administration

SYNOPSIS

sacadm -a -p *pmtag* -t *type* -c *cmd* -v *ver* [-f dx] [-n *count*] \
   [-y *comment*] [-z script]

sacadm -r -p *pmtag*

sacadm -s -p *pmtag*

sacadm -k -p *pmtag*

sacadm -e -p *pmtag*

sacadm -d -p *pmtag*

sacadm -l [-p *pmtag* | -t *type*]

sacadm -L [-p *pmtag* | -t *type*]

sacadm -g -p *pmtag* [-z *script*]

sacadm -G [-z script]

sacadm -x [-p *pmtag*]

DESCRIPTION

sacadm is the administrative command for the upper level of the Service Access
Facility hierarchy, that is, for port monitor administration. sacadm performs the
following functions:

- adds or removes a port monitor

- starts or stops a port monitor

- enables or disables a port monitor

- installs or replaces a per-system configuration script

- installs or replaces a per-port monitor configuration script

- prints requested port monitor information

Requests about the status of port monitors (-l and -L) and requests to print per-
port monitor and per-system configuration scripts (-g and -G without the -z
option) may be executed by any user on the system. Other sacadm commands may
be executed only by a privileged user.

The options have the following meanings:

-a   Add a port monitor. When adding a port monitor, sacadm creates the sup-
        porting directory structure in /etc/saf and /var/saf and adds an entry
        for the new port monitor to /etc/saf/_sactab. The file _sactab already
        exists on the delivered system. Initially, it is empty except for a single line,
        which contains the version number of the Service Access Controller.

        Unless the command line that adds the new port monitor includes a -f
        option with the argument x, the new port monitor will be started. Because
        of the complexity of the options and arguments that follow the -a option,
        it may be convenient to use a command script or the menu system to add
        port monitors. If you use the menu system, enter sysadm ports and then
        choose the port_monitors option.

-c *cmd*   Execute the command string *cmd* to start a port monitor. The -c option may be used only with a -a. A -a option requires a -c.

-d   Disable the port monitor *pmtag*.

-e   Enable the port monitor *pmtag*.

-f dx   The -f option specifies one or both of the following two flags which are then included in the flags field of the _sactab entry for the new port monitor. If the -f option is not included on the command line, no flags are set and the default conditions prevail. By default, a port monitor is started. A -f option with no following argument is illegal.

        d   Do not enable the new port monitor.

        x   Do not start the new port monitor.

-g   The -g option is used to request output or to install or replace the per-port monitor configuration script /etc/saf/*pmtag*/_config. -g requires a -p option. The -g option with only a -p option prints the per-port monitor configuration script for port monitor *pmtag*. The -g option with a -p option and a -z option installs the file script as the per-port monitor configuration script for port monitor *pmtag*. Other combinations of options with -g are invalid.

-G   The -G option is used to request output or to install or replace the per-system configuration script /etc/saf/_sysconfig. The -G option by itself prints the per-system configuration script. The -G option in combination with a -z option installs the file script as the per-system configuration script. Other combinations of options with a -G option are invalid.

-k   Stop port monitor *pmtag*.

-l   The -l option is used to request port monitor information. The -l by itself lists all port monitors on the system. The -l option in combination with the -p option lists only the port monitor specified by *pmtag*. A -l in combination with the -t option lists all port monitors of type *type*. Any other combination of options with the -l option is invalid.

-L   The -L option is identical to the -l option except that the output appears in a condensed format.

-n *count*

    Set the restart count to *count*. If a restart count is not specified, count is set to 0. A count of 0 indicates that the port monitor is not to be restarted if it fails.

-p *pmtag*

    Specifies the tag associated with a port monitor.

-r   Remove port monitor *pmtag*. sacadm removes the port monitor entry from /etc/saf/_sactab. If the removed port monitor is not running, then no further action is taken. If the removed port monitor is running, the Service Access Controller (SAC) sends it SIGTERM to indicate that it should shut down. Note that the port monitor's directory structure remains intact.

-s   Start a port monitor. The SAC starts the port monitor *pmtag*.

-t *type*   Specifies the port monitor type.

-v *ver*   Specifies the version number of the port monitor. This version number may be given as

> -v `pmspec -V`

where *pmspec* is the special administrative command for port monitor *pmtag*. This special command is ttyadm for ttymon and nlsadmin for listen. The version stamp of the port monitor is known by the command and is returned when *pmspec* is invoked with a -V option.

-x   The -x option by itself tells the SAC to read its database file (_sactab). The -x option with the -p option tells port monitor *pmtag* to read its administrative file.

-y *comment*
> Include *comment* in the _sactab entry for port monitor *pmtag*.

-z script
> Used with the -g and -G options to specify the name of a file that contains a configuration script. With the -g option, script is a per-port monitor configuration script; with -G it is a per-system configuration script. Modifying a configuration script is a three-step procedure. First a copy of the existing script is made (-g or -G). Then the copy is edited. Finally, the copy is put in place over the existing script (-g or -G with -z).

OUTPUT

If successful, sacadm will exit with a status of 0. If sacadm fails for any reason, it will exit with a nonzero status. Options that request information will write the information on the standard output. In the condensed format (-L), port monitor information is printed as a sequence of colon-separated fields; empty fields are indicated by two successive colons. The standard format (-l) prints a header identifying the columns, and port monitor information is aligned under the appropriate headings. In this format, an empty field is indicated by a hyphen. The comment character is #.

EXAMPLES

The following command line adds a port monitor. The port monitor tag is npack; its type is listen; if necessary, it will restart three times before failing; its administrative command is nlsadmin; and the configuration script to be read is in the file script:

```
sacadm -a -p npack -t listen -c /usr/lib/saf/listen npack \
    -v `nlsadmin -V` -n 3 -z script
```

Remove a port monitor whose tag is pmtag:

```
sacadm -r -p pmtag
```

Start the port monitor whose tag is pmtag:

```
sacadm -s -p pmtag
```

Stop the port monitor whose tag is pmtag:

```
sacadm -k -p pmtag
```

Enable the port monitor whose tag is pmtag:

```
sacadm -e -p pmtag
```

Disable the port monitor whose tag is pmtag:

```
sacadm -d -p pmtag
```

List status information for all port monitors:

```
sacadm -l
```

List status information for the port monitor whose tag is pmtag:

```
sacadm -l -p pmtag
```

List the same information in condensed format:

```
sacadm -L -p pmtag
```

List status information for all port monitors whose type is listen:

```
sacadm -l -t listen
```

Replace the per-port monitor configuration script associated with the port monitor whose tag is pmtag with the contents of the file file.config:

```
sacadm -g -p pmtag -z file.config
```

SEE ALSO

doconfig(3N), pmadm(1M), sac(1M)

FILES

```
/etc/saf/_sactab
/etc/saf/_sysconfig
/etc/saf/pmtag/_config
```

NAME

sact - print current SCCS file editing activity

SYNOPSIS

sact *files*

DESCRIPTION

sact informs the user of any impending deltas to a named SCCS file. This situation occurs when get with the -e option has been previously executed without a subsequent execution of delta. If a directory is named on the command line, sact behaves as though each file in the directory were specified as a named file, except that non-SCCS files and unreadable files are silently ignored. If a name of − is given, the standard input is read with each line being taken as the name of an SCCS file to be processed.

The output for each named file consists of five fields separated by spaces.

Field 1	specifies the SID of a delta that currently exists in the SCCS file to which changes will be made to make the new delta.
Field 2	specifies the SID for the new delta to be created.
Field 3	contains the logname of the user who will make the delta (that is, executed a get for editing).
Field 4	contains the date that get -e was executed.
Field 5	contains the time that get -e was executed.

SEE ALSO

delta(1), diff(1), get(1), help(1), unget(1)

DIAGNOSTICS

Use help(1) for explanations.

NAME

sadc: sa1, sa2, sadc - system activity report package

SYNOPSIS

/usr/lib/sa/sadc [*t n*] [*ofile*]

/usr/lib/sa/sa1 [*t n*]

/usr/lib/sa/sa2 [-ubdycwaqvmpgrkxDSAC] [-s *time*] [-e *time*] [-i *sec*]
[-P *processor-id*]

DESCRIPTION

System activity data can be accessed at the special request of a user (see sar(1M))
and automatically on a routine basis. The operating system contains several
counters that are incremented as various system actions occur. These include
counters for processor utilization, buffer usage, disk and tape I/O activity, TTY
device activity, switching and system-call activity, file-access, queue activity,
inter-process communications, paging and Remote File Sharing.

Some of these counters (those in the si member of the binary activity record produced by sadc) are maintained separately for each processor that is or has been
online in the system. For each separately maintained counter, the system also
maintains a corresponding aggregate counter. The per-processor counters are a
measure of the actions performed by each processor in the system. The corresponding aggregate counters represent a measure of the same actions performed by the
system as a whole. For uni-processing, there is only one per-processor set of data.

sadc and shell procedures, sa1 and sa2, are used to sample, save, and process data.

sadc, the data collector, samples system data *n* times, with an interval of *t* seconds
between samples. The sampling interval *t* should be greater than 5 seconds; otherwise, the activity of sadc itself may affect the sample. If *t* and *n* are omitted, a special record is written. This facility is used at system boot time, when booting to a
multiuser state, to mark the time at which the counters restart from zero. For example, the /sbin/init.d/perf file writes the restart mark to the daily data by the
command entry:

```
su sys -c "/usr/lib/sa/sadc /var/adm/sa/sadate +%d"
```

sadc writes system activity records in binary format. This format includes information describing per processor system activity and counters describing aggregate
system activity. If *ofile* is not specified, sadc writes this data to standard output. If
ofile is specified, sadc writes the data to *ofile*.

If the -P option is used, sa2 reports system activity information that applies to the
processor specified by *processor-id* to standard output. The -P option applies to
multi-processing only.

The shell script sa1, a variant of sadc, is used to collect and store data in binary file /var/adm/sa/sa*dd* where *dd* is the current day. The arguments *t* and *n* cause records to be written *n* times at an interval of *t* seconds, or once if omitted. The following entries in /var/spool/cron/crontabs/sys will produce records every 20 minutes during working hours and hourly otherwise:

```
0 * * * 0-6 /usr/lib/sa/sa1
20,40 8-17 * * 1-5 /usr/lib/sa/sa1
```

See crontab(1) for details.

EXAMPLE

The shell script sa2, a variant of sar, writes a daily report in the file /var/adm/sa/sar*dd*. The options are explained in sar(1). The following entry in /var/spool/cron/crontabs/sys will report important activities hourly during the working day:

```
5 18 * * 1-5 /usr/lib/sa/sa2 -s 8:00 -e 18:01 -i 1200 -A
```

FILES

/var/adm/sa/sa*dd*	daily data file for system as a whole
/var/adm/sa/sar*dd*	daily report file
/tmp/sa.adrfl	address file

SEE ALSO

crontab(1), timex(1), sar(1M)

NAME

    sadp - disk access profiler

SYNOPSIS

    sadp [-th] [-d *drive*] *s* [*n*]

DESCRIPTION

    sadp reports disk access location and seek distance, in tabular or histogram form. It samples disk activity once every second during an interval of s seconds. This is done n times if n is specified. Cylinder usage and disk distance are recorded in units of sectors.

    The drive name must be the filename of a raw device in the form of *prefix_cXdYsZ*, where *prefix* uniquely defines the type of device, X specifies the controller number (starting from zero) of the stated device type, Y specifies the logical device number (starting from zero) for the device attached to the stated controller, and Z specifies the device dependent information. For a SCSI disk, Z is the slice number for the whole disk, usually 7.

    If *drive* is not specified, sadp profiles all the disk drives present.

    The -t flag causes the data to be reported in tabular form. The -h flag produces a histogram of the data. The default is -t.

EXAMPLE

    The command:

        sadp 900 4

    will generate four tabular reports, each describing slice usage and seek distance of all disk drives during a 15-minute interval.

SEE ALSO

    mem(7).

NAME

sag - system activity graph

SYNOPSIS

sag [*options*]

DESCRIPTION

sag graphically displays the system activity data stored in a binary data file by a previous sar(1M) run. Any of the sar data items may be plotted singly, or in combination; as cross plots, or versus time. Simple arithmetic combinations of data may be specified. sag invokes sar and finds the desired data by string-matching the data column header (run sar to see what is available). These *options* are passed through to sar:

-s *time*   Select data later than *time* in the form *hh* [: *mm*]. The default is 08:00.

-e *time*   Select data up to *time*. The default is 18:00.

-i *sec*   Select data at intervals as close as possible to *sec* seconds.

-f *file*   Use *file* as the data source for sar. The default value is the current daily data file (/usr/adm/sa/sa*dd*).

Other *options*:

-T *term*   Produce output suitable for terminal *term*. The default value is $TERM. The only terminal type that is supported for making line graphs is the Tektronix 4014 (can be emulated by xterm(1)). If any other terminal type is used, an ASCII graph is printed.

-x *spec*   x axis specification with *spec* in the form:
            "*name* [*op name*] . . . [*lo hi*]"

-y *spec*   y axis specification with *spec* in the same form as above.

Name is either a string that will match a column header in the sar report, with an optional device name in square brackets, (such as r+w/s[dsk-1], or an integer value. *Op* is one of four characters ("+", "-", "*", or "/"), surrounded by blanks. (Parentheses are not recognized.) Up to five names may be specified. Contrary to custom, + and - have precedence over * and /". Evaluation is done from left to right. Thus $A / A + B * 100$ is evaluated $(A/(A+B))*100$, and $A + B / C + D$ is $(A+B)/(C+D)$. *Lo* and *hi* are optional numeric scale limits. If unspecified, they are deduced from the data.

A single *spec* is permitted for the x axis; if unspecified, *time* is used. For the y axis, specify up to five *specs*, separated by semi-colons (;). If you specify more than one argument to -x or -y, and leave one or more blank spaces between list items, enclose the list in double quotes (" "). The default value for the -y option is

```
-y "%usr 0 100; %usr + %sys 0 100; %usr + %sys + %wio 0 100"
```

EXAMPLES

For a report on today's CPU utilization:

```
sag
```

For a report on the activity of all disk drives over a 15-minute period:

When used with -D, buffer caching is reported for locally-mounted remote resources.

-d   Report activity for each block device which provides this support. The device name is reported for each device. The activity data reported is:

%busy   percentage of time device was busy servicing a transfer request.

avque   average number of requests outstanding during the monitored period.

r+w/s   number of data transfers to or from device per second.

blks/s   number of 512-byte blocks transferred to or from the device per second.

avwait   average time in milliseconds that transfer requests wait idly on queue.

avserv   average time in milliseconds for a transfer request to be completed by the device (for disks includes seek, rotational latency and data transfer times).

-y   Report TTY device activity (per second):

rawch/s   input characters.

canch/s   input characters processed by canon.

outch/s   output characters.

rcvin/s   receiver hardware interrupts.

xmtin/s   transmitter hardware interrupts.

mdmin/s   modem interrupts.

-c   Report system calls (per second):

scall/s   system calls of all types.

sread/s, swrit/s, fork/s, exec/s
    specific system calls.

rchar/s   characters (bytes) transferred by read system calls.

wchar/s   characters (bytes) transferred by write system calls.

When used with -D, the system calls are split into incoming, outgoing, and strictly local calls. No incoming or outgoing fork and exec calls are reported.

-w   Report system swapping and switching activity (per second):

swpin/s, swpot/s
    number of transfers to and from memory

pswin/s, pswot/s
    number of 512-byte blocks transferred for swapins and swapouts (including initial loading of some programs).

pswch/s   process switches.

-a   Report use of file access system routines (per second):

iget/s   number of S5 and UFS files located by inode entry.

namei/s   number of file system path searches.

dirblk/s   number of S5 and UFS directory block reads issued.

-q   Report average queue length while occupied, and percentage of time occupied:

runq-sz   run queue of processes in memory and runnable.

%runocc   percentage of time run queue is occupied.

swpq-sz, %swpocc
the average number of processes in the swap queue when there were processes in the queue and the percent of time during the sample that there were processes in the swap queue. If there are no processes in the swap queue, these fields are blank.

-v   Report status of process, i-node, file and file lock record tables. Only S5 file system inode information is reported. The maximum number of files open is reported as inf if it depends only on available memory.

proc-sz, inod-sz, file-sz, lock-sz
entries/size for each table, evaluated once at sampling point.

ov   overflows that occur between sampling points for each table.

-m   Report message and semaphore activities:

msg/s, sema/s
primitives per second.

-p   Report paging activities:

atch/s   page faults per second that are satisfied by reclaiming a page currently in memory (attaches per second).

pgin/s   page-in requests per second.

ppgin/s   pages paged-in per second.

pflt/s   page faults from protection errors per second (invalid access to page) or "copy-on-writes."

vflt/s   address translation page faults per second (valid page not in memory).

slock/s   faults per second caused by software lock requests requiring physical I/O.

-g   Report paging activities:

pgout/s   page-out requests per second.

ppgout/s   pages paged-out per second.

pgfree/s   pages per second placed on the freelist by the page stealing daemon.

pgscan/s   pages per second scanned by the page stealing daemon.

%s5ipf   the percentage of S5 inodes taken off the freelist by iget which had reusable pages associated with it. These pages are flushed and cannot be reclaimed by processes. Thus, this is the percentage of igets with page flushes.

-r   Report unused memory pages and disk blocks:

freemem   average pages available to user processes.

freeswap   disk blocks available for page swapping.

-k   Report kernel memory allocation (KMA) activities:

Information about the memory pool reserving and allocating space for small requests (less than 256 bytes):

sml_mem   the amount of memory in bytes KMA has for the small pool.

alloc   the number of bytes allocated to satisfy requests for small amounts of memory.

fail   the number of requests for small amounts of memory that were not satisfied (failed).

Information for the large memory pool:

lg_mem, alloc, fail
           (analogous to the information for the small memory pool.)

Information for oversized requests (because oversized memory is allocated dynamically, there is not a pool):

ovsz_alloc
           the amount of memory allocated for oversize requests.

fail   the number of oversize requests that could not be satisfied.

-x   Report remote file sharing (RFS) operations:

open/s   the number of open operations made per second by clients (incoming) and by the server (outgoing).

create/s   the number of create operations made per second by clients (incoming) and by the server (outgoing).

lookup/s   the number of lookup operations made per second by clients (incoming) and by the server (outgoing).

readdir/s the number of readdir operations made per second by clients (incoming) and by the server (outgoing).

getpage/s the number of getpage operations made per second by clients (incoming) and by the server (outgoing).

putpage/s the number of putpage operations made per second by clients (incoming) and by the server (outgoing).

other/s   the number of other operations made per second by clients (incoming) and by the server (outgoing).

    -D   Report Remote File Sharing activity:

When used in combination with -u, -b or -c, it causes sar to produce the remote file sharing version of the corresponding report. -Du is assumed when only -D is specified.

    -S   Report server and request queue status:

serv/lo-hi   average number of Remote File Sharing servers on the system (lo and hi are the minimum and maximum number of servers respectively).

request %busy   percentage of time receive descriptors are on the request queue.

request avg lgth
        average number of receive descriptors waiting for service when queue is occupied.

server %avail   percentage of time there are idle servers.

server avg avail
        average number of idle servers when idle ones exist.

    -A   Without the -P option, this is equivalent to -udqbwcayvmpgrkxCSD. With the -P option, this is equivalent to -ubwcaymgD.

    -C   Report Remote File Sharing data caching overhead:

snd-inv/s   number of invalidation messages per second sent by your machine as a server.

snd-msg/s   total outgoing RFS messages sent per second.

rcv-inv/s   number of invalidation messages received from the remote server.

rcv-msg/s   total number of incoming RFS messages received per second.

dis-bread/s   number of read messages that would be eligible for caching if caching had not been turned off because of an invalidation message. (Indicates the penalty incurred because of the invalidation message).

blk-inv/s   number of pages removed from the client cache in response to cache invalidation messages.

EXAMPLES

To see today's processor activity so far:

```
sar
```

To see the system call activity so far for processor 0:

```
sar -c -P0
```

To watch processor activity evolve for 10 minutes and save data:

```
sar -o temp 60 10
```

To later review disk and tape activity from that period:

```
sar -d -f temp
```

FILES

/var/adm/sa/sa*dd*   daily data file, where *dd* are digits representing the day of the month

SEE ALSO

sadc(1M), sag(1M)

NAME

sccs - front end for the Source Code Control System (SCCS)

SYNOPSIS

/usr/ucb/sccs [-r] [-d*prefixpath*] [-p*finalpath*] *command*
[*SCCS-flags* . . .] [*filename* . . .]

DESCRIPTION

The sccs command is a front end to the utility programs of the Source Code Control System (SCCS).

sccs normally prefixes each *filename*, or the last component of each *filename*, with
the string 'SCCS/s.', because you normally keep your SCCS database files in a
directory called SCCS, and each database file starts with an 's.' prefix. If the
environment variable PROJECTDIR is set, and is an absolute pathname (that is,
begins with a slash) sccs will search for SCCS files in the directory given by that
variable. If it is a relative pathname (that is, does not begin with a slash), it is
treated as the name of a user, and sccs will search in that user's home directory for
a directory named src or source. If that directory is found, sccs will search for
SCCS files in the directory given by that variable.

sccs program options must appear before the *command* argument. Flags to be
passed to the actual SCCS command (utility program) must appear after the *command* argument. These flags are specific to the *command* being used.

sccs also includes the capability to run "set user ID" to another user to provide
additional protection. Certain commands (such as admin(1)) cannot be run "set
user ID" by all users, since this would allow anyone to change the authorizations.
Such commands are always run as the real user.

OPTIONS

-r   Run sccs as the real user rather than as whatever effective user sccs is "set
        user ID" to.

-d*prefixpath*
        Define the prefix portion of the pathname for the SCCS database files. The
        default prefix portion of the pathname is the current directory. *prefixpath* is
        prefixed to the entire pathname. See EXAMPLE.

        This flag overrides any directory specified by the PROJECTDIR environment
        variable.

-p*finalpath*
        Define the name of a lower directory in which the SCCS files will be found;
        SCCS is the default. *finalpath* is appended before the final component of the
        pathname. See EXAMPLE.

USAGE

Additional sccs Commands

Several "pseudo-commands" are available in addition to the usual SCCS commands. These are:

create   create is used when creating new s. files. For example, given a C
            source language file called 'obscure.c', create would perform the
            following actions: (1) create the 's.' file called 's.obscure.c' in the
            SCCS directory; (2) rename the original source file to ',obscure.c'; (3)
            do an 'sccs get' on 'obscure.c'. Compared to the SCCS admin

command, `create` does more of the startup work for you and should be used in preference to `admin`.

enter
: `enter` is just like `create`, except that it does not do the final 'sccs get'. It is usually used if an 'sccs edit' is to be performed immediately after the `enter`.

edit
: Get a file for editing.

delget
: Perform a `delta` on the named files and then `get` new versions. The new versions have ID keywords expanded, and so cannot be edited.

deledit
: Same as `delget`, but produces new versions suitable for editing. `deledit` is useful for making a "checkpoint" of your current editing phase.

fix
: Remove the named delta, but leaves you with a copy of the delta with the changes that were in it. `fix` must be followed by a `-r` flag. `fix` is useful for fixing small compiler bugs, etc. Since `fix` does not leave audit trails, use it carefully.

clean
: Remove everything from the current directory that can be recreated from SCCS files. `clean` checks for and does not remove any files being edited. If 'clean -b' is used, branches are not checked to see if they are currently being edited. Note: -b is dangerous if you are keeping the branches in the same directory.

unedit
: "Undo" the last `edit` or 'get -e' and return a file to its previous condition. If you `unedit` a file being edited, all changes made since the beginning of the editing session are lost.

info
: Display a list of all files being edited. If the -b flag is given, branches (that is, SID's with two or fewer components) are ignored. If the -u flag is given (with an optional argument), only files being edited by you (or the named user) are listed.

check
: Check for files currently being edited, like `info`, but returns an exit code rather than a listing: nothing is printed if nothing is being edited, and a non-zero exit status is returned if anything is being edited. `check` may thus be included in an "install" entry in a makefile, to ensure that everything is included in an SCCS file before a version is installed.

tell
: Display a list of files being edited on the standard output. Filenames are separated by NEWLINE characters. Take the -b and -u flags like `info` and `check`.

diffs
: Compare (in `diff`-like format) the current version of the program you have out for editing and the versions in SCCS format. `diffs` accepts the same arguments as `diff`, except that the -c flag must be specified as -C instead, because the -c flag is taken as a flag to `get` indicating which version is to be compared with the current version.

print
: Print verbose information about the named files. `print` does an 'sccs prs -e' followed by an 'sccs get -p -m' on each file.

EXAMPLE

The command:

```
sccs  -d/usr/include  get sys/inode.h
```

converts to:

```
get  /usr/include/sys/SCCS/s.inode.h
```

The intent here is to create aliases such as:

```
alias  syssccs  sccs  -d/usr/src
```

which will be used as:

```
syssccs  get  cmd/who.c
```

The command:

```
sccs  -pprivate  get  usr/include/stdio.h
```

converts to:

```
get  usr/include/private/s.stdio.h
```

To put a file called `myprogram.c` into SCCS format for the first time, assuming also that there is no SCCS directory already existing:

```
$ mkdir SCCS
$ sccs create myprogram.c
$ myprogram.c:
1.1
14 lines
```
after you have verified that everything is all right
you remove the version of the file that starts with a comma:
```
$ rm myprogram.c
$
```

To get a copy of `myprogram.c` for editing, edit that file, then place it back in the SCCS database:

```
$ sccs edit myprogram.c
1.1
new delta 1.2
14 lines
$ vi myprogram.c
```
your editing session
```
$ sccs delget myprogram.c
comments? Added abusive responses for compatibility
1.2
7 inserted
7 deleted
7 unchanged
1.2
14 lines
$
```

To get a file from another directory:

```
sccs -p/usr/src/sccs/  get cc.c
```

or:

```
sccs get /usr/src/sccs/cc.c
```

To make a delta of a large number of files in the current directory:

```
sccs delta *.c
```

To get a list of files being edited that are not on branches:

```
sccs info -b
```

To delta everything that you are editing:

```
$ sccs delta `sccs tell -u`
```

In a makefile, to get source files from an SCCS file if it does not already exist:

```
SRCS = <list of source files>
$(SRCS):
        sccs get $(REL) $@
```

Regular sccs Commands

The "regular" SCCS commands are described very briefly below. It is unlikely that you ever need to use these commands because the user interface is so complicated, and the `sccs` front end command does 99.9% of the interesting tasks for you.

admin
: Create new SCCS files and changes parameters of existing SCCS files. You can use 'sccs create' to create new SCCS files, or use 'sccs admin' to do other things.

cdc
: Change the commentary material in an SCCS delta.

comb
: Combine SCCS deltas and reconstructs the SCCS files.

delta
: Permanently introduces changes that were made to a file previously retrieved using 'sccs get'. You can use 'sccs delget' as the more useful version of this command since 'sccs delget' does all of the useful work and more.

get
: Extract a file from the SCCS database, either for compilation, or for editing when the -e option is used. Use 'sccs get' if you really need it, but 'sccs delget' will normally have done this job for you. Use sccs edit instead of get with the -e option.

help
: Supposed to help you interpret SCCS error messages.

prs
: Display information about what is happening in an SCCS file.

rmdel
: Remove a delta from an SCCS file.

sccsdiff
: Compare two versions of an SCCS file and generates the differences between the two versions.

val
: Determine if a given SCCS file meets specified criteria. If you use the sccs command, you should not need to use val, because its user interface is unbelievable.

what   Display SCCS identification information.

FILES

`/usr/sccs/*`

SEE ALSO

`admin`(1), `cdc`(1), `comb`(1), `delta`(1), `get`(1), `help`(1), `prs`(1), `rmdel`(1), `sact`(1), `sccsdiff`(1), `unget`(1), `val`(1), `what`(1), `sccsfile`(5).

NOTES

The `help` command usually just parrots SCCS error messages and is generally not considered very helpful.

NAME

sccsdiff - compare two versions of an SCCS file

SYNOPSIS

sccsdiff -r*SID1* -r*SID2* [-p] [-s*n*] *files*

DESCRIPTION

sccsdiff compares two versions of an SCCS file and generates the differences between the two versions. Any number of SCCS files may be specified, but arguments apply to all files.

-r*SID1* -r*SID2*	*SID1* and *SID2* specify the deltas of an SCCS file that are to be compared. Versions are passed to bdiff in the order given.
-p	pipe output for each file through pr.
-s*n*	*n* is the file segment size that bdiff will pass to diff. This option is useful when diff fails due to a high system load.

FILES

/var/tmp/get?????   temporary files

SEE ALSO

get(1), help(1)

diff(1), bdiff(1), pr(1).

NAME

`script` - make typescript of a terminal session

SYNOPSIS

`script` [`-a`] [*filename*]

DESCRIPTION

`script` makes a typescript of everything printed on your terminal. The typescript is written to *filename*, or appended to *filename* if the `-a` option is given. If no file name is given, the typescript is saved in the file `typescript`.

The script ends when the forked shell exits or when ctrl-D is typed.

NOTES

`script` places *everything* that appears on the screen in the log file, including prompts.

NAME

scsi1x7 - add /dev entries for SCSI devices in the Equipped Device Table (EDT)

SYNOPSIS

/sbin/auto-device/scsi1x7

DESCRIPTION

scsi1x7 performs the following steps:

1. Searches the EDT to determine if the scsi1x7 SCSI host adapter support is configured. If it is not found, the program deletes any existing related device nodes and exits.

2. Examines the Extended EDT information to determine the peripheral complement attached to the host adapter. All non-present devices with existing device nodes have their device nodes deleted.

3. Compares the existing device nodes against the Extended EDT information, and device nodes are created for all devices that do not have device nodes. Devices that may have changed type (for example, tape to disk) will have their device nodes deleted and recreated.

FILES

/dev/dsk/*	entries for the hard disk and floppies for general use
/dev/rdsk/*	
/dev/rmt/*	entries for the tapes for general use
/dev/generic/*	entries for pass-through support

SEE ALSO

makedev(1M), mvme328(1M), sysadm(1M), intro(7)

NAME

scsifmt - format a SCSI hard disk or floppy

SYNOPSIS

scsifmt [-p *info-file*] /dev/rdsk/*

DESCRIPTION

scsifmt will attempt to format the specified device by invoking the dinit(1M) command with the ddef file that is correct for the device. This is done by comparing the vendor and product ID fields of the SCSI inquiry information returned from the device against the contents of the identification database file (by default /etc/scsifmt.info).

The -p option specifies the path name of an alternate identification database file.

An identification database file is composed of one or more lines, each of which identifies the information about a single device. Any line starting with a # is treated as a comment. Device entries may appear in any order and each entry is separated into five white-space separated fields.

The first field should contain the vendor ID information enbedded in double quotes. The field only needs to be long enough to uniquely identify the device.

The second field should contain the product ID information enbedded in double quotes. The field only needs to be long enough to uniquely identify the device.

The third field should contain the name of the ddef file appropriate for the entry.

The fourth field should contain the slice number associated with the ddef file. For hard disks this is typically slice 7.

The fifth field should contain a brief (30 characters or less) description of the disk embedded in quotes.

FILES

/dev/rdsk/*
/etc/scsifmt.info

SEE ALSO

dinit(1M)

NAME

scsiscan - locate and describe SCSI devices

SYNOPSIS

scsiscan [-c] [-h] [-p delimiter]

DESCRIPTION

scsiscan attempts to locate and describe all Small Computer System Interface (SCSI) devices connected to Motorola supported host adapters.

If the -p option is not used, the output will be in tabular form. If the -p option is used, the information will be output one device per line with the fields separated by the specified single character delimiter. If the -h option is used, the table header will not be printed.

If the -c option is used, the host adapter name, board number, board revision string, and firmware revision string will be printed.

If the -c option is not used, the generic device description, device identifier, vendor name, product ID, and revision number will be printed.

SEE ALSO

prtconf(1M), intro(7)

NAME

sdiff - print file differences side-by-side

SYNOPSIS

sdiff [*options*] *file1 file2*

DESCRIPTION

sdiff uses the output of the diff command to produce a side-by-side listing of two files indicating lines that are different. Lines of the two files are printed with a blank gutter between them if the lines are identical, a < in the gutter if the line appears only in *file1*, a > in the gutter if the line appears only in *file2*, and a | for lines that are different. For example:

```
x       |       y
a               a
b       <
c       <
d               d
        >       c
```

Valid options are:

-w *n*   Use the argument *n* as the width of the output line. The default line length is 130 columns. Multicolumn characters that cross the right margin of a file are displayed as ASCII spaces.

-l   Print only the left side of any lines that are identical.

-s   Do not print identical lines.

-o *output*   Use the argument *output* as the name of a third file that is created as a user-controlled merge of *file1* and *file2*. Identical lines of *file1* and *file2* are copied to *output*. Sets of differences, as produced by diff, are printed; where a set of differences share a common gutter character. After printing each set of differences, sdiff prompts the user with a % and waits for one of the following user-typed commands:

    l   Append the left column to the output file.
    r   Append the right column to the output file.
    s   Turn on silent mode; do not print identical lines.
    v   Turn off silent mode.
    e l   Call the editor with the left column.
    e r   Call the editor with the right column.
    e b   Call the editor with the concatenation of left and right.
    e   Call the editor with a zero length file.
    q   Exit from the program.

On exit from the editor, the resulting file is concatenated to the end of the *output* file.

INTERNATIONAL FUNCTIONS

sdiff can process files containing characters from supplementary code sets.

SEE ALSO

diff(1), ed(1)

NAME

sed - stream editor

SYNOPSIS

sed [-n] [-e *script*] [-f *sfile*] [*file* ...]

DESCRIPTION

sed copies the named *file* (standard input default) to the standard output, edited according to a script of commands. The -f option causes the script to be taken from file *sfile*; these options accumulate. If there is just one -e option and no -f options, the flag -e may be omitted. The -n option suppresses the default output. A script consists of editing commands, one per line, of the following form:

> [*address* [, *address*]] *function* [*arguments*]

In normal operation, sed cyclically copies a line of input into a *pattern space* (unless there is something left after a D command), applies in sequence all commands whose *addresses* select that pattern space, and at the end of the script copies the pattern space to the standard output (except under -n) and deletes the pattern space.

Some of the commands use a *hold space* to save all or part of the *pattern space* for subsequent retrieval.

An *address* is either a decimal number that counts input lines cumulatively across files, a $ that addresses the last line of input, or a context address, i.e., a /*regular expression*/ in the style of ed(1) modified thus:

> In a context address, the construction \?*regular expression*?, where ? is any character, is identical to /*regular expression*/. Note that in the context address \xabc\xdefx, the second x stands for itself, so that the regular expression is abcxdef.
> The escape sequence \n matches a new-line *embedded* in the pattern space.
> A period (.) matches any character except the *terminal* new-line of the pattern space.
> A command line with no addresses selects every pattern space.
> A command line with one address selects each pattern space that matches the address.
> A command line with two addresses selects the inclusive range from the first pattern space that matches the first address through the next pattern space that matches the second address. (If the second address is a number less than or equal to the line number selected by the first address, only the line corresponding to the first address is selected.) Thereafter the process is repeated, looking again for the first address.

Editing commands can be applied only to non-selected pattern spaces by use of the negation function ! (below).

In the following list of functions the maximum number of permissible addresses for each function is indicated in parentheses.

The *text* argument consists of one or more lines, all but the last of which end with \ to hide the new-line. Backslashes in text are treated like backslashes in the replacement string of an s command, and may be used to protect initial blanks and tabs against the stripping that is done on every script line. The *rfile* or *wfile* argument must terminate the command line and must be preceded by exactly one blank.

Each *wfile* is created before processing begins. There can be at most 10 distinct *wfile* arguments.

(1) a\		
text	Append. Place *text* on the output before reading the next input line.	

(2) b *label*   Branch to the : command bearing the *label*. If *label* is empty, branch to the end of the script.

(2) c\
text   Change. Delete the pattern space. Place *text* on the output. Start the next cycle.

(2) d   Delete the pattern space. Start the next cycle.

(2) D   Delete the initial segment of the pattern space through the first new-line. Start the next cycle.

(2) g   Replace the contents of the pattern space by the contents of the hold space.

(2) G   Append the contents of the hold space to the pattern space.

(2) h   Replace the contents of the hold space by the contents of the pattern space.

(2) H   Append the contents of the pattern space to the hold space.

(1) i\
text   Insert. Place *text* on the standard output.

(2) l   List the pattern space on the standard output in an unambiguous form. Non-printable characters are displayed in octal notation and long lines are folded.

(2) n   Copy the pattern space to the standard output. Replace the pattern space with the next line of input.

(2) N   Append the next line of input to the pattern space with an embedded new-line. (The current line number changes.)

(2) p   Print. Copy the pattern space to the standard output.

(2) P   Copy the initial segment of the pattern space through the first new-line to the standard output.

(1) q   Quit. Branch to the end of the script. Do not start a new cycle.

(2) r *rfile*   Read the contents of *rfile*. Place them on the output before reading the next input line.

(2) s / *regular expression* / *replacement* / *flags*
       Substitute the *replacement* string for instances of the *regular expression* in the pattern space. Any character may be used instead of /. For a fuller description see ed(1). *flags* is zero or more of:

       n   *n* = 1 - 512. Substitute for just the *n*th occurrence of the *regular expression*.

       g   Global. Substitute for all nonoverlapping instances of the *regular expression* rather than just the first one.

       p   Print the pattern space if a replacement was made.

  w *wfile* Write. Append the pattern space to *wfile* if a replacement was made.

(2) t *label* Test. Branch to the : command bearing the *label* if any substitutions have been made since the most recent reading of an input line or execution of a t. If *label* is empty, branch to the end of the script.

(2) w *wfile* Write. Append the pattern space to *wfile*. The first occurrence of w will cause *wfile* to be cleared. Subsequent invocations of w will append. Each time the sed command is used, *wfile* is overwritten.

(2) x   Exchange the contents of the pattern and hold spaces.

(2) y / *string1* / *string2* /
      Transform. Replace all occurrences of characters in *string1* with the corresponding characters in *string2*. *string1* and *string2* must have the same number of characters.

(2) ! *function*
      Don't. Apply the *function* (or group, if *function* is { }) only to lines *not* selected by the address(es).

(0) : *label* This command does nothing; it bears a *label* for b and t commands to branch to.

(1) =   Place the current line number on the standard output as a line.

(2) {   Execute the following commands through a matching } only when the pattern space is selected.

(0)   An empty command is ignored.

(0) #   If a # appears as the first character on a line of a script file, then that entire line is treated as a comment, with one exception: if a # appears on the first line and the character after the # is an n, then the default output will be suppressed. The rest of the line after #n is also ignored. A script file must contain at least one non-comment line.

INTERNATIONAL FUNCTIONS

sed can process characters from supplementary code sets as well as ASCII characters.

Searches and pattern matching with regular expressions are performed on characters, not bytes.

Comments in *script* files can contain charcters from supplementary code sets.

WARNING

When characters from supplementary code sets are specified for *string1* and *string2* of the y command, the results of processing cannot be guaranteed.

sed allows only one comment line in a script file, and the comment line must be the first physical line in the file. sed treats all other comment lines as unknown commands.

SEE ALSO

    awk(1), ed(1), grep(1)

NAME

sendmail - send mail over the internet

SYNOPSIS

/usr/ucblib/sendmail [-ba] [-bd] [-bi] [-bm] [-bp] [-bs] [-bt] [-bv]
[-bz] [-C*file*] [-d*X*] [-F*fullname*] [-f*name*] [-h*N*] [-n] [-o *xvalue*]
[-q[*time*]] [-r*name*] [-t] [-v] [*address . . .*]

DESCRIPTION

sendmail sends a message to one or more people, routing the message over whatever networks are necessary. sendmail does internetwork forwarding as necessary
to deliver the message to the correct place.

sendmail is not intended as a user interface routine; other programs provide user-
friendly front ends; sendmail is used only to deliver pre-formatted messages.

With no flags, sendmail reads its standard input up to an EOF, or a line with a single dot and sends a copy of the letter found there to all of the addresses listed. It
determines the network to use based on the syntax and contents of the addresses.

Local addresses are looked up in the local aliases(4) file, or by using the YP name
service, and aliased appropriately. In addition, if there is a .forward file in a
recipient's home directory, sendmail forwards a copy of each message to the list of
recipients that file contains. Aliasing can be prevented by preceding the address
with a backslash. Normally the sender is not included in alias expansions, for
example, if 'john' sends to 'group', and 'group' includes 'john' in the expansion,
then the letter will not be delivered to 'john'.

sendmail will also route mail directly to other known hosts in a local network. The
list of hosts to which mail is directly sent is maintained in the file
/usr/lib/mailhosts.

The following options are available:

-ba	Go into ARPANET mode. All input lines must end with a CR-LF, and all messages will be generated with a CR-LF at the end. Also, the "From:" and "Sender:" fields are examined for the name of the sender.
-bd	Run as a daemon, waiting for incoming SMTP connections.
-bi	Initialize the alias database.
-bm	Deliver mail in the usual way (default).
-bp	Print a summary of the mail queue.
-bs	Use the SMTP protocol as described in RFC 821. This flag implies all the operations of the -ba flag that are compatible with SMTP.
-bt	Run in address test mode. This mode reads addresses and shows the steps in parsing; it is used for debugging configuration tables.
-bv	Verify names only — do not try to collect or deliver a message. Verify mode is normally used for validating users or mailing lists.
-bz	Create the configuration freeze file.

−C*file*	Use alternate configuration file.
−d*X*	Set debugging value to X.
−F*fullname*	Set the full name of the sender.
−f*name*	Sets the name of the "from" person (that is, the sender of the mail). −f can only be used by "trusted" users (who are listed in the config file).
−h*N*	Set the hop count to N. The hop count is incremented every time the mail is processed. When it reaches a limit, the mail is returned with an error message, the victim of an aliasing loop.
−M*id*	Attempt to deliver the queued message with message-id id.
−n	Do not do aliasing.
−o*x value*	Set option *x* to the specified *value*. Options are described below.
−q[*time*]	Processed saved messages in the queue at given intervals. If *time* is omitted, process the queue once. *time* is given as a tagged number, with s being seconds, m being minutes, h being hours, d being days, and w being weeks. For example, −q1h30m or −q90m would both set the timeout to one hour thirty minutes.
−r*name*	An alternate and obsolete form of the −f flag.
−R*string*	Go through the queue of pending mail and attempt to deliver any message with a recipient containing the specified string. This is useful for clearing out mail directed to a machine which has been down for awhile.
−t	Read message for recipients. "To:", "Cc:", and "Bcc:" lines will be scanned for people to send to. The "Bcc:" line will be deleted before transmission. Any addresses in the argument list will be suppressed.
−v	Go into verbose mode. Alias expansions will be announced, etc.

PROCESSING OPTIONS

There are also a number of processing options that may be set. Normally these will only be used by a system administrator. Options may be set either on the command line using the −o flag or in the configuration file. The options are:

A*file*	Use alternate alias file.
c	On mailers that are considered "expensive" to connect to, do not initiate immediate connection. This requires queueing.
d*x*	Set the delivery mode to *x*. Delivery modes are i for interactive (synchronous) delivery, b for background (asynchronous) delivery, and q for queue only — that is, actual delivery is done the next time the queue is run.
D	Run newaliases(1M) to automatically rebuild the alias database, if necessary.
e*x*	Set error processing to mode *x*. Valid modes are m to mail back the error message, w to "write" back the error message (or mail it back if the sender is not logged in), p to print the errors on the terminal (default), 'q' to throw away error messages (only exit status is returned), and 'e' to do special processing for the BerkNet. If the text

	of the message is not mailed back by modes m or w and if the sender is local to this machine, a copy of the message is appended to the file `dead.letter` in the sender's home directory.
F*mode*	The mode to use when creating temporary files.
f	Save -system-style "From" lines at the front of messages.
g*N*	The default group ID to use when calling mailers.
H*file*	The SMTP help file.
i	Do not take dots on a line by themselves as a message terminator.
L*n*	The log level.
m	Send to "me" (the sender) also if I am in an alias expansion.
o	If set, this message may have old style headers. If not set, this message is guaranteed to have new style headers (that is, commas instead of spaces between addresses). If set, an adaptive algorithm is used that will correctly determine the header format in most cases.
Q*queuedir*	Select the directory in which to queue messages.
r*timeout*	The timeout on reads; if none is set, `sendmail` will wait forever for a mailer.
S*file*	Save statistics in the named file.
s	Always instantiate the queue file, even under circumstances where it is not strictly necessary.
T*time*	Set the timeout on messages in the queue to the specified time. After sitting in the queue for this amount of time, they will be returned to the sender. The default is three days.
t*stz,dtz*	Set the name of the time zone.
u*N*	Set the default user id for mailers.

If the first character of the user name is a vertical bar, the rest of the user name is used as the name of a program to pipe the mail to. It may be necessary to quote the name of the user to keep `sendmail` from suppressing the blanks from between arguments.

`sendmail` returns an exit status describing what it did. The codes are defined in *sysexits.h*

EX_OK	Successful completion on all addresses.
EX_NOUSER	User name not recognized.
EX_UNAVAILABLE	Catchall meaning necessary resources were not available.
EX_SYNTAX	Syntax error in address.
EX_SOFTWARE	Internal software error, including bad arguments.
EX_OSERR	Temporary operating system error, such as cannot fork.
EX_NOHOST	Host name not recognized.
EX_TEMPFAIL	Message could not be sent immediately, but was queued.

If invoked as *newaliases,* `sendmail` rebuilds the alias database. If invoked as *mailq,* `sendmail` prints the contents of the mail queue.

FILES

Except for `/etc/sendmail.cf`, these pathnames are all specified in `/etc/sendmail.cf`. Thus, these values are only approximations.

`/usr/bin/uux`	to deliver uucp mail
`/usr/bin/mail`	to deliver local mail
`/var/spool/mqueue/*`	temp files and queued mail
`~/.forward`	list of recipients for forwarding messages

SEE ALSO

`biff`(1), `aliases`(4)

Su, Zaw-Sing, and Jon Postel, *The Domain Naming Convention for Internet User Applications*, RFC 819, Network Information Center, SRI International, Menlo Park, Calif., August 1982
Postel, Jon, *Simple Mail Transfer Protocol*, RFC 821, Network Information Center, SRI International, Menlo Park, Calif., August 1982
Crocker, Dave, *Standard for the Format of ARPA-Internet Text Messages*, RFC 822, Network Information Center, SRI International, Menlo Park, Calif., August 1982

NAME

    `set`, `unset` - set and unset local or global environment variables

SYNOPSIS

    `set` [`-l` *variable*[=*value*]] ...
    `set` [`-e` *variable*[=*value*]] ...
    `set` [`-f`*file variable*[=*value*]] ...

    `unset` `-l` *variable* ...
    `unset` `-f`*file variable* ...

DESCRIPTION

The `set` command sets *variable* in the environment, or adds *variable=value* to *file*. If *variable* is not equated it to a value, `set` expects the value to be on standard input. The `unset` command removes *variable*. Note that the FMLI predefined, read-only variables (such as `ARG1`), may not be set or unset.

FMLI inherits the UNIX environment when invoked:

`-l`   sets or unsets the specified variable in the local environment. Variables set with `-l` will not be inherited by processes invoked from FMLI.

`-e`   sets the specified variable in the UNIX environment. Variables set with `-e` will be inherited by any processes started from FMLI. Note that these variables cannot be `unset`.

`-f`*file*

    sets or unsets the specified variable in the global environment. The argument *file* is the name, or pathname, of a file containing lines of the form *variable=value*. *file* will be created if it does not already exist. Note that no space intervenes between `-f` and *file*.

Note that at least one of the above options must be used for each variable being set or unset. If you set a variable with the `-f`*filename* option, you must thereafter include *filename* in references to that variable. For example, $\{\ (\textit{file})\ \textit{VARIABLE}\}$.

EXAMPLE

Storing a selection made in a menu:

```
name=Selection 2
action=`set -l SELECTION=2`close
```

NOTES

Variables set to be available to the UNIX environment (those set using the `-e` option) can only be set for the current `fmli` process and the processes it calls.

When using the `-f` option, unless *file* is unique to the process, other users of FMLI on the same machine will be able to expand these variables, depending on the read/write permissions on *file*.

A variable set in one frame may be referenced or unset in any other frame. This includes local variables.

When a variable is evaluated that does not specifically reference a file, the local environment and UNIX system environment are searched in that order. (When a `set -l` and a `set -e` is done for the same variable, the variable evaluates to the value used in the `set -l` command.)

SEE ALSO
env(1), sh(1)

setany (1M)

NAME

setany - program to retrieve and set variables in an SNMP entity

SYNOPSIS

setany *entity_addr community_name* [*variable name* -<i/o/d/a/c/g/t> *value*] ...

DESCRIPTION

setany does a GET request to get the current values of the variables to be set, then performs a SET request on the variables. The arguments are the entity name or address in internet dot notation, the community name for access to the SNMP entity, and a triplet for each variable to be set consisting of: the variable name in dot notation, an i, o, d, a, c, g, or t preceeded by a dash to indicate if the variable's value is being given as an integer, an octet string (in hex notation), an object identifier (in dot notation), an IP address (in dot notation), a counter, a gauge, or time-ticks, followed by the value. For example:

```
setany 128.169.1.1 suranet0 "ifAdminStatus.2" -i 3
```

to set the adminstrative status of interface 2 to 3 (down).

The actions that take place during a SET request are that a GET request is issued for the variable. The variable name returned from this request is used in the SET request.

SEE ALSO

getmany(1M), getone(1M), getnext(1M)
RFC 1155, RFC 1156, RFC 1157

NAME

    setclk - set system time from hardware clock

SYNOPSIS

    /sbin/setclk

DESCRIPTION

    setclk is used to set the internal system time from the hardware time-of-day clock. The command can be used only by the super-user. It is normally executed by an entry in the /etc/inittab file when the system is initialized at boot time. Note that setclk checks the Nonvolatile Random Access Memory (NVRAM) only for the date. If the date is set, setclk runs silently. If the date is not set, setclk prompts the user to use sysadm datetime [see sysadm(1)] for the proper setting of the hardware clock.

SEE ALSO

    sysadm(1).

NAME

setcolor - redefine or create a color

SYNOPSIS

setcolor *color red_level green_level blue_level*

DESCRIPTION

The setcolor command takes four arguments: *color*, which must be a string naming the color; and the arguments *red_level*, *green_level*, and *blue_level*, which must be integer values defining, respectively, the intensity of the red, green, and blue components of *color*. Intensities must be in the range of 0 to 1000. If you are redefining an existing color, you must use its current name (default color names are: black, blue, green, cyan, red, magenta, yellow, and white). setcolor returns the color's name string.

EXAMPLE

`` `setcolor blue 100 24 300` ``

NAME

setmnt - establish mount table

SYNOPSIS

`/sbin/setmnt`

DESCRIPTION

`setmnt` creates the `/etc/mnttab` table which is needed for both the `mount` and `umount` commands. `setmnt` reads standard input and creates a `mnttab` entry for each line. Input lines have the format:

filesys node

where *filesys* is the name of the file system's "special file" (such as `/dev/dsk/c?d?s?`) and *node* is the root name of that file system. Thus *filesys* and *node* become the first two strings in the mount table entry.

FILES

`/etc/mnttab`

SEE ALSO

`mount`(1M)

NOTES

Problems may occur if *filesys* or *node* are longer than 32 characters.

`setmnt` silently enforces an upper limit on the maximum number of `mnttab` entries.

NAME
     settime - change the access and modification dates of files

SYNOPSIS
     settime *mmddhhmm*[*yy*] [-f *fname*] *name. . .*

DESCRIPTION
     settime sets the access and modification dates for one or more files. The dates are
     set to the specified date, or to the access and modification dates of the file specified
     via -f. Exactly one of these methods must be used to specify the new date(s). The
     first *mm* is the month number; *dd* is the day number in the month; *hh* is the hour
     number (24 hour system); the second *mm* is the minute number; *yy* is the last two
     digits of the year and is optional. For example:

          settime 1008004583 ralph pete

     sets the access and modification dates of files ralph and pete to Oct. 8, 12:45 AM,
     1983. Another example:

          settime -f ralph john

     This sets the access and modification dates of the file john to those of the file
     ralph.

NOTES
     Use of touch in place of settime is encouraged.

NAME

setuname - changes machine information

SYNOPSIS

setuname [-s *name*] [-n *node*] [-t]

DESCRIPTION

setuname changes the parameter value for the system name and node name. Each parameter can be changed using setuname and the appropriate option.

The options and arguments for this command are:

-s   Changes the system name. *name* specifies new system name and can consist of alphanumeric characters and the special characters dash, underbar, and dollar sign.

-n   Changes the node name. *node* specifies the new network node name and can consist of alphanumeric characters and the special characters dash, underbar, and dollar sign.

-t   Temporary change. No attempt will be made to create a permanent change.

Either or both the -s and -n options must be given when invoking setuname.

The system architecture may place requirements on the size of the system and network node name. The command will issue a fatal warning message and an error message if the name entered is incompatible with the system requirements.

NOTES

setuname attempts to change the parameter values in two places: the running kernel and, as necessary per implementation, to cross system reboots. A temporary change changes only the running kernel.

NAME

setup - initialize system for first user

SYNOPSIS

setup

DESCRIPTION

The setup command, which is also accessible as a login by the same name, allows the first user to be established as the owner of the machine.

The user can then set the date, time and time zone of the machine.

The user can then set the node name of the machine.

The user can then protect the system from unauthorized modification of the machine configuration and software by giving passwords to the administrative and maintenance functions. Normally, the first user of the machine enters this command through the setup login, which initially has no password, and then gives passwords to the various functions in the system. Any that the user leaves without password protection can be exercised by anyone.

The user can then give passwords to system logins such as root, bin, etc. (*provided they do not already have passwords*). Once given a password, each login can only be changed by that login or root.

Finally, the user is permitted to add the first logins to the system, usually starting with his or her own.

INTERNATIONAL FUNCTIONS

With setup, the time zone can be changed only to the zones in the time zone menu displayed by setup. Other time zones should be specified using the environment variable TZ in the file /etc/TIMEZONE.

SEE ALSO

passwd(1), timezone(4).

DIAGNOSTICS

The passwd(1) command complains if the password provided does not meet its standards.

NOTES

If the setup login is not under password control, anyone can put passwords on the other functions.

NAME

sh, jsh, rsh - shell, the standard, job control, and restricted command interpreter

SYNOPSIS

```
sh [ -acefhiknprstuvx ] [ args ]
jsh [ -acefhiknprstuvx ] [ args ]
rsh [ -acefhiknprstuvx ] [ args ]
```

DESCRIPTION

sh is a command programming language that executes commands read from a terminal or a file. The command jsh is an interface to the shell which provides all of the functionality of sh and enables Job Control (see "Job Control," below). rsh is a restricted version of the standard command interpreter sh; It is used to restrict logins to execution environments whose capabilities are more controlled than those of the standard shell. See "Invocation," below for the meaning of arguments to the shell.

Definitions

A *blank* is a tab or a space. A *name* is a sequence of ASCII letters, digits, or underscores, beginning with a letter or an underscore. A *parameter* is a name, a digit, or any of the characters *, @, #, ?, -, $, and ! \ ^.

Commands

A *simple-command* is a sequence of non-blank *word*s separated by *blank*s. The first *word* specifies the name of the command to be executed. Except as specified below, the remaining *word*s are passed as arguments to the invoked command. The command name is passed as argument 0 [see exec(2)]. The *value* of a *simple-command* is its exit status if it terminates normally, or (octal) 200+*status* if it terminates abnormally; see signal(5) for a list of status values.

A *pipeline* is a sequence of one or more *command*s separated by |. The standard output of each *command* but the last is connected by a pipe(2) to the standard input of the next *command*. Each *command* is run as a separate process; the shell waits for the last *command* to terminate. The exit status of a *pipeline* is the exit status of the last command in the *pipeline*.

A *list* is a sequence of one or more *pipeline*s separated by ;, &, &&, or | |, and optionally terminated by ; or &. Of these four symbols, ; and & have equal precedence, which is lower than that of && and | |. The symbols && and | | also have equal precedence. A semicolon (;) causes sequential execution of the preceding *pipeline* (i.e., the shell waits for the *pipeline* to finish before executing any commands following the semicolon); an ampersand (&) causes asynchronous execution of the preceding pipeline (i.e., the shell does *not* wait for that pipeline to finish). The symbol && (| |) causes the *list* following it to be executed only if the preceding pipeline returns a zero (non-zero) exit status. An arbitrary number of new-lines may appear in a *list*, instead of semicolons, to delimit commands.

A *command* is either a *simple-command* or one of the following. Unless otherwise stated, the value returned by a command is that of the last *simple-command* executed in the command.

for *name* [in *word* ...] do *list* done

         Each time a for command is executed, *name* is set to the next *word* taken from the in *word* list. If in *word* ... is omitted, then the for command executes the do *list* once for each positional parameter that is set (see

"Parameter Substitution," below). Execution ends when there are no more words in the list.

case *word* in [*pattern* [| *pattern*] ...) *list* ;;] ... esac
> A case command executes the *list* associated with the first *pattern* that matches *word*. The form of the patterns is the same as that used for file-name generation (see "File Name Generation") except that a slash, a leading dot, or a dot immediately following a slash need not be matched explicitly.

if *list* then *list* [elif *list* then *list*] ... [else *list*] fi
> The *list* following if is executed and, if it returns a zero exit status, the *list* following the first then is executed. Otherwise, the *list* following elif is executed and, if its value is zero, the *list* following the next then is executed. Failing that, the else *list* is executed. If no else *list* or then *list* is executed, then the if command returns a zero exit status.

while *list* do *list* done
> A while command repeatedly executes the while *list* and, if the exit status of the last command in the list is zero, executes the do *list*; otherwise the loop terminates. If no commands in the do *list* are executed, then the while command returns a zero exit status; until may be used in place of while to negate the loop termination test.

(*list*)
> Execute *list* in a sub-shell.

{ *list* ; }
> *list* is executed in the current (that is, parent) shell. The { must be followed by a space.

name () { *list* ; }
> Define a function which is referenced by *name*. The body of the function is the *list* of commands between { and }. The { must be followed by a space. Execution of functions is described below (see "Execution"). The { and } are unnecessary if the body of the function is a *command* as defined above, under "Commands."

The following words are only recognized as the first word of a command and when not quoted:

```
if then else elif fi case esac for while until do done {  }
```

Comments

A word beginning with # causes that word and all the following characters up to a new-line to be ignored.

Command Substitution

The shell reads commands from the string between two grave accents (` `) and the standard output from these commands may be used as all or part of a word. Trailing new-lines from the standard output are removed.

No interpretation is done on the string before the string is read, except to remove backslashes (\) used to escape other characters. Backslashes may be used to escape a grave accent (`) or another backslash (\) and are removed before the command string is read. Escaping grave accents allows nested command substitution. If the command substitution lies within a pair of double quotes (" ...` ...` ... "), a backslash used to escape a double quote (\") will be removed; otherwise, it will be left intact.

If a backslash is used to escape a new-line character (\new-line), both the backslash and the new-line are removed (see the later section on "Quoting"). In addition, backslashes used to escape dollar signs (\$) are removed. Since no parameter substitution is done on the command string before it is read, inserting a backslash to escape a dollar sign has no effect. Backslashes that precede characters other than \, `` ` ``, ", new-line, and $ are left intact when the command string is read.

Parameter Substitution

The character $ is used to introduce substitutable *parameters*. There are two types of parameters, positional and keyword. If *parameter* is a digit, it is a positional parameter. Positional parameters may be assigned values by set. Keyword parameters (also known as variables) may be assigned values by writing:

> *name=value* [*name=value*] ...

Pattern-matching is not performed on *value*. There cannot be a function and a variable with the same *name*.

$ { *parameter* }

> The value, if any, of the parameter is substituted. The braces are required only when *parameter* is followed by a letter, digit, or underscore that is not to be interpreted as part of its name. If *parameter* is * or @, all the positional parameters, starting with $1, are substituted (separated by spaces). Parameter $0 is set from argument zero when the shell is invoked.

$ { *parameter* : -*word* }

> If *parameter* is set and is non-null, substitute its value; otherwise substitute *word*.

$ { *parameter* : =*word* }

> If *parameter* is not set or is null set it to *word*; the value of the parameter is substituted. Positional parameters may not be assigned in this way.

$ { *parameter* : ?*word* }

> If *parameter* is set and is non-null, substitute its value; otherwise, print *word* and exit from the shell. If *word* is omitted, the message "parameter null or not set" is printed.

$ { *parameter* : +*word* }

> If *parameter* is set and is non-null, substitute *word*; otherwise substitute nothing.

In the above, *word* is not evaluated unless it is to be used as the substituted string, so that, in the following example, pwd is executed only if d is not set or is null:

```
echo ${d:-'pwd'}
```

If the colon (:) is omitted from the above expressions, the shell only checks whether *parameter* is set or not.

The following parameters are automatically set by the shell.

> #   The number of positional parameters in decimal.
>
> -   Flags supplied to the shell on invocation or by the set command.

?   The decimal value returned by the last synchronously executed command.

\$ The process number of this shell.

!   The process number of the last background command invoked.

The following parameters are used by the shell. The parameters in this section are also referred to as environment variables.

HOME   The default argument (home directory) for the cd command, set to the user's login directory by login(1) from the password file [see passwd(4)].

PATH   The search path for commands (see "Execution," below). The user may not change PATH if executing under rsh.

CDPATH
      The search path for the cd command.

MAIL   If this parameter is set to the name of a mail file *and* the MAILPATH parameter is not set, the shell informs the user of the arrival of mail in the specified file.

MAILCHECK
      This parameter specifies how often (in seconds) the shell will check for the arrival of mail in the files specified by the MAILPATH or MAIL parameters. The default value is 600 seconds (10 minutes). If set to 0, the shell will check before each prompt.

MAILPATH
      A colon (:) separated list of file names. If this parameter is set, the shell informs the user of the arrival of mail in any of the specified files. Each file name can be followed by % and a message that will be printed when the modification time changes. The default message is you have mail.

PS1   Primary prompt string, by default "\$ ".

PS2   Secondary prompt string, by default "> ".

IFS   Internal field separators, normally space, tab, and new-line (see "Blank Interpretation").

LANG   If this parameter is set, the shell will use it to determine the current locale; see environ(5), setlocale(3C).

SHACCT
      If this parameter is set to the name of a file writable by the user, the shell will write an accounting record in the file for each shell procedure executed.

SHELL   When the shell is invoked, it scans the environment (see "Environment," below) for this name. If it is found and rsh is the file name part of its value, the shell becomes a restricted shell.

The shell gives default values to PATH, PS1, PS2, MAILCHECK, and IFS. HOME and MAIL are set by login(1).

Blank Interpretation

After parameter and command substitution, the results of substitution are scanned for internal field separator characters (those found in IFS) and split into distinct arguments where such characters are found. Explicit null arguments (" " or ´ ´)

are retained. Implicit null arguments (those resulting from *parameters* that have no values) are removed.

Input/Output

A command's input and output may be redirected using a special notation interpreted by the shell. The following may appear anywhere in a *simple-command* or may precede or follow a *command* and are *not* passed on as arguments to the invoked command. Note that parameter and command substitution occurs before *word* or *digit* is used.

<word   Use file *word* as standard input (file descriptor 0).

>word   Use file *word* as standard output (file descriptor 1). If the file does not exist, it is created; otherwise, it is truncated to zero length.

>>word   Use file *word* as standard output. If the file exists, output is appended to it (by first seeking to the end-of-file); otherwise, the file is created.

<<[-]word   After parameter and command substitution is done on *word*, the shell input is read up to the first line that literally matches the resulting *word*, or to an end-of-file. If, however, - is appended to *<<*:

      1)   leading tabs are stripped from *word* before the shell input is read (but after parameter and command substitution is done on *word*),

      2)   leading tabs are stripped from the shell input as it is read and before each line is compared with *word*, and

      3)   shell input is read up to the first line that literally matches the resulting *word*, or to an end-of-file.

      If any character of *word* is quoted (see "Quoting," later), no additional processing is done to the shell input. If no characters of *word* are quoted:

      1)   parameter and command substitution occurs,

      2)   (escaped) `\new-line`s are removed, and

      3)   `\` must be used to quote the characters `\`, `$`, and `'`.

      The resulting document becomes the standard input.

<&digit   Use the file associated with file descriptor *digit* as standard input. Similarly for the standard output using *>&digit*.

<&-   The standard input is closed. Similarly for the standard output using *>&-*.

If any of the above is preceded by a digit, the file descriptor which will be associated with the file is that specified by the digit (instead of the default 0 or 1). For example:

```
    . . .  2>&1
```

associates file descriptor 2 with the file currently associated with file descriptor 1.

The order in which redirections are specified is significant. The shell evaluates redirections left-to-right. For example:

    . . . 1>*xxx* 2>&1

first associates file descriptor 1 with file *xxx*. It associates file descriptor 2 with the file associated with file descriptor 1 (i.e., *xxx*). If the order of redirections were reversed, file descriptor 2 would be associated with the terminal (assuming file descriptor 1 had been) and file descriptor 1 would be associated with file *xxx*.

Using the terminology introduced on the first page, under "Commands," if a *command* is composed of several *simple commands*, redirection will be evaluated for the entire *command* before it is evaluated for each *simple command*. That is, the shell evaluates redirection for the entire *list*, then each *pipeline* within the *list*, then each *command* within each *pipeline*, then each *list* within each *command*.

If a command is followed by & the default standard input for the command is the empty file /dev/null. Otherwise, the environment for the execution of a command contains the file descriptors of the invoking shell as modified by input/output specifications.

Redirection of output is not allowed in the restricted shell.

File Name Generation

Before a command is executed, each command *word* is scanned for the characters *, ?, and [. If one of these characters appears the word is regarded as a *pattern*. The word is replaced with alphabetically sorted file names that match the pattern. If no file name is found that matches the pattern, the word is left unchanged. The character . at the start of a file name or immediately following a /, as well as the character / itself, must be matched explicitly.

*	Matches any string, including the null string.
?	Matches any single character.
[...]	Matches any one of the enclosed characters. A pair of characters separated by – matches any character lexically between the pair, inclusive. If the first character following the opening [is a !, any character not enclosed is matched.

Note that all quoted characters (see below) must be matched explicitly in a filename.

Quoting

The following characters have a special meaning to the shell and cause termination of a word unless quoted:

    ; & ( ) | ^ < > new-line space tab

A character may be *quoted* (i.e., made to stand for itself) by preceding it with a backslash (\) or inserting it between a pair of quote marks (´ ´ or " "). During processing, the shell may quote certain characters to prevent them from taking on a special meaning. Backslashes used to quote a single character are removed from the word before the command is executed. The pair \new-line is removed from a word before command and parameter substitution.

All characters enclosed between a pair of single quote marks (´ ´), except a single quote, are quoted by the shell. Backslash has no special meaning inside a pair of single quotes. A single quote may be quoted inside a pair of double quote marks (for example, " ´ "), but a single quote can not be quoted inside a pair of single quotes.

Inside a pair of double quote marks (" "), parameter and command substitution occurs and the shell quotes the results to avoid blank interpretation and file name generation. If $* is within a pair of double quotes, the positional parameters are substituted and quoted, separated by quoted spaces ("$1 $2 ..."); however, if $@ is within a pair of double quotes, the positional parameters are substituted and quoted, separated by unquoted spaces ("$1" "$2" ...). \ quotes the characters \, ´, ", and $. The pair \new-line is removed before parameter and command substitution. If a backslash precedes characters other than \, ´, ", $, and new-line, then the backslash itself is quoted by the shell.

Prompting

When used interactively, the shell prompts with the value of PS1 before reading a command. If at any time a new-line is typed and further input is needed to complete a command, the secondary prompt (i.e., the value of PS2) is issued.

Environment

The *environment* [see environ(5)] is a list of name-value pairs that is passed to an executed program in the same way as a normal argument list. The shell interacts with the environment in several ways. On invocation, the shell scans the environment and creates a parameter for each name found, giving it the corresponding value. If the user modifies the value of any of these parameters or creates new parameters, none of these affects the environment unless the export command is used to bind the shell's parameter to the environment (see also set -a). A parameter may be removed from the environment with the unset command. The environment seen by any executed command is thus composed of any unmodified name-value pairs originally inherited by the shell, minus any pairs removed by unset, plus any modifications or additions, all of which must be noted in export commands.

The environment for any *simple-command* may be augmented by prefixing it with one or more assignments to parameters. Thus:

```
TERM=450 cmd                    and
(export TERM; TERM=450; cmd)
```

are equivalent as far as the execution of *cmd* is concerned if *cmd* is not a Special Command. If *cmd* is a Special Command, then

```
TERM=450 cmd
```

will modify the TERM variable in the current shell.

If the -k flag is set, *all* keyword arguments are placed in the environment, even if they occur after the command name. The following first prints a=b c and c:

```
echo a=b c
set -k
echo a=b c
```

Signals

The INTERRUPT and QUIT signals for an invoked command are ignored if the command is followed by `&`; otherwise signals have the values inherited by the shell from its parent, with the exception of signal 11 (but see also the `trap` command below).

Execution

Each time a command is executed, the command substitution, parameter substitution, blank interpretation, input/output redirection, and filename generation listed above are carried out. If the command name matches the name of a defined function, the function is executed in the shell process (note how this differs from the execution of shell procedures). If the command name does not match the name of a defined function, but matches one of the *Special Commands* listed below, it is executed in the shell process. The positional parameters $1, $2, ... are set to the arguments of the function. If the command name matches neither a *Special Command* nor the name of a defined function, a new process is created and an attempt is made to execute the command via `exec`(2).

The shell parameter `PATH` defines the search path for the directory containing the command. Alternative directory names are separated by a colon (`:`). The default path is `/usr/bin`. The current directory is specified by a null path name, which can appear immediately after the equal sign, between two colon delimiters anywhere in the path list, or at the end of the path list. If the command name contains a `/` the search path is not used; such commands will not be executed by the restricted shell. Otherwise, each directory in the path is searched for an executable file. If the file has execute permission but is not an `a.out` file, it is assumed to be a file containing shell commands. A sub-shell is spawned to read it. A parenthesized command is also executed in a sub-shell.

The location in the search path where a command was found is remembered by the shell (to help avoid unnecessary *execs* later). If the command was found in a relative directory, its location must be re-determined whenever the current directory changes. The shell forgets all remembered locations whenever the `PATH` variable is changed or the `hash -r` command is executed (see below).

Special Commands

Input/output redirection is now permitted for these commands. File descriptor 1 is the default output location. When Job Control is enabled, additional *Special Commands* are added to the shell's environment (see ''Job Control'').

`:`   No effect; the command does nothing. A zero exit code is returned.

`. `*file*   Read and execute commands from *file* and return. The search path specified by `PATH` is used to find the directory containing *file*.

`break` [*n*]

> Exit from the enclosing `for` or `while` loop, if any. If *n* is specified, break *n* levels.

`continue` [*n*]

> Resume the next iteration of the enclosing `for` or `while` loop. If *n* is specified, resume at the *n*-th enclosing loop.

cd [*arg*]
> Change the current directory to *arg*. The shell parameter HOME is the default *arg*. The shell parameter CDPATH defines the search path for the directory containing *arg*. Alternative directory names are separated by a colon (:). The default path is <null> (specifying the current directory). Note that the current directory is specified by a null path name, which can appear immediately after the equal sign or between the colon delimiters anywhere else in the path list. If *arg* begins with a / the search path is not used. Otherwise, each directory in the path is searched for *arg*. The cd command may not be executed by rsh.

echo [*arg* ...]
> Echo arguments. See echo(1) for usage and description.

eval [*arg* ...]
> The arguments are read as input to the shell and the resulting command(s) executed.

exec [*arg* ...]
> The command specified by the arguments is executed in place of this shell without creating a new process. Input/output arguments may appear and, if no other arguments are given, cause the shell input/output to be modified.

exit [*n*]
> Causes a shell to exit with the exit status specified by *n*. If *n* is omitted the exit status is that of the last command executed (an end-of-file will also cause the shell to exit.)

export [*name* ...]
> The given *name*s are marked for automatic export to the *environment* of subsequently executed commands. If no arguments are given, variable names that have been marked for export during the current shell's execution are listed. (Variable names exported from a parent shell are listed only if they have been exported again during the current shell's execution.) Function names are *not* exported.

getopts
> Use in shell scripts to support command syntax standards [see intro(1)]; it parses positional parameters and checks for legal options. See getopts(1) for usage and description.

hash [-r] [*name* ...]
> For each *name*, the location in the search path of the command specified by *name* is determined and remembered by the shell. The -r option causes the shell to forget all remembered locations. If no arguments are given, information about remembered commands is presented. *Hits* is the number of times a command has been invoked by the shell process. *Cost* is a measure of the work required to locate a command in the search path. If a command is found in a "relative" directory in the search path, after changing to that directory, the stored location of that command is recalculated. Commands for which this will be done are indicated by an asterisk (*) adjacent to the *hits* information. *Cost* will be incremented when the recalculation is done.

newgrp [*arg*]
> Equivalent to exec newgrp *arg*. See newgrp(1M) for usage and description.

pwd   Print the current working directory. See pwd(1) for usage and description.

read *name* ...
> One line is read from the standard input and, using the internal field separator, IFS (normally space or tab), to delimit word boundaries, the first word is assigned to the first *name*, the second word to the second *name*, etc., with leftover words assigned to the last *name*. Lines can be continued using \new-line. Characters other than new-line can be quoted by preceding them with a backslash. These backslashes are removed before words are assigned to *names*, and no interpretation is done on the character that follows the backslash. The return code is 0, unless an end-of-file is encountered.

readonly [*name* ...]
> The given *names* are marked *readonly* and the values of the these *names* may not be changed by subsequent assignment. If no arguments are given, a list of all *readonly* names is printed.

return [*n*]
> Causes a function to exit with the return value specified by *n*. If *n* is omitted, the return status is that of the last command executed.

set [--aefhkntuvx [*arg* ...]]
> | | |
> |---|---|
> | -a | Mark variables which are modified or created for export. |
> | -e | Exit immediately if a command exits with a non-zero exit status. |
> | -f | Disable file name generation |
> | -h | Locate and remember function commands as functions are defined (function commands are normally located when the function is executed). |
> | -k | All keyword arguments are placed in the environment for a command, not just those that precede the command name. |
> | -n | Read commands but do not execute them. |
> | -t | Exit after reading and executing one command. |
> | -u | Treat unset variables as an error when substituting. |
> | -v | Print shell input lines as they are read. |
> | -x | Print commands and their arguments as they are executed. |
> | -- | Do not change any of the flags; useful in setting $1 to -. |
>
> Using + rather than - causes these flags to be turned off. These flags can also be used upon invocation of the shell. The current set of flags may be found in $-. The remaining arguments are positional parameters and are assigned, in order, to $1, $2, ... If no arguments are given the values of all names are printed.

shift [*n*]
> The positional parameters from $*n*+1 ... are renamed $1 .... If *n* is not given, it is assumed to be 1.

    test
        Evaluate conditional expressions. See test(1) for usage and description.
    times
        Print the accumulated user and system times for processes run from the
        shell.
    trap [*arg*] [*n*] ...
        The command *arg* is to be read and executed when the shell receives
        numeric or symbolic signal(s) (*n*). (Note that *arg* is scanned once when the
        trap is set and once when the trap is taken.) Trap commands are executed
        in order of signal number or corresponding symbolic names. Any attempt
        to set a trap on a signal that was ignored on entry to the current shell is
        ineffective. An attempt to trap on signal 11 (memory fault) produces an
        error. If *arg* is absent all trap(s) *n* are reset to their original values. If *arg* is
        the null string this signal is ignored by the shell and by the commands it
        invokes. If *n* is 0 the command *arg* is executed on exit from the shell. The
        trap command with no arguments prints a list of commands associated
        with each signal number.
    type [*name* ...]
        For each *name*, indicate how it would be interpreted if used as a command
        name.
    ulimit [-[HS][a | cdfnstv]]
    ulimit [-[HS][c | d | f | n | s | t | v]] *limit*
        ulimit prints or sets hard or soft resource limits. These limits are described
        in getrlimit(2).

        If *limit* is not present, ulimit prints the specified limits. Any number of
        limits may be printed at one time. The -a option prints all limits.

        If *limit* is present, ulimit sets the specified limit to *limit*. The string unlim-
        ited requests the largest valid limit. Limits may be set for only one
        resource at a time. Any user may set a soft limit to any value below the
        hard limit. Any user may lower a hard limit. Only a super-user may raise a
        hard limit; see su(1).

        The -H option specifies a hard limit. The -S option specifies a soft limit. If
        neither option is specified, ulimit will set both limits and print the soft
        limit.

        The following options specify the resource whose limits are to be printed or
        set. If no option is specified, the file size limit is printed or set.

-c	maximum core file size (in 512-byte blocks)
-d	maximum size of data segment or heap (in kbytes)
-f	maximum file size (in 512-byte blocks)
-n	maximum file descriptor plus 1
-s	maximum size of stack segment (in kbytes)
-t	maximum CPU time (in seconds)
-v	maximum size of virtual memory (in kbytes)

umask [*nnn*]
> The user file-creation mask is set to *nnn* [see umask(1)]. If *nnn* is omitted, the current value of the mask is printed.

unset [*name* ...]
> For each *name*, remove the corresponding variable or function value. The variables PATH, PS1, PS2, MAILCHECK, and IFS cannot be unset.

wait [*n*]
> Wait for your background process whose process id is *n* and report its termination status. If *n* is omitted, all your shell's currently active background processes are waited for and the return code will be zero.

Invocation

If the shell is invoked through exec(2) and the first character of argument zero is -, commands are initially read from /etc/profile and from $HOME/.profile, if such files exist. Thereafter, commands are read as described below, which is also the case when the shell is invoked as /usr/bin/sh. The flags below are interpreted by the shell on invocation only. Note that unless the -c or -s flag is specified, the first argument is assumed to be the name of a file containing commands, and the remaining arguments are passed as positional parameters to that command file:

-c *string*   If the -c flag is present commands are read from *string*.

-i   If the -i flag is present or if the shell input and output are attached to a terminal, this shell is *interactive*. In this case TERMINATE is ignored (so that kill 0 does not kill an interactive shell) and INTERRUPT is caught and ignored (so that wait is interruptible). In all cases, QUIT is ignored by the shell.

-p   If the -p flag is present, the shell will not set the effective user and group IDs to the real user and group IDs.

-r   If the -r flag is present the shell is a restricted shell.

-s   If the -s flag is present or if no arguments remain, commands are read from the standard input. Any remaining arguments specify the positional parameters. Shell output (except for *Special Commands*) is written to file descriptor 2.

The remaining flags and arguments are described under the set command above.

Job Control (jsh)

When the shell is invoked as jsh, Job Control is enabled in addition to all of the functionality described previously for sh. Typically Job Control is enabled for the interactive shell only. Non-interactive shells typically do not benefit from the added functionality of Job Control.

With Job Control enabled every command or pipeline the user enters at the terminal is called a *job*. All jobs exist in one of the following states: foreground, background or stopped. These terms are defined as follows: 1) a job in the foreground has read and write access to the controlling terminal; 2) a job in the background is denied read access and has conditional write access to the controlling terminal [see stty(1)]; 3) a stopped job is a job that has been placed in a suspended state, usually as a result of a SIGTSTP signal [see signal(5)].

Every job that the shell starts is assigned a positive integer, called a *job number* which is tracked by the shell and will be used as an identifier to indicate a specific job. Additionally the shell keeps track of the *current* and *previous* jobs. The *current job* is the most recent job to be started or restarted. The *previous job* is the first non-current job.

The acceptable syntax for a Job Identifier is of the form:

    %jobid

where, *jobid* may be specified in any of the following formats:

    % or +   for the current job

    −   for the previous job

    ?*<string>*   specify the job for which the command line uniquely contains *string*.

    n   for job number *n*, where *n* is a job number

    pref   where *pref* is a unique prefix of the command name (for example, if the command `ls −l foo` were running in the background, it could be referred to as `%ls`); *pref* cannot contain blanks unless it is quoted.

When Job Control is enabled, the following commands are added to the user's environment to manipulate jobs:

`bg` [*%jobid* ...]
    Resumes the execution of a stopped job in the background. If *%jobid* is omitted the current job is assumed.

`fg` [*%jobid* ...]
    Resumes the execution of a stopped job in the foreground, also moves an executing background job into the foreground. If *%jobid* is omitted the current job is assumed.

`jobs` [-p|-l] [*%jobid* ...]

`jobs` -x *command* [*arguments*]
    Reports all jobs that are stopped or executing in the background. If *%jobid* is omitted, all jobs that are stopped or running in the background will be reported. The following options will modify/enhance the output of `jobs`:

    -l   Report the process group ID and working directory of the jobs.

    -p   Report only the process group ID of the jobs.

    -x   Replace any *jobid* found in *command* or *arguments* with the corresponding process group ID, and then execute *command* passing it *arguments*.

`kill` [-signal] *%jobid*
    Builtin version of `kill` to provide the functionality of the `kill` command for processes identified with a *jobid*.

`stop` *%jobid* ...
    Stops the execution of a background job(s).

suspend
> Stops the execution of the current shell (but not if it is the login shell).

wait [%*jobid* ...]
> wait builtin accepts a job identifier. If %*jobid* is omitted wait behaves as described above under Special Commands.

Restricted Shell (rsh) Only

rsh is used to set up login names and execution environments whose capabilities are more controlled than those of the standard shell. The actions of rsh are identical to those of sh, except that the following are disallowed:

> changing directory [see cd(1)],
> setting the value of $PATH,
> specifying path or command names containing /,
> redirecting output (> and >>).

The restrictions above are enforced after *.profile* is interpreted.

A restricted shell can be invoked in one of the following ways: (1) rsh is the file name part of the last entry in the */etc/passwd* file [see passwd(4)]; (2) the environment variable SHELL exists and rsh is the file name part of its value; (3) the shell is invoked and rsh is the file name part of argument 0; (4) the shell is invoke with the -r option.

When a command to be executed is found to be a shell procedure, rsh invokes sh to execute it. Thus, it is possible to provide to the end-user shell procedures that have access to the full power of the standard shell, while imposing a limited menu of commands; this scheme assumes that the end-user does not have write and execute permissions in the same directory.

The net effect of these rules is that the writer of the *.profile* [see profile(4)] has complete control over user actions by performing guaranteed setup actions and leaving the user in an appropriate directory (probably *not* the login directory).

The system administrator often sets up a directory of commands (i.e., /usr/rbin) that can be safely invoked by a restricted shell. Some systems also provide a restricted editor, red.

EXIT STATUS

Errors detected by the shell, such as syntax errors, cause the shell to return a non-zero exit status. If the shell is being used non-interactively execution of the shell file is abandoned. Otherwise, the shell returns the exit status of the last command executed (see also the exit command above).

jsh Only

If the shell is invoked as jsh and an attempt is made to exit the shell while there are stopped jobs, the shell issues one warning:

There are stopped jobs.

This is the only message. If another exit attempt is made, and there are still stopped jobs they will be sent a SIGHUP signal from the kernel and the shell is exited.

FILES

```
/etc/profile
$HOME/.profile
/tmp/sh*
/dev/null
```

SEE ALSO

cd(1), echo(1), getopts(1), intro(1), login(1), newgrp(1M), pwd(1), stty(1), test(1), umask(1), wait(1) dup(2), exec(2), fork(2), getrlimit(2), pipe(2), ulimit(2), setlocale(3C), profile(4), environ(5), signal(5).

NOTES

Words used for filenames in input/output redirection are not interpreted for filename generation (see "File Name Generation," above). For example, cat file1 >a* will create a file named a*.

Because commands in pipelines are run as separate processes, variables set in a pipeline have no effect on the parent shell.

If you get the error message *cannot fork, too many processes*, try using the wait(1) command to clean up your background processes. If this doesn't help, the system process table is probably full or you have too many active foreground processes. (There is a limit to the number of process ids associated with your login, and to the number the system can keep track of.)

Only the last process in a pipeline can be waited for.

If a command is executed, and a command with the same name is installed in a directory in the search path before the directory where the original command was found, the shell will continue to exec the original command. Use the hash command to correct this situation.

INTERNATIONAL FUNCTIONS

sh can process characters from supplementary code sets in addition to ASCII characters. Characters from supplementary code sets can be used for command arguments, as values of variables and field separators, and in prompt strings, comments and pipes.

Searches and pattern matching using metacharacters are performed in character units, not bytes.

?   Matches an character from supplementary code sets.

*   Matches any string, including the null string.

[ ]   Matches any one character in the string enclosed by square brackets, or any one character with a code value within the range designated using a minus (-) sign. When the characters in the range are from different code sets, one of the characters specified in the range is matched.

[!]   Excludes the specified character from all characters from supplementary code sets matched.

Shell scripts may also contain characters from supplementary code sets.

NAME

`share` - make local resource available for mounting by remote systems

SYNOPSIS

`share` [-F *fstype*] [-o *specific_options*] [-d *description*] [*pathname* [*resourcename*]]

DESCRIPTION

The `share` command makes a resource available for mounting through a remote file system of type *fstype*. If the option -F *fstype* is omitted, the first file system type listed in file `/etc/dfs/fstypes` will be used as the default. *Specific_options* as well as the semantics of *resourcename* are specific to particular distributed file systems. When invoked with only a file system type, `share` displays all resources shared by the given file system to the local system. When invoked with no arguments, `share` displays all resources shared by the local system. See `share_FSType`(1M) for details.

The *access_spec* is used to control access of the shared resource. It may be one of the following:

`rw`   *pathname* is shared read/write to all clients. This is also the default behavior.

`rw`=*client*[:*client*]
pathname is shared read/write only to the listed clients. No other systems can access *resourcename*.

`ro`   *pathname* is shared read-only to all clients.

`ro`=*client*[:*client*]
pathname is shared read-only only to the listed clients. No other systems can access *pathname*.

The -d flag may be used to provide a description of the resource being shared.

FILES

```
/etc/dfs/dfstab
/etc/dfs/sharetab
/etc/dfs/fstypes
```

SEE ALSO

`share_nfs`(1M), `share_rfs`(1M), `unshare`(1M).

NAME

share - make local NFS resource available for mounting by remote systems

SYNOPSIS

share [-F nfs] [-o *specific_options*] [-d *description*] *pathname*

DESCRIPTION

The share command makes local resources available for mounting by remote systems.

If no argument is specified, then share displays all resources currently shared, including NFS resources and resources shared through other distributed file system packages.

The following options are recognized:

-o *specific_options*

> Specify options in a comma-separated list of keywords and attribute-value-assertions for interpretation by the file-system-type-specific command.

> *specific_options* can be any combination of the following:

> rw
>> Sharing will be read-write to all clients.

> rw=*client*[:*client*]...
>> Sharing will be read-write to the listed clients; overrides the ro suboption for the clients specified.

> ro
>> Sharing will be read-only to all clients.

> ro=*client*[:*client*]...
>> Sharing will be read-only to the listed clients; overrides the rw suboption for the clients specified.

> anon=*uid*
>> Set *uid* to be the effective user ID of unathenticated users if AUTH_DES authentication is used, or to be root if AUTH_UNIX authentication is used. By default, unknown users are given the effective user ID UID_NOBODY. If *uid* is set to -1, access is denied.

> root=*host*[:*host*]...
>> Only root users from the specified hosts will have root access. By default, no host has root access.

> secure
>> Clients must use the AUTH_DES authentication of RPC. AUTH_UNIX authentication is the default.

> If *specific_options* is not specified, then by default sharing will be read-write to all clients.

-d *description*

> Provide a comment that describes the resource to be shared.

pathname   Specify the pathname of the resource to be shared.

FILES

    /etc/dfs/fstypes
    /etc/dfs/sharetab

SEE ALSO

    unshare(1M)

NOTES

The command will fail if both `ro` and `rw` are specified. If the same client name exists in both the `ro=` and `rw=` lists, the `rw` will override the `ro`, giving read/write access to the client specified.

`ro=`, `rw=`, and `root=` are guaranteed to work over UDP but may not work over other transport providers.

If a resource is shared with a `ro=` list and a `root=` list, any host that is on the `root=` list will be given only read-only access, regardless of whether that host is specified in the `ro=` list, unless `rw` is declared as the default, or the host is mentioned in a `rw=` list. The same is true if the resource is shared with `ro` as the default. For example, the following `share` commands will give read-only permissions to `hostb`:

    share -F nfs -oro=hosta,root=hostb /var

    share -F nfs -oro,root=hostb /var

While the following will give read/write permissions to hostb:

    share -F nfs -oro=hosta,rw=hostb,root=hostb /var

    share -F nfs -oroot=hostb /var

NAME

share - make local RFS resource available for mounting by remote systems

SYNOPSIS

share [-F rfs] [-o *access_spec*] [-d *description*] [*pathname resourcename*]

DESCRIPTION

The share command makes a resource available for mounting through Remote File Sharing. The -F flag may be omitted if rfs is the first file system type listed in the file /etc/dfs/fstypes. When invoked with only a file system type (or no arguments), share displays all local resources shared through Remote File Sharing.

The *access_spec* is used to control client access of the shared resource. Clients may be specified in any of the following forms:

> *domain.*
> *domain.system*
> *system*

The *access_spec* can be one of the following:

rw
: *resourcename* is shared read/write to all clients. This is also the default behavior.

rw=*client*[*:client*]...
: *resourcename* is shared read/write only to the listed clients. No other systems can access *resourcename*.

ro
: *resourcename* is shared read-only to all clients.

ro=*client*[*:client*]...
: *resourcename* is shared read-only only to the listed clients. No other systems can access *resourcename*.

The -d flag may be used to provide a description of the resource being shared.

ERRORS

If the network is not up and running or *pathname* is not a full path, an error message will be sent to standard error. If *pathname* isn't on a file system mounted locally or the *client* is specified but syntactically incorrect, an error message will be sent to standard error. If the same *resource* name in the network over the same transport provider is to be shared more than once, an error message will be sent to standard error.

FILES

/etc/dfs/dfstab
/etc/dfs/sharetab
/etc/dfs/fstypes

SEE ALSO

unshare(1M)

NAME

shareall, unshareall - share, unshare multiple resources

SYNOPSIS

shareall [-F *fstype*[,*fstype*...]] [- | *file*]

unshareall [-F *fstype*[,*fstype*...]]

DESCRIPTION

When used with no arguments, shareall shares all resources from *file*, which contains a list of share command lines. If the operand is a hyphen (-), then the share command lines are obtained from the standard input. Otherwise, if neither a *file* nor a hyphen is specified, then the file /etc/dfs/dfstab is used as the default.

Resources may be shared to specific file systems by specifying the file systems in a comma-separated list as an argument to -F.

unshareall unshares all currently shared resources. Without a -F flag, it unshares resources for all distributed file system types.

FILES

/etc/dfs/dfstab

SEE ALSO

share(1M), unshare(1M).

NAME

shell - run a command using shell

SYNOPSIS

shell *command* [*command*] . . .

DESCRIPTION

The shell function concatenates its arguments, separating each by a space, and passes this string to the UNIX system shell ($SHELL if set, otherwise /usr/bin/sh).

EXAMPLES

Since the Form and Menu Language does not directly support background processing, the shell function can be used instead.

```
'shell "build prog > /dev/null &"'
```

If you want the user to continue to be able to interact with the application while the background job is running, the output of an executable run by shell in the background must be redirected: to a file if you want to save the output, or to /dev/null if you don't want to save it (or if there is no output), otherwise your application may appear to be hung until the background job finishes processing.

shell can also be used to execute a command that has the same name as an FMLI built-in function.

NOTES

The arguments to shell will be concatenated using spaces, which may or may not do what is expected. The variables set in local environments will not be expanded by the shell because "local" means "local to the current process."

SEE ALSO

sh(1)

NAME

shl - shell layer manager

SYNOPSIS

shl

DESCRIPTION

shl allows a user to interact with more than one shell from a single terminal. The user controls these shells, known as layers, using the commands described below.

The *current layer* is the layer which can receive input from the keyboard. Other layers attempting to read from the keyboard are blocked. Output from multiple layers is multiplexed onto the terminal. To have the output of a layer blocked when it is not current, the stty option loblk may be set within the layer.

The stty character swtch (set to ˆZ if NUL) is used to switch control to shl from a layer. shl has its own prompt, >>>, to help distinguish it from a layer.

A *layer* is a shell which has been bound to a virtual tty device (/dev/sxt???). The virtual device can be manipulated like a real tty device using stty(1) and ioctl(2). Each layer has its own process group id.

Definitions

A *name* is a sequence of characters delimited by a blank, tab or new-line. Only the first eight characters are significant. The *name*s (1) through (7) cannot be used when creating a layer. They are used by shl when no name is supplied. They may be abbreviated to just the digit.

Commands

The following commands may be issued from the shl prompt level. Any unique prefix is accepted.

create [*name*]

> Create a layer called *name* and make it the current layer. If no argument is given, a layer will be created with a name of the form *(#)* where # is the last digit of the virtual device bound to the layer. The shell prompt variable PS1 is set to the name of the layer followed by a space. A maximum of seven layers can be created.

block *name* [*name* ...]

> For each *name*, block the output of the corresponding layer when it is not the current layer. This is equivalent to setting the stty option -loblk within the layer.

delete *name* [*name* ...]

> For each *name*, delete the corresponding layer. All processes in the process group of the layer are sent the SIGHUP signal (see signal(2)).

help (or ?)

> Print the syntax of the shl commands.

layers [-l] [*name* ...]

> For each *name*, list the layer name and its process group. The -l option produces a ps(1)-like listing. If no arguments are given, information is presented for all existing layers.

resume [*name*]

> Make the layer referenced by *name* the current layer. If no argument is given, the last existing current layer will be resumed.

```
toggle
```
Resume the layer that was current before the last current layer.

`unblock` *name* [*name* ...]

For each *name*, do not block the output of the corresponding layer when it is not the current layer. This is equivalent to setting the `stty` option `-loblk` within the layer.

`quit`   Exit `shl`. All layers are sent the SIGHUP signal.

name   Make the layer referenced by *name* the current layer.

FILES

`/dev/sxt???`   Virtual tty devices

`$SHELL`   Variable containing path name of the shell to use (default is `/bin/sh`).

SEE ALSO

sh(1), `stty`(1), `ioctl`(2), `signal`(2), `sxt`(7).

NOTES

To avoid disabling the suspend character when in the job control environment, the *swtch* character must be redefined.

INTERNATIONAL FUNCTIONS

shells managed with `shl` provide the same functionality with characters from supplementary code sets as the current shell.

Layer names must be specified using ASCII characters only.

NAME
showmount - show all remote mounts

SYNOPSIS
/usr/sbin/showmount [-ade] [*hostname*]

DESCRIPTION
showmount lists all the clients that have remotely mounted a filesystem from *host*. This information is maintained by the mountd(1M) server on *host*, and is saved across crashes in the file /etc/rmtab. The default value for *host* is the value returned by hostname(1).

OPTIONS
-a   Print all remote mounts in the format:

       hostname : directory

where *hostname* is the name of the client, and *directory* is the root of the file system that has been mounted.

-d   List directories that have been remotely mounted by clients.

-e   Print the list of exported file systems.

FILES
/etc/rmtab

SEE ALSO
hostname(1), exportfs(1M), mountd(1M)

NOTES
If a client crashes, its entry will not be removed from the list until it reboots and executes umount -a.

NAME

shutdown - shut down system, change system state

SYNOPSIS

shutdown [-y] [-g*grace_period* [-i*init_state*]

DESCRIPTION

This command is executed by the super-user to change the state of the machine. In most cases, it is used to change from the multi-user state (state 2) to another state (see below).

By default, it brings the system to a state where only the console has access to the UNIX system. This state is called single-user (see below).

The command sends a warning message and a final message before it starts actual shutdown activities. By default, the command asks for confirmation before it starts shutting down daemons and killing processes. The options are used as follows:

-y
> pre-answers the confirmation question so the command can be run without user intervention. A default of 60 seconds is allowed between the warning message and the final message. Another 60 seconds is allowed between the final message and the confirmation.

-g*grace_period*
> allows the super-user to change the number of seconds from the 60-second default.

-i*init_state* specifies the state that init is to be put
> in following the warnings, if any. By default, system state "s" is used.

Other recommended system state definitions are:

state 0
> Shut the machine down so it is safe to remove the power. Have the machine remove power if it can. The rc0 procedure is called to do this work.

state 1
> State 1 is referred to as the administrative state. In state 1 filesystems required for multi-user operations are mounted, and logins requiring access to multi-user filesystems can be used. When the system comes up from firmware mode into state 1, only the console is active and other multi-user (state 2) services are unavailable. Note that not all user processes are stopped when transitioning from multi-user state to state 1.

state s, S
> State s (or S) is referred to as the single-user state. All user processes are stopped on transitions to this state. In the single-user state, filesystems required for multi-user logins are unmounted and the system can only be accessed through the console. Logins requiring access to multi-user file systems cannot be used.

state 5
> Stop the UNIX system and go to firmware mode.

state 6
> Stop the UNIX system and reboot to the state defined by the initdefault entry in /etc/inittab; configure a new bootable operating system, if necessary, before the reboot. The rc6 procedure is called to do this work.

NOTES

shutdown(1M) behaves differently depending on the number of users logged in. If several users are logged in, three messages are displayed, warning, final and confirmation, with grace period between each message. If only the user issuing shutdown(1M) is logged in, two messages are displayed, the final and confirmation message, with grace period between them.

If the system is being shutdown to state 0 or state 6, you may see warning messages like the one below.

WARNING: dis_vfs: dounmount() [error # = 16]; filesystem [major = 116, minor = 256] not unmounted

One of these messages will be output for each file system that could not be unmounted because a process held some resource(s) found in that file system at the time of the shutdown. Each file system that fails to be unmounted at shutdown time will have to be checked before it can be used, typically via the fsck(1M) program. If these messages occur, notify your system administrator so the errant process(es) can be fixed.

SEE ALSO

init(1M), rc0(1M), rc2(1M), rc6(1M), inittab(4), fsck(1M)

NAME

shutdown - close down the system at a given time

SYNOPSIS

/usr/ucb/shutdown [-fhknr] *time* [*warning-message* ...]

DESCRIPTION

shutdown provides an automated procedure to notify users when the system is to be shut down. *time* specifies when shutdown will bring the system down; it may be the word now (indicating an immediate shutdown), or it may specify a future time in one of two formats: *+number* and *hour*:*min*. The first form brings the system down in *number* minutes, and the second brings the system down at the time of day indicated in 24-hour notation.

At intervals that get closer as the apocalypse approaches, warning messages are displayed at terminals of all logged-in users, and of users who have remote mounts on that machine. Five minutes before shutdown, or immediately if shutdown is in less than 5 minutes, logins are disabled by creating /etc/nologin and writing a message there. If this file exists when a user attempts to log in, login(1M) prints its contents and exits. The file is removed just before shutdown exits.

At shutdown time a message is written to the system log daemon, syslogd(1M), containing the time of shutdown, the instigator of the shutdown, and the reason. Then a terminate signal is sent to init, which brings the system down to single-user mode.

The time of the shutdown and the warning message are placed in /etc/nologin, which should be used to inform the users as to when the system will be back up, and why it is going down (or anything else).

OPTIONS

As an alternative to the above procedure, these options can be specified:

-f   Arrange, in the manner of fastboot(1M), that when the system is rebooted, the file systems will not be checked.

-h   Execute halt(1M).

-k   Simulate shutdown of the system. Do not actually shut down the system.

-n   Prevent the normal sync(2) before stopping.

-r   Execute reboot(1M).

FILES

/etc/nologin   tells login not to let anyone log in
/etc/xtab   list of remote hosts that have mounted this host

SEE ALSO

fastboot(1M), halt(1M), login(1), reboot(1M), syslogd(1M), sync(2).

NOTES

Only allows you to bring the system down between now and 23:59 if you use the absolute time for shutdown.

NAME

size - print section sizes in bytes of object files

SYNOPSIS

size [-F -f -n -o -V -x] *files*

DESCRIPTION

The size command produces segment or section size information in bytes for each loaded section in ELF or COFF object files. size prints out the size of the text, data, and bss (uninitialized data) segments (or sections) and their total.

size processes ELF and COFF object files entered on the command line. If an archive file is input to the size command, the information for each object file in the archive is displayed.

When calculating segment information, the size command prints out the total file size of the non-writable segments, the total file size of the writable segments, and the total memory size of the writable segments minus the total file size of the writable segments.

If it cannot calculate segment information, size calculates section information. When calculating section information, it prints out the total size of sections that are allocatable, non-writable, and not NOBITS, the total size of the sections that are allocatable, writable, and not NOBITS, and the total size of the writable sections of type NOBITS. (NOBITS sections do not actually take up space in the *file*.)

If size cannot calculate either segment or section information, it prints an error message and stops processing the file.

-F   Prints out the size of each loadable segment, the permission flags of the segment, then the total of the loadable segment sizes. If there is no segment data, size prints an error message and stops processing the file.

-f   Prints out the size of each allocatable section, the name of the section, and the total of the section sizes. If there is no section data, size prints out an error message and stops processing the file.

-n   Prints out non-loadable segment or non-allocatable section sizes. If segment data exists, size prints out the memory size of each loadable segment or file size of each non-loadable segment, the permission flags, and the total size of the segments. If there is no segment data, size prints out, for each allocatable and non-allocatable section, the memory size, the section name, and the total size of the sections. If there is no segment or section data, size prints an error message and stops processing.

-o   Prints numbers in octal, not decimal.

-V   Prints the version information for the size command on the standard error output.

-x   Prints numbers in hexadecimal; not decimal.

EXAMPLES

The examples below are typical `size` output.

```
size file          2724 + 88 + 0 =   2812
size -f file       26(.text) + 5(.init) + 5(.fini)  = 36
size -F file       2724(r-x) + 88(rwx) + 0(rwx) = 2812
```

SEE ALSO

as(1), cc(1), ld(1), a.out(4), ar(4)

NOTES

Since the size of bss sections is not known until link-edit time, the `size` command does not give the true total size of pre-linked objects.

NAME

slattach - attach serial lines as network interfaces

SYNOPSIS

slattach [{ + | - } { c | e | i | m *mtu* | v } . . .] *tty_name* *source_address* *destination_address* [*baud_rate*]

DESCRIPTION

The slattach command is used for assigning the tty line *tty_name* to a network interface, as well as for defining the network *source_address* and *destination_address* values. The *tty_name* parameter is the name of the serial line over which the Serial Line Interface Protocol (SLIP) will run; if the *tty_name* parameter does not begin with /dev/, then /dev/ will be prepended to *tty_name*. The optional *baud_rate* parameter is used to set the speed of the connection. If not specified, the default value of 9600 will be used.

Only the super-user may attach (or detach) a network interface.

The following optional arguments can be used to fine tune how the network interface is to behave:

{ + | - } c   turns the TCP/IP header compression mode on or off (the default setting is off).

{ + | - } e   turns the automatic detection and the use of TCP/IP header compression on or off (the default setting is off). If the flag +c is given, then this flag (either +e or -e) has no effect. When the flag +e is given, the SLIP module will not send any compressed TCP/IP headers until it has received and successfully uncompressed a compressed TCP/IP packet.

{ + | - } i   turns the suppression of ICMP packets on or off (the default setting is off).

{ + | - }m *mtu*

     sets the maximum transmission unit (''mtu'') of the network interface to *mtu* (the default ''mtu'' value is 296).

{ + | - }v   print or don't print various messages about the interface as it is being brought up (the default setting is to not print messages).

To detach a SLIP interface, simply kill the slattach process and then use the following command to remove this Point-to-Point route from the Routing Table:

route delete *destination_address* *gateway_address*

EXAMPLES

```
slattach contty 128.211.8.4 128.211.8.186
slattach +c /dev/contty percival zapranoth 2400
```

DIAGNOSTICS

The following error messages may occur:

- The specified interface does not exist.
- The requested address is unknown.
- A non-privileged user tried to alter the configuration for an interface.

SEE ALSO

netstat(1M), ifconfig(1M), rc2(1M), route(1M), slip(7).
RFC 1144.

NOTES

If both ends of the connection use the flag +e and if neither end uses +c, then the TCP/IP header compression mode will never get turned on because neither end will take the initiative to send a compressed packet.

It is suggested that the *mtu* value for the TCP/IP packet header be 40 plus some power of 2 (for example, 296 = 40 + 2**8).

NAME

    `sleep` - suspend execution for an interval

SYNOPSIS

    `sleep` *time*

DESCRIPTION

    `sleep` suspends execution for *time* seconds. It is used to execute a command after a certain amount of time, as in:

```
(sleep 105; command)&
```

or to execute a command every so often, as in:

```
while true
do
        command
        sleep 37
done
```

SEE ALSO

    `alarm`(2), `sleep`(3C).

NAME

slink - streams linker

SYNOPSIS

slink [-v] [-p] [-u] [-f] [-c *file*] [func [*arg1 arg2 . . .*]]

DESCRIPTION

slink is a STREAMS configuration utility which is used to link together the various STREAMS modules and drivers required for STREAMS TCP/IP. Input to slink is in the form of a script specifying the STREAMS operations to be performed. Input is normally taken from the file /etc/strcf.

The following options may be specified on the slink command line:

-c *file*   Use *file* instead of /etc/strcf.

-v   Verbose mode (each operation is logged to stderr).

-p   Don't use persistent links (i.e., slink will remain in the background).

-f   Don't use persistent links and don't fork (i.e., slink will remain in foreground).

-u   Unlink persistent links (i.e., shut down network).

The configuration file contains a list of *functions*, each of which is composed of a list of *commands*. Each command is a call to one of the functions defined in the configuration file or to one of a set of built-in functions. Among the built-in functions are the basic STREAMS operations open, link, and push, along with several TCP/IP-specific functions.

slink processing consists of parsing the input file, then calling the user-defined function boot, which is normally used to set up the standard configuration at boot time. If a function is specified on the slink command line, that function will be called instead of boot.

By default, slink establishes streams with persistent links (I_PLINK) and exits following the execution of the specified function. If the -p flag is specified, slink establishes streams with regular links (I_LINK) and remains idle in the background, holding open whatever file descriptors have been opened by the configuration commands. If the -f flag is specified, slink establishes streams with regular links (I_LINK) and remains in the foreground, holding open whatever file descriptors have been opened by the configuration commands.

A function definition has the following form:

```
function-name {
    command1
    command2
    . . .
}
```

The syntax for commands is:

> *function arg1 arg2 arg3 . . .*

or

> var = *function arg1 arg2 arg3 . . .*

The placement of newlines is important: a newline must follow the left and right braces and every command. Extra newlines are allowed, i.e. where one newline is required, more than one may be used. A backslash (\) followed immediately by a newline is considered equivalent to a space, i.e. may be used to continue a command on a new line. The use of other white space characters (spaces and tabs) is at the discretion of the user, except that there must be white space separating the function name and the arguments of a command.

Comments are delimited by # and newline, and are considered equivalent to a newline.

Function and variable names may be any string of characters taken from A-Z, a-z, 0-9, and _, except that the first character cannot be a digit. Function names and variable names occupy separate name spaces. All functions are global and may be forward referenced. All variables are local to the functions in which they occur.

Variables are defined when they appear to the left of an equals (=) on a command line; for example,

```
tcp = open /dev/tcp
```

The variable acquires the value returned by the command. In the above example, the value of the variable `tcp` will be the file descriptor returned by the `open` call.

Arguments to a command may be either variables, parameters, or strings.

A variable that appears as an argument must have been assigned a value on a previous command line in that function.

Parameters take the form of a dollar sign ($) followed by one or two decimal digits, and are replaced with the corresponding argument from the function call. If a given parameter was not specified in the function call, an error results (e.g. if a command references $3 and only two arguments were passed to the function, an execution error will occur).

Strings are sequences of characters optionally enclosed in double quotes ("). Quotes may be used to prevent a string from being interpreted as a variable name or a parameter, and to allow the inclusion of spaces, tabs, and the special characters {, }, =, and #. The backslash (\) may also be used to quote the characters {, }, =, #, ", and \ individually.

The following built-in functions are provided by `slink`:

open *path*	Open the device specified by pathname *path*. Returns a file descriptor referencing the open stream.
link *fd1 fd2*	Link the stream referenced by *fd2* beneath the stream referenced by *fd1*. Returns the link identifier associated with the link. Unless the -f or -p flag is specified on the command line, the streams will be linked with persistent links. Note: *fd2* cannot be used after this operation.
push *fd module*	Push the module *module* onto the stream referenced by *fd*.
sifname *fd link name*	Send a SIOCSIFNAME (set interface name) ioctl down the stream referenced by *fd* for the link associated with link identifier *link* specifying the name *name*.

unitsel *fd unit*   Send a IF_UNITSEL (unit select) ioctl down the stream
                          referenced by *fd* specifying unit *unit*.

dlattach *fd unit*   Send a DL_ATTACH_REQ message down the stream refer-
                          enced by *fd* specifying unit *unit*.

initqp *path qname lowat hiwat ...*

                          Send an INITQPARMS (initialize queue parameters) ioctl to
                          the driver corresponding to pathname *path*. *qname*
                          specifies the queue for which the low and high water
                          marks will be set, and must be one of:

hd	stream head
rq	read queue
wq	write queue
muxrq	multiplexor read queue
muxwq	multiplexor write queue

                          lowat and *hiwat* specify the new low and high water marks
                          for the queue. Both *lowat* and *hiwat* must be present. To
                          change only one of these parameters, the other may be
                          replaced with a dash (–). Up to five *qname lowat hiwat* tri-
                          plets may be present.

strcat *str1 str2*   Concatenate strings *str1* and *str2* and return the resulting
                          string.

return *val*   Set the return value for the current function to *val*.
                          Note: executing a return command does not terminate
                          execution of the current function.

FILES
     /etc/strcf

SEE ALSO
     strcf(4)

NAME

smtp - send SMTP mail to a remote host using Simple Mail Transfer Protocol

SYNOPSIS

smtp [-D] [-u] [-d *domain*] [-H *helohost*] *sender host recip* ...

DESCRIPTION

smtp sends a message to a remote host *host* using the Simple Mail Transfer Protocol (SMTP). The message is read from standard input. *sender* is used to identify the sender of the message and the *recip*s are used as the recipients.

When establishing a connection, smtp will use the first transport for which netdir_getbyname(3) returns an address, based on hostname, transport [returned from getnetpath(3)], and service smtp. Normally, this will be the "tcp" transport.

The options to smtp and their meanings are as follows:

-D   This option turns on debugging. Debugging information is printed on standard error.

-H *helohost*   This option can be used to set the hostname used in SMTP HELO message (this defaults to the system's name).

-d *domain*   This option can be used to set the domain name to be used for this host.

-u   This option is for UNIX System V format: Do no conversion to RFC822 format.

smtp is normally run by the smtpsched process to deliver mail queued in /var/spool/smtpq.

FILES

/var/spool/smtpq   where messages are queued

SEE ALSO

smtpsched(1M)
RFC821 - Simple Mail Transfer Protocol

NAME

smtpd - receive incoming SMTP messages

SYNOPSIS

smtpd [-n] [-H *helohost*] [-h *thishost*] [-L *loadlim*] [-l *maxprocs*]

DESCRIPTION

smtpd is a daemon that normally runs while in multi-user mode, waiting for requests from remote hosts to send mail. smtpd listens for these requests on any TLI-based network for which the SMTP service is defined (to netdir_getbyname(3)). Normally, this will only be the "tcp" network. As requests are received, smtpd will fork off child smtpd processes to handle each individual SMTP transaction.

The options to smtpd and their meanings are as follows:

-n   Do not create smtpsched processes to process the incoming mail. Rely on the hourly cron(1) invocation of smtpsched instead.

-H *helohost*   This option can be used to specify the name to be used for the host in the initial SMTP HELO message. If it is not specified, the name used in the HELO message defaults to the system node name.

-h *thishost*   Specify the network name to be prepended onto the sender path in the From line of the message. This option is passed through to the fromsmtp program.

-L *loadlim*   Specify the maximum load at which smtpd will create children. If this option is not specified, there is no limit to the load at which children may run. The load is determined by reading the kernel variable avenrun.

-l *maxprocs*   This option is used to specify the maximum number of children of smtpd that can be running at once. Each child handles one SMTP conversation. If this option is not specified, there is no limit to the number of children that may run.

Mail that is successfully received is piped to the fromsmtp command, which in turn delivers the mail by piping it to rmail. A log of all smtpd's activities is kept in the file /var/spool/smtpq/LOG.

FILES

/dev/kmem	To get the current machine load (avenrun)
/etc/services	List of TCP/UDP services (SMTP should be 25/tcp)
/etc/net/*/services	List of other TLI networks' services
/usr/lib/mail/surrcmd/fromsmtp	
	Where incoming mail is piped to
/var/spool/smtpq/LOG	Log of smtpd transactions

SEE ALSO

cron(1M), fromsmtp(1M), smtp(1M)

NAME

`smtpqer` - queue mail for delivery by SMTP

SYNOPSIS

`smtpqer` [`-nu`] [`-a` *toaddr*] [`-d` *domain*] [`-H` *helohost*] *sender host recip* ...

DESCRIPTION

`smtpqer` queues the mail message it reads from standard input for eventual delivery by `smtp`. The message is queued for delivery to the host specified in the *to* address.

`smtpqer` should normally be invoked by the `mail` command by placing the following line in `/etc/mail/mailsurr`:

```
´.+´  ´([^!@]+)!(.+)´  ´< /usr/lib/mail/surrcmd/smtpqer %R \\1 \\2´
```

`smtpqer` will check the host name in the *to* address. If it is one that can be reached (i.e., if `netdir_getbyname`(3) can find it on at least one TLI network), the message will be queued, and `smtpqer` will exit with a return code of 0 (which means the mail was successfully queued). Otherwise, it will return with an exit code of 1, and the message will not be queued.

Messages that are queued are stored in a file under the SMTP queue directory (`/var/spool/smtpq`). If the `-u` option is not used, they are first converted to RFC822 format, by filtering them through the program `tosmtp`. Finally, `smtpqer` invokes the `smtpsched` program to deliver the mail.

The `-H` option is used to specify the host name that should be used in the SMTP HELO message. This option is passed to both the `tosmtp` and `smtp` programs.

The `-d` option is used to specify the domain name that should be used for your host. This option is passed to the `tosmtp` program. If this option is not used, and a domain has been specified in the mail configuration file *mailcnfg*, that domain will be used instead.

The `-a` option is used to specify the "to address" that is passed to the `smtp` program. Finally, the `-n` option is used to prevent `smtpqer` from starting an `smtpsched` process to deliver the mail.

FILES

`/usr/bin/rmail`	where mail originates from
`/etc/hosts`	database of remote hosts (for TCP/IP)
`/etc/mail/mailcnfg`	mail configuration file
`/etc/net/*/hosts`	database of remote hosts (for other TLI networks)
`/etc/mail/mailsurr`	control file containing rule to invoke `smtpqer`
`/usr/lib/mail/surrcmd/smtpsched`	
	program to process message queues
`/usr/lib/mail/surrcmd/smtp`	
	program that passes message to remote host
`/usr/lib/mail/surrcmd/tosmtp`	
	filter to convert to RFC822 format

       /var/spool/smtpq   where messages are queued

SEE ALSO

       rmail(1M), smtpsched(1M), smtp(1M), tosmtp(1M), getdomainname(3).
       RFC822 - Standard for the Format of ARPA Internet Text Messages

NAME

smtpsched - process messages queued in the SMTP mail queue

SYNOPSIS

smtpsched [-c] [-v] [-t] [-s *scheds*] [-r *days*] [-w *days*] [*qnames*]

DESCRIPTION

smtpsched is used to process the messages queued up in the SMTP mail queue /var/spool/smtpq. It is invoked automatically by the SMTP mail surrogate smtpqer, whenever mail is queued for SMTP delivery to a remote host, and by smtpd whenever incoming mail arrives. It should also be run once per hour (from cron) to attempt delivery of any mail that cannot be delivered immediately.

smtpsched will normally attempt to send all messages queued under all subdirectories of /var/spool/smtpq. However, if *qnames* are specified, only those listed subdirectories of /var/spool/smtpq will be searched for messages to deliver. The subdirectories each refer to a different remote host.

The options to smtpsched are as follows:

-c   Causes empty queue directories to be removed.

-v   Causes verbose logging to occur.

-t   Test mode. The actions smtpsched would take are logged but not performed.

-s *scheds*   Specifies the maximum number of concurrent smtpscheds that may be running at once. If more than this number is running, smtpsched will exit.

-r *days*   Causes mail older than *days* days to be returned.

-w *days*   Any mail older than *days* days will trigger a warning message, which is sent to the originator.

FILES

/usr/lib/mail/surrcmd/smtp	delivers the mail
/usr/lib/mail/surrcmd/smtpqer	queues the mail
/var/spool/smtpq	queued mail messages
/var/spool/smtpq/LOG*	log files
/var/spool/smtpq/*host*	mail messages queued for *host*

SEE ALSO

cron(1M), smtp(1M), smtpqer(1M)

NAME

snmp: `/etc/snmp` - SNMP start/stop script

SYNOPSIS

`/etc/snmp` start
`/etc/snmp` stop

DESCRIPTION

`/etc/snmp` is used to start or stop the SNMP software. SNMP will start automatically at system startup time if `/etc/snmp` is linked to `/etc/rc2.d/S` *name*`snmp` (*name* is installed as 73 by default). Similarly, SNMP will stop automatically at system shutdown time if `/etc/snmp` is linked to `/etc/rc0.d/K` *name*`snmp` (*name* is installed as 67 by default). See `rc0`(1M) and `rc2`(1M) for further information.

A transport service for SNMP may have to be initialized before SNMP is started. Conversely, the service have to be turned off after SNMP is brought down.

SEE ALSO

`getid`(1M), `getmany`(1M), `getnext`(1M), `getone`(1M), `getroute`(1M), `setany`(1M), `snmpd`(1M), `trap_rece`(1M), `trap_send`(1M), `rc0`(1M), `rc2`(1M), `sh`(1).

NAME
    snmpd - SNMP daemon

SYNOPSIS
    `/usr/sbin/snmpd [-v]`

DESCRIPTION
    snmpd is the Internet Simple Network Management Protocol server process. The
    server uses the UDP protocol and listens at the port specified in the "snmp" service
    specification; see `services`(4).

    snmpd uses three configuration files. They are `/etc/snmp.d/snmpd.conf`,
    `/etc/snmp.d/snmpd.comm`, and `/etc/snmp.d/snmpd.trap`.
    `/etc/snmp.d/snmpd.conf` is read to initialize the elements in the `system` group.
    The other two files, `/etc/snmp.d/snmpd.comm` and `/etc/snmp.d/snmpd.trap`,
    are used to initialize the lists of systems in the communities that will be allowed
    access the Management Information Base on the local system. See `snmpd.conf`(4),
    `snmpd.comm`(4), and `snmpd.trap`(4) for more information on the format and uses of
    these files.

    The optional argument, `-v`, is used to enable debugging output. Debugging infor-
    mation is written to standard output.

FILES
    `/etc/snmp.d/snmpd.conf`
    `/etc/snmp.d/snmpd.comm`
    `/etc/snmp.d/snmpd.trap`

SEE ALSO
    `getid`(1M), `getmany`(1M), `getnext`(1M), `getone`(1M), `getroute`(1M),
    `setany`(1M), snmpd(1M), `trap_rece`(1M), `trap_send`(1M), snmp(1M),
    `snmpd.conf`(4), `snmpd.comm`(4), `snmpd.trap`(4).
    RFC 1155, RFC 1156, RFC 1157.

NAME

snmpstat - show network status using SNMP

SYNOPSIS

snmpstat [-trasin] [*host*] [*session*]

DESCRIPTION

The snmpstat command symbolically displays the contents of various network-related data structures. The options have the following meanings:

-t   show the complete transport endpoint table

-r   show the routing table

-a   show the address translation table

-s   show the variables comprising the system group of the MIB

-i   show the status of active interfaces

-n   display addresses and port numbers numerically instead of symbolically

The arguments *host* and *session* allow substitutes for the defaults localhost and public. *Session* refers the SNMP session or community in which to make the specified requests.

There are a number of display formats, depending on the information presented.

By default, active transport endpoints are displayed. The -t flag is used to display all transport endpoints including servers. Active transport endpoints are those whose local address portions have been set to a specific address. The protocol, local and remote address, and the internal state of the protocol (if applicable) are shown.

Address formats are of the form "host.port" or "network.port" if an endpoint's address specifies a network but no specific host address. If the -n flag is not used, the host and network addresses and port numbers are displayed symbolically according to the data bases /etc/hosts , /etc/networks , and /etc/services , respectively. If a symbolic name for an address is unknown or if the -n flag has been used, the address is printed in the Internet "dot format". Unspecified, or "wildcard," addresses and ports appear as " * ".

The routing table display indicates the available routes and their status. Each route consists of a destination host or network and a gateway to use in forwarding packets. The "metric" field shows the metric associated with the route. The "type" field displays what kind of route this is, whether for a directly connected network or a remote network, etc. The "proto" field indicates the mechanism by which the route was learned. The "interface" shows the name of the interface with which this route is associated. The "type" and "proto" fields are displayed symbolically.

The address translation display indicates the current knowledge regarding address translations for remote hosts which have been communicated with recently. Entries in the address translation table consist of a host address, its physical address (typically an ethernet address), and the name of the interface for which this translation is valid.

The system display contains the description of the entity being managed, the object identifier describing the management subsystem on the entity, and the duration of time since the management subsystem was re-initialized.

The interface display provides a table of cumulative statistics regarding packets transferred, errors, and queue lengths. The "name", "address", and "mtu" (maximum transmission unit) of the interface are also displayed.

SEE ALSO

getid(1M), getroute(1M), snmpd(1M), hosts(4), networks(4).
RFC 1155, RFC 1156, RFC 1157.

NAME

    `soelim` - resolve and eliminate .so requests from nroff or troff input

SYNOPSIS

    `/usr/ucb/soelim` [*filename . . .*]

DESCRIPTION

    The `soelim` command reads the specified files or the standard input and performs the textual inclusion implied by the `nroff`(1) directives of the form

        `.so` *somefile*

    when they appear at the beginning of input lines. This is useful since programs such as `tbl`(1) do not normally do this; it allows the placement of individual tables in separate files to be run as a part of a large document.

    An argument consisting of '−' is taken to be a file name corresponding to the standard input.

    Note: inclusion can be suppressed by using ' ´ ' instead of ' . ', that is,

        `´ so /usr/ucblib/doctools/tmac/tmac.s`

EXAMPLE

    A sample usage of `soelim` would be

        `soelim exum?.n | tbl | nroff -ms | col | lpr`

SEE ALSO

    `more`(1), `nroff`(1), `tbl`(1).

NAME

sort - sort and/or merge files

SYNOPSIS

sort [-cmu] [-o*output*] [-y*kmem*] [-z*recsz*] [-dfiMnr] [-btx]
[+*pos1* [-*pos2*]] [*files*]

DESCRIPTION

The sort command sorts lines of all the named files together and writes the result on the standard output. The standard input is read if - is used as a filename or no input files are named.

Comparisons are based on one or more sort keys extracted from each line of input. By default, there is one sort key, the entire input line, and ordering is lexicographic by bytes in machine collating sequence.

The following options alter the default behavior:

-c   Check that the input file is sorted according to the ordering rules; give no output unless the file is out of sort.

-m   Merge only, the input files are already sorted.

-u   Unique: suppress all but one in each set of lines having equal keys.

-o*output*
    The argument given is the name of an output file to use instead of the standard output. This file may be the same as one of the inputs. There may be optional blanks between -o and *output*.

-y*kmem*
    The amount of main memory used by sort has a large impact on its performance. Sorting a small file in a large amount of memory is a waste. If this option is omitted, sort begins using a system default memory size, and continues to use more space as needed. If this option is presented with a value, kmem, sort will start using that number of kilobytes of memory, unless the administrative minimum or maximum is violated, in which case the corresponding extremum will be used. Thus, -y0 is guaranteed to start with minimum memory. By convention, -y (with no argument) starts with maximum memory.

-z*recsz*
    The size of the longest line read is recorded in the sort phase so buffers can be allocated during the merge phase. If the sort phase is omitted via the -c or -m options, a popular system default size will be used. Lines longer than the buffer size will cause sort to terminate abnormally. Supplying the actual number of bytes in the longest line to be merged (or some larger value) will prevent abnormal termination.

The following options override the default ordering rules.

-d   Dictionary order: only letters, digits, and blanks (spaces and tabs) are significant in comparisons. No comparison is performed for multibyte characters.

-f   Fold lower-case letters into upper case. Only applies to single byte characters.

-i   Ignore non-printable characters. All multibyte characters are also ignored.

-M   Compare as months. The first three non-blank characters of the field are folded to upper case and compared. For example, in English the sorting order is "JAN" < "FEB" < ... < "DEC". Invalid fields compare low to "JAN". The -M option implies the -b option (see below).

-n   An initial numeric string, consisting of optional blanks, optional minus sign, and zero or more digits with optional decimal point, is sorted by arithmetic value. The -n option implies the -b option (see below). Note that the -b option is only effective when restricted sort key specifications are in effect.

-r   Reverse the sense of comparisons.

When ordering options appear before restricted sort key specifications, the requested ordering rules are applied globally to all sort keys. When attached to a specific sort key (described below), the specified ordering options override all global ordering options for that key.

The notation +*pos1* -*pos2* restricts a sort key to one beginning at *pos1* and ending just before *pos2*. The characters at position *pos1* and just before *pos2* are included in the sort key (provided that *pos2* does not precede *pos1*). A missing -*pos2* means the end of the line.

Specifying *pos1* and *pos2* involves the notion of a field, a minimal sequence of characters followed by a field separator or a newline. By default, the first blank (space or tab) of a sequence of blanks acts as the field separator. All blanks in a sequence of blanks are considered to be part of the next field; for example, all blanks at the beginning of a line are considered to be part of the first field. The treatment of field separators can be altered using the options:

-b   Ignore leading blanks when determining the starting and ending positions of a restricted sort key. If the -b option is specified before the first +*pos1* argument, it will be applied to all +*pos1* arguments. Otherwise, the b flag may be attached independently to each +*pos1* or -*pos2* argument (see below).

-t*x*   Use *x* as the field separator character; *x* is not considered to be part of a field (although it may be included in a sort key). Each occurrence of *x* is significant (for example, *xx* delimits an empty field). A character from supplementary code sets can be specified in *x* as the field separator.

pos1 and *pos2* each have the form $m.n$ optionally followed by one or more of the flags `bdfinr`. A starting position specified by +$m.n$ is interpreted to mean the n+1st column in the m+1st field. A missing .n means .0, indicating the first column of the m+1st field. If the b flag is in effect, n is counted from the first non-blank column in the m+1st field; +$m.$0b refers to the first non-blank column in the m+1st field.

A last position specified by -$m.n$ is interpreted to mean the nth column (including separators) after the last character of the mth field. A missing .n means .0, indicating the last column of the mth field. If the b flag is in effect, n is counted from the last leading blank in the m+1st field; -$m.$1b refers to the first non-blank in the m+1st field.

When there are multiple sort keys, later keys are compared only after all earlier keys compare equally. Lines that otherwise compare equally are ordered with all significant bytes.

EXAMPLES

Sort the contents of *infile* with the second field as the sort key:

```
sort +1 -2 infile
```

Sort, in reverse order, the contents of *infile1* and *infile2*, placing the output in *outfile* and using the first column of the second field as the sort key:

```
sort -r -o outfile +1.0 -1.2 infile1 infile2
```

Sort, in reverse order, the contents of *infile1* and *infile2* using the first non-blank column of the second field as the sort key:

```
sort -r +1.0b -1.1b infile1 infile2
```

Print the password file [see `passwd`(4)] sorted by the numeric user ID (the third colon-separated field):

```
sort -t: +2n -3 /etc/passwd
```

Print the lines of the already sorted file *infile*, suppressing all but the first occurrence of lines having the same third field (the options -um with just one input file make the choice of a unique representative from a set of equal lines predictable):

```
sort -um +2 -3 infile
```

FILES

```
/var/tmp/stm???
```

INTERNATIONAL FUNCTIONS

`sort` can process characters from supplementary code sets. Specifying the -o option allows output of characters from supplementary code sets.

Characters from supplementary code sets are collated in code order.

SEE ALSO

`comm`(1), `join`(1), `uniq`(1).

NOTES

`sort` comments and exits with non-zero status for various trouble conditions (for example, when input lines are too long), and for disorder discovered under the -c option. When the last line of an input file is missing a newline character, `sort` appends one, prints a warning message, and continues.

`sort` does not guarantee preservation of relative line ordering on equal keys.

NAME

sortbib - sort a bibliographic database

SYNOPSIS

/usr/ucb/sortbib [-s*key-letters*] *database* . . .

DESCRIPTION

The sortbib command sorts files of records containing refer key-letters by user-specified keys. Records may be separated by blank lines, or by '. [' and '.]' delimiters, but the two styles may not be mixed together. This program reads through each *database* and pulls out key fields, which are sorted separately. The sorted key fields contain the file pointer, byte offset, and length of corresponding records. These records are delivered using disk seeks and reads, so sortbib may not be used in a pipeline to read standard input.

By default, sortbib alphabetizes by the first %A and the %D fields, which contain the senior author and date. The -s option is used to specify new *key-letters*. See addbib for a list of the most common key letters. For instance, -sATD will sort by author, title, and date, while -sA+D will sort by all authors, and date. Sort keys past the fourth are not meaningful. No more than 16 databases may be sorted together at one time. Records longer than 4096 characters will be truncated.

sortbib sorts on the last word on the %A line, which is assumed to be the author's last name. A word in the final position, such as 'jr.' or 'ed.', will be ignored if the name beforehand ends with a comma. Authors with two-word last names or unusual constructions can be sorted correctly by using the nroff convention '\0' in place of a blank. A %Q field is considered to be the same as %A, except sorting begins with the first, not the last, word. sortbib sorts on the last word of the %D line, usually the year. It also ignores leading articles (like 'A' or 'The') when sorting by titles in the %T or %J fields; it will ignore articles of any modern European language. If a sort-significant field is absent from a record, sortbib places that record before other records containing that field.

SEE ALSO

addbib(1), indxbib(1), lookbib(1), refer(1), roffbib(1)

NOTES

Records with missing author fields should probably be sorted by title.

NAME

spell, hashmake, spellin, hashcheck - find spelling errors

SYNOPSIS

spell [-v] [-b] [-x] [-l] [+*local_file*] [*files*]

/usr/lib/spell/hashmake

/usr/lib/spell/spellin *n*

/usr/lib/spell/hashcheck *spelling_list*

DESCRIPTION

spell collects words from the named *files* and looks them up in a spelling list. Words that neither occur among nor are derivable (by applying certain inflections, prefixes, and/or suffixes) from words in the spelling list are printed on the standard output. If no *files* are named, words are collected from the standard input.

spell ignores most troff(1), tbl(1), and eqn(1) constructions.

-v	All words not literally in the spelling list are printed, and plausible derivations from the words in the spelling list are indicated.
-b	British spelling is checked. Besides preferring centre, colour, programme, speciality, travelled, and so on, this option insists upon *-ise* in words like standardise, Fowler and the OED (Oxford English Dictionary) to the contrary notwithstanding.
-x	Every plausible stem is displayed, one per line, with = preceding each word.
-l	Follow the chains of *all* included files. By default, spell (like deroff(1)) follows chains of included files (.so and .nx troff(1) requests), *unless* the names of such included files begin with /usr/lib.
+*local_file*	Words found in *local_file* are removed from spell's output. *local_file* is the name of a user-provided file that contains a sorted list of words, one per line. The list must be sorted with the ordering used by sort(1) (for example, upper case preceding lower case). If this ordering is not followed, some entries in *local_file* may be ignored. With this option, the user can specify a set of words that are correct spellings (in addition to spell's own spelling list) for each job.

The spelling list is based on many sources, and while more haphazard than an ordinary dictionary, is also more effective with respect to proper names and popular technical words. Coverage of the specialized vocabularies of biology, medicine, and chemistry is light.

Alternate auxiliary files (spelling lists, stop list, history file) may be specified on the command line by using environment variables. These variables and their default settings are shown in the FILES section. Copies of all output are accumulated in the *history* file. The *stop list* filters out misspellings (for example, thier=thy-y+ier) that would otherwise pass.

Three routines help maintain and check the hash lists used by spell:

`hashmake`	Reads a list of words from the standard input and writes the corresponding nine-digit hash code on the standard output. This is the first step in creating a new spelling list or adding words to an existing list; it must be used prior to using `spellin`.
`spellin`	Reads *n* hash codes (created by `hashmake`) from the standard input and writes a compressed spelling list on the standard output. Use `spellin` to add words to an existing spelling list or create a new spelling list.
`hashcheck`	Reads a compressed *spelling_list* and recreates the nine-digit hash codes for all the words in it; it writes these codes on the standard output. It takes as input an existing spelling list (`hlista` or `hlistb`) or a list created or modified by `spellin`. By using `hashcheck` on an existing compressed *spelling_list* and `hashmake` on a file of selected words, you can compare the two output files to determine if the selected words are present in the existing *spelling_list*.

FILES

`D_SPELL=/usr/share/lib/spell/hlist[ab]`	hashed spelling lists, American & British
`S_SPELL=/usr/share/lib/spell/hstop`	hashed stop list
`H_SPELL=/var/adm/spellhist`	history file
`/usr/lib/spell/spellprog`	program

SEE ALSO

`deroff`(1), `sed`(1), `sort`(1), `tee`(1), `eqn`(1), `tbl`(1), `troff`(1).

NOTES

The spelling list's coverage is uneven; new installations will probably wish to monitor the output for several months to gather local additions; typically, these are kept in a separate local file that is added to the hashed *spelling_list* via `spellin`.

NAME

    `spline` - interpolate smooth curve

SYNOPSIS

    `spline` [*option*] ...

DESCRIPTION

    `spline` takes pairs of numbers from the standard input as abcissas and ordinates of a function. It produces a similar set, which is approximately equally spaced and includes the input set, on the standard output. The cubic spline output (R. W. Hamming, *Numerical Methods for Scientists and Engineers*, 2nd ed., 349ff) has two continuous derivatives, and sufficiently many points to look smooth when plotted. See `graph`(1G).

    The following options are recognized, each as a separate argument:

-a   Supply abscissas automatically (they are missing from the input); spacing is given by the next argument, or is assumed to be 1 if the next argument is not a number.

-k   The constant `k` used in the boundary value computation

$$y_0'' = ky_1'', \quad y_n'' = ky_{n-1}''$$

    is set by the next argument. By default, $k = 0$.

-n   Space output points so that approximately n intervals occur between the lower and upper x limits. (Default $n = 100$.)

-p   Make output periodic, i.e., match derivatives at ends. First and last input values should agree.

-x   Next 1 (or 2) arguments are lower (and upper) x limits. Normally these limits are calculated from the data. Automatic abcissas start at lower limit (default 0).

SEE ALSO

    `graph`(1G), `plot`(1G).

DIAGNOSTICS

    When data is not strictly monotone in x, `spline` reproduces the input without interpolating extra points.

BUGS

    A limit of 1000 input points is enforced silently.

NAME

split - split a file into pieces

SYNOPSIS

split [-n] [*file* [*name*]]

DESCRIPTION

split reads *file* and writes it in *n*-line pieces (default 1000 lines) onto a set of output files. The name of the first output file is *name* with aa appended, and so on lexicographically, up to zz (a maximum of 676 files). The maximum length of *name* is 2 characters less than the maximum filename length allowed by the filesystem. See statvfs(2). If no output name is given, x is default.

If no input file is given, or if - is given in its stead, then the standard input file is used.

SEE ALSO

bfs(1), csplit(1)

statvfs(2).

NAME

spray - spray packets

SYNOPSIS

/usr/sbin/spray [-c *count*] [-d *delay*] [-l *length*] [-t *nettype host*]

DESCRIPTION

spray sends a one-way stream of packets to *host* using RPC, and reports how many were received, as well as the the transfer rate. The *host* argument can be either a name or an Internet address.

The following options are available:

-c *count*   Specify how many packets to send. The default value of *count* is the number of packets required to make the total stream size 100000 bytes.

-d *delay*   Specify how many microseconds to pause between sending each packet. The default is 0.

-l *length*   The *length* parameter is the numbers of bytes in the Ethernet packet that holds the RPC call message. Since the data is encoded using XDR, and XDR only deals with 32 bit quantities, not all values of *length* are possible, and spray rounds up to the nearest possible value. When *length* is greater than 1514, then the RPC call can no longer be encapsulated in one Ethernet packet, so the *length* field no longer has a simple correspondence to Ethernet packet size. The default value of *length* is 86 bytes (the size of the RPC and UDP headers).

-t *nettype*   Specify clas of transports. Defaults to netpath. See rpc(3N) for a description of supported classes.

SEE ALSO

sprayd(1M), rpc(3N)

NAME

    `rpc.sprayd` - spray server

SYNOPSIS

    `/usr/lib/netsvc/spray/rpc.sprayd`

DESCRIPTION

    `rpc.sprayd` is a server which records the packets sent by `spray`(1M). The `rpc.sprayd` daemon may be started by `inetd`(1M) or `listen`(1M).

SEE ALSO

    `inetd`(1M) `listen`(1M), `pmadm`(1M), `sacadm`(1M), `spray`(1M)

NAME

srchtxt - display contents of, or search for a text string in, message data bases

SYNOPSIS

srchtxt [-s] [-l *locale*] [-m *msgfile*, ...] [*text*]

DESCRIPTION

The srchtxt utility is used to display all the text strings in message data bases, or to search for a text string in message data bases (see mkmsgs(1)). These data bases are files in the directory /usr/lib/locale/*locale*/LC_MESSAGES (see setlocale(3C)), unless a file name given with the -m option contains a /. The directory *locale* can be viewed as the name of the language in which the text strings are written. If the -l option is not specified, the files accessed will be determined by the value of the environment variable LC_MESSAGES. If LC_MESSAGES is not set, the files accessed will be determined by the value of the environment variable LANG. If LANG is not set, the files accessed will be in the directory /usr/lib/locale/C/LC_MESSAGES, which contains default strings.

If no *text* argument is present, then all the text strings in the files accessed will be displayed.

The meanings of the options are as follows:

-s   suppress printing of the message sequence numbers of the messages being displayed

-l *locale*   access files in the directory /usr/lib/locale/*locale*/LC_MESSAGES. If -m *msgfile* is also supplied, *locale* is ignored for *msgfile*s containing a /.

-m *msgfile*   access file(s) specified by one or more *msgfile*s. If *msgfile* contains a / character, then *msgfile is* interpreted as a pathname; otherwise, it will be assumed to be in the directory determined as described above. To specify more than one *msgfile*, separate the file names using commas.

text   search for the text string specified by *text* and display each one that matches. *text* can take the form of a regular expression (see ed(1)).

If the -s option is not specified, the displayed text is prefixed by message sequence numbers. The message sequence numbers are enclosed in angle brackets: <*msgfile*:*msgnum*>.

msgfile   name of the file where the displayed text occurred

msgnum   sequence number in *msgfile* where the displayed text occurred

This display is in the format used by gettxt(1) and gettxt(3C).

EXAMPLES

The following examples show uses of srchtxt.

Example 1:

> If message files have been installed in a locale named french by using mkmsgs(1), then you could display the entire set of text strings in the french locale (/usr/lib/locale/french/LC_MESSAGES/*) by typing:

```
srchtxt -l french
```

Example 2:

>   If a set of error messages associated with the UNIX operating system have been installed in the file UX in the french locale (`/usr/lib/locale/french/LC_MESSAGES/UX`), then, using the value of the LANG environment variable to determine the locale to be searched, you could search that file in that locale for all error messages dealing with files by typing:

```
LANG=french; export LANG
srchtxt -m UX "[Ff]ichier"
```

If `/usr/lib/locale/french/LC_MESSAGES/UX` contained the following strings:

```
Erreur E/S\n
Liste d'arguments trop longue\n
Fichier inexistant\n
Argument invalide\n
Trop de fichiers ouverts\n
Fichier trop long\n
Trop de liens\n
Argument hors du domaine\n
Identificateur supprim\n
Etreinte fatale\n
          .
          .
          .
```

then the following strings would be displayed:

```
<UX:3>Fichier inexistant\n
<UX:5>Trop de fichiers ouverts\n
<UX:6>Fichier trop long\n
```

Example 3:

>   If a set of error messages associated with the UNIX operating system have been installed in the file UX and a set of error messages associated with the INGRESS data base product have been installed in the file ingress, both in the german locale, then you could search for the pattern [Dd]atei in both the files UX and ingress in the german locale by typing:

```
srchtxt -l german -m UX,ingress "[Dd]atei"
```

FILES

`/usr/lib/locale/C/LC_MESSAGES/*`   default files created by mkmsgs(1)

`/usr/lib/locale/`*locale*`/LC_MESSAGES/*`   message files created by mkmsgs(1)

SEE ALSO

ed(1), exstr(1), gettxt(1), mkmsgs(1)
gettxt(3C), setlocale(3C)

DIAGNOSTICS

The error messages produced by srchtxt are intended to be self-explanatory. They indicate an error in the command line or errors encountered while searching for a particular locale and/or message file.

NOTES

srchtxt can search the characters from supplementary code sets of text strings in the message handling facility for a text string.

NAME

statd - network status monitor

SYNOPSIS

/usr/lib/nfs/statd

DESCRIPTION

statd is an intermediate version of the status monitor. It interacts with lockd(1M) to provide the crash and recovery functions for the locking services on NFS.

FILES

/etc/sm
/etc/sm.bak
/etc/state

SEE ALSO

lockd(1M)

NOTES

The crash of a site is only detected upon its recovery.

NAME

`strace` - print STREAMS trace messages

SYNOPSIS

`strace` [*mid sid level*] . . .

DESCRIPTION

`strace` without arguments writes all STREAMS event trace messages from all drivers and modules to its standard output. These messages are obtained from the STREAMS log driver [`log`(7)]. If arguments are provided they must be in triplets of the form *mid, sid, level*, where *mid* is a STREAMS module ID number, *sid* is a sub-ID number, and *level* is a tracing priority level. Each triplet indicates that tracing messages are to be received from the given module/driver, sub-ID (usually indicating minor device), and priority level equal to or less than the given level. The token `all` may be used for any member to indicate no restriction for that attribute.

The format of each trace message output is:

<seq> *<time>* *<ticks>* *<level>* *<flags>* *<mid>* *<sid>* *<text>*

<seq>	trace sequence number
<time>	time of message in *hh:mm:ss*
<ticks>	time of message in machine ticks since boot
<level>	tracing priority level
<flags>	`E` : message is also in the error log `F` : indicates a fatal error `N` : mail was sent to the system administrator
<mid>	module ID number of source
<sid>	sub-ID number of source
<text>	formatted text of the trace message

Once initiated, `strace` will continue to execute until terminated by the user.

EXAMPLES

Output all trace messages from the module or driver whose module ID is 41:

```
strace  41 all all
```

Output those trace messages from driver/module ID 41 with sub-IDs 0, 1, or 2:

```
strace  41 0 1  41 1 1  41 2 0
```

Messages from sub-IDs 0 and 1 must have a tracing level less than or equal to 1. Those from sub-ID 2 must have a tracing level of 0.

SEE ALSO

`log`(7).

NOTES

Due to performance considerations, only one `strace` process is permitted to open the STREAMS log driver at a time. The log driver has a list of the triplets specified in the command invocation, and compares each potential trace message against this list to decide if it should be formatted and sent up to the `strace` process. Hence, long lists of triplets will have a greater impact on overall STREAMS performance. Running `strace` will have the most impact on the timing of the modules and drivers generating the trace messages that are sent to the strace process. If trace messages are generated faster than the strace process can handle them, then some of the messages will be lost. This last case can be determined by examining the sequence numbers on the trace messages output.

NAME

strchg, strconf - change or query stream configuration

SYNOPSIS

```
strchg  -h module1 [, module2  ...]
strchg  -p  [-a  |  -u module]
strchg  -f file
strconf  [-t  |  -m module]
```

DESCRIPTION

These commands are used to alter or query the configuration of the stream associated with the user's standard input. The strchg command pushes modules on and/or pops modules off the stream. The strconf command queries the configuration of the stream. Only the super-user or owner of a STREAMS device may alter the configuration of that stream.

With the -h option, strchg pushes modules onto a stream; it takes as arguments the names of one or more pushable streams modules. These modules are pushed in order; that is, *module1* is pushed first, *module2* is pushed second, etc.

The -p option pops modules off the stream. With the -p option alone, strchg pops the topmost module from the stream. With the -p and -a options, all the modules above the topmost driver are popped. When the -p option is followed by -u *module*, then all modules above but not including *module* are popped off the stream. The -a and -u options are mutually exclusive.

With the -f option, the user can specify a *file* that contains a list of modules representing the desired configuration of the stream. Each module name must appear on a separate line where the first name represents the topmost module and the last name represents the module that should be closest to the driver. The strchg command will determine the current configuration of the stream and pop and push the necessary modules in order to end up with the desired configuration.

The -h, -f and -p options are mutually exclusive.

Invoked without any arguments, strconf prints a list of all the modules in the stream as well as the topmost driver. The list is printed with one name per line where the first name printed is the topmost module on the stream (if one exists) and the last item printed is the name of the driver. With the -t option, only the topmost module (if one exists) is printed. The -m option determines if the named *module* is present on a stream. If it is, strconf prints the message yes and returns zero. If not, strconf prints the message no and returns a non-zero value. The -t and -m options are mutually exclusive.

EXAMPLES

The following command pushes the module ldterm on the stream associated with the user's standard input:

```
strchg -h ldterm
```

The following command pops the topmost module from the stream associated with /dev/term/24. The user must be the owner of this device or the super-user.

```
strchg -p < /dev/term/24
```

If the file `fileconf` contains the following:

```
compat
ldterm
ptem
```

then the command

```
strchg -f fileconf
```

will configure the user's standard input stream so that the module `ptem` is pushed over the driver, followed by `ldterm` and `compat` closest to the stream head.

The `strconf` command with no arguments lists the modules and topmost driver on the stream; for a stream that has only the module `ldterm` pushed above the `ports` driver, it would produce the following output:

```
ldterm
ports
```

The following command asks if `ldterm` is on the stream

```
strconf -m ldterm
```

and produces the following output while returning an exit status of 0:

```
yes
```

SEE ALSO

`streamio`(7).

DIAGNOSTICS

`strchg` returns zero on success. It prints an error message and returns non-zero status for various error conditions, including usage error, bad module name, too many modules to push, failure of an ioctl on the stream, or failure to open *file* from the `-f` option.

`strconf` returns zero on success (for the `-m` or `-t` option, "success" means the named or topmost module is present). It returns a non-zero status if invoked with the `-m` or `-t` option and the module is not present. It prints an error message and returns non-zero status for various error conditions, including usage error or failure of an `ioctl` on the stream.

NOTES

If the user is neither the owner of the stream nor the super-user, the `strchg` command will fail. If the user does not have read permissions on the stream and is not the super-user, the `strconf` command will fail.

If modules are pushed in the wrong order, one could end up with a stream that does not function as expected. For ttys, if the line discipline module is not pushed in the correct place, one could have a terminal that does not respond to any commands.

NAME
strclean - STREAMS error logger cleanup program

SYNOPSIS
strclean [-d *logdir*] [-a *age*]

DESCRIPTION
strclean is used to clean up the STREAMS error logger directory on a regular basis (for example, by using cron). By default, all files with names matching error.* in /var/adm/streams that have not been modified in the last three days are removed. A directory other than /var/adm/streams can be specified using the -d option. The maximum age in days for a log file can be changed using the -a option.

EXAMPLE
```
strclean -d /var/adm/streams -a 3
```
has the same result as running strclean with no arguments.

FILES
/var/adm/streams/error.*

SEE ALSO
cron(1M), strerr(1M).

NOTES
strclean is typically run from cron on a daily or weekly basis.

NAME

strerr - STREAMS error logger daemon

SYNOPSIS

strerr

DESCRIPTION

strerr receives error log messages from the STREAMS log driver [log(7)] and appends them to a log file. The error log files produced reside in the directory /var/adm/streams, and are named error.*mm-dd*, where *mm* is the month and *dd* is the day of the messages contained in each log file.

The format of an error log message is:

<seq> <time> <ticks> <flags> <mid> <sid> <text>

<seq>	error sequence number
<time>	time of message in hh:mm:ss
<ticks>	time of message in machine ticks since boot priority level
<flags>	T : the message was also sent to a tracing process F : indicates a fatal error N : send mail to the system administrator
<mid>	module ID number of source
<sid>	sub-ID number of source
<text>	formatted text of the error message

Messages that appear in the error log are intended to report exceptional conditions that require the attention of the system administrator. Those messages which indicate the total failure of a STREAMS driver or module should have the F flag set. Those messages requiring the immediate attention of the administrator will have the N flag set, which causes the error logger to send the message to the system administrator via mail. The priority level usually has no meaning in the error log but will have meaning if the message is also sent to a tracer process.

Once initiated, strerr continues to execute until terminated by the user. It is commonly executed asynchronously.

FILES

/var/adm/streams/error.*mm-dd*

SEE ALSO

log(7).

NOTES

Only one strerr process at a time is permitted to open the STREAMS log driver.

If a module or driver is generating a large number of error messages, running the error logger will cause a degradation in STREAMS performance. If a large burst of messages are generated in a short time, the log driver may not be able to deliver some of the messages. This situation is indicated by gaps in the sequence numbering of the messages in the log files.

NAME

strings - find printable strings in an object file or binary

SYNOPSIS

strings [-a] [-o] [-n *number* | -*number*] *filename* . . .

DESCRIPTION

The `strings` command looks for ASCII strings in a binary file. A string is any sequence of 4 or more printing characters ending with a newline or a null character.

`strings` is useful for identifying random object files and many other things.

The following options are available:

-a   Look everywhere in the file for strings. If this flag is omitted, `strings` only looks in the initialized data space of object files.

-o   Precede each string by its offset in the file.

-n *number*   Use *number* as the minimum string length rather than 4.

SEE ALSO

od(1)

NOTES

The algorithm for identifying strings is extremely primitive.

For backwards compatibility, -*number* can be used in place of -n *number*. Similarly, the -a and a - option are interchangeable. The - and the -*number* variations are obsolescent.

NAME

strip - strip symbol table, debugging and line number information from an object file.

SYNOPSIS

strip [-blrVx] *file* ...

DESCRIPTION

The strip command strips the symbol table, debugging information, and line number information from ELF object files; COFF object files can no longer be stripped. Once this stripping process has been done, no symbolic debugging access will be available for that file; therefore, this command is normally run only on production modules that have been debugged and tested.

If strip is executed on a common archive file [see ar(4)] in addition to processing the members, strip will remove the archive symbol table. The archive symbol table must be restored by executing the ar(1) command with the -s option before the archive can be linked by the ld(1) command. strip will produce appropriate warning messages when this situation arises.

The amount of information stripped from the ELF object file can be controlled by using any of the following options:

-b   Same effect as the default behavior. This option is obsolete and will be removed in the next release.

-l   Strip line number information only; do not strip the symbol table or debugging information.

-r   Same effect as the default behavior. This option is obsolete and will be removed in the next release.

-V   Print, on standard error, the version number of strip.

-x   Do not strip the symbol table; debugging and line number information may be stripped.

strip is used to reduce the file storage overhead taken by the object file.

FILES

TMPDIR/strp*   temporary files

TMPDIR   usually /var/tmp but can be redefined by setting the environment variable TMPDIR [see tempnam() in tmpnam(3S)].

SEE ALSO

ar(1), as(1), cc(1), ld(1), tmpnam(3S), a.out(4), ar(4)

NOTES

The symbol table section will not be removed if it is contained within a segment, or the file is either a relocatable or dynamic shared object.

The line number and debugging sections will not be removed if they are contained within a segment, or their associated relocation section is contained within a segment.

NAME

stty - set the options for a terminal

SYNOPSIS

stty [-a] [-g] [*options*]

DESCRIPTION

stty sets certain terminal I/O options for the device that is the current standard input; without arguments, it reports the settings of certain options.

In this report, if a character is preceded by a caret (ˆ), then the value of that option is the corresponding control character (for example, "ˆh" is CTRL-h; in this case, recall that CTRL-h is the same as the "back-space" key.) The sequence "ˆ ´" means that an option has a null value.

-a   reports all of the option settings;

-g   reports current settings in a form that can be used as an argument to another stty command.

For detailed information about the modes listed from Control Modes through Local Modes, below, see termio(7). For detailed information about the modes listed under Hardware Flow Control Modes and Clock Modes, below, see termiox(7). Please refer to the device specific man pages of the device being utilized to determine whether hardware flow control is supported. Options described in the Combination Modes section are implemented using options in the earlier sections. Note that many combinations of options make no sense, but no sanity checking is performed. Hardware flow control and clock modes options may not be supported by all hardware interfaces. The options are selected from the following:

Control Modes

parenb (-parenb)   enable (disable) parity generation and detection.

parext (-parext)   enable (disable) extended parity generation and detection for mark and space parity.

parodd (-parodd)   select odd (even) parity, or mark (space) parity if parext is enabled.

cs5 cs6 cs7 cs8   select character size [see termio(7)].

0   hang up line immediately.

110 300 600 1200 1800 2400 4800 9600 19200 38400
      Set terminal baud rate to the number given, if possible. (All speeds are not supported by all hardware interfaces.)

ispeed 0 110 300 600 1200 1800 2400 4800 9600 19200 38400
      Set terminal input baud rate to the number given, if possible. (Not all hardware supports split baud rates.) If the input baud rate is set to zero, the input baud rate will be specified by the value of the output baud rate.

ospeed 0 110 300 600 1200 1800 2400 4800 9600 19200 38400
      Set terminal output baud rate to the number given, if possible. (Not all hardware supports split baud rates.) If the output baud rate is set to zero, the line will be hung up immediately.

hupcl (-hupcl)	hang up (do not hang up) connection on last close.
hup (-hup)	same as hupcl (-hupcl).
cstopb (-cstopb)	use two (one) stop bits per character.
cread (-cread)	enable (disable) the receiver.
clocal (-clocal)	n assume a line without (with) modem control.
loblk (-loblk)	block (do not block) output from a non-current layer.

Input Modes

ignbrk (-ignbrk)	ignore (do not ignore) break on input.
brkint (-brkint)	signal (do not signal) INTR on break.
ignpar (-ignpar)	ignore (do not ignore) parity errors.
parmrk (-parmrk)	mark (do not mark) parity errors [see termio(7)].
inpck (-inpck)	enable (disable) input parity checking.
istrip (-istrip)	strip (do not strip) input characters to seven bits.
inlcr (-inlcr)	map (do not map) NL to CR on input.
igncr (-igncr)	ignore (do not ignore) CR on input.
icrnl (-icrnl)	map (do not map) CR to NL on input.
iuclc (-iuclc)	map (do not map) upper-case alphabetics to lower case on input.
ixon (-ixon)	enable (disable) START/STOP output control. Output is stopped by sending STOP control character and started by sending the START control character.
ixany (-ixany)	allow any character (only DC1) to restart output.
ixoff (-ixoff)	request that the system send (not send) START/STOP characters when the input queue is nearly empty/full.
imaxbel (-imaxbel)	echo (do not echo) BEL when the input line is too long.

Output Modes

opost (-opost)	post-process output (do not post-process output; ignore all other output modes).
olcuc (-olcuc)	map (do not map) lower-case alphabetics to upper case on output.
onlcr (-onlcr)	map (do not map) NL to CR-NL on output.
ocrnl (-ocrnl)	map (do not map) CR to NL on output.
onocr (-onocr)	do not (do) output CRs at column zero.
onlret (-onlret)	on the terminal NL performs (does not perform) the CR function.

`ofill (-ofill)`	use fill characters (use timing) for delays.
`ofdel (-ofdel)`	fill characters are DELs (NULs).
`cr0 cr1 cr2 cr3`	select style of delay for carriage returns [see `termio(7)`].
`nl0 nl1`	select style of delay for line-feeds [see `termio(7)`].
`tab0 tab1 tab2 tab3`	select style of delay for horizontal tabs [see `termio(7)`].
`bs0 bs1`	select style of delay for backspaces [see `termio(7)`].
`ff0 ff1`	select style of delay for form-feeds [see `termio(7)`].
`vt0 vt1`	select style of delay for vertical tabs [see `termio(7)`].

Local Modes

`isig (-isig)`	enable (disable) the checking of characters against the special control characters INTR, QUIT, and SWTCH.
`icanon (-icanon)`	enable (disable) canonical input (ERASE and KILL processing).
`xcase (-xcase)`	canonical (unprocessed) upper/lower-case presentation.
`echo (-echo)`	echo back (do not echo back) every character typed.
`echoe (-echoe)`	echo (do not echo) ERASE character as a backspace-space-backspace string. Note: this mode will erase the ERASEed character on many CRT terminals; however, it does not keep track of column position and, as a result, may be confusing on escaped characters, tabs, and backspaces.
`echok (-echok)`	echo (do not echo) NL after KILL character.
`lfkc (-lfkc)`	the same as `echok (-echok)`; obsolete.
`echonl (-echonl)`	echo (do not echo) NL.
`noflsh (-noflsh)`	disable (enable) flush after INTR, QUIT, or SWTCH.
`stwrap (-stwrap)`	disable (enable) truncation of lines longer than 79 characters on a synchronous line.
`tostop (-tostop)`	send (do not send) SIGTTOU when background processes write to the terminal.
`echoctl (-echoctl)`	echo (do not echo) control characters as `^`*char*, delete as `^?`
`echoprt (-echoprt)`	echo (do not echo) erase character as character is "erased".
`echoke (-echoke)`	BS-SP-BS erase (do not BS-SP-BS erase) entire line on line kill.
`flusho (-flusho)`	output is (is not) being flushed.
`pendin (-pendin)`	retype (do not retype) pending input at next read or input character.
`iexten (-iexten)`	enable (disable) extended (implementation-defined) functions for input data.

stflush (-stflush)   enable (disable) flush on a synchronous line after every write(2).

stappl (-stappl)   use application mode (use line mode) on a synchronous line.

Hardware Flow Control Modes

rtsxoff (-rtsxoff)   enable (disable) RTS hardware flow control on input.

ctsxon (-ctsxon)   enable (disable) CTS hardware flow control on output.

dtrxoff (-dtrxoff)   enable (disable) DTR hardware flow control on input.

cdxon (-cdxon)   enable (disable) CD hardware flow control on output.

isxoff (-isxoff)   enable (disable) isochronous hardware flow control on input.

Clock Modes

xcibrg   get transmit clock from internal baud rate generator.

xctset   get the transmit clock from transmitter signal element timing (DCE source) lead, CCITT V.24 circuit 114, EIA-232-D pin 15.

xcrset   get transmit clock from receiver signal element timing (DCE source) lead, CCITT V.24 circuit 115, EIA-232-D pin 17.

rcibrg   get receive clock from internal baud rate generator.

rctset   get receive clock from transmitter signal element timing (DCE source) lead, CCITT V.24 circuit 114, EIA-232-D pin 15.

rcrset   get receive clock from receiver signal element timing (DCE source) lead, CCITT V.24 circuit 115, EIA-232-D pin 17.

tsetcoff   transmitter signal element timing clock not provided.

tsetcrbrg   output receive baud rate generator on transmitter signal element timing (DTE source) lead, CCITT V.24 circuit 113, EIA-232-D pin 24.

tsetctbrg   output transmit baud rate generator on transmitter signal element timing (DTE source) lead, CCITT V.24 circuit 113, EIA-232-D pin 24.

tsetctset   output tranmitter signal element timing (DCE source) on transmitter signal element timing (DTE source) lead, CCITT V.24 circuit 113, EIA-232-D pin 24.

tsetcrset   output receiver signal element timing (DCE source) on transmitter signal element timing (DTE source) lead, CCITT V.24 circuit 113, EIA-232-D pin 24.

rsetcoff   receiver signal element timing clock not provided.

rsetcrbrg   output receive baud rate generator on receiver signal element timing (DTE source) lead, CCITT V.24 circuit 128, no EIA-232-D pin.

`rsetctbrg`	output transmit baud rate generator on receiver signal element timing (DTE source) lead, CCITT V.24 circuit 128, no EIA-232-D pin.
`rsetctset`	output transmitter signal element timing (DCE source) on receiver signal element timing (DTE source) lead, CCITT V.24 circuit 128, no EIA-232-D pin.
`rsetcrset`	output receiver signal element timing (DCE source) on receiver signal element timing (DTE source) lead, CCITT V.24 circuit 128, no EIA-232-D pin.

Control Assignments

control-character c	set *control-character* to *c*, where *control-character* is `ctab`, `discard`, `dsusp`, `eof`, `eol`, `eol2`, `erase`, `intr`, `kill`, `lnext`, `quit`, `reprint`, `start`, `stop`, `susp`, `swtch`, or `werase`. [`ctab` is used with `-stappl` [see `termio`(7)]. If *c* is preceded by a caret (^) indicating an escape from the shell, then the value used is the corresponding control character (for example, "^d" is a CTRL-d). "^?" is interpreted as DEL and "^-" is interpreted as undefined.

In some circumstances the character *c* will have to be escaped by preceding it with a backslash (\) character. An example of this would be setting a control-character to the octothorpe (#) character. The command "`stty` *control-character* #" will be interpreted by the shell as "`stty` *control-character*" since everything after and including the octothorpe will be ignored by the shell. The correct syntax for this would be "`stty` *control-character* \#." Other instances of needing to escape the *c* character occur when setting a *control-character* to the same value as the *control-character* `erase`, `intr`, `kill`, or `eof`.

`min`, `time` *number*	Set the value of `min` or `time` to *number*. MIN and TIME are used in Non-Canonical mode input processing (`-icanon`).
`line` *i*	set line discipline to *i* ($0 < i < 127$).

Combination Modes

`evenp` or `parity`	enable `parenb` and `cs7`.
`oddp`	enable `parenb`, `cs7`, and `parodd`.
`spacep`	enable `parenb`, `cs7`, and `parext`.
`markp`	enable `parenb`, `cs7`, `parodd`, and `parext`.
`-parity`, or `-evenp`	disable `parenb`, and set `cs8`.
`-oddp`	disable `parenb` and `parodd`, and set `cs8`.

-spacep	disable parenb and parext, and set cs8.
-markp	disable parenb, parodd, and parext, and set cs8.
raw (-raw or cooked)	enable (disable) raw input and output (no ERASE, KILL, INTR, QUIT, SWTCH, EOT, or output post processing).
nl (-nl)	unset (set) icrnl, onlcr. In addition -nl unsets inlcr, igncr, ocrnl, and onlret.
lcase (-lcase)	set (unset) xcase, iuclc, and olcuc.
LCASE (-LCASE)	same as lcase (-lcase).
tabs (-tabs or tab3)	preserve (expand to spaces) tabs when printing.
ek	reset ERASE and KILL characters back to normal # and @.
sane	resets all modes to some reasonable values.
term	set all modes suitable for the terminal type *term*, where *term* is one of tty33, tty37, vt05, tn300, ti700, or tek.
async	set normal asynchronous communications where clock settings are xcibrg, rcibrg, tsetcoff and rsetcoff.

Window Size

rows *n*	set window size to *n* rows.
columns *n*	set window size to *n* columns.
ypixels *n*	set vertical window size to *n* pixels.
xpixels *n*	set horizontal window size to *n* pixels.

SEE ALSO

tabs(1), ioctl(2), termio(7), termiox(7).

NAME

stty - set the options for a terminal

SYNOPSIS

/usr/ucb/stty [-a] [-g] [-h] [*options*]

DESCRIPTION

stty sets certain terminal I/O options for the device that is the current standard input; without arguments, it reports the settings of certain options.

In this report, if a character is preceded by a caret (^), then the value of that option is the corresponding CTRL character (for example, "^h" is CTRL-h; in this case, recall that CTRL-h is the same as the "back-space" key.) The sequence "^ ´" means that an option has a null value.

-a   reports all of the option settings;

-g   reports current settings in a form that can be used as an argument to another *stty* command.

-h   reports all the option settings with the control characters in an easy to read column format.

Options in the last group are implemented using options in the previous groups. Note that many combinations of options make no sense, but no sanity checking is performed. Hardware flow control and clock modes options may not be supported by all hardware interfaces. The options are selected from the following:

Special Requests

all	Reports the same option settings as stty without arguments, but with the control characters in column format.
everything	Everything stty knows about is printed. Same as -h option.
speed	The terminal speed alone is reported on the standard output.
size	The terminal (window) sizes are printed on the standard output, first rows and then columns. This option is only appropriate if currently running a window system.
	size and speed always report on the settings of /dev/tty, and always report the settings to the standard output.

Control Modes

parenb (-parenb)	enable (disable) parity generation and detection.
parext (-parext)	enable (disable) extended parity generation and detection for mark and space parity.
parodd (-parodd)	select odd (even) parity, or mark (space) parity if parext is enabled.
cs5 cs6 cs7 cs8	select character size [see termio(7)].
0	hang up line immediately.
110 300 600 1200 1800 2400 4800 9600 19200 exta 38400 extb	Set terminal baud rate to the number given, if possible. (All speeds are not supported by all hardware interfaces.)

ispeed 0 110 300 600 1200 1800 2400 4800 9600 19200 exta 38400 extb
> Set terminal input baud rate to the number given, if possible. (Not all hardware supports split baud rates.) If the input baud rate is set to zero, the input baud rate will be specified by the value of the output baud rate.

ospeed 0 110 300 600 1200 1800 2400 4800 9600 19200 exta 38400 extb
> Set terminal output baud rate to the number given, if possible. (Not all hardware supports split baud rates.) If the baud rate is set to zero, the line will be hung up immediately.

hupcl (-hupcl)	hang up (do not hang up) connection on last close.
hup (-hup)	same as hupcl (-hupcl).
cstopb (-cstopb)	use two (one) stop bits per character.
cread (-cread)	enable (disable) the receiver.
clocal (-clocal)	assume a line without (with) modem control.
loblk (-loblk)	block (do not block) output from a non-current layer.

Input Modes

ignbrk (-ignbrk)	ignore (do not ignore) break on input.
brkint (-brkint)	signal (do not signal) INTR on break.
ignpar (-ignpar)	ignore (do not ignore) parity errors.
parmrk (-parmrk)	mark (do not mark) parity errors [see termio(7)].
inpck (-inpck)	enable (disable) input parity checking.
istrip (-istrip)	strip (do not strip) input characters to seven bits.
inlcr (-inlcr)	map (do not map) NL to CR on input.
igncr (-igncr)	ignore (do not ignore) CR on input.
icrnl (-icrnl)	map (do not map) CR to NL on input.
iuclc (-iuclc)	map (do not map) upper-case alphabetics to lower case on input.
ixon (-ixon)	enable (disable) START/STOP output control. Output is stopped by sending an STOP and started by sending an START.
ixany (-ixany)	allow any character (only START) to restart output.
decctlq (-decctlq)	Same as -ixany.
ixoff (-ixoff)	request that the system send (not send) START/STOP characters when the input queue is nearly empty/full.
tandem (-tandem)	Same as ixoff.
imaxbel (-imaxbel)	echo (do not echo) BEL when the input line is too long.
iexten (-iexten)	enable (disable) extended (implementation-defined) functions for input data.

Output Modes

opost (-opost)	post-process output (do not post-process output; ignore all other output modes).
olcuc (-olcuc)	map (do not map) lower-case alphabetics to upper case on output.
onlcr (-onlcr)	map (do not map) NL to CR-NL on output.
ocrnl (-ocrnl)	map (do not map) CR to NL on output.
onocr (-onocr)	do not (do) output CRs at column zero.
onlret (-onlret)	on the terminal NL performs (does not perform) the CR function.
ofill (-ofill)	use fill characters (use timing) for delays.
ofdel (-ofdel)	fill characters are DELs (NULs).
cr0 cr1 cr2 cr3	select style of delay for carriage returns [see termio(7)].
nl0 nl1	select style of delay for line-feeds [see termio(7)].
tab0 tab1 tab2 tab3	select style of delay for horizontal tabs [see termio(7)].
bs0 bs1	select style of delay for backspaces [see termio(7)].
ff0 ff1	select style of delay for form-feeds [see termio(7)].
vt0 vt1	select style of delay for vertical tabs [see termio(7)].

Local Modes

isig (-isig)	enable (disable) the checking of characters against the special control characters INTR, QUIT, and SWTCH.
icanon (-icanon)	enable (disable) canonical input (ERASE and KILL processing).
cbreak (-cbreak)	Same as -icanon.
xcase (-xcase)	canonical (unprocessed) upper/lower-case presentation.
echo (-echo)	echo back (do not echo back) every character typed.
echoe (-echoe)	echo (do not echo) ERASE character as a backspace-space-backspace string. Note: this mode will erase the ERASEed character on many CRT terminals; however, it does *not* keep track of column position and, as a result, may be confusing on escaped characters, tabs, and backspaces.
crterase (-crterase)	Same as echoe.
echok (-echok)	echo (do not echo) NL after KILL character.
lfkc (-lfkc)	the same as echok (-echok); obsolete.
echonl (-echonl)	echo (do not echo) NL.
noflsh (-noflsh)	disable (enable) flush after INTR, QUIT, or SWTCH.

stwrap (-stwrap)	disable (enable) truncation of lines longer than 79 characters on a synchronous line.
tostop (-tostop)	send (do not send) SIGTTOU for background processes.
echoctl (-echoctl)	echo (do not echo) control characters as ^*char*, delete as ^?
ctlecho (-ctlecho)	Same as echoctl.
echoprt (-echoprt)	echo (do not echo) erase character as character is "erased".
prterase (-prterase)	Same as echoprt.
echoke (-echoke)	BS-SP-BS erase (do not BS-SP-BS erase) entire line on line kill.
crtkill (-crtkill)	Same as echoke.
flusho (-flusho)	output is (is not) being flushed.
pendin (-pendin)	retype (do not retype) pending input at next read or input character.
stflush (-stflush)	enable (disable) flush on a synchronous line after every *write*(2).
stappl (-stappl)	use application mode (use line mode) on a synchronous line.

Hardware Flow Control Modes

rtsxoff (-rtsxoff)	enable (disable) RTS hardware flow control on input.
ctsxon (-ctsxon)	enable (disable) CTS hardware flow control on output.
dterxoff (-dterxoff)	enable (disable) DTER hardware flow control on input.
rlsdxon (-rlsdxon)	enable (disable) RLSD hardware flow control on output.
isxoff (-isxoff)	enable (disable) isochronous hardware flow control on input.

Clock Modes

xcibrg	get transmit clock from internal baud rate generator.
xctset	get the transmit clock from transmitter signal element timing (DCE source) lead, CCITT V.24 circuit 114, EIA-232-D pin 15.
xcrset	get transmit clock from receiver signal element timing (DCE source) lead, CCITT V.24 circuit 115, EIA-232-D pin 17.
rcibrg	get receive clock from internal baud rate generator.
rctset	get receive clock from transmitter signal element timing (DCE source) lead, CCITT V.24 circuit 114, EIA-232-D pin 15.
rcrset	get receive clock from receiver signal element timing (DCE source) lead, CCITT V.24 circuit 115, EIA-232-D pin 17.
tsetcoff	transmitter signal element timing clock not provided.
tsetcrc	output receive clock on transmitter signal element timing (DTE source) lead, CCITT V.24 circuit 113, EIA-232-D pin 24, clock source.

`tsetcxc`	output transmit clock on transmitter signal element timing (DTE source) lead, CCITT V.24 circuit 113, EIA-232-D pin 24, clock source.
`rsetcoff`	receiver signal element timing clock not provided.
`rsetcrc`	output receive clock on receiver signal element timing (DTE source) lead, CCITT V.24 circuit 128, no EIA-232-D pin, clock source.
`rsetcxc`	output transmit clock on receiver signal element timing (DTE source) lead, CCITT V.24 circuit 128, no EIA-232-D pin, clock source.

Control Assignments

control-character c	set *control-character* to *c*, where *control-character* is `intr`, `quit`, `erase`, `kill`, `eof`, `eol`, `eol2`, `swtch`, `start`, `stop`, `susp`, `dsusp`, `rprnt`, `flush`, `werase`, `lnext min`, `ctab`, `time`, or `brk`) [`ctab` is used with `-stappl`; `min` and `time` are used with `-icanon`; see `termio`(7)]. If *c* is preceded by an (escaped from the shell) caret (^), then the value used is the corresponding CTRL character (for example, "^d" is a `CTRL-d`); "^?" is interpreted as DEL and "^-" is interpreted as undefined.
`line` *i*	set line discipline to *i* ($0 < i < 127$).

Combination Modes

`evenp` or `parity`	enable `parenb` and `cs7`.
`-evenp`, or `-parity`	disable `parenb`, and set `cs8`.
`even` (`-even`)	Same as `evenp` (`-evenp`).
`oddp`	enable `parenb`, `cs7`, and `parodd`.
`-oddp`	disable `parenb` and `parodd`, and set `cs8`.
`odd` (`-odd`)	Same as `oddp` (`-oddp`).
`spacep`	enable `parenb`, `cs7`, and `parext`.
`-spacep`	disable `parenb` and `parext`, and set `cs8`.
`markp`	enable `parenb`, `cs7`, `parodd`, and `parext`.
`-markp`	disable `parenb`, `parodd`, and `parext`, and set `cs8`.
`raw` (`-raw` or `cooked`)	enable (disable) raw input and output (no ERASE, KILL, INTR, QUIT, SWTCH, EOT, or output post processing).
`nl` (`-nl`)	unset (set) `icrnl`, `onlcr`. In addition `-nl` unsets `inlcr`, `igncr`, `ocrnl`, and `onlret`.
`lcase` (`-lcase`)	set (unset) `xcase`, `iuclc`, and `olcuc`.
`LCASE` (`-LCASE`)	same as `lcase` (`-lcase`).
`tabs` (`-tabs` or `tab3`)	preserve (expand to spaces) tabs when printing.

`ek`	reset ERASE and KILL characters back to normal # and @.
`sane`	resets all modes to some reasonable values.
`term`	set all modes suitable for the terminal type *term*, where *term* is one of `tty33`, `tty37`, `vt05`, `tn300`, `ti700`, or `tek`.
`async`	set normal asynchronous communications where clock settings are `xcibrg`, `rcibrg`, `tsetcoff` and `rsetcoff`.
`litout` (`-litout`)	Disable (enable) `parenb`, `istrip`, and `opost`, and set `cs8` (`cs7`).
`pass8` (`-pass8`)	Disable (enable) `parenb` and `istrip`, and set `cs8` (`cs7`).
`crt`	Set options for a CRT (`echoe`, `echoctl`, and, if >= 1200 baud, `echoke`.)
`dec`	Set all modes suitable for Digital Equipment Corp. operating systems users (ERASE, KILL, and INTR characters to `^?`, `^U`, and `^C`, `decctlq`, and `crt`.)

Window Size

`rows` *n*	set window size to *n* rows.
`columns` *n*	set window size to *n* columns.
`cols` *n*	An alias for `columns` *n*.
`ypixels` *n*	set vertical window size to *n* pixels.
`xpixels` *n*	set horizontal window size to *n* pixels.

SEE ALSO

`tabs`(1), `ioctl`(2), `termio`(7), `termiox`(7).

NAME

sttydefs - maintain line settings and hunt sequences for TTY ports

SYNOPSIS

/usr/sbin/sttydefs -a *ttylabel* [-b] [-n *nextlabel*] [-i *initial-flags*] [-f *final-flags*]

/usr/sbin/sttydefs -l [*ttylabel*]

/usr/sbin/sttydefs -r *ttylabel*

DESCRIPTION

sttydefs is an administrative command that maintains the line settings and hunt sequences for the system's TTY ports by making entries in and deleting entries from the /etc/ttydefs file.

sttydefs with a -a or -r option may be invoked only by a privileged user. sttydefs with -l may be invoked by any user on the system.

The options have the following meanings:

-l   If a *ttylabel* is specified, sttydefs will display the record from /etc/ttydefs whose TTY label matches the specified *ttylabel*. If no *ttylabel* is specified, sttydefs will display the entire contents of /etc/ttydefs. sttydefs will verify that each entry it displays is correct and that the entry's *nextlabel* field references an existing *ttylabel*.

-a *ttylabel*   Adds a record to the ttydefs file, using *ttylabel* as its label. The following describes the effect of the -b, -n, -i, or -f options when used in conjunction with the -a option:

-b   Specifies that autobaud should be enabled. Autobaud allows the system to set the line speed of a given TTY port to the line speed of the device connected to the port without the user's intervention.

-n *nextlabel*   Specifies the value to be used in the *nextlabel* field in /etc/ttydefs. If this option is not specified, sttydefs will set *nextlabel* equal to *ttylabel*.

-i *initial-flags* Specifies the value to be used in the *initial-flags* field in /etc/ttydefs. *initial-flags* must be in a format recognized by the stty command. These flags are used by ttymon when searching for the correct baud rate. They are set prior to writing the prompt.

                     If this option is not specified, sttydefs will set *initial-flags* equal to the termio(7) flag 9600.

-f *final-flags*   Specifies the value to be used in the *final-flags* field in /etc/ttydefs. *final-flags* must be in a format recognized by the stty command. *final-flags* are the termio(7) settings used by ttymon after receiving a successful connection request and immediately before invoking the service on the port. If this option is not specified, sttydefs will set *final-flags* equal to the termio(7) flags 9600 and sane.

-r *ttylabel*   Removes any record in the `ttydefs` file that has *ttylabel* as its label.

OUTPUT

If successful, `sttydefs` will exit with a status of `0`. `sttydefs -l` will generate the requested information and send it to the standard output.

EXAMPLES

The following command will list all the entries in the `ttydefs` file and print an error message for each invalid entry that is detected.

```
sttydefs -l
```

The following shows a command that requests information for a single label and its output:

```
# sttydefs -l 9600

------------------------------------------------------------------
9600:9600 hupcl erase ^h:9600 sane ixany tab3 hupcl erase ^h::4800
------------------------------------------------------------------

ttylabel:       9600
initial flags:  9600 hupcl erase ^h
final flags:    9600 sane ixany tab3 hupcl erase ^h
autobaud:       no
nextlabel:      4800
```

The following sequence of commands will add the labels 1200, 2400, 4800, and 9600 and put them in a circular list:

```
sttydefs -a 1200 -n 2400 -i 1200 -f "1200 sane"
sttydefs -a 2400 -n 4800 -i 2400 -f "2400 sane"
sttydefs -a 4800 -n 9600 -i 4800 -f "4800 sane"
sttydefs -a 9600 -n 1200 -i 9600 -f "9600 sane"
```

FILES

```
/etc/ttydefs
```

NAME

su - become super-user or another user

SYNOPSIS

su [-] [*name* [*arg* ...]]

DESCRIPTION

su allows one to become another user without logging off. The default user *name* is root (that is, super-user).

To use su, the appropriate password must be supplied (unless one is already root). If the password is correct, su will execute a new shell with the real and effective user and group IDs and supplementary group list set to that of the specified user. The new shell will be the optional program named in the shell field of the specified user's password file entry [see passwd(4)] or /usr/bin/sh if none is specified [see sh(1)]. Note that if /usr/bin/sh is not available, /sbin/sh will be used as the default. To restore normal user ID privileges, type an EOF character (CTRL-d) to the new shell.

Any additional arguments given on the command line are passed to the program invoked as the shell. When using programs such as sh, an *arg* of the form -c *string* executes *string* via the shell and an arg of -r gives the user a restricted shell.

The following statements are true only if the optional program named in the shell field of the specified user's password file entry is like sh. If the first argument to su is a -, the environment will be changed to what would be expected if the user actually logged in as the specified user. This is done by invoking the program used as the shell with an *arg0* value whose first character is -, thus causing first the system's profile (/etc/profile) and then the specified user's profile (.profile in the new HOME directory) to be executed. Otherwise, the environment is passed along with the possible exception of $PATH, which is set to /sbin:/usr/sbin:/usr/bin:/etc for root. Note that if the optional program used as the shell is /usr/bin/sh, the user's .profile can check *arg0* for -sh or -su to determine if it was invoked by login or su, respectively. If the user's program is other than /usr/bin/sh, then .profile is invoked with an *arg0* of *-program* by both login and su.

All attempts to become another user using su are logged in the log file /var/adm/sulog.

EXAMPLES

To become user bin while retaining your previously exported environment, execute:

```
su bin
```

To become user bin but change the environment to what would be expected if bin had originally logged in, execute:

```
su - bin
```

To execute *command* with the temporary environment and permissions of user bin, type:

```
su - bin -c "command args"
```

FILES

`/etc/passwd`	system's password file
`/etc/profile`	system's profile
`$HOME/.profile`	user's profile
`/var/adm/sulog`	log file
`/etc/default/su`	the default parameters that live here are:

         `SULOG`:   If defined, all attempts to `su` to another user are logged in the indicated file.

         `CONSOLE`:   If defined, all attempts to `suroot` are logged on the console.

         `PATH`:   Default path.

         `SUPATH`:   Default path for a user invoking `suroot`.

SEE ALSO

     `env`(1), `login`(1), `sh`(1), `passwd`(4), `profile`(4), `environ`(5).

NAME

sulogin - access single-user mode

SYNOPSIS

sulogin

DESCRIPTION

sulogin is automatically invoked by init when the system is first started. It prompts the user to type the root password to enter system maintenance mode (single-user mode) or to type EOF (typically CTRL-d) for normal startup (multi-user mode). sulogin should never be directly invoked by the user.

FILES

/sbin/sulogin

SEE ALSO

init(1M).

NAME

sum - print checksum and block count of a file

SYNOPSIS

sum [-r] *file*

DESCRIPTION

sum calculates and prints a 16-bit checksum for the named file, and also prints the number of 512 byte blocks in the file. It is typically used to look for bad spots, or to validate a file communicated over some transmission line. The option -r causes an alternate algorithm to be used in computing the checksum.

SEE ALSO

wc(1).

DIAGNOSTICS

"Read error" is indistinguishable from end of file on most devices; check the block count.

NAME

sum - calculate a checksum for a file

SYNOPSIS

/usr/ucb/sum *filename*

DESCRIPTION

sum calculates and displays a 16-bit checksum for the named file, and also displays
the size of the file in kilobytes. It is typically used to look for bad spots, or to validate a file communicated over some transmission line. The checksum is calculated
by an algorithm which may yield different results on machines with 16-bit ints and
machines with 32-bit ints, so it cannot always be used to validate that a file has
been transferred between machines with different-sized ints.

SEE ALSO

sum(1), wc(1).

DIAGNOSTICS

Read error is indistinguishable from EOF on most devices; check the block count.

NOTES

Obsolescent.

NAME
swap - swap administrative interface

SYNOPSIS
    /usr/sbin/swap -a *swapname swaplow swaplen*
    /usr/sbin/swap -d *swapname swaplow*
    /usr/sbin/swap -l [-s]
    /usr/sbin/swap -s

DESCRIPTION
swap provides a method of adding, deleting, and monitoring the system swap areas used by the memory manager. The following options are recognized:

-a   Add the specified swap area. *swapname* is the name of the block special slice, e.g., /dev/dsk/m328_c0d2s7 or a regular file. *swaplow* is the offset in 512-byte blocks into the slice where the swap area should begin. *swaplen* is the length of the swap area in 512-byte blocks. This option can only be used by the super-user. If additional swap areas are added, it is normally done during the system start up routine /etc/rc when going into multi-user mode.

-d   Delete the specified swap area. *swapname* is the name of block special slice, e.g., /dev/dsk/m328_c0d2s7 or a regular file. *swaplow* is the offset in 512-byte blocks into the the swap area to be deleted. Using this option marks the swap area as "INDEL" (in the process of being deleted). The system will not allocate any new blocks from the area, and will try to free swap blocks from it. The area will remain in use until all blocks from it are freed. This option can be used only by the super-user.

-l   List the status of all the swap areas. The output has five columns:

   path   The path name for the swap area.

   dev   The major/minor device number in decimal if it is a block special device; zeros otherwise.

   swaplo The *swaplow* value for the area in 512-byte blocks.

   blocks The *swaplen* value for the area in 512-byte blocks.

   free   The number of free 512-byte blocks in the area. If the swap area is being deleted, the word INDEL will be printed to the right of this number.

-s   Print the following information about total swap space usage:

   allocated The amount of swap space (in 512-byte blocks) allocated to private pages.

   reserved   The number of swap space (in 512-bytes blocks) not currently allocated, but claimed by memory mappings that have not yet created private pages.

   used   The total amount of swap space, in 512-byte blocks, that is either allocated or reserved.

   available The total swap space, in 512-byte blocks, that is currently available for future reservation and allocation.

WARNINGS

No check is done to see if a swap area being added overlaps with an existing file system.

NAME

sync - update the super block

SYNOPSIS

sync

DESCRIPTION

sync executes the sync system primitive. If the system is to be stopped, sync must be called to insure file system integrity. It will flush all previously unwritten system buffers out to disk, thus assuring that all file modifications up to that point will be saved. See sync(2) for details.

NOTE

If you have done a write to a file on a remote machine in a Remote File Sharing environment, you cannot use sync to force buffers to be written out to disk on the remote machine. sync will only write local buffers to local disks.

SEE ALSO

sync(2).

NAME

sysadm - visual interface to perform system administration

SYNOPSIS

sysadm [*menu name* | *task name*]

DESCRIPTION

This command, when invoked without an argument, presents a set of menus that help you do administrative work. If you specify a menu or task on the command line, one of two things happens: if the requested menu or task is unique, it is immediately displayed; if the menu or task is not unique, a menu of choices is displayed.

The sysadm command may be given a password. To assign a password, use the password task under the system_setup menu. To change a password after it is assigned, use the passwd command.

The following menus, which appear on the main sysadm menu, are available on the current release of this product.

UNIX System V Administration

Menu Name	Description
applications	Administration for Available Applications
backup_service	Backup Scheduling, Setup, and Control
diagnostics	Diagnosing System Errors
file_systems	File System Creation, Checking and Mounting
machine	Machine Configuration, Display and Powerdown
network_services	Network Services Administration
ports	Port Access Services and Monitors
printers	Printer Configuration and Services
restore_service	Restore From Backup Data
schedule_task	Schedule Automatic Task
software	Software Installation and Removal
storage_devices	Storage Device Operations and Definitions
system_setup	System Name, Date/Time and Initial Password Setup
users	User Login and Group Administration

If you install FACE or X11 software packages, the applications option will appear as part of the main sysadm menu. If neither package is present, the applications option will not appear.

The rest of this section describes each menu listed on the main menu.

Backup Service Management

This menu lists four areas of administrative support for the backup services.

basic (Backup to Removable Media)

This menu contains subtasks to perform the following: display backup history of operations, make personal backups, schedule backups for automatic execution, and make system backups.

Diagnosing System Errors

This menu provides two tasks, diskreport and diskrepair, which allow you to look for and sometimes repair problems in the system.

diskrepair (Advises on Disk Error Repairs)
This task advises you on how to repair errors that occur on a hard disk.

WARNING: Because this is a repair function, it should be performed only by qualified service personnel.

NOTE: Disk errors often cause files to be lost and/or data to be damaged. Be sure to restore a repaired disk from backup copies.

diskreport (Reports Disk Errors)
This task shows you if the system has collected any information indicating that there have been errors while reading the hard disk. You can request either summary or full reports. A summary report provides sufficient information about disk errors to determine if a repair should be attempted. If the message no errors logged is part of the report, then there is probably no damage. If a number of errors are reported, there is damage and you should call for service. The full report gives additional details for qualified service personnel who are trouble-shooting complicated problems.

Manage File Systems

This menu provides eleven tasks that are part of file system management. These tasks include checking for and repairing errors on a specific file system, monitoring disk usage for all file systems, tracking files based on age or size, listing all file systems currently mounted on your system, creating a new file system, and mounting and unmounting file systems.

check (Check a File System)
This task lets you check a file system for errors and fix them, either interactively or automatically.

defaults (Manage Defaults)
This task identifies the percentage of hard disks currently occupied by files.

diskuse (Display Disk Usage)
This task identifies the percentage of hard disks currently occupied by files. The information is presented as a list, organized by file system name.

display (Display Installed Types)
This task displays a list of the file system types installed on your system.

fileage (List Files by Age)
This task lets you print the names of old files in the directory you specify. If you do not specify an age, files older than 90 days are listed.

`filesize`(List Files by Size)
> This task lets you print the names of the largest files in a specific directory. If you do not request a particular number of files, the ten largest files are listed.

`identify`(Identify File System Type)
> This task tries to determine the type of any unmounted file system without damaging the data or the medium of the file system.

`list`(List Mounted File Systems)
> This task lets you list all file systems mounted on your computer.

`make`(Create a File System)
> This task lets you create a new file system on a removable medium which can then store data you do not want to keep on hard disk. When mounted, the file system has all the properties of a file kept on hard disk.

`mount`(Mount a File System)
> This task lets you mount a file system located on a removable medium and make it available to users on your system. The file system may be unmounted using the `unmount` task.
>
> WARNING: The medium must not be removed while the file system is still mounted.

`unmount`(Unmount a File System)
> This task lets you unmount a file system and thus lets you remove the medium on which it resides. Both `/` and `/usr` are excluded because unmounting these file systems would cause a system crash. Once a file system has been unmounted, you may remove the medium on which it resided.

Machine Configuration Display and Powerdown

This menu provides seven tasks for functions such as turning off the computer, rebooting it, and changing to firmware mode.

`configuration`(Display System Configuration)
> This task lets you display the system information or summary information.

`reboot`(Stops All Running Programs and Reboots Machine)
> This task lets you reboot the computer after all running programs have been stopped, any open files have been closed, and any necessary information (such as directory information) has been written out to disk. This procedure can be used to resolve some types of system trouble, such as a process that cannot be killed.

`shutdown`(Stops All Running Programs and Turns Off Machine)
> This task lets you stop all running programs, close any open files, write out information (such as directory information) to disk, and then turn off the power in the machine.

`whos on` (Displays List of Users Logged onto Machine)
This task prints the login ID, terminal device number, and sign-on time of all users who are currently using the computer.

Network Services Management

This menu provides four functions for managing networks.

`basic_networking` (Basic Networking Utilities Management)
This menu allows you to set up administrative files for UUCP utilities.

`remote_files` (Distributed File System Management)
This menu allows you to set up administrative files for the Remote File Sharing (RFS) Utilities or the Network File Sharing (NFS) Utilities.

`selection` (Network Selection Management)
This menu allows you to set up administrative files for Network Selection; that is, for dynamically selecting a transport protocol.

`name_to_address` (Machine and Service Address Management)
This menu allows you to define machine addresses and service port information for the protocols that exist on the machine.

Service Access Management

This menu provides functions for managing service access to the system.

`port_monitors` (Port Monitor Management)
This menu provides functions for managing port monitors under the Service Access Facility. Specifically, it allows you to add, disable, enable, list, modify, remove, start, and stop port monitors.

`port_services` (Port Service Management)
This menu provides functions for managing port services provided by port monitors. Specifically, it allows you to add, disable, enable, list, modify, and remove port services.

`quick_terminal` (Setup a quick terminal)
This menu enables you to quickly add or remove a terminal from a port.

`tty_settings` (Terminal Line Setting Management)
This menu provides functions for managing tty line settings. Specifically, it allows you to create new tty settings and hunt sequences, and to display (on your screen) and remove those settings. It also allows you to modify an existing tty line setting, remove the entry for it and then recreate it, including the modifications.

Line Printer Services Configuration and Operation

This menu provides functions for managing the printers and print services you can make available to your users through the LP print service. Specifically, this menu can help you do the following: set up and control the LP print service; start and stop the print service, check the status of the print service and, if necessary, stop and start it; add new printers to your system, and change the configuration of existing printers; add, change, and mount forms; add, change, and change filters; and monitor users' print requests.

classes (Manage Classes of Related Printers)
> This menu allows you to add new classes and to display a list of the current classes.

filters (Manage Filters for Special Processing)
> This menu allows you to manage filters for special processing.

forms (Manage Pre-Printed Forms)
> This menu allows you to manage pre-printed forms.

operations (Perform Daily Printer Service Operations)
> This menu allows you to perform daily printer operations such as enabling printers, starting the print service, and mounting forms.

printers (Configure Printers for the Printer Service)
> This menu allows you to configure printers for the LP print service.

priorities (Assign Print Queue Priorities to Users)
> This menu allows you to assign priority in the queue for print requests.

requests (Manage Active Print Requests)
> This menu allows you to hold and release pending print requests, to move print requests to new destinations, and to cancel print requests.

status (Display Status of Printer Service)
> This menu allows you to display the current status of the LP print service.

systems (Configure Connections to Remote Systems)
> This menu allows you to configure the connections between your LP print service system and any other LP print service.

Restore Service Management

basic (Restore from Removable Media)
> This menu contains subtasks for restoring personal files, directories, system restores, and selective system restores.

Schedule Automatic Task

This menu contains subtasks to add, change, delete, and display tasks bound for automatic execution.

Software Installation and Information Management

The tasks in this menu provide functions for software package installation, removal, and management of information pertaining to software packages. They include the ability to install and remove packages, and to check the accuracy of package installation. In addition, they include the ability to set installation defaults, store interactions with a particular package, store a package without actually installing it, and to list all installed packages.

check (Checks Accuracy of Installation)
> This task lets you check installed software packages for consistency, correct for inconsistencies, check for hidden files, and check the contents of files which are likely to have changed.

defaults (Sets Installation Defaults)
> This task allows you to decide, ahead of time, the way that the system should respond to an installation problem.

install (Installs Software Packages)
> This task lets you install software packages onto a spool, a hard disk, or a floppy diskette, and select the method that the system will use to respond to installation problems.

interact (Stores Interactions with Package)
> This task allows you to interact with the software installation process.

list (Displays Information about Packages)
> This task shows you the software packages that are installed on your system and tells you the name, location, and category of each.

read_in (Stores Packages Without Installing)
> This task lets you read in software packages without installing them.

remove (Removes Packages)
> This task lets you remove installed software packages.

Storage Device Operations and Definitions

This menu contains tasks for getting descriptions of device aliases and attributes and for assigning device groups.

add   This menu lets you add a storage device to the system.

> This menu lets you copy volumes from one device to another.

devices
> This menu lets you manage devices in the datebase.

display
> This task will display information about devices.

groups
> This menu lets you manage device groups in the Device management feature.

remove
> This menu lets you remove a device from the system.

System Name, Date Time and Initial Password Setup

This menu lets you set up your machine. The tasks in this menu include setting the system date and time, setting the node name of your system, doing initial system setup, and assigning passwords to administrative logins on the system.

datetime (System Date and Time Information)
: This task lets you tell the computer the date, time, time zone, and whether you observe Daylight Savings Time (DST). It is normally run once when the machine is first set up. If you observe DST, the computer automatically starts to observe it in the spring and returns to standard time in the fall. The machine must be turned off and turned back on again to guarantee that all times are reported correctly. Most times are correct the next time a user logs in.

nodename (System Name and Network Node Name of the Machine)
: This task lets you change the node name and system name of this machine. These names are used by various communications networks to identify this machine.

password (Assigns Administrative Login Passwords)
: This task lets you assign passwords to administrative logins.

setup (Sets up System Information for First Time)
: This task lets you define the first login, set the initial passwords on administration logins, and set the time zone for your location.

User Login and Group Administration

This menu lets you manage the user IDs and groups on your machine. Tasks include the ability to add, modify, and delete users or groups defined on your machine. You can place users in groups so that they can share access to files belonging to members of the group but protect these files from access by members of other groups. In addition, you can set defaults that are used for subsequent user definitions on your machine, and you can define or redefine user password information.

add (Adds Users or Groups)
: This task lets you define either a new user or a new group on your system.

defaults (Defines Defaults for Adding Users)
: This task lets you change some of the default values used when the add user task creates a new login. Changing the default values does not affect any existing logins; it affects only those added subsequently.

list (Lists Users or Groups)
: This task lets you examine the attributes of the users and groups on your system.

modify (Modifies Attributes of Users or Groups)
: This task lets you modify either a user definition or a group definition on your system.

password ((Re-)defines User Password Information)
: This task lets you define or change a user's password.

remove (Removes Users or Groups)
: This task lets you remove a user from your system.

ALTERNATE KEYSTROKES

For terminals that do not support function keys, the Form and Menu Language Interpreter provides alternate keystrokes to perform these functions, as described in the following table. These keystrokes perform different functions depending upon whether you are working within a text, a form, or a menu.

FMLI Alternate Keystrokes

Name	Keystroke	Name	Keystroke
BACKSPACE	CTRL-h	LEFT-ARROW	CTRL-i
BACKTAB	CTRL-t	MARK	CTRL-f m
BEG	CTRL-b	NEXT	CTRL-n
CLEAR	CTRL-y	PAGE-DOWN	CTRL-w
CLEAR-LINE	CTRL-y	PAGE-UP	CTRL-v
CLEAR-EOL	CTRL-f y	PREV	CTRL-p
COMMAND LINE	CTRL-j, CTRL-f c	RESET	CTRL-f r
DEL	CTRL-x	RETURN	CTRL-m
DELETE-CHAR	CTRL-x	RIGHT-ARROW	CTRL-r
DELETE-LINE	CTRL-k	SELECT FUNCTION BOX	CTRL-f [1-8]
DOWN-ARROW	CTRL-d	SCROLL-DOWN	CTRL-f d
END	CTRL-e	SCROLL-UP	CTRL-f u
HOME	CTRL-f b	SPACEBAR	none
HOME-DOWN	CTRL-f e	TAB	CTRL-i
INSERT-CHAR	CTRL-a	UP-ARROW	CTRL-u
INSERT-LINE	CTRL-o		

DIAGNOSTICS

The `sysadm` command exits with one of the following values:

0   Normal exit.

2   Invalid command syntax. Usage message of the `sysadm` command is displayed.

4   The menu or task name given as an argument does not exist.

5   The menu name given as an argument is an empty placeholder menu, and therefore not available for use.

7   The `sysadm` command is not available because it cannot invoke `fmli`. (The FMLI package may be corrupt or it may not have been installed.)

EXAMPLE

`sysadm nodename`

INTERNATIONAL FUNCTIONS

Some messages output by `sysadm` use the word *character(s)*, however, this actually means *byte(s)*.

SEE ALSO

`checkfsys`(1M), `cpio`(1), `delsysadm`(1M), `edsysadm`(1M), `groupadd`(1M), `groupdel`(1M), `groupmod`(1M), `makefsys`(1M), `mountfsys`(1M), `password`(1M), `setup`(1M), `shutdown`(1M), `useradd`(1M), `userdel`(1M), `usermod`(1M).

NOTES

When `sysadm` is executed, a 'stty -tabs' is invoked on the current terminal, to ensure proper tabs. If the user had no tabs set prior to running `sysadm`, invoking 'stty tabs' after leaving `sysadm` will return the terminal to its previous state.

NAME

sysdef - output system definition

SYNOPSIS

/usr/sbin/sysdef [-n *namelist* [-m *master*]]
/usr/sbin/sysdef -i

DESCRIPTION

sysdef outputs the current system definition in tabular form. It lists all hardware devices as well as pseudo devices, system devices, loadable modules, and the values of selected kernel tunable parameters.

It generates the output by analyzing the named bootable operating system file (*namelist*) and extracting the configuration information from it and files in the master directory. This directory contains the system configuration files used to build *namelist*.

The default system *namelist* is /stand/unix; the default *master* directory is /etc/master.d.

Valid options and parameters are:

-n *namelist*

Specifies a *namelist* other than the default (/stand/unix). The *namelist* specified must be a valid bootable operating system [see cunix(1M)].

-m *master*

Specifies a *master* directory other than the default (/etc/master.d). Can only be used with the -n option.

-i   Allows you read the configuration information from the kernel that is currently in memory (that is, from /dev/kmem) rather than from a file.

DIAGNOSTICS

internal name list overflow

If the master table contains more than an internally specified number of entries for use by nlist(3C).

FILES

/stand/unix   default operating system file (file that contains the system namelist)

/etc/master.d/*   default directory containing master files

SEE ALSO

cunix(1M), nlist(3C), master(4).

NAME

`syslogd` - log system messages

SYNOPSIS

`/usr/sbin/syslogd` [`-d`] [`-f`*configfile*] [`-m` *interval*]

DESCRIPTION

`syslogd` reads and forwards system messages to the appropriate log files and/or users, depending upon the priority of a message and the system facility from which it originates. The configuration file `/etc/syslog.conf` [see `syslog.conf`(4)] controls where messages are forwarded. `syslogd` logs a mark (timestamp) message every *interval* minutes (default 20) at priority `LOG_INFO` to the facility whose name is given as `mark` in the `syslog.conf` file.

A system message consists of a single line of text, which may be prefixed with a priority code number enclosed in angle-brackets (`<>`); priorities are defined in `sys/syslog.h`.

`syslogd` reads from the STREAMS log driver, `/dev/log`, from any transport provider specified in `/etc/netconfig`, `/etc/net/`*transport*`/hosts`, and `/etc/net/`*transport*`/services`, and from the special device `/dev/klog` (for kernel messages).

`syslogd` reads the configuration file when it starts up, and again whenever it receives a HUP signal, at which time it also closes all files it has open, re-reads its configuration file, and then opens only the log files that are listed in that file. `syslogd` exits when it receives a TERM signal.

As it starts up, `syslogd` creates the file `/etc/syslog.pid`, if possible, containing its process ID (PID).

The following options are available:

`-d`   Turn on debugging.

`-f`*configfile*   Specify an alternate configuration file.

`-m` *interval*   Specify an interval, in minutes, between mark messages.

FILES

`/etc/syslog.conf`	configuration file
`/etc/syslog.pid`	process ID
`/dev/log`	STREAMS log driver
`/etc/netconfig`	specifies the transport providers available on the system
`/etc/net/`*transport*`/hosts`	
	network hosts for each transport
`/etc/net/`*transport*`/services`	
	network services for each transport

SEE ALSO

`logger`(1), `syslog`(3), `syslog.conf`(4), `log`(7).

NAME

tabs - set tabs on a terminal

SYNOPSIS

tabs [*tabspec*] [-T*type*] [+m*n*]

DESCRIPTION

tabs sets the tab stops on the user's terminal according to the tab specification *tabspec*, after clearing any previous settings. The user's terminal must have remotely settable hardware tabs.

tabspec   Four types of tab specification are accepted for *tabspec*. They are described below: canned (-*code*), repetitive (-*n*), arbitrary (*n1,n2, . . .*), and file (--*file*). If no *tabspec* is given, the default value is -8, that is, UNIX system "standard" tabs. The lowest column number is 1. Note that for tabs, column 1 always refers to the leftmost column on a terminal, even one whose column markers begin at 0, for example, the DASI 300, DASI 300s, and DASI 450.

-*code*   Use one of the codes listed below to select a *canned* set of tabs. The legal codes and their meanings are as follows:

    -a   1,10,16,36,72
            Assembler, IBM S/370, first format

    -a2   1,10,16,40,72
            Assembler, IBM S/370, second format

    -c   1,8,12,16,20,55
            COBOL, normal format

    -c2   1,6,10,14,49
            COBOL compact format (columns 1-6 omitted). Using this code, the first typed character corresponds to card column 7, one space gets you to column 8, and a tab reaches column 12. Files using this tab setup should include a format specification as follows (see fspec(4)):

                <:t-c2 m6 s66 d:>

    -c3   1,6,10,14,18,22,26,30,34,38,42,46,50,54,58,62,67
            COBOL compact format (columns 1-6 omitted), with more tabs than -c2. This is the recommended format for COBOL. The appropriate format specification is [see fspec(4)]:

                <:t-c3 m6 s66 d:>

    -f   1,7,11,15,19,23
            FORTRAN

    -p   1,5,9,13,17,21,25,29,33,37,41,45,49,53,57,61
            PL/I

    -s   1,10,55
            SNOBOL

-u   1,12,20,44
UNIVAC 1100 Assembler

-n   A *repetitive* specification requests tabs at columns $1+n$, $1+2*n$, etc. Of particular importance is the value 8: this represents the UNIX system "standard" tab setting, and is the most likely tab setting to be found at a terminal. Another special case is the value 0, implying no tabs at all.

n1 , n2 , . . .

The *arbitrary* format permits the user to type any chosen set of numbers, separated by commas, in ascending order. Up to 40 numbers are allowed. If any number (except the first one) is preceded by a plus sign, it is taken as an increment to be added to the previous value. Thus, the formats 1,10,20,30, and 1,10,+10,+10 are considered identical.

--file   If the name of a *file* is given, tabs reads the first line of the file, searching for a format specification [see fspec(4)]. If it finds one there, it sets the tab stops according to it, otherwise it sets them as -8. This type of specification may be used to make sure that a tabbed file is printed with correct tab settings, and would be used with the pr command:

             tabs *-- file*; pr *file*

Any of the following also may be used; if a given flag occurs more than once, the last value given takes effect:

-Ttype   tabs usually needs to know the type of terminal in order to set tabs and always needs to know the type to set margins. *type* is a name listed in term(5). If no -T flag is supplied, tabs uses the value of the environment variable TERM. If TERM is not defined in the *environment* [see environ(5)], tabs tries a sequence that will work for many terminals.

+mn   The margin argument may be used for some terminals. It causes all tabs to be moved over *n* columns by making column *n+1* the left margin. If +m is given without a value of *n*, the value assumed is 10. For a TermiNet, the first value in the tab list should be 1, or the margin will move even further to the right. The normal (leftmost) margin on most terminals is obtained by +m0. The margin for most terminals is reset only when the +m flag is given explicitly.

Tab and margin setting is performed via the standard output.

EXAMPLES

tabs -a   example using *-code* (*canned* specification) to set tabs to the settings required by the IBM assembler: columns 1, 10, 16, 36, 72.

tabs -8   example of using *-n* (*repetitive* specification), where *n* is 8, causes tabs to be set every eighth position:
1+(1*8), 1+(2*8), . . . which evaluate to columns 9, 17, . . .

tabs 1,8,36   example of using *n1 , n2 , . . .* (*arbitrary* specification) to set tabs at columns 1, 8, and 36.

```
tabs --$HOME/fspec.list/att4425
```
example of using *--file* (*file* specification) to indicate that tabs should be set according to the first line of `$HOME/fspec.list/att4425` [see `fspec`(4)].

DIAGNOSTICS

`illegal tabs`   when arbitrary tabs are ordered incorrectly

`illegal increment`

when a zero or missing increment is found in an arbitrary specification

`unknown tab code`   when a *canned* code cannot be found

`can't open`   if *--file* option used, and file can't be opened

`file indirection`   if *--file* option used and the specification in that file points to yet another file. Indirection of this form is not permitted

SEE ALSO

`newform`(1), `pr`(1), `tput`(1)
`fspec`(4), `terminfo`(4), `environ`(5), `term`(5).

NOTES

There is no consistency among different terminals regarding ways of clearing tabs and setting the left margin.

`tabs` clears only 20 tabs (on terminals requiring a long sequence), but is willing to set 64.

The *tabspec* used with the `tabs` command is different from the one used with the `newform` command. For example, `tabs -8` sets every eighth position; whereas `newform -i-8` indicates that tabs are set every eighth position.

NAME

`tail` - deliver the last part of a file

SYNOPSIS

`tail` [± *number* `lbcr`] [*file*]
`tail` [`-lbcr`] [*file*]
`tail` [± *number* `lbcf`] [*file*]
`tail` [`-lbcf`] [*file*]

DESCRIPTION

`tail` copies the named file to the standard output beginning at a designated place. If no file is named, the standard input is used.

Copying begins at distance +*number* from the beginning, or −*number* from the end of the input (if *number* is null, the value 10 is assumed). *Number* is counted in units of lines, blocks, or characters, according to the appended option `l`, `b`, or `c`. When no units are specified, counting is by lines.

With the `-f` (follow) option, if the input file is not a pipe, the program will not terminate after the line of the input file has been copied, but will enter an endless loop, wherein it sleeps for a second and then attempts to read and copy further records from the input file. Thus it may be used to monitor the growth of a file that is being written by some other process. For example, the command:

```
tail -f fred
```

will print the last ten lines of the file `fred`, followed by any lines that are appended to `fred` between the time `tail` is initiated and killed. As another example, the command:

```
tail -15cf fred
```

will print the last 15 characters of the file `fred`, followed by any lines that are appended to `fred` between the time `tail` is initiated and killed.

The `r` option copies lines from the specified starting point in the file in reverse order. The default for `r` is to print the entire file in reverse order.

The `r` and `f` options are mutually exclusive.

INTERNATIONAL FUNCTIONS

`tail` can process files containing characters from supplementary code sets.

Characters from supplementary code sets may not be displayed correctly when options `-b` or `-c` are specified, as they are processed byte-by-byte.

SEE ALSO

`cat`(1), `dd`(1M), `head`(1), `more`(1), `pg`(1), `tail`(1).

NOTES

Tails relative to the end of the file are stored in a buffer, and thus are limited in length. Various kinds of anomalous behavior may happen with character special files.

The `tail` command will only tail the last 4096 bytes of a file regardless of its line count.

NAME

`talk` - talk to another user

SYNOPSIS

`talk` *username* [*ttyname*]

DESCRIPTION

`talk` is a visual communication program that copies lines from your terminal to that of a user on the same or on another host. *username* is that user's login name.

The program is architecture dependent; it works only between machines of the same architecture.

If you want to talk to a user who is logged in more than once, the *ttyname* argument may be used to indicate the appropriate terminal name.

When first called, `talk` sends the message:

```
Message from TalkDaemon@ her_machine at time ...
talk: connection requested by your_name@your_machine
talk: respond with: talk your_name@your_machine
```

to the user you want to talk to. At this point, the recipient of the message should reply by typing:

```
talk your_name@your_machine
```

It does not matter from which machine the recipient replies, as long as the login name is the same. Once communication is established, the two parties may type simultaneously, with their output appearing in separate windows. Typing CTRL-1 redraws the screen, while your erase, kill, and word kill characters will work in `talk` as normal. To exit, just type your interrupt character; `talk` then moves the cursor to the bottom of the screen and restores the terminal.

Permission to talk may be denied or granted by use of the `mesg`(1) command. At the outset talking is allowed. Certain commands, such as `pr`(1), disallow messages in order to prevent messy output.

FILES

`/etc/hosts`	to find the recipient's machine
`/var/adm/utmp`	to find the recipient's tty

SEE ALSO

`mail`(1), `mesg`(1), `pr`(1), `who`(1), `write`(1), `talkd`(1M)

NAME

> `talkd`, `in.talkd` - server for talk program

SYNOPSIS

> `in.talkd`

DESCRIPTION

> `talkd` is a server used by the `talk`(1) program. It listens at the UDP port indicated in the "talk" service description; see `services`(4). The actual conversation takes place on a TCP connection that is established by negotiation between the two machines involved.

SEE ALSO

> `talk`(1), `inetd`(1M), `services`(4)

NOTES

> The protocol is architecture dependent.

NAME

tar - tape file archiver

SYNOPSIS

/usr/sbin/tar -c[vwfbLkFDhienA#] *device block files tapesize incfile* ...
/usr/sbin/tar -c[vwfbLkXDhienA#] *device block files tapesize excfile* ...
/usr/sbin/tar -r[vwfbLkFDhienA#] *device block files tapesize incfile* ...
/usr/sbin/tar -r[vwfbLkXDhienA#] *device block files tapesize excfile* ...
/usr/sbin/tar -t[vfLXien#] *device* [*files* ...] *excfile*
/usr/sbin/tar -u[vwfbLkXDhienA#] *device block files tapesize excfile* ...
/usr/sbin/tar -u[vwfbLkFDhienA#] *device block files tapesize incfile* ...
/usr/sbin/tar -x[lmovwfLXpienA#] *device* [*files* ...] *excfile*

DESCRIPTION

tar saves and restores files on magnetic tape. Its actions are controlled by a string
of characters containing one option (c, r, t, u, or x), and possibly followed by one
or more modifiers (v, w, f, b, L, k, F, X, D, h, i, e, n, A, l, m, o, p and #). Other arguments to the command are *files* (or directory names) specifying which files are to be
dumped or restored. In all cases, appearance of a directory name refers to the files
and (recursively) subdirectories of that directory.

The options are as follows:

-c   Create a new tape; writing begins at the beginning of the tape, instead of
            after the last file. The -c option implies the -r option.

-r   Replace. The named *files* are written on the end of the tape. The -c and -u
            options imply the -r option.

-t   Table. The names and other information for the specified files are listed
            each time that they occur on the tape. The listing is similar to the format
            produced by the ls -l command [see ls(1)]. If no *files* argument is given,
            all the names on the tape are listed.

-u   Update. The named *files* are added to the tape if they are not already
            there, or have been modified since last written on that tape. The -u option
            implies the -r option.

-x   Extract. The named *files* are extracted from the tape. If a named file
            matches a directory whose contents had been written onto the tape, this
            directory is (recursively) extracted. Use the file or directory's relative path
            when appropriate, or tar will not find a match. The owner, modification
            time, and mode are restored (if possible). If no *files* argument is given, the
            entire contents of the tape is extracted. Note that if several files with the
            same name are on the tape, the last one overwrites all earlier ones.

The modifiers below may be used in the order shown in the synopsis.

This modifier determines the drive on which the tape is mounted (replace
            # with the drive number) The modifier tells tar to use a drive other than
            the default drive. The defaults are listed in /etc/default/tar.

            The following criteria, listed in order of precedence, to determine which
            device to use.

        -f *device* present on command line

        TAPE environment variable set

        # option used on command line

        the 0 device in /etc/default/tar

v   Verbose. Normally, tar does its work silently. The v (verbose) modifier causes it to print the name of each file it treats, preceded by the option. With the -t option, v gives more information about the tape entries than just the name.

w   What. This modifier causes tar to print the action to be taken, followed by the name of the file, and then wait for your confirmation. If a word beginning with y is given, the action is performed. Any other input means no. This is not valid with the -t option.

f   File. This causes tar to use the *device* argument as the name of the archive instead of the default. If the name of the file is -, tar writes to the standard output or reads from the standard input, whichever is appropriate. Thus, tar can be used as the head or tail of a pipeline. tar can also be used to move hierarchies with the command:

        cd *fromdir*; tar cf - . | (cd *todir*; tar xf -)

b   Blocking Factor. This modifier causes tar to use the *block* argument as the blocking factor for tape records. The default is 20. This modifier should not be supplied when operating on regular archives or block special devices. It is mandatory however, when reading archives on raw magnetic tape archives (see f above). The block size is determined automatically when reading tapes created on block special devices (options x and t).

1   Link. This modifier causes tar to complain if it cannot resolve all of the links to the files being dumped. If the 1 modifier is not specified, no error messages are printed.

m   Modify. This modifier causes tar to not restore the modification times. The modification time of the file will be the time of extraction.

o   Ownership. This modifier causes extracted files to take on the user and group identifier of the user running the program, rather than those on tape. This is only valid with the -x option.

L   Follow symbolic links. This modifier causes symbolic links to be followed. By default, symbolic links are not followed.

k   This modifier uses the *tapesize* argument as the size in bytes per volume for non-tape devices (such as a floppy drive). A value of 0 for *tapesize* causes multi-volume mode to be disabled (interpreted as an infinite volume size). This modifier may be used with the -c, -r, and -u options.

F   This modifier uses the *incfile* argument as a file containing a list of named files (or directories) to be included on the tape. This modifier may only be used with the -c, -r, and -u options. This modifier may not be used with the X modifier.

X   This modifier uses the *excfile* argument as a file containing a list of named files (or directories) to be excluded. This modifier may not be used with the F modifier.

h   This modifier causes tar to follow symbolic links as if they were normal files or directories. Normally tar does not follow symbolic links. The h modifier may be used with the -c, -r, and -u options.

p   This modifier restores the named *file* arguments to their original modes, ignoring the present value returned by umask [see umask(2)]. setuid and sticky bit information are also restored if the effective user ID is root. This modifier may only be used with the -x option.

i   This modifier causes tar to ignore directory checksum errors.

e   This modifier causes tar to quit when certain minor errors are encountered. Otherwise tar will continue when minor errors are encountered.

n   This modifier must be used when the *device* argument is for a non-tape device (for example, a floppy drive).

A   This modifier causes absolute pathnames for files to be suppressed, and may be used with the -r, -c, -u, and -x options. This causes all pathnames to be interpreted as relative to the current working directory.

D   By default tar uses the industry standard POSIX 1003.1 archive format. The POSIX format for directory entries is not understood by older BSD-derived tar programs. The D option causes directories to be archived in a format which is compatible with these tar programs. This compatible format is achieved by appending a '/' character to all directories in the archive. This option should be used with the -r, -c and -u options.

EXAMPLES

Two examples using the TAPE environment variable:

```
TAPE=/dev/rmt/ctape1n
tar -cf /dev/rmt/ctape1
```

will use /dev/rmt/ctape1.

```
TAPE=/dev/rmt/ctape1n
tar -c0h
```

will use /dev/rmt/ctape1n rather than the 0 entry of /etc/default/tar.

FILES

/etc/default/tar

/tmp/tar*

/usr/lib/locale/*locale*/LC_MESSAGES/uxcore
        language-specific message file [see LANG on environ(5)]

SEE ALSO

ar(1), cpio(1), ls(1), umask(2)

DIAGNOSTICS

Complains about tape read/write errors.
Complains if insufficient memory is available to hold the link tables.

NOTES

There is no way to ask for the *n*-th occurrence of a file.

The -b modifier should not be used with archives that are going to be updated. The current magnetic tape driver cannot backspace raw magnetic tape. If the archive is on a disk file, the -b modifier should not be used at all, because updating an archive stored on disk can destroy it.

The current limit on file name length is 100 characters.

When UNIX System V Release 4.0 `tar` is used on pre-Release 4.0 archives, a false warning message that file permissions have changed will be issued.

If you use `tar`(1) to extract files from a tape archive, the following warnings will be printed if the user or group of the file being restored do not exist on the system.

```
tar: problem reading passwd entry
tar: file: owner not changed
tar: problem reading group entry
tar: file: group not changed/f1
```

The file will be properly extracted, but it will be owned by `root` and belong to group `root` instead of the owner and group of the file on the archive.

NAME

tbl - format tables for nroff or troff

SYNOPSIS

/usr/ucb/tbl [-me] [-ms] [-mm] [-TX] [*filename*] ...

DESCRIPTION

The tbl command is a preprocessor for formatting tables for nroff or troff. The input *filename*s are copied to the standard output, except that lines between .TS and .TE command lines are assumed to describe tables and are reformatted.

If no arguments are given, tbl reads the standard input, so tbl may be used as a filter. When tbl is used with eqn or neqn the tbl command should be first, to minimize the volume of data passed through pipes.

The -me option copies the -me macro package to the front of the output file.

The -ms option copies the -ms macro package to the front of the output file.

The -mm option copies the -mm macro package to the front of the output file.

The -TX option produces output that does not have fractional line motions in it.

EXAMPLE

As an example, letting \t represent a TAB (which should be typed as a genuine TAB) the input

```
.TS
c s s
c c s
c c c
l n n.
Household\tPopulation
Town\tHouseholds
\tNumber\tSize
Bedminster\t789\t3.26
Bernards Twp.\t3087\t3.74
Bernardsville\t2018\t3.30
.TE
```

yields

| Household Population | | |
| Town | Households | |
	Number	Size
Bedminster	789	3.26
Bernards Twp.	3087	3.74
Bernardsville	2018	3.30

SEE ALSO

eqn(1), nroff(1), troff(1)

NAME

tbx/ctbx - DeltaPRO Toolbox

SYNOPSIS

tbx [-c *corefile*] [-p *source_path_list*] [-w] [-G] [-+] [-?] [-h] [*objfile*]

ctbx [-c *corefile*] [-p *source_path_list*] [-w] [-G] [-+] [-I] [-C] [-?] [-h] [*objfile*]

DESCRIPTION

tbx is a utility for source-level debugging and execution of programs written in C, Fortran, and C++. ctbx accepts the same commands as tbx, but uses the curses tty interface.

objfile is an executable object file produced by cc, f77, or CC (the C++ compiler). For full debugging capabilities, the -g option should be specified for all compilations.

If no *objfile* is specified, a.out will be the default. If the object file cannot be found, a usage message is printed.

Each time you start a debugging session, tbx looks for a file named .tbxinit. The user's home directory is searched first. If the file is not found, the current working directory is then searched. If a .tbxinit file can be found, all commands in the file will be executed prior to the start of tbx.

OPTIONS

-c corefile

        Specify an alternate core file. The default is core. Use -c *none* to ignore an existing core file. To use a core file called none, use -c ./none.

-p *dir_list*   Add *dir_list* to the search path for source files. *dir_list* can be a single path or a list of paths separated by colons. On System V Release 4, tbx will normally find source files, regardless of their location, because of path information generated by the DeltaPRO compilers. Therefore, this option is normally only needed on System V Release 3 systems unless source files have been moved since compilation.

-w   Toggle warning reports. This includes various problems that tbx finds, primarily during the startup procedure. If warnings are enabled, tbx also shows the name of each source file as it finds it during startup. By default, warnings are enabled.

-G   Toggle Fortran END or ERR goto interception. When debugging Fortran programs compiled by the DeltaPRO Fortran compiler, tbx will intercept execution of Fortran ERR= or END= I/O specifiers and report that program control was transferred abnormally. If you do not want this to occur, specify the -G option. If you are debugging a C program or a Fortran program compiled with a different compiler, this option has no effect.

-I   Toggle terminal I/O intercept (ctbx only). When you are using ctbx, any terminal I/O performed by your program will be intercepted by the debugger by default. If you are debugging a program which makes minimal use of terminal I/O, or debugging an attached program, you may wish to disable this feature. If you use this feature, any terminal I/O that your program writes will overwrite the TBX display. For attached processes, I/O will happen in the window in which the process is running.

-+   Use C++ name demangling.

-C   Toggle `curses application` mode (ctbx only). If you are debugging an application which uses the curses library with ctbx, you need to specify this option to prevent conflicts between the tbx curses interface and your program. Note that this option implicitly turns on the -I option. When the tbx display is disrupted by the actions of your program, you can use the `update` command to correct the problem.

All of the standard X command line options (`-geometry`, `-fg`, `-display`, etc...) are also available with tbx. Refer to the *X Window System User's Guide* for complete details.

ENVIRONMENT VARIABLES

The environment variable TBXOPTIONS can be used to toggle the default state of the flags controlled by the -w , -G , -I , and -C options. To do this, initialize the TBXOPTIONS variable to contain the option flags. For example, to have tbx not report warnings and not intercept END and ERR gotos, you could specify the following command (from ksh):

```
export TBXOPTIONS="-w -G"
```

If this is done, the options can still be toggled back to their original state by using the same options on the tbx command line.

Environment variables that are used by X (such as $DISPLAY) can also be used to modify the behavior of tbx. Refer to the *X Window System User's Guide* for complete details.

USAGE

For a detailed discussion of the .tbxinit file, the command interface, and the graphic interface refer to the tbx manual.

FILES

`core`	default core file
`a.out`	default executable target program
`.tbxinit`	local tbx initialization file
`$HOME/.tbxinit`	user's tbx initialization file
`/usr/lib/X11/app-defaults/Tbx`	X window resource file for tbx
`/usr/TARs/TBX`	a directory containing two files: list of unknown problems, and list of problems fixed since last release

SEE ALSO

cc(1), csh(1), kill(1), lex(1), make(1), yacc(1).

BUGS

Refer to the files in /usr/TARs/TBX for a list of known bugs in tbx.

NAME

tcopy - copy a magnetic tape

SYNOPSIS

/usr/ucb/tcopy *source* [*destination*]

DESCRIPTION

tcopy copies the magnetic tape mounted on the tape drive specified by the *source* argument. The only assumption made about the contents of a tape is that there are two tape marks at the end.

When only a source drive is specified, tcopy scans the tape, and displays information about the sizes of records and tape files. If a destination is specified, tcopy makes a copies the source tape onto the *destination* tape, with blocking preserved. As it copies, tcopy produces the same output as it does when only scanning a tape.

SEE ALSO

mt(1), ioctl(2).

NOTES

tcopy will only run on systems supporting an associated set of ioctl(2) requests.

NAME

   tee - pipe fitting

SYNOPSIS

   tee [-i] [-a] [*file*] ...

DESCRIPTION

   tee transcribes the standard input to the standard output and makes copies in the *files*. The

   -i   ignore interrupts;

   -a   causes the output to be appended to the *files* rather than overwriting them.

NAME

telnet - User interface to a remote system using the TELNET protocol

SYNOPSIS

telnet [-d] [-n *tracefile*] [-a] [-l *user*] [-e *escape_char*] [*host*] [*port*]

DESCRIPTION

The telnet command is used to communicate with another host using the TEL-NET protocol. If telnet is invoked without the *host* argument, it will enter command mode as indicated by its prompt telnet >. In this mode, telnet will accept and execute the commands listed below; if telnet is invoked with arguments, it will perform an open command (see "TELNET COMMANDS" below) with those arguments.

The following options are available:

-d   Sets the initial value of the debug toggle to TRUE.

-n *tracefile*   Opens *tracefile* for recording the trace information. (See the set *tracefile* command below.)

-a   Automatic login into the remote system. If the remote system understands the ENVIRON option, then the variable USER will be sent to the remote system. This option may also be used with the open command.

-l *user*   When connecting to the remote system and if the remote system understands the ENVIRON option, then *user* will be sent to the remote system as the value for the variable *user*. This option may also be used with the open command.

-e [*escape_char*]
            Sets the initial TELNET escape character to *escape_char*. If *escape_char* is omitted, then there will be no pre-defined escape character.

host   Indicates the host's official name: an alias or the Internet address of a remote host.

port   Indicates a port number (i.e., the address of an application). If a number is not specified, the default TELNET port will be used.

Once a connection has been opened, TELNET will enter the "input mode". TELNET will attempt to enable the TELNET LINEMODE option. If this fails, then TELNET will revert to one of two input modes: either the "character at a time" mode or the "old line by line" mode, depending on what the remote system supports.

When LINEMODE is enabled, character processing will be done on the local system while under the control of the remote system. When input editing or character echoing is to be disabled, the remote system will relay that information. The remote system will also relay changes to any special characters that happen on the remote system, so that they can take effect on the local system.

In the "character at a time" mode, most entered text will be sent immediately to the remote host for processing.

In the "old line by line" mode, all text will be echoed locally, but (normally) only completed lines will be sent to the remote host. The "local echo character" (initially ``"^E"``) may be used to enable and disable the local echo mode; normally, this would be used only for entering passwords so that the password will not be echoed.

If the LINEMODE option is enabled or if the `localchars` toggle is TRUE (the default value for the "old line by line" mode; see below), the user's `quit`, `intr`, and `flush` characters will be trapped locally and sent as TELNET protocol sequences to the remote machine. If LINEMODE had been enabled at any earlier time, then the user's `susp` and `eof` characters will also be sent as TELNET protocol sequences; `quit` will be sent as a TELNET ABORT instead of BREAK. There are options (see "toggle" `autoflush` and "toggle" `autosynch` below) which cause this action to flush any subsequent output to the terminal (until the remote host acknowledges the TELNET sequence) and to flush previous terminal input (in the case of `quit` and `intr`).

While connected to a remote host, the `telnet` command mode may be entered by typing the TELNET "escape character" (initially "^E").

When in command mode, the normal terminal editing conventions will be available.

TELNET COMMANDS

The following TELNET commands are available, but only enough of each command need be typed to uniquely identify it (this is also true for arguments pertaining to the `mode`, `set`, `toggle`, `unset`, `slc`, `environ`, and `display` commands).

`close`   Close a TELNET session and return to command mode.

`display` *argument* ...

         Displays all, or some, of the `set` and `toggle` values (see description below).

`mode` [*type*]

         Depending on the state of the TELNET session, the *type* argument is one of several available options. The remote host will be asked for permission to go into the requested mode. If the remote host is capable of entering that mode, the requested mode will be entered.

         `character`   Disable the TELNET LINEMODE option; or, if the remote side does not understand the LINEMODE option, then enter the "character at a time" mode.

         `line`   Enable the TELNET LINEMODE option; or, if the remote side does not understand the TELNET LINEMODE option, then attempt to enter the "old line by line" mode.

         `isig`

         `-isig`   Attempt to enable (disable) the TRAPSIG mode of the TELNET LINEMODE option. This requires that the LINEMODE option be enabled.

         `edit`

         `-edit`   Attempt to enable (disable) the EDIT mode of the LINEMODE option. This requires that the LINEMODE option be enabled.

```
softtabs
```

```
-softtabs
```
Attempt to enable (disable) the SOFT_TAB mode of the LINEMODE option. This requires that the LINEMODE option be enabled.

```
litecho
```

```
-litecho
```
Attempt to enable (disable) the LIT_ECHO mode of the LINEMODE option. This requires that the LINEMODE option be enabled.

? Prints out help information for the mode command.

open *host* [*user*] [[-] *port*] [-a] [-l *user*]

Open a connection to the named *host*. If no *port* number is specified, telnet will attempt to contact a TELNET server at the default port. The *host* specification may be either a host name [see hosts(4N)] or an Internet address specified in the "dot notation" [see inet(3)].

The -l or the -a option may be used to specify the *user* name to be passed to the remote system via the ENVIRON option.

When connecting to a non-standard port, telnet will omit the automatic initiation of any TELNET options. When the port number is preceded by a minus sign, the initial option negotiation will be done as follows: After establishing a connection, the file .telnetrc in the user's home directory will be opened. Lines beginning with a # will be treated as comment lines; blank lines will be ignored. Lines that begin without whitespace will be the start of a machine entry. The first thing on the line will the name of the machine to which this host is being connected. The rest of the line - and successive lines which begin with whitespace - will be assumed to be telnet commands and will be processed as if they had been entered manually in response to the telnet command prompt.

quit Close any open TELNET session and exit telnet. When in command mode, an End-of-File (EOF) will also close a session and exit.

send *arguments*

Sends one (or more) special character sequences to the remote host. The following are the arguments which may be specified (more than one argument may be specified at a given time):

abort Sends the TELNET ABORT (ABORT processes) sequence.

ao Sends the TELNET AO (Abort Output) sequence which should cause the remote system to flush all output from the remote system to the user's terminal.

ayt Sends the TELNET AYT ("Are You There?") sequence; the remote system may or may not choose to respond to this transmission.

brk Sends the TELNET BRK (Break) sequence which may have significance to the remote system.

ec   Sends the TELNET EC (Erase Character) sequence which should cause the remote system to erase the last character entered.

el   Sends the TELNET EL (Erase Line) sequence which should cause the remote system to erase the line currently being entered.

eof   Sends the TELNET EOF (End Of File) sequence.

eor   Sends the TELNET EOR (End Of Record) sequence.

escape
     Sends the current TELNET escape character (initially "^E").

ga   Sends the TELNET GA (Go Ahead) sequence, which probably has no significance to the remote system.

getstatus
     If the remote side supports the TELNET STATUS command, getstatus will send the subnegotiation request that the server send its current option status.

ip   Sends the TELNET IP (Interrupt Process) sequence, which should cause the remote system to abort the currently running process.

nop   Sends the TELNET NOP (No OPeration) sequence.

susp   Sends the TELNET SUSP (SUSPend process) sequence.

synch   Sends the TELNET SYNCH sequence. This sequence causes the remote system to discard all previously typed (but not yet read) input. This sequence will be sent as TCP urgent data (and may not work if the remote system is a 4.2 BSD system; if it doesn't work, a lower case " l " may be echoed on the terminal).

?   Prints out help information for the send command.

set *argument value*

unset *argument value*
     The set command will set anyone of a number of TELNET variables to a specific value or to TRUE. The special value off will turn off the function associated with this variable; this is equivalent to using the unset command. The unset command will disable (or set to FALSE) any of the specified functions. The values of variables may be interrogated with the aid of the display command. The variables which may be set or unset - but not toggled - are listed here. In addition, any of the variables for the toggle command may be explicitly enabled or disabled using the set and unset commands.

echo   This is the value (initially "^E") which, when in the "line by line" mode, will toggle between doing local echoing of entered characters (for normal processing) and suppressing echoing of entered characters (for example, for entering a password).

`eof` If `telnet` is operating in LINEMODE or in the "old line by line" mode, entering this character as the first character on a line will cause this character to be sent to the remote system. The initial value of the "eof" character is taken to be the terminal's `eof` character.

`erase` If `telnet` is in `localchars` mode (see "toggle" `localchars` below), and if `telnet` is operating in the "character at a time" mode, then when this character is entered, a TELNET EC sequence (see `send ec` above) will be sent to the remote system. The initial value for the erase character is taken to be the terminal's `erase` character.

`escape`
    This is the TELNET escape character (initially "`^[`") which causes entry into the TELNET command mode when connected to a remote system.

`flushoutput`
    If `telnet` is in `localchars` mode (see "toggle" `localchars` below) and the `flushoutput` character is entered, a TELNET AO sequence (see `send ao` above) will be sent to the remote host. The initial value for the flush character is taken to be the terminal's `flush` character.

`interrupt`
    If TELNET AO is in `localchars` mode (see "toggle" `localchars` below) and the `interrupt` character is entered, a TELNET IP sequence (see `send ip` above) will be sent to the remote host. The initial value for the interrupt character is taken to be the terminal's `intr` character.

`kill` If TELNET IP is in `localchars` mode (see "toggle" `localchars` below), and if TELNET IP is operating in the "character at a time" mode, then when this character is entered, a TELNET EL sequence (see `send el` above) will be sent to the remote system. The initial value for the kill character is taken to be the terminal's `kill` character.

`lnext` If TELNET EL is operating in LINEMODE or in the "old line by line" mode, then this character is taken to be the terminal's `lnext` character. The initial value for the `lnext` character is taken to be the terminal's `lnext` character.

`quit` If TELNET EL is in `localchars` mode (see "toggle" `localchars` below) and the `quit` character is entered, a TELNET BRK sequence (see `send brk` above) will be sent to the remote host. The initial value for the `quit` character is taken to be the terminal's `quit` character.

`reprint`
    If TELNET BRK is operating in LINEMODE or in the "old line by line" mode, then this character is taken to be the terminal's `reprint` character. The initial value for the `reprint` character is taken to be the terminal's `reprint` character.

start If the TELNET TOGGLE-FLOW-CONTROL option has been enabled, then this character is taken to be the terminal's `start` character. The initial value for the `start` character is taken to be the terminal's `start` character.

stop If the TELNET TOGGLE-FLOW-CONTROL option has been enabled, then this character is taken to be the terminal's `stop` character. The initial value for the `stop` character is taken to be the terminal's `stop` character.

susp If TELNET is in the `localchars` mode or if the LINEMODE is enabled and the suspend character is entered, a TELNET SUSP sequence (see `send susp` above) will be sent to the remote host. The initial value for the `suspend` character is taken to be the terminal's `suspend` character.

tracefile
This is the file to which the output generated by the `netdata` command will be written.

worderase
If TELNET is operating in LINEMODE or in the "old line by line" mode, then this character is taken to be the terminal's `worderase` character. The initial value for the `worderase` character is taken to be the terminal's `worderase` character.

? Displays the legal `set` and `unset` commands.

slc [*state*]
The `slc` command ("Set Local Characters") is used to set (or change) the state of the special characters when the TELNET LINEMODE option has been enabled. The "Special Characters" are characters that get mapped to TELNET commands sequences (like `ip` or `quit`) or line-editing characters (like `erase` and `kill`). By default, the "local special characters" are exported.

export
Switch to the local defaults for the "special characters". The "local default characters" are those of the local terminal at the time when `telnet` was started.

import
Switch to the remote defaults for the "special characters". The remote default characters are those of the remote system at the time when the TELNET connection was established.

check Verify the current settings for the current "special characters". The remote side is requested to send all the current special character settings; if there are any discrepancies with the local side, the local side will switch to the set of remote values.

? Prints out help information for the `slc` command.

environ [*arguments* [...]]
The `environ` command is used to manipulate the variables that may be sent through the TELNET ENVIRON option. The initial set of variables is taken from the user's environment; with only the USER and DISPLAY variables

being exported.

The valid arguments for the `environ` command are:

`define` *variable value*
> Define the variable *variable* to have a value of *value*. Any variables defined by this command are automatically exported. The *value* may be enclosed in single or double quotes so that tabs and embedded spaces may be included.

`undefine` *variable*
> Remove *variable* from the list of environment variables.

`export`
> *variable* Mark the variable *variable* to be exported to the remote side.

`unexport`
> *variable*
> Mark the variable *variable* to not be exported unless explicitly requested by the remote side.

`list`   List the current set of environment variables. Those marked with a * will be sent automatically; any other variables will be sent only if requested explicitly.

`?`   Prints out help information for the `environ` command.

`toggle` *arguments* [...]
> Toggle various flags (between TRUE and FALSE) that control how TELNET responds to events. These flags may be set explicitly to TRUE or FALSE using the `set` and `unset` commands listed above. More than one argument may be specified. The state of these flags may be interrogated with the aid of the `display` command. The valid arguments are:

`autoflush`
> If `autoflush` and `localchars` are both TRUE, then when the `ao` or the `quit` characters are recognized (and transformed into TELNET sequences; see `set` above for details), TELNET will refuse to display any data on the user's terminal until the remote system acknowledges (via a TELNET TIMING MARK option) that it has processed those TELNET sequences. The initial value for this toggle is TRUE if the terminal user had not executed an "stty noflsh"; otherwise FALSE [see `stty`(1)].

`autosynch`
> If `autosynch` and `localchars` are both TRUE, then when either the `intr` or `quit` character is entered (see `set` above for descriptions of the `intr` and `quit` characters), the resulting TELNET sequence sent will be followed by the TELNET SYNCH sequence. This procedure "should" cause the remote system to begin throwing away all previously entered input until both of the TELNET sequences have been read and acted upon. The initial value of this toggle is FALSE.

`binary`
> Enable or disable the TELNET BINARY option on both the input and output.

`inbinary`
> Enable or disable the TELNET BINARY option on input.

`outbinary`
> Enable or disable the TELNET BINARY option on output.

`crlf`   If this "toggle" value is TRUE, then Carriage Returns will be sent as <CR> <LF>. If this is FALSE, then Carriage Returns will be sent as <CR><NUL>. The initial value for this toggle is FALSE.

`crmod` Toggle the Carriage Return mode. When this mode is enabled, most Carriage Return characters received from the remote host will be mapped into a Carriage Return followed by a Line Feed. This mode does not affect those characters entered by the user, but only those received from the remote host. This mode is not very useful unless the remote host only sends Carriage Return, but never any Line Feeds. The initial value for this toggle is FALSE.

`debug` Toggles the socket level debugging mode (useful only to the super-user). The initial value for this toggle is FALSE.

`localchars`
> If this is TRUE, then the `flush`, `interrupt`, `quit`, `erase`, and `kill` characters (see `set` above) are recognized locally and then transformed into (hopefully) appropriate TELNET control sequences (respectively `ao`, `ip`, `brk`, `ec`, and `el`; see `send` above). The initial value for this toggle is TRUE in "old line by line" mode and FALSE in "character at a time" mode.
>
> When the LINEMODE option is enabled, the value of `localchars` is ignored and assumed to always be TRUE. If LINEMODE has ever been enabled, then `quit` will be sent as `abort`; `eof` and `suspend` will be sent as `eof` and `susp`; (see `send` above).

`netdata`
> Toggles the display of all network data (in hexadecimal format). The initial value for this toggle is FALSE.

`options`
> Toggles the display of some internal `telnet` protocol processing which pertain to TELNET options. The initial value for this toggle is FALSE.

`prettydump`
> When the `netdata` toggle is enabled and if `prettydump` is enabled, the output from the `netdata` command will be reorganized into a more user-friendly format. Spaces will be put between each character in the output and the beginning of any TELNET escape sequence will be preceded by a '`*`' to aid in locating them.

`?`   Displays the legal `toggle` commands.

`Ctrl-z`
Suspend `telnet`. This command will work only when the user is using `csh`(1) or `ksh`(1).

! [command]
> Execute a single command in a subshell on the local system. If command is omitted, then an interactive subshell will be invoked.

status
> Show the current status of telnet. This includes the peer to which one is connected, as well as the current mode.

? [command]
> Get help. When no command is specified, telnet will print a summary for the help command. If a command is specified, telnet will print the help information for just that command.

ENVIRONMENT

The telnet command uses at least the following environent variables: HOME, SHELL, USER, DISPLAY, and TERM. Other environment variables may be propagated to the other side via the TELNET ENVIRON option.

FILES

$HOME/.telnetrc   user-customized telnet startup values

HISTORY

The telnet command appeared in 4.2 BSD.

USER CONSIDERATIONS

On some remote systems, the echo command has to be turned off manually when in the "old line by line" mode.

When in the "old line by line" mode or in LINEMODE, the terminal's eof character is only recognized (and sent to the remote system) when it is the first character in a line.

NAME

`telnetd` - DARPA TELNET protocol server

SYNOPSIS

`in.telnetd` [`-debug` [*port*]] [`-h`] [`-D` (*options* | *report* | *exercise* | *netdata* | *ptydata*)]

DESCRIPTION

`telnetd` is a server which supports the DARPA standard TELNET virtual terminal protocol. `telnetd` is invoked by the internet server [see `inetd`(1M)], normally for requests to connect to the TELNET port as indicated by the `/etc/services` file [see `services`(4)]. The `-debug` option can be used to start up `telnetd` manually, instead of through `inetd`(8). If started up in this manner, *port* may be specified to run `telnetd` on this alternate TCP port number.

The `-h` option stops `telnetd` printing a login banner.

The `-D` option can be used for debugging purposes. This will allow *telnet* to print out debugging information to the connection, thus enabling the user to see what `telnetd` is doing. Several modifiers are available for the debugging mode:

options	prints information about the negotiation of the TELNET options,
report	prints the *options* information, as well as some additional information about what processing is going on,
netdata	displays the data stream received by `telnetd`,
ptydata	displays data written to the pty, and
exercise	has not been implemented yet.

The `telnetd` command operates by allocating a pseudo-terminal device [see `pty`(4)] for a client, thereby creating a login process which has the slave side of the pseudo-terminal serving as `stdin`, `stdout`, and `stderr`. The `telnetd` command will manipulate the master side of the pseudo-terminal by implementing the TEL-NET protocol and by passing characters between the remote client and the login process.

When a TELNET session is started up, `telnetd` will send TELNET options to the client side which will indicate a willingness

- to do *remote echo* of characters,
- to *suppress go ahead,*
- to do *remote flow control,* as well as
- to receive *terminal type information,*
- to receive *terminal speed information,* and
- to receive *window size information* from the remote client.

If the remote client is willing, the remote terminal type will be propagated to the environment of the created login process. The pseudo-terminal allocated to the client will be configured to operate in "cooked" mode, with XTABS and CRMOD enabled [see `termio`(4)].

telnetd is willing to do: *echo, binary, suppress go ahead*, and *timing mark*. telnetd is willing to have the remote client do: *linemode, binary1, terminal type, terminal speed, window size, toggle flow control, environment, X display location*, and *suppress go ahead*.

SEE ALSO

telnet(1), resolv.conf(4).
RFC 854.

NOTES

Some TELNET commands are only partially implemented.

Because of bugs in the original 4.2 BSD telnet(1), telnetd performs some dubious protocol exchanges to try to discover if the remote client is, in fact, a 4.2 BSD telnet(1).

Binary mode has no common interpretation except between similar operating systems

The terminal type name received from the remote client is converted to lower case.

telnetd never sends TELNET *go ahead* commands.

It is possible for telnetd to respond slowly when Domain Name Service is in place and the primary nameserver is unreachable or slow to respond. If your nameserver or network is heavily loaded, refer to the resolv.conf(4) man page for details on how to configure DNS under these conditions.

NAME

term - conventional names for terminals

DESCRIPTION

Terminal names are maintained as part of the shell environment in the environment variable TERM [see sh(1), profile(4), and environ(5)]. These names are used by certain commands [for example, tabs, tput, and vi] and certain functions [for example, see curses(3X)].

Files under /usr/share/lib/terminfo are used to name terminals and describe their capabilities. These files are in the format described in terminfo(4). Entries in terminfo source files consist of a number of comma-separated fields. To print a description of a terminal *term*, use the command infocmp -I *term* [see infocmp(1M)]. White space after each comma is ignored. The first line of each terminal description in the terminfo database gives the names by which terminfo knows the terminal, separated by bar (|) characters. The first name given is the most common abbreviation for the terminal [this is the one to use to set the environment variable TERMINFO in $HOME/.profile; see profile(4)], the last name given should be a long name fully identifying the terminal, and all others are understood as synonyms for the terminal name. All names but the last should contain no blanks and must be unique in the first 14 characters; the last name may contain blanks for readability.

Terminal names (except for the last, verbose entry) should be chosen using the following conventions. The particular piece of hardware making up the terminal should have a root name chosen, for example, for the AT&T 4425 terminal, att4425. This name should not contain hyphens, except that synonyms may be chosen that do not conflict with other names. Up to 8 characters, chosen from the set a through z and 0 through 9, make up a basic terminal name. Names should generally be based on original vendors rather than local distributors. A terminal acquired from one vendor should not have more than one distinct basic name. Terminal sub-models, operational modes that the hardware can be in, or user preferences should be indicated by appending a hyphen and an indicator of the mode. Thus, an AT&T 4425 terminal in 132 column mode is att4425-w. The following suffixes should be used where possible:

Suffix	Meaning	Example
-w	Wide mode (more than 80 columns)	att4425-w
-am	With auto. margins (usually default)	vt100-am
-nam	Without automatic margins	vt100-nam
-*n*	Number of lines on the screen	aaa-60
-na	No arrow keys (leave them in local)	c100-na
-np	Number of pages of memory	c100-4p
-rv	Reverse video	att4415-rv

To avoid conflicts with the naming conventions used in describing the different modes of a terminal (for example, -w), it is recommended that a terminal's root name not contain hyphens. Further, it is good practice to make all terminal names used in the terminfo(4) database unique. Terminal entries that are present only for inclusion in other entries via the use= facilities should have a '+' in their name, as in 4415+nl.

Here are some of the known terminal names: (For a complete list, enter the command `ls -C /usr/share/lib/terminfo/?.`)

`2621,hp2621`	Hewlett-Packard 2621 series
`2631`	Hewlett-Packard 2631 line printer
`2631-c`	Hewlett-Packard 2631 line printer, compressed mode
`2631-e`	Hewlett-Packard 2631 line printer, expanded mode
`2640,hp2640`	Hewlett-Packard 2640 series
`2645,hp2645`	Hewlett-Packard 2645 series
`3270`	IBM Model 3270
`33,tty33`	AT&T Teletype Model 33 KSR
`35,tty35`	AT&T Teletype Model 35 KSR
`37,tty37`	AT&T Teletype Model 37 KSR
`4000a`	Trendata 4000a
`4014,tek4014`	TEKTRONIX 4014
`40,tty40`	AT&T Teletype Dataspeed 40/2
`43,tty43`	AT&T Teletype Model 43 KSR
`4410,5410`	AT&T 4410/5410 in 80-column mode, version 2
`4410-nfk,5410-nfk`	AT&T 4410/5410 without function keys, version 1
`4410-nsl,5410-nsl`	AT&T 4410/5410 without pln defined
`4410-w,5410-w`	AT&T 4410/5410 in 132-column mode
`4410v1,5410v1`	AT&T 4410/5410 in 80-column mode, version 1
`4410v1-w,5410v1-w`	AT&T 4410/5410 in 132-column mode, version 1
`4415,5420`	AT&T 4415/5420 in 80-column mode
`4415-nl,5420-nl`	AT&T 4415/5420 without changing labels
`4415-rv,5420-rv`	AT&T 4415/5420 80 columns in reverse video
`4415-rv-nl,5420-rv-nl`	AT&T 4415/5420 reverse video without changing labels
`4415-w,5420-w`	AT&T 4415/5420 in 132-column mode
`4415-w-nl,5420-w-nl`	AT&T 4415/5420 in 132-column mode without changing labels
`4415-w-rv,5420-w-rv`	AT&T 4415/5420 132 columns in reverse video
`4418,5418`	AT&T 5418 in 80-column mode

`4418-w,5418-w`	AT&T 5418 in 132-column mode
`4420`	AT&T Teletype Model 4420
`4424`	AT&T Teletype Model 4424
`4424-2`	AT&T Teletype Model 4424 in display function group ii
`4425,5425`	AT&T 4425/5425
`4425-fk,5425-fk`	AT&T 4425/5425 without function keys
`4425-nl,5425-nl`	AT&T 4425/5425 without changing labels in 80-column mode
`4425-w,5425-w`	AT&T 4425/5425 in 132-column mode
`4425-w-fk,5425-w-fk`	AT&T 4425/5425 without function keys in 132-column mode
`4425-nl-w,5425-nl-w`	AT&T 4425/5425 without changing labels in 132-column mode
`4426`	AT&T Teletype Model 4426S
`450`	DASI 450 (same as Diablo 1620)
`450-12`	DASI 450 in 12-pitch mode
`500,att500`	AT&T-IS 500 terminal
`510,510a`	AT&T 510/510a in 80-column mode
`513bct,att513`	AT&T 513 bct terminal
`5320`	AT&T 5320 hardcopy terminal
`5420_2`	AT&T 5420 model 2 in 80-column mode
`5420_2-w`	AT&T 5420 model 2 in 132-column mode
`5620,dmd`	AT&T 5620 terminal 88 columns
`5620-24,dmd-24`	AT&T Teletype Model DMD 5620 in a 24x80 layer
`5620-34,dmd-34`	AT&T Teletype Model DMD 5620 in a 34x80 layer
`610,610bct`	AT&T 610 bct terminal in 80-column mode
`610-w,610bct-w`	AT&T 610 bct terminal in 132-column mode
`630,630MTG`	AT&T 630 Multi-Tasking Graphics terminal
`7300,pc7300,unix_pc`	AT&T UNIX PC Model 7300
`735,ti`	Texas Instruments TI735 and TI725
`745`	Texas Instruments TI745
`dumb`	generic name for terminals that lack reverse line-feed and other special escape sequences
`hp`	Hewlett-Packard (same as 2645)
`lp`	generic name for a line printer
`pt505`	AT&T Personal Terminal 505 (22 lines)
`pt505-24`	AT&T Personal Terminal 505 (24-line mode)

sync   generic name for synchronous Teletype
                                Model 4540-compatible terminals

Commands whose behavior depends on the type of terminal should accept arguments of the form -T*term* where *term* is one of the names given above; if no such argument is present, such commands should obtain the terminal type from the environment variable TERM, which, in turn, should contain *term*.

FILES
/usr/share/lib/terminfo/?/*   compiled terminal description database

SEE ALSO
infocmp(1M), sh(1), stty(1), tabs(1), tput(1), vi(1) curses(3X) profile(4), terminfo(4), environ(5).

NAME

    `test` - condition evaluation command

SYNOPSIS

    `test` *expr*

    [*expr*]

DESCRIPTION

    `test` evaluates the expression *expr* and, if its value is true, sets a zero (true) exit status; otherwise, a non-zero (false) exit status is set; `test` also sets a non-zero exit status if there are no arguments. When permissions are tested, the effective user ID of the process is used.

    All operators, flags, and brackets (brackets used as shown in the second SYNOPSIS line) must be separate arguments to the `test` command; normally these items are separated by spaces.

    The following primitives are used to construct *expr*:

`-r` *file*	true if *file* exists and is readable.
`-w` *file*	true if *file* exists and is writable.
`-x` *file*	true if *file* exists and is executable.
`-f` *file*	true if *file* exists and is a regular file. Alternatively, if `/usr/sh` users specify `/usr/ucb` before `/usr/bin` in their PATH environment variable, then `test` will return true if *file* exists and is `(not-a-directory)`. This is also the default for `/usr/bin/csh` users.
`-d` *file*	true if *file* exists and is a directory.
`-h` *file*	true if *file* exists and is a symbolic link. With all other primitives (except `-L` *file*), the symbolic links are followed by default.
`-c` *file*	true if *file* exists and is a character special file.
`-b` *file*	true if *file* exists and is a block special file.
`-p` *file*	true if *file* exists and is a named pipe (fifo).
`-u` *file*	true if *file* exists and its set-user-ID bit is set.
`-g` *file*	true if *file* exists and its set-group-ID bit is set.
`-k` *file*	true if *file* exists and its sticky bit is set.
`-s` *file*	true if *file* exists and has a size greater than zero.
`-t` [*fildes*]	true if the open file whose file descriptor number is *fildes* (1 by default) is associated with a terminal device.
`-z` *s1*	true if the length of string *s1* is zero.
`-n` *s1*	true if the length of the string *s1* is non-zero.
s1 `=` *s2*	true if strings *s1* and *s2* are identical.
s1 `!=` *s2*	true if strings *s1* and *s2* are *not* identical.
s1	true if *s1* is *not* the null string.

n1 -eq *n2*   true if the integers *n1* and *n2* are algebraically equal. Any of the comparisons -ne, -gt, -ge, -lt, and -le may be used in place of -eq.

-L *file*   true if *file* exists and is a symbolic link. With all other primitives (except -h *file*), the symbolic links are followed by default.

These primaries may be combined with the following operators:

!   unary negation operator.

-a   binary *and* operator.

-o   binary *or* operator (-a has higher precedence than -o).

(expr)   parentheses for grouping. Notice also that parentheses are meaningful to the shell and, therefore, must be quoted.

INTERNATIONAL FUNCTIONS

test can process characters from supplementary code sets in expr.

SEE ALSO

find(1), sh(1).

NOTES

The not-a-directory alternative to the -f option is a transition aid for BSD applications and may not be supported in future releases.

The -L option is a migration aid for users of other shells which have similar options and may not be supported in future releases.

If you test a file you own (the *-r*, *-w*, or *-x* tests), but the permission tested does not have the *owner* bit set, a non-zero (false) exit status will be returned even though the file may have the group or *other* bit set for that permission. The correct exit status will be set if you are super-user.

The = and != operators have a higher precedence than the -r through -n operators, and = and != always expect arguments; therefore, = and != cannot be used with the -r through -n operators.

If more than one argument follows the -r through -n operators, only the first argument is examined; the others are ignored, unless a -a or a -o is the second argument.

NAME

    `test` - condition evaluation command

SYNOPSIS

    `test` *expr*

    [*expr*]

DESCRIPTION

    `test` evaluates the expression *expr* and if its value is true, sets a zero (TRUE) exit status; otherwise, a non-zero (FALSE) exit status is set; `test` also sets a non-zero exit status if there are no arguments. When permissions are tested, the effective user ID of the process is used.

    All operators, flags, and brackets (brackets used as shown in the second SYNOPSIS line) must be separate arguments to `test`. Normally these items are separated by spaces.

    The following primitives are used to construct *expr*:

`-r` *file*	true if *file* exists and is readable.
`-w` *file*	true if *file* exists and is writable.
`-x` *file*	true if *file* exists and is executable.
`-f` *file*	true if *file* exists and is a regular file.
`-d` *file*	true if *file* exists and is a directory.
`-c` *file*	true if *file* exists and is a character special file.
`-b` *file*	true if *file* exists and is a block special file.
`-p` *file*	true if *file* exists and is a named pipe (fifo).
`-u` *file*	true if *file* exists and its set-user-ID bit is set.
`-g` *file*	true if *file* exists and its set-group-ID bit is set.
`-k` *file*	true if *file* exists and its sticky bit is set.
`-s` *file*	true if *file* exists and has a size greater than zero.
`-t` [*fildes*]	true if the open file whose file descriptor number is *fildes* (1 by default) is associated with a terminal device.
`-z` *s1*	true if the length of string *s1* is zero.
`-n` *s1*	true if the length of the string *s1* is non-zero.
s1 `=` *s2*	true if strings *s1* and *s2* are identical.
s1 `!=` *s2*	true if strings *s1* and *s2* are *not* identical.
s1	true if *s1* is *not* the null string.
n1 `-eq` *n2*	true if the integers *n1* and *n2* are algebraically equal. Any of the comparisons `-ne`, `-gt`, `-ge`, `-lt`, and `-le` may be used in place of `-eq`.

    These primaries may be combined with the following operators:

!	unary negation operator.
-a	binary and operator.
-o	binary or operator (-a has higher precedence than -o).
`( expr )`	parentheses for grouping. Notice also that parentheses are meaningful to the shell and, therefore, must be quoted.

NOTES

If you test a file you own (the -r, -w , or -x tests), but the permission tested does not have the *owner* bit set, a non-zero (false) exit status will be returned even though the file may have the *group* or *other* bit set for that permission. The correct exit status will be set if you are super-user.

The = and ! = operators have a higher precedence than the -r through -n operators, and = and ! = always expect arguments; therefore, = and ! = cannot be used with the -r through -n operators.

If more than one argument follows the -r through -n operators, only the first argument is examined; the others are ignored, unless a -a or a -o is the second argument.

SEE ALSO

find(1), sh(1).

NAME

`test` - condition evaluation command

SYNOPSIS

`/usr/ucb/test` *expr*

[*expr*]

DESCRIPTION

test evaluates the expression *expr* and, if its value is true, sets a zero (true) exit status; otherwise, a non-zero (false) exit status is set; *test* also sets a non-zero exit status if there are no arguments. When permissions are tested, the effective user ID of the process is used.

All operators, flags, and brackets (brackets used as shown in the second SYNOPSIS line) must be separate arguments to the *test* command; normally these items are separated by spaces.

The following primitives are used to construct *expr*:

`-r` *file*	true if *file* exists and is readable.
`-w` *file*	true if *file* exists and is writable.
`-x` *file*	true if *file* exists and is executable.
`-f` *file*	true if *file* exists and is a regular file. Alternatively, if `/usr/sh` users specify `/usr/ucb` before `/usr/bin` in their PATH environment variable, then *test* will return true if *file* exists and is (`not-a-directory`). This is also the default for `/usr/bin/csh` users.
`-d` *file*	true if *file* exists and is a directory.
`-c` *file*	true if *file* exists and is a character special file.
`-b` *file*	true if *file* exists and is a block special file.
`-p` *file*	true if *file* exists and is a named pipe (fifo).
`-u` *file*	true if *file* exists and its set-user-ID bit is set.
`-g` *file*	true if *file* exists and its set-group-ID bit is set.
`-k` *file*	true if *file* exists and its sticky bit is set.
`-s` *file*	true if *file* exists and has a size greater than zero.
`-t` [*fildes*]	true if the open file whose file descriptor number is *fildes* (1 by default) is associated with a terminal device.
`-z` *s1*	true if the length of string *s1* is zero.
`-n` *s1*	true if the length of the string *s1* is non-zero.
s1 `=` *s2*	true if strings *s1* and *s2* are identical.
s1 `!=` *s2*	true if strings *s1* and *s2* are *not* identical.
s1	true if *s1* is *not* the null string.
n1 `-eq` *n2*	true if the integers *n1* and *n2* are algebraically equal. Any of the comparisons `-ne`, `-gt`, `-ge`, `-lt`, and `-le` may be used in place of `-eq`.

-L*file*   true if `file` exists and is a symbolic link. With all other primitives, the symbolic links are followed by default.

These primaries may be combined with the following operators:

!   unary negation operator.

-a   binary *and* operator.

-o   binary *or* operator (-a has higher precedence than -o).

(*expr*)   parentheses for grouping. Notice also that parentheses are meaningful to the shell and, therefore, must be quoted.

SEE ALSO

`find`(1), `sh`(1).

NOTES

The 'not-a-directory' alternative to the -f option is a transition aid for BSD applications and may not be supported in future releases.

The -L option is a migration aid for users of other shells which have similar options and may not be supported in future releases.

If you test a file you own (the *-r*, *-w*, or *-x* tests), but the permission tested does not have the *owner* bit set, a non-zero (false) exit status will be returned even though the file may have the *group* or *other* bit set for that permission. The correct exit status will be set if you are super-user.

The = and ! = operators have a higher precedence than the -r through -n operators, and = and ! = always expect arguments; therefore, = and ! = cannot be used with the -r through -n operators.

If more than one argument follows the -r through -n operators, only the first argument is examined; the others are ignored, unless a -a or a -o is the second argument.

NAME

`tftp` - trivial file transfer program

SYNOPSIS

`tftp` [*host*]

DESCRIPTION

`tftp` is the user interface to the Internet TFTP (Trivial File Transfer Protocol), which allows users to transfer files to and from a remote machine. The remote *host* may be specified on the command line, in which case `tftp` uses *host* as the default host for future transfers (see the `connect` command below).

USAGE

Commands

Once `tftp` is running, it issues the prompt `tftp>` and recognizes the following commands:

`connect` *host-name* [*port*]

> Set the *host* (and optionally *port*) for transfers. The TFTP protocol, unlike the FTP protocol, does not maintain connections between transfers; thus, the `connect` command does not actually create a connection, but merely remembers what host is to be used for transfers. You do not have to use the `connect` command; the remote host can be specified as part of the `get` or `put` commands.

`mode` *transfer-mode*

> Set the mode for transfers; *transfer-mode* may be one of `ascii` or `binary`. The default is `ascii`.

`put` *filename*
`put` *localfile remotefile*
`put` *filename1 filename2 ... filenameN remote-directory*

> Transfer a file, or a set of files, to the specified remote file or directory. The destination can be in one of two forms: a filename on the remote host if the host has already been specified, or a string of the form
>
> > *host* : *filename*
>
> to specify both a host and filename at the same time. If the latter form is used, the specified host becomes the default for future transfers. If the remote-directory form is used, the remote host is assumed to be running the UNIX system.

`get` *filename*
`get` *remotename localname*
`get` *filename1 filename2 filename3 ... filenameN*

> Get a file or set of files (three or more) from the specified remote *sources*. *source* can be in one of two forms: a filename on the remote host if the host has already been specified, or a string of the form
>
> > *host* : *filename*
>
> to specify both a host and filename at the same time. If the latter form is used, the last host specified becomes the default for future transfers.

quit   Exit `tftp`. An EOF also exits.

verbose
        Toggle verbose mode.

trace   Toggle packet tracing.

status
        Show current status.

rexmt *retransmission-timeout*
        Set the per-packet retransmission timeout, in seconds.

timeout *total-transmission-timeout*
        Set the total transmission timeout, in seconds.

ascii   Shorthand for `mode ascii`.

binary
        Shorthand for `mode binary`.

? [*command-name* . . .]
        Print help information.

NOTES

Because there is no user-login or validation within the TFTP protocol, many remote sites restrict file access in various ways. Approved methods for file access are specific to each site, and therefore cannot be documented here.

When using the `get` command to transfer multiple files from a remote host, three or more files must be specified. The command returns an error message if only two files are specified.

Due to the limitations of the TFTP protocol, the integrity of the data cannot be guaranteed for multiple file transfers using the `get` or `put` commands.

NAME

tftpd - DARPA Trivial File Transfer Protocol server

SYNOPSIS

in.tftpd [-s] [*homedir*]

DESCRIPTION

tftpd is a server that supports the DARPA Trivial File Transfer Protocol (TFTP). This server is normally started by inetd(1M) and operates at the port indicated in the tftp Internet service description in the /etc/inetd.conf file. By default, the entry for tftpd in etc/inetd.conf is commented out. To make tftpd operational, the comment character(s) must be deleted from the file. See inetd.conf(4) for details.

Before responding to a request, the server attempts to change its current directory to *homedir*; the default value is /tftpboot.

OPTIONS

-s   Secure. When specified, the directory change must succeed; and the daemon also changes its root directory to *homedir*.

The use of tftp does not require an account or password on the remote system. Due to the lack of authentication information, tftpd will allow only publicly readable files to be accessed. Files may be written only if they already exist and are publicly writable. Note that this extends the concept of public to include all users on all hosts that can be reached through the network; this may not be appropriate on all systems, and its implications should be considered before enabling this service.

tftpd runs with the user ID and group ID set to [GU]ID_NOBODY. -2, under the assumption that no files exist with that owner or group. However, nothing checks this assumption or enforces this restriction.

NOTES

Due to the limitations of the TFTP protocol, the integrity of the data cannot be guaranteed for multiple file transfers using the get or put commands.

SEE ALSO

tftp(1), inetd(1M), ipallocd(1M), netconfig(4).
RFC 783.

NAME

tic - terminfo compiler

SYNOPSIS

tic [-v[*n*]] [-c] *file*

DESCRIPTION

The command tic translates a terminfo file from the source format into the compiled format. The results are placed in the directory /usr/share/lib/terminfo. The compiled format is necessary for use with the library routines in curses(3X).

-v*n* Specifies that (verbose) output be written to standard error trace information showing tic's progress. The optional integer *n* is a number from 1 to 10, inclusive, indicating the desired level of detail of information. If *n* is omitted, the default level is 1. If *n* is specified and greater than 1, the level of detail is increased.

-c Specifies to check only *file* for errors. Errors in use= links are not detected.

file Contains one or more terminfo terminal descriptions in source format [see terminfo(4)]. Each description in the file describes the capabilities of a particular terminal. When a use=*entry-name* field is discovered in a terminal entry currently being compiled, tic reads in the binary from /usr/share/lib/terminfo to complete the entry. (Entries created from *file* will be used first. If the environment variable TERMINFO is set, that directory is searched instead of /usr/share/lib/terminfo.) tic duplicates the capabilities in *entry-name* for the current entry, with the exception of those capabilities that explicitly are defined in the current entry.

If the environment variable TERMINFO is set, the compiled results are placed there instead of /usr/share/lib/terminfo.

Total compiled entries cannot exceed 4096 bytes. The name field cannot exceed 128 bytes. Terminal names exceeding 14 characters will be truncated to 14 characters and a warning message will be printed.

FILES

/usr/share/lib/terminfo/?/* compiled terminal description database

NOTES

When an entry, e.g., entry_name_1, contains a use=*entry_name_2* field, any canceled capabilities in *entry_name_2* must also appear in entry_name_1 before use= for these capabilities to be canceled in entry_name_1.

INTERNATIONAL FUNCTIONS

tic can translate a terminfo(4) file including variables for international functionality from the source format to the compiled format.

tic also recognizes the environment variable TERMINFO with a value that includes characters from the supplementary code sets as the path name for the compiled result.

Entry names in terminfo(4) files must be in single-byte characters, since the compiled result will be placed in a directory named using the first byte of the entry name.

SEE ALSO
    captoinfo(1M), infocmp(1M), curses(3X), terminfo(4).

NAME

    `time` - time a command

SYNOPSIS

    `time` *command*

DESCRIPTION

The *command* is executed; after it is complete, `time` prints the elapsed time during the command, the time spent in the system, and the time spent in execution of the command. Times are reported in seconds.

The times are printed on standard error.

SEE ALSO

    `timex`(1)
    `time`(2).

NAME
      timedc - timed control program

SYNOPSIS
      timedc [*command* [*argument ...*]]

DESCRIPTION
      The timedc command is used to control the operation of the timed(1M) program.
      It may be used to:

      • measure the differences between machines' clocks,
      • find the location where the master time server is running,
      • enable or disable tracing of messages received by timed, and
      • perform various debugging actions.

      Without any arguments, timedc will prompt for commands from the standard
      input. If any arguments are supplied, timedc will interpret the first argument as a
      command and the remaining arguments as the parameters to this command. The
      standard input may be redirected causing timedc to read commands from a file.

      A timedc command may be abbreviated while maintaining its uniqueness; the
      recognized command are:

      ? [*command* ...]

      help [*command* ...]
                  Print a short description of each command specified in the argument
                  list; a list of the recognized commands will be generated if no argu-
                  ments are specified.

      clockdiff *host* ...
                  Compute the differences between the clock of the host machine and
                  the clocks of the machines given as the argument(s).

      trace on

      trace off   Enable or disable the tracing of incoming messages to timed in the
                  file /var/log/timed.log .

      quit   Exit from timedc .

      Other timedc commands may be included for use in testing and debugging timed
      (consult the help command and the program source for details).

FILES
      /var/adm/timed.masterlog log file for master timed
      /var/log/timed.log   System V tracing file for timed
      /usr/adm/timed.log   BSD tracing file for timed

SEE ALSO
      date(1), adjtime(2), icmp(7), rdate(1M), timed(1M).

DIAGNOSTICS
      ?Ambiguous command   an abbreviation matches more than one command
      ?Invalid command   no match found
      ?Privileged command   this command can be executed by root only

NAME

timex - time a command; report process data and system activity

SYNOPSIS

timex [*options*] *command*

DESCRIPTION

The given *command* is executed; the elapsed time, user time and system time spent in execution are reported in seconds. Optionally, process accounting data for the *command* and all its children can be listed or summarized, and total system activity during the execution interval can be reported.

The output of timex is written on standard error.

The *options* are:

-p   List process accounting records for *command* and all its children. This option works only if the process accounting software is installed. Suboptions f, h, k, m, r, and t modify the data items reported. The options are as follows:

       -f   Print the fork(2)/ exec(2) flag and system exit status columns in the output.

       -h   Instead of mean memory size, show the fraction of total available CPU time consumed by the process during its execution. This "hog factor" is computed as (total CPU time)/(elapsed time).

       -k   Instead of memory size, show total kcore-minutes.

       -m   Show mean core size (the default).

       -r   Show CPU factor (user time/(system-time + user-time).

       -t   Show separate system and user CPU times. The number of blocks read or written and the number of characters transferred are always reported.

-o   Report the total number of blocks read or written and total characters transferred by *command* and all its children. This option works only if the process accounting software is installed.

-s   Report total system activity (not just that due to *command*) that occurred during the execution interval of *command*. All the data items listed in sar(1) are reported.

EXAMPLES

A simple example:

```
timex -ops sleep 60
```

A terminal session of arbitrary complexity can be measured by timing a sub-shell:

```
timex -opskmt sh
```

       session commands

     EOT

NOTES

Process records associated with *command* are selected from the accounting file /var/adm/pacct by inference, since process genealogy is not available. Background processes having the same user ID, terminal ID, and execution time window will be spuriously included.

SEE ALSO
    time(1), sar(1), times(2).

NAME

`tnamed`, `in.tnamed` - DARPA trivial name server

SYNOPSIS

`in.tnamed [ -v ]`

DESCRIPTION

`tnamed` is a server that supports the DARPA Name Server Protocol. The name server operates at the port indicated in the name service description [see `services`(4)], and is invoked by `inetd`(1M) when a request is made to the name server.

OPTIONS

`-v`   Invoke the daemon in verbose mode.

SEE ALSO

`uucp`(1C), `inetd`(1M), `services`(4)

Postel, Jon, *Internet Name Server*, IEN 116, SRI International, Menlo Park, California, August 1979

NOTES

The protocol implemented by this program is obsolete. Its use should be phased out in favor of the Internet Domain Name Service (DNS) protocol. See `named`(1M).

NAME

tosmtp - send mail to SMTP

SYNOPSIS

tosmtp [-f] [-n] [-u] [-d *domain*] [-H *helohost*] *sender host recip* . . .

DESCRIPTION

tosmtp translates a UNIX System mail message (read from standard input), into an RFC822 mail message, which can then be delivered with SMTP. tosmtp is normally invoked by smtpqer as part of the process of queueing mail for delivery.

The options to tosmtp and their meanings are as follows:

-d *domain*   Pass the specified *domain* directly to the smtp program.

-f   Act as a filter. The RFC822 message is sent to the standard output.

-H *helohost*   This option can be used to specify the name to be used for the host in the initial SMTP HELO message. This option is also passed to the smtp program.

-n   Do not place a To: line in the resulting RFC822 header.

-u   Do no conversion. The standard input is sent directly to the standard output.

FILES

/usr/lib/mail/surrcmd/smtp   Where the message is piped to

SEE ALSO

smtp(1M), smtpqer(1M)
RFC822 - Standard for the Format of ARPA Internet Text Messages

NAME

touch - update access and modification times of a file

SYNOPSIS

touch [-amc] [*mmddhhmm*[*yy*]] *files*

DESCRIPTION

touch causes the access and modification times of each argument to be updated. The file name is created if it does not exist. If no time is specified [see date(1)] the current time is used. The -a and -m options cause touch to update only the access or modification times respectively (default is -am). The -c option silently prevents touch from creating the file if it did not previously exist.

The return code from touch is the number of files for which the times could not be successfully modified (including files that did not exist and were not created).

SEE ALSO

date(1), utime(2).

NOTES

Users familiar with the BSD environment will find that the -f option is accepted, but ignored. The -f option is unnecessary since touch will succeed for all files owned by the user regardless of the permissions on the files.

NAME

tput - initialize a terminal or query `terminfo` database

SYNOPSIS

tput [-T*type*] *capname* [*parms* ...]

tput [-T*type*] init

tput [-T*type*] reset

tput [-T*type*] longname

tput -S <<

DESCRIPTION

tput uses the `terminfo` database to make the values of terminal-dependent capabilities and information available to the shell [see sh(1)], to initialize or reset the terminal, or return the long name of the requested terminal type. tput outputs a
string if the attribute (*capability name*) is of type string, or an integer if the attribute
is of type integer. If the attribute is of type boolean, tput simply sets the exit code
(0 for TRUE if the terminal has the capability, 1 for FALSE if it does not), and produces no output. Before using a value returned on standard output, the user
should test the exit code [$?, see sh(1)] to be sure it is 0. (See the **EXIT CODES** and
DIAGNOSTICS sections.) For a complete list of capabilities and the *capname* associated with each, see `terminfo`(4).

-T*type*   Indicates the *type* of terminal. Normally this option is unnecessary,
              because the default is taken from the environment variable TERM. If -T
              is specified, the shell variables LINES and COLUMNS and the layer size
              [see layers(1)] will not be referenced.

capname   Indicates the attribute from the `terminfo` database.

parms   If the attribute is a string that takes parameters, the arguments *parms*
              will be instantiated into the string. An all-numeric argument will be
              passed to the attribute as a number.

-S   Allows more than one capability per invocation of tput. The capabili-
              ties must be passed to tput from the standard input instead of from
              the command line (see example). Only one *capname* is allowed per line.
              The -S option changes the meaning of the 0 and 1 boolean and string
              exit codes (see the **EXIT CODES** section).

init   If the `terminfo` database is present and an entry for the user's terminal
              exists (see -T*type*, above), the following will occur: (1) if present, the
              terminal's initialization strings will be output (is1, is2, is3, if,
              iprog), (2) any delays (for example, newline) specified in the entry will
              be set in the tty driver, (3) tabs expansion will be turned on or off
              according to the specification in the entry, and (4) if tabs are not
              expanded, standard tabs will be set (every 8 spaces). If an entry does
              not contain the information needed for any of the four above activities,
              that activity will silently be skipped.

reset   Instead of putting out initialization strings, the terminal's reset strings
              will be output if present (rs1, rs2, rs3, rf). If the reset strings are not
              present, but initialization strings are, the initialization strings will be
              output. Otherwise, reset acts identically to init.

longname   If the `terminfo` database is present and an entry for the user's terminal exists (see -T*type* above), the long name of the terminal will be put out. The long name is the last name in the first line of the terminal's description in the `terminfo` database [see term(5)].

EXAMPLES

`tput init`   Initialize the terminal according to the type of terminal in the environmental variable TERM. This command should be included in everyone's `.profile` after the environmental variable TERM has been exported, as illustrated on the `profile`(4) manual page.

`tput -T5620 reset`
         Reset an AT&T 5620 terminal, overriding the type of terminal in the environmental variable TERM.

`tput cup 0 0`   Send the sequence to move the cursor to row 0, column 0 (the upper left corner of the screen, usually known as the home cursor position).

`tput clear`   Echo the clear-screen sequence for the current terminal.

`tput cols`   Print the number of columns for the current terminal.

`tput -T450 cols`   Print the number of columns for the 450 terminal.

`bold='tput smso'`

`offbold='tput rmso'`
         Set the shell variables `bold`, to begin stand-out mode sequence, and `offbold`, to end standout mode sequence, for the current terminal. This might be followed by a prompt:
`echo "${bold}Please type in your name: ${offbold}\c"`

`tput hc`   Set exit code to indicate if the current terminal is a hardcopy terminal.

`tput cup 23 4`   Send the sequence to move the cursor to row 23, column 4.

`tput longname`   Print the long name from the `terminfo` database for the type of terminal specified in the environmental variable TERM.

```
tput -S <<!
> clear
> cup 10 10
> bold
> !
```
         This example shows `tput` processing several capabilities in one invocation. This example clears the screen, moves the cursor to position 10, 10 and turns on bold (extra bright) mode. The list is terminated by an exclamation mark (!) on a line by itself.

FILES

`/usr/share/lib/terminfo/?/*`	compiled terminal description database
`/usr/include/curses.h`	curses(3X) header file
`/usr/include/term.h`	`terminfo` header file
`/usr/lib/tabset/*`	tab settings for some terminals, in a format appropriate to be output to the terminal (escape sequences that set margins and tabs); for more information, see the "Tabs and Initialization" section of `terminfo`(4)

INTERNATIONAL FUNCTIONS

capnames for international functionality can also be specified.

SEE ALSO

`clear`(1), `stty`(1), `tabs`(1), `tic`(1M)
`profile`(4), `terminfo`(4).

EXIT CODES

If *capname* is of type boolean, a value of 0 is set for TRUE and 1 for FALSE unless the `-S` option is used.

If *capname* is of type string, a value of 0 is set if the *capname* is defined for this terminal *type* (the value of *capname* is returned on standard output); a value of 1 is set if *capname* is not defined for this terminal *type* (a null value is returned on standard output).

If *capname* is of type boolean or string and the `-S` option is used, a value of 0 is returned to indicate that all lines were successful. No indication of which line failed can be given so exit code 1 will never appear. Exit codes 2, 3, and 4 retain their usual interpretation.

If *capname* is of type integer, a value of 0 is always set, whether or not *capname* is defined for this terminal *type*. To determine if *capname* is defined for this terminal *type*, the user must test the value of standard output. A value of -1 means that *capname* is not defined for this terminal *type*.

Any other exit code indicates an error; see the **DIAGNOSTICS** section.

DIAGNOSTICS

`tput` prints the following error messages and sets the corresponding exit codes.

Exit Code	Error Message
0	-1 (*capname* is a numeric variable that is not specified in the `terminfo`(4) database for this terminal type, for example `tput -T450 lines` and `tput -T2621 xmc`)
1	no error message is printed; see the **EXIT CODES** section
2	usage error
3	unknown terminal *type* or no `terminfo` database
4	unknown `terminfo` capability *capname*

NAME

tr - translate characters

SYNOPSIS

tr [-cds] [*string1* [*string2*]]

DESCRIPTION

tr copies the standard input to the standard output with substitution or deletion of selected characters. Input characters found in *string1* are mapped into the corresponding characters of *string2*. Any combination of the options -cds may be used:

-c   Complements the set of characters in *string1* with respect to the universe of characters whose ASCII codes are 001 through 377 octal.

-d   Deletes all input characters in *string1*.

-s   Squeezes all strings of repeated output characters that are in *string2* to single characters.

The following abbreviation conventions may be used to introduce ranges of characters or repeated characters into the strings:

[a-z]   Stands for the string of characters whose ASCII codes run from character a to character z, inclusive.

[a*n]   Stands for *n* repetitions of a. If the first digit of *n* is 0, *n* is considered octal; otherwise, *n* is taken to be decimal. A zero or missing *n* is taken to be huge; this facility is useful for padding *string2*.

The escape character \ may be used as in the shell to remove special meaning from any character in a string. In addition, \ followed by 1, 2, or 3 octal digits stands for the character whose ASCII code is given by those digits.

EXAMPLE

The following example creates a list of all the words in *file1* one per line in *file2*, where a word is taken to be a maximal string of alphabetics. The strings are quoted to protect the special characters from interpretation by the shell; 012 is the ASCII code for newline.

```
tr -cs "[A-Z][a-z]" "[\012*]" <file1>file2
```

INTERNATIONAL FUNCTIONS

tr can process characters from supplementary code sets. Characters specified are searched for and translated in character units, not bytes.

The semantics of the "[x-y]" notation takes after the range specification of the regular expression syntax.

When octal notation with the backslash (\) escape character is used, a backslash is placed before each byte of characters from supplementary code set.

SEE ALSO

ed(1), sh(1)
ascii(5).

NOTES

Will not handle ASCII NUL in *string1* or *string2*; always deletes NUL from input.

NAME

tr - translate characters

SYNOPSIS

/usr/ucb/tr [-cds] [*string1* [*string2*]]

DESCRIPTION

tr copies the standard input to the standard output with substitution or deletion of selected characters. The arguments *string1* and *string2* are considered sets of characters. Any input character found in *string1* is mapped into the character in the corresponding position within *string2*. When *string2* is short, it is padded to the length of *string1* by duplicating its last character.

In either string the notation:

    a–b

denotes a range of characters from *a* to *b* in increasing ASCII order. The character \ , followed by 1, 2 or 3 octal digits stands for the character whose ASCII code is given by those digits. As with the shell, the escape character \ , followed by any other character, escapes any special meaning for that character.

OPTIONS

Any combination of the options -c, -d, or -s may be used:

-c   Complement the set of characters in *string1* with respect to the universe of characters whose ASCII codes are 01 through 0377 octal.

-d   Delete all input characters in *string1*.

-s   Squeeze all strings of repeated output characters that are in *string2* to single characters.

EXAMPLE

The following example creates a list of all the words in *filename1* one per line in *filename2*, where a word is taken to be a maximal string of alphabetics. The second string is quoted to protect ' \ ' from the shell. 012 is the ASCII code for NEWLINE.

    tr -cs A-Za-z '\012' <*filename1*>*filename2*

SEE ALSO

ed(1), ascii(5).

NOTES

Will not handle ASCII NUL in *string1* or *string2*. tr always deletes NUL from input.

NAME

traceroute - traces the route packets take to reach a network host

SYNOPSIS

traceroute [-dnrv] [-w *wait*] [-m *max_ttl*] [-p *port #*] [-q *nqueries*] [-t *tos*]
[-s *src_addr*] [-g *gateway*] *host* [*data size*]

DESCRIPTION

The traceroute command utilizes the "time-to-live" field of the IP protocol to elicit an ICMP TIME_EXCEEDED response from each gateway along the path to some host.

host is the destination host name or the IP number of the host to reach; *packetsize* is the packet size (in bytes) of the probe datagram (*packetsize* defaults to 38 bytes).

The available options are:

-d	Turns on socket level debugging (useful only to the *super-user*).
-n	Print the hop addresses numerically (rather than symbolically); the numeric lookup procedure will avoid a nameserver address-to-name lookup for each gateway found along the path.
-r	Bypass the normal Routing Tables and send directly to a host on an attached network. If the host is not on a directly-attached network, an error is returned. This option can be used to "ping" a local host through an interface that has no route through it [for example, after the interface was dropped by routed(1M)].
-v	Verbose output: The received ICMP packets - other than TIME_EXCEEDED and PORT_UNREACHABLE - will be listed.
-w *wait*	Set the time to wait for a response to an outgoing probe packet to *wait time* seconds (the default value is 3 seconds).
-m *max_ttl*	Set the maximum time-to-live (that is, the maximum number of hops) used in outgoing probe packets to *max-ttl* hops. The default value is 30 hops (the same default value as used for TCP connections).
-n	Print the hop addresses numerically (rather than symbolically); the numeric lookup procedure will avoid a nameserver address-to-name lookup for each gateway found along the path.
-p *port*	Set the base UDP port number used for probe packets to *port* (the default value is (decimal) 33434). traceroute hopes that nothing is listening on UDP ports *base* to *base+nhops-1* at the destination host so that an ICMP PORT_UNREACHABLE message will be returned to terminate the route tracing process. If something is listening on a port in the default range, this option can be used to pick an unused port range.
-q *nqueries*	Set the number of probe packets for each time-to-live ("ttl") setting to the value *n* (the default value is 3).
-s *src_addr*	Use *src_addr* as the IP address (which must be given as an IP number, not as a hostname) which will serve as the source address for outgoing probe packets. On hosts with more than one IP address, this option can be used to force the source address to be something other

than the IP address of the interface on which the probe packets are being sent.

If the IP address is not one of this machine's interface addresses, an error will be returned and nothing will be sent.

-g *addr*   Enable the IP LSRR (Loose Source Record Route) option in addition to the TTL tests. This is useful for asking how somebody else - at IP address *addr* - can reach a particular target.

-t *tos*   Set the *type-of-service* ("TOS") in probe packets to the value defined below (the default value is zero). The value must be a decimal integer in the range from 0 - 255. This option can be used to see if different *types-of-service* will result in different paths.

Not all values of *tos* will be legal or meaningful; see the IP specification for definitions. Probably the useful values will be -t 16 (low delay) and -t 8 (high throughput).

This program attempts to trace the route which an IP packet would follow to some internet host by launching UDP probe packets with a small "ttl" (time-to-live) value and then listens for an ICMP TIME EXCEEDED reply from a gateway. The probes will be started with a "ttl" of one and then increased by one until an ICMP PORT UNREACHABLE message is received or until the maximum number of probes has been sent. Three probes will be sent at each "ttl" setting; a line will be printed to show:

> the "ttl" value
> the address of the gateway
> the round-trip time for each probe

If the probe answers come from different gateways, the address of each responding system will be printed. If there is no response within 3 seconds, an "*" will be printed for that probe.

A sample use of traceroute and of its output might be:

```
[yak 71]% traceroute nis.nsf.net.
traceroute to nis.nsf.net (35.1.1.48), 30 hops max, 56 byte packet
 1  helios.ee.lbl.gov (128.3.112.1)  19 ms  19 ms   0 ms
 2  lilac-dmc.Berkeley.EDU (128.32.216.1)  39 ms  39 ms  19 ms
 3  lilac-dmc.Berkeley.EDU (128.32.216.1)  39 ms  39 ms  19 ms
 4  ccngw-ner-cc.Berkeley.EDU (128.32.136.23)  39 ms  40 ms  39 ms
 5  ccn-nerif22.Berkeley.EDU (128.32.168.22)  39 ms  39 ms  39 ms
 6  128.32.197.4 (128.32.197.4)  40 ms  59 ms  59 ms
 7  131.119.2.5 (131.119.2.5)  59 ms  59 ms  59 ms
 8  129.140.70.13 (129.140.70.13)  99 ms  99 ms  80 ms
 9  129.140.71.6 (129.140.71.6)  139 ms  239 ms  319 ms
10  129.140.81.7 (129.140.81.7)  220 ms  199 ms  199 ms
11  nic.merit.edu (35.1.1.48)  239 ms  239 ms  239 ms
```

Note that lines 2 and 3 are the same. This is due to a buggy kernel on the 2nd hop system - lbl-csam.arpa - that forwards packets with a zero ttl (a bug in the distributed version of 4.3BSD).

A more interesting example is:

```
[yak 72]% traceroute allspice.lcs.mit.edu.
traceroute to allspice.lcs.mit.edu (18.26.0.115), 30 hops max
 1  helios.ee.lbl.gov (128.3.112.1)  0 ms  0 ms  0 ms
 2  lilac-dmc.Berkeley.EDU (128.32.216.1)  19 ms  19 ms  19 ms
 3  lilac-dmc.Berkeley.EDU (128.32.216.1)  39 ms  19 ms  19 ms
 4  ccngw-ner-cc.Berkeley.EDU (128.32.136.23)  19 ms  39 ms  39 ms
 5  ccn-nerif22.Berkeley.EDU (128.32.168.22)  20 ms  39 ms  39 ms
 6  128.32.197.4 (128.32.197.4)  59 ms  119 ms  39 ms
 7  131.119.2.5 (131.119.2.5)  59 ms  59 ms  39 ms
 8  129.140.70.13 (129.140.70.13)  80 ms  79 ms  99 ms
 9  129.140.71.6 (129.140.71.6)  139 ms  139 ms  159 ms
10  129.140.81.7 (129.140.81.7)  199 ms  180 ms  300 ms
11  129.140.72.17 (129.140.72.17)  300 ms  239 ms  239 ms
12  * * *
13  128.121.54.72 (128.121.54.72)  259 ms  499 ms  279 ms
14  * * *
15  * * *
16  * * *
17  * * *
18  ALLSPICE.LCS.MIT.EDU (18.26.0.115)  339 ms  279 ms  279 ms
```

Note that the gateways 12, 14, 15, 16 & 17 hops away either do not send ICMP TIME EXCEEDED messages or send them with a ''ttl'' too small to reach us. Gateways 14 - 17 are running the MIT C Gateway code that does not send ICMP TIME EXCEEDED packets.

The silent gateway 12 in the above example may be the result of a bug in the 4.[23]BSD network code (and its derivatives): 4.x (x <= 3) will send an unreachable message using whatever ''ttl'' remains in the original datagram. Since, for gateways, the remaining ''ttl'' is zero, the ICMP TIME EXCEEDED is guaranteed to not make it back to the sending host.

The behavior of this particular bug is slightly more interesting when it appears on the destination system:

```
 1  helios.ee.lbl.gov (128.3.112.1)  0 ms  0 ms  0 ms
 2  lilac-dmc.Berkeley.EDU (128.32.216.1)  39 ms  19 ms  39 ms
 3  lilac-dmc.Berkeley.EDU (128.32.216.1)  19 ms  39 ms  19 ms
 4  ccngw-ner-cc.Berkeley.EDU (128.32.136.23)  39 ms  40 ms  19 ms
 5  ccn-nerif35.Berkeley.EDU (128.32.168.35)  39 ms  39 ms  39 ms
 6  csgw.Berkeley.EDU (128.32.133.254)  39 ms  59 ms  39 ms
 7  * * *
 8  * * *
 9  * * *
10  * * *
11  * * *
12  * * *
13  rip.Berkeley.EDU (128.32.131.22)  59 ms !  39 ms !  39 ms !
```

Notice that there are 12 "gateways" (13 is the final destination) and that exactly the last half of them are "missing". What is really happening here is that `rip` (a Sun-3 running SunOS 3.5) is using the "ttl" from the arriving datagram as the "ttl" in its ICMP reply. Therefore, the reply will time out on the return path until a probe with a "ttl" that is at least twice the path length is sent. `rip` is really only 7 hops away. A reply that returns with a "ttl" of 1 is an indication that this problem exists. `traceroute` will print a "!" after the time if the "ttl" is <= 1.

The possible annotations after the time are:

"!"   the "ttl" in return packet is <= 1.

"!H" An ICMP HOST_UNREACHABLE packet was received.

"!N" An ICMP NETWORK_UNREACHABLE packet was received.

"!P" An ICMP PROTOCOL_UNREACHABLE packet was received.

"!S" An ICMP SOURCE_ROUTE_FAILED packet was received. This response should never occur: it indicates that the gateway is broken.

"!F" An ICMP FRAGMENTATION_NEEDED packet was received. This response should never occur: it indicates that the gateway is broken.

This program is intended for use in network testing, measurement, and management. It should be used primarily for manual fault isolation. Because of the extra load it could impose on the network, it will be unwise to use `traceroute` during normal operations or from automated scripts.

SEE ALSO

`netstat`(1), `ping`(1M).

NAME

trap_rece - program to receive traps from a remote trap generating entity

SYNOPSIS

trap_rece

DESCRIPTION

trap_rece is a program to receive traps from remote SNMP trap generating entities. It binds to the SNMP trap port (udp/162) to listen for the traps and thus must be run as root. It prints to standard output messages corresponding to the traps it has received. The primary purpose of this program is to demonstrate how traps are parsed using the SNMP library.

SEE ALSO

trap_send(1M).
RFC 1155, RFC 1156, RFC 1157.

NAME

    trap_send - program to generate traps

SYNOPSIS

    trap_send [*ip_address*] [*trap_type*]

DESCRIPTION

    trap_send is a program to send trap messages to trap monitoring stations. It takes as arguments the IP address of the monitoring station and the integer number that corresponds to the trap to be sent.

SEE ALSO

    trap_rece(1M).
    RFC 1155, RFC 1156, RFC 1157.

NAME

troff - typeset or format documents

SYNOPSIS

/usr/ucb/troff [-afiz] [-F*dir*] [-m*name*] [-n*N*] [-o*list*] [-r*aN*] [-s*N*]
      [-T*dest*] [-u*N*] [*filename*] ...

DESCRIPTION

troff formats text in the *filename*s. Input to troff is expected to consist of text interspersed with formatting requests and macros. If no *filename* argument is present, troff reads standard input. A - as a *filename* argument indicates that standard input is to be read at that point in the list of input files; troff reads the files named ahead of the - in the arguments list, then text from the standard input, and then text from the files named after the -.

The following options may appear in any order, but they all must appear before the first *filename*.

-a
    Send a printable approximation of the formatted output to the standard output file.

-f
    Do not print a trailer after the final page of output or cause the postprocessor to relinquish control of the device.

-i
    Read the standard input after the input files are exhausted.

-z
    Suppress formatted output. Only diagnostic messages and messages output using the .tm request are output.

-F*dir*
    Search the directory *dir* for font width tables instead of the system-dependent default directory.

-m*name*
    Prepend the macro file /usr/ucblib/doctools/tmac/tmac.*name* to the input *filename*s. Note: most references to macro packages include the leading m as part of the name; for example, the man macro package resides in /usr/ucblib/doctools/tmac/tmac.an.

-n*N*
    Number first generated page *N*.

-o*list*
    Print only pages whose page numbers appear in the comma-separated *list* of numbers and ranges. A range *N-M* means pages *N* through *M*; an initial *-N* means from the beginning to page *N*; and a final *N-* means from *N* to the end.

-r*aN*
    Set register *a* (one-character) to *N*.

-s*N*
    Stop the phototypesetter every *N* pages. On some devices, troff produces a trailer so you can change cassettes; resume by pressing the typesetter's start button.

-T*dest*
    Prepare output for typesetter *dest*. The following values can be supplied for *dest*:

        202   Mergenthaler Linotron 202. This is the default value.
        cat   Graphics Systems C/A/T.
        aps   Autologic APS-5.

    $-uN$ Set the emboldening factor for the font mounted in position 3 to N. If N is missing, then set the emboldening factor to 0.

FILES

`/tmp/trtmp`	temporary file
`/usr/ucblib/doctools/tmac/tmac.*`	standard macro files
`/usr/ucblib/doctools/font/*`	font width tables for alternate mounted `troff` fonts

SEE ALSO

checknr(1), chmod(1), col(1), eqn(1), lpd(1M), lpr(1), nroff(1), tbl(1), man(7), me(7), ms(7).

NAME

`trpt` - transliterate protocol trace

SYNOPSIS

`trpt` [`-afjst`] [`-p` *hex-address*] [*system* [*core*]]

DESCRIPTION

`trpt` interrogates the buffer of TCP trace records created when a socket is marked for debugging [see `getsockopt`(3N)], and prints a readable description of these records. When no options are supplied, `trpt` prints all the trace records found in the system grouped according to TCP connection protocol control block (PCB). The following options may be used to alter this behavior.

OPTIONS

`-a` In addition to the normal output, print the values of the source and destination addresses for each packet recorded.

`-f` Follow the trace as it occurs, waiting a short time for additional records each time the end of the log is reached.

`-j` Just give a list of the protocol control block addresses for which there are trace records.

`-s` In addition to the normal output, print a detailed description of the packet sequencing information.

`-t` In addition to the normal output, print the values for all timers at each point in the trace.

`-p` *hex-address*
 Show only trace records associated with the protocol control block, the address of which follows.

The recommended use of `trpt` is as follows. Isolate the problem and enable debugging on the `socket`(s) involved in the connection. Find the address of the protocol control blocks associated with the sockets using the `-A` option to `netstat`(1M). Then run `trpt` with the `-p` option, supplying the associated protocol control block addresses. The `-f` option can be used to follow the trace log once the trace is located. If there are many sockets using the debugging option, the `-j` option may be useful in checking to see if any trace records are present for the socket in question.

If debugging is being performed on a system or core file other than the default, the last two arguments may be used to supplant the defaults.

FILES

`/stand/unix`
`/dev/kmem`

SEE ALSO

`netstat`(1M), `getsockopt`(3N)

DIAGNOSTICS

`no namelist`
 When the system image does not contain the proper symbols to find the trace buffer; others which should be self explanatory.

NOTES

Should also print the data for each input or output, but this is not saved in the trace record.

The output format is inscrutable and should be described here.

NAME

true, false - provide truth values

SYNOPSIS

```
true

false
```

DESCRIPTION

true does nothing, successfully. false does nothing, unsuccessfully. They are typically used in input to sh such as:

```
while true
do
        command
done
```

SEE ALSO

sh(1)

DIAGNOSTICS

true has exit status zero, false nonzero.

NAME

truss - trace system calls and signals

SYNOPSIS

truss [-p] [-f] [-c] [-a] [-e] [-i] [-[tvx] [!] *syscall...*] [-s [!] *signal...*] [-m [!] *fault...*] [-[rw] [!] *fd...*] [-o *outfile*] *command*

DESCRIPTION

truss executes the specified command and produces a trace of the system calls it performs, the signals it receives, and the machine faults it incurs. Each line of the trace output reports either the fault or signal name or the system call name with its arguments and return value(s). System call arguments are displayed symbolically when possible using defines from relevant system header files; for any pathname pointer argument, the pointed-to string is displayed. Error returns are reported using the error code names described in intro(2).

The following options are recognized. For those options which take a list argument, the name all can be used as a shorthand to specify all possible members of the list. If the list begins with a !, the meaning of the option is negated (for example, exclude rather than trace). Multiple occurrences of the same option may be specified. For the same name in a list, subsequent options (those to the right) override previous ones (those to the left).

-p
Interpret the arguments to truss as a list of process-ids for existing processes [see ps(1)] rather than as a command to be executed. truss takes control of each process and begins tracing it provided that the userid and groupid of the process match those of the user or that the user is a privileged user. Processes may also be specified by their names in the /proc directory, for example, /proc/1234; this works for remotely-mounted /proc directories as well.

-f
Follow all children created by fork and include their signals, faults, and system calls in the trace output. Normally, only the first-level command or process is traced. When -f is specified, the process-id is included with each line of trace output to indicate which process executed the system call or received the signal.

-c
Count traced system calls, faults, and signals rather than displaying the trace line-by-line. A summary report is produced after the traced command terminates or when truss is interrupted. If -f is also specified, the counts include all traced system calls, faults, and signals for child processes.

-a
Show the argument strings which are passed in each exec system call.

-e
Show the environment strings which are passed in each exec system call.

-i
Don't display interruptible sleeping system calls. Certain system calls, such as open and read on terminal devices or pipes can sleep for indefinite periods and are interruptible. Normally, truss reports such sleeping system calls if they remain asleep for more than one second. The system call is reported again a second time when it completes. The -i option causes such system calls to be reported only once, when they complete.

-t [!] *syscall,...*   System calls to trace or exclude. Those system calls specified in the comma-separated list are traced. If the list begins with a '!', the specified system calls are excluded from the trace output. Default is -tall.

-v [!] *syscall,...*   Verbose. Display the contents of any structures passed by address to the specified system calls (if traced). Input values as well as values returned by the operating system are shown. For any field used as both input and output, only the output value is shown. Default is -v!all.

-x [!] *syscall,...*   Display the arguments to the specified system calls (if traced) in raw form, usually hexadecimal, rather than symbolically. Default is -x!all.

-s [!] *signal,...*   Signals to trace or exclude. Those signals specified in the comma-separated list are traced. The trace output reports the receipt of each specified signal, even if the signal is being ignored (not blocked) by the process. (Blocked signals are not received until the process releases them.) Signals may be specified by name or number (see sys/signal.h). If the list begins with a '!', the specified signals are excluded from the trace output. Default is -sall.

-m [!] *fault,...*   Machine faults to trace or exclude. Those machine faults specified in the comma-separated list are traced. Faults may be specified by name or number (see sys/fault.h). If the list begins with a '!', the specified faults are excluded from the trace output. Default is -mall -m!fltpage.

-r [!] *fd,...*   Show the full contents of the I/O buffer for each read on any of the specified file descriptors. The output is formatted 32 bytes per line and shows each byte as an ascii character (preceded by one blank) or as a 2-character C language escape sequence for control characters such as horizontal tab (\ t) and newline (\ n). If ascii interpretation is not possible, the byte is shown in 2-character hexadecimal representation. (The first 16 bytes of the I/O buffer for each traced read are shown even in the absence of -r.) Default is -r!all.

-w [!] *fd,...*   Show the contents of the I/O buffer for each write on any of the specified file descriptors (see -r). Default is -w!all.

-o *outfile*   File to be used for the trace output. By default, the output goes to standard error.

See syscall for names accepted by the -t, -v, and -x options. System call numbers are also accepted.

If truss is used to initiate and trace a specified command and if the -o option is used or if standard error is redirected to a non-terminal file, then truss runs with hangup, interrupt, and quit signals ignored. This facilitates tracing of interactive programs which catch interrupt and quit signals from the terminal.

If the trace output remains directed to the terminal, or if existing processes are traced (the -p option), then `truss` responds to hangup, interrupt, and quit signals by releasing all traced processes and exiting. This enables the user to terminate excessive trace output and to release previously-existing processes. Released processes continue normally, as though they had never been touched.

EXAMPLES

This example produces a trace of the `find`(1) command on the terminal:

```
truss find . -print >find.out
```

Or, to see only a trace of the open, close, read, and write system calls:

```
truss -t open,close,read,write find . -print >find.out
```

This produces a trace of the `spell`(1) command on the file truss.out:

```
truss -f -o truss.out spell document
```

`spell` is a shell script, so the `-f` flag is needed to trace not only the shell but also the processes created by the shell. (The spell script runs a pipeline of eight concurrent processes.)

A particularly boring example is:

```
truss nroff -mm document >nroff.out
```

because 97% of the output reports `lseek`, `read`, and `write` system calls. To abbreviate it:

```
truss -t !lseek,read,write nroff -mm document >nroff.out
```

This example verbosely traces the activity of process #1, `init`(1M) (provided you are a privileged user):

```
truss -p -v all 1
```

Interrupting `truss` returns `init` to normal operation.

FILES

`/proc/`*nnnnn*   process files

NOTES

Some of the system calls described in the manpages differ from the actual operating system interfaces. Do not be surprised by minor deviations of the trace output from the descriptions in Section 2.

Every machine fault (except a page fault) results in the posting of a signal to the process which incurred the fault. A report of a received signal will immediately follow each report of a machine fault (except a page fault) unless that signal is being blocked by the process.

The operating system enforces certain security restrictions on the tracing of processes. In particular, any command whose object file (a.out) cannot be read by a user cannot be traced by that user; set-uid and set-gid commands can be traced only by a privileged user. Unless it is run by a privileged user, truss loses control of any process which performs an exec(2) of a set-id or unreadable object file; such processes continue normally, though independently of truss, from the point of the exec.

To avoid collisions with other controlling processes, truss will not trace a process which it detects is being controlled by another process via the /proc interface. This allows truss to be applied to *proc*(4)-based debuggers as well as to another instance of itself.

The trace output contains tab characters under the assumption that standard tab stops are set (every eight positions).

The trace output for multiple processes is not produced in strict time order. For example, a read on a pipe may be reported before the corresponding write. For any one process, the output is strictly time-ordered.

The system may run out of per-user process slots when tracing of children is requested. When tracing more than one process, truss runs as one controlling process for each process being traced. For the example of the spell command shown above, spell itself uses 9 process slots, one for the shell and 8 for the 8-member pipeline, while truss adds another 9 processes, for a total of 18. This is perilously close to the usual system-imposed limit of 25 processes per user.

truss uses shared memory and semaphores when dealing with more than one process (-f option or -p with more than one pid). It issues a warning message and proceeds when these are needed but not configured in the system. However, the trace output may become garbled in this case and the output of the -c option reports only the top-level command or first pid and no children are counted.

Not all possible structures passed in all possible system calls are displayed under the -v option.

On M88000 family of processors systems supporting the M88000 family of processors Binary Compatible Standard, BCS, truss may not correctly trace programs compiled and linked on a pre System V Release 4 system.

SEE ALSO

    intro(2), proc(4).

NAME

tset, reset - establish or restore terminal characteristics

SYNOPSIS

tset [-InQrs] [-ec] [-kc] [-m [port-ID [baudrate] : type] ...] [type]

reset [-] [-ec] [-I] [-kc] [-n] [-Q] [-r] [-s]
　　　[-m [indent] [test baudrate]: type] ... [type]

DESCRIPTION

tset sets up your terminal, typically when you first log in. It does terminal dependent processing such as setting erase and kill characters, setting or resetting delays, sending any sequences needed to properly initialized the terminal, and the like. tset first determines the type of terminal involved, and then does necessary initializations and mode settings. If a port is not wired permanently to a specific terminal (not hardwired) it is given an appropriate generic identifier such as dialup.

reset clears the terminal settings by turning off CBREAK and RAW modes, output delays and parity checking, turns on NEWLINE translation, echo and TAB expansion, and restores undefined special characters to their default state. It then sets the modes as usual, based on the terminal type (which will probably override some of the above). See stty(1) for more information. All arguments to tset may be used with reset. reset also uses rs= and rf= to reset the initialization string and file. This is useful after a program dies and leaves the terminal in a funny state. Often in this situation, characters will not echo as you type them. You may have to type '<LINEFEED>reset<LINEFEED>' since '<RETURN>' may not work.

When no arguments are specified, tset reads the terminal type from the TERM environment variable and re-initializes the terminal, and performs initialization of mode, environment and other options at login time to determine the terminal type and set up terminal modes.

When used in a startup script (.profile for sh(1) users or .login for csh(1) users) it is desirable to give information about the type of terminal you will usually use on ports that are not hardwired. Any of the alternate generic names given in /etc/terminfo may be used for the identifier. Refer to the -m option below for more information. If no mapping applies and a final type option, not preceded by a -m, is given on the command line then that type is used.

It is usually desirable to return the terminal type, as finally determined by tset, and information about the terminal's capabilities, to a shell's environment. This can be done using the -, -s, or -S options.

For the Bourne shell, put this command in your .profile file:

```
cval `tset -s options...`
```

or using the C shell, put this command in your .login file:

```
eval `tset -s options...`
```

With the C shell, it is also convenient to make an alias in your .cshrc file:

```
alias tset 'eval `tset -s \!*`'
```

This also allows the command:

```
tset 2621
```

to be invoked at any time to set the terminal and environment. It is not possible to get this aliasing effect with a Bourne shell script, because shell scripts cannot set the environment of their parent. If a process could set its parent's environment, none of this nonsense would be necessary in the first place.

Once the terminal type is known, `tset` sets the terminal driver mode. This normally involves sending an initialization sequence to the terminal, setting the single character erase (and optionally the line-kill (full line erase)) characters, and setting special character delays. TAB and NEWLINE expansion are turned off during transmission of the terminal initialization sequence.

On terminals that can backspace but not overstrike (such as a CRT), and when the erase character is '#', the erase character is changed as if `-e` had been used.

The following options are available with `tset`:

`-`	The name of the terminal finally decided upon is output on the standard output. This is intended to be captured by the shell and placed in the TERM environment variable.
`-e`c	Set the erase character to be the named character c on all terminals. Default is the BACKSPACE key on the keyboard, usually ^H (CTRL-H). The character c can either be typed directly, or entered using the circumflex-character notation used here.
`-i`c	Set the interrupt character to be the named character c on all terminals. Default is ^C (CTRL-C). The character c can either be typed directly, or entered using the circumflex-character notation used here.
`-I`	Suppress transmitting terminal-initialization strings.
`-k`c	Set the line kill character to be the named character c on all terminals. Default is ^U (CTRL-U). The kill character is left alone if `-k` is not specified. Control characters can be specified by prefixing the alphabetical character with a circumflex (as in CTRL-U) instead of entering the actual control key itself. This allows you to specify control keys that are currently assigned.
`-n`	
`-Q`	Suppress printing the 'Erase set to' and 'Kill set to' messages.
`-r`	In addition to other actions, reports the terminal type.
`-s`	Output commands to set and export TERM. This can be used with

```
set noglob
eval `tset -s . . .`
unset noglob
```

to bring the terminal information into the environment. Doing so makes programs such as `vi`(1) start up faster. If the SHELL environment variable ends with `csh`, C shell commands are output, otherwise Bourne shell commands are output.

–m [*port*-ID[*baudrate*]: *type*] ...

Specify (map) a terminal type when connected to a generic port (such as *dialup* or *plugboard*) identified by *port-ID*. The *baudrate* argument can be used to check the baudrate of the port and set the terminal type accordingly. The target rate is prefixed by any combination of the following operators to specify the conditions under which the mapping is made:

>   Greater than
@   Equals or "at"
<   Less than
!   It is not the case that (negates the above operators)
?   Prompt for the terminal type. If no response is given, then *type* is selected by default.

In the following example, the terminal type is set to adm3a if the port is a dialup with a speed of greater than 300 or to dw2 if the port is a dialup at 300 baud or less. In the third case, the question mark preceding the terminal type indicates that the user is to verify the type desired. A NULL response indicates that the named type is correct. Otherwise, the user's response is taken to be the type desired.

```
tset -m 'dialup>300:adm3a' -m 'dialup:dw2' -m \
    'plugboard:?adm3a'
```

To prevent interpretation as metacharacters, the entire argument to –m should be enclosed in single quotes. When using the C shell, exclamation points should be preceded by a backslash (\).

EXAMPLES

These examples all use the '–' option. A typical use of tset in a .profile or .login will also use the –e and –k options, and often the –n or –Q options as well. These options have been omitted here to keep the examples short.

To select a 2621, you might put the following sequence of commands in your .login file (or .profile for Bourne shell users).

```
set noglob
eval `tset -s 2621`
unset noglob
```

If you have a switch which connects to various ports (making it impractical to identify which port you may be connected to), and use various terminals from time to time, you can select from among those terminals according to the *speed* or baud rate. In the example below, tset will prompt you for a terminal type if the baud rate is greater than 1200 (say, 9600 for a terminal connected by an RS-232 line), and use a Wyse® 50 by default. If the baud rate is less than or equal to 1200, it will select a 2621. Note the placement of the question mark, and the quotes to protect the > and ? from interpretation by the shell.

```
set noglob
eval `tset -s -m 'switch>1200:?wy' -m 'switch<=1200:2621'`
unset noglob
```

The following entry is appropriate if you always dial up, always at the same baud rate, on many different kinds of terminals, and the terminal you use most often is an adm3a.

```
set noglob
```

```
      eval `tset -s ?adm3a`
      unset noglob
```
If you want to make the selection based only on the baud rate, you might use the
following:
```
      set noglob
      eval `tset -s -m '>1200:wy' 2621`
      unset noglob
```

The following example quietly sets the erase character to BACKSPACE, and kill to
CTRL-U. If the port is switched, it selects a Concept™ 100 for speeds less than or
equal to 1200, and asks for the terminal type otherwise (the default in this case is a
Wyse 50). If the port is a direct dialup, it selects Concept 100 as the terminal type.
If logging in over the ARPANET, the terminal type selected is a Datamedia® 2500
terminal or emulator. Note the backslash escaping the NEWLINE at the end of the
first line in the example.

```
      set noglob
      eval `tset -e -k^U -Q -s -m 'switch<=1200:concept100' -m \
            'switch:?wy' -m dialup:concept100 -m arpanet:dm2500`
      unset noglob
```

FILES
```
.login
.profile
```

SEE ALSO
csh(1), sh(1), vi(1), stty(1), terminfo(4), ttytab(5), environ(5).

NOTES
The `tset` command is one of the first commands a user must master when getting
started on a UNIX system. Unfortunately, it is one of the most complex, largely
because of the extra effort the user must go through to get the environment of the
login shell set. Something needs to be done to make all this simpler, either the
`login` program should do this stuff, or a default shell alias should be made, or a
way to set the environment of the parent should exist.

This program cannot intuit personal choices for erase, interrupt and line kill characters, so it leaves these set to the local system standards.

It could well be argued that the shell should be responsible for ensuring that the
terminal remains in a sane state; this would eliminate the need for the `reset` program.

NAME

tset - provide information for setting terminal modes

SYNOPSIS

tset [*options*] [*type*]

DESCRIPTION

tset allows the user to set a terminal's ERASE and KILL characters, and define the terminal's type and capabilities by creating values for the TERM and TERMCAP environment variables. If a *type* is given with the -s option, tset creates information for a terminal of the specified type. The type may be any type given in /usr/share/lib/termcap. If the *type* is not specified with the -s option, tset creates information for a terminal of the type defined by the value of the environment variable, TERM unless the -h or -m option is given. If the TERM variable is undefined, tset looks in /usr/share/lib/termcap for the appropriate information. If these options are used, tset searches the /etc/ttytype file for the terminal type corresponding to the current serial port; it then creates information for a terminal based on this type. If the serial port is not found in /etc/ttytype, the terminal type is set to dumb.

tset displays the created information on the standard output. The information is in a form that can be used to set the current environment variables. The exact form depends on the login shell from which tset was invoked. The examples below illustrate how to use this information to change the variables.

The following options are valid:

-e[*c*]   Sets the ERASE character to [*c*] on all terminals. The default setting is BACKSPACE, or CTRL-H.

-E[*c*]   Identical to the -e optino except that it only operates on terminals that can backspace.

-k[*c*]   Sets the KILL character to *c*, defaulting to CTRL-U.

-    Prints the terminal type on the standard output.

-s   Outputs the "setenv" commands [for csh(1)], or "export" and assignment commands [for sh(1)]. The type of commands are determined by the user's login shell.

-S   Only outputs the strings to be placed in the environment variables.

-r   Prints the terminal type on the diagnostic output.

-Q   Suppresses the printing of the "Erase set to" and "Kill set to" messages.

-I   Suppresses printing of the terminal initialization strings.

tset is most useful when included in the .login [for csh] or .profile [for sh] file executed automatically at login, with -m option is given, the first correct mapping prevails.

EXAMPLES

```
tset gt42
tset - mdialup>300:adm3a-mdialup:dw2-Qr-e#
tset -mdial:ti733-mplug:?hp2621-munknown:?-e-k^U
```

To use the information created by the `-s` option for the Bourne shell, (`sh`), repeat these commands:

```
tset -s...>/tmp/tset$$
/tmp/tset$$
rm/tmp/tset$$
```

To use the information for `csh`, use:

```
set noglob
set term=('tset-S...')
setenv TERM$term[1]
setenv TERMCAP"$term[2]"
unset term
unset noglob
```

FILES

    `/usr/share/lib/termcap`   Terminal capability database.

SEE ALSO

    `stty`(1), `termcap`(1), `tty`(1)

NAME

     tsort - topological sort

SYNOPSIS

     tsort [*file*]

DESCRIPTION

The tsort command produces on the standard output a totally ordered list of items consistent with a partial ordering of items mentioned in the input *file*. If no *file* is specified, the standard input is understood.

The input consists of pairs of items (nonempty strings) separated by blanks. Pairs of different items indicate ordering. Pairs of identical items indicate presence, but not ordering.

SEE ALSO

     lorder(1)

DIAGNOSTICS

     Odd data: there is an odd number of fields in the input file.

NAME

　　`tty` - get the name of the terminal

SYNOPSIS

　　`tty [ -l ] [ -s ]`

DESCRIPTION

　　`tty` prints the path name of the user's terminal.

　　`-l`　　prints the synchronous line number to which the user's terminal is connected, if it is on an active synchronous line.

　　`-s`　　inhibits printing of the terminal path name, allowing one to test just the exit code.

EXIT CODES

　　2　　if invalid options were specified,
　　0　　if standard input is a terminal,
　　1　　otherwise.

DIAGNOSTICS

　　`''not on an active synchronous line''` if the standard input is not a synchronous terminal and `-l` is specified.

　　`''not a tty''` if the standard input is not a terminal and `-s` is not specified.

NAME

ttyadm - format and output port monitor-specific information

SYNOPSIS

/usr/sbin/ttyadm [-b] [-c] [-r *count*] [-h] [-i *msg*] [-m *modules*]
    -p *prompt*] [-t *timeout*] -d *device* -l *ttylabel* -s *service*

/usr/sbin/ttyadm -V

DESCRIPTION

The ttyadm command is an administrative command that formats ttymon-specific
information and writes it to the standard output. The Service Access Facility (SAF)
requires each port monitor to provide such a command. Note that the port monitor
administrative file is updated by the Service Access Controller's administrative
commands, sacadm and pmadm. ttyadm provides a means of presenting formatted
port monitor-specific (that is, ttymon-specific) data to these commands.

-b	Sets the "bidirectional port" flag. When this flag is set, the line can be used in both directions. ttymon will allow users to connect to the service associated with the port, but if the port is free, uucico, cu, or ct can use it for dialing out.
-c	Sets the connect-on-carrier flag for the port. If the -c flag is set, ttymon will invoke the port's associated service immediately when a connect indication is received (that is, no prompt is printed and no baud-rate searching is done).
-d *device*	*device* is the full pathname of the device file for the TTY port.
-h	Sets the hangup flag for the port. If the -h flag is not set, ttymon will force a hangup on the line by setting the speed to zero before setting the speed to the default or specified value.
-i *message*	Specifies the inactive (disabled) response message. This message will be sent to the TTY port if the port is disabled or the ttymon monitoring the port is disabled.
-l *ttylabel*	Specifies which *ttylabel* in the /etc/ttydefs file to use as the starting point when searching for the proper baud rate.
-m *modules*	Specifies a list of pushable STREAMS modules. The modules will be pushed, in the order in which they are specified, before the service is invoked. *modules* must be a comma-separated list of modules, with no white space included. Any modules currently on the stream will be popped before these modules are pushed.
-r *count*	When the -r option is invoked, ttymon will wait until it receives data from the port before it displays a prompt. If *count* is equal to zero, ttymon will wait until it receives any character. If *count* is greater than zero, ttymon will wait until *count* newlines have been received.
-p *prompt*	Specifies the prompt message, for example, "login:."

`-s` *service*	*service* is the full pathname of the service to be invoked when a connection request is received. If arguments are required, the command and its arguments must be enclosed in double quotes.
`-t` *timeout*	Specifies that `ttymon` should close a port if the open on the port succeeds and no input data is received in *timeout* seconds.
`-V`	Displays the version number of the current `/usr/lib/saf/ttymon` command.

OUTPUT

If successful, `ttyadm` will generate the requested information, write it on the standard output, and exit with a status of `0`. If `ttyadm` is invoked with an invalid number of arguments or invalid arguments, or if an incomplete option is specified, an error message will be written to the standard error and `ttymon` will exit with a non-zero status.

FILES

`/etc/ttydefs`

SEE ALSO

`pmadm`(1M), `sacadm`(1M), `ttymon`(1M).

NAME

ttymon - port monitor for terminal ports

SYNOPSIS

/usr/lib/saf/ttymon

/usr/lib/saf/ttymon -g [-h] [-d *device*] [-l *ttylabel*] [-t *timeout*] \
    [-p *prompt*] [-m *modules*]

DESCRIPTION

ttymon is a STREAMS-based TTY port monitor. Its function is to monitor ports, to
set terminal modes, baud rates, and line disciplines for the ports, and to connect
users or applications to services associated with the ports. Normally, ttymon is
configured to run under the Service Access Controller, sac, as part of the Service
Access Facility (SAF). It is configured using the sacadm command. Each instance
of ttymon can monitor multiple ports. The ports monitored by an instance of
ttymon are specified in the port monitor's administrative file. The administrative
file is configured using the pmadm and ttyadm commands. When an instance of
ttymon is invoked by the sac command, it starts to monitor its ports. For each
port, ttymon first initializes the line disciplines, if they are specified, and the speed
and terminal settings. The values used for initialization are taken from the
appropriate entry in the TTY settings file. This file is maintained by the sttydefs
command. Default line disciplines on ports are usually set up by the autopush
command of the Autopush Facility.

ttymon then writes the prompt and waits for user input. If the user indicates that
the speed is inappropriate by pressing the BREAK key, ttymon tries the next speed
and writes the prompt again. When valid input is received, ttymon interprets the
per-service configuration file for the port, if one exists, creates a utmp entry if
required, establishes the service environment, and then invokes the service associated with the port. Valid input consists of a string of at least one non-newline character, terminated by a carriage return. After the service terminates, ttymon cleans
up the utmp entry, if one exists, and returns the port to its initial state.

If *autobaud* is enabled for a port, ttymon will try to determine the baud rate on the
port automatically. Users must enter a carriage return before ttymon can recognize
the baud rate and print the prompt. Currently, the baud rates that can be determined by *autobaud* are 110, 1200, 2400, 4800, and 9600.

If a port is configured as a bidirectional port, ttymon will allow users to connect to
a service, and, if the port is free, will allow uucico, cu or ct to use it for dialing out.
If a port is bidirectional, ttymon will wait to read a character before it prints a
prompt.

If the *connect-on-carrier* flag is set for a port, ttymon will immediately invoke the
port's associated service when a connection request is received. The prompt message will not be sent.

If a port is disabled, ttymon will not start any service on that port. If a disabled
message is specified, ttymon will send out the disabled message when a connection
request is received. If ttymon is disabled, all ports under that instance of ttymon
will also be disabled.

SERVICE INVOCATION

The service `ttymon` invokes for a port is specified in the `ttymon` administrative file. `ttymon` will scan the character string giving the service to be invoked for this port, looking for a `%d` or a `%%` two-character sequence. If `%d` is found, `ttymon` will modify the service command to be executed by replacing those two characters by the full path name of this port (the device name). If `%%` is found, they will be replaced by a single `%`.

When the service is invoked, file descriptor 0, 1, and 2 are opened to the port device for reading and writing. The service is invoked with the user ID, group ID and current home directory set to that of the user name under which the service was registered with `ttymon`. Two environment variables, HOME and TTYPROMPT, are added to the service's environment by `ttymon`. HOME is set to the HOME directory of the user name under which the service is invoked. TTYPROMPT is set to the prompt string configured for the service on the port. This is provided so that a service invoked by `ttymon` has a means of determining if a prompt was actually issued by `ttymon` and, if so, what that prompt actually was.

See `ttyadm`(1M) for options that can be set for ports monitored by `ttymon` under the Service Access Controller.

INVOKING A STAND-ALONE `ttymon` **PROCESS**

A special invocation of `ttymon` is provided with the `-g` option. This form of the command should only be called by applications that need to set the correct baud rate and terminal settings on a port and then connect to `login` service, but that cannot be pre-configured under the SAC. The following combinations of options can be used with `-g`:

`-d` *device*	*device* is the full path name of the port to which `ttymon` is to attach. If this option is not specified, file descriptor 0 must be set up by the invoking process to a TTY port.
`-h`	If the -h flag is not set, `ttymon` will force a hangup on the line by setting the speed to zero before setting the speed to the default or specified speed.
`-t` *timeout*	Specifies that `ttymon` should exit if no one types anything in *timeout* seconds after the prompt is sent.
`-l` *ttylabel*	*ttylabel* is a link to a speed and TTY definition in the `ttydefs` file. This definition tells `ttymon` at what speed to run initially, what the initial TTY settings are, and what speed to try next if the user indicates that the speed is inappropriate by pressing the BREAK key. The default speed is 9600 baud.
`-p` *prompt*	Allows the user to specify a prompt string. The default prompt is "Login: ".
`-m` *modules*	When initializing the port, `ttymon` will pop all modules on the port, and then push *modules* in the order specified. *modules* is a comma-separated list of pushable modules. Default modules on the ports are usually set up by the Autopush Facility.

SEE ALSO

pmadm(1M), sac(1M), sacadm(1M), ttyadm(1M).

NOTES

If a port is monitored by more than one ttymon, it is possible for the ttymons to send out prompt messages in such a way that they compete for input.

NAME

tunefs - tune up an existing file system

SYNOPSIS

tunefs [-a *maxcontig*] [-d *rotdelay*] [-e *maxbpg*] [-m *minfree*] [-o [s | space | t | time]] *special* | *filesystem*

DESCRIPTION

tunefs is designed to change the dynamic parameters of a file system which affect the layout policies. The file system must be unmounted before using tunefs. The parameters which are to be changed are indicated by the options given below:

The options are:

-a *maxcontig*   Specify the maximum number of contiguous blocks that will be laid out before forcing a rotational delay (see -d below). The default value is one, since most device drivers require an interrupt per disk transfer. Device drivers that can chain several buffers together in a single transfer should set this to the maximum chain length.

-d *rotdelay*   Specify the expected time (in milliseconds) to service a transfer completion interrupt and initiate a new transfer on the same disk. It is used to decide how much rotational spacing to place between successive blocks in a file.

-e *maxbpg*   Indicate the maximum number of blocks any single file can allocate out of a cylinder group before it is forced to begin allocating blocks from another cylinder group. Typically this value is set to approximately one quarter of the total blocks in a cylinder group. The intent is to prevent any single file from using up all the blocks in a single cylinder group, thus degrading access times for all files subsequently allocated in that cylinder group. The effect of this limit is to cause big files to do long seeks more frequently than if they were allowed to allocate all the blocks in a cylinder group before seeking elsewhere. For file systems with exclusively large files, this parameter should be set higher.

-m *minfree*   Specify the percentage of space held back from normal users; the minimum free space threshold. The default value used is 10%. This value can be set to zero, however up to a factor of three in throughput will be lost over the performance obtained at a 10% threshold. Note: if the value is raised above the current usage level, users will be unable to allocate files until enough files have been deleted to get under the higher threshold.

-o [s | space | t | time]

Change optimization strategy for the file system. s and space are interchangeable, and t and time are interchangeable.

s or space - conserve space.
t or time - attempt to organize file layout to minimize access time.

Generally one should optimize for time unless the file system is over 90% full.

SEE ALSO
    mkfs(1M)

NAME

uadmin - administrative control

SYNOPSIS

`/sbin/uadmin` *cmd fcn*

DESCRIPTION

The `uadmin` command provides control for basic administrative functions. This command is tightly coupled to the System Administration procedures and is not intended for general use. It may be invoked only by the super-user.

The arguments *cmd* (command) and *fcn* (function) are converted to integers and passed to the `uadmin` system call.

SEE ALSO

`uadmin`(2).

NAME

udpublickey - updater for NIS public key database

SYNOPSIS

cd /var/yp ; udpublickey *publickeymap command*

DESCRIPTION

The NIS utility udpublickey is not intended to be invoked directly by a user but rather to be run by ypupdated(1M) based on the target *publickey.byname* in the makefile /var/up/updaters. This is done indirectly in response to a ypmake publickey request or by a newkey(1) or chkey(1) request.

ypupdated updates the NIS public key database *publickeymap* by reading from standard input and interpreting secure RPC protocol messages generated by ypupdate(3N) as specified in updaters(4). It validates the user making the request, makes the requested changes to the *publickeymap* file and then invokes a shell to run the command specified in the *command* argument. The *command* is expected to invoke make(1) with an argument that is the target *publickey*. This will use /var/yp/Makefile to build the NIS public key database.

udpublickey exits with status zero if successful, with status YPERR_KEY if changing or deleting a key that is not in the map, with status YPERR_ACCESS if the user is nobody or updating another's key, or with status YPERR_YPERR if it cannot find or update the *publickeymap* file or detects a protocol error.

FILES

/var/yp/updaters
/var/yp/Makefile

SEE ALSO

chkey(1), keyserv(1M), make(1), newkey(1), ypmake(1M), ypupdated(1M), ypupdate(3N), updaters(4).

NAME

ufsdump - incremental file system dump

SYNOPSIS

ufsdump [*options*] *filesystem*

DESCRIPTION

ufsdump backs up all files in *filesystem*, or files changed after a certain date, to magnetic tape; *options* is a string that specifies ufsdump options, as shown below.

Filesystem may be specified as the full special file name, the full special file name without the leading '/', the suffix of the full special file name, the directory mount point on which *filesystem* is mounted, or the directory mount point on which *filesystem* is mounted without the leading '/'. The only requirement is that *filesystem* must exist in at least one of either *mnttab* or *vfstab*. e.g. Assuming that the appropriate entry is in at least one of *mnttab* or *vfstab*, any of the following are acceptable *filesystem* specifications:

- /usr2
- usr2
- /dev/dsk/m328_c0d0s6
- dev/dsk/m328_c0d0s6
- /dev/rdsk/m328_c0d0s6
- dev/rdsk/m328_c0d0s6
- m328_c0d0s6
- /dev/SA/disk1s6
- dev/SA/disk1s6
- /dev/rSA/disk1s6
- dev/rSA/disk1s6
- disk1s6

The options are:

0-9   The dump level. All files in the *filesystem* that have been modified since the last ufsdump at a lower dump level are copied to the volume. For instance, if you did a level 2 dump on Monday, followed by a level 4 dump on Tuesday, a subsequent level 3 dump on Wednesday would contain all files modified or added since the level 2 (Monday) backup. A level 0 dump copies the entire filesystem to the dump volume.

-b *factor*
Blocking factor. Specify the blocking factor for tape writes. The default is 20 blocks per write. Note: the blocking factor is specified in terms of 512 bytes blocks, for compatibility with tar. The default blocking factor for tapes of density 6250BPI and greater is 64. The default blocking factor for cartridge tapes (-c option specified) is 126. The highest blocking factor available with most tape drives is 126.

c   Cartridge. Use a cartridge instead of the standard half-inch reel. This sets the density to 1000BPI and the blocking factor to 126. The length is set to 425 feet. This option is incompatible with the -d option, unless you specify a density of 1000BPI with that option.

-d *bpi*   Tape density. The density of the tape, expressed in BPI, is taken from *bpi*. This is used to keep a running tab on the amount of tape used per reel. The default density is 1600 except for cartridge tape. Unless a higher density is specified explicitly, `ufsdump` uses its default density — even if the tape drive is capable of higher-density operation (for instance, 6250BPI). Note: the density specified should correspond to the density of the tape device being used, or `ufsdump` will not be able to handle end-of-tape properly.

-f *dump-file*
> Dump file. Use *dump-file* as the file to dump to, instead of `/dev/rmt/ctape1`. If *dump-file* is specified as -, dump to the standard output.

-n   Notify all operators in the operator group that `ufsdump` requires attention by sending messages to their terminals, in a manner similar to that used by the `wall` command.

-s *size*   Specify the *size* of the volume being dumped to. When the specified size is reached, `ufsdump` waits for you to change the volume. `ufsdump` interprets the specified size as the length in feet for tapes and cartridges. The following are defaults:

> tape   2300 feet
> cartridge   425 feet

-t *tracks*
> Specify the number of tracks for a cartridge tape. The default is 9 tracks. The -t option is not compatible with the -D option.

-u   Update the dump record. Add an entry to the file `/etc/dumpdates`, for each filesystem successfully dumped that includes the filesystem name, date, and dump level. This file can be edited by the super-user.

-w   List the file systems that need backing up. This information is gleaned from the files `/etc/dumpdates` and `/etc/vfstab`. When the -w option is used, all other options are ignored. After reporting, `ufsdump` exits immediately.

W   Similar to the -w option, except that the -W option includes all file systems that appear in `/etc/dumpdates`, along with information about their most recent dump dates and levels. Filesystems that need backing up are highlighted.

If no *options* are given, the default is 9u.

NOTES

Fewer than 32 read errors on the filesystem are ignored.

Each reel requires a new process, so parent processes for reels already written just hang around until the entire tape is written.

It is recommended that incremental dumps also be performed with the system running in single-user mode.

FILES

    `/dev/rmt/ctape1`   default unit to dump to

```
/etc/dumpdates      dump date record
/etc/group          to find group operator
/etc/hosts
```

SEE ALSO

`tar`(1), `wall`(1), `shutdown`(1M), `ufsrestore`(1M).

NAME

ufsrestore - incremental file system restore

SYNOPSIS

ufsrestore *options* [*filename...*]

DESCRIPTION

ufsrestore restores files from backup tapes created with the ufsdump. command. *options* is a string of at least one of the options listed below, along with any modifiers and arguments you supply. Remaining arguments to ufsrestore are the names of files (or directories whose files) are to be restored to disk. Unless the h modifier is in effect, a directory name refers to the files it contains, and (recursively) its subdirectories and the files they contain.

The options are:

-i   Interactive. After reading in the directory information from the tape, ufsrestore invokes an interactive interface that allows you to browse through the dump tape's directory hierarchy and select individual files to be extracted. See Interactive Commands, below, for a description of available commands.

-r   Restore the entire tape. Load the tape's full contents into the current directory. This option should be used only to restore a complete dump tape onto a clear filesystem, or to restore an incremental dump tape after a full level 0 restore.

-R   Resume restoring. ufsrestore requests a particular tape of a multivolume set from which to resume a full restore (see the -r option above). This allows ufsrestore to start from a checkpoint when it is interrupted in the middle of a full restore.

-t   Table of contents. List each *filename* that appears on the tape. If no *filename* argument is given, the root directory is listed. This results in a list of all files on the tape, unless the -h modifier is in effect.

-x   Extract the named files from the tape. If a named file matches a directory whose contents were written onto the tape, and the -h modifier is not in effect, the directory is recursively extracted. The owner, modification time, and mode are restored (if possible). If no *filename* argument is given, the root directory is extracted. This results in the entire tape being extracted unless the -h modifier is in effect.

-c   Convert the contents of the dump tape to the new filesystem format.

-d   Debug. Turn on debugging output.

h   Extract the actual directory, rather than the files that it references. This prevents hierarchical restoration of complete subtrees from the tape.

m   Extract by inode numbers rather than by filename to avoid regenerating complete pathnames. This is useful if only a few files are being extracted.

v   Verbose. ufsrestore displays the name of each file it restores, preceded by its file type.

y   Do not ask whether to abort the restore in the event of tape errors. ufsrestore tries to skip over the bad tape block(s) and continue as best it can.

b *factor*
> Blocking factor. Specify the blocking factor for tape reads. By default, `ufsre-store` will attempt to figure out the block size of the tape. Note: a tape block is 512 bytes.

f *dump-file*
> Use *dump-file* instead of `/dev/rmt/ctape1` as the file to restore from. If *dump-file* is specified as '-', `ufsrestore` reads from the standard input. This allows, `ufsdump(1M)` and `ufsrestore` to be used in a pipeline to dump and restore a file system:
>
>   example# ufsdump 0f - /dev/rmt/ctape1 | (cd /mnt;
>   ufsrestore xf -)
>
> If the name of the file is of the form *machine*:*device* the restore is done from the specified machine over the network using `rmt(1M)`. Since `ufsrestore` is normally run by root, the name of the local machine must appear in the `.rhosts` file of the remote machine. If the file is specified as *user*!*machine*:*device*, `ufsrestore` will attempt to execute as the specified user on the remote machine. The specified user must have a `.rhosts` file on the remote machine that allows root from the local machine. If `ufsrestore` is called as `ufsrre-store`, the tape defaults to `dumphost:/dev/rmt/ctape1`. To direct the input from a desired remote machine, set up an alias for `dumphost` in the file `/etc/hosts`.

s *n*
> Skip to the *n*'th file when there are multiple dump files on the same tape. For example, the command:
>
>   example# ufsrestore xfs /dev/rmt/ctape1 5
>
> would position you at the fifth file on the tape.

`ufsrestore` enters interactive mode when invoked with the i option. Interactive commands are reminiscent of the shell. For those commands that accept an argument, the default is the current directory.

ls[*directory*]
> List files in `directory` or the current directory, represented by a '.' (period). Directories are appended with a '/' (backslash). Entries marked for extraction are prefixed with a '*' (asterisk). If the verbose option is in effect, inode numbers are also listed.

cd *directory*
> Change to directory `directory` (within the dump-tape).

pwd
> Print the full pathname of the current working directory.

add[*filename*]
> Add the current directory, or the named file or directory `directory` to the list of files to extract. If a directory is specified, add that directory and its files (recursively) to the extraction list (unless the h modifier is in effect).

delete[*filename*]
> Delete the current directory, or the named file or directory from the list of files to extract. If a directory is specified, delete that directory and all its descendents from the extraction list (unless the h modifier is in

effect). The most expedient way to extract a majority of files from a directory is to add that directory to the extraction list, and then delete specific files to omit.

extract   Extract all files on the extraction list from the dump tape. `ufsrestore` asks which volume the user wishes to mount. The fastest way to extract a small number of files is to start with the last tape volume and work toward the first.

verbose   Toggle the status of the v modifier. While v is in effect, the `ls` command lists the inode numbers of all entries, and `ufsrestore` displays information about each file as it is extracted.

help   Display a summary of the available commands.

quit   `ufsrestore` exits immediately, even if the extraction list is not empty.

NOTES

`ufsrestore` can get confused when doing incremental restores from dump tapes that were made on active file systems.

A level 0 dump must be done after a full restore. Because `ufsrestore` runs in user mode, it has no control over inode allocation; this means that `ufsrestore` repositions the files, although it does not change their contents. Thus, a full dump must be done to get a new set of directories reflecting the new file positions, so that later incremental dumps will be correct.

DIAGNOSTICS

`ufsrestore` complains about bad option characters.

Read errors result in complaints. If y has been specified, or the user responds y, `ufsrestore` will attempt to continue.

If the dump extends over more than one tape, `ufsrestore` asks the user to change tapes. If the x or i option has been specified, `ufsrestore` also asks which volume the user wishes to mount.

There are numerous consistency checks that can be listed by `ufsrestore`. Most checks are self-explanatory or can never happen. Common errors are given below.

`Converting to new file system format.`
> A dump tape created from the old file system has been loaded. It is automatically converted to the new file system format.

filename`: not found on tape`
> The specified file name was listed in the tape directory, but was not found on the tape. This is caused by tape read errors while looking for the file, and from using a dump tape created on an active file system.

`expected next file` *inumber*`, got` *inumber*
> A file that was not listed in the directory showed up. This can occur when using a dump tape created on an active file system.

`Incremental tape too low`
> When doing an incremental restore, a tape that was written before the previous incremental tape, or that has too low an incremental level has been loaded.

```
Incremental tape too high
```
When doing incremental restore, a tape that does not begin its coverage where the previous incremental tape left off, or one that has too high an incremental level has been loaded.

```
Tape read error while restoring filename
Tape read error while skipping over inode  inumber
Tape read error while trying to resynchronize
A tape read error has occurred.
```
If a file name is specified, then its contents are probably partially wrong. If an inode is being skipped or the tape is trying to resynchronize, then no extracted files have been corrupted, though files may not be found on the tape.

```
resync ufsrestore, skipped num
```
After a tape read error, `ufsrestore` may have to resynchronize itself. This message lists the number of blocks that were skipped over.

FILES

`/dev/rmt/ctape1`	the default tape drive
`dumphost:/dev/rmt/ctape1`	
	the default tape drive if called as `ufsrrestore`
`/tmp/rstdir*`	file containing directories on the tape
`/tmp/rstmode*`	owner, mode, and timestamps for directories
`./restoresymtable`	information passed between incremental restores

SEE ALSO

`ufsdump`(1M), `mkfs`(1M), `mount`(1M).

NAME

ul - underline

SYNOPSIS

/usr/ucb/ul [-i] [-t *terminal*] [*filename* ...]

DESCRIPTION

The ul command reads the named *filenames* (or the standard input if none are given) and translates occurrences of underscores to the sequence which indicates underlining for the terminal in use, as specified by the environment variable TERM. ul uses the /usr/share/lib/termcap file to determine the appropriate sequences for underlining. If the terminal is incapable of underlining, but is capable of a standout mode then that is used instead. If the terminal can overstrike, or handles underlining automatically, ul degenerates to cat. If the terminal cannot underline, underlining is ignored.

The following options are available:

-t *terminal*   Override the terminal kind specified in the environment. If the terminal cannot underline, underlining is ignored.

-i   Indicate underlining by a separate line containing appropriate dashes -; this is useful when you want to look at the underlining which is present in an nroff output stream on a CRT-terminal.

SEE ALSO

cat(1), man(1), nroff(1).

NAME

umask - set file-creation mode mask

SYNOPSIS

umask [*ooo*]

DESCRIPTION

The user file-creation mode mask is set to *ooo*. The three octal digits refer to read/write/execute permissions for *owner*, group, and *others*, respectively (see chmod(2) and umask(2)). The value of each specified digit is subtracted from the corresponding "digit" specified by the system for the creation of a file (see creat(2)). For example, umask 022 removes group and *others* write permission (files normally created with mode 777 become mode 755; files created with mode 666 become mode 644).

If *ooo* is omitted, the current value of the mask is printed.

umask is recognized and executed by the shell.

umask can be included in the user's .profile (see profile(4)) and invoked at login to automatically set the user's permissions on files or directories created.

SEE ALSO

chmod(1), sh(1).
chmod(2), creat(2), umask(2),
profile(4).

NAME

uname - print name of current UNIX system

SYNOPSIS

uname [-amnprsv]
uname [-S *system_name*]

DESCRIPTION

uname prints the current system name of the UNIX system to standard output. It is mainly useful to determine which system one is using. The options cause selected information returned by uname(2) and/or sysinfo(2) to be printed:

-a   Print all information.

-m   Print the machine hardware name.

-n   Print the nodename (the nodename is the name by which the system is known to a communications network).

-p   Print the current host's processor type.

-r   Print the operating system release.

-s   Print the name of the operating system (e.g. UNIX System V). This is the default.

-v   Print the operating system version.

On the computer, the nodename may be changed by specifying a system name argument to the -S option. The system name argument is restricted to SYS_NMLN characters. SYS_NMLN is an implementation specific value defined in sys/utsname.h. Only the super-user is allowed this capability.

SEE ALSO

sysinfo(2), uname(2).

NAME

unget - undo a previous get of an SCCS file

SYNOPSIS

unget [-r*SID*] [-s] [-n] *files*

DESCRIPTION

unget undoes the effect of a get -e done prior to creating the intended new delta. If a directory is named, unget behaves as though each file in the directory were specified as a named file, except that non-SCCS files and unreadable files are silently ignored. If a name of - is given, the standard input is read with each line being taken as the name of an SCCS file to be processed.

Keyletter arguments apply independently to each named file.

-r*SID*	Uniquely identifies which delta is no longer intended. (This would have been specified by get as the "new delta"). The use of this keyletter is necessary only if two or more outstanding gets for editing on the same SCCS file were done by the same person (login name). A diagnostic results if the specified *SID* is ambiguous, or if it is necessary and omitted on the command line.
-s	Suppresses the printout, on the standard output, of the intended delta's *SID*.
-n	Causes the retention of the gotten file, which would normally be removed from the current directory.

unget must be performed by the same user who performed the original get -e.

FILES

p-file	[see delta(1)]
q-file	[see delta(1)]
z-file	[see delta(1)]

SEE ALSO

delta(1), get(1), help(1), sact(1)

DIAGNOSTICS

Use help(1) for explanations.

NAME

unifdef - resolve and remove ifdef'ed lines from C program source

SYNOPSIS

/usr/ucb/unifdef [-clt] [-D*name*] [-U*name*] [-iD*name*] [-iU*name*]
... [*filename*]

DESCRIPTION

unifdef removes ifdefed lines from a file while otherwise leaving the file alone.
It is smart enough to deal with the nested ifdefs, comments, single and double
quotes of C syntax, but it does not do any including or interpretation of macros.
Neither does it strip out comments, though it recognizes and ignores them. You
specify which symbols you want defined with -D options, and which you want
undefined with -U options. Lines within those ifdefs will be copied to the output,
or removed, as appropriate. Any ifdef, ifndef, else, and endif lines associated
with *filename* will also be removed.

ifdefs involving symbols you do not specify are untouched and copied out along
with their associated ifdef, else, and endif lines.

If an ifdef*X* occurs nested inside another ifdef*X*, then the inside ifdef is treated
as if it were an unrecognized symbol. If the same symbol appears in more than one
argument, only the first occurrence is significant.

unifdef copies its output to the standard output and will take its input from the
standard input if no *filename* argument is given.

The following options are available:

-c   Complement the normal operation. Lines that would have been
            removed or blanked are retained, and vice versa.

-l   Replace "lines removed" lines with blank lines.

-t   Plain text option. unifdef refrains from attempting to recognize com-
            ments and single and double quotes.

-iD*name*   Ignore, but print out, lines associated with the defined symbol *name*. If
            you use ifdefs to delimit non-C lines, such as comments or code which
            is under construction, then you must tell unifdef which symbols are
            used for that purpose so that it will not try to parse for quotes and com-
            ments within them.

-iU*name*   Ignore, but print out, lines associated with the undefined symbol *name*.

SEE ALSO

cc(1), diff(1).

DIAGNOSTICS

Premature EOF   Inappropriate else or endif.

Exit status is 0 if output is exact copy of input, 1 if not, 2 if unifdef encounters
problems.

NAME

uniq - report repeated lines in a file

SYNOPSIS

uniq [-udc [+n] [-n]] [*input* [*output*]]

DESCRIPTION

uniq reads the input file comparing adjacent lines. In the normal case, the second and succeeding copies of repeated lines are removed; the remainder is written on the output file. *Input* and *output* should always be different. Note that repeated lines must be adjacent in order to be found; see sort(1). If the -u flag is used, just the lines that are not repeated in the original file are output. The -d option specifies that one copy of just the repeated lines is to be written. The normal mode output is the union of the -u and -d mode outputs.

The -c option supersedes -u and -d and generates an output report in default style but with each line preceded by a count of the number of times it occurred.

The *n* arguments specify skipping an initial portion of each line in the comparison:

-*n*   The first *n* fields together with any blanks before each are ignored. A field is defined as a string of non-space, non-tab characters separated by tabs and spaces from its neighbors.

+*n*   The first *n* columns are ignored. Fields are skipped before columns.

INTERNATIONAL FUNCTIONS

uniq can process characters from supplementary code sets.

SEE ALSO

comm(1), sort(1).

NAME

units - conversion program

SYNOPSIS

units

DESCRIPTION

units converts quantities expressed in various standard scales to their equivalents in other scales. It works interactively in this fashion:

```
You have: inch
You want: cm
        * 2.540000e+00
        / 3.937008e-01
```

A quantity is specified as a multiplicative combination of units optionally preceded by a numeric multiplier. Powers are indicated by suffixed positive integers, division by the usual sign:

```
You have: 15 lbs force/in2
You want: atm
        * 1.020689e+00
        / 9.797299e-01
```

units only does multiplicative scale changes; thus it can convert Kelvin to Rankine, but not Celsius to Fahrenheit. Most familiar units, abbreviations, and metric prefixes are recognized, together with a generous leavening of exotica and a few constants of nature including:

pi	ratio of circumference to diameter,
c	speed of light,
e	charge on an electron,
g	acceleration of gravity,
force	same as g,
mole	Avogadro's number,
water	pressure head per unit height of water,
au	astronomical unit.

Pound is not recognized as a unit of mass; lb is. Compound names are run together, (for example, lightyear). British units that differ from their U.S. counterparts are prefixed thus: brgallon. For a complete list of units, type:

```
cat /usr/share/lib/unittab
```

FILES

/usr/lib/unittab

NAME

unshare - make local resource unavailable for mounting by remote systems

SYNOPSIS

unshare [-F *fstype*] [-o *specific_options*] [*pathname* | *resourcename*]

DESCRIPTION

The unshare command makes a shared local resource unavailable to file system type *fstype*. If the option -F *fstype* is omitted, then the first file system type listed in file /etc/dfs/fstypes will be used as the default. *Specific_options*, as well as the semantics of *resourcename*, are specific to particular distributed file systems. See unshare_*FSType*(1M) for details.

FILES

/etc/dfs/fstypes
/etc/dfs/sharetab

SEE ALSO

share(1M), shareall(1M), unshare_nfs(1M), unshare_rfs(1M).

NOTES

If *pathname* or *resourcename* is not found in the shared information, an error message will be sent to standard error.

NAME

unshare - make local NFS resource unavailable for mounting by remote systems

SYNOPSIS

unshare [-F nfs] *pathname*

DESCRIPTION

The unshare command makes local resources unavailable for mounting by remote systems. The shared resource must correspond to a line with NFS as the *fstype* in the file /etc/dfs/sharetab. The -F option may be omitted if NFS is the first file system type listed in the files /etc/dfs/fstypes.

FILES

/etc/dfs/fstypes
/etc/dfs/sharetab

SEE ALSO

share(1M)

NAME

unshare - make local RFS resource unavailable for mounting by remote systems

SYNOPSIS

unshare [-F rfs] {*pathname* | *resourcename*}

DESCRIPTION

The unshare command makes a shared resource unavailable through Remote File Sharing. The shared resource must correspond to a line with rfs as the *fstype* in the file /etc/dfs/sharetab. The -F flag may be omitted if RFS is the first file system type listed in the file /etc/dfs/fstypes.

FILES

/etc/dfs/dfstab
/etc/dfs/fstypes
/etc/dfs/sharetab

SEE ALSO

unshare(1M), share(1M)

NAME

uptime - show how long the system has been up

SYNOPSIS

`/usr/ucb/uptime`

DESCRIPTION

The `uptime` command prints the current time, the length of time the system has been up. It is the first line of a w(1) command.

EXAMPLE

Below is an example of the output `uptime` provides:

```
uptime
6:47am  up 6 days, 16:38,  1 users
```

SEE ALSO

w(1), who(1), whodo(1).

NOTES

`who -b` gives the time the system was last booted.

NAME

urestore - request restore of files and directories

SYNOPSIS

urestore [-mn] [-s | v] [-o *target*] [-d *date*] -F *file* . . .

urestore [-mn] [-s | v] [-o *target*] [-d *date*] -D *dir* . . .

urestore -c *jobid*

DESCRIPTION

urestore posts requests for files or directories to be restored from system-maintained archives. If the appropriate archive containing the requested files or directories is on-line, the files or directories are restored immediately. If not, a request to restore the specified files or directories is posted to a restore status table, /etc/bkup/rsstatus.tab. A restore request that has been posted must later be resolved by an operator (see rsoper(1M)). Each file or directory to be restored is assigned a restore job ID that can be used to monitor the progress of the restore (see ursstatus(1M)) or to cancel it.

The user must have write permission for the current directory and any subdirectories to be traversed in storing the restored files or directories. Requests for restores may be made only by the user who owned the files or directories at the time the archive containing the files or directories was made, or by a user with superuser privileges.

Options

-c *jobid*	Cancels a previously issued restore request.
-d *date*	Restores the filesystem or directory as of *date*. (This may or may not be the latest archive.) See getdate(3C) for valid date formats.
-m	If the restore cannot be carried out immediately, this option notifies the invoking user (via mail) when the request has been completed.
-n	Displays a list of all archived versions of the filesystem or directory contained in the backup history log but does not attempt to restore the filesystem or directory.
-o *target*	Instead of restoring directly to the specified file or directory, this option replaces the file or directory *target* with the archive of the specified file or directory.
-s	While a restore operation is occurring, displays a "." for each 100 (512-byte) blocks transferred from the destination device.
-v	Displays the name of each object as it is restored. Only those archiving methods that restore named directories and files (incfile, ffile) support this option.
-D	Initiates a restore operation for directories.
-F	Initiates a restore operation for files.

DIAGNOSTICS

The exit codes for urestore are the following:

    0 = the task completed successfully
    1 = one or more parameters to `urestore` are invalid
    2 = an error has occurred, causing `urestore` to fail to
       complete *all* portions of its task.

EXAMPLES

Example 1:

```
urestore -m -F bigfile
```

posts a request to restore the most current archived version of the file `bigfile`. If the restore operation cannot be carried out immediately, it notifies the invoking user when the request has been completed.

Example 2:

```
urestore -c rest-256a,rest-256b
```

cancels restore requests with job ID numbers `rest-256a` and `rest-256b`.

Example 3:

```
urestore -o /testfiles/myfile.b -F /testfiles/myfile.a
```

posts a request for the archived file `/testfiles/myfile.a` to be restored as `/testfiles/myfile.b`

Example 4:

```
urestore -d "december 1, 1987" -D /user1 -v
```

posts a request for the archived directory structure `/user1`, with all its files and subdirectories, to be restored as of December 1, 1987. If the restore is done immediately from an on-line archive, the name of each file will be displayed on standard output while the restore is underway.

Example 5:

```
urestore -n -D /pr3/reports
```

requests the system to display the backup dates and an `ls -l` listing from the backup history log of all archived versions of the directory `/pr3/reports`. The directory is not restored.

FILES

`/etc/bkup/bkhist.tab`	-	contains the labels of all volumes that have been used for backup operations
`/etc/bkup/rsstatus.tab`	-	contains status information about all restore requests from users
`/etc/bkup/rsnotify.tab`	-	contains the electronic mail address of the operator to be notified whenever restore requests require operator intervention

SEE ALSO

`restore`(1M), `ursstatus`(1M), `mail`(1), `getdate`(3C).

NAME

ursstatus - report the status of posted user restore requests

SYNOPSIS

ursstatus [-h] [-j *jobids*] [-f *field_separator*] [-d *ddev*] [-u *users*]

DESCRIPTION

With no options, ursstatus reports the status of all pending user restore requests that are posted in the restore status table.

This command can request a status report for only those restore requests that the user has initiated.

Options

-h   Suppresses header for the report.

-j *jobids*   Restricts the report to the specified jobs. *jobids* is a list of restore job IDs (either comma-separated or blank-separated and surrounded by quotes). *jobids* must be valid for the user invoking the command.

-f *field_separator*

         Suppresses field wrap and specifies an output field separator to be used. *field_separator* is the character that will appear as the field separator in the output displayed. A null *field_separator* will use a tab character as a separator.

-d *ddev*   Restricts the report to pending restore jobs that could be satisfied by the specified device type or volumes. *ddev* describes the device or volumes used to select requests to be restored. *ddev* is of the form:

         [*dtype*][: *dlabels*]

dtype is a device type (such as diskette, cartridge tape, or 9-track tape). If specified, restrict the report to posted requests that could be satisfied by volumes of the type specified.

dlabels is a list of volume names corresponding to the *volumename* displayed by the labelit command. *dlabels* may be either comma-separated or blank-separated and surrounded by quotes. If specified, restrict the report to posted requests that could be satisfied by an archive residing on the specified volumes.

-u *users*   Restricts the report to requests submitted by the specified *users* (either comma-separated or blank-separated and surrounded by quotes). *users* must be listed in the passwd file.

DIAGNOSTICS

The exit codes for ursstatus are the following:

0 = successful completion of the task
1 = one or more parameters to ursstatus are invalid.
2 = an error has occurred which caused ursstatus to fail to
      complete *all* portions of its task.

EXAMPLE

```
ursstatus -j rest-354a,rest-429b
```

reports the status of only the two posted restore requests with the specified job IDs.

FILES

`/etc/bkup/rsstatus.tab`   contains status report information for all restore requests from users

SEE ALSO

`restore`(1M), `rsstatus`(1M), `urestore`(1M).

NAME

useradd - administer a new user login on the system

SYNOPSIS

useradd [-u *uid* [-o]] [-g *group*] [-G *group*[, *group*...]] [-d *dir*] [-s *shell*]
[-c *comment*] [-m [-k *skel_dir*]] [-f *inactive*] [-e *expire*] *login*

useradd -D [-g *group*] [-b *base_dir*] [-f *inactive*] [-e *expire*]

DESCRIPTION

Invoking useradd without the -D option adds a new user entry to the /etc/passwd and /etc/shadow files. It also creates supplementary group memberships for the user (-G option) and creates the home directory (-m option) for the user if requested. The new login remains locked until the passwd(1M) command is executed.

Invoking useradd -D with no additional options displays the default values for *group, base_dir, shel_dir, shell, inactive,* and *expire.* The values for *group, base_dir, inactive, expire,* and *shell* are used for invocations without the -D option.

Invoking useradd -D with -g, -b, -f, or -e (or any combination of these) sets the default values for the respective fields. (As installed, the default group is other (group ID of 1) and the default value of *base_dir* is /home). Subsequent invocations of useradd without the -D option use these arguments.

The system file entries created with this command have a limit of 512 characters per line. Specifying long arguments to several options may exceed this limit.

The following options are available:

-u *uid*   The UID of the new user. This UID must be a non-negative decimal integer below MAXUID as defined in param.h. The UID defaults to the next available (unique) number above the highest number currently assigned. For example, if UIDs 100, 105, and 200 are assigned, the next default UID number will be 201. (UIDs from 0-99 are reserved.)

-o   This option allows a UID to be duplicated (non-unique).

-g *group*   An existing group's integer ID or character-string name. Without the -D option, it defines the new user's primary group membership and defaults to the default group. You can reset this default value by invoking useradd -D -g *group.*

-G *group*   An existing group's integer ID or character-string name. It defines the new user's supplementary group membership. Duplicates between *group* with the -g and -G options are ignored. No more than NGROUPS_MAX groups may be specified.

-d *dir*   The home directory of the new user. It defaults to *base_dir/login,* where *base_dir* is the base directory for new login home directories and *login* is the new login.

-s *shell*   Full pathname of the program used as the user's shell on login. It defaults to an empty field causing the system to use /sbin/sh as the default. The value of *shell* must be a valid executable file.

-c *comment*
>   Any text string. It is generally a short description of the login, and is currently used as the field for the user's full name. This information is stored in the user's /etc/passwd entry.

-m
>   Create the new user's home directory if it doesn't already exist. If the directory already exists, it must have read, write, and execute permissions by *group*, where *group* is the user's primary group.

-k *skel_dir*
>   A directory that contains skeleton information (such as .profile) that can be copied into a new user's home directory. This directory must exist. The system provides a "skel" directory (/etc/skel) that can be used for this purpose.

-e *expire*
>   The date on which a login can no longer be used; after this date, no user will be able to access this login. (This option is useful for creating temporary logins.) You may type the value of the argument *expire* (which is a date) in any format you like (except a Julian date). For example, you may enter 10/6/90 or October 6, 1990. A value of ' ' ' ' defeats the status of the expired date.

-f *inactive*
>   The maximum number of days allowed between uses of a login ID before that login ID is declared valid. Normal values are positive integers. A value of -1 defeats the status.

login
>   A string of printable characters that specifies the existing login name of the user. It must exist and may not contain a colon (:) or a newline (\n).

login
>   A string of printable characters that specifies the new login name of the user. It may not contain a colon (:) or a newline (\n).

-b *base_dir*
>   The default base directory for the system. If -d *dir* is not specified. *base_dir* is concatenated with the user's login to define the home directory. If the -m option is not used, base_dir must exist.

FILES

/etc/passwd
/etc/shadow
/etc/group
/etc/skel

SEE ALSO

groupadd(1M),   groupdel(1M),   groupmod(1M),   logins(1M),   passwd(1),
passwd(1M), userdel(1M), usermod(1M), users(1)

DIAGNOSTICS

The `useradd` command exits with one of the following values:

0	The command was executed successfully.
2	The command line syntax was invalid. A usage message for the `useradd` command is displayed.
3	An invalid argument was provided with an option.
4	The *uid* specified with the `-u` option is already in use.
6	The *group* specified with the `-g` option does not exist.
9	The specified *login* is not unique.
10	Cannot update `/etc/group`. The login was added to the `/etc/passwd` file but not to the `/etc/group` file.
12	Unable to create the home directory (with the `-m` option) or unable to complete the copy of *skel_dir* to the home directory.

NAME

userdel - delete a user's login from the system

SYNOPSIS

userdel [-r] *login*

DESCRIPTION

The userdel command deletes a user's login from the system and makes the appropriate login-related changes to the system file and file system.

The following options are available:

-r   Remove the user's home directory from the system. This directory must exist. The files and directories under the home directory will no longer be accessible following successful execution of the command.

login A string of printable characters that specifies an existing login on the system. It may not contain a colon (:), or a newline (\n).

FILES

/etc/passwd
/etc/shadow
/etc/group
/etc/security/ia/index
/etc/security/ia/master
/etc/security/ia/uidage

SEE ALSO

groupadd(1M), groupdel(1M), groupmod(1M), logins(1M), passwd(1), passwd(1M), useradd(1M), usermod(1M), users(1).

DIAGNOSTICS

The userdel command exits with one of the following values:

0   Success.

2   Invalid command syntax. A usage message for the userdel command is displayed.

6   The login to be removed does not exist.

8   The login to be removed is in use.

10   Cannot update the /etc/group file but the login is removed from the /etc/passwd file.

12   Cannot remove or otherwise modify the home directory.

NAME

usermod - modify a user's login information on the system

SYNOPSIS

usermod [-u *uid* [-o]] [-g *group*] [-G *group*[, *group* . . .]   [-d *dir* [-m]] [-s *shell*]
[-c *comment*] [-l *new_logname*] [-f *inactive*] [-e *expire*] *login*

DESCRIPTION

The usermod command modifies a user's login definition on the system. It changes the definition of the specified login and makes the appropriate login-related system file and file system changes.

The system file entries created with this command have a limit of 512 characters per line. Specifying long arguments to several options may exceed this limit.

The following options are available:

-u *uid* New UID for the user. It must be a non-negative decimal integer below MAXUID as defined in param.h.

-o   This option allows the specified UID to be duplicated (non-unique).

-g *group*
An existing group's integer ID or character-string name. It redefines the user's primary group membership.

-G *group*
An existing group's integer "ID" "," or character string name. It redefines the user's supplementary group membership. Duplicates between group with the -g and -G options are ignored. No more than NGROUPS_UMAX groups may be specified as defined in param.h.

-d *dir* The new home directory of the user. It defaults to *base_dir/login*, where *base_dir* is the base directory for new login home directories, and *login* is the new login.

-m   Move the user's home directory to the new directory specified with the -d option. If the directory already exists, it must have permissions read/write/execute by *group*, where *group* is the user's primary group.

-s *shell*
Full pathname of the program that is used as the user's shell on login. The value of *shell* must be a valid executable file.

-c *comment*
Any text string. It is generally a short description of the login, and is currently used as the field for the user's full name. This information is stored in the user's /etc/passwd entry.

-l *new_logname*
A string of printable characters that specifies the new login name for the user. It may not contain a colon (:) or a newline (\n).

-e *expire*
The date on which a login can no longer be used; after this date, no user will be able to access this login. (This option is useful for creating temporary logins.) You may type the value of the argument *expire* (which is a date) in any format you like (except a Julian date). For example, you may enter 10/6/90 or October 6, 1990. A value of ' ' ' ' defeats the status of the

expired date.

-f *inactive*
> The maximum number of days allowed between uses of a login ID before that login ID is declared valid. Normal values are positive integers. A value of -1 defeats the status.

login   A string of printable characters that specifies the existing login name of the user. It must exist and may not contain a colon (:), or a newline (\n).

FILES

/etc/passwd, /etc/shadow, /etc/group

SEE ALSO

groupadd(1M), groupdel(1M), groupmod(1M), logins(1M), passwd(1), passwd(1M), useradd(1M), userdel(1M), users(1)

DIAGNOSTICS

The usermod command exits with one of the following values:

0   The command was executed successfully.

2   The command syntax was invalid. A usage message for the usermod command is displayed.

3   An invalid argument was provided to an option.

4   The *uid* given with the -u option is already in use.

6   The login to be modified does not exist or *group* does not exist.

8   The login to be modified is in use.

9   The *new_logname* is already in use.

10   Cannot update the /etc/group file. Other update requests will be implemented.

11   Insufficient space to move the home directory (-m option). Other update requests will be implemented.

12   Unable to complete the move of the home directory to the new home directory.

NAME

users - display a compact list of users logged in

SYNOPSIS

/usr/ucb/users [*file*]

DESCRIPTION

users lists the login names of the users currently on the system in a compact, one-line format.

Specifying *file*, tells users where to find its information; by default it checks /var/adm/utmp.

Typing *users* is equivalent to typing who -q.

EXAMPLE

```
users
paul george ringo
```

FILES

/var/adm/utmp

SEE ALSO

who(1).

NAME

uucheck - check the uucp directories and permissions file

SYNOPSIS

`/usr/lib/uucp/uucheck` [options]

DESCRIPTION

uucheck checks for the presence of the uucp system required files and directories. uucheck also does error checking of the *Permissions* file (`/etc/uucp/Permissions`). uucheck has the following options:

-v   Give a detailed (verbose) explanation of how the uucp programs will interpret the *Permissions* file.

-x*debug_level*

debug_level is a number from 0 to 9. Higher numbers give more detailed debugging information.

uucheck is executed during package installation. Note that uucheck can only be used by the super-user or uucp.

FILES

```
/etc/uucp/Systems
/etc/uucp/Permissions
/etc/uucp/Devices
/etc/uucp/Limits
/var/spool/uucp/*
/var/spool/locks/*
/var/spool/uucppublic/*
```

SEE ALSO

uucico(1M), uusched(1M).
uucp(1C), uustat(1C), uux(1C).

NOTES

The program does not check file/directory modes or some errors in the *Permissions* file such as duplicate login or machine name.

NAME

uucico, in.uucpd - file transport programs for the uucp system

SYNOPSIS

/usr/lib/uucp/uucico [*options*]

/usr/sbin/in.uucpd

DESCRIPTION

uucico is the file transport program for uucp work file transfers. The following options are available.

-c*type*	The first field in the Devices file is the "Type" field. The -c option forces uucico to only use entries in the "Type" field that match the user specified *type*. The specified *type* is usually the name of a local area network.
-d*spool_directory*	This option specifies the directory *spool_directory* that contains the uucp work files to be transferred. The default spool directory is /var/spool/uucp.
-f	This option is used to "force execution" of uucico by ignoring the limit on the maximum number of uucicos defined in the /etc/uucp/Limits file.
-i*interface*	This option defines the *interface* used with uucico. The interface only affects slave mode. Known interfaces are UNIX (default), TLI (basic Transport Layer Interface), and TLIS (Transport Layer Interface with Streams modules, read/write).
-r*role_number*	The *role_number* 1 is used for master mode. *role_number* 0 is used for slave mode (default). When uucico is started by a program or cron, *role_number* 1 should be used for master mode.
-s*system_name*	The -s option defines the remote system (*system_name*) that uucico will try to contact. It is required when the role is master; *system_name* must be defined in the Systems file.
-x*debug_level*	Both uux and uucp queue jobs that will be transferred by uucico. These jobs are normally started by the uusched scheduler, for debugging purposes, and can be started manually. For example, the shell Uutry starts uucico with debugging turned on. The *debug_level* is a number between 0 and 9. Higher numbers give more detailed debugging information.

in.uucpd is provided strictly for BSD compatabilty. Uucp communication over the TCP protocol between System V machines should use the TLI listener. However, this is not possible when the remote machine is a BSD system. The in.uucpd daemon accepts incoming uucp requests over the network and starts uucico to handle the job. in.uucpd is faithful to the original BSD version, which means that it can only be used for file transfers - login facilities such as cu will not function.

FILES

/etc/uucp/Systems
/etc/uucp/Permissions
/etc/uucp/Devices
/etc/uucp/Devconfig

```
/etc/uucp/Sysfiles
/etc/uucp/Limits
/var/spool/uucp/*
/var/spool/locks/*
/var/spool/uucppublic/*
```

SEE ALSO
cron(1M), uusched(1M), Uutry(1M) , listen(1M).
uucp(1C), uustat(1C), uux(1C), cu(1C).

NAME

uucleanup - uucp spool directory clean-up

SYNOPSIS

/usr/lib/uucp/uucleanup [*options*]

DESCRIPTION

uucleanup will scan the spool directories for old files and take appropriate action to remove them in a useful way:

Inform the requester of send/receive requests for systems that cannot be reached.

Return undeliverable mail to the sender.

Deliver rnews files addressed to the local system.

Remove all other files.

In addition, there is a provision to warn users of requests that have been waiting for a given number of days (default 1). Note that uucleanup will process as if all option times were specified to the default values unless *time* is specifically set.

The following options are available.

-C*time*   Any C. files greater or equal to *time* days old will be removed with appropriate information to the requester. (Default 7 days.)

-D*time*   Any D. files greater or equal to *time* days old will be removed. An attempt will be made to deliver mail messages and execute rnews when appropriate. (Default 7 days.)

-W*time*   Any C. files equal to *time* days old will cause a mail message to be sent to the requester warning about the delay in contacting the remote. The message includes the *JOBID*, and in the case of mail, the mail message. The administrator may include a message line telling whom to call to check the problem (-m option). (Default 1 day.)

-X*time*   Any X. files greater or equal to *time* days old will be removed. The D. files are probably not present (if they were, the X. could get executed). But if there are D. files, they will be taken care of by D. processing. (Default 2 days.)

-m*string*   Include *string* in the warning message generated by the -W option. Characters from supplementary code sets can be used for the warning message contained in *string*.

-o*time*   Other files whose age is more than *time* days will be deleted. (Default 2 days.) The default line is See your local administrator to locate the problem.

-s*system*   Execute for system spool directory only.

-x*debug_level*

The -x debug level is a single digit between 0 and 9; higher numbers give more detailed debugging information. (This option may not be available on all systems.)

This program is typically started by the shell *uudemon.cleanup*, which should be started by cron(1M).

FILES

> /usr/lib/uucp   directory with commands used by uucleanup internally
>
> /var/spool/uucp   spool directory

SEE ALSO

> cron(1M), uucp(1C), uux(1C).

NAME

uucp, uulog, uuname - UNIX-to-UNIX system copy

SYNOPSIS

uucp [*options*] *source-files destination-file*
uulog [*options*] *system*
uuname [*options*]

DESCRIPTION

uucp

uucp copies files named by the *source-file* arguments to the *destination-file* argument.
A source filename may be a path name on your machine, or, may have the form:

> *system-name* ! *pathname*

where *system-name* is taken from a list of system names that uucp knows about.
The destination *system-name* may also include a list of system names such as:

> *system-name* ! *system-name* ! . . . ! *system-name* ! *pathname*

In this case, an attempt is made to send the file, via the specified route, to the destination. Care should be taken to ensure that intermediate nodes in the route are willing to forward information (see **NOTES** below for restrictions).

The shell metacharacters ?, * and [. . .] appearing in *pathname* will be expanded on the appropriate system.

Path names may be one of:

(1)　　a full path name;

(2)　　a path name preceded by ~*user* where *user* is a login name on the specified system and is replaced by that user's login directory;

(3)　　a path name preceded by ~/*destination* where *destination* is appended to /var/spool/uucppublic; (NOTE: This destination will be treated as a filename unless more than one file is being transferred by this request or the destination is already a directory. To ensure that it is a directory, follow the destination with a '/'. For example ~/*dan*/ as the destination will make the directory /var/spool/uucppublic/dan if it does not exist and put the requested file(s) in that directory).

(4)　　anything else is prefixed by the current directory.

If the result is an erroneous path name for the remote system, the copy will fail. If the *destination-file* is a directory, the last part of the *source-file* name is used.

uucp removes execute permissions across the transmission and gives 0666 read and write permissions [see chmod(2)].

The following options are interpreted by uucp:

-c　　　　Do not copy local file to the spool directory for transfer to the remote machine (default).

-C　　　　Force the copy of local files to the spool directory for transfer.

`-d`	Make all necessary directories for the file copy (default).
`-f`	Do not make intermediate directories for the file copy.
`-g`*grade*	*grade* can be either a single letter/number or a string of alphanumeric characters defining a service grade. The `uuglist` command can determine whether it is appropriate to use the single letter/number or a string of alphanumeric characters as a service grade. The output from the `uuglist` command will be a list of service grades that are available or a message that says to use a single letter/number as a grade of service.
`-j`	Output the `uucp` job identification string on the standard output. This job identification can be used by `uustat` to obtain the status of a `uucp` job or to terminate a `uucp` job. It is valid as long as the job remains queued on the local system.
`-m`	Send mail to the requester when the copy is completed.
`-n`*user*	Notify *user* on the remote system that a file was sent.
`-r`	Do not start the file transfer, just queue the job.
`-s`*file*	Report status of the transfer to *file*. This option overrides the -m option.
`-x`*debug_level*	Produce debugging output on standard output. *debug_level* is a number between 0 and 9; as it increases to 9, more detailed debugging information is given. This option may not be available on all systems.

uulog

`uulog` queries a log file of `uucp` or `uuxqt` transactions in file `/var/uucp/.Log/uucico/`*system* or `/var/uucp/.Log/uuxqt/`*system*.

These options cause `uulog` to print logging information:

`-s`*sys*	Print information about file transfer work involving system *sys*.
`-f`*system*	Does a `tail -f` of the file transfer log for `system`. (You must enter BREAK to exit this function.)

Other options used in conjunction with the above options are:

`-x`	Look in the `uuxqt` log file for the given system.
`-`*number*	Indicates that a `tail` command of *number* lines should be executed.

uuname

`uuname` lists the names of systems known to `uucp`. `uuname` recognizes the following options:

`-c`	Returns the names of systems known to `cu`. (The two lists are the same, unless your machine is using different *Systems* files for `cu` and `uucp`. See the *Sysfiles* file.)
`-l`	Return the local system name.

FILES

    `/var/spool/uucp`   spool directories

`/var/spool/uucppublic/*`	public directory for receiving and sending
`/usr/lib/uucp/*`	other program files
`/etc/uucp/*`	other data files

INTERNATIONAL FUNCTIONS

uucp can process files containing characters from supplementary code sets.

System dependent names (for example, user names) and the *grade* with options -g must be in ASCII characters.

When using shell metacharacters, the target system must also be able to support international functions.

SEE ALSO

mail(1), uuglist(1C), uustat(1C), uux(1C), uuxqt(1M), chmod(2).

NOTES

For security reasons, the domain of remotely accessible files may be severely restricted. You will very likely not be able to access files by path name; ask a responsible person on the remote system to send them to you. For the same reasons, you will probably not be able to send files to arbitrary path names. As distributed, the remotely accessible files are those whose names begin with `/var/spool/uucppublic` (equivalent to ~/).

All files received by uucp will be owned by uucp.

The -m option will only work sending files or receiving a single file. Receiving multiple files specified by special shell characters ? * [. . .] will not activate the -m option.

The forwarding of files through other systems may not be compatible with the previous version of uucp. If forwarding is used, all systems in the route must have compatible versions of uucp.

Protected files and files that are in protected directories that are owned by the requester can be sent by uucp. However, if the requester is root, and the directory is not searchable by other or the file is not readable by other, the request will fail.

NAME

uuencode, uudecode - encode a binary file, or decode its ASCII representation

SYNOPSIS

uuencode [*source-file*] *file-label*

uudecode [*encoded-file*]

DESCRIPTION

uuencode converts a binary file into an ASCII-encoded representation that can be sent using mail(1). It encodes the contents of *source-file*, or the standard input if no *source-file* argument is given. The *file-label* argument is required. It is included in the encoded file's header as the name of the file into which uudecode is to place the binary (decoded) data. uuencode also includes the ownership and permission modes of *source-file*, so that *file-label* is recreated with those same ownership and permission modes.

uudecode reads an *encoded-file*, strips off any leading and trailing lines added by mailer programs, and recreates the original binary data with the filename and the mode and owner specified in the header.

The encoded file is an ordinary ASCII text file; it can be edited by any text editor. But it is best only to change the mode or file-label in the header to avoid corrupting the decoded binary.

SEE ALSO

mail(1), uucp(1C), uux(1C), uuencode(5) .

NOTES

The encoded file's size is expanded by 35% (3 bytes become 4, plus control information), causing it to take longer to transmit than the equivalent binary.

The user on the remote system who is invoking uudecode (typically uucp) must have write permission on the file specified in the *file-label*.

Since both uuencode and uudecode run with user ID set to uucp, uudecode can fail with permission denied when attempted in a directory that does not have write permission allowed for other.

NAME

uuglist - print the list of service grades that are available on this UNIX system

SYNOPSIS

uuglist [-u]

DESCRIPTION

uuglist prints the list of service grades that are available on the system to use with the -g option of uucp(1C) and uux(1C). The -u option lists the names of the service grades that the user is allowed to use with the -g option of the uucp and uux commands.

FILES

/usr/lib/uucp/Grades   contains the list of service grades

SEE ALSO

uucp(1C), uux(1C).

NAME

uusched - the scheduler for the uucp file transport program

SYNOPSIS

/usr/lib/uucp/uusched [*options*]

DESCRIPTION

uusched is the uucp(1C) file transport scheduler. It is usually started by the daemon *uudemon.hour* that is started by cron(1M) from an entry in
/var/spool/cron/crontab:

```
41,11 * * * * /usr/bin/su uucp -c "/usr/lib/uucp/uudemon.hour >
/dev/null"
```

The options are for debugging purposes only. *debug_level* are numbers between 0
and 9. Higher numbers give more detailed debugging information:

-u*debug_level*   The -u *debug_level* option is passed to uucico(1M) as -x
                     debug_level.

-x*debug_level*   Outputs debugging messages from uusched(1M).

FILES

/etc/uucp/Systems
/etc/uucp/Permissions
/etc/uucp/Devices
/var/spool/uucp/*
/var/spool/locks/*
/var/spool/uucppublic/*

SEE ALSO

cron(1M), uucico(1M), uucp(1C), uustat(1C), uux(1C).

NAME

uustat - uucp status inquiry and job control

SYNOPSIS

uustat [-q] or [-m] or [-k*jobid* [-n]] or [-r*jobid* [-n]] or [-p]
uustat [-a [-j]] [-u*user*] [-S*qric*]
uustat [-s*system* [-j]] [-u*user*] [-S*qric*]
uustat -t*system* [-d*number*] [-c]

DESCRIPTION

uustat functions in the following three areas: displays the general status of, or cancels, previously specified uucp commands; provides remote system performance information, in terms of average transfer rates or average queue times; provides general remote system-specific and user-specific status of uucp connections to other systems.

Here are the options that obtain general status of, or cancel, previously specified uucp commands; uustat allows only one of these options to appear on each uustat command line execution:

-a
    List all jobs in queue.

-j
    List the total number of jobs displayed. The -j option can only be used in conjunction with the -a or the -s option.

-k*jobid*
    Kill the uucp request whose job identification is *jobid*. The killed uucp request must belong to the person issuing the uustat command unless one is the super-user or uucp administrator. If the job is killed by the super-user or uucp administrator, electronic mail is sent to the user.

-m
    Report the status of accessibility of all machines.

-n
    Suppress all standard out output, but not standard error. The -n option is used in conjunction with the -k and -r options.

-p
    Execute the command ps -flp for all the process-ids that are in the lock files.

-q
    List the jobs queued for each machine. If a status file exists for the machine, its date, time and status information are reported. In addition, if a number appears in parentheses next to the number of C or X files, it is the age in days of the oldest C./X. file for that system. The Retry field represents the number of hours until the next possible call. The Count is the number of failure attempts. NOTE: for systems with a moderate number of outstanding jobs, this could take 30 seconds or more of real-time to execute. Here is an example of the output produced by the -q option:

```
eagle      3C     04/07-11:07    NO DEVICES AVAILABLE
mh3bs3     2C     07/07-10:42    SUCCESSFUL
```

The above output tells how many command files are waiting for each system. Each command file may have zero or more files to be sent (zero means to call the system and see if work is to be done). The date and time refer to the previous interaction with the system followed by the status of the interaction.

-rjobid   Rejuvenate *jobid*. The files associated with *jobid* are touched so that their modification time is set to the current time. This prevents the cleanup daemon from deleting the job until the jobs' modification time reaches the limit imposed by the daemon.

Here are the options that provide remote system performance information, in terms of average transfer rates or average queue times; the -c and -d options can only be used in conjunction with the -t option:

-tsystem   Report the average transfer rate or average queue time for the past 60 minutes for the remote *system*. The following parameters can only be used with this option:

-dnumber   *number* is specified in minutes. Used to override the 60 minute default used for calculations. These calculations are based on information contained in the optional performance log and therefore may not be available. Calculations can only be made from the time that the performance log was last cleaned up.

-c   Average queue time is calculated when the -c parameter is specified and average transfer rate when -c is not specified. For example, the command

```
uustat -teagle -d50 -c
```

produces output in the following format:

```
average queue time to eagle for last 50 minutes: 5 seconds
```

The same command without the -c parameter produces output in the following format:

```
average transfer rate with eagle for last 50 minutes: 2000.88
bytes/sec
```

Here are the options that provide general remote system-specific and user-specific status of uucp connections to other systems. Either or both of the following options can be specified with *uustat*. The -j option can only be used in conjunction with the -s or -a option to list the total number of jobs displayed:

-ssystem   Report the status of all uucp requests for remote system *system*.

-uuser   Report the status of all uucp requests issued by *user*.

Output for both the -s and -u options has the following format:

```
eagleN1bd7   4/07-11:07  S   eagle   dan   522     /home/dan/A
eagleC1bd8   4/07-11:07  S   eagle   dan   59      D.3b2al2ce4924
             4/07-11:07  S   eagle   dan   rmail   mike
```

With the above two options, the first field is the *jobid* of the job. This is followed by the date/time. The next field is an S if the job is sending a file or an R if the job is requesting a file. The next field is the machine where the file is to be transferred. This is followed by the user-id of the user who queued the job. The next field contains the size of the file, or in the case of a remote execution (rmail is the command used for remote mail), the name of the command. When the size appears in this field, the file name is also given. This can either be the name given by the user or an internal name (for example, D.3b2alce4924) that is created for data files associated with remote executions (rmail in this example).

-S*qric* Report the job state: q for queued jobs, r for running jobs, i for interrupted jobs, and c for completed jobs.

A job is queued if the transfer has not started. A job is running when the transfer has begun. A job is interrupted if the transfer began but was terminated before the file was completely transferred. A completed job, of course, is a job that successfully transferred. The completed state information is maintained in the accounting log, which is optional and therefore may be unavailable. The parameters can be used in any combination, but at least one parameter must be specified. The -S option can also be used with -s and -u options. The output for this option is exactly like the output for -s and -u except that the job states are appended as the last output word. Output for a completed job has the following format:

```
eagleC1bd3 completed
```

When no options are given, uustat outputs the status of all uucp requests issued by the current user.

FILES

```
/var/spool/uucp/*          spool directories
/var/uucp/.Admin/account   accounting log
/var/uucp/.Admin/perflog   performance log
```

SEE ALSO

uucp(1C)

DIAGNOSTICS

The -t option produces no message when the data needed for the calculations is not being recorded.

NOTES

After the user has issued the uucp request, if the file to be transferred is moved or deleted or was not copied to the spool directory with the -C option when the uucp request was made, uustat reports a file size of -99999. This job will eventually fail because the file(s) to be transferred can not be found.

NAME

uuto, uupick - public UNIX-to-UNIX system file copy

SYNOPSIS

uuto [*options*] *source-files destination*
uupick [-s *system*]

DESCRIPTION

uuto sends *source-files* to *destination*. uuto uses the uucp(1C) facility to send files, while it allows the local system to control the file access. A source-file name is a path name on your machine. Destination has the form:

system[! *system*] ... ! *user*

where system is taken from a list of system names that uucp knows about [see uuname(1C)]. *user* is the login name of someone on the specified system.

Two options are available:

-p   Copy the source file into the spool directory before transmission.
-m   Send mail to the sender when the copy is complete.

The files (or sub-trees if directories are specified) are sent to *PUBDIR* on system, where *PUBDIR* is a public directory defined in the uucp source. By default, this directory is /var/spool/uucppublic. Specifically the files are sent to

PUBDIR/receive/*user*/*mysystem*/files.

The destined recipient is notified by mail(1) of the arrival of files.

uupick accepts or rejects the files transmitted to the user. Specifically, uupick searches *PUBDIR* for files destined for the user. For each entry (file or directory) found, the following message is printed on the standard output:

from system *sysname* : [file *file-name*] [dir *dirname*] ?

uupick then reads a line from the standard input to determine the disposition of the file:

<new-line>	Go on to next entry.
d	Delete the entry.
m [*dir*]	Move the entry to named directory *dir*. If *dir* is not specified as a complete path name (in which $HOME is legitimate), a destination relative to the current directory is assumed. If no destination is given, the default is the current directory.
a [*dir*]	Same as m except moving all the files sent from system.
p	Print the content of the file.
q	Stop.
EOT (CTRL-d)	Same as q.
! *command*	Escape to the shell to do *command*.
*	Print a command summary.

uupick invoked with the -s *system* option will only search the *PUBDIR* for files sent from system.

FILES

PUBDIR   `/var/spool/uucppublic`   public directory

SEE ALSO

`mail`(1), `uucp`(1C), `uustat`(1C), `uucleanup`(1M), `uux`(1C).

NOTES

In order to send files that begin with a dot (for example, .profile), the files must be qualified with a dot. For example, the following files are correct:

```
.profile
.prof*
.profil?
```

The following files are incorrect:

```
*prof*
?profile
```

NAME

uux - UNIX-to-UNIX system command execution

SYNOPSIS

uux [*options*] *command-string*

DESCRIPTION

uux will gather zero or more files from various systems, execute a command on a specified system and then send standard output to a file on a specified system.

NOTE: For security reasons, most installations limit the list of commands executable on behalf of an incoming request from uux, permitting only the receipt of mail [see mail(1)]. Remote execution permissions are defined in /etc/uucp/Permissions.

The *command-string* is made up of one or more arguments that look like a shell command line, except that the command and filenames may be prefixed by *system-name!*. A null *system-name* is interpreted as the local system.

File names may be one of:

    (1)   a full path name;

    (2)   a path name preceded by ~*xxx*, where *xxx* is a login name on the specified system and is replaced by that user's login directory;

    (3)   anything else is prefixed by the current directory.

As an example, the command

```
uux    "!diff   sys1!/home/dan/file1   sys2!/a4/dan/file2   >
!~/dan/file.diff"
```

will get the *file1* and *file2* files from the sys1 and sys2 machines, execute a diff(1) command and put the results in *file.diff* in the local *PUBDIR*/dan/ directory. *PUBDIR* is a public directory defined in the uucp source. By default, this directory is /var/spool/uucppublic.

Any special shell characters such as <, >, ;, | should be quoted either by quoting the entire *command-string*, or quoting the special characters as individual arguments.

uux will attempt to get all appropriate files to the specified system where they will be processed. For files that are output files, the filename must be escaped using parentheses. For example, the command:

```
uux "a!cut -f1 b!/usr/file > c!/usr/file"
```

gets /usr/file from system b and sends it to system a performs a cut command on that file and sends the result of the cut command to system c.

uux will notify you if the requested command on the remote system was disallowed. This notification can be turned off by the -n option. The response comes by remote mail from the remote machine.

The following *options* are interpreted by uux:

    −   The standard input to uux is made the standard input to the *command-string*.

-a*name*   Use *name* as the user job identification replacing the initiator user-ID. (Notification will be returned to user-ID *name*.)

-b   Return whatever standard input was provided to the uux command if the exit status is non-zero.

-c   Do not copy local file to the spool directory for transfer to the remote machine (default).

-C   Force the copy of local files to the spool directory for transfer.

-g*grade*   *grade* can be either a single letter, number, or a string of alphanumeric characters defining a service grade. The *uuglist*(1C) command determines whether it is appropriate to use the single letter, number, or a string of alphanumeric characters as a service grade. The output from the *uuglist* command will be a list of service grades that are available or a message that says to use a single letter or number as a grade of service.

-j   Output the job ID string on the standard output which is the job identification. This job identification can be used by uustat(1C) to obtain the status or terminate a job.

-n   Do not notify the user if the command fails.

-p   Same as -: The standard input to uux is made the standard input to the *command-string*.

-r   Do not start the file transfer, just queue the job.

-s*file*   Report status of the transfer in *file*.

-x*debug_level*
           Produce debugging output on the standard output. *debug_level* is a number between 0 and 9; as it increases to 9, more detailed debugging information is given.

-z   Send success notification to the user.

FILES

```
/var/spool/uucp           spool directories
/etc/uucp/Permissions     remote execution permissions
/usr/lib/uucp/*           other programs
/etc/uucp/*               other data and programs
```

NOTES

Only the first command of a shell pipeline may have a *system-name!*. All other commands are executed on the system of the first command.

The use of the shell metacharacter * will probably not do what you want it to do. The shell tokens << and >> are not implemented.

The execution of commands on remote systems takes place in an execution directory known to the uucp system. All files required for the execution will be put into this directory unless they already reside on that machine. Therefore, the simple filename (without path or machine reference) must be unique within the uux request. The following command will not work:

```
uux "a!diff b!/home/dan/xyz c!/home/dan/xyz > !xyz.diff"
```

The following command will work if `diff` is a permitted command:

```
uux "a!diff a!/home/dan/xyz c!/home/dan/xyz > !xyz.diff"
```

Protected files and files that are in protected directories that are owned by the requester can be sent in commands using uux. However, if the requester is `root`, and the directory is not searchable by `other`, the request will fail.

INTERNATIONAL FUNCTIONS

uux can process characters from supplementary code sets.

SEE ALSO

cut(1), mail(1), uuglist(1C), uucp(1C), uustat(1C).

NAME

uuxqt - execute remote command requests

SYNOPSIS

/usr/lib/uucp/uuxqt [*options*]

DESCRIPTION

uuxqt is the program that executes remote job requests from remote systems generated by the use of the uux command. (mail uses uux for remote mail requests). uuxqt searches the spool directories looking for execution requests. For each request, uuxqt checks to see if all the required data files are available, accessible, and the requested commands are permitted for the requesting system. The Permissions file is used to validate file accessibility and command execution permission.

There are two environment variables that are set before the uuxqt command is executed:

UU_MACHINE is the machine that sent the job (the previous one).
UU_USER is the user that sent the job.

These can be used in writing commands that remote systems can execute to provide information, auditing, or restrictions. uuxqt has the following options:

-s*system*   Specifies the remote system name.

-x*debug_level*   *debug_level* is a number from 0 to 9. Higher numbers give more detailed debugging information.

FILES

/etc/uucp/Permissions
/etc/uucp/Limits
/var/spool/uucp/*
/var/spool/locks/*

SEE ALSO

mail(1), uucico(1M), uucp(1C), uustat(1C), uux(1C).

NAME

vacation - automatically respond to incoming mail messages

SYNOPSIS

`vacation` [-M *canned_msg_file*] [-l *logfile*] [-m *savefile*] [-d] [-f *forward-id*] [-F *forward-id*]

`vacation -n`

DESCRIPTION

When a new mail message arrives, the `mail` command first checks the recipient's forwarding file, `/var/mail/:forward/`*user*, to see if the message is to be forwarded elsewhere (to some other recipient or as the input to some command). `vacation` is used to set up forwarding via a Post-Processing Personal Surrogate so that the new message is both saved into the user's mailbox and a canned response is sent to the message's originator.

NOTE: If you are using `/usr/bin/vacation`, you must use `/bin/mail/` as the mail delivery agent. `/usr/bin/vacation` does not work with the default delivery agents used by `sendmail`(1M).

Command-line options are:

-l *logfile*   File to keep track of which originators have already seen the canned response. If not specified, it defaults to `$HOME/.maillog`. The log file prevents the originator from seeing the vacation message multiple times.

-M *canned_msg_file*
File to send back as the canned response. If *canned_msg_file* is not specified, it defaults to `/usr/share/lib/mail/std_vac_msg`, which contains:

```
Subject: AUTOANSWERED!!!

I am on vacation. I will read (and answer if necessary)
your e-mail message when I return.

This message was generated automatically and you will
receive it only once, although all messages you send
me while I am away WILL be saved.
```

-m *savefile*   Normally, the user's mailbox is used to store the mail. This option allows a different filename to be specified. If the file cannot be written, the user's mailbox will be used.

-f *forwarding-id*
The mail will be forwarded to this user id in addition to being stored in the user's mailbox.

-i *forwarding-id*
The mail will be forwarded to this user id *instead* of being stored in the user's mailbox. If both -f and -i are given, the mail will not be stored in the user's mailbox.

-d   The day's date will be appended to the filename specified by -m.

    -n   Remove the `vacation` processing. It is equivalent to using

                    `mail -F " "`

FILES

    /usr/share/lib/mail/std_vac_msg   default canned response
    /var/mail/*   users' standard mailboxes
    /var/mail/:forward/*   users' forwarding information
    /usr/lib/mail/vacation2   program that actually sends back the
                                         canned response

SEE ALSO

    `mail`(1), `vacation_bsd`(1).

NOTES

vacation uses the personal surrogate facility of `mail` to implement notifications.

If you are using `/usr/bin/vacation`, you must use `/bin/mail` as the mail delivery agent.

NAME

vacation - reply to mail automatically

SYNOPSIS

/usr/ucb/vacation [-I]
/usr/ucb/vacation [-j] [-a*alias*] [-t*N*] *username*

DESCRIPTION

vacation automatically replies to incoming mail. The reply is contained in the file
.vacation.msg, that you create in your home directory.

NOTE: If you are using /usr/ucb/vacation, you must use
/usr/ucblib/sendmail as the mail delivery agent.

This file should include a header with at least a 'Subject:' line (it should not
include a 'From:' or a 'To:' line). For example:

```
Subject: I am on vacation
I am on vacation until July 22.  If you have something urgent,
please contact Joe Jones (jones@f40).
        --John
```

If the string $SUBJECT appears in the .vacation.msg file, it is replaced with the
subject of the original message when the reply is sent; thus, a .vacation.msg file
such as

```
Subject: I am on vacation
I am on vacation until July 22.
Your mail regarding "$SUBJECT" will be read when I return.
If you have something urgent, please contact
Joe Jones (jones@f40).
        --John
```

will include the subject of the message in the reply.

No message is sent if the 'To:' or the 'Cc:' line does not list the user to whom the
original message was sent or one of a number of aliases for them, if the initial From
line includes the string -REQUEST@, or if a 'Precedence: bulk' or 'Precedence:
junk' line is included in the header.

The following options are available:

-I   Initialize the .vacation.pag and .vacation.dir files and start
           /usr/ucb/vacation.

If the -I flag is not specified, and a *user* argument is given, /usr/ucb/vacation
reads the first line from the standard input (for a 'From:' line, no colon). If absent,
it produces an error message. The following options may be specified:

-a*alias* Indicate that *alias* is one of the valid aliases for the user running
           /usr/ucb/vacation, so that mail addressed to that alias generates a
           reply.

-j   Do not check whether the recipient appears in the 'To: ' or the 'Cc:'
           line.

> `-tN`   Change the interval between repeat replies to the same sender. The default is 1 week. A trailing `s`, `m`, `h`, `d`, or `w` scales *N* to seconds, minutes, hours, days, or weeks respectively.

USAGE

To start `/usr/ucb/vacation`, create a `.forward` file in your home directory containing a line of the form:

> `\`*username*, `"|/usr/ucb/vacation` *username*`"`

where *username* is your login name.

Then type in the command:

> `/usr/ucb/vacation -I`

To stop `/usr/ucb/vacation`, remove the `.forward` file, or move it to a new name.

If `/usr/ucb/vacation` is run with no arguments, it will permit you to interactively turn `/usr/ucb/vacation` on or off. It will create a `.vacation.msg` file for you, or edit an existing one, using the editor specified by the `VISUAL` or `EDITOR` environment variable, or `vi`(1) if neither of those environment variables are set. If a `.forward` file is present in your home directory, it will ask whether you want to remove it and turn off `/usr/ucb/vacation`. If it is not present in your home directory, it creates it for you, and automatically performs a '`/usr/ucb/vacation -I`' function, turning on `/usr/ucb/vacation`.

FILES

`~/.forward`
`~/.vacation.mesg`

A list of senders is kept in the files `.vacation.pag` and `.vacation.dir` in your home directory.

SEE ALSO

`sendmail`(1M), `vi`(1).

NAME

val - validate an SCCS file

SYNOPSIS

val -

val [-s] [-r*SID*] [-m*name*] [-y*type*] *files*

DESCRIPTION

val determines if the specified *file* is an SCCS file meeting the characteristics specified by the optional argument list. Arguments to val may appear in any order. The arguments consist of keyletter arguments, which begin with a -, and named files.

val has a special argument, -, which causes reading of the standard input until an end-of-file condition is detected. Each line read is independently processed as if it were a command line argument list.

val generates diagnostic messages on the standard output for each command line and file processed, and also returns a single 8-bit code on exit as described below.

The keyletter arguments are defined as follows. The effects of any keyletter argument apply independently to each named file on the command line.

-s   The presence of this argument silences the diagnostic message normally generated on the standard output for any error that is detected while processing each named file on a given command line.

-r*SID*   The argument value *SID* (SCCS identification string) is an SCCS delta number. A check is made to determine if the *SID* is ambiguous (for example, -r1 is ambiguous because it physically does not exist but implies 1.1, 1.2, and so on, which may exist) or invalid (for example, r1.0 or r1.1.0 are invalid because neither can exist as a valid delta number). If the *SID* is valid and not ambiguous, a check is made to determine if it actually exists.

-m*name*   The argument value *name* is compared with the SCCS %M% keyword in *file*.

-y*type*   The argument value *type* is compared with the SCCS %Y% keyword in *file*.

The 8-bit code returned by val is a disjunction of the possible errors; it can be interpreted as a bit string where (moving from left to right) set bits are interpreted as follows:

> bit 0 = missing file argument
> bit 1 = unknown or duplicate keyletter argument
> bit 2 = corrupted SCCS file
> bit 3 = cannot open file or file not SCCS
> bit 4 = *SID* is invalid or ambiguous
> bit 5 = *SID* does not exist
> bit 6 = %Y%, -y mismatch
> bit 7 = %M%, -m mismatch

val can process two or more files on a given command line and in turn can process multiple command lines (when reading the standard input). In these cases an aggregate code is returned: a logical OR of the codes generated for each command line and file processed.

SEE ALSO

admin(1), delta(1), get(1), help(1, prs(1)

DIAGNOSTICS

Use help(1) for explanations.

NOTES

val can process up to 50 files on a single command line.

NAME

vc - version control

SYNOPSIS

vc [-a] [-t] [-c*char*] [-s] [*keyword=value ... keyword=value*]

DESCRIPTION

This command is obsolete and will be removed in the next release.

The vc command copies lines from the standard input to the standard output under control of its arguments and of control statements encountered in the standard input. In the process of performing the copy operation, user-declared *keyword*s may be replaced by their string *value* when they appear in plain text and/or control statements.

The copying of lines from the standard input to the standard output is conditional, based on tests (in control statements) of keyword values specified in control statements or as vc command arguments.

A control statement is a single line beginning with a control character, except as modified by the -t keyletter (see below). The default control character is colon (:), except as modified by the -c keyletter (see below). Input lines beginning with a backslash (\) followed by a control character are not control lines and are copied to the standard output with the backslash removed. Lines beginning with a backslash followed by a non-control character are copied in their entirety.

A keyword is composed of 9 or less alphanumerics; the first must be alphabetic. A value is any ASCII string that can be created with ed; a numeric value is an unsigned string of digits. Keyword values may not contain blanks or tabs.

Replacement of keywords by values is done whenever a keyword surrounded by control characters is encountered on a version control statement. The -a keyletter (see below) forces replacement of keywords in all lines of text. An uninterpreted control character may be included in a value by preceding it with \. If a literal \ is desired, then it too must be preceded by \.

The following options are valid:

-a   Forces replacement of keywords surrounded by control characters with their assigned value in all text lines and not just in vc statements.

-t   All characters from the beginning of a line up to and including the first tab character are ignored for the purpose of detecting a control statement. If a control statement is found, all characters up to and including the tab are discarded.

-c*char*   Specifies a control character to be used in place of the " : " default.

-s   Silences warning messages (not error) that are normally printed on the diagnostic output.

vc recognizes the following version control statements:

:dcl *keyword*[, ..., *keyword*]
          Declare keywords. All keywords must be declared.

`:asg` *keyword=value*

> Assign values to keywords. An `asg` statement overrides the assignment for the corresponding keyword on the `vc` command line and all previous `asg` statements for that keyword. Keywords that are declared but are not assigned values have null values.

`:if` *condition*

   ...

`:end`

> Skip lines of the standard input. If the condition is true, all lines between the `if` statement and the matching `end` statement are copied to the standard output. If the condition is false, all intervening lines are discarded, including control statements. Note that intervening `if` statements and matching `end` statements are recognized solely for the purpose of maintaining the proper `if-end` matching.
>
> The syntax of a condition is:

$$
\begin{array}{lll}
<cond> & ::= & [\ "not"\ ]\ <or> \\
<or> & ::= & <and>\ |\ <and>\ "|"\ <or> \\
<and> & ::= & <exp>\ |\ <exp>\ "\&"\ <and> \\
<exp> & ::= & "("\ <or>\ ")"\ |\ <value>\ <op>\ <value> \\
<op> & ::= & "="\ |\ "!="\ |\ "<"\ |\ ">" \\
<value> & ::= & <arbitrary\ ASCII\ string>\ |\ <numeric\ string>
\end{array}
$$

> The available operators and their meanings are:

=	equal
!=	not equal
&	and
|	or
>	greater than
<	less than
( )	used for logical groupings
not	may only occur immediately after the `if`, and when present, inverts the value of the entire condition

The `>` and `<` operate only on unsigned integer values (for example, `: 012 > 12` is false). All other operators take strings as arguments (for example, `: 012 != 12` is true).

The precedence of the operators (from highest to lowest) is:

> `= != > <` all of equal precedence
>
> `&`
>
> `|`

Parentheses may be used to alter the order of precedence.

Values must be separated from operators or parentheses by at least one blank or tab.

`::` *text*

> Replace keywords on lines that are copied to the standard output. The two leading control characters are removed, and keywords surrounded by

control characters in text are replaced by their value before the line is copied
to the output file. This action is independent of the -a keyletter.

`:on`
`:off` Turn on or off keyword replacement on all lines.

`:ctl` *char*
> Change the control character to *char*.

`:msg` *message*
> Print *message* on the diagnostic output.

`:err` *message*
> Print *message* followed by :
>
>   ERROR: err statement on line ... (915)

on the diagnostic output. vc halts execution and returns an exit code of 1.

EXAMPLE

If you have a file named `note` containing,

```
:dcl NAME PLACE
   :NAME:,
   Just a note to remind you that we
   have a meeting scheduled Monday
   morning at :PLACE:,
```

The command,

```
VC -a NAME=JOE PLACE=WIDGET INC. < note
```

will produce,

```
Joe
Just a note to remind you that we have
a meeting Monday morning at Widget Inc..
```

INTERNATIONAL FUNCTIONS

No international capability. *keyword* and *value* cannot be specified using characters
from supplementary code sets.

SEE ALSO

ed(1), help(1).

NAME

vi - screen-oriented (visual) display editor based on ex

SYNOPSIS

vi [-t *tag*] [-r *file*] [-l] [-L] [-w*n*] [-R] [-x] [-C] [-c *command*] *file*...
view [-t *tag*] [-r *file*] [-l] [-L] [-w*n*] [-R] [-x] [-C] [-c *command*] *file*...
vedit [-t *tag*] [-r *file*] [-l] [-L] [-w*n*] [-R] [-x] [-C] [-c *command*] *file*...

DESCRIPTION

vi (visual) is a display-oriented text editor based on an underlying line editor ex. It is possible to use the command mode of ex from within vi and vice-versa. The visual commands are described on this manual page; how to set options (like automatically numbering lines and automatically starting a new output line when you type carriage return) and all ex line editor commands are described on the ex(1) manual page.

When using vi, changes you make to the file are reflected in what you see on your terminal screen. The position of the cursor on the screen indicates the position within the file.

Invocation Options

The following invocation options are interpreted by vi (previously documented options are discussed in the NOTES section of this manual page):

-t *tag*　　　　　Edit the file containing the *tag* and position the editor at its definition.

-r *file*　　　　　Edit *file* after an editor or system crash. (Recovers the version of *file* that was in the buffer when the crash occurred.)

-l　　　　　　　Set up for editing LISP programs.

-L　　　　　　　List the name of all files saved as the result of an editor or system crash.

-w*n*　　　　　Set the default window size to *n*. This is useful when using the editor over a slow speed line.

-R　　　　　　Readonly mode; the readonly flag is set, preventing accidental overwriting of the file.

-x　　　　　　Encryption option; when used, vi simulates the X command of ex and prompts the user for a key. This key is used to encrypt and decrypt text using the algorithm of the crypt command. The X command makes an educated guess to determine whether text read in is encrypted or not. The temporary buffer file is encrypted also, using a transformed version of the key typed in for the -x option. See crypt(1). Also, see the WARNING section at the end of this manual page.

-C　　　　　　Encryption option; same as the -x option, except that vi simulates the C command of ex. The C command is like the X command of ex, except that all text read in is assumed to have been encrypted.

-c *command*　　Begin editing by executing the specified editor *command* (usually a search or positioning command).

The *file* argument indicates one or more files to be edited.

The *view* invocation is the same as vi except that the readonly flag is set.

The *vedit* invocation is intended for beginners. It is the same as vi except that the report flag is set to 1, the showmode and novice flags are set, and magic is turned off. These defaults make it easier to learn how to use vi.

vi Modes

Command	Normal and initial mode. Other modes return to command mode upon completion. ESC (escape) is used to cancel a partial command.
Input	Entered by setting any of the following options: a A i I o O c C s S R . Arbitrary text may then be entered. Input mode is normally terminated with ESC character, or, abnormally, with an interrupt.
Last line	Reading input for : / ? or !; terminate by typing a carriage return; an interrupt cancels termination.

COMMAND SUMMARY

In the descriptions, CR stands for carriage return and ESC stands for the escape key.

Sample commands

← ↓ ↑ →	arrow keys move the cursor
h j k l	same as arrow keys
i*text*ESC	insert *text*
cw*new*ESC	change word to *new*
ea*s*ESC	pluralize word (end of word; append s; escape from input state)
x	delete a character
dw	delete a word
dd	delete a line
3dd	delete 3 lines
u	undo previous change
ZZ	exit vi, saving changes
:q!CR	quit, discarding changes
/*text*CR	search for *text*
^U ^D	scroll up or down
:*cmd*CR	any ex or ed command

Counts before vi commands

Numbers may be typed as a prefix to some commands. They are interpreted in one of these ways.

line/column number	z G |
scroll amount	^D ^U
repeat effect	most of the rest

Interrupting, canceling

ESC	end insert or incomplete cmd
DEL	(delete or rubout) interrupts

File manipulation

ZZ	if file modified, write and exit; otherwise, exit
:wCR	write back changes
:w ! CR	forced write, if permission originally not valid
:qCR	quit
:q ! CR	quit, discard changes
:e *name*CR	edit file *name*
:e ! CR	reedit, discard changes
:e + *name*CR	edit, starting at end
:e +*n*CR	edit starting at line *n*
:e #CR	edit alternate file
:e ! #CR	edit alternate file, discard changes
:w *name*CR	write file *name*
:w ! *name*CR	overwrite file *name*
:shCR	run shell, then return
: ! *cmd*CR	run *cmd*, then return
:nCR	edit next file in arglist
:n *args*CR	specify new arglist
^G	show current file and line
:ta *tag*CR	position cursor to *tag*

In general, any ex or ed command (such as *substitute* or *global*) may be typed, preceded by a colon and followed by a carriage return.

Positioning within file

^F	forward screen
^B	backward screen
^D	scroll down half screen
^U	scroll up half screen
*n*G	go to the beginning of the specified line (end default), where *n* is a line number
/*pat*	next line matching *pat*
?*pat*	previous line matching *pat*
n	repeat last / or ? command
N	reverse last / or ? command
/*pat*/+*n*	nth line after *pat*
?*pat*?-*n*	nth line before *pat*
]]	next section/function
[[	previous section/function
(	beginning of sentence
)	end of sentence
{	beginning of paragraph
}	end of paragraph
%	find matching ( ) { or }

Adjusting the screen

^L	clear and redraw window
^R	clear and redraw window if ^L is → key
zCR	redraw screen with current line at top of window
z-CR	redraw screen with current line at bottom of window
z.CR	redraw screen with current line at center of window
/*pat*/z-CR	move *pat* line to bottom of window
z*n*.CR	use *n*-line window
^E	scroll window down 1 line
^Y	scroll window up 1 line

Marking and returning

`` ` ` ``	move cursor to previous context
´ ´	move cursor to first non-white space in line
m*x*	mark current position with the ASCII lower-case letter *x*
`` `x ``	move cursor to mark *x*
´*x*	move cursor to first non-white space in line marked by *x*

Line positioning

H	top line on screen
L	last line on screen
M	middle line on screen
+	next line, at first non-white
–	previous line, at first non-white
CR	return, same as +
↓ or j	next line, same column
↑ or k	previous line, same column

Character positioning

^	first non white-space character
0	beginning of line
$	end of line
h or →	forward
l or ←	backward
^H	same as←(backspace)
space	same as→(space bar)
f*x*	find next *x*
F*x*	find previous x
t*x*	move to character prior to next *x*
T*x*	move to character following previous *x*
;	repeat last f F t or T
´	repeat inverse of last f F t or T
n|	move to column *n*
%	find matching ({) or }

Words, sentences, paragraphs

w	forward a word
b	back a word
e	end of word
)	to next sentence
}	to next paragraph
(	back a sentence
{	back a paragraph
W	forward a blank-delimited word
B	back a blank-delimited word
E	end of a blank-delimited word

Corrections during insert

^H	erase last character (backspace)
^W	erase last word
erase	your erase character, same as ^H (backspace)
kill	your kill character, erase this line of input
\\	quotes your erase and kill characters
ESC	ends insertion, back to command mode
DEL	interrupt, terminates insert mode
^D	backtab one character; reset left margin of *autoindent*
^^D	caret (^) followed by control-d (^D); backtab to beginning of line; do not reset left margin of *autoindent*
0^D	backtab to beginning of line; reset left margin of *autoindent*
^V	quote non-printable character

Insert and replace

a	append after cursor
A	append at end of line
i	insert before cursor
I	insert before first non-blank
o	open line below
O	open above
r*x*	replace single char with *x*
R*text*ESC	replace characters

Operators

Operators are followed by a cursor motion, and affect all text that would have been moved over. For example, since w moves over a word, dw deletes the word that would be moved over. Double the operator, for example, dd to affect whole lines.

d	delete
c	change
y	yank lines to buffer
<	left shift
>	right shift
!	filter through command

Miscellaneous Operations

C	change rest of line (c$)
D	delete rest of line (d$)
s	substitute chars (c1)
S	substitute lines (cc)
J	join lines
x	delete characters (d1)
X	delete characters before cursor (dh)
Y	yank lines (yy)

Yank and Put

Put inserts the text most recently deleted or yanked; however, if a buffer is named (using the ASCII lower-case letters a - z), the text in that buffer is put instead.

3yy	yank 3 lines
3yl	yank 3 characters
p	put back text after cursor
P	put back text before cursor
"xp	put from buffer x
"xy	yank to buffer x
"xd	delete into buffer x

Undo, Redo, Retrieve

u	undo last change
U	restore current line
.	repeat last change
"dp	retrieve d'th last delete

AUTHOR

vi and ex were developed by The University of California, Berkeley California, Computer Science Division, Department of Electrical Engineering and Computer Science.

FILES

/tmp   default directory where temporary work files are placed; it can be changed using the directory option [see the ex(1) set command]

/usr/share/lib/terminfo/?/*
     compiled terminal description database

/usr/lib/.COREterm/?/*
     subset of compiled terminal description database

NOTES

Two options, although they continue to be supported, have been replaced in the documentation by options that follow the Command Syntax Standard [see intro(1)]. A -r option that is not followed with an option-argument has been replaced by -L and +*command* has been replaced by -c *command*.

The encryption options are provided with the Security Administration Utilities package, which is available only in the United States.

Tampering with entries in /usr/share/lib/terminfo/?/* or /usr/share/lib/terminfo/?/* (for example, changing or removing an entry) can affect programs such as vi that expect the entry to be present and correct. In particular, removing the "dumb" terminal may cause unexpected problems.

Software tabs using ^T work only immediately after the *autoindent*.

Left and right shifts on intelligent terminals do not make use of insert and delete character operations in the terminal.

INTERNATIONAL FUNCTIONS

vi can process and display characters from supplementary character sets using a consistant user interface.

All processing is in character units, not columns or bytes. Accordingly, in *command mode*, vi recognizes arguments to indicate the number of characters.

In regular expressions, also, processing is performed on characters, not bytes.

Multi-column characters are split over two lines when using the full screen width. vi displays the same number of ASCII > characters as the split character's display width.

For the commands r*x*, f*x*, F*x*, t*x*, and T*x*, the accompanying argument *x* must be a single-byte character.

SEE ALSO

ed(1), edit(1), ex(1)

NAME

volcopy (generic) - make literal copy of file system

SYNOPSIS

volcopy [-F *FSType*] [-V] [*current_options*] [-o *specific_options*] *operands*

DESCRIPTION

volcopy makes a literal copy of the file system.

current_options are options supported by the s5-specific module of volcopy. Other FSTypes do not necessarily support these options. *specific_options* indicate suboptions specified in a comma-separated list of suboptions and/or keyword-attribute pairs for interpretation by the *FSType*-specific module of the command. See volcopy_*FSType*(1M) for details.

operands generally include the device and volume names and are file system specific. See volcopy_*FSType*(1M) for details.

The options are:

-F   Specify the *FSType* on which to operate. The *FSType* should either be specified here or be determinable from /etc/vfstab by matching the *operands* with an entry in the table.

-V   Echo the complete command line, but do not execute the command. The command line is generated by using the options and arguments provided by the user and adding to them information derived from /etc/vfstab. This option should be used to verify and validate the command line.

-o   Specify *FSType*-specific options.

NOTE

This command may not be supported for all FSTypes.

FILES

/etc/vfstab   list of default parameters for each file system

SEE ALSO

volcopy_s5(1M), volcopy_ufs(1M), vfstab(4).

NAME

volcopy (s5) - make a literal copy of an s5 file system

SYNOPSIS

volcopy [-F s5] [*generic_options*] [-a] *fsname srcdevice volname1 destdevice volname2*

DESCRIPTION

generic_options are options supported by the generic volcopy command.

volcopy makes a literal copy of the s5 file system using a blocksize matched to the device.

The options are:

-F s5   Specify the s5-FSType.

-a   Invoke a verification sequence requiring a positive operator response instead of the standard 10 second delay before the copy is made.

The *fsname* argument represents the mounted name (e.g.: root, u1, etc.) of the file system being copied.

The *srcdevice* or *destdevice* should be the disk slice or tape (e.g.: /dev/rdsk/m328_c1d0s8, /dev/rdsk/m328_c1d1s8, etc.).

The *volname* is the physical volume name. Such label names are limited to six or fewer characters. *Volname* may be - to use the existing volume name.

Srcdevice and *volname1* are the device and volume from which the copy of the file system is being extracted. *Destdevice* and *volname2* are the target device and volume.

Fsname and *volname* are recorded in the superblock (char fsname[6], volname[6];).

NOTE

volcopy does not support tape-to-tape copying. Use dd(1M) for tape-to-tape copying.

FILES

/var/adm/log/filesave.log   a record of file systems/volumes copied

SEE ALSO

dd(1M), labelit(1M), generic volcopy(1M), cpio(4), fs(4).
cpio(1), sh(1).

NAME

volcopy (ufs) - make a literal copy of a ufs file system

SYNOPSIS

volcopy [-F ufs] [*generic_options*] [-a] *fsname srcdevice volname1 destdevice volname2*

DESCRIPTION

generic_options are options supported by the generic volcopy command.

volcopy makes a literal copy of the ufs file system using a blocksize matched to the device.

The *fsname* argument represents the mounted name (for example, root, u1, and so on) of the file system being copied.

The *srcdevice* or *destdevice* should be the physical disk section or tape (for example, /dev/rdsk/m328_c1d0s8, /dev/rdsk/m328_c1d1s8, etc.).

The *volname* is the physical volume name. Such label names are limited to six or fewer characters. *volname* may be '-' to use the existing volume name.

srcdevice and *volname1* are the device and volume from which the copy of the file system is being extracted. *destdevice* and *volname2* are the target device and volume.

fsname and *volname* are recorded in the superblock.

The options are:

-F ufs

        Specifies the ufs-FSType.

-a   Invoke a verification sequence requiring a positive operator response instead of the standard ten-second delay before the copy is made.

NOTE

volcopy does not support tape-to-tape copying. Use dd(1M) for tape-to-tape copying.

FILES

/var/adm/filesave.log   a record of file systems/volumes copied

SEE ALSO

cpio(1), dd(1M), labelit(1M), generic volcopy(1M), cpio(4), ufs(4).

NAME

vsig - synchronize a co-process with the controlling FMLI application

SYNOPSIS

vsig

DESCRIPTION

The vsig executable sends a SIGUSR2 signal to the controlling FMLI process. This signal/alarm causes FMLI to execute the FMLI built-in command checkworld which causes all posted objects with a reread descriptor evaluating to TRUE to be reread. vsig takes no arguments.

EXAMPLES

The following is a segment of a shell program:

```
echo "Sending this string to an FMLI process"
vsig
```

The vsig executable will flush the output buffer *before* it sends the SIGUSR2 signal to make sure the string is actually in the pipe created by the cocreate function.

NOTES

Because vsig synchronizes with FMLI, it should be used rather than kill to send a SIGUSR2 signal to FMLI.

SEE ALSO

coproc(1F), kill(1), kill(2), signal(2).

NAME

w - who is logged in, and what are they doing

SYNOPSIS

`/usr/ucb/w` [`-hls`] [*user*]

DESCRIPTION

The `w` command displays a summary of the current activity on the system, including what each user is doing. The heading line shows the current time of day, how long the system has been up, and the number of users logged into the system.

The fields displayed are: the users login name, the name of the tty the user is on, the time of day the user logged on (in *hours:minutes*), the idle time—that is, the number of minutes since the user last typed anything (in *hours:minutes*), the CPU time used by all processes and their children on that terminal (in *minutes:seconds*), the CPU time used by the currently active processes (in *minutes:seconds*), the name and arguments of the current process.

If a *user* name is included, output is restricted to that user.

The following options are available:

`-h`　　　Suppress the heading.

`-l`　　　Produce a long form of output, which is the default.

`-s`　　　Produce a short form of output. In the short form, the tty is abbreviated, the login time and CPU times are left off, as are the arguments to commands.

EXAMPLE

```
w
7:36am  up 6 days, 16:45,   1 users
User tty   login@      idle  JCPU  PCPU  what
ralph console    7:10am         1  10:05 4:31  w
```

FILES

`/var/adm/utmp`

SEE ALSO

`ps`(1), `who`(1), `whodo`(1M), `utmp`(4).

NOTES

The notion of the "current process" is muddy. The current algorithm is 'the highest numbered process on the terminal that is not ignoring interrupts, or, if there is none, the highest numbered process on the terminal'. This fails, for example, in critical sections of programs like the shell and editor, or when faulty programs running in the background fork and fail to ignore interrupts. In cases where no process can be found, `w` prints –.

The CPU time is only an estimate, in particular, if someone leaves a background process running after logging out, the person currently on that terminal is "charged" with the time.

Background processes are not shown, even though they account for much of the load on the system.

Sometimes processes, typically those in the background, are printed with null or garbaged arguments. In these cases, the name of the command is printed in parentheses.

w does not know about the conventions for detecting background jobs. It will sometimes find a background job instead of the right one.

NAME

wait - await completion of process

SYNOPSIS

wait [*n*]

DESCRIPTION

Wait for your background process whose process id is *n* and report its termination status. If *n* is omitted, all your shell's currently active background processes are waited for and the return code will be zero.

When the wait(1) command is invoked with an argument that is not a valid pid of a background process, wait exits immediately with a return value of 0. This differs from the System V Release 3 behavior of the command.

The shell itself executes wait, without creating a new process.

EXAMPLE

```
command1 &
c1_pid=$!
command2
wait $c1_pid
```

This sequence will start command1 running in the background and remember its process ID in c1_pid, then execute command2. When command2 finishes, the shell will wait until command1 is also finished before continuing.

SEE ALSO

sh(1).

NOTES

If you get the error message cannot fork, too many processes, try using the wait command to clean up your background processes. If this doesn't help, the system process table is probably full or you have too many active foreground processes. (There is a limit to the number of process ids associated with your login, and to the number the system can keep track of.)

Not all the processes of a 3- or more-stage pipeline are children of the shell, and thus cannot be waited for.

NAME

`wall` - write to all users

SYNOPSIS

`/usr/sbin/wall`

DESCRIPTION

`wall` reads its standard input until an end-of-file. It then sends this message to all currently logged-in users preceded by:

```
Broadcast Message from . . .
```

It is used to warn all users, typically prior to shutting down the system.

The sender must be super-user to override any protections the users may have invoked [see `mesg`(1)].

`wall` runs `setgid( )` [see `setuid`(2)] to the group ID `tty`, in order to have write permissions on other user's terminals.

`wall` will detect non-printable characters before sending them to the user's terminal. Control characters will appear as a '^' followed by the appropriate ASCII character; characters with the high-order bit set will appear in meta notation. For example, '`\003`' is displayed as '`^C`' and '`\372`' as '`M-z`'.

FILES

`/dev/tty*`

SEE ALSO

`mesg`(1), `write`(1)

NOTES

"Cannot send to . . ." when the open on a user's tty file fails.

NAME

wc - word count

SYNOPSIS

wc [-lwc] [*names*]

DESCRIPTION

wc counts lines, words, and characters in the named files, or in the standard input if no *names* appear. It also keeps a total count for all named files. A word is a maximal string of characters delimited by spaces, tabs, or newlines.

The options l, w, and c may be used in any combination to specify that a subset of lines, words, and characters are to be reported. The default is -lwc.

When *names* are specified on the command line, they will be printed along with the counts.

INTERNATIONAL FUNCTIONS

Files can contain characters from supplementary code sets.

With the -c option, characters from supplementary code sets are counted in bytes, not characters. With the -w option, characters from supplementary code sets are ignored during counting.

NAME

wchrtbl - generate character classification and conversion tables for ASCII and supplementary code sets

SYNOPSIS

```
wchrtbl [file]
```

DESCRIPTION

`wchrtbl` creates tables containing information on character classification, character conversion, character set width and numeric editing. The first table is a byte-sized array encoded such that a table lookup can be used to determine the character classification of a character, convert a character [see ctype(3C) and wctype(3W)] and find the byte and screen width of a character in one of the supplementary code sets. The size of the array is (257*2) + 7 bytes: 257 bytes are required for the 8-bit code set character classification table, 257 bytes for the upper- to lower-case and lower- to upper-case conversion table, and 7 bytes for character set width information. The second table is 2 bytes long and is encoded such that the first byte is used to specify the decimal delimiter and the second byte the thousand delimiter. If supplementary code sets are specified, additional variable sized tables are generated for multibyte character classification and conversion.

`wchrtbl` reads the user-defined character classification and conversion information from *file* and creates three output files in the current directory. One output file, `wctype.c` (a C-language source file), contains the variable sized array generated from processing the information from *file*. You should review the content of `wctype.c` to verify that the array is set up as you had planned. The first 257 bytes of the array in `wctype.c` are used for character classification for single byte characters. The characters used for initializing these bytes of the array represent character classifications that are defined in `/usr/include/ctype.h`; for example, `_L` means a character is lower case and `_S | _B` means the character is both a spacing character and a blank. The second 257 bytes of the array are used for character conversion. These bytes of the array are initialized so that characters for which you do not provide conversion information will be converted to themselves. When you do provide conversion information, the first value of the pair is stored where the second one would be stored normally, and vice versa; for example, if you provide `<0x41 0x61>`, then `0x61` is stored where `0x41` would be stored normally, and `0x61` is stored where `0x41` would be stored normally. The last 7 bytes are used for character width information. Up to three supplementary code sets can be specified.

For supplementary code sets, there are three sets of tables. The first set is three pointer arrays which point to supplementary code set information tables. If the corresponding supplementary code set information is not specified, the contents of the pointers are zeros. The second one is a set of three supplementary code set information tables. Each table contains minimum and maximum code values to be classified and converted, and also contains pointers to character classification and conversion tables. If there is no corresponding table, the contents of the pointers are zeros. The last one is a set of character classification and conversion tables which contain the same information as the single byte table except that the codes are represented as process codes and the table size is variable. The characters used for initializing values of the character classification table represent character classifications that are defined in `/usr/include/ctype.h` and `/usr/include/wctype.h`. `_E1` through `_E8` are for international use and `_E9` through `_E24` are for language dependent use.

The second output file (a data file) contains the same information, but is structured for efficient use by the character classification and conversion routines [see ctype(3C) and wctype(3W)]. The name of this output file is the value of the character classification LC_CTYPE read in from *file*. This output file must be copied to the /usr/lib/locale/*locale*/LC_CTYPE file by someone who is super-user or a member of group bin. This file must be readable by user, group, and other; no other permissions should be set. To use the character classification and conversion tables on this file, set the LC_CTYPE category of setlocale() [see setlocale(3C)] appropriately.

The third output file (a data file) is created only if numeric editing information is specified in the input file. The name of the file is the value of the character classification LC_NUMERIC read from the *file*. This output file must be copied to the /usr/lib/locale/*locale*/LC_NUMERIC file by someone who is super-user or a member of group bin. This file must be readable by user, group, and other; no other permissions should be set. To use the numeric editing information on this file, set the LC_NUMERIC category of setlocale() appropriately.

If no input file is given, or if the argument - is encountered, wchrtbl reads from standard input.

The syntax of *file* allows the user to define the name of the data file created by wchrtbl, the assignment of characters to character classifications, the relationship between conversion letters, and byte and screen widths for up to three supplementary code sets. The keywords recognized by wchrtbl are:

LC_CTYPE	name of the first data file to be created by wchrtbl
isupper	character codes to be classified as upper-case letters
islower	character codes to be classified as lower-case letters
isdigit	character codes to be classified as numeric
isspace	character codes to be classified as spacing (delimiter) characters
ispunct	character codes to be classified as punctuation characters
iscntrl	character codes to be classified as control characters
isblank	character code for the space character
isxdigit	character codes to be classified as hexadecimal digits
ul	relationship between conversion characters
cswidth	byte and screen width information
LC_NUMERIC	name of the second data file created by wchrtbl
decimal_point	decimal delimiters
thousands_sep	thousands delimiters
LC_CTYPE1	specify that functions for specification of supplementary code set 1 follows

`LC_CTYPE2`	specify that functions for specification of supplementary code set 2 follows
`LC_CTYPE3`	specify that functions for specification of supplementary code set 3 follows
`isphonogram(iswchar1)`	character codes to be classified as phonograms in supplementary code sets
`isideogram(iswchar2)`	character codes to be classified as ideograms in supplementary code sets
`isenglish(iswchar3)`	character codes to be classified as English letters in supplementary code sets
`isnumber(iswchar4)`	character codes to be classified as numeric in supplementary code sets
`isspecial(iswchar5)`	character codes to be classified as special letters in supplementary code sets
`iswchar6`	character codes to be classified as other printable letters in supplementary code sets
`iswchar7 - iswchar8`	reserved for international use
`iswchar9 - iswchar24`	character codes to be classified as language dependent letters/characters

The keywords `iswchar1` through `iswchar24` correspond to bit names `_E1` through `_E24` defined in `wctype.h`

Any lines with the number sign (#) in the first column are treated as comments and are ignored. Blank lines are also ignored.

Characters for `isupper`, `islower`, `isdigit`, `isspace`, `ispunct`, `iscntl`, `isblank`, `isxdigit`, `ul`, `isphonogram`, `isideogram`, `isenglish`, `isnumber`, `isspecial` and `iswchar1-iswchar24` can be represented as hexadecimal or octal constants (for example, the letter a can be represented as `0x61` in hexadecimal or `0141` in octal) and must be up to two byte process codes. Hexadecimal and octal constants may be separated by one or more space and tab characters.

The following is the format of an input specification for `cswidth` (byte widths for supplementary code sets 2 and 3 are exlusive of the Single Shift characters):

```
cswidth n1[[:s1][,n2[:s2][,n3[:s3]]]]
```

where,
`n1`	byte width for supplementary code set 1
`s1`	screen width for supplementary code set 1
`n2`	byte width for supplementary code set 2
`s2`	screen width for supplementary code set 2
`n3`	byte width for supplementary code set 3
`s3`	screen width for supplementary code set 3

The dash character (-) may be used to indicate a range of consecutive numbers (inclusive of the characters delimiting the range). Zero or more space characters may be used for separating the dash character from the numbers.

The backslash character (\) is used for line continuation. Only a carriage return is permitted after the backslash character.

The relationship between conversion letters (ul) is expressed as ordered pairs of octal or hexadecimal constants: *<converting-character converted-character>*. These two constants must be up to two byte process codes and may be separated by one or more space characters. Zero or more space characters may be used for separating the angle brackets (< >) from the numbers.

EXAMPLE

The following is an example of an input file used to create the JAPAN code set definition table on a file named LC_CTYPE and LC_NUMERIC.

```
#
# locale JAPAN
#
LC_CTYPE     LC_CTYPE
#
# specification for single byte characters
#
isupper        0x41 - 0x5a
islower        0x61 - 0x7a
isdigit        0x30 - 0x39
isspace        0x20    0x9 - 0xd
ispunct        0x21 - 0x2f      0x3a - 0x40   \
               0x5b - 0x60      0x7b - 0x7e
iscntrl        0x0 - 0x1f       0x7f - 0x9f
isblank        0x20
isxdigit  0x30 - 0x39    0x61 - 0x66 0x41 - 0x46
ul             <0x41 0x61> <0x42 0x62> <0x43 0x63> \
               <0x44 0x64> <0x45 0x65> <0x46 0x66> \
               <0x47 0x67> <0x48 0x68> <0x49 0x69> \
               <0x4a 0x6a> <0x4b 0x6b> <0x4c 0x6c> \
               <0x4d 0x6d> <0x4e 0x6e> <0x4f 0x6f> \
               <0x50 0x70> <0x51 0x71> <0x52 0x72> \
               <0x53 0x73> <0x54 0x74> <0x55 0x75> \
               <0x56 0x76> <0x57 0x77> <0x58 0x78> \
               <0x59 0x79> <0x5a 0x7a>
cswidth            2:2,1:1,2:2
LC_NUMERIC   LC_NUMERIC
decimal_point        .
thousands_sep
#
# specification for supplementary code set 1
#
LC_CTYPE1
isupper              0xa3c1 - 0xa3da
```

```
            islower          0xa3e1 - 0xa3fa
            isdigit          0xa3b0 - 0xa3b9
            isspace          0xa1a1
            isphonogram 0xa4a1 - 0xa4f3 0xa5a1 - 0xa5f6
            isideogram  0xb0a1 - 0xb0fe 0xb1a1 - 0xb1fe 0xb2a1 - 0xb2fe \
                        0xb3a1 - 0xb3fe 0xb4a1 - 0xb4fe 0xb5a1 - 0xb5fe \
                        0xb6a1 - 0xb6fe 0xb7a1 - 0xb7fe 0xb8a1 - 0xb8fe \
                        0xb9a1 - 0xb9fe 0xbaa1 - 0xbafe 0xbba1 - 0xbbfe \
                        0xbca1 - 0xbcfe 0xbda1 - 0xbdfe 0xbea1 - 0xbefe \
                        0xbfa1 - 0xbffe 0xc0a1 - 0xc0fe 0xc1a1 - 0xc1fe \
                        0xc2a1 - 0xc2fe 0xc3a1 - 0xc3fe 0xc4a1 - 0xc4fe \
                        0xc5a1 - 0xc5fe 0xc6a1 - 0xc6fe 0xc7a1 - 0xc7fe \
                        0xcca1 - 0xccfe 0xcda1 - 0xcdfe 0xcea1 - 0xcefe \
                        0xcfa1 - 0xcffe 0xd0a1 - 0xd0fe 0xd1a1 - 0xd1fe \
                        0xd2a1 - 0xd2fe 0xd3a1 - 0xd3fe 0xd4a1 - 0xd4fe \
                        0xd5a1 - 0xd5fe 0xd6a1 - 0xd6fe 0xd7a1 - 0xd7fe \
                        0xd8a1 - 0xd8fe 0xd9a1 - 0xd9fe 0xdaa1 - 0xdafe \
                        0xdba1 - 0xdbfe 0xdca1 - 0xdcfe 0xdda1 - 0xddfe \
                        0xdea1 - 0xdefe 0xdfa1 - 0xdffe 0xe0a1 - 0xe0fe \
                        0xe1a1 - 0xe1fe 0xe2a1 - 0xe2fe 0xe3a1 - 0xe3fe \
                        0xe4a1 - 0xe4fe 0xe5a1 - 0xe5fe 0xe6a1 - 0xe6fe \
                        0xe7a1 - 0xe7fe 0xe8a1 - 0xe8fe 0xe9a1 - 0xe9fe \
                        0xeaa1 - 0xeafe 0xeba1 - 0xebfe 0xeca1 - 0xecfe \
                        0xeda1 - 0xedfe 0xeea1 - 0xeefe 0xefa1 - 0xeffe \
                        0xf0a1 - 0xf0fe 0xf1a1 - 0xf1fe 0xf2a1 - 0xf2fe \
                        0xf3a1 - 0xf3fe 0xf4a1 - 0xf4fe 0xf5a1 - 0xf5fe \
                        0xf6a1 - 0xf6fe 0xf7a1 - 0xf7fe 0xf8a1 - 0xf8fe \
                        0xf9a1 - 0xf9fe 0xfaa1 - 0xfafe 0xfba1 - 0xfbfe \
                        0xfca1 - 0xfcfe 0xfda1 - 0xfdfe 0xfea1 - 0xfefe \
            isenglish   0xa3c1 - 0xa3da 0xa3e1 - 0xa3fa
            isnumber    0xa3b0 - 0xa3b9
            isspecial   0xa1a2 - 0xa1fe 0xa2a1 - 0xa2ae 0xa2ba - 0xa2c1 \
                        0xa2ca - 0xa2d0 0xa2dc - 0xa2ea 0xa2f2 - 0xa2f9 \
                        0xa2fe
            iswchar6    0xa6a1 - 0xa6b8 0xa6c1 - 0xa6d8 0xa7a1 - 0xa7c1 \
                        0xa7d1 - 0xa7f1
            #
            #           JIS X0208 whole code set
            #
            iswchar9    0xa1a1 - 0xa1fe 0xa2a1 - 0xa2fe 0xa3a1 - 0xa3fe \
                        0xa4a1 - 0xa4fe 0xa5a1 - 0xa5fe 0xa6a1 - 0xa6fe \
                        0xa7a1 - 0xa7fe 0xa8a1 - 0xa8fe 0xa9a1 - 0xa9fe \
                        0xaaa1 - 0xaafe 0xaba1 - 0xabfe 0xaca1 - 0xacfe \
                        0xada1 - 0xadfe 0xaea1 - 0xaefe 0xafa1 - 0xaffe \
                        0xb0a1 - 0xb0fe 0xb1a1 - 0xb1fe 0xb2a1 - 0xb2fe \
                        0xb3a1 - 0xb3fe 0xb4a1 - 0xb4fe 0xb5a1 - 0xb5fe \
                        0xb6a1 - 0xb6fe 0xb7a1 - 0xb7fe 0xb8a1 - 0xb8fe \
                        0xb9a1 - 0xb9fe 0xbaa1 - 0xbafe 0xbba1 - 0xbbfe \
                        0xbca1 - 0xbcfe 0xbda1 - 0xbdfe 0xbea1 - 0xbefe \
                        0xbfa1 - 0xbffe 0xc0a1 - 0xc0fe 0xc1a1 - 0xc1fe \
```

```
                    0xc2a1 - 0xc2fe 0xc3a1 - 0xc3fe 0xc4a1 - 0xc4fe \
                    0xc5a1 - 0xc5fe 0xc6a1 - 0xc6fe 0xc7a1 - 0xc7fe \
                    0xc8a1 - 0xc8fe 0xc9a1 - 0xc9fe 0xcaa1 - 0xcafe \
                    0xcba1 - 0xcbfe 0xcca1 - 0xccfe 0xcda1 - 0xcdfe \
                    0xcea1 - 0xcefe 0xcfa1 - 0xcffe 0xd0a1 - 0xd0fe \
                    0xd1a1 - 0xd1fe 0xd2a1 - 0xd2fe 0xd3a1 - 0xd3fe \
                    0xd4a1 - 0xd4fe 0xd5a1 - 0xd5fe 0xd6a1 - 0xd6fe \
                    0xd7a1 - 0xd7fe 0xd8a1 - 0xd8fe 0xd9a1 - 0xd9fe \
                    0xdaa1 - 0xdafe 0xdba1 - 0xdbfe 0xdca1 - 0xdcfe \
                    0xdda1 - 0xddfe 0xdea1 - 0xdefe 0xdfa1 - 0xdffe \
                    0xe0a1 - 0xe0fe 0xe1a1 - 0xe1fe 0xe2a1 - 0xe2fe \
                    0xe3a1 - 0xe3fe 0xe4a1 - 0xe4fe 0xe5a1 - 0xe5fe \
                    0xe6a1 - 0xe6fe 0xe7a1 - 0xe7fe 0xe8a1 - 0xe8fe \
                    0xe9a1 - 0xe9fe 0xeaa1 - 0xeafe 0xeba1 - 0xebfe \
                    0xeca1 - 0xecfe 0xeda1 - 0xedfe 0xeea1 - 0xeefe \
                    0xefa1 - 0xeffe 0xf0a1 - 0xf0fe 0xf1a1 - 0xf1fe \
                    0xf2a1 - 0xf2fe 0xf3a1 - 0xf3fe 0xf4a1 - 0xf4fe \
                    0xf5a1 - 0xf5fe 0xf6a1 - 0xf6fe 0xf7a1 - 0xf7fe \
                    0xf8a1 - 0xf8fe 0xf9a1 - 0xf9fe 0xfaa1 - 0xfafe \
                    0xfba1 - 0xfbfe 0xfca1 - 0xfcfe 0xfda1 - 0xfdfe \
                    0xfea1 - 0xfefe
#
#                   JIS X0208 parentheses
#
iswchar10           0xa1c6 - 0xa1db
#
#                   JIS X0208 hiragana
#
iswchar11           0xa4a1 - 0xa4f3
#
#                   JIS X0208 katakana
#
iswchar12           0xa5a1 - 0xa5f6
#
#                   JIS X0208 other characters
#
iswchar13           0xa6a1 - 0xa6b8 0xa6c1 - 0xa6d8 0xa7a1 - 0xa7c1 \
                    0xa7d1 - 0xa7f1 0xa8a1 - 0xa8bf
#
#                   English letter translation table
#
ul                  <0xa3c1 0xa3e1> <0xa3c2 0xa3e2> <0xa3c3 0xa3e3> \
                    <0xa3c4 0xa3e4> <0xa3c5 0xa3e5> <0xa3c6 0xa3e6> \
                    <0xa3c7 0xa3e7> <0xa3c8 0xa3e8> <0xa3c9 0xa3e9> \
                    <0xa3ca 0xa3ea> <0xa3cb 0xa3eb> <0xa3cc 0xa3ec> \
                    <0xa3cd 0xa3ed> <0xa3ce 0xa3ee> <0xa3cf 0xa3ef> \
                    <0xa3d0 0xa3f0> <0xa3d1 0xa3f1> <0xa3d2 0xa3f2> \
                    <0xa3d3 0xa3f3> <0xa3d4 0xa3f4> <0xa3d5 0xa3f5> \
                    <0xa3d6 0xa3f6> <0xa3d7 0xa3f7> <0xa3d8 0xa3f8> \
                    <0xa3d9 0xa3f9> <0xa3da 0xa3fa> \
```

```
#
#               kana translation table
#
                <0xa4a1 0xa5a1> <0xa4a2 0xa5a2> <0xa4a3 0xa5a3> \
                <0xa4a4 0xa5a4> <0xa4a5 0xa5a5> <0xa4a6 0xa5a6> \
                <0xa4a7 0xa5a7> <0xa4a8 0xa5a8> <0xa4a9 0xa5a9> \
                <0xa4aa 0xa5aa> <0xa4ab 0xa5ab> <0xa4ac 0xa5ac> \
                <0xa4ad 0xa5ad> <0xa4ae 0xa5ae> <0xa4af 0xa5af> \
                <0xa4b0 0xa5b0> <0xa4b1 0xa5b1> <0xa4b2 0xa5b2> \
                <0xa4b3 0xa5b3> <0xa4b4 0xa5b4> <0xa4b5 0xa5b5> \
                <0xa4b6 0xa5b6> <0xa4b7 0xa5b7> <0xa4b8 0xa5b8> \
                <0xa4b9 0xa5b9> <0xa4ba 0xa5ba> <0xa4bb 0xa5bb> \
                <0xa4bc 0xa5bc> <0xa4bd 0xa5bd> <0xa4be 0xa5be> \
                <0xa4bf 0xa5bf> <0xa4c0 0xa5c0> <0xa4c1 0xa5c1> \
                <0xa4c2 0xa5c2> <0xa4c3 0xa5c3> <0xa4c4 0xa5c4> \
                <0xa4c5 0xa5c5> <0xa4c6 0xa5c6> <0xa4c7 0xa5c7> \
                <0xa4c8 0xa5c8> <0xa4c9 0xa5c9> <0xa4ca 0xa5ca> \
                <0xa4cb 0xa5cb> <0xa4cc 0xa5cc> <0xa4cd 0xa5cd> \
                <0xa4ce 0xa5ce> <0xa4cf 0xa5cf> <0xa4d0 0xa5d0> \
                <0xa4d1 0xa5d1> <0xa4d2 0xa5d2> <0xa4d3 0xa5d3> \
                <0xa4d4 0xa5d4> <0xa4d5 0xa5d5> <0xa4d6 0xa5d6> \
                <0xa4d7 0xa5d7> <0xa4d8 0xa5d8> <0xa4d9 0xa5d9> \
                <0xa4da 0xa5da> <0xa4db 0xa5db> <0xa4dc 0xa5dc> \
                <0xa4dd 0xa5dd> <0xa4de 0xa5de> <0xa4df 0xa5df> \
                <0xa4e0 0xa5e0> <0xa4e1 0xa5e1> <0xa4e2 0xa5e2> \
                <0xa4e3 0xa5e3> <0xa4e4 0xa5e4> <0xa4e5 0xa5e5> \
                <0xa4e6 0xa5e6> <0xa4e7 0xa5e7> <0xa4e8 0xa5e8> \
                <0xa4e9 0xa5e9> <0xa4ea 0xa5ea> <0xa4eb 0xa5eb> \
                <0xa4ec 0xa5ec> <0xa4ed 0xa5ed> <0xa4ee 0xa5ee> \
                <0xa4ef 0xa5ef> <0xa4f0 0xa5f0> <0xa4f1 0xa5f1> \
                <0xa4f2 0xa5f2> <0xa4f3 0xa5f3>
#
# specification for supplementary code set 2
#
LC_CTYPE2
iswchar6        0xa1 - 0xdf
iswchar14       0xa1 - 0xdf
```

FILES

`/usr/lib/locale/`*locale*`/LC_CTYPE`
>   data files containing character classification and conversion
>   tables and character set width information created by `chrtbl` or
>   `wchrtbl`.

`/usr/lib/locale/`*locale*`/LC_NUMERIC`
>   data files containing numeric editing information.

`/usr/include/ctype.h`
>   header file containing information used by character
>   classification and conversion routines for single byte characters.

`/usr/include/wctype.h`
> header file containing information used by international charac-
> ter classification and conversion routines for supplementary code
> sets.

`/usr/include/xctype.h`
> header file containing information used by language dependent
> character classification and conversion routines for supplemen-
> tary code sets.

SEE ALSO

ctype(3C), wctype(3W), setlocale(3C), environ(5).

DIAGNOSTICS

The error messages produced by `wchrtbl` are intended to be self-explanatory.
They indicate errors in the command line or syntactic errors encountered within the
input file.

WARNING

The `numeric` entry is used to specify decimal and thousands delimiters by
`wchrtbl` of the previous release of *MNLS*. In *SVR4 MNLS*, the `decimal_point` and
`thousands_sep` entries are used instead of the `numeric`, to adopt its syntax with
that of chrtbl(1).

NAME

what - print identification strings

SYNOPSIS

what [-s] *files*

DESCRIPTION

what searches the given files for all occurrences of the pattern that the get command substitutes for %Z% (this is @ (#) at this printing) and prints out what follows
until the first ", >, new-line, \, or null character. For example, if the C program in
file f.c contains:

        #ident " @(#) *identification information* "

and f.c is compiled to yield f.o and a.out, the command:

        what f.c f.o a.out

prints:

        f.c:
                identification information

        f.o:
                identification information

        a.out:
                identification information

what is intended to be used in conjunction with the get command, which automatically inserts identifying information, but it can also be used where the information
is inserted manually. Only one option exists:

        -s   quit after finding the first occurrence of pattern in each file

EXAMPLE

If test1.c has the following string:

        #ident "@(#)1 test1.c2";

entering:

        what test1.c

would print the following:

        test1.c:
                1 test1.c2

INTERNATIONAL FUNCTIONS

files can be specified using characters from supplementary code sets.

Characters from supplementary code sets can be used for *identification information*.

SEE ALSO

get(1), help(1), mcs(1).

DIAGNOSTICS

Exit status is 0 if any matches are found, otherwise 1. See help(1) for explanations.

NAME

whatis - display a one-line summary about a keyword

SYNOPSIS

`/usr/ucb/whatis` *command* ...

DESCRIPTION

`whatis` looks up a given *command* and displays the header line from the manual section. You can then run the man(1) command to get more information. If the line starts '*name*(*section*) ...' you can do 'man *section name*' to get the documentation for it. Try 'whatis ed' and then you should do 'man 1 ed' to get the manual page for ed(1).

`whatis` is actually just the `-f` option to the man command.

FILES

`/usr/share/man/whatis`   data base

SEE ALSO

`man(1)`, `catman(1M)`

NAME

which - locate a command; display its pathname or alias

SYNOPSIS

/usr/ucb/which [*filename*] . . .

DESCRIPTION

which takes a list of names and looks for the files which would be executed had these names been given as commands. Each argument is expanded if it is aliased, and searched for along the user's path. Both aliases and path are taken from the user's .cshrc file.

FILES

~/.cshrc　　　　　　　　source of aliases and path values

SEE ALSO

csh(1), ksh(1), sh(1).

DIAGNOSTICS

A diagnostic is given for names which are aliased to more than a single word, or if an executable file with the argument name was not found in the path.

NOTES

Only aliases and paths from ~/.cshrc are used; importing from the current environment is not attempted.

which must be executed by csh(1), since only csh knows about aliases. If you are using sh instead of csh, whence -v provides similar functionality.

To compensate for ~/.cshrc files in which aliases depend upon the prompt variable being set, which sets this variable. If the ~/.cshrc produces output or prompts for input when prompt is set, which may produce some strange results.

NAME

who - who is on the system

SYNOPSIS

who [-uTlHqpdbrtas] [*file*]

who -qn *x* [*file*]

who am i

who am I

DESCRIPTION

who can list the user's name, terminal line, login time, elapsed time since activity occurred on the line, and the process-ID of the command interpreter (shell) for each current UNIX system user. It examines the /var/adm/utmp file to obtain its information. If *file* is given, that file (which must be in utmp(4) format) is examined. Usually, *file* will be /var/adm/wtmp, which contains a history of all the logins since the file was last created.

who with the am i or am I option identifies the invoking user.

The general format for output is:

name [*state*] *line* *time* [*idle*] [*pid*] [*comment*] [*exit*]

The *name*, *line*, and *time* information is produced by all options except -q; the *state* information is produced only by -T; the *idle* and *pid* information is produced only by -u and -l; and the *comment* and exit information is produced only by -a. The information produced for -p, -d, and -r is explained during the discussion of each option, below.

With options, who can list logins, logoffs, reboots, and changes to the system clock, as well as other processes spawned by the init process. These options are:

-u   This option lists only those users who are currently logged in. The *name* is the user's login name. The *line* is the name of the line as found in the directory /dev. The *time* is the time that the user logged in. The *idle* column contains the number of hours and minutes since activity last occurred on that particular line. A dot (.) indicates that the terminal has seen activity in the last minute and is therefore "current". If more than twenty-four hours have elapsed or the line has not been used since boot time, the entry is marked old. This field is useful when trying to determine whether a person is working at the terminal or not. The *pid* is the process-ID of the user's shell. The *comment* is the comment field associated with this line as found in /etc/inittab [see inittab(4)]. This can contain information about where the terminal is located, the telephone number of the dataset, type of terminal if hard-wired, etc.

-T   This option is the same as the -s option, except that the *state* of the terminal line is printed. The *state* describes whether someone else can write to that terminal. A + appears if the terminal is writable by anyone; a - appears if it is not. root can write to all lines having a + or a - in the *state* field. If a bad line is encountered, a ? is printed.

-l This option lists only those lines on which the system is waiting for someone to login. The *name* field is LOGIN in such cases. Other fields are the same as for user entries except that the *state* field does not exist.

-H This option will print column headings above the regular output.

-q This is a quick who, displaying only the names and the number of users currently logged on. When this option is used, all other options are ignored.

-p This option lists any other process which is currently active and has been previously spawned by init. The *name* field is the name of the program executed by init as found in /etc/inittab. The *state*, line, and *idle* fields have no meaning. The *comment* field shows the id field of the line from /etc/inittab that spawned this process. See inittab(4).

-d This option displays all processes that have expired and not been respawned by init. The exit field appears for dead processes and contains the termination and exit values [as returned by wait(2)], of the dead process. This can be useful in determining why a process terminated.

-b This option indicates the time and date of the last reboot.

-r This option indicates the current *run-level* of the init process. In addition, it produces the process termination status, process id, and process exit status [see utmp(4)] under the *idle*, *pid*, and *comment* headings, respectively.

-t This option indicates the last change to the system clock (via the date command) by root. See su(1M).

-a This option processes /var/adm/utmp or the named *file* with all options turned on.

-s This option is the default and lists only the *name*, line, and *time* fields.

-n *x* This option takes a numeric argument, *x*, which specifies the number of users to display per line. *x* must be at least 1. The -n option must be used with -q.

Note to the super-user: after a shutdown to the single-user state, who returns a prompt; the reason is that since /var/adm/utmp is updated at login time and there is no login in single-user state, who cannot report accurately on this state. who am i, however, returns the correct information.

FILES

    /var/adm/utmp
    /var/adm/wtmp
    /etc/inittab

SEE ALSO

    date(1), login(1), mesg(1), su(1M), init(1M), wait(2), inittab(4), utmp(4).

NAME

whoami - display the effective current username

SYNOPSIS

/usr/ucb/whoami

DESCRIPTION

whoami displays the login name corresponding to the current effective user ID. If you have used su to temporarily adopt another user, whoami will report the login name associated with that user ID. whoami gets its information from the geteuid and getpwuid library routines (see getuid and getpwent, respectively).

FILES

/etc/passwd　　　　　　　username data base

SEE ALSO

su(1), who(1), getuid(2), getpwent(3).

NAME

whodo - who is doing what

SYNOPSIS

`/usr/sbin/whodo` [-h] [-l] [*user*]

DESCRIPTION

`whodo` produces formatted and dated output from information in the `/var/adm/utmp`, `/etc/ps_data`, and `/proc/pid` files.

The display is headed by the date, time, and machine name. For each user logged in, device name, user ID and login time is shown, followed by a list of active processes associated with the user ID. The list includes the device name, process ID, CPU minutes and seconds used, and process name.

If *user* is specified, output is restricted to all sessions pertaining to that user.

The following options are available:

-h   Suppress the heading.

-l   Produce a long form of output. The fields displayed are: the user's login name, the name of the tty the user is on, the time of day the user logged in (in *hours*:*minutes*), the idle time — that is, the time since the user last typed anything (in *hours*:*minutes*), the CPU time used by all processes and their children on that terminal (in *minutes*:*seconds*), the CPU time used by the currently active processes (in *minutes*:*seconds*), and the name and arguments of the current process.

EXAMPLE

The command:

```
whodo
```

produces a display like this:

```
Tue Mar 12 15:48:03 1985
bailey

tty09     mcn           8:51
    tty09    28158     0:29 sh

tty52     bdr          15:23
    tty52    21688     0:05 sh
    tty52    22788     0:01 whodo
    tty52    22017     0:03 vi
    tty52    22549     0:01 sh

xt162     lee          10:20
    tty08     6748     0:01 layers
    xt162     6751     0:01 sh
    xt163     6761     0:05 sh
    tty08     6536     0:05 sh
```

FILES

```
/etc/passwd
/etc/ps_data
/var/adm/utmp
/proc/pid
```

DIAGNOSTICS

If the PROC driver is not installed or configured or if /proc is not mounted, a message to that effect is issued and whodo will fail.

The exit status is zero on success, non-zero on failure.

SEE ALSO

ps(1), who(1).

NAME

whois - Internet user name directory service

SYNOPSIS

whois [-h *host*] *identifier*

DESCRIPTION

whois searches for an Internet directory entry for an *identifier* which is either a name (such as "Smith") or a handle (such as "SRI-NIC"). The default is for whois to search the Internet directory, sri_nic.arpa. For users who do not have direct access to Internet, whois provides the -h option, which allows users to specify a host from which to request information.

To force a name-only search, precede the name with a period; to force a handle-only search, precede the handle with an exclamation point.

To search for a group or organization entry, precede the argument with * (an asterisk). The entire membership list of the group will be displayed with the record.

You can use an exclamation point and asterisk, or a period and asterisk together.

EXAMPLES

The command

    whois Smith

looks for the name or handle SMITH.

The command

    whois !SRI-NIC

looks for the handle SRI-NIC only.

The command

    whois .Smith, John

looks for the name JOHN SMITH only.

Adding . . . to the name or handle argument will match anything from that point; that is, ZU . . . will match ZUL, ZUM, and so on.

NOTES

Any host specified with the -h option must be running some kind of a server on the whois port specified in /etc/services, and you must have a connection to the host. Such a server is not supplied with this system. To use the default host, sri_nic.arpa, you must have a connection to it, which generally means that you must be on the Internet.

NAME

write - write to another user

SYNOPSIS

write *user* [*line*]

DESCRIPTION

write copies lines from your terminal to that of another user. When first called, it sends the message:

    Message from *yourname* (tty??) [*date*]. . .

to the person you want to talk to. When it has successfully completed the connection, it also sends two bells to your own terminal to indicate that what you are typing is being sent.

The recipient of the message should write back at this point. Communication continues until an end of file is read from the terminal, an interrupt is sent, or the recipient has executed "mesg n". At that point write writes EOT on the other terminal and exits.

If you want to write to a user who is logged in more than once, the line argument may be used to indicate which line or terminal to send to (for example, term/12); otherwise, the first writable instance of the user found in /var/adm/utmp is assumed and the following message posted:

    user is logged on more than one place.
    You are connected to ''terminal''.
    Other locations are:
    terminal

Permission to write may be denied or granted by use of the mesg command. Writing to others is normally allowed by default. Certain commands, such as the pr command, disallow messages in order to prevent interference with their output. However, if the user has super-user permissions, messages can be forced onto a write-inhibited terminal.

If the character ! is found at the beginning of a line, write calls the shell to execute the rest of the line as a command.

write runs setgid( ) [see setuid(2)] to the group ID tty, in order to have write permissions on other user's terminals.

write will detect non-printable characters before sending them to the user's terminal. Control characters will appear as a '^' followed by the appropriate ASCII character; characters with the high-order bit set will appear in meta notation. For example, '\003' is displayed as '^C' and '\372' as 'M-z'.

The following protocol is suggested for using write: when you first write to another user, wait for them to write back before starting to send. Each person should end a message with a distinctive signal (that is, (o) for "over") so that the other person knows when to reply. The signal (oo) (for "over and out") is suggested when conversation is to be terminated.

FILES

```
/var/adm/utmp
        to find user
/usr/bin/sh
        to execute !
```

SEE ALSO

mail(1), mesg(1), pr(1), sh(1), who(1), setuid(2)

DIAGNOSTICS

`user is not logged on`	if the person you are trying to `write` to is not logged on.
`Permission denied`	if the person you are trying to `write` to denies that permission (with `mesg`).
`Warning: cannot respond, set mesg -y`	if your terminal is set to `mesg n` and the recipient cannot respond to you.
`Can no longer write to user`	if the recipient has denied permission (`mesg n`) after you had started writing.

NAME

xargs - construct argument list(s) and execute command

SYNOPSIS

xargs [*flags*] [*command* [*initial-arguments*]]

DESCRIPTION

xargs combines the fixed *initial-arguments* with arguments read from standard input to execute the specified *command* one or more times. The number of arguments read for each *command* invocation and the manner in which they are combined are determined by the flags specified.

command, which may be a shell file, is searched for, using one's $PATH. If *command* is omitted, /usr/bin/echo is used.

Arguments read in from standard input are defined to be contiguous strings of characters delimited by one or more blanks, tabs, or new-lines; empty lines are always discarded. Blanks and tabs may be embedded as part of an argument if escaped or quoted. Characters enclosed in quotes (single or double) are taken literally, and the delimiting quotes are removed. Outside of quoted strings a backslash (\) escapes the next character.

Each argument list is constructed starting with the *initial-arguments*, followed by some number of arguments read from standard input (Exception: see -i flag). Flags -i, -l, and -n determine how arguments are selected for each command invocation. When none of these flags are coded, the *initial-arguments* are followed by arguments read continuously from standard input until an internal buffer is full, and then *command* is executed with the accumulated args. This process is repeated until there are no more args. When there are flag conflicts (for example, -l vs. -n), the last flag has precedence. Valid *flags* are:

-l*number*　　　　　*command* is executed for each non-empty *number* lines of arguments from standard input. The last invocation of *command* will be with fewer lines of arguments if fewer than *number* remain. A line is considered to end with the first new-line *unless* the last character of the line is a blank or a tab; a trailing blank/tab signals continuation through the next non-empty line. If *number* is omitted, 1 is assumed. Option -x is forced.

-i*replstr*　　　　　Insert mode: *command* is executed for each line from standard input, taking the entire line as a single arg, inserting it in *initial-arguments* for each occurrence of *replstr*. A maximum of five arguments in *initial-arguments* may each contain one or more instances of *replstr*. Blanks and tabs at the beginning of each line are thrown away. Constructed arguments may not grow larger than 255 characters, and option -x is also forced. { } is assumed for *replstr* if not specified.

-n*number*　　　　　Execute *command* using as many standard input arguments as possible, up to *number* arguments maximum. Fewer arguments are used if their total size is greater than *size* characters, and for the last invocation if there are fewer than *number* arguments remaining. If option -x is also coded, each *number* arguments must fit in the *size* limitation, else xargs terminates execution.

-t	Trace mode: The *command* and each constructed argument list are echoed to file descriptor 2 just prior to their execution.
-p	Prompt mode: The user is asked whether to execute *command* each invocation. Trace mode (-t) is turned on to print the command instance to be executed, followed by a ?. . . prompt. A reply of y (optionally followed by anything) executes the command; anything else, including just a carriage return, skips that particular invocation of *command*.
-x	Causes xargs to terminate if any argument list would be greater than *size* characters; -x is forced by the options -i and -l. When neither of the options -i, -l, or -n are coded, the total length of all arguments must be within the *size* limit.
-s*size*	The maximum total size of each argument list is set to *size* characters; *size* must be a positive integer less than or equal to 470. If -s is not coded, 470 is taken as the default. Note that the character count for *size* includes one extra character for each argument and the count of characters in the command name.
-e*eofstr*	*eofstr* is taken as the logical end-of-file string. Underbar (_) is assumed for the logical EOF string if -e is not coded. The value -e with no *eofstr* coded turns off the logical EOF string capability (underbar is taken literally). xargs reads standard input until either end-of-file or the logical EOF string is encountered.

xargs terminates if either it receives a return code of -1 from, or if it cannot execute, *command*. When *command* is a shell program, it should explicitly exit (see sh(1)) with an appropriate value to avoid accidentally returning with -1.

EXAMPLES

The following examples moves all files from directory $1 to directory $2, and echo each move command just before doing it:

```
ls $1 | xargs -i -t mv $1/{} $2/{}
```

The following example combines the output of the parenthesized commands onto one line, which is then echoed to the end of file log:

```
(logname; date; echo $0 $*) | xargs >>log
```

The user is asked which files in the current directory are to be archived and archives them into arch (1.) one at a time, or (2.) many at a time.

```
1.   ls | xargs -p -l ar r arch
2.   ls | xargs -p -l | xargs ar r arch
```

The following example executes diff(1) with successive pairs of arguments originally typed as shell arguments:

```
echo $* | xargs -n2 diff
```

SEE ALSO

sh(1)

NAME

xbackup - performs backup functions

SYNOPSIS

xbackup [-t] [-p | -c | -f <files> | -u "<user1> [user2]"] -d <device>

xbackup -h

DESCRIPTION

-h produces a history of backups. Tells the user when the last complete and incremental/partial backups were done.

-c complete backup. All files changed since the system was installed are backed up. If an incremental/partial backup was done, all files modified since that time are backed up, otherwise all files modified since the last complete backup are backed up. A complete backup must be done before a partial backup.

-f backup files specified by the *<files>* argument. file names may contain characters to be expanded (i.e., *, .) by the shell. The argument must be in quotes.

-u backup a user's home directory. All files in the user's home directory will be backed up. At least one user must be specified but there can be more. The argument must be in quotes if more than one user is specified. If the user name is "all", then all the user's home directories will be backed up.

-d used to specify the device to be used. It defaults to /dev/rmt/ctape1.

-t used when the device is a tape. This option must be used with the -d option when the tape device is specified.

-p used to specify a partial backup. A complete backup must be done before an incremental backup is made. The partial backup is always based on the date of the last backup whether complete or partial.

A complete backup must be done before a partial backup can be done. Raw devices rather than block devices should always be used. The program can handle multi-volume backups. The program will prompt the user when it is ready for the next medium. The program will give you an estimated number of tapes that will be needed to do the backup. Tapes do not need to be formatted. If backup is done to tape, the tape must be rewound.

SEE ALSO

sh(1).

NAME

xformtrk - convert bad track list from one format to another

SYNOPSIS

xformtrk -I *opt* -O *opt* [-t *file*] [-d *ddefsdir*] *devtype*

DESCRIPTION

xformtrk converts the input data, in any of the four input formats (bad blocks; track; head,cylinder pairs; logical-device,block pairs) to a file containing values in either track or head,cylinder format. All input entries must be in the same format and, for any format, must be one number or pair per line. For example:

bad blocks:	tracks:	head,cyl pair:	logical-dev,block offset pair:
23348	1501	4 1234	11 1234
207608	2345	6 9182	73 5678

The output from xformtrk is displayed on stdout.

The options are:

-I *opt*
Specify the input as either t for track; b for bad blocks; c for head,cylinder sector; or d for logical-device,block pairs, one entry per line. For head,cylinder pairs, do not input the byte offset or BFI (bytes from index).

-O *opt*
Specify the output as either t for track or c for head,cylinder, sector, one entry per line.

-t *file*
Use the named file as input. The format is either bad block numbers; single track numbers; head,cylinder pairs; or logical-device,block offset pairs, one number or pair per line. For head,cylinder pairs, do not input the byte offset or BFI (bytes from index). When the -t option is omitted, you are prompted to enter the data manually.

-d *ddefsdir*
Use the directory ddefsdir rather than /etc/dskdefs/ to find the entry for *devtype*.

devtype
This is the device type found in /etc/dskdefs which uniquely identifies the device (for example, mcdcV). See ddefs(1M).

EXAMPLE

Convert the file badtrkfile from bad block numbers to head, cylinder, sector with the numbers referencing the first CDC WREN disk attached to the MVME323 controller (the MVME323 controller is supported only on the M68000 family of processors).

```
xformtrk -I t -O c -t badtrkfile mcdcV
```

FILES

/etc/dskdefs/*
/tmp/xf.*device*

DIAGNOSTICS

Exit Codes:

0 - success

1 - internal failure	unknown type or device, general error
2 - I/O failure	files not found, read/write failure, etc.
3 - bad command usage	syntax error within command line
4 - user interrupt	

NOTES

Currently only the b (bad block number) input option is supported. The output format corresponding to the bad block number input format should be c (head, cylinder, sector).

NAME

xinstall - installs commands

SYNOPSIS

xinstall [-c *dira*] [-f *dirb*] [-n *dirc*] [-o] [-a] *file* [*dirz* ...]

DESCRIPTION

xinstall is a command most commonly used in "makefiles" [see make(1)] to xinstall a file (updated target file) in a specific place within a file system. Each file is installed by copying it into the appropriate directory, thereby retaining the mode and owner of the original command file. The program prints messages telling you exactly what files it is replacing or creating and where they are going.

If no options or directories (*dirz* ...) are given, xinstall will search [using find(1)] a set of default directories (/usr/bin/usr/usr/bin, /etc, /usr/lib, and /usr/usr/lib, in that order) for a file with the same name as *file*. When the first occurrence is found, xinstall issues a message saying that it is overwriting that file with *file*, and proceeds to do so. If the file is not found, the program states this and exits without further action.

If one or more directories (*dirz* ...) are specified after *file*, those directories will be searched before the directories specified in the default list.

The meanings of the options are:

-c *dira*   Installs a new command file in the directory specified in *dira*. Looks for *file* in *dira* and installs it there if it is not found. If it is found, xinstall issues a message saying that the file already exists, and exits without overwriting it. May be used alone or with the -s option.

-f *dirb*   Forces *file* to be installed in given directory, whether or not one already exists. if the file being installed does not already exist, the mode and owner of the new file will be set to 755 and bin, respectively. If the file exists, the mode and owner will be that of the existing file. May be used alone or with the -o or -s options.

-1   Ignores default directory list, searching only through the given directories (*dirz* ...). May be used alone or with any other options except -c and -f.

-n *dirc*   If *file* is not found in any of the searched directories, it is put in the directory specified in *dirc*. The mode and owner of the new file will be set to 755 and bin, respectively. May be used alone or with any other options except -c and -f.

-o   If *file* is found, this option saves the "found" file by copying it to *oldfile* in the directory in which is was found. May be used alone or with any other options except -c.

-s   Suppresses printing of messages other than error messages. May be used alone or with any other options.

SEE ALSO

find(1), make(1)

NAME

xrestore - restore file to original directory

SYNOPSIS

xrestore [-c] [-i] [-o] [-t] [-d *device*] | [*pattern* [*pattern*]. . .]

DESCRIPTION

-c   complete restore. All files on the tape are restored.

-i   gets the index file off of the medium. This only works when the archive was created using xbackup. The output is a list of all the files on the medium. No files are actually restored.

-o   overwrite existing files. If the file being restored already exists it will not be restored unless this option is specified.

-t   indicates that the tape device is to be used. Must be used with the -d option when restoring from tape.

-d   *device* is the raw device to be used. It defaults to dev/rmt/ctape1

When doing a restore, one or more patterns can be specified. These patterns are matched against the files on the tape. When a match is found, the file is restored. Since backups are done using full pathnames, the file is restored to its original directory. Metacharacters can be used to match multiple files. The patterns should be in quotes to prevent the characters from being expanded before they are passed to the command. If no patterns are specified, it defaults to restoring all files. If a pattern does not match any file on the tape, a message is printed.

When end of medium is reached, the user is prompted for the next media. The user can exit at this point by typing q. (This may cause files to be corrupted if a file happens to span a medium.) In general, quitting in the middle is not a good idea.

If the file already exists and an attempt is made to restore it without the -o option, the file name will be printed on the screen followed by a question mark. This file will not be restored.

In order for multi-volume restores to work correctly, the raw device must be used.

SEE ALSO

sh(1), xbackup(1).

NAME

yacc - yet another compiler-compiler

SYNOPSIS

yacc [-vVdlt] [-Q[y|n]] *file*

DESCRIPTION

The yacc command converts a context-free grammar into a set of tables for a simple automaton that executes an LALR(1) parsing algorithm. The grammar may be ambiguous; specified precedence rules are used to break ambiguities.

The output file, y.tab.c, must be compiled by the C compiler to produce a program yyparse. This program must be loaded with the lexical analyzer program, yylex, as well as main and yyerror, an error handling routine. These routines must be supplied by the user; the lex(1) command is useful for creating lexical analyzers usable by yacc.

-v   Prepares the file y.output, which contains a description of the parsing tables and a report on conflicts generated by ambiguities in the grammar.

-d   Generates the file y.tab.h with the #define statements that associate the yacc-assigned "token codes" with the user-declared "token names." This association allows source files other than y.tab.c to access the token codes.

-l   Specifies that the code produced in y.tab.c will not contain any #line constructs. This option should only be used after the grammar and the associated actions are fully debugged.

-Q[y | n]
            The -Qy option puts the version stamping information in y.tab.c. This allows you to know what version of yacc built the file. The -Qn option (the default) writes no version information.

-t   Compiles runtime debugging code by default. Runtime debugging code is always generated in y.tab.c under conditional compilation control. By default, this code is not included when y.tab.c is compiled. Whether or not the -t option is used, the runtime debugging code is under the control of YYDEBUG, a preprocessor symbol. If YYDEBUG has a non-zero value, then the debugging code is included. If its value is zero, then the code will not be included. The size and execution time of a program produced without the runtime debugging code will be smaller and slightly faster.

-V   Prints on the standard error output the version information for yacc.

FILES

```
y.output
y.tab.c
y.tab.h                        defines for token names
yacc.tmp,
yacc.debug, yacc.acts          temporary files
LIBDIR/yaccpar                 parser prototype for C programs
```

LIBDIR   usually /usr/ccs/lib

SEE ALSO

lex(1).

DIAGNOSTICS

The number of reduce-reduce and shift-reduce conflicts is reported on the standard error output; a more detailed report is found in the y.output file. %Similarly, if some rules are not reachable from the start symbol, this instance is also reported.

NOTES

Because file names are fixed, at most one yacc process can be active in a given directory at a given time.

NAME

yes - print string repeatedly

SYNOPSIS

yes [*string*]

DESCRIPTION

yes repeatedly outputs "y", or if a single string argument is given, *string* is output repeatedly. The command continues indefinitely unless aborted. yes is useful in pipes to commands that prompt for input and require a "y" response for a yes. In this case, yes terminates when the command that it pipes to terminates so that no infinite loop occurs.

NAME

ypcat - print values in a YP data base

SYNOPSIS

ypcat [-k] [-d *ypdomain*] [-t] *mname*
ypcat [-x]

DESCRIPTION

The ypcat command prints out values in the YP name service map specified by
mname, which may be either a map name or a map nickname. Since ypcat uses the
YP network services, no YP server is specified.

Refer to ypfiles(4) and ypserv(1M) for an overview of the YP name service.

The following options are available:

-d *ypdomain*
    Specify a domain other that the default domain.

-k   Display the keys for those maps in which the values are null or the key is
not part of the value. None of the maps derived from files that have an
ASCII version in /etc fall into this class.

-t   Inhibit map nickname translation.

-x   Dump the map nickname translation table.

SEE ALSO

ypmatch(1), ypserv(1M), ypfiles(4), Network Information Service Administration guide

NOTE

NIS package should be installed to be able to use the nickname features.

NAME

`ypinit` - build and install YP database

SYNOPSIS

```
/usr/sbin/ypinit -c
/usr/sbin/ypinit -m
/usr/sbin/ypinit -s master-name
```

DESCRIPTION

`ypinit` sets up a YP name service database on a YP server. It can be used to set up a master or a slave server, or a client system. You must be the privileged user to run it. It asks a few self-explanatory questions, and reports success or failure to the terminal.

It sets up a master server using the simple model in which that server is master to all maps in the data base. This is the way to bootstrap the YP system; later if you want you can change the association of maps to masters.

All databases are built from scratch, either from information available to the program at runtime, or from the ASCII data base files in `/etc`. These files should be in their traditional form, rather than the abbreviated form used on client machines.

A YP database on a slave server is set up by copying an existing database from a running server. The *master-name* argument should be the hostname of a YP server (either the master server for all the maps, or a server on which the data base is up-to-date and stable).

To set up a client, `ypinit` prompts for a list of YP servers to bind the client to, this list should be ordered from closest to farthest server.

Read `ypfiles`(4) and `ypserv`(1M) for an overview of the YP name service.

The following options are available:

`-c`	Set up a client system.
`-m`	Indicate that the local host is to be the YP master.
`-s` *master-name*	Set up a slave database.

SEE ALSO

`makedbm`(1M), `ypmake`(1M), `yppush`(1M), `ypserv`(1M), `ypxfr`(1M), `ypfiles`(4)

FILES

`/var/yp/binding/`*domainname*`/ypservers`

NAME

ypmake - rebuild NIS database

SYNOPSIS

`cd /var/yp ; make [ map ... ]`

DESCRIPTION

The file `/var/yp/Makefile` is used by `make` to build the NIS name service database. With no arguments, `make` creates `ndbm` databases for any NIS maps that are out-of-date.

If any *map* names are supplied on the command line, `make` will update only those map(s).

There are several variables used in the makefile `/var/yp/Makefile` which can be set on the command line or by editing the makefile itself. See the makefile for descriptions of each variable which can be modified and the variable's value are before attempting to make the NIS database.

`ypmake` also creates an entry in `/var/yp/aliases` for converting canonoical NIS network names to the actual `ndbm` file names used to store the data for that particular map. Refer to `ypfiles`(4) and `ypserv`(1M) for an overview of the NIS database and directory structure.

FILES

`/var/yp`
`/var/yp/aliases`
`/var/yp/Makefile`

SEE ALSO

`make`(1), `makedbm`(1M), `yppush`(1M), `ypserv`(1M), `ndbm`(3), `ypfiles`(4)

NAME

ypmatch - print the value of one or more keys from the NIS map

SYNOPSIS

ypmatch [-d *ypdomain*] [-t] [-k] *key* [*key...*] *mname*
ypmatch [-x]

DESCRIPTION

ypmatch prints the values associated with one or more keys from the NIS name services map specified by *mname*, which may be either a *mapname* or a map nickname.

Multiple keys can be specified; the same map will be searched for all keys. The keys must be exact values insofar as capitalization and length are concerned. No pattern matching is available. If a key is not matched, a diagnostic message is produced.

The following options are available:

-d *ypdomain*	Specify a domain other than the default domain.
-k	Before printing the value of a key, print the key itself, followed by a colon (":"). This is useful only if the keys are not duplicated in the values, or so many keys were specified that the output could be confusing.
-t	Inhibit map nickname translation.
-x	Dump the map nickname translation table.

SEE ALSO

ypcat(1), ypfiles(4), Network Information Service Administration guide

NOTE

NIS package should be installed to be able to use the nickname features.

NAME

yppoll - return current version of the map at the NIS server host

SYNOPSIS

/usr/sbin/yppoll [-d *ypdomain*] [-h *host*] *mapname*

DESCRIPTION

The yppoll command asks a ypserv(1M) process what the order number is, and which host is the master NIS server for the named map.

The following options are available:

-d *ypdomain*   Use *ypdomain* instead of the default domain.

-h *host*   Ask the ypserv process at *host* about the map parameters. If *host* is not specified, the NIS server for the local host is used. That is, the default host is the one returned by ypwhich(1).

SEE ALSO

ypserv(1M), ypwhich(1), ypfiles(4)

NAME

yppush - force propagation of a changed NIS map

SYNOPSIS

/usr/sbin/yppush [-v] [-d *ypdomain*] *mapname*

DESCRIPTION

yppush copies a new version of the NIS name service map from the master NIS server to the slave NIS servers. It is normally run only on the master NIS server by the Makefile in /var/yp after the master databases are changed. It first constructs a list of NIS server hosts by reading the NIS map ypservers within the *ypdomain*, or if the map is not set up, the local file is used. Keys within the map ypservers are the ASCII names of the machines on which the NIS servers run.

A transfer map request is sent to the NIS server at each host, along with the information needed by the transfer agent (the program that actually moves the map) to call back the yppush. When the attempt has completed (successfully or not), and the transfer agent has sent yppush a status message, the results may be printed to stdout. Messages are also printed when a transfer is not possible; for instance when the request message is undeliverable, or when the timeout period on responses has expired.

Refer to ypfiles(4) and ypserv(1M) for an overview of the NIS name service.

The following options are available:

-v   Verbose. Print messages when each server is called, and for each response. If this flag is omitted, only error messages are printed.

-d *ypdomain*   Specify a *ypdomain* other than the default domain.

FILES

/var/yp/*ypdomain*/ypservers.{*dir,pag*}   local file
/var/yp

SEE ALSO

ypserv(1M), ypxfr(1M), ypfiles(4)

NAME

ypserv, ypbind - NIS server and binder processes

SYNOPSIS

/usr/lib/netsvc/yp/ypserv

/usr/lib/netsvc/yp/ypbind [-ypset | -ypsetme]

DESCRIPTION

The NIS provides a simple network lookup service consisting of databases and processes. The databases are dbm(3) files in a directory tree rooted at /var/yp. These files are described in ypfiles(4). The processes are /usr/lib/netsvc/yp/ypserv, the NIS database lookup server, and /usr/lib/netsvc/yp/ypbind, the NIS binder. The programmatic interface to NIS is described in ypclnt(3N). Administrative tools are described in yppush(1M), ypxfr(1M), yppoll(1M), ypwhich(1), and ypset(1M). Tools to see the contents of NIS maps are described in ypcat(1), and ypmatch(1). Database generation and maintenance tools are described in ypinit(1M), ypmake(1M), and makedbm(1M).

Both ypserv and ypbind are daemon processes typically activated at system startup time. ypserv runs only on NIS server machines with a complete NIS database. ypbind runs on all machines using NIS services, both NIS servers and clients.

The ypserv daemon's primary function is to look up information in its local database of NIS maps. Communication to and from ypserv is by means of RPC calls. Lookup functions are described in ypclnt(3N), and are supplied as C-callable functions in the NIS library. There are four lookup functions, all of which are performed on a specified map within some NIS domain: *Match*, *"Get_first"*, *"Get_next"*, and *"Get_all"*. The *Match* operation takes a key, and returns the associated value. The *"Get_first"* operation returns the first key-value pair from the map, and *"Get_next"* can be used to enumerate the remainder. *"Get_all"* ships the entire map to the requester as the response to a single RPC request.

Two other functions supply information about the map, rather than map entries: *"Get_order_number"*, and *"Get_master_name"*. In fact, both order number and master name exist in the map as key-value pairs, but the server will not return either through the normal lookup functions. If you examine the map with makedbm(1M), however, they will be visible.

The function of ypbind is to remember information that lets client processes on a single node communicate with some ypserv process. ypbind must run on every machine which has NIS client processes; ypserv may or may not be running on the same node, but must be running somewhere on the network.

The information ypbind remembers is called a *binding*—the association of a domain name with a NIS server.

The process of binding is driven by client requests. As a request for an unbound domain comes in, the ypbind process steps through the ypservers list (last entry first) trying to find a ypserv process that serves maps within that domain. There must be a ypserv process on at least one of the hosts in the ypservers file. Once a domain is bound by a particular ypbind, that same binding is given to every client process on the node. The ypbind process on the local node or a remote node may be queried for the binding of a particular domain by using the ypwhich(1) command.

If ypbind is unable to speak to the ypserv process it is bound to, it marks the domain as unbound, tells the client process that the domain is unbound, and tries to bind the domain once again. Requests received for an unbound domain will wait until the domain requested is bound. In general, a bound domain is marked as unbound when the node running ypserv crashes or gets overloaded. In such a case, ypbind will try to bind to another NIS server listed in /var/yp/binding/*domainname*/ypservers.

ypbind also accepts requests to set its binding for a particular domain. The request is usually generated by the NIS subsystem itself. ypset(1M) is a command to access the *"Set_domain"* facility. Note: the *Set Domain* procedure only accepts requests from processes with appropriate privileges, and the -ypset or -ypsetme flags must have been set for ypbind.

The following options are available for the ypbind command only:

-ypset   Allow any user to call ypset(1M). By default, no one can call ypset(1M).

-ypsetme   Only allow root on local machines to call ypset(1M). By default, no one can call ypset(1M).

FILES

If the file /var/yp/ypserv.log exists when ypserv starts up, log information will be written to this file when error conditions arise.
/var/yp
/var/yp/binding/*ypdomain*/ypservers

SEE ALSO

makedbm(1M), ypcat(1), ypinit(1M), ypmake(1M), ypmatch(1), yppoll(1M), yppush(1M), ypset(1M), ypwhich(1), ypxfr(1M), dbm(3X), ypclnt(3N), ypfiles(4)

NOTES

Both ypbind and ypserv support multiple domains. The ypserv process determines the domains it serves by looking for directories of the same name in the directory /var/yp. Additionally, the ypbind process can maintain bindings to several domains and their servers.

NAME

ypset - point ypbind at a particular server

SYNOPSIS

/usr/sbin/ypset [-d *ypdomain*] [-h *host*] *server*

DESCRIPTION

In order to run ypset, ypbind must be initiated with the -ypset or -ypsetme options. See ypserv(1M). ypset tells ypbind to get NIS services for the specified *ypdomain* from the ypserv process running on *server*. If *server* is down, or is not running ypserv, this is not discovered until the NIS client process tries to get a binding for the domain. At this point, the binding set by ypset will be tested by ypbind. If the binding is invalid, ypbind will attempt to rebind for the same domain.

ypset is useful for binding a client node which is not on a broadcast net, or is on a broadcast net which is not running the NIS server host. It also is useful for debugging NIS client applications, for instance where the NIS map only exists at a single NIS server host.

In cases where several hosts on the local net are supplying NIS services, it is possible for ypbind to rebind to another host even while you attempt to find out if the ypset operation succeeded. For example, you can type:

```
# ypset host1
# ypwhich
host2
```

which can be confusing. This is a function of the NIS subsystem's attempt to load-balance among the available NIS servers, and occurs when *host1* does not respond to ypbind because it is not running ypserv (or is overloaded), and *host2*, running ypserv, gets the binding.

server indicates the NIS server to bind to, and must be specified as a name. This will work only if the node has a current valid binding for the domain in question, and ypbind has been set to allow use of ypset. In most cases, *server* should be specified as an IP address.

ypset tries to bind ypbind over a datagram transport first. Datagram Transports are recommended for higher performance. The NIS library calls, yp_enum( ), yp_all( ), yp_next( ), and yp_first( ) use circuit transports regardless of the main transport being used.

Refer to ypfiles(4) and ypserv(1M) for an overview of the NIS name service.

The following options are available:

-h *host*   Set ypbind's binding on *host*, instead of locally. *host* must be specified as a name.

-d *ypdomain* Use *ypdomain*, instead of the default domain.

SEE ALSO

ypserv(1M), ypwhich(1), ypfiles(4)

NAME

ypupdated - server for changing NIS information

SYNOPSIS

/usr/lib/netsvc/yp/ypupdated [-is]

DESCRIPTION

ypupdated is a daemon that updates information in the NIS name service, normally started up by inetd(1M). ypupdated consults the file updaters(4) in the directory /var/yp to determine which NIS maps should be updated and how to change them.

By default, the daemon requires the most secure method of authentication available to it, either DES (secure) or UNIX (insecure).

The following options are available:

-i   Accept RPC calls with the insecure AUTH_UNIX credentials. This allows programmatic updating of NIS maps in all networks.

-s   Only accept calls authenticated using the secure RPC mechanism (AUTH_DES authentication). This disables programmatic updating of NIS maps unless the network supports these calls.

FILES

/var/yp/updaters

SEE ALSO

inetd(1M), keyserv(1M), updaters(4)

NAME

ypwhich - return name of NIS server or map master

SYNOPSIS

ypwhich [-d *ypdomain*] [[-t] -m [*mname*] | [-V2 | -V3] *hostname*]
ypwhich [-x]

DESCRIPTION

ypwhich tells which NIS server supplies the NIS name services to the NIS client, or
which is the master for a map. If invoked without arguments, it gives the NIS
server for the local machine. If *hostname* is specified, that machine is queried to find
out which NIS master it is using. While searching for the server to which the client
is bound, if either -V2 or -V3 is specified, the search is made only for protocol version 2 or version 3 respectively. Otherwise, the search will start with the current
version, and then drop to the previous version.

Refer to ypfiles(4) and ypserv(1M) for an overview of the NIS name services.

The following options are available:

-d *ypdomain*	Use *ypdomain* instead of the default domain.
-m *mname*	Find the master NIS server for a map. No *hostname* can be specified with -m. *mname* can be a mapname, or a nickname for a map. When *mname* is omitted, produce a list available maps.
-t	Inhibit map nickname translation.
-x	Dump the map nickname translation table.

SEE ALSO

ypserv(1M), ypset(1M), ypfiles(4), Network Information Service Administration guide

NOTE

NIS package should be installed to be able to use the nickname features.

NAME

ypxfr - transfer YP map from a YP server to host

SYNOPSIS

/usr/sbin/ypxfr [-c] [-f] [-d *ypdomain*] [-h *host*] [-s *ypdomain*]
　　[-C *tid prog server*] *mapname*

DESCRIPTION

The ypxfr command moves a YP map in the default domain for the local host to
the local host by making use of normal YP services. It creates a temporary map in
the directory /var/yp/*ypdomain* (this directory must already exist; *ypdomain* is the
default domain for the local host), fills it by enumerating the map's entries, fetches
the map parameters (master and order number), and loads them. It then deletes
any old versions of the map and moves the temporary map to the real *mapname*.

If run interactively, ypxfr writes its output to the terminal. However, if it is started
without a controlling terminal, and if the log file /var/yp/ypxfr.log exists, it
appends all its output to that file. Since ypxfr is most often run from the privileged
user's crontab file, or by ypserv, the log file can be used to retain a record of what
was attempted, and what the results were.

For consistency between servers, ypxfr should be run periodically for every map in
the YP data base. Different maps change at different rates: a map may not change
for months at a time, for instance, and may therefore be checked only once a day.
Some maps may change several times per day. In such a case, you may want to
check hourly for updates. A crontab(1) entry can be used to perform periodic
updates automatically. Rather than having a separate crontab entry for each map,
you can group commands to update several maps in a shell script. Examples
(mnemonically named) are in /usr/sbin/yp: ypxfr_1perday, and
ypxfr_1perhour. They can serve as reasonable first cuts.

Refer to ypfiles(4) and ypserv(1M) for an overview of the YP name service.

The following options are available:

-c　　　　　　　　　Do not send a Clear current map request to the local ypserv pro-
　　　　　　　　　　cess. Use this flag if ypserv is not running locally at the time you
　　　　　　　　　　are running ypxfr. Otherwise, ypxfr complains that it cannot
　　　　　　　　　　talk to the local ypserv, and the transfer fails.

-f　　　　　　　　　Force the transfer to occur even if the version at the master is not
　　　　　　　　　　more recent than the local version.

-C *tid prog server*　This option is *only* for use by ypserv. When ypserv starts
　　　　　　　　　　ypxfr, it specifies that ypxfr should call back a yppush process
　　　　　　　　　　at the host *server*, registered as program number *prog*, and waiting
　　　　　　　　　　for a response to transaction *tid*.

-d *ypdomain*　　　Specify a domain other than the default domain.

-h *host*　　　　　　Get the map from *host*, regardless of what the map says the mas-
　　　　　　　　　　ter is. If *host* is not specified, ypxfr asks the YP service for the
　　　　　　　　　　name of the master, and try to get the map from there. *host* must
　　　　　　　　　　be a name.

-s *ypdomain*   Specify a source domain from which to transfer a map that should be the same across domains.

FILES

`/var/yp/ypxfr.log`	log file
`/usr/sbin/yp/ypxfr_1perday`	`cron`(1M) script to run one transfer per day
`/usr/sbin/yp/ypxfr_1perhour`	script for hourly transfers of volatile maps
`/var/yp/ypdomain`	YP domain
`/usr/spool/cron/crontabs/root`	privileged user's `crontab` file

SEE ALSO

`cron`(1M), `crontab`(1), `ypserv`(1M), `yppush`(1M), `ypfiles`(4)

NAME

zdump - time zone dumper

SYNOPSIS

zdump [-v] [-c *cutoffyear*] [*zonename* . . .]

DESCRIPTION

The zdump command prints the current time in each *zonename* named on the command line.

The following options are available:

-v　　　　　For each *zonename* on the command line, print the current time, the time at the lowest possible time value, the time one day after the lowest possible time value, the times both one second before and exactly at each time at which the rules for computing local time change, the time at the highest possible time value, and the time at one day less than the highest possible time value. Each line ends with isdst=1 if the given time is Daylight Saving Time or isdst=0 otherwise.

-c *cutoffyear*　　Cut off the verbose output near the start of the year *cutoffyear*.

FILES

/usr/lib/locale/TZ　　　standard zone information directory

SEE ALSO

zic(1M), ctime(3C)

NAME

zic - time zone compiler

SYNOPSIS

`zic [ -v ] [ -d directory ] [ -l localtime ] [ `*filename*` ... ]`

DESCRIPTION

`zic` reads text from the file(s) named on the command line and creates the time conversion information files specified in this input. If a *filename* is '-', the standard input is read.

Input lines are made up of fields. Fields are separated by any number of white space characters. Leading and trailing white space on input lines is ignored. A pound sign (#) in the input introduces a comment which extends to the end of the line the pound sign appears on. White space characters and pound signs may be enclosed in double quotes (") if they're to be used as part of a field. Any line that is blank (after comment stripping) is ignored. Non-blank lines are expected to be of one of three types: rule lines, zone lines, and link lines.

A rule line has the form

> **Rule** *NAME FROM   TO   TYPE IN   ON   AT   SAVE LETTER/S*

For example:

```
Rule   USA    1969 1973    -   Apr lastSun 2:00 1:00      D
```

The fields that make up a rule line are:

NAME
    Gives the (arbitrary) name of the set of rules this rule is part of.

FROM
    Gives the first year in which the rule applies. The word `minimum` (or an abbreviation) means the minimum year with a representable time value. The word `maximum` (or an abbreviation) means the maximum year with a representable time value.

TO
    Gives the final year in which the rule applies. In addition to `minimum` and `maximum` (as above), the word `only` (or an abbreviation) may be used to repeat the value of the FROM field.

TYPE
    Gives the type of year in which the rule applies. If TYPE is '-' then the rule applies in all years between FROM and TO inclusive; if TYPE is `uspres`, the rule applies in U.S. Presidential election years; if TYPE is `nonpres`, the rule applies in years other than U.S. Presidential election years. If TYPE is something else, then `zic` executes the command

> `yearistype` *year type*

    to check the type of a year: an exit status of zero is taken to mean that the year is of the given type; an exit status of one is taken to mean that the year is not of the given type.

IN
    Names the month in which the rule takes effect. Month names may be abbreviated.

ON
    Gives the day on which the rule takes effect. Recognized forms include:

5	the fifth of the month
`lastSun`	the last Sunday in the month
`lastMon`	the last Monday in the month
`Sun>=8`	first Sunday on or after the eighth
`Sun<=25`	last Sunday on or before the 25th

Names of days of the week may be abbreviated or spelled out in full. Note: there must be no spaces within the ON field.

AT Gives the time of day at which the rule takes effect. Recognized forms include:

2	time in hours
`2:00`	time in hours and minutes
`15:00`	24-hour format time (for times after noon)
`1:28:14`	time in hours, minutes, and seconds

Any of these forms may be followed by the letter w if the given time is local "wall clock" time or s if the given time is local "standard" time; in the absence of w or s, wall clock time is assumed.

SAVE Gives the amount of time to be added to local standard time when the rule is in effect. This field has the same format as the AT field (although, of course, the w and s suffixes are not used).

LETTER/S
Gives the "variable part" (for example, the "S" or "D" in "EST" or "EDT") of time zone abbreviations to be used when this rule is in effect. If this field is '−', the variable part is null.

A zone line has the form

Zone   *NAME*   *GMTOFF   RULES/SAVE   FORMAT   [UNTIL]*

For example:

```
Zone Australia/South-west  GMTOFF   RULES/SAVE   FORMAT
```

The fields that make up a zone line are:

NAME The name of the time zone. This is the name used in creating the time conversion information file for the zone.

GMTOFF The amount of time to add to GMT to get standard time in this zone. This field has the same format as the AT and SAVE fields of rule lines; begin the field with a minus sign if time must be subtracted from GMT.

RULES/SAVE
The name of the rule(s) that apply in the time zone or, alternately, an amount of time to add to local standard time. If this field is '−' then standard time always applies in the time zone.

FORMAT The format for time zone abbreviations in this time zone. The pair of characters %s is used to show where the "variable part" of the time zone abbreviation goes. UNTIL The time at which the GMT offset or the rule(s) change for a location. It is specified as a year, a month, a day, and a time of day. If this is specified, the time zone information is generated from the given GMT offset and rule change until the time specified.

The next line must be a "continuation" line; this has the same form as a zone line except that the string "Zone" and the name are omitted, as the continuation line will place information starting at the time specified as the UNTIL field in the previous line in the file used by the previous line. Continuation lines may contain an UNTIL field, just as zone lines do, indicating that the next line is a further continuation.

A link line has the form

```
Link   LINK-FROM      LINK-TO
```

For example:

```
Link   US/Eastern    EST5EDT
```

The LINK-FROM field should appear as the NAME field in some zone line; the LINK-TO field is used as an alternate name for that zone.

Except for continuation lines, lines may appear in any order in the input.

OPTIONS

-v   Complain if a year that appears in a data file is outside the range of years representable by system time values (0:00:00 AM GMT, January 1, 1970, to 3:14:07 AM GMT, January 19, 2038).

-d directory
    Create time conversion information files in the directory directory rather than in the standard directory /usr/share/lib/zoneinfo.

-l timezone
    Use the time zone timezone as local time. zic will act as if the file contained a link line of the form

```
Link   timezone                          localtime
```

FILES
    /usr/share/lib/zoneinfo   standard directory used for created files

SEE ALSO
    time(1), ctime(3)

NOTE
    For areas with more than two types of local time, you may need to use local standard time in the AT field of the earliest transition time's rule to ensure that the earliest transition time recorded in the compiled file is correct.

Permuted Index

Commands Reference Manual